LIVING LITURGY

LIVING ✠ LITURGY

Spirituality, Celebration, and Catechesis for Sundays and Solemnities

Year C • 2019

UK–Ireland Edition

Brian Schmisek
Katy Beedle Rice
Diana Macalintal

CATHOLIC TRUTH SOCIETY
London

www.ctsbooks.org

LITURGICAL PRESS
Collegeville, Minnesota

www.litpress.org

Published in the UK and Republic of Ireland 2018
by the Incorporated Catholic Truth Society, London
ISBN 9781784695699
www.ctsbooks.org

CONTENTS

CONTRIBUTORS

Brian Schmisek is professor and dean of the Institute of Pastoral Studies at Loyola University Chicago. Prior to coming to Chicago in 2012, he was the founding dean of the School of Ministry at the University of Dallas. His published works include *The Rome of Peter and Paul: A Pilgrim's Handbook to New Testament Sites in the Eternal City* (Pickwick), *Ancient Faith for the Modern World: A Brief Guide to the Apostles' Creed* (ACTA), *Resurrection of the Flesh or Resurrection from the Dead: Implications for Theology* (Liturgical Press), many other books coauthored for biblical study, and articles.

Katy Beedle Rice is a catechist and writer who lives with her husband and three children in Boise, Idaho. She is a formation leader for the National Association of the Catechesis of the Good Shepherd, training catechists who work with children ages three through six. Rice is also a contributing preacher for the Dominican Podcast *the Word* (https://word.op.org), writes for Celebration Publications, a division of the National Catholic Reporter Publishing Company, and blogs about motherhood, ministry, and the Eucharist at blessedbrokenshared.blogspot.com.

Diana Macalintal has served as a liturgist, musician, author, speaker, and composer for the last twenty-five years, and her work can be found in *Give Us This Day* and many other publications. She is the author of *The Work of Your Hands: Prayers for Ordinary and Extraordinary Moments of Grace, Joined by the Church, Sealed by a Blessing: Couples and Communities Called to Conversion Together*, and *Your Parish* Is *the Curriculum: RCIA in the Midst of the Community* (Liturgical Press). Macalintal is a cofounder of TeamRCIA.com with her husband, Nick Wagner.

PREFACE

Renewal

Last year Liturgical Press gave a new look and feel to this popular resource. We spoke of it with the metaphor of a new house, or even a renovation. So we have been in this renovated house for a year now, and so begins year two. With the renewed look and feel of *Living Liturgy*™ last year, we heard many good things including some constructive feedback. We remain indebted to the work that Sr. Joyce Ann Zimmerman, CPPS, director of the Institute for Liturgical Ministry (now closed, unfortunately), and Sr. Kathleen Harmon, SNDdeN, did by launching this resource nearly twenty years ago. Much of the structure they gave the work has remained the same. In fact, in this 2019 edition we largely return to the format they were using, especially concerning "Focusing the Gospel, Connecting the Gospel, and Connecting the Responsorial Psalm." We tried a slightly different model in 2018 but now return to the tried-and-true earlier format for those sections. It's worth another look at this new home as it were.

Artwork

We like the artwork in this new edition and received positive reviews. So it stays! Liturgical Press brought back the three artists from the 2018 edition: Deborah Luke, Tanja Butler, and Ned Bustard. The artwork, like that for 2018, is new and original, commissioned especially for this 2019 edition. We hope you enjoy this as much as you did the artwork in last year's edition.

Reflecting on the Gospel and Living the Paschal Mystery

Based on surveys and feedback, we know that the most frequented part of the book is "Reflecting on the Gospel," followed by "Living the Paschal Mystery," true to Sr. Joyce Ann's insight. Brian Schmisek wrote these pieces again, as he did last year, with that in mind. Especially because we are in the year of Luke, many of the themes tend to reflect the social tradition of the church, as well as Pope Francis's focus on mercy.

Focusing the Gospel, Connecting the Gospel, Connecting the Responsorial Psalm, Prompts for Faith Sharing, and Homily Points

Pages 2–3 of the material each week remain widely used. Katy Beedle Rice, an author new to this project, wrote these sections, drawing on the former structure including "Key words and phrases" and "To the point," as well as model prayers. Her insights as a mother, wife, and catechist shine through these sections.

Liturgy

Liturgy remains a primary focus of the book, and it is our good fortune to have Diana Macalintal's experience and knowledge forming the gist of this section. She continues to share her insight and practical advice honed by years of parish and diocesan ministry. From musical selections to commentary on the General Instruction of the Roman Missal, her words are filled with wisdom.

Purpose

The three authors for this book, Brian, Katy, and Diana, continue to retain its original and primary purpose: "to help people prepare for liturgy and live a liturgical spirituality (that is, a way of living that is rooted in liturgy), opening their vision to their baptismal identity as the Body of Christ and shaping their living according to the rhythm of paschal mystery dying and rising. The paschal mystery is the central focus of liturgy, of the gospels, and of this volume." We are humbled and privileged to be carrying on this task. We hope this work with its artful imagery assists many in living a liturgical spirituality. We are open to feedback and look forward to hearing from you about this renovated home for *Living Liturgy*™.

SEASON OF ADVENT

SPIRITUALITY

GOSPEL ACCLAMATION
Ps 84:8

R̦. Alleluia, alleluia.
Let us see, O Lord, your mercy
and give us your saving help.
R̦. Alleluia, alleluia.

Gospel

Luke 21:25-28, 34-36

Jesus said to his disciples: 'There will be signs in the sun and moon and stars; on earth nations in agony, bewildered by the clamour of the ocean and its waves; men dying of fear as they await what menaces the world, for the powers of heaven will be shaken. And then they will see the Son of Man coming in a cloud with power and great glory. When these things begin to take place, stand erect, hold your heads high, because your liberation is near at hand.

'Watch yourselves, or your hearts will be coarsened with debauchery and drunkenness and the cares of life, and that day will be sprung on you suddenly, like a trap. For it will come down on every living man on the face of the earth. Stay awake, praying at all times for the strength to survive all that is going to happen, and to stand with confidence before the Son of Man.'

Reflecting on the Gospel

Most of us look for meaning in the signs and events of daily life. We wonder how God might be acting in our lives. Was this a chance meeting with an old friend, or part of something greater? Was it a coincidence that I was thinking of this person when I received a call from him or her? Did the inclement weather keep me at home so I was able to spend time with my family? Not only we, but generations of those who have gone before us, discerned meaning in the events of daily life. The ancient pagan Romans looked at the sky for omens, and read the entrails of slaughtered chickens to discern how the gods were acting in their world.

The gospel reading for today gives the reader signs that will accompany the end times, the coming of the Son of Man. But we would be mistaken if we took these passages literally. And it's certainly true that hundreds if not thousands of people have done just that – looked for these signs to be fulfilled literally.

The message of this passage sought to give hope to a beleaguered people, the Christians, who anticipated their redemption. Many of them desperately wanted to see the coming of the Son of Man who would establish justice and peace. Many of the early Christians were on the bottom of the social ladder, experiencing tribulations and trials. Jesus himself had faced a violent end at the hands of the state. The Christians needed to be reminded that their salvation would come, and that they also needed to be vigilant, watching for that same salvation. And at the time this gospel was written there were many other Christians who may have lost hope or grown weary of waiting. This message was for them; and the message is also for us.

For us, the watching for the coming of the Son of Man has been not merely decades, as it was for the early Christians, but two millennia! Do we really believe that the end is near? that Jesus might return any day? It might be more worthwhile for me to imagine my own personal end (death) rather than the end of the world. In that way, it might be easier to see that my own personal end could catch me by surprise 'like a trap'. And when I live with the expectation that my end is near, or at least unknown, it can be easier for daily anxieties to dissipate. This is not to say we have no cares for the world, but rather, we have our eyes set on something greater as we live by a different set of values. Ideally, we serve more than we are served; we give more than we receive. And in that way we imitate Christ, whose disciples we are.

Living the Paschal Mystery

How would I live today if I knew it was my last day on the earth? What priorities would guide my choices and decisions? The church gives us the reading from Luke to start this Advent season in part so that we might call to mind the 'end times' and the concurrent coming of the Son of Man. When our minds are drowning in lists, shopping, groceries, and gifts, we might pause, raise our head above these pressing concerns, and reflect from another point of view. In the end, what does it all mean? What is driving my actions and behaviours? Am I watchful, vigilant for the Lord's coming? And what would such watchfulness look like? The dying and rising of Christ gives meaning to my own personal death and resurrection each season, when I set aside my own desires and aims and focus on something eternal, something lasting. It is then that we recall the relationships forged and celebrated on this earth endure forever. The coming of the Son of Man means death to an old way of life, and resurrection of hope and life everlasting.

Focusing the Gospel

Key words and phrases: When these things begin to take place, stand erect, hold your heads high, because your liberation is near at hand.

To the point: We begin a new church year with a gospel that seems intent upon shocking and startling us out of complacency. Jesus speaks of signs that will accompany the coming of the Son of Man. These signs are so terrifying that people are 'dying of fear', and yet, in the midst of it, we hear a word of hope: though these calamities may occur, 'stand erect, hold your heads high, because your liberation is near at hand'. To prepare for this redemption, Jesus counsels us to be vigilant in waiting and in prayer.

Connecting the Gospel

to the first reading: The prophet Jeremiah also preaches a word of hope, this time to the people of Israel in exile in Babylon. Even though they have seen their homeland taken over by foreign armies and their temple destroyed, Jeremiah reminds the people that their God has not forgotten them. Indeed, 'the days are coming – it is the Lord who speaks – when I am going to fulfil the promise I made to the House of Israel and the House of Judah'.

to experience: Jeremiah proclaims that God has a plan for Judah to be saved and for Jerusalem to dwell in safety. When we hear these words of comfort, taken together with today's gospel that speaks of calamities and dismay, we can know that the God of Jeremiah and Jesus, our God, is one who desires peace and for all people to dwell in safety. How might we preach peace, safety, and hope when we encounter panic, chaos, and despair?

Connecting the Responsorial Psalm

to the readings: The theme of hope and trust is evident in today's psalm. The psalmist prays, 'Lord, teach me your paths. / Make me walk in your truth, and teach me: / for you are God my saviour'. Like the prophet Jeremiah, the psalmist proclaims the constancy of God who is eager to guide the humble along the path of life. And how might we characterise this path of life in its essence? In the second reading, Paul, writing to the community in Thessalonica, gives us a clue. He concludes a prayer for their community by stating, 'May the Lord be generous in increasing your love and make you love one another and the whole human race'. This abounding love will strengthen the hearts of the community and shape them in holiness. It is abounding love that will allow them (and us) to stand erect to greet the Son of Man when he comes.

to psalmist preparation: This psalm is one of deep longing to know the ways of the Lord and to live in God's covenant. We are called to a practice of waiting within Advent – to live in the here and now, and also to yearn and work for the coming of the kingdom of God in its fulness. How do you practise a spirituality of waiting? How do you come to know the Lord?

PROMPTS FOR FAITH-SHARING

What is an action or practice of preparation you can embrace this Advent? It could be an action of preparing for Christmas, preparing for Jesus's second coming, or preparing our world to become more like the kingdom of God.

As Christians living in the year 2018 we realise that our own personal end will likely come before the second coming of Jesus. Thinking about your own mortality, how would you live this coming year if you knew it was your last on earth?

Advent is a time of preparation and a time of waiting. What spiritual practices make waiting fruitful for you?

Though today's gospel can seem disturbing, we are called to be people of hope and joy. As a Christian, how do you preach safety, peace, and hope when you encounter panic, chaos, and despair?

CELEBRATION

Model Penitential Act

Presider: In today's gospel Jesus speaks of the coming of the Son of Man. As we begin a new church year, let us ask for God's mercy and forgiveness, so as to be ready to greet Jesus when he comes again . . . [*pause*]

Lord Jesus, you are Son of God and Son of Man: Lord, have mercy.

Christ Jesus, you are the fulfilment of God's promise: Christ, have mercy.

Lord Jesus, you show us the path of holiness: Lord, have mercy.

Homily Points

• Advent is a season of preparation. We prepare our hearts and homes to celebrate the feast of Christmas. We prepare spiritually to greet Christ when he comes again. And we also look to how we can prepare our world to become more and more like the kingdom of God where love and justice rule. Advent is a time when we live this preparation in an intentional manner, but waiting and preparing are constant hallmarks of the Christian life.

• In the second reading, the apostle Paul reminds us that we have never arrived in this life. Our preparation is never complete. He exhorts the community in Thessalonica that even as they are conducting themselves in a way pleasing to God, that they 'make more and more progress'. The conduct that Paul calls the community to is one that has abounding love as its foundation and guide. As Christians, we never have a reason to be bored or complacent. Our work is never finished as we collaborate with Jesus in building a kingdom of love and peace.

• Despite the foreboding nature of our gospel reading today, as Christians we believe in a radical promise – that light is stronger than darkness, love is stronger than hate, and life is stronger than death. We are called to be signs of hope in a world at times overcome with fear. As we begin the physical preparations for Christmas by lighting our Advent wreaths, buying gifts, planning our feasts and parties for the Christmas season, let us also consider, how might we prepare ourselves to be light, love, and life to those around us?

Model Universal Prayer (Prayer of the Faithful)

Presider: Let us present our needs to the Lord, confident in his love and mercy.

Response: Lord, hear our prayer.

That the church be a beacon of hope in troubled times . . .

That all people throughout the world dwell in safety and work for justice . . .

That those who suffer from depression, anxiety, and mental illness might know the love and tender care of the God of hope . . .

That each of us here might give up our daily anxieties so as to live more fully into God's promise of peace . . .

Presider: God of abounding love, you call us to live with you in holiness and peace. Grant our prayers that we might grow closer to you each day. We ask this through Christ our Lord. Amen.

COLLECT

Let us pray.

Pause for silent prayer

Grant your faithful, we pray, almighty God,
the resolve to run forth to meet your Christ
with righteous deeds at his coming,
so that, gathered at his right hand,
they may be worthy to possess
the heavenly Kingdom.
Through our Lord Jesus Christ, your Son,
who lives and reigns with you
in the unity of the Holy Spirit,
one God, for ever and ever. **Amen.**

FIRST READING
Jer 33:14-16

See, the days are coming – it is the Lord who speaks – when I am going to fulfil the promise I made to the House of Israel and the House of Judah:

'In those days and at that time,
I will make a virtuous Branch grow
    for David,
who shall practise honesty and integrity
    in the land.
In those days Judah shall be saved
and Israel shall dwell in confidence.
And this is the name the city will
    be called:
The Lord-our-integrity.'

CATECHESIS

RESPONSORIAL PSALM
Ps 24:4-5, 8-9, 10, 14 (1)

R︎. To you, O Lord, I lift up my soul.

Lord, make me know your ways.
Lord, teach me your paths.
Make me walk in your truth, and teach me:
for you are God my saviour.

R︎. To you, O Lord, I lift up my soul.

The Lord is good and upright.
He shows the path to those who stray,
he guides the humble in the right path;
he teaches his way to the poor.

R︎. To you, O Lord, I lift up my soul.

His ways are faithfulness and love
for those who keep his covenant and will.
The Lord's friendship is for those who
    revere him;
to them he reveals his covenant.

R︎. To you, O Lord, I lift up my soul.

SECOND READING
1 Thess 3:12-4:2

May the Lord be generous in increasing your love and make you love one another and the whole human race as much as we love you. And may he so confirm your hearts in holiness that you may be blameless in the sight of our God and Father when our Lord Jesus Christ comes with all his saints.

Finally, brothers, we urge you and appeal to you in the Lord Jesus to make more and more progress in the kind of life that you are meant to live: the life that God wants, as you learnt from us, and as you are already living it. You have not forgotten the instructions we gave you on the authority of the Lord Jesus.

About Liturgy
Be vigilant: We may be able to control our own personal practices and even our parish culture, but we will never be able to control how other people observe the weeks leading up to Christmas. We can ensure that we omit the Gloria at Mass during Advent (except for solemnities, weddings, and confirmation), but people will still sing and play Christmas songs in their households and social gatherings. No matter how long you refrain from putting up your own Christmas tree, many others will have theirs fully decorated in November! And no amount of preaching will convince the majority of your parishioners that they should be spending more time in quiet prayer than in shopping for gifts and going to Christmas parties.

As much as we want all Christians to keep prayerful, sober watch in anticipation of the coming of the Lord, we cannot become 'Advent police', because the exhortation to vigilance goes both ways. We, too, must be vigilant that our behaviour and attitudes help us with 'increasing [our] love and make [us] love one another and the whole human race' (1 Thess 3:12). One way you can do this is to learn and participate in some of the Advent practices of cultures that are different from yours. For many Hispanic and Asian communities, Advent is a time of prayer and parties, of joyful music and quiet contemplation. There is a beautiful grace, too, in this kind of waiting for the day of the Lord.

As those who help shape the unique spirit of Advent in our communities, let us help one another be attentive to God's presence all around us so that our hearts may not become 'coarsened with the cares of life'.

About Initiation
Today is not a beginning: Although today is the beginning of the new liturgical year, it is not the beginning of RCIA. There is no formal 'beginning' to the first period of the Rite of Christian Initiation of Adults, which is the period of evangelisation and precatechumenate. We should be evangelising all year long and be ready to meet seekers every day of the year! To help your community understand that evangelisation is year-round and to avoid any misconception that catechumens are formed on a school-year calendar, do not schedule a Rite of Acceptance for this Sunday. Instead, plan to celebrate it a few times during Ordinary Time throughout the year.

About Liturgical Music
Metre and melody: Because the Advent season is so short, it is a good time to incorporate seasonal songs that are used every Sunday of Advent. This helps your assembly become more familiar with the music over the weeks, especially if you may have more visitors and newcomers this time of year. It also sets a musical 'environment' that is both constant and developing. One way to strike this balance is to use a seasonal hymn tune for the entrance song, such as CONDITOR ALME SIDERUM (more correctly CREATOR ALME SIDERUM), and each week pair it with different texts. To do this, find texts that match the tune's metre, which is LM (or 88 88, meaning there are four phrases of eight syllables each). Some text examples from *Laudate* might be 'Creator of the Stars of Night', which is the most common for this tune; 'Before the Earth' by David M. Young; 'Lift Up Your Heads, You Mighty Gates', translated by Catherine Winkworth; 'On Jordan's Bank', translated by John Chandler. As you explore your own music resources, be sure that the stressed syllables of the text match the natural stresses of the tune.

2 DECEMBER 2018
FIRST SUNDAY OF ADVENT

GOSPEL ACCLAMATION
Cf. Luke 1:28

R̸. Alleluia, alleluia.
Hail, Mary, full of grace; the Lord is with thee!
Blessed art thou among women.
R̸. Alleluia, alleluia.

Gospel

Luke 1:26-38

**The angel Gabriel was sent by God
to a town in Galilee called Nazareth,
to a virgin betrothed to a man named
Joseph, of the house of David; and the
virgin's name was Mary. He went in and
said to her, 'Rejoice, so highly favoured!
The Lord is with you.' She was deeply
disturbed by these words and asked
herself what this greeting could mean,
but the angel said to her, 'Mary, do not
be afraid; you have won God's favour.
Listen! You are to conceive and bear a
son, and you must name him Jesus. He
will be great and will be called Son of
the Most High. The Lord God will give
him the throne of his ancestor David;
he will rule over the House of Jacob
for ever and his reign will have no end.'**

Continued in Appendix, p. 269.

See Appendix, p. 269, for the other readings.

Reflecting on the Gospel

The immaculate conception is a difficult concept for adults to grasp, much less children. Though it is a basic element of faith, it is the source of never-ending confusion and much explanatory catechesis. Frankly, the issue is not made easier when the reading for this solemnity narrates the conception of Jesus (also known as the annunciation) and not the immaculate conception (the conception of Mary). But as we know, there is no scriptural passage that narrates the conception of Mary, so the church gives us the story about the conception of Jesus! No wonder confusion abounds.

We recall that every Marian title ultimately says more about Jesus than it does about Mary. And that is certainly true with the immaculate conception, which claims that the salvific effects of what God has done in Christ preserved Mary from sin from the moment of her conception. Thus, the salvific power of the Christ-event transcends time, reaches back as it were, and has an effect on Mary herself as she is conceived.

For most of the history of the church this doctrine remained in the realm of theological inquiry and/or speculation. Not until the mid-nineteenth century was this formally proclaimed as doctrine by Pope Pius IX.

Upon reading the gospel for the day we may turn our attention to Mary's faith in God and her openness to the Lord's will. Mary is known and celebrated throughout the world for this characteristic, among many others. Her yes (in Latin, *fiat*, or 'let what you have said be done to me') shows her willingness to cooperate with God for the salvation of humanity. Her attitude and character were called 'immaculate' by many early church fathers even if they were not referring to her conception. She was so open, pure, and devoted to God that she was willing to become an unwed mother in an age when that meant punishment and death under the law. Her character was understood to be immaculate from the moment of her conception by a singularly unique gift.

We can understand and appreciate some confusion regarding the meaning of this feast, which celebrates Mary's immaculate character from the moment of conception, by reading from the gospel about the conception of Jesus by Mary's own word of *fiat*.

Living the Paschal Mystery

Ours is an adult faith with fairly sophisticated concepts and theological insights. Not only do we have sacred texts, but we have a tradition of faith with a capital 'T' carried through the ages by saints, martyrs, popes, and the people of God. For some it becomes something of a theological parlour game to know and recite Catholic trivia with names, dates, historical underpinnings, and whimsical theories consigned to the dustbin of theological inquiry. But our faith is much more than an intellectual head-trip. Faith in Christ is about doing much more than knowing, though both have their rightful place. Never once in the gospels does Jesus say people will be judged by what they know. Instead, he often admonishes his audiences about what they do, or rather, do not do. On this feast day of the Immaculate Conception we certainly nod to the theological history and development of doctrine that gives us today's celebration. But we might also remind ourselves that we are to be doers of the word, and not mere hearers.

Focusing the Gospel

Key words and phrases: [F]or nothing is impossible to God.

To the point: In the second reading we hear God's plan of salvation, which is '[b]efore the world was made, he chose us, chose us in Christ, / to be holy and spotless, and to live through love in his presence'. In Mary we see this plan perfected. She is sustained by Gabriel's promise that 'nothing is impossible to God'. We, too, believe in a God of infinite possibilities and can trust in this plan of salvation.

Model Penitential Act

Presider: In today's second reading we hear that we have been chosen before the foundation of the world to be holy and without blemish before God. Let us pause to ask for God's mercy and pardon for the times we have not lived up to this call . . . [*pause*]

Lord Jesus, you are Son of God and son of Mary: Lord, have mercy.

Christ Jesus, you have blessed us with every spiritual blessing: Christ, have mercy.

Lord Jesus, you call us to holiness: Lord, have mercy.

Model Universal Prayer (Prayer of the Faithful)

Presider: Let us bring our intentions before the Lord, believing as Mary did that nothing is impossible for God.

Response: Lord, hear our prayer.

That the church be a spiritual mother for all who seek comfort and shelter within her arms . . .

That all people might know of the love and mercy of God . . .

That those in need, especially pregnant women, might find support and security . . .

That all those gathered here might renew their commitment to 'let what you have said be done to me' . . .

Presider: God of infinite love, for whom all things are possible, you call us to be holy and without blemish in your sight. Hear the prayers we bring to you today for ourselves and for our world, through Christ Jesus our Lord. Amen.

COLLECT

Let us pray.

Pause for silent prayer

O God, who by the Immaculate Conception of the Blessed Virgin
prepared a worthy dwelling for your Son,
grant, we pray,
that, as you preserved her from every stain
by virtue of the Death of your Son, which you foresaw,
so, through her intercession,
we, too, may be cleansed and admitted to your presence.
Through our Lord Jesus Christ, your Son,
who lives and reigns with you in the unity of the Holy Spirit,
one God, for ever and ever. **Amen.**

FOR REFLECTION

• In Mary we find a model of discipleship. Just as Mary was invited to bear Christ to the world, we are also called to be Christ-bearers. How do you bear Christ to the world?

• The angel Gabriel proclaims to Mary, '[N]othing is impossible to God'. Where do you need to hear this proclamation in your own life?

• As God protected Mary from sin from the moment of her conception, he also desires to wash all sin from us. What spiritual practices reveal God's forgiveness to you?

Homily Points

• The church fathers have taught us that in her immaculate conception the Blessed Virgin Mary was protected from Original Sin from the very moment of her creation in the womb of her mother Anne. In the first reading today we witness Adam and Eve in the Garden of Eden making choices that separate them from the ideal relationship they enjoyed with God up to that point. Now, instead of walking with God in the garden, Adam hides as God calls, 'Where are you'?

• In our lives as Christians we, too, are invited to walk with God. In what areas in our lives does God call to us, 'Where are you'?

SPIRITUALITY

℞. Alleluia, alleluia.
Prepare a way for the Lord,
make his paths straight,
and all mankind shall see the salvation of God.
℞. Alleluia, alleluia.

Gospel

Luke 3:1-6

**In the fifteenth year of
Tiberius Caesar's reign,
when Pontius Pilate was
governor of Judaea, Herod
tetrarch of Galilee, his brother
Philip tetrarch of the lands of Ituraea
and Trachonitis, Lysanias tetrarch
of Abilene, during the pontificate of
Annas and Caiaphas, the word of God
came to John son of Zechariah, in the
wilderness. He went through the whole
Jordan district proclaiming a baptism
of repentance for the forgiveness of
sins, as it is written in the book of
sayings of the prophet Isaiah:**

> **A voice cries in the wilderness:
> Prepare a way for the Lord,
> make his paths straight.
> Every valley will be filled in,
> every mountain and hill be laid low,
> winding ways will be straightened
> and rough roads made smooth.
> And all mankind shall see the
> salvation of God.**

Reflecting on the Gospel

After his introductory material, including the infancy narratives in chapters 1 and 2, Luke picks up the gospel story he inherited from Mark. That is, today's reading from Luke is based on the opening verses of the Gospel of Mark with important additions. Beginning with John the Baptist's preaching, Luke situates the Christ-event in a particular historical time and place, for, as he tells us in Acts 26:26, these things did not happen in a corner. And it is precisely because of Luke's desire to give us the historical details that scholars can be fairly confident of their dating. Luke cites both civil and religious leaders to situate the Christ-event in history. The Emperor Tiberius, who reigned from AD 14 to 36, succeeded Caesar Augustus, which means that the fifteenth year of Tiberius's reign could be anywhere from AD 27 to 29 depending on how one counts the years. This is the most specific date given by Luke in this passage; the other figures named by Luke all fall within a wider range than that. For example, Pontius Pilate served from AD 26 to 36.

The historical details do much for the modern Christian (and ancient Christian for that matter) in demonstrating that Jesus was a historical figure. The Christ-event is not a mere myth like so many other Greek and Roman tales. Jesus was a living, breathing Jewish human being who lived in the Roman Empire in the province of Judea. These things did not happen in a corner (cf. Acts 26:26).

Once the events are situated in their historical setting, Luke continues the narrative with the story about John the Baptist, whose birth is recounted in the first chapter. There we hear the story of Zechariah and Elizabeth having a child even though Elizabeth is barren. It is Luke who essentially makes John a cousin of Jesus, a detail found nowhere else in the New Testament. The appellation of John as 'son of Zechariah' (Luke 3:2) is a nod to the story in the first chapter.

These details alone – the historical setting and the familial relationship between John and Jesus – tell us we are dealing with a unique author who has his own theological insights to convey. Luke is a gifted storyteller, theologian, and evangelist. We do well to read his story carefully.

Living the Paschal Mystery

Christians believe in the person Jesus, the Christ, the son of the Living God. Jesus walked this earth, breathed the air, enjoyed the sunshine, had meaningful relationships, and ultimately suffered death at the hands of the state. His story really happened: it is not myth, make believe, or something we simply tell children so they will be nice to one another. Luke is an evangelist who gives us the details, which allow scholars to situate the life of Jesus in a historical context. The names of civil and religious leaders like Tiberius, Pontius Pilate, Herod, Philip, and others throughout the gospel are known by ancient pagan sources as well. They form something of an anchor or peg upon which to hang a timeline for Jesus and his ministry. In the language of another gospel, this is the story of the Word made flesh in a given time and place.

Jesus lived in a province ruled by Rome and was executed by that ruling power. Though put to death by the state he was raised up by God, giving us the paschal mystery. On this Second Sunday of Advent we pause to reflect on Jesus's historical circumstances and our own, knowing that death is not the end.

Focusing the Gospel

Key words and phrases: [T]he word of God came to John son of Zechariah, in the wilderness [desert]. . . . Prepare a way for the Lord.

To the point: Earlier in the Gospel of Luke we hear of John the Baptist's childhood in which '[t]he child grew and became strong in spirit, and he was in the desert until the day of his manifestation to Israel' (1:80; NABRE). This desert time is important for John's formation as the preacher we hear in the gospel today. In the desert one must listen. John proclaims the words of the prophet Isaiah to the people, 'Prepare a way for the Lord'. These words were addressed originally to the Israelites in exile in Babylon. The way being prepared was the way the Lord would lead them out of exile and restore them to their homeland. Now John invites his listeners to undertake an interior way of repentance.

Connecting the Gospel

to the first and second readings: In the gospel we hear of John the Baptist drawing close to God in the desert. In the first two readings both the apostle Paul and the prophet Baruch are undergoing their own 'desert' experiences. Paul is writing to the Christian community at Philippi from a prison. Baruch preaches a word of hope to the people of Israel in exile in Babylon.

to experience: While difficult, desert experiences often serve to sharpen our faith and put our lives into focus. Where is the desert in your life right now? How might God be speaking to you in the desert?

Connecting the Responsorial Psalm

to the readings: Psalm 125 is one of pure joy and exultation. A people that were taken captive and exiled to another land are restored to security and prosperity in their homeland. This exultation is echoed by the prophet Baruch in the first reading. Baruch speaks to the city of Jerusalem mourning the loss of her children in the Babylonian exile. Baruch reassures her, saying, '[T]urn your eyes to the east: / see your sons reassembled from west and east / at the command of the Holy One, jubilant that God has remembered them'. Another prophet raises his voice in the gospel reading: John the Baptist. Unlike the psalm and the first reading, the gospel sounds harsher in some ways. Broaching no nonsense, John calls the people to a baptism of repentance. His call, though, is also reason to rejoice. Our God is one who does not turn his back on sinners. Instead, God wishes to restore all those who have fallen 'captive' to sin. And when that happens '[t]hose who are sowing in tears / will sing when they reap'.

to psalmist preparation: As you prepare to sing this psalm, reflect on moments of great joy in your own life. When has your mouth been filled with laughter and your tongue sung for joy? How might you express this overflowing joy to those in the assembly?

PROMPTS FOR FAITH-SHARING

As we prepare the way for Jesus to be born anew into our hearts this Christmas, what are the valleys we are called to fill in? Which mountains within our lives (pride, greed, anger) must be made low?

In his letter to the Philippians St. Paul writes, 'My prayer is that your love for each other may increase more and more and never stop improving your knowledge and deepening your perception so that you can always recognise what is best' (1:9-10). How might we fulfill that prayer within our own lives?

Both John and Jesus experience a period of time in the desert before taking on their public ministry. Where might you cultivate desert places in your life where you go to be with God in solitude and prayer?

As a parish how might you prepare to welcome with love and joy the people who will join your community to celebrate Christmas?

CELEBRATION

Model Penitential Act

Presider: In today's gospel John the Baptist proclaims a baptism of repentance for the forgiveness of sins. For the areas in our own lives crying for repentance and forgiveness, we ask for God's mercy. . . [*pause*]

Lord Jesus, you are the way, the truth and the life: Lord, have mercy.

Christ Jesus, you show us the way of salvation: Christ, have mercy.

Lord Jesus, you call us to repentance: Lord, have mercy.

Homily Points

• The word of God comes to John the Baptist in the desert. We are not told what this word is but we see the result: John leaves his life of solitude and prayer to proclaim a baptism of repentance for the forgiveness of sins. As the forerunner of Jesus, John's work is to prepare the people to receive the one who is coming, the one who is 'the salvation of God'. John has been prepared for his mission by his life in the desert. Later Jesus will also follow this path. After being baptised in the Jordan, he will be led into the desert by the Spirit where he will fast and pray for forty days and forty nights.

• A few hundred years later, around the third century AD, a group of monks and nuns return to the desert to live lives of solitude and prayer. These Desert Fathers and Mothers left behind words of wisdom and a model for living the spiritual life. Although we may not be able to follow their austere example, we can cultivate areas of stillness and quiet in our own lives.

• Advent and Lent, our two seasons of preparation in the church year, provide annual opportunities for us to enter into the desert on retreat. We are given time to follow in the footsteps of Jesus, John, and the Desert Fathers and Mothers to listen to God away from all distractions. Where can you find space in your life to cultivate interior silence and contemplation? How might you set aside time for deep listening to the word of God?

Model Universal Prayer (Prayer of the Faithful)

Presider: Heeding the call of John the Baptist, we pray for the strength and wisdom to '[p]repare a way for the Lord'.

Response: Lord, hear our prayer.

That the Church offer welcome to those seeking the way of repentance . . .

That all peoples of the world realign their lives with mercy and justice . . .

That those who are experiencing imprisonment or exile might know the unchanging love of God. . .

That each of us here may undertake the work of preparing a way for the Lord in our own lives. . .

Presider: God of justice and mercy, you speak a word of hope and promise to us in the desert areas of our lives. Hear our prayers that we might draw ever nearer to you in this season of Advent. Through Christ our Lord. Amen.

COLLECT

Let us pray.

Pause for silent prayer

Almighty and merciful God,
may no earthly undertaking
    hinder those
who set out in haste to meet
    your Son,
but may our learning
of heavenly wisdom
gain us admittance to his company.
Who lives and reigns with you
    in the unity of the Holy Spirit,
one God, for ever and ever. **Amen.**

FIRST READING
Bar 5:1-9

Jerusalem, take off your dress of sorrow
    and distress,
put on the beauty of the glory of God
    for ever,
wrap the cloak of the integrity of God
    around you,
put the diadem of the glory of the Eternal
    on your head:
since God means to show your splendour
    to every nation under heaven,
since the name God gives you for ever
    will be,
'Peace through integrity, and honour
    through devotedness.'
Arise, Jerusalem, stand on the heights
and turn your eyes to the east:
see your sons reassembled from west
    and east
at the command of the Holy One, jubilant
    that God has remembered them.
Though they left you on foot,
with enemies for an escort,
now God brings them back to you
like royal princes carried back in glory.
For God has decreed the flattening
of each high mountain, of the
    everlasting hills,
the filling of the valleys to make the
    ground level
so that Israel can walk in safety under the
    glory of God.
And the forests and every fragrant tree
    will provide shade
for Israel at the command of God;
for God will guide Israel in joy by the light
    of his glory
with his mercy and integrity for escort.

CATECHESIS

RESPONSORIAL PSALM
Ps 125 (3)

R℣. What marvels the Lord worked for us!
Indeed we were glad.

When the Lord delivered Zion
　　from bondage
it seemed like a dream.
Then was our mouth filled with laughter,
on our lips there were songs.

R℣. What marvels the Lord worked for us!
Indeed we were glad.

The heathens themselves said:
　　'What marvels
the Lord worked for them!'
What marvels the Lord worked for us!
Indeed we were glad.

R℣. What marvels the Lord worked for us!
Indeed we were glad.

Deliver us, O Lord, from our bondage
as streams in dry land.
Those who are sowing in tears
will sing when they reap.

R℣. What marvels the Lord worked for us!
Indeed we were glad.

They go out, they go out, full of tears
carrying seed for the sowing:
they come back, they come back, full
　　of song,
carrying their sheaves.

R℣. What marvels the Lord worked for us!
Indeed we were glad.

SECOND READING
Phil 1:4-6, 8-11

Every time I pray for all of you, I pray with joy, remembering how you have helped to spread the Good News from the day you first heard it right up to the present. I am quite certain that the One who began this good work in you will see that it is finished when the Day of Christ Jesus comes. God knows how much I miss you all, loving you as Christ Jesus loves you. My prayer is that your love for each other may increase more and more and never stop improving your knowledge and deepening your perception so that you can always recognise what is best. This will help you to become pure and blameless, and prepare you for the Day of Christ, when you will reach the perfect goodness which Jesus Christ produces in us for the glory and praise of God.

About Liturgy

Prepare the way: I do a lot of airline travel so I'm quite familiar with airport security protocols and I know the best ways to get through screening lines quickly and without much hassle. Except during the holidays. That's when all the once- or twice-a-year travellers come out. They always bring way too much luggage, never have their IDs and boarding passes ready, and usually end up right in front of me in the security queue. I used to roll my eyes every time I saw them and grumble under my breath. Why couldn't they know more about airport etiquette and be a road warrior like me?

That is until I had a conversation with a harried single mom while waiting at security. She was taking three excited kids and a sullen teenager to Disneyland. She had scraped and sacrificed for several years to save up just enough to pay for the entire trip on her own. Yet the airport was the hardest part of the journey for her because she was deathly afraid to fly. None of her kids had been on a plane before, and she hadn't flown since she was a child herself, but she was determined to give her children a bit of joy after so many years of just getting by. Her story, grit, and courage helped me see my inexperienced travel companions with a bit more compassion and even admiration.

How might it change our perception of those Christmas and Easter Catholics who start making their way to our parishes this time of year if we saw them less as a nuisance or burden and more like Christ for whom we wait? What if the road we are called to make straight is meant to be for them? What if we made every effort to ease their path to Christ with sincere and radical hospitality? We will not know how many obstacles they have had to navigate just to get to our doors unless we long for them with the affection of Christ. Then perhaps all those of us who are travellers on the road will see the salvation of God together.

About Liturgical Music

Singing by ear and by heart: Many people today do not read music. It is simply a reality. While we need to do our part to promote more music-reading literacy in our communities, we should also aid those who may feel discouraged or put off by music they perceive to be complicated. This doesn't mean that we need to water down our liturgical music. It simply challenges us to look for melodies that can be learned easily by ear and are grounded in strong texts, and with settings that are flexible enough to be enhanced by a choir or additional instruments. Two such pieces for this Sunday are found in *Music from Taizé* and the *Psallite* project. First, 'Prepare the Way of the Lord' (Taizé Community) is a four-part round that can be learned quickly by an assembly. Once the assembly is confident with the melody, the choir can complement the assembly line with the canon. You could even invite the entire assembly to join in the canon as well, dividing parts by men and women or by sections of the church. The refrain of 'Arise Jerusalem, Stand on the Height' (Collegeville Composers Group), with its exhortation to 'open your hearts', can be a powerful antiphon the assembly sings during the communion procession while cantors or a schola lead the verses.

9 DECEMBER 2018
SECOND SUNDAY OF ADVENT

SPIRITUALITY

GOSPEL ACCLAMATION
Isa 61:1 (Luke 4:18)

R̷. Alleluia, alleluia.
The spirit of the Lord has been given to me.
He has sent me to bring good news to the poor.
R̷. Alleluia, alleluia.

Gospel   Luke 3:10-18

When all the people asked John, 'What must we do?' he answered, 'If anyone has two tunics he must share with the man who has none, and the one with something to eat must do the same.' There were tax collectors too who came for baptism, and these said to him, 'Master what must we do?' He said to them, 'Exact no more than your rate.' Some soldiers asked him in their turn, 'What about us? What must we do?' He said to them, 'No intimidation! No extortion! Be content with your pay!'

A feeling of expectancy had grown among the people, who were beginning to think that John might be the Christ, so John declared before them all, 'I baptise you with water, but someone is coming, someone who is more powerful than I am, and I am not fit to undo the strap of his sandals; he will baptise you with the Holy Spirit and fire. His winnowing-fan is in his hand to clear his threshing-floor and to gather the wheat into his barn; but the chaff he will burn in a fire that will never go out.' As well as this, there were many other things he said to exhort the people and to announce the Good News to them.

Reflecting on the Gospel

We hear the preaching of John the Baptist today, the Third Sunday of Advent. We are moving towards the imminent coming of the Son of Man. John would have been a fine preacher of the fire and brimstone variety, motivating his audience to action. Three times different groups ask him, 'What must we do?' And three times John has an answer founded in justice and mercy. Follow the rules; share with those who have not. This is fairly simple and straightforward advice. And because of it he was thought to be the Messiah.

We can almost feel the crowd's anticipation and excitement. Here is someone who is preaching justice and mercy. By the crowd's ready reception of this message we might imagine that justice and mercy were in short supply. Soldiers might have taken more than their due, as did the tax collectors. Mercy, giving another a cloak when you have two, seems to have been wanting. The reception of the message tells us something about the crowds, who likely were on the lower economic rungs of society.

Furthermore, John tells them that this is only the beginning. Another is coming. Rather than a message of peace, John tells them that the one to come bears a winnowing fan. Though today many might not be familiar with the term, a winnowing fan was a fork-like shovel. The winnower used the fan to throw wheat grains into the air. The heavy kernels would fall to the ground and the lighter chaff would be blown away, gathered up, and burned. John the Baptist used this vivid image to speak of what the 'one who is to come' would do.

Being burned in an 'in a fire that will never go out' seems a distant image from the 'lilies of the field' Jesus that Luke will narrate later in his gospel. This might cause us to wonder, were John's expectations met? Perhaps in his fire-and-brimstone preaching he was hoping for a fiery judgement. And this could be the reason he sent messengers to Jesus later in the gospel asking him, 'Are you the one who is to come, or should we look for another'? (Luke 7:19; NABRE). John's own expectation of a Messiah who would bring judgement, wrath, and 'a fire that will never go out' might not have been met by Jesus. John would not be the first to have dashed expectations and hopes. Jesus has another way. Still, John's essential message of practising justice and mercy are good ways to prepare for Christ's coming.

Living the Paschal Mystery

John the Baptist's simple message of justice and mercy has global ramifications in the modern world. Though it's easy to glance backward and recognise the challenges faced by those in the ancient world, John's message is for us too. There are those today who are cheated out of wages and/or benefits by others who game the system. Many of us might even benefit (intentionally or not) from a system that encourages unjust practices when it comes to labour conditions or wages and benefits. Those in the developed world have the equivalent of multiple cloaks while many throughout the world go without. While it might be rare for us to see outright pilfering of wages, more often we can encounter poor working conditions, a minimum wage that requires 120 hours of work each week to support a family, or cheap goods whose real costs are borne far away. What are the values that guide our lives? How are we to live in preparation for the coming of the Son of Man? Justice and mercy are a sure foundation.

Focusing the Gospel

Key words and phrases: '[A]ll the people asked John, "What must we do?"'

To the point: After hearing John's preaching, the people who have gathered around him are inspired to take action in their own lives. Three times we hear the question repeated in this gospel passage, 'What must we do?' The crowds, then the tax collectors, and finally the soldiers ask. And three times John replies to this question. He tells the crowds to share their excess with those that have nothing. He instructs the tax collectors and soldiers to practise fairness and prudence in their professions. John's good news requires action and sows seeds for the kingdom of God of which Jesus will preach.

Connecting the Gospel

to the first and second readings: In today's set of readings we have an unusual situation where the Old Testament and epistle connect seamlessly with each other while the gospel seems to be on its own. In the first two readings we hear the theme of rejoicing loud and clear. The prophet Zephaniah tells us to '[s]hout for joy . . .'! while the apostle Paul exhorts, 'I want you to be happy, always happy in the Lord'. Both readings announce the nearness of God and tell us not to be afraid. In the gospel, John the Baptist strikes a sterner tone. He gives clear examples of the actions the people must take in order to demonstrate their repentance. He ends with a powerful image of Jesus with winnowing fan in hand ready to gather the harvest while destroying the chaff. This gospel, however sombre, is also a reason to rejoice. John's call from God to preach to the people shows that it is not too late for them to return to God. They, too, can have lives free from fear and full of rejoicing. The One who is the source of complete joy and peace calls to them.

to experience: The season of Advent is halfway over and Christmas is drawing near. How does God call to you to let go of anxieties and make room for the joy of Christmas?

Connecting the Responsorial Psalm

to the readings: The psalm today comes from the book of the prophet Isaiah. These verses cap off a section in Isaiah called the Book of Emmanuel (6:1-12:6). The name Emmanuel, which means 'God with us', is not directly heard in the psalm or the readings for today, but we hear echoes of this theme. The prophet Zephaniah proclaims, 'The Lord your God is in your midst'. The apostle Paul writes, 'the Lord is very near'. And in the psalm itself we hear, 'People of Zion, sing and shout for joy / for great in your midst is the Holy One of Israel'.

to psalmist preparation: We are approaching Christmas, the feast of the Incarnation, when God chose to become a human being to draw near to us. As you prepare to proclaim this psalm of thanksgiving and joy, pause to reflect on how you have experienced Emmanuel, 'God with us', in your own life.

Model Penitential Act

PROMPTS FOR FAITH-SHARING

The prophet Zephaniah tells us, 'The Lord your God is in your midst'. How have you experienced God in your midst this past week?

In today's second reading St. Paul exhorts us, 'There is no need to worry'. What anxieties are you dealing with right now in your life? How might you give these anxieties over to God?

In today's gospel the people ask John the Baptist, 'What must we do?' As you enter into the final nine days of Advent, what is one action you might take to serve Jesus's mission of mercy and justice?

This is Gaudete Sunday, a Sunday for joy even as we continue the season of Advent preparing our hearts and minds for Christmas. Are there Christmas preparations that are causing you stress and worry? Can you trade them in or let go of them in order to allow room for more joy?

CELEBRATION

Presider: On this Gaudete Sunday, we are reminded to rejoice always in the Lord. As we prepare to enter into this celebration, we reflect on how we have lived this call to joy. . . [*pause*]

    Lord Jesus, you baptise with the holy Spirit and fire: Lord, have mercy.

    Christ Jesus, you are the promised Messiah: Christ, have mercy.

    Lord Jesus, you show us the way of kindness and joy: Lord, have mercy.

Homily Points

• In her book, *The Religious Potential of the Child*, theologian Sofia Cavalletti says, 'It is only in love, and not in fear, that one may have a moral life worthy of the name'. In the gospel we hear the people gathered around John the Baptist ask him, 'What must we do?' They want to offer a fitting response to the baptism of repentance they have experienced. Today we have the stern exhortations of John paired with the injunction from the apostle Paul, 'I want you to be happy, always happy in the Lord; I repeat, what I want is your happiness'. We are called not only to do good but to do good with joy and love.

• In today's readings we hear the source of our joy proclaimed: 'the Lord is very near' and God is in our midst. Our belief in Emmanuel, 'God with us', is central to our lives as Christians. It shapes our relationship with God and others and calls us to be living signs of God's presence in the world. When we live from this central belief we naturally desire to do what is right in honour of our relationship with God.

• John the Baptist lifts up the image of Jesus with winnowing fan in hand, ready to 'gather the wheat into his barn' and burn the chaff with 'a fire that will never go out'. Advent can be seen as a time to clear away the chaff in our own lives. Out of love for God and for our neighbour we can ask, what are the things that separate us from experiencing God in our daily lives? Where have we failed to live the moral life with joy and love? We are now over halfway through with Advent. As Christmas draws closer may we intensify our prayer for Jesus to send the fire of his love to purify our hearts and minds anew.

Model Universal Prayer (Prayer of the Faithful)

Presider: Today St. Paul exhorts us, 'There is no need to worry; but if there is anything you need, pray for it, asking God for it with prayer and thanksgiving'. In this spirit let us offer our petitions.

Response: Lord, hear our prayer.

That the church may be a sign of joy in the world . . .

That all people may know the 'peace of God, which is so much greater than we can understand' . . .

That those who are experiencing loneliness and despair in this Advent season might be comforted . . .

That each of us here may open ourselves to the question, 'what must I do'? and be prepared to take action to spread joy and kindness in our families and communities . . .

Presider: God of joy, you call us to let go of our anxieties and to trust in your bountiful love and peace. Hear our prayers that we may become living signs of your tender care for all. Through Christ our Lord. Amen.

COLLECT

Let us pray.

Pause for silent prayer

O God, who see how your people
faithfully await the feast
    of the Lord's Nativity,
enable us, we pray,
to attain the joys of so great
    a salvation
and to celebrate them always
with solemn worship
    and glad rejoicing.
Through our Lord Jesus Christ, your Son,
who lives and reigns with you
    in the unity of the Holy Spirit,
one God, for ever and ever. **Amen.**

FIRST READING

Zeph 3:14-18

Shout for joy, daughter of Zion,
Israel, shout aloud!
Rejoice, exult with all your heart,
daughter of Jerusalem!
The Lord has repealed your sentence;
he has driven your enemies away.
The Lord, the king of Israel, is in
    your midst;
you have no more evil to fear.
When that day comes, word will come
    to Jerusalem:
Zion, have no fear,
do not let your hands fall limp.
The Lord your God is in your midst,
a victorious warrior.
He will exult with joy over you,
he will renew you by his love;
he will dance with shouts of joy for you
as on a day of festival.

RESPONSORIAL PSALM

Isa 12:2-6 (6)

R̸. Sing and shout for joy for great in your midst is the Holy One of Israel.

Truly, God is my salvation,
I trust, I shall not fear.
For the Lord is my strength, my song,
he became my saviour.
With joy you will draw water
from the wells of salvation.

R̸. Sing and shout for joy for great in your midst is the Holy One of Israel.

Give thanks to the Lord, give praise to his name!
Make his mighty deeds known to the peoples!
Declare the greatness of his name.

R̸. Sing and shout for joy for great in your midst is the Holy One of Israel.

Sing a psalm to the Lord
for he has done glorious deeds,
make them known to all the earth!
People of Zion, sing and shout for joy
for great in your midst is the Holy One
of Israel.

R̸. Sing and shout for joy for great in your midst is the Holy One of Israel.

SECOND READING

Phil 4:4-7

I want you to be happy, always happy in the Lord; I repeat, what I want is your happiness. Let your tolerance be evident to everyone: the Lord is very near. There is no need to worry; but if there is anything you need, pray for it, asking God for it with prayer and thanksgiving, and that peace of God, which is so much greater than we can understand, will guard your hearts and your thoughts, in Christ Jesus.

About Liturgy

No sourpusses allowed: In Joy of the Gospel, Pope Francis quotes Pope John XXIII's speech at the opening of Vatican II and his statement that we must disagree with 'those prophets of doom' who see nothing hopeful in the world. Then Francis says, 'One of the more serious temptations which stifles boldness and zeal is a defeatism which turns us into querulous and disillusioned pessimists, "sourpusses"' (85). You have to love a pope that uses the word 'sourpusses' in an official papal exhortation! Earlier that year, in one of his intimate daily Mass homilies at the Vatican's Casa Santa Marta, Francis said, 'We can't proclaim Jesus with funeral faces' (May 31, 2013). And still again at an earlier homily, 'Sometimes these melancholic Christians' faces have more in common with pickled peppers than the joy of having a beautiful life' (May 10, 2013).

I wonder if someone took a picture of your liturgical ministers at Sunday Mass, would the pope's words ring true? Would you see sourpusses and pickled peppers? I know I have at many of the Masses I've been to in my life and I was probably one of those pickled peppers! When we get so focused on the details of doing the liturgy and getting it all just right, sometimes we can look like those melancholy Christians. We don't mean to, but often our faces don't match what we're trying to communicate, that is, glad tidings and good news.

Pope Francis's entire pontificate has been marked by joy. It is one of the four behaviours, the pope says, by which Christians will be known. (The other three are love, harmony, and suffering.) The pope also says that the Spirit is the 'author of joy, the creator of joy' and this joy of the Spirit 'gives us true Christian freedom' (May 31, 2013). Today of all days, Gaudete 'Rejoice' Sunday, we must keep the sourpusses and prophets of doom in ourselves at bay. As you prepare to minister today pray to the Spirit to free you from any anxiety, worry, or sadness that might dampen the good news you want to communicate through your words and actions. Your prayer might even be a simple refrain from today's second reading: 'I want you to be happy, always happy in the Lord; I repeat, what I want is your happiness' (Phil 4:4).

About Initiation

The parish is *the curriculum:* In their 1999 pastoral plan on adult faith formation the United States bishops said, '[W]hile the parish may *have an* adult faith formation programme, it is no less true that the parish *is* an adult faith formation programme' (Our Hearts Were Burning Within Us 121, emphasis original). Although they weren't referring specifically to the RCIA, this statement gives catechumenate teams a deeper understanding of what the Rite of Christian Initiation of Adults means when it says that the initiation of catechumens 'takes place within the community of the faithful' (4).

Formation of those preparing to live the Christian way of life doesn't happen in a classroom. It happens where other Christians are doing what Christians do: wherever they reflect on the Word together, strive to live and work in harmony and joy with one another, gather to pray, and especially, proclaim the good news to those in need.

About Liturgical Music

Suggestions: These last nine days before Christmas are the traditional times for singing the O Antiphons. Today 'O Come, O Come, Emmanuel' with a joyfully sung refrain at a non-funereal tempo, would be an appropriate song to conclude the Mass and begin this final period of Advent. Also, look at *Psallite*'s 'Rejoice in the Lord, Again Rejoice'! as a possible communion procession.

SPIRITUALITY

GOSPEL ACCLAMATION
Luke 1:38

R̸. Alleluia, alleluia.
I am the handmaid of the Lord:
let what you have said be done to me.
R̸. Alleluia, alleluia.

Gospel

Luke 1:39-45

Mary set out and went as quickly as she could to a town in the hill country of Judah. She went into Zechariah's house and greeted Elizabeth. Now as soon as Elizabeth heard Mary's greeting, the child leapt in her womb and Elizabeth was filled with the Holy Spirit. She gave a loud cry and said, 'Of all women you are the most blessed, and blessed is the fruit of your womb. Why should I be honoured with a visit from the mother of my Lord? For the moment your greeting reached my ears, the child in my womb leapt for joy. Yes, blessed is she who believed that the promise made her by the Lord would be fulfilled.'

Reflecting on the Gospel

We are only days away from Christmas when we celebrate the fourth Sunday of Advent this year. This season is especially short and can make for a hectic, frenetic pace as we consider all that needs to happen before the holiday. Some are preparing households to receive guests, others are preparing meals, and many are doing both! Still others are setting out on their travels to see loved ones during these holy days. We are busy with many tasks.

We might imagine Mary and Elizabeth sharing these feelings in this reading from Luke. Mary visits her cousin and Elizabeth has certainly been preparing for her guest. The greeting is joyful and Luke tells us that Elizabeth was filled with the Holy Spirit. For Luke the evangelist the Holy Spirit is active not only in Jesus's ministry but before Jesus was born, in preparation for it. Recall that Mary conceives by the power of the Holy Spirit, and after Jesus is raised from the dead Luke will recount how the Holy Spirit was poured out on the assembled disciples at Pentecost as tongues of fire. Some have even said Luke's Acts of the Apostles would be better termed the Acts of the Holy Spirit. So it is significant here that Elizabeth, too, is filled with the Holy Spirit. Not only that but essentially she proclaims the baby in Mary's womb to be 'Lord'. Here again Luke is displaying his theological insight that Jesus was not merely Lord at the moment of his baptism (as Mark might have it), but he could rightfully be called Lord before he was even born. Even the baby John in Elizabeth's womb shares the joy.

This gospel passage calls to mind for us how important human relationships are. Amidst all the travel, preparation, meals, and general business, the bonds of human love bind us together. When we consider the holiday season with its pressing demands let us recall the ultimate reason for our cares and concerns. We have in mind those we love and care for. May the relationships we celebrate this season, especially the relationships we have in Christ, inspire us to live in a meaningful way.

Living the Paschal Mystery

In this the first chapter of Luke's gospel we learn that Elizabeth was filled with the Holy Spirit. Luke has a concern for women as we shall see in reading his gospel. Luke often gives women pride of place, or at least shows them with a status equal to that of men. This story is an example of that. We hear virtually nothing about Zechariah, who has been struck speechless. Instead, this is an encounter between two women, each filled with the Holy Spirit, having a profound meeting and reflecting theologically on that.

Like these women, we are to recognise the work of the Holy Spirit in our lives. Whether it may be the miraculous birth of a child or the bringing forth of other new life, the Holy Spirit is as active today as in days of old.

When the daily activities of life seem to overwhelm us, as they might at this time of year, it is good to pause and to reflect on the lives of these women who were open to God's activity in their lives.

Focusing the Gospel

Key words and phrases: Mary set out and went as quickly as she could to a town in the hill country of Judah.

To the point: Our gospel today begins with a journey. Mary, having heard from the angel Gabriel of Elizabeth's pregnancy, sets out to visit her kinswoman. This was no small expedition. Tradition holds that Zechariah and Elizabeth lived in Ain Karim, a little town in the hill country of Judea about five miles from Jerusalem. The journey from Nazareth was nearly one hundred miles: travelling on foot or by caravan, it would have taken three to five days. Not only did Mary believe the news Gabriel had brought her, but she puts this faith into action immediately, travelling in haste to be close to Elizabeth and to share the good news that invites us all to '[leap] for joy'.

Connecting the Gospel

to the first reading: The prophet Micah speaks to the people of Israel exiled in Babylon and tells them of a leader who will be raised up for them. This ruler will be a shepherd who 'will extend his power / to the ends of the land'. Finally, Micah tells us, '[h]e himself will be peace'. In the gospel we see this prophecy coming true. When Mary reaches Elizabeth's house, Elizabeth is alerted to the presence of Jesus by the infant leaping within her own womb. By the Holy Spirit she proclaims that this is, indeed, 'the mother of my Lord'. John the Baptist, who will later point to Jesus with words and actions, begins his task of pointing to Jesus by leaping for joy.

to experience: As we near the end of Advent our joy grows ever greater. We, too, prepare to herald Jesus, the Prince of Peace, in word and action.

Connecting the Responsorial Psalm

to the readings: The first reading and the gospel speak of God's promise (first reading) and the fulfilment of that promise (gospel) to send a saviour to God's people. Micah prophesies a ruler who will shepherd the people out of exile into a place of security and peace. John the Baptist announces the presence of this ruler in the womb of the Virgin Mary when he leaps for joy. Today's psalm has a different tone, however. As a lament, it calls upon God to come to the aid of a nation in shambles. The psalmist demands that God 'rouse up your might, . . . come to our help'.

to psalmist preparation: This is a song of faith and of desperation. The psalmist demands that God protect God's people in a time of near annihilation. As you proclaim this psalm to the people of God today, think of a time when you yourself have been desperate for God's protection, love, and care. Use this experience to convey both the urgency in the psalm as well as the faith that God will do what God has promised and restore the people once again.

PROMPTS FOR FAITH-SHARING

In the second reading, the letter to the Hebrews proclaims that we have been 'made holy by the offering of his body made once and for all by Jesus Christ'. How do our lives give testimony to being holy?

Just as in the birth of Jesus, the Holy Spirit is active in our own time. How do you experience the Holy Spirit working in your life?

John the Baptist first prophesies to Jesus's presence by leaping for joy in Elizabeth's womb. In this season of Advent and Christmas does your joy point to the risen Lord? How?

Mary and Elizabeth share each other's joy and offer strength to one another in their pregnancies. In our spiritual life we need companions who can point out where God is working in our lives. Other times we are called to be the one who bears witness to Christ's presence in another. How might we cultivate these spiritual friendships?

CELEBRATION

Model Penitential Act

Presider: In today's gospel Elizabeth tells Mary, 'blessed is she who believed that the promise made her by the Lord would be fulfilled'. Let us prepare to enter into this liturgy by opening ourselves up to the transformative word of God. . . [*pause*]

Lord Jesus, you are Son of God and son of Mary: Lord, have mercy.

Christ Jesus, you shepherd us into life: Christ, have mercy.

Lord Jesus, you are the Prince of Peace: Lord, have mercy.

Homily Points

• There is a theme that runs throughout all salvation history of God choosing the small and humble to do great things. We see this in the gospel where the woman chosen to be Jesus's mother is not the wife of the high priest who lives close to Jerusalem, but is instead a young unmarried woman from Nazareth, a small settlement in the northern part of Israel. And yet it is this woman who says 'yes' to the angel's request that she bear a child who will be, 'Son of the Most High'.

• In the first reading the prophet Micah calls Bethlehem-Ephrathah 'the least of the clans of Judah', but then goes on to say 'out of you will be born for me / the one who is to rule over Israel'. Jesus will be born not in Jerusalem, the holiest and most important city in Israel, but in little Bethlehem. When we gather together in a few days to celebrate the Nativity of the Lord we will hear that arriving in Bethlehem, with no room available at the inn, his family must seek shelter in the place where animals are kept. The first people to visit his manger-cradle are not the local elite or dignitaries but shepherds fresh from the fields.

• All of these details of Jesus's conception and birth reveal to us the character of God. If it is God's way to choose the small and humble, then it must be ours as well. How might we find a way to embrace this preference in our own lives and in our celebration of Christmas?

Model Universal Prayer (Prayer of the Faithful)

Presider: Let us pray for the faith of Mary, who believed that what was spoken to her by the Lord would be fulfilled.

Response: Lord, hear our prayer.

That all members of the church may faithfully follow Jesus, the Shepherd . . .

That all people of the world might dwell in peace . . .

That those who are shut-in or experience isolation might be embraced in the community of God's love . . .

That each of us here may joyfully recognise Jesus within the small and humble of society . . .

Presider: Faithful God, you gave us Mary as a model of belief and discipleship. Hear our prayers that we might follow her example. Through Christ our Lord. Amen.

COLLECT

Let us pray.

Pause for silent prayer

Pour forth, we beseech you, O Lord,
your grace into our hearts,
that we, to whom the Incarnation of Christ
    your Son
was made known by
    the message of an Angel,
may by his Passion and Cross
be brought to the glory
    of his Resurrection.
Who lives and reigns with you
    in the unity of the Holy Spirit,
one God, for ever and ever.

FIRST READING
Mic 5:1-4

The Lord says this:

You, Bethlehem Ephrathah,
the least of the clans of Judah,
out of you will be born for me
the one who is to rule over Israel;
his origin goes back to the distant past,
to the days of old.
The Lord is therefore going to
    abandon them
till the time when she who is to give
    birth gives birth.
Then the remnant of his brothers will
    come back
to the sons of Israel.
He will stand and feed his flock
with the power of the Lord,
with the majesty of the name of his God.
They will live secure, for from then on
    he will extend his power
to the ends of the land.
He himself will be peace.

CATECHESIS

RESPONSORIAL PSALM
Ps 79:2-3, 15-16, 18-19 (4)

R︎︎. God of hosts, bring us back; let your
    face shine on us and we shall be saved.

O shepherd of Israel, hear us,
shine forth from your cherubim throne.
O Lord, rouse up your might,
O Lord, come to our help.

R︎. God of hosts, bring us back; let your
    face shine on us and we shall be saved.

God of hosts, turn again, we implore,
look down from heaven and see.
Visit this vine and protect it,
the vine your right hand has planted.

R︎. God of hosts, bring us back; let your
    face shine on us and we shall be saved.

May your hand be on the man you
    have chosen,
the man you have given your strength.
And we shall never forsake you again:
give us life that we may call upon
    your name.

R︎. God of hosts, bring us back; let your
    face shine on us and we shall be saved.

SECOND READING
Heb 10:5-10

This is what Christ said, on coming into
the world:

    You who wanted no sacrifice
        or oblation,
    prepared a body for me.
    You took no pleasure in holocausts or
        sacrifices for sin;
    then I said,
    just as I was commanded in the scroll
        of the book,
    'God, here I am! I am coming to obey
        your will.'

Notice that he says first: You did not want what the Law lays down as the things to be offered, that is: the sacrifices, the oblations, the holocausts and the sacrifices for sin, and you took no pleasure in them; and then he says: Here I am! I am coming to obey your will. He is abolishing the first sort to replace it with the second. And this will was for us to be made holy by the offering of his body made once and for all by Jesus Christ.

About Liturgy
Hail, Mary: The gospel for the Fourth Sunday of Advent in each liturgical year focuses on Mary, the Mother of God. Today's passage from Luke gives us a Marian set of beatitudes: 'Of all women you are the most blessed'; 'blessed is the fruit of your womb'; and 'blessed is she who believed'. What an overwhelming and powerful way to be greeted – with blessing after blessing!

This visitation scene reminds us that greetings are opportunities for blessings and for recognising the presence of Christ in one another. How appropriate then that in the days when we give our season's greetings that we take time to recognise these as more than just mere formality or holiday tradition.

First, in the liturgy we have the ritual greeting and response, 'The Lord be with you'; 'And with your spirit'. Here presider and people recognise the presence of Christ in one another and bless each other for the work that they are about to perform. This dialogue occurs at five key moments of the Mass: at the beginning, before the gospel proclamation, at the start of the eucharistic prayer, just before Communion, and at the dismissal. Each of these moments requires focused attention and commitment from all the people of God whatever their role is in the body of Christ. This ritual dialogue does not serve as a nicety like 'Good morning'. Rather they are words reminding us of the profound responsibility we each have in bearing Christ to the world. As Christians we are called to do this through our witness in communal prayer, proclamation of the good news, priestly offering of ourselves in union with Christ's sacrifice, working for peace, and finally, by bringing that peace to the ends of the earth.

Second, we can bring this blessing through the greetings we share each day, whether spoken, written, or silent. If we can make these few seconds moments of intentional connection and blessing, we, too, just might leap for joy.

Marian prayers at Mass: In some places it has become a practice to insert the Hail Mary as a prayer of the assembly during Mass. Often this happens as a conclusion to the universal prayer or perhaps after Communion. This practice, however, does not align with any rubrics from the Roman Missal. The Mass is always christological in that our prayer reflects on our salvation in Christ. Even when our readings or the liturgical feast emphasise Mary the Mother of God, our praise is centred on Christ. We might use Mary's own words, as in, for example, the *Magnificat*, but the focus remains on God.

About Liturgical Music
Suggestions: Any setting of the *Magnificat* would be appropriate for today, even though we do not get that specific text in this part of the gospel reading. The *Psallite* setting 'My soul rejoices in God' includes assembly friendly mini antiphons within the verses, while the Alstott/Farrell version, 'My soul proclaims the greatness of the Lord', uses the same music as the *Benedictus* setting, 'Blest be the Lord, the God of Israel', itself very appropriate for the season of Advent. One image that we do get from today's readings is Mary as the one who does God's will. One lovely piece that communicates the joy of doing God's will is *Psallite*'s 'Come, All You Good and Faithful Servants'. The refrain text is 'Come, all you good and faithful servants, share in the joy, the joy of the Lord'. This is interspersed with verses from Psalm 34, which makes it a perfect communion processional. Another possible *Psallite* antiphon is 'Let the Word Make a Home in Your Heart', which serves as a connection to the Word made flesh we will hear in John's gospel on Christmas Day and with Mary who pondered all these things in her heart.

23 DECEMBER 2018
FOURTH SUNDAY OF ADVENT

SEASON OF CHRISTMAS

The Lord entered her, and became a servant;
the Word entered her, and became silent within her;
thunder entered her, and his voice was still;
the Shepherd of all entered her;
he became a Lamb in her, and came forth bleating.

– St. Ephrem the Syrian

SPIRITUALITY

The Vigil Mass

GOSPEL ACCLAMATION
John 8:31-32

R. Alleluia, alleluia!
Tomorrow there will be an end to the sin of
    the world
and the saviour of the world will be
    our king.
R. Alleluia!

Gospel

Matt 1:1-25

**A genealogy of Jesus
Christ, the son of David,
son of Abraham:**

**Abraham was the father
    of Isaac,
Isaac the father of Jacob,
Jacob the father of Judah and
    his brothers,
Judah the father of Perez and Zerah,
    Tamar being their mother,
Perez the father of Hezron,
Hezron the father of Ram,
Ram the father of Amminadab,
Amminadab the father of Nahshon,
Nahshon the father of Salmon,
Salmon was the father of Boaz, Rahab
    being his mother,
Boaz the father of Obed, Ruth being
    his mother,
Obed was the father of Jesse;
and Jesse was the father of King David.**

**David was the father of Solomon, whose
    mother had been Uriah's wife,
Solomon was the father of Rehoboam,
Rehoboam the father of Abijah,
Abijah the father of Asa,**

Continued in Appendix, p. 270, or
Matt 1:18-25 *in Appendix, p. 270.*

See Appendix, p. 270, for the other readings.

Reflecting on the Gospel and Living the Paschal Mystery
Key words and phrases:
Jesus Christ, the son of David, son of Abraham. Emmanuel, / a name which means 'God-is-with-us'.

To the point: This evening's reading gives lectors trouble. It is worth taking time to practise the pronunciation of the names – while also learning rhythm and emphasis – in proclaiming Matthew's three sets of fourteen generations. All too often the names are lost in the struggle to pronounce them properly. It is critical that those who proclaim the Word of God practise their proclamation skills.

All that being noted, it is significant that Matthew traces Jesus's lineage to Abraham, the father in faith. When Luke has the chance to convey Jesus's lineage he traces it back to Adam! Each evangelist is writing for his own audience: Matthew for a Jewish Christian audience (thus Abraham) and Luke for a Gentile Christian audience (thus Adam). Moreover, Matthew values an orderly and numerically significant count of generations that Luke does not address at all. Neither agrees on his genealogy, the number of generations, or even the names in the generations, including the name of Jesus's paternal grandfather (the father of Joseph)! In fact, students of Scripture are often given the task of comparing the genealogies of Matthew and Luke to recognise these significant and irreconcilable differences. But the differences point to something more profound, which is each evangelist's theological perspective on Jesus.

One important matter to learn by a compare-and-contrast exercise is not the names of the generations, but rather that Jesus was born of human stock, in a human lineage. He was a human being (Adam), Jewish (Abraham) of the tribe of Judah, and in the line of David. Though David lived one thousand years before Jesus, the promise of a new David is fulfilled in Jesus.

To ponder and pray: How many of us remember waiting as children for Christmas morning, or waiting for a special birthday, or a visit from family or friends? The wait seemed interminable. And yet the object of our anticipation finally and inevitably arrived. In one sense this evening's gospel tells the story of another wait, but this time for one thousand years! The promised Son of David, the sprout from the stump of Jesse, has appeared. Jesus, the fulfilment of the promises made of old, is Son of David and also Emmanuel, God with us. The divine has become human and humanity is thereby infused with divinity.

This opening chapter of Matthew sets the stage for the theological understanding of Jesus. At the conclusion of the gospel Jesus will tell his disciples that he will be with them always. He who bears the title Emmanuel is 'God with us' not only once two thousand years ago but also now and eternally. When we celebrate the birth of the Messiah we recognise the fulfilment of all of our longings, all of our anticipation, all of our expectations. Only Emmanuel, God with us, can satisfy these existential yearnings. For that, we celebrate and are grateful.

SPIRITUALITY

Mass at Midnight

GOSPEL ACCLAMATION
Luke 2:10-11

℟. Alleluia, alleluia!
I bring you news of great joy:
today a saviour has been born to us,
    Christ the Lord.
℟. Alleluia!

Gospel

Luke 2:1-14

Caesar Augustus issued a decree for a census of the whole world to be taken. This census – the first – took place while Quirinius was governor of Syria, and everyone went to his own town to be registered. So Joseph set out from the town of Nazareth in Galilee and travelled up to Judaea, to the town of David called Bethlehem, since he was of David's House and line, in order to be registered together with Mary, his betrothed, who was with child. While they were there the time came for her to have her child, and she gave birth to a son, her first-born. She wrapped him in swaddling clothes, and laid him in a manger because there was no room for them at the inn.

Continued in Appendix, p. 271.

See Appendix, p. 271, for the other readings.

Reflecting on the Gospel and Living the Paschal Mystery
Key words and phrases: She wrapped him in swaddling clothes, and laid him in a manger.

To the point: The gospel for midnight Mass contains the scene we connect most readily with Christmas. Jesus, Son of God and son of Mary, is born in Bethlehem, but since there is no room at the inn he has no cradle for a bed. Instead, a feedbox becomes his resting place. We've pictured this scene so many times that maybe it has stopped shocking us. It certainly would have shocked Jesus's first visitors. This baby, whose birth is proclaimed by an angel, is to be found with his mother and father sleeping among the animals. This one, whom the shepherds are told is 'Saviour', 'Messiah', and 'Lord', enters the world as a helpless baby who must depend on others for all of his physical needs.

To ponder and pray: That God chose to become a human being is remarkable, but that God chose to become a human being born in a barn to poor parents is even more so. This child of whom angels sing is born into the messiness of human life. Can we also find him there?

SPIRITUALITY

Mass at Dawn

GOSPEL ACCLAMATION
Luke 2:14

℟. Alleluia, alleluia!
Glory to God in the highest heaven,
and peace to men who enjoy his favour.
℟. Alleluia!

Gospel

Luke 2:15-20

Now when the angels had gone from them into heaven, the shepherds said to one another, 'Let us go to Bethlehem and see this thing that has happened which the Lord has made known to us.' So they hurried away and found Mary and Joseph, and the baby lying in the manger. When they saw the child they repeated what they had been told about him, and everyone who heard it was astonished at what the shepherds had to say. As for Mary, she treasured all these things and pondered them in her heart. And the shepherds went back glorifying and praising God for all they had heard and seen; it was exactly as they had been told.

See Appendix, p. 272, for the other readings.

Reflecting on the Gospel and Living the Paschal Mystery

Key words and phrases: [T]hey hurried away. [T]hey repeated what they had been told about him. [P]ondered them in her heart.

To the point: The story of Christmas does not end with the angels' song glorifying God. Here we see the shepherds' response to the revelation given to them by that heavenly host. They 'hurried away', which echoes Mary's swift response after her own angelic visit in the previous chapter. Having seen for themselves what had been revealed to them, the shepherds did not stay long at the manger despite what our nativity scenes capture. The shepherds keep moving, making known the message about the child Jesus and glorifying God as they returned to their flocks. Although they remained shepherds, they had been changed. They were now the first evangelists of the in-breaking of God into human history.

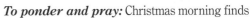

In this same passage, we see another kind of response to the message of salvation. Mary's silent contemplation, we know, will not remain silent for long. Though she has few words recorded in the gospels after the birth of her son, she, too, communicated the saving message not only by her words but also by her presence at the cross and among the apostles.

On this Christmas morning the gospel calls us to respond to God's action in our lives. That response requires both quiet contemplation and bold proclamation.

To ponder and pray: Christmas morning finds many of us unwrapping gifts that have been waiting all Advent to be opened. Once the adrenaline of surprise and wonder has passed, we experience a 'gift coma' that lulls us into a pleasant and carefree mood.

In this time with family and friends we can bask in their presence and take pleasure in the things we have received from loved ones. However, a true gift given in love is one that obligates the receiver to action, that is, to return the gift – not as a kind of payment or equal exchange but as a loving response of thanksgiving, acknowledging both the gift and the giver.

When our heavenly Father is the one who bestows the gift, and the gift given is Jesus his only Son, what 'return gift' could we possibly give?

Today we can look to the humble shepherds who had nothing to give but their presence and their courageous witness to any who would hear their message – that God is with us! We also can follow the example of Mary whose 'return gift' was her very heart in which she allowed the message to dwell and shape her life and actions.

In his famous poem Howard Thurman says, 'When the song of the angels is stilled . . . the work of Christmas begins' ('The Work of Christmas', *The Mood of Christmas and Other Celebrations*). We still have much work to do this Christmas.

SPIRITUALITY

Mass during the Day

GOSPEL ACCLAMATION
R̂. Alleluia, alleluia!
A hallowed day has dawned upon us.
Come, you nations, worship the Lord,
for today a great light has shone down upon
    the earth.
R̂. Alleluia!

Gospel

John 1:1-18

In the beginning was the Word:
the Word was with God
and the Word was God.
He was with God in the beginning.
Through him all things came to be,
not one thing had its being but
        through him.
All that came to be had life in him
and that life was the light of men,
a light that shines in the dark,
a light that darkness could not overpower.

A man came, sent by God.
His name was John.
He came as a witness,
as a witness to speak for the light,
so that everyone might believe through him.
He was not the light,
only a witness to speak for the light.

The Word was the true light
that enlightens all men;
and he was coming into the world.
He was in the world
that had its being through him,
and the world did not know him.
He came to his own domain
and his own people did not accept him.
But to all who did accept him
he gave power to become children of God,
to all who believe in the name of him
who was born not out of human stock
or urge of the flesh
or will of man
but of God himself.

Continued in Appendix, p. 272, or
John 1:1-5, 9-14 *in Appendix, p. 272.*

See Appendix, p. 273, for the other readings.

Reflecting on the Gospel and Living the Paschal Mystery
Key words and phrases:
In the beginning was the Word. The Word was made flesh.

To the point: Those expecting a gospel reading about the nativity may be surprised to hear high-minded, sophisticated, theological discourse from John's prologue. This is perhaps the most subtle, nuanced, and erudite expression of the dynamic relationship between the Word and God. A pinnacle is reached when we read, 'The Word was made flesh', which is true incarnation theology. The eternal unchanging word underwent change and became time-bound flesh. There is nothing here about Mary, Joseph, angels, or shepherds. Instead, we have refined theology, which is not wedded to story.

To ponder and pray: The incarnation is a central mystery of faith and belief in it marks one as Christian. In Jesus the divine becomes human, raising humanity to divinity. Lowly, changing, finite flesh is the place of the exalted, unchanging, eternal God. This central insight from John's prologue means that all humanity, as well as each human person, is worthy of respect, dignity, and care because every human person is the reflection of and dwelling place of the divine. How we treat our fellow human beings is therefore an expression of our worship of God. It is not possible to worship God and mistreat our fellows. By the incarnation our humanity is exalted to divinity.

CELEBRATION

Model Penitential Act

Presider: We gather to celebrate the birth of Emmanuel, God with us, now and forever. As we prepare to enter into the mystery of the incarnation let us pause to ask for pardon and healing . . . [*pause*]

Lord Jesus, you bring light into gloom and darkness: Lord, have mercy.

Christ Jesus, wrapped in swaddling clothes and laid in a manger, you are the saviour of the world: Christ, have mercy.

Lord Jesus, you fill the earth with glory: Lord, have mercy.

Model Universal Prayer (Prayer of the Faithful)

Presider: With hearts full of gratitude for the gift of Jesus, we lift our prayers to God.

Response: Lord, hear our prayer.

That the church be a sign of peace and hope within a world in need of healing . . .

That the rulers of the world might lead with justice and peace . . .

That those in need may have shelter and food, and find a generous welcome this Christmas . . .

That each of us here might be renewed in our lives as Christians this Christmas by accepting anew God's gift of love . . .

Presider: Glorious God, we praise you for the gift of your Son, the saviour who came for all people to bring peace and justice. We ask you to hear our prayers and grant them through Jesus Christ, Lord forever and ever. Amen.

About Liturgy

Facets of the Nativity: There are four different sets of readings and prayers assigned to four different times of day in the Roman Missal and the Lectionary for the celebration of the nativity. The Vigil Mass is used in the evening on December 24, and the gospel comes from Matthew's genealogy. On Christmas Day there are three options: the Mass during the Night, which proclaims the beginning of Luke's nativity narrative; the Mass at Dawn, which continues Luke's account; and the Mass during the Day, which gives us John's prologue.

Although the Roman Missal prayers are set for each time of day, the readings may be chosen from among the various options given. Many will choose to proclaim Luke's gospel at all the Masses on these two days because it gives the Christmas story that most people expect. However, there is great wisdom in using each assigned set of readings at their proper times because these give us a fuller picture of who this newborn king truly is. By bookending the Nativity feast with the complexity of Jesus's family tree and John's poetic description of the Logos, one sees a deeper way of understanding Christmas that goes beyond the familiar manger scene.

FOR REFLECTION

• Sometime during Christmas Eve, Christmas Day, or throughout the Christmas season you will likely sing 'Silent Night.' Where and when do you find silence to celebrate the birth of Christ?

• On Christmas we celebrate how 'The Word was made flesh, / he lived among us'. How do you experience Jesus as flesh and blood in your own life?

Homily Points

• On this feast of the Nativity of the Lord we are given four different gospels to be read on the vigil, midnight, dawn, and day of Christmas. Each reading invites us into a unique facet of the mystery of the incarnation. The vigil reading from Matthew shows Jesus as the pinnacle of a long line of ancestors from Abraham through forty-two generations to the Messiah, the long-awaited one. The gospels for midnight and dawn contain the birth of Jesus and the adoration of the shepherds found in Luke. Luke's historical details assure us that this event actually took place in Bethlehem over two thousand years ago. He also shows us that the Saviour of the world made his dwelling first among the poor and lowly. In John's gospel, Jesus's genesis is told in a different way: the Word that was with God from the very beginning 'was made flesh, / he lived among us'.

SPIRITUALITY

GOSPEL ACCLAMATION
Cf. Ac 16:14

℟. Alleluia, alleluia.
Open our heart, O Lord,
to accept the words of your Son.
℟. Alleluia, alleluia.

Gospel   Luke 2:41-52

Every year the parents of Jesus used to go to Jerusalem for the feast of the Passover. When he was twelve years old, they went up for the feast as usual. When they were on their way home after the feast, the boy Jesus stayed behind in Jerusalem without his parents knowing it. They assumed he was with the caravan, and it was only after a day's journey that they went to look for him among their relations and acquaintances. When they failed to find him they went back to Jerusalem looking for him everywhere.

Three days later, they found him in the Temple, sitting among the doctors, listening to them, and asking them questions; and all those who heard him were astounded at his intelligence and his replies. They were overcome when they saw him, and his mother said to him, 'My child, why have you done this to us? See how worried your father and I have been, looking for you.' 'Why were you looking for me?' he replied. 'Did you not know that I must be busy with my Father's affairs?' But they did not understand what he meant.

He then went down with them and came to Nazareth and lived under their authority. His mother stored up all these things in her heart. And Jesus increased in wisdom, in stature, and in favour with God and men.

Reflecting on the Gospel

A missing child is a parent's worst fear. We can imagine being in a grocery store, a department store, or even an amusement park and the panic that would overtake us if a child in our care was nowhere to be found. We might have been relying on someone else to keep an eye on this young one, only to realise that was a misunderstanding. Such things happen occasionally and often the child is found shortly thereafter. Other times it results in tragedy. But in today's gospel story the Holy Family had lost Jesus in the capital city of Jerusalem! This is a reminder that though Jesus's family is holy it was not without challenges, like any family. Joseph and Mary dealt with parenting a preteen who thought he was fine on his own. Obviously miscommunication was a challenge for them as it might be for us as well.

It can be simple for us to imagine that the Holy Family was perfect, something to which we could never measure up. But Luke gives us a story of a family with real-life challenges and problems. In fact, this is a challenge we would not wish upon anyone, losing track of a child for days in a major city.

Even so, such a story might give us hope as we deal with daily activities in family life, striving not for perfection, which is an unattainable ideal. But instead, we recognise that family life can be messy, punctuated with misunderstandings, miscommunication, and mistakes. Such events are not 'sinful' and they were obviously part of life for the Holy Family. It is significant that Luke tells us not only that Jesus was obedient to his parents but that he also grew in wisdom. He was not born fully formed and all knowing. As a human being he naturally learned things. And simply reflecting on this fact can be the source of profound meditation on our part. We who believe that Jesus was divine also believe that he was human. He was not a divine puppet but a flesh-and-blood human being who was raised in a family and grew in wisdom. Our own families are places of sanctity. We will have challenges as the Holy Family did. But we can deal with them forthrightly, knowing that the relationships we have in this most basic human unit are a means of sanctification.

Living the Paschal Mystery

The family has been called the 'domestic church' as it is the first encounter children have with the Gospel, and it is the dwelling place of faith and lived Christian relationships. But often we hear such ideas and think that a family must therefore be a place of perfection, and we all know from our own experiences that families (or churches for that matter) are anything but places of perfection. So the idea can be daunting and seem unattainable. But Luke gives us an image of family life that might be more relatable. Even the Holy Family had their share of challenges, and so we have hope for ourselves and our own family situations. We know from experience – confirmed by research – that we learn more by imitation and example than we do by preaching and teaching. In other words, our actions speak more loudly than words. How we live the gospel message in the midst of family life says much more about our faith commitment than what we say about the Gospel. Our homes and families ought to be places of security, welcome, love, care, concern, and forgiveness. Speaking about such things does not mean as much as living them. The same can be said for the Holy Family. Their behaviours spoke more loudly than their words. Today on this feast of the Holy Family, we might pause to consider what message we convey by our actions.

Focusing the Gospel

Key words and phrases: 'Did you not know that I must be busy with my Father's affairs?'

To the point: In many ways this seems like an odd gospel to choose for the feast of the Holy Family. Mary and Joseph lose their adolescent son in a big city not just for an hour or an afternoon but for three days. This hardly seems like an example to lift up or emulate for tranquil family life. But perhaps that is part of the point. Jesus is born into a human family. Out of all of the places in the world God chose a faithful Jewish couple living in Israel to raise his son. Jesus's growing up years are often called the 'hidden life in Nazareth'. Much of family life is hidden and often involves misunderstandings and anxieties. Can we claim all parts of this life as holy?

Connecting the Gospel

to the first reading: In the first reading from First Samuel we see many parallels to the gospel. Another mother and another son approach the 'temple of the Lord'. Hannah, who was also only able to conceive through the intervention of God, now takes this long-awaited child (for whom she prayed for so fervently that the high priest accused her of being intoxicated) and gives him to the Lord. Whereas Mary and Joseph find their son in the temple, Hannah leaves her child in the temple of the Lord. In toddlerhood (Samuel) and early adolescence (Jesus) each son was unique, set apart for a special purpose and consecrated to the Lord.

to experience: In Hannah's devotion and Mary and Joseph's anxiety and misunderstanding we see the struggle of parents who love their child but also know this child is not theirs but God's. Within the Holy Family, Mary and Joseph were blessed with closeness to Jesus but also challenged and at times saddened by his vocation that would take him away from them. In our own lives, how can we follow the examples of Hannah and Mary and Joseph and hold those that we love most dear gently, realising that they are gifts that do not belong to us but to God?

Connecting the Responsorial Psalm

to the readings: Today's psalm is one of joy and anticipation, fitting for a pilgrim to Jerusalem who longs to dwell in the house of the Lord. Jesus also finds joy and contentment in the temple, not wanting to leave after journeying to Jerusalem for the feast of Passover.

to psalmist preparation: For the pilgrim there is joy in the journey and joy in the ultimate destination. This psalm is a prayer for pilgrims going up to Jerusalem for one of the three pilgrimage feasts of the year. As you proclaim it, infuse your words with longing and with joy so as to remind the assembly of where their true home lies – in the house of the Lord.

PROMPTS FOR FAITH-SHARING

How do you experience your family as a 'domestic church?'

Where do you find 'holy imperfection' in your own family?

How does your family support each other in times of stress and sadness?

Do you feel at home in your church community? How do you experience it as a place of shelter and welcome? How might you help it grow to be even more a house of God?

CELEBRATION

Model Penitential Act

Presider: Today we celebrate the Holy Family of Jesus, Mary, and Joseph. We also remember that we are children of God and therefore members of God's family. For the times that have not lived up to this identity, we ask for pardon and healing . . . [*pause*]

Lord Jesus, you command us to love one another: Lord, have mercy.

Christ Jesus, you are a member of the Holy Family with Mary and Joseph: Christ, have mercy.

Lord Jesus, you call us to remain in you: Lord, have mercy.

Homily Points

• Even in the Holy Family there were misunderstandings and anxieties. We are told in the gospel that after Mary and Joseph found Jesus in the temple and questioned him, they did not understand it when he said, 'Did you not know that I must be busy with my Father's affairs?' If Mary and Joseph did not always understand Jesus, we can be assured that misunderstandings will occur among our own family members. What is most important is how we respond to these misunderstandings. How might we practise love and respect, especially when confusion and anxiety arise?

• In the 1930s a new religious community grew up in the Roman Catholic Church called the Little Brothers of Jesus and the Little Sisters of Jesus. These communities, inspired by the work and writing of Blessed Charles de Foucald, take as their model the hidden life of Jesus of Nazareth. Brother Charles wrote, 'I did not feel that I was called to imitate Jesus in his public life and preaching, but understood that I should imitate the hidden life of the humble and poor workman of Nazareth'. How might we also take as our model the hidden life of Nazareth where Jesus lived with Mary and Joseph and 'increased in wisdom, in stature, and in favour with God and men'?

• Mary, Joseph, and Jesus were a family deeply immersed in the rituals and traditions of their people. In today's gospel we hear of how they keep the feast of Passover by travelling to Jerusalem to celebrate this holy day. In our own lives we are given a family and also the family of the church, the people of God. In both our domestic family and our church family relationships are strengthened through the celebration of rituals. How might we invite more ritual into the life of our families?

Model Universal Prayer (Prayer of the Faithful)

Presider: As children of God, we bring our intercessions to the Lord with confidence, knowing we will receive what we need.

Response: Lord, hear our prayer.

That all members of the church seek to live out in peace and tranquility their call to be the family of God . . .

That the countries of the world seek to safeguard and protect the earth, our common home . . .

That families in crisis might find the help and support they need to flourish and thrive . . .

That all gathered here might strive to be faithful and loving members of the families we belong to . . .

Presider: God, Father of all, through your son Jesus, you invite us to claim our rightful places as your beloved sons and daughters. Hear the prayers we bring before you, that through the intercession of the Holy Family we might become a sign of your love in the world, through Jesus Christ our Lord. Amen.

RESPONSORIAL PSALM
Ps 83:2-3, 5-6, 9-10 (5)

R℣. They are happy who dwell in your
house, O Lord.

How lovely is your dwelling place,
Lord, God of hosts.
My soul is longing and yearning,
is yearning for the courts of the Lord.
My heart and my soul ring out their joy
to God, the living God.

R℣. They are happy who dwell in your
house, O Lord.

They are happy, who dwell in your house,
for ever singing your praise.
They are happy, whose strength is in you;
they walk with ever growing strength.

R℣. Blessed are they who dwell in your
house, O Lord.

O Lord, God of hosts, hear my prayer,
give ear, O God of Jacob.
Turn your eyes, O God, our shield,
look on the face of your anointed.

R℣. They are happy who dwell in your
house, O Lord.

SECOND READING
1 John 3:1-2, 21-24

Think of the love that the Father has
        lavished on us,
by letting us be called God's children;
and that is what we are.
Because the world refused to
        acknowledge him,
therefore it does not acknowledge us.
My dear people, we are already the
        children of God
but what we are to be in the future has not
        yet been revealed,
all we know is, that when it is revealed
we shall be like him
because we shall see him as he really is.
My dear people,
if we cannot be condemned by our
        own conscience,
we need not be afraid in God's presence,
and whatever we ask him,
we shall receive,
because we keep his commandments
and live the kind of life that he wants.
His commandments are these:
that we believe in the name of his Son
        Jesus Christ
and that we love one another
as he told us to.
Whoever keeps his commandments
lives in God and God lives in him.
We know that he lives in us
by the Spirit that he has given us.

About Liturgy

The domestic church: This Sunday is a good time to help your households reflect on how they are the church in miniature. The Dogmatic Constitution on the Church says that the family is 'regarded as the domestic church' (*Lumen Gentium* 11). In the family Christian spouses signify the unity between Christ and the church, help one another attain holiness through the love they share in their marriage, and build up the church by raising children in the faith.

These kinds of households, made up of married spouses with children, hold a special place among the people of God. This does not mean, however, that other kinds of households cannot be holy as well. Homilists and liturgy planners need to be aware that many in their assemblies today will not reflect this 'ideal' image of a holy family. Thankfully, today's gospel reading can give us a glimpse into the 'holy imperfection' even the Holy Family experienced! For what makes a family holy is not perfection but love that is shown in compassion, kindness, humility, gentleness, patience, perseverance, and forgiveness. All of us in our own households can surely reflect and inspire that kind of holiness.

A domestic church calendar: As we near the end of the calendar year and the solemnity of the Epiphany when calendars might be blessed, you could invite all your households to prepare their own domestic church calendar. In addition to Sunday, the premier holy day, and the holy days of obligation, this calendar would have all the spiritual days that are important for that specific household to remember and observe with prayer. Here are some days that could be included in a domestic church calendar: birthdays of family members, baptismal anniversaries, wedding anniversaries, death anniversaries of loved ones, first Communion and confirmation anniversaries, patron saint days, and parish or diocesan patron saint day. Invite households to bring their domestic church calendar to the Epiphany Masses next week to be blessed.

About Initiation

Formation at home: Although you might not be meeting with catechumens and candidates during this Christmas season, you can still help them to be formed in the Christian faith. Give them 'mystagogical' questions they can reflect on by themselves or with their family and sponsors during the holidays. These are questions that prompt them to look for Christ in their daily lives and to reflect on what their encounters with Christ mean. When you come together again you can share your responses.

Here are some question ideas: Read through your Christmas cards. How do you hear 'good news' in those greetings? How did you see God today, and did it remind you of a story from the Bible? What was the most memorable moment from church in these past few weeks, and what did that say to you about who Jesus is?

About Liturgical Music

Singing at home: Today's second reading option from Colossians invites us to sing psalms, hymns, and spiritual songs with gratitude to God in our hearts. As music ministers we do this mostly at church in the liturgy. Yet we can also be models of sung prayer at home as well.

One place where communal singing can easily be incorporated into home life is at mealtime prayer. You can help your parish households sing their table blessings by teaching them simple refrains they could use at home. One such refrain that would be appropriate as a communion song for today is *Psallite*'s 'We Receive from Your Fulness'.

30 DECEMBER 2018
THE HOLY FAMILY OF JESUS, MARY, AND JOSEPH

GOSPEL ACCLAMATION
Heb 1:1-2

℟. Alleluia, alleluia!
At various times in the past
and in various different ways,
God spoke to our ancestors through
    the prophets;
but in our own time, the last days,
he has spoken to us through his Son.
℟. Alleluia!

Gospel

Luke 2:16-21

The shepherds hurried away to Bethlehem and found Mary and Joseph, and the baby lying in the manger. When they saw the child they repeated what they had been told about him, and everyone who heard it was astonished at what the shepherds had to say. As for Mary, she treasured all these things and pondered them in her heart. And the shepherds went back glorifying and praising God for all they had heard and seen; it was exactly as they had been told.

When the eighth day came and the child was to be circumcised, they gave him the name Jesus, the name the angel had given him before his conception.

See Appendix, p. 273, for the other readings.

Reflecting on the Gospel

Catholics are known for having a devotion to Mary, the mother of Jesus. In many RCIA classes the topic of Mary consumes a great deal of the room's oxygen. Mary's role is also a flashpoint in discussions between Catholics and other Christians, especially Protestants. There is much room for confusion over Marian titles; in fact, they are often misunderstood. A good rule of thumb is that any title for Mary says much more about Jesus than it does about Mary. And that is certainly the case today when we celebrate the solemnity of Mary, the Mother of God.

On its face such a title, Mother of God, can be perplexing. How can God, who exists from all eternity, have a mother? Where is that in the Scriptures? But of course, the statement says more about Jesus, who is the enfleshment (incarnation) of the Word of God.

These questions also perplexed the church fathers who were debating the terms 'Mother of God' or, literally, 'God-bearer' (*Theotokos* in Greek), and whether it was appropriate to apply them to Mary. Many theologians objected to 'Theotokos' (bearer of God) being applied to Mary and instead preferred 'Christotokos' (bearer of Christ). These theologians said it was better to refer to Mary as the one who bore Christ rather than as the one who bore God. On the other side of the argument were theologians who said that Jesus was the incarnation of God to such a degree that Mary could legitimately be called 'bearer of God'. And to make a long story short, the latter group carried the day as our commemorating this feast today certainly indicates.

But it would be too easy to become caught up in this Marian title as another example of outsized Catholic devotion to Mary. Instead, this title has its roots in the fifth century, one thousand years before Catholics and Protestants. Ultimately, like so many other Marian titles, this says more about Jesus and his identity than it does about Mary. And the claim is simply and profoundly this: that Jesus was the incarnation of God from the moment of his conception so that Mary can rightly be said to have borne the divine. Christianity is an incarnational and sacramental faith. Matter, earth, and world are the place of divine revelation. It is not that humanity must raise itself up to divinity, but rather, divinity humbles itself and enters into humanity to become human. All the created world, most especially each human being, is a locus of the divine.

Living the Paschal Mystery

When we recognise that all of creation is a place for God's indwelling we see that the sacred is infused within the secular. There is not such a sharp distinction any longer between the holy and the profane, for by the incarnation the divine has become human, the eternal time-bound, and the immortal mortal.

We now treat not only humans but all creation with the respect and humility that it deserves as a place for the divine. Despite all the evidence to the contrary – wars, disease, poverty, selfishness, and even death itself – God has the last word, which is eternal life. God who is all powerful is also all vulnerable. God suffers with creation when it is desecrated. God is not far removed and otherworldly. God intimately knows human life and the human struggle for justice, dignity, and equality. Jesus, the incarnation of the Word of God underwent the paschal mystery of dying and rising. By so doing he gave new meaning to these most fundamental aspects of our world. Death now leads to life, as the created world is infused with the divine.

Focusing the Gospel

Key words and phrases: [S]he treasured all these things and pondered them in her heart.

To the point: On this solemnity of Mary we are given only a small snippet of her life. In the gospel all we hear is that she 'treasured all these things and pondered them in her heart'. Many times there will be things we don't understand in life. Today Mary's response is lifted up for us to contemplate. When faced with the infinite mystery of God become human, Mary holds it close to her very core, safe in the centre of her heart.

Model Penitential Act

Presider: As we gather today to consecrate this New Year to God through the intercession of Mary, the Holy Mother of God, let us pause to acknowledge our own sinfulness and need of God's mercy. . .[*pause*]

Lord Jesus, you are Son of God and son of Mary: Lord, have mercy.

Christ Jesus, through you we are able to call God 'Abba, Father!': Christ, have mercy.

Lord Jesus, you give us every spiritual blessing: Lord, have mercy.

Model Universal Prayer (Prayer of the Faithful)

Presider: As we enter into this New Year let us offer our intentions to God, assured of his love and faithful blessing.

Response: Lord, hear our prayer.

That the church might be a sign of the merciful, compassionate, parental love of God . . .

That this New Year might bring peace and overflowing blessings to all the nations of the world . . .

That, through the intercession of Mary, those who have lost their way might come home to God. . .

That each of us here might be a tangible blessing to all we meet . . .

Presider: Loving God, we commend this New Year to your merciful care, along with all of our needs, hopes, and dreams. We ask this through Jesus Christ our Lord. Amen.

About Liturgy

Blessings: Today's readings give us an opportunity to reflect on what the church teaches us about blessings. You may already know about the *Book of Blessings*, which is the universal church's official ritual text for blessings used throughout the liturgical year and for specific occasions in a parish's or household's life. To get a substantial understanding of the theology of blessings, read the 'General Introduction' to this ritual book. From those introductory notes we learn that God has been blessing us from the very beginning of creation. It is simply what God does. 'He who is all good has made all things good, so that he might fill his creatures with blessings' (1). Christ is 'the Father's supreme blessing upon us' (3); and those who become God's children through Christ are given the Spirit of Christ 'in order to bring God's healing blessings to the world' (3).

On this first day of the year, when we give praise to God for the blessings we have received through Christ by his coming into human history through the life of a woman, Mary, let us recommit to being a blessing for others and to bring God's healing blessings to the world.

COLLECT

Let us pray.

Pause for silent prayer

O God, who through the fruitful virginity of
      Blessed Mary
bestowed on the human race
the grace of eternal salvation,
grant, we pray,
that we may experience the intercession of her,
through whom we were found worthy
to receive the author of life,
our Lord Jesus Christ, your Son.
Who lives and reigns with you in the unity of
      the Holy Spirit,
one God, for ever and ever. **Amen.**

FOR REFLECTION

• In the first reading Aaron is instructed by God on how to bless the people. In this New Year, how might we dedicate our lives to be a blessing for all those around us?

• In the second reading from Galatians we hear God referred to as 'Abba, Father'. In your prayer life how do you address God?

• We can imagine how the shepherds' lives might have changed that night they drew close to Jesus in the manger. How has your faith grown and deepened this Christmas season?

Homily Points

• In the gospel we are told the shepherds 'hurried away' to confirm the angel's message to them. Mary, after hearing her own earth-shattering news from an angel, 'hurried' to visit her cousin Elizabeth. The good news shared with Mary at Jesus's conception and with the shepherds at Jesus's birth motivates the ones who hear it to immediate action. This overflowing joy and wonder demands to be shared.

• This haste is counterbalanced by Mary's response to the shepherds' news: '[S]he treasured all these things and pondered them in her heart'. How in our lives as Christians can we balance the need for haste and the need for reflection? How might we invite both of these states into our lives this New Year?

SPIRITUALITY

GOSPEL ACCLAMATION
Matt 2:2

℟. Alleluia, alleluia!
We saw his star as it rose
and have come to do the Lord homage.
℟. Alleluia!

Gospel

Matt 2:1-12

After Jesus had been born at Bethlehem in Judaea during the reign of King Herod, some wise men came to Jerusalem from the east. 'Where is the infant king of the Jews?' they asked. 'We saw his star as it rose and have come to do him homage.' When King Herod heard this he was perturbed, and so was the whole of Jerusalem. He called together all the chief priests and the scribes of the people, and enquired of them where the Christ was to be born. 'At Bethlehem in Judaea,' they told him 'for this is what the prophet wrote:

And you, Bethlehem, in the land of Judah
you are by no means least among the leaders of Judah,
for out of you will come a leader who will shepherd my people Israel.'

Continued in Appendix, p. 274.

Reflecting on the Gospel

The feast of the Epiphany is celebrated in many cultures and often more prominently than Christmas! At a time when many households have taken down decorations and put away special dishes from the season, we are reminded that there are still celebrations to be had. This story of the visit from the magi is unique to Matthew's gospel and when read on its own terms it can be especially revealing. Often, however, we read this gospel with preconceived notions. For example, the text doesn't say how many magi there were but because they gave three gifts (gold, frankincense, and myrrh) artists, preachers, and homilists through the centuries talk about there being three kings. Aside from fulfilling Scripture (e.g., Isa 60:6), the gifts are symbolic, as they were given to kings or divinities in antiquity. Gold is a precious element representing kingship, frankincense a perfume, and myrrh a costly balm or ointment.

And this leads to the term, 'king', which is not used in the gospel text. Instead, the term is 'wise men' ['magi'; NABRE], which designated the Persian (modern-day Iran) priestly caste. Thus, Matthew foreshadows the postresurrection mission to the Gentiles by showing Gentiles (Persians) coming to worship the child Jesus. Ultimately, this is a story about who Jesus is and what his mission will be.

It is also significant that the magi worship the *child* Jesus. Matthew does not use the term infant here for Jesus is no longer an infant. And it's clear from the story that Mary is at her *house*, not in a manger as Luke would have it. Again, when we read these stories on their own terms without importing 'what we know' from other stories, a different picture emerges, and that can be a picture that conforms more closely to the theology that the evangelist wanted to impart.

In the story following today's gospel, Matthew tells us of the Holy Family's flight into Egypt to escape Herod slaughtering all the male children in Bethlehem up to two years old (Matt 2:16; NABRE). This is a clear indication that the magi visited the home about two years after the birth of Jesus. And the point here is theological. Jesus is brought to Egypt so that the Scripture passage might be fulfilled, 'Out of Egypt I called my son' (Matt 2:15; Hos 11:1; NABRE). So in today's gospel reading we see the mission to the Gentiles and the universal scope of salvation foreshadowed by the visit of the magi to worship the child Jesus. Salvation knows no bounds. This is a cause for celebration indeed!

Living the Paschal Mystery

Both children and adults enjoy giving and receiving gifts: it seems to be part of the human condition. For the receiver there is an element of surprise. What could it be? Perhaps some anticipation comes with opening the gift and there is a sense of wonder. For the giver there is the joy of generosity, in seeing the look on the face of the one who receives. There is the joy that comes in simply thinking of the other and providing something for the other not because it was earned, but instead because it comes from a place of generosity. Stories of gifts given and received are numerous in the Scriptures, antiquity, and history. They come to be part of family and friend lore as well. It's likely that many of us can quickly call to mind gifts that we've given or received. The gifts given by the magi in some way represent or symbolise the best physical objects that humanity has to offer. And Jesus is the best that God has to offer. By the conclusion of the gospel story humanity will have executed Jesus, the gift of God, only to have God raise him up from the dead. This expression of the paschal mystery guides our thoughts today when the magi present the best of human intentions.

Focusing the Gospel

Key words and phrases: The sight of the star filled them with delight.

To the point: In today's gospel creation itself proclaims the birth of Jesus to the magi, the kings who are strangers in the land of Israel. They follow the star in their search for this newborn king, and when they find him not in the palace in Jerusalem but in a humble home in Bethlehem, they worship this baby and offer him kingly gifts. The magi respond with joy to the revelation of Jesus, unlike Herod who is 'perturbed'. Unable to receive the gift of Jesus or to offer Jesus the gift of himself he remains hostage to his greed and lust for power.

Connecting the Gospel

to the first and second readings: For the first time in our Advent and Christmas gospel readings the gift of Jesus is extended to the Gentiles. This is foreshadowed in Isaiah's prophecy to the people of Israel, 'The nations come to your light'. Jesus, the light of the world, born to the Jewish people, invites everyone, Jews and Gentiles, into the light of God's love. The apostle Paul proclaims in his letter to the Ephesians, 'pagans now share the same inheritance, that they are parts of the same body, and that the same promise has been made to them, in Christ Jesus, through the gospel'.

to experience: Paul proclaims the radical inclusivity of God's kingdom ushered in by the mystery of the incarnation: God become human, longing to draw all of creation to God-self. How do we practise this radical inclusivity in our own lives? How might we not only welcome the stranger but also reverence the stranger's wisdom, understanding, and right to be among us?

Connecting the Responsorial Psalm

to the readings: Psalm 71 is a prayer for the king of Israel, asking that the entire world might receive blessing through him as a representative of God and God's divine judgement and justice. In the gospel we see this prayer brought to fulfilment. The psalmist prays, 'Before him all kings shall fall prostrate, / all nations shall serve him'. In the gospel the magi (representatives from foreign lands) come and do just this – prostrate themselves before Jesus and do him homage. The psalmist proclaims that this king of great glory who rules all nations is concerned with the poor and the lowly, and then in the gospel we see that the king is in fact one of the poor and the lowly. Jesus is not found in a lavish palace with guards, wealth, and an army at his command. He is a defenceless child born to commoners.

to psalmist preparation: Today's feast marks the opening of the covenant to all the people of the world. Just as the magi welcomed the sight of the star with great joy, we, too, are invited to joyfully accept this humble child as our king and Lord. The psalm you proclaim today lauds the glory of this king and also extolls his compassion to the poor and the oppressed. How might you proclaim God's glory and compassion within the acts of your daily life?

PROMPTS FOR FAITH-SHARING

The prophet Isaiah tells us, 'Arise, . . . for your light has come'. When have you had the opportunity to be a light for others?

The magi follow a star that leads them to Jesus, God with us. In your life, how has creation helped you to know God?

The magi, strangers from a foreign country, travel to the land of Israel and are welcomed into Jesus's home. In your life of faith when have you encountered different cultures and/or religions? How has this experience changed your understanding of God and humanity?

In today's second reading St. Paul proclaims the inclusivity of God's kingdom where both Jews and Gentiles are welcome. How do you welcome those of different backgrounds into your home or parish?

CELEBRATION

Model Penitential Act

Presider: On this great feast of Epiphany we are invited anew to walk in the light of the Lord. Let us seek God's mercy for the times we have preferred the darkness to this saving light . . . [*pause*]

> Lord Jesus, you are the light of the world: Lord, have mercy.
>
> Christ Jesus, creation itself heralds you as the king: Christ, have mercy.
>
> Lord Jesus, you are ruler and shepherd of the world: Lord, have mercy.

Homily Points

• Throughout the Advent and Christmas gospels we have seen God communicate with people in many different ways. Mary, Joseph, and the shepherds in the fields of Bethlehem all receive angelic visitors to tell them of Jesus's birth. Elizabeth and John the Baptist know of Jesus's presence in the womb of Mary by the power of the Holy Spirit. In today's gospel the scribes and priests know the Messiah's birthplace through the prophecies they have studied their entire lives. For the magi, creation itself points the way to God through their study of the stars and the new star they have charted and followed.

• Of the many people who hear of the Messiah's arrival, there is one who does not receive the news with joy and wonder. The magi arrive in Jerusalem looking for the newborn king of the Jews and instead they find Herod, a power-hungry ruler. It has been said that the gospel is meant to 'comfort the afflicted and afflict the comfortable'. Herod is certainly not comforted by the news of a newborn king but instead is 'perturbed'. In the gospel Herod becomes the first of many who will reject Jesus's light, life, and love.

• The gifts of the magi reveal the nature of Jesus to us. Gold is a gift befitting a king. Frankincense was a precious incense burned at the temple as a sign of the presence of God. Myrrh is mentioned in the gospels surrounding Jesus's death. It is offered to Jesus on the cross mixed with wine, which he refuses to drink, and it is among the perfumes and spices that Nicodemus brings to prepare Jesus's body for burial. The gifts proclaim Jesus king, God, and human. From creation to angelic messages to small details in the gospel, it seems that God desires to communicate God-self to us through whatever means available. The question is, are we listening?

Model Universal Prayer (Prayer of the Faithful)

Presider: On this feast of Epiphany we lift up our prayers and petitions to the God of light.

Response: Lord, hear our prayer.

That the church might shine as a light, inviting all nations into the peace and justice of the Lord . . .

That the nations of the world might attend to the oppressed and needy within their midst . . .

That those who walk in the darkness of greed, jealousy, and lust for power might be touched by the merciful light of God . . .

That all of us gathered here might welcome the light of God into our lives to eradicate the darkness of sin . . .

Presider: God of creation, you call to us through the radiance of the sun and the stars to fashion our lives after that of your son Jesus, the light of the world. Hear and grant our prayers through Christ our Lord. Amen.

COLLECT

(from the Mass during the Day)
Let us pray

Pause for silent prayer

O God, who on this day
revealed your Only Begotten Son to
    the nations
by the guidance of a star,
grant in your mercy
that we, who know you already by faith,
may be brought to behold the beauty of
    your sublime glory.
Through our Lord Jesus Christ, your Son,
who lives and reigns with you in the unity
    of the Holy Spirit,
one God, for ever and ever. Amen.

FIRST READING

Isa 60:1-6

Arise, shine out Jerusalem, for your light
    has come,
the glory of the Lord is rising on you,
though night still covers the earth
and darkness the peoples.
Above you the Lord now rises
and above you his glory appears.
The nations come to your light
and kings to your dawning brightness.

Lift up your eyes and look around:
all are assembling and coming
    towards you,
your sons from far away
and daughters being tenderly carried.

At this sight you will glow radiant,
your heart throbbing and full;
since the riches of the sea will flow to you;
the wealth of the nations come to you;

camels in throngs will cover you,
and dromedaries of Midian and Ephah;
everyone in Sheba will come,
bringing gold and incense
and singing the praise of the Lord.

RESPONSORIAL PSALM
Ps 71:1-2, 7-8, 10-13 (11)

R̸. All nations shall fall prostrate before
    you, O Lord.

O God, give your judgement to the king,
to a king's son your justice,
that he may judge your people in justice
and your poor in right judgement.

R̸. All nations shall fall prostrate before
    you, O Lord.

In his days justice shall flourish
and peace till the moon fails.
He shall rule from sea to sea,
from the Great River to earth's bounds.

R̸. All nations shall fall prostrate before
    you, O Lord.

The Kings of Tarshish and the sea coasts
shall pay him tribute.
The kings of Sheba and Seba
shall bring him gifts.
Before him all kings shall fall prostrate,
all nations shall serve him.

R̸. All nations shall fall prostrate before
    you, O Lord.

For he shall save the poor when they cry
and the needy who are helpless.
He will have pity on the weak
and save the lives of the poor.

R̸. All nations shall fall prostrate before
    you, O Lord.

SECOND READING
Eph 3:2-3, 5-6

You have probably heard how I have been entrusted by God with the grace he meant for you, and that it was by a revelation that I was given the knowledge of the mystery. This mystery that has now been revealed through the Spirit to his holy apostles and prophets was unknown to any men in past generations; it means that pagans now share the same inheritance, that they are parts of the same body, and that the same promise has been made to them, in Christ Jesus, through the gospel.

About Liturgy

Blessing of calendars: Closely connected to this solemnity of the Epiphany is the focus on the blessing of time. We see this in the tradition of the announcement of Easter and the moveable feasts, sung this day after the proclamation of the gospel. We also see it in the traditional inscription used to bless a house at Epiphany, in which the date of the new calendar year is written above a house's door, along with the initials of the wise men's names: 'C', 'M', and 'B' according to tradition. Perhaps it is because of the beginning of the new year, or because the magi used their keen observation of the movement of the stars that we mark the passage of time with blessings on this day.

If you had invited your community to create their own domestic church calendar (see feast of the Holy Family), today might be a good day to bless these calendars or to send home a blessing prayer people can use to bless their daily calendars. There is no official text found in the Book of Blessings for such a blessing, but you can find a 'Blessing of Calendars on the Feast of the Epiphany' in *The Work of Your Hands* (Liturgical Press).

About Initiation

Copartners in the promise: Today's second reading from Ephesians gives us the crux of the meaning of Epiphany. The revelation given to St. Paul to steward is this: 'pagans now share the same inheritance, that they are parts of the same body, and that the same promise has been made to them, in Christ Jesus, through the gospel' (Eph 3:6). No longer is God's chosen limited to only one people: God's promise is given to all who seek God in Christ, and they become members of the same body of Christ. In light of this revelation, today may be an opportune time to celebrate a Rite of Reception of Baptised Christians into the Full Communion of the Catholic Church. The ritual may take place within or outside of Mass; however, it is preferable that the newly received also celebrate the Eucharist. Although the rite is relatively simple and does not take too much time, it is best to schedule this rite for a Mass at which there are no other additional rites, blessings, or lengthy presentations.

About Liturgical Music

Beyond 'We Three Kings': No Epiphany celebration can go by without singing 'We Three Kings'. However there are many other carols that can take us beyond the literal retelling of the magi story. Songs to look for are those that focus on the promise of God given to all people, such as those that complement the message of today's psalm response, 'All nations shall fall prostrate before you, O Lord' (Ps 72), such as 'O Worship the Lord in the Beauty of Holiness'. Also look for songs that pick up the images from today's first reading of light rising over all.

Some song suggestions are: 'The Race That Long in Darkness Pined'; 'Bethlehem, of Noblest Cities'; *Psallite*'s 'Our City Has No Need of Sun or Moon'.

Announcing Easter: Even though we're not done with Christmas yet, the church reminds us today that the fulcrum of the entire liturgical year is the Easter celebration of the Lord's resurrection. Don't forget to consider preparing to sing the Announcement of Easter and the Moveable Feasts, which are found in appendix I of the Roman Missal. This may be led by the deacon or a cantor.

SPIRITUALITY

GOSPEL ACCLAMATION
Cf. Luke 3:13

℟. Alleluia, alleluia.
Someone is coming, said John,
    someone greater than I.
He will baptise you with the
    Holy Spirit and with fire.
℟. Alleluia, alleluia.

Gospel

Luke 3:15-16, 21-22

**A feeling of expectancy
had grown among
the people, who were
beginning to think that
John might be the Christ,
so John declared before
them all, 'I baptise you
with water, but someone
is coming, someone who
is more powerful than
I am and I am not fit to
undo the strap of his
sandals; he will baptise
you with the Holy Spirit and fire.'**

**Now when all the people had been
baptised and while Jesus after his own
baptism was at prayer, heaven opened
and the Holy Spirit descended on him in
bodily shape, like a dove. And a voice
came from heaven, 'You are my Son, the
Beloved; my favour rests on you.'**

Reflecting on the Gospel

The baptism of an infant is the cause of much joy, celebration, and love among family and friends. The baby is welcomed into the Christian community, a community of grace, support, and encouragement in the face of all that life can bring. This ritual action has its roots not only in Jesus but in John, 'the Baptist' who was so named precisely because of this action he performed at the Jordan River. The early followers of Jesus recognised that Jesus's own ministry began after he was baptised by John, a story first recounted in the Gospel of Mark, which states that John preached a baptism of 'forgiveness of sins'. This story is echoed in Luke as well (Luke 3:3).

Thus, we (and the early Christians) experience a theological quandary. Why did Jesus, who is said to be without sin, submit to baptism by John? To what purpose or to what end is a baptism of forgiveness of sins to one without sin? Responses to this question were as varied as the gospel writers and church fathers themselves. Matthew says that it is 'to fulfill all righteousness' (Matt 3:15; NABRE). The Gospel of John simply neglects to say that Jesus was baptised by John. Instead, John the Baptist merely testifies to Jesus without baptising him at all. Luke places the baptism of Jesus in the passive voice and almost as an afterthought: 'Now when all the people had been baptised and while Jesus after his own baptism . . .' (Luke 3:21). Other than the Synoptics, neither Paul nor any other New Testament authors mention Jesus being baptised.

As indicated by the gospels, the ministry of Jesus began at or shortly after his baptism. And Luke shows that the Holy Spirit was active at this time, descending upon Jesus 'in bodily shape, like a dove'. Though Matthew says the Spirit descended upon him like a dove, only Luke says, 'in *bodily shape*, like a dove'. This phrase reflects Luke's tendency to objectivise the supernatural and it is something we will notice throughout this gospel. Further, Luke is also the only evangelist to say that Jesus was at prayer during this event. Prayer is another Lucan theme that we will see throughout his gospel: Luke shows Jesus at prayer more than any other evangelist. Luke will also show the early Christian community at prayer in the Acts of the Apostles.

So in these four short verses we have Lucan theology bursting from the page. Jesus is baptised by John (passive voice) though John preaches a baptism of forgiveness of sins. Luke objectivises the supernatural by saying the Holy Spirit descended in bodily form like a dove, and Luke shows Jesus at prayer.

Living the Paschal Mystery

When we are about to make an important or life-altering decision we certainly pause to give it some thought. Before accepting a new position, a big move, or making a commitment to someone or something we likely ask God's guidance and wisdom. Some state simply that this is a prayer. And it seems Jesus did the same: he prayed before he embarked on his ministry.

If Luke is certain to show us that Jesus prayed, we are sure to see this as an example for our own lives. We are to pray. Significantly, Luke does not tell us what Jesus prayed only *that* he prayed. And this has ramifications for us too. We are to be a people of prayer who consult and communicate with the Almighty, seeking direction, guidance, wisdom, and insight before embarking on our way.

When we pray we imitate Jesus and the relationship he lived with the Father. We also imitate the early Christians. We recognise that prayer is not limited to the liturgy or to formal recitation of memorised texts. Instead, it is a reflection of the relationship we have with God.

Focusing the Gospel

Key words and phrases: You are my Son, the Beloved; my favour rests on you.

To the point: In the beginning of Luke's gospel Jesus is named 'Son of God' by the angel Gabriel, 'my Lord' by Elizabeth, and 'Messiah' by the angel of the Lord. Now, after being baptised in the River Jordan, Jesus is given another name, 'my Son, the Beloved'. Assured of God's love and approval, Jesus is ready to begin his public ministry.

Connecting the Gospel

to the second reading: In the Acts of the Apostles we see the moment of the baptism of Jesus, which was first witnessed by the people of Israel and then opened up to all people. Peter, the quintessential Jewish apostle, is called to visit the Roman centurion Cornelius, a Gentile. Through prayer, mystical vision, and meeting with Cornelius, Peter is finally able to proclaim, 'God does not have favourites'. Even though the good news of Jesus first came to the people of Israel, it is meant as a gift for all.

to experience: It is easy in life to want to divide the world into 'us' and 'them'. As human beings we are naturally more comfortable when surrounded by people and places that are familiar to us. As Christians, however, we are called to proclaim a God who shows no favouritism. How might we live this good news in our lives?

Connecting the Responsorial Psalm

to the readings: This psalm gives praise to God, whose might and glory is shown by his command of the waters of the earth. This water is destructive at times through flooding, but water also brings life into the dry desert. We hear that '[t]he Lord's voice [is] resounding on the waters' and remember how in the beginning the Holy Spirit hovered over the waters of the earth. We hear that '[t]he Lord sat enthroned over the flood' and remember God promising Noah and his descendants never again to send water to wipe out creation. In the gospel a new moment in salvation history is narrated and it, too, contains water. Jesus steps forwards to be baptised in the waters of the Jordan River and when he comes out we again hear the 'Lord's voice resounding on the waters'. This heavenly voice proclaims, 'You are my Son, the Beloved; my favour rests on you', and we can picture Jesus at prayer 'enthroned' at the Jordan River as he lives more fully into his kingship as God's beloved.

to psalmist preparation: Proclaim this psalm with awe and wonder. The God we serve and worship is the God of all creation. Remember a time when you were awestruck by nature. Perhaps it was during a beautiful sunset, seeing the view from a mountaintop or gazing out at the ocean for the first time. Our God is creator and ruler of all this. As part of his creation let us, too, cry, 'Glory'!

PROMPTS FOR FAITH-SHARING

On this feast of the Baptism of the Lord, consider your own baptismal day. What do you remember or what have you been told about the day you were baptised?

This feast day officially marks the last day of the Christmas season. Looking back on the weeks since December 25th, what has been most meaningful for you this Christmas? What traditions would you like to continue? Looking forwards to next year, what would you like to do differently?

After being baptised, Jesus prays. In Luke's gospel we often see Jesus in prayer. How would you like to enrich your own prayer life this year?

At his baptism Jesus hears the voice of God saying, 'You are my Son, the Beloved; my favour rests on you'. Is it easy or difficult for you to believe that you are God's beloved? Why do you think this is?

CELEBRATION

Model Rite for the Blessing and Sprinkling of Water

Presider: On this feast of the Baptism of the Lord we recall the grace of our own baptism. As we are sprinkled with holy water let us prepare ourselves to enter into this celebration with joy and a renewed commitment to our own baptismal promises . . . [*pause*]

[*continue with* The Roman Missal, *Appendix II*]

Homily Points

• The baptism that John preaches in Luke's gospel is 'a baptism of repentance for the forgiveness of sins' (3:3; NABRE). Having no need for repentance, conversion, or forgiveness, Jesus nevertheless joins the crowds on the banks of the Jordan River.

• In an action that prefigures the cross and resurrection, Jesus bears the sins of all others as he goes down into the Jordan and then reemerges to be named the 'beloved Son' of God. Pope Benedict XVI tells us, 'To accept the invitation to be baptised now means to go to the place of Jesus's Baptism. It is to go where he identifies himself with us and to receive there our identification with him. The point where he anticipates death has now become the point where we anticipate rising again with him' (*Jesus of Nazareth*). In Jesus's baptism and our own, we touch the place where humanity and divinity, as well as mortality and immortality, meet.

• Jesus's baptism also marks the beginning of his public ministry. In his book *Life of the Beloved*, Henri Nouwen says, 'Self-rejection is the greatest enemy of the spiritual life because it contradicts the sacred voice that calls us the "Beloved".' When we embrace and live into the reality that 'being the Beloved expresses the core truth of our existence', we are ready to go forth, following in the footsteps of Jesus to love and serve others. In baptism we are configured to Jesus, named children of the light, and commissioned to go forth as beloved sons and daughters of God.

Model Universal Prayer (Prayer of the Faithful)

Presider: As beloved sons and daughters of God we dare to bring our petitions before the Lord.

Response: Lord, hear our prayer.

That the church might be a voice of justice for those neglected and oppressed in the world . . .

That nations might work together to protect clean water sources and provide adequate drinking water for all people . . .

That the forgotten of society, especially prisoners, the mentally ill, and the disabled might be treated as beloved sons and daughters of God . . .

That all of us here might be renewed in the grace of our own Baptism to follow in the footsteps of Jesus . . .

Presider: God of mercy, you never cease to call us to repentance and fulness of life. Hear our prayers as we strive to follow the way of Jesus. We ask this through Christ our Lord. Amen.

COLLECT
Let us pray

Pause for silent prayer

Almighty ever-living God,
who, when Christ had been baptised in the
    River Jordan
and as the Holy Spirit descended upon him,
solemnly declared him your beloved Son,
grant that your children
    by adoption,
reborn of water and the Holy Spirit,
may always be well pleasing to you.
Through our Lord Jesus Christ, your Son,
who lives and reigns with you in the unity
    of the Holy Spirit,
one God, for ever and ever. **Amen.**

FIRST READING
Isa 42:1-4, 6-7

Thus says the Lord:

Here is my servant whom I uphold,
    my chosen one in whom my soul
        delights.
I have endowed him with my spirit
    that he may bring true justice to the
        nations.

He does not cry out or shout aloud,
    or make his voice heard in the streets.
He does not break the crushed reed,
    nor quench the wavering flame.

Faithfully he brings true justice;
    he will neither waver, nor be crushed
until true justice is established on earth,
    for the islands are awaiting his law.

I, the Lord, have called you to serve the
        cause of right;
I have taken you by the hand and
        formed you;
I have appointed you as covenant of the
        people and light of the nations,
to open the eyes of the blind
to free captives from prison,
    and those who live in darkness from the
        dungeon.

CATECHESIS

RESPONSORIAL PSALM
Ps 28:1-4, 9-10 (11)

R℣. The Lord will bless his people with peace.

O give the Lord you sons of God,
give the Lord glory and power;
give the Lord the glory of his name.
Adore the Lord in his holy court.

R℣. The Lord will bless his people with peace.

The Lord's voice resounding on the waters,
the Lord on the immensity of waters;
the voice of the Lord, full of power,
the voice of the Lord, full of splendour.

R℣. The Lord will bless his people with peace.

The God of glory thunders.
In his temple they all cry: 'Glory!'
The Lord sat enthroned over the flood;
the Lord sits as king for ever.

R℣. The Lord will bless his people with peace.

SECOND READING
Acts 10:34-38

Peter addressed Cornelius and his household: 'The truth I have now come to realise' he said 'is that God does not have favourites, but that anybody of any nationality who fears God and does what is right is acceptable to him.

'It is true, God sent his word to the people of Israel, and it was to them that the good news of peace was brought by Jesus Christ-but Jesus Christ is Lord of all men. You must have heard about the recent happenings in Judaea; about Jesus of Nazareth and how he began in Galilee, after John had been preaching baptism. God had anointed him with the Holy Spirit and with power, and because God was with him, Jesus went about doing good and curing all who had fallen into the power of the devil.'

About Liturgy

Epiphany, part two: In the Eastern church Epiphany (or Theophany, meaning 'manifestation of God') evokes three different scenes in the life of Christ. First is the visitation of the magi and the epiphany that God's promise is given to all people. Second is today's manifestation at the Jordan of God's chosen one in Jesus. Third is next week's revelation of God's glory made visible in the first public miracle of Christ at a wedding at Cana. This triptych is often seen together in religious art and gives us a profound insight into the meaning of Christmas.

For most people Christmas is a children's holiday and a time for adults to return to the innocence and joy of their childhood. The emphasis in both secular and religious imagery on the Christ-child in Bethlehem reinforces this idea. However, the Christmas feast of the Baptism of the Lord counterbalances that notion. It reminds us that the child in the manger becomes an adult on mission, and that mission will eventually lead not only to a feast filled with rich food and choice wine but also to suffering and death. This is one reason why it is important that we mark this Sunday as the final day of Christmas.

This triple-revelation gives us a summary of Christ's mission and, thus, the mission of every disciple who follows him into those same baptismal waters. As we memorialise the baptism of Jesus today let us also remember our own baptism and call to mind our participation in Christ's mission 'to open the eyes of the blind to free captives from prison, / and those who live in darkness from the dungeon' (Isa 42:7).

About Initiation

Remembering our baptism: The Rite of Christian Initiation of Adults (RCIA) is primarily for the initiation of those who are unbaptised. However, baptised persons who were baptised as infants as Roman Catholics or in another Christian community but did not receive any further formation in the Christian way of life may benefit from a similar process for catechesis as that of the catechumens. Nonetheless, their formation must always be seen as post-baptismal and mystagogical, recalling that they already are members of the church and children of God by their baptism. (See especially RCIA 400 to 403.)

One way to honour the baptism of these candidates preparing for reception or for confirmation and Eucharist is to help them recall their baptism. Although some may have no actual memory of the event, you can still help them through their imagination to picture some of the symbols of their baptism: water, light, oil, name, garment, godparent, minister. Then have a prayerful discussion on what each of these symbols means to them and to the church. This is also a good exercise for all the baptised to do today!

If you have baptised *uncatechised* adults (as described in RCIA 400), today might be a good day to celebrate the optional Rite of Welcoming. If you have baptised *catechised* adults preparing for reception or confirmation, today might be a good time do a simple blessing for them as they continue in their preparation. Although both of these groups are baptised, you should not combine uncatechised and catechised persons together in the rituals because they are at different levels in their journey of conversion.

About Liturgical Music

Christmas isn't over yet: The Christmas season officially ends after the Baptism of the Lord. Although it may seem strange to sing Christmas carols in the middle of January, be sure to include at least a few songs that mark this day as the last day of Christmas. *Laudate* and *Celebration Hymnal for Everyone* include extensive selections for this day. Try 'When Jesus comes to be baptised' for a good recent LM text.

13 JANUARY 2019
THE BAPTISM OF THE LORD

ORDINARY
TIME I

SPIRITUALITY

GOSPEL ACCLAMATION
Cf. Jn 6:63, 68

℟. Alleluia, alleluia.
Your words are spirit, Lord,
and they are life:
you have the message of eternal life.
℟. Alleluia, alleluia.

Gospel

John 2:1-11

There was a wedding at Cana in Galilee. The mother of Jesus was there, and Jesus and his disciples had also been invited. When they ran out of wine, since the wine provided for the wedding was all finished, the mother of Jesus said to him, 'They have no wine.' Jesus said, 'Woman why turn to me? My hour has not come yet.' His mother said to the servants, 'Do whatever he tells you.' There were six stone water jars standing there, meant for the ablutions that are customary among the Jews; each could hold twenty or thirty gallons. Jesus said to the servants, 'Fill the jars with water,' and they filled them to the brim. 'Draw some out now' he told them 'and take it to the steward.' They did this; the steward tasted the water, and it had turned into wine. Having no idea where it came from – only the servants who had drawn the water knew – the steward called the bridegroom and said, 'People generally serve the best wine first, and keep the cheaper sort till the guests have plenty to drink; but you have kept the best wine till now.'

This was the first of the signs given by Jesus: it was given at Cana in Galilee. He let his glory be seen, and his disciples believed in him.

Reflecting on the Gospel

How many of us have been to a wedding party preceded by the groom's dinner, which is itself preceded by a number of festivities celebrating the bride and groom and their new life together? There are standard elements in most wedding celebrations, including the exchanging of vows (within a Mass or not) and usually a dinner or some food is served to the guests. Quite often there is dancing or some other activity. It's a day to remember for the guests, the hosts, the bride and groom, and their families. Family stories will be told for many years after each wedding, as legends become lore.

In antiquity, marriage celebrations followed a pattern as well, as reflected in today's gospel. One such cultural element that is still followed today(!) is that the best wine is served before a lesser quality wine. Such norms are the background setting for Jesus's first sign, as narrated by the Gospel of John. (In the Gospel of John, Jesus performs seven signs rather than a myriad of miracles, and the signs are indications of his true identity.) Interestingly, this gospel is the only one to tell this story. The Synoptic Gospel writers neglect this story: they may not have been aware of it.

Although liturgically we are in Year (or Cycle) C when we read from the Gospel of Luke, we begin Ordinary Time with this reading from the Gospel of John, which does not refer to Jesus's mother by name, for she is never named in this gospel, but rather, Mary is called 'the mother of Jesus's. According to this gospel, not only is she present at the beginning of Jesus's ministry, but she will be present at the cross too, accompanied by the Beloved Disciple (who, like the mother of Jesus, remains nameless). For the Gospel of John, the emphasis is on Jesus to such a degree that the other characters do not even have names!

And this is a good point for us. Namely, our emphasis should be on Jesus and his true identity. It is easy to be drawn away from him and look to novelties or curiosities. But in the Fourth Gospel we have stories of seven signs that Jesus performs, each revealing his identity as Son of God, the Word made flesh. We need look no further. For the disciple, and certainly for the evangelist, the focus is on Jesus for he is the incarnation of the Word of God and his words are life eternal.

Living the Paschal Mystery

Jesus was a living, breathing human being with a mother, father (Joseph), brothers, and sisters according to the Synoptics. According to today's gospel reading, he attended a wedding feast, and we can probably assume this was not his first or last wedding feast. In the shortest of all the Bible verses, according to many translations, the Gospel of John later tells us, 'And Jesus wept' (11:35; NABRE). In sum, Jesus was a human being rather than a divine puppet. He experienced emotions from celebrating at a wedding to weeping at the death of a friend. Ultimately, he faced death itself, as each of us will. By undergoing his passion and death, which led to resurrection and life, he gives us the promise of life eternal. In Jesus, divinity became humanity thus exalting humanity to the divine. The paschal mystery nourishes our faith with the knowledge that our own personal death will lead to eternal life because of what God has done in Christ.

Focusing the Gospel

Key words and phrases: This was the first of the signs given by Jesus: it was given at Cana in Galilee. He let his glory be seen, and his disciples believed in him.

To the point: In the Gospel of John we do not hear of Jesus performing 'miracles'; instead he offers 'signs' that reveal his own identity and the nature of the kingdom of God. From this first sign in Cana we can glean that the kingdom is like a wedding feast where the wine will never run out and the joy grows ever deeper.

Connecting the Gospel

to the first reading: The wedding theme of today's gospel is echoed in the first reading in which the prophet Isaiah assures Israel, 'Like a young man marrying a virgin, / so will the one who built you wed you, / and as the bridegroom rejoices in his bride, / so will your God rejoice in you'. Just as a wedding feast is an apt image for the kingdom of God, marriage is a metaphor used in both the Old and New Testaments to symbolise the relationship God desires with God's people. This relationship is not without its difficulties. But even after infidelity – when the people of God turned away from the covenant and worshipped idols – God remains faithful.

to experience: All relationships, especially marriage, require work and celebration to keep the relationship vital. How do you set aside time to nurture and celebrate your relationship with God?

Connecting the Responsorial Psalm

to the readings: The psalmist enjoins us, 'O sing a new song to the Lord'. In the first reading from Isaiah, the prophet announces that Israel will receive a new name. Instead of '[a]bandoned' or '[f]orsaken', Israel shall now be called 'The Wedded'. Isaiah tells the nation, recently brought out of exile in Babylon, to begin again in their homeland to live out the covenant with their God. At the wedding feast in Cana we encounter Jesus who is also on the edge of something new. At the behest of his mother, he performs his first public sign and begins to reveal his identity to those closest to him. Our God is one of new beginnings and we are called to be a people of hope who believe that newness is possible: new behaviours, new actions, new love, and new life.

to psalmist preparation: In worship, we often return to the songs that we know and love to express our adoration for God. Today the psalmist reminds us to sing something new. The creator God invites us to embrace our own God-given creativity. Where are you being called to newness in your own life?

PROMPTS FOR FAITH-SHARING

In the first reading from Isaiah we see our relationship to God as that of a bride and bridegroom. One metaphor alone cannot contain the mystery of our covenant with God. In what ways is this metaphor helpful and true for you in your spiritual journey?

In the psalm we are encouraged to 'sing a new song to the Lord'. Where might God be calling you to 'newness' in your own life?

Read through the list of spiritual gifts in the second reading (1 Cor 12:8-10). What gifts do you recognise in your own life and community? Which gifts are your community in need of at this moment in time?

Jesus's signs disclose himself and the kingdom of God to us. What does today's gospel about the wedding feast in Cana reveal to you about Jesus's nature and kingdom?

CELEBRATION

Model Penitential Act

Presider: In today's gospel reading Mary instructs the servers at the wedding feast in Cana, 'Do whatever he tells you'. These words are addressed to us as well in the life of faith. For the times that we have not listened attentively to the voice of Jesus calling us to righteousness, we ask for God's pardon and healing . . . [*pause*]

Lord Jesus, you invite us to collaborate in your saving work: Lord, have mercy.

Christ Jesus, you call us to newness of life: Christ, have mercy.

Lord Jesus, you provide for all our needs: Lord, have mercy.

Homily Points

• In the first half of the Gospel of John, Jesus performs seven signs that reveal Jesus's identity to us, as well as the nature of the kingdom of God. In these signs Jesus turns an abundance of water into wine, cures the sick and the lame, feeds the hungry, walks on water, and raises Lazarus from the dead. Through these signs we see that the kingdom of God is one where there will be no more illness, hunger, grief, destruction, or death. As children of the kingdom we are called to be signs of this kingdom of peace and abundance.

• We are given direction in becoming 'kingdom people' in today's second reading. As human persons we've all experienced moments of feeling self-righteous about our own talents or envious of another's. St. Paul counsels us against this mind-set. When we compare ourselves to others we set up distinctions. We are either better or worse and we are usually not peaceful about either. St. Paul offers us another way: all abilities are given as gifts by the Holy Spirit, and all gifts are meant to be used for the good of the community.

• Mary also shows us the way to the kingdom. Despite Jesus's first dismissive remarks to his mother, Mary tells the waiters at the wedding feast, 'Do whatever he tells you'. Mary knows Jesus's generous nature. She probably wasn't surprised when her son, instead of supplying a small portion of wine for the wedding feast, converted upward of 120 gallons of water into wine. Later, Jesus will tell his disciples, 'I came so that they might have life and have it more abundantly' (10:10; NABRE). When we listen to Mary's command, we, too, encounter life in abundance.

Model Universal Prayer (Prayer of the Faithful)

Presider: With confidence in the God of abundance who provides for our every need we bring our prayers before the Lord.

Response: Lord, hear our prayer.

That the church be a sign of the joy of the Kingdom of God by providing hospitality and welcome to all seekers . . .

That the nations of the world adopt a spirit of cooperation and generosity in dealing with both need and plenty . . .

That married couples renew their commitment to each other and find an abundance of joy in their covenant relationship . . .

That all of us here strive to use the spiritual gifts we have been given for the good of all . . .

Presider: God of the covenant, you invite us to live as people of the Kingdom of God in joy and hope. Increase our confidence in your goodness and help us see the abundance that surrounds us spiritually and materially, and to use it for your glory. We ask these prayers through Christ Jesus our Lord. Amen.

COLLECT

Let us pray.

Pause for silent prayer

Almighty ever-living God,
who govern all things,
both in heaven and on earth,
mercifully hear the pleading
      of your people
and bestow your peace on
      our times.
Through our Lord Jesus Christ, your Son,
who lives and reigns with you
      in the unity of the Holy Spirit,
one God, for ever and ever. **Amen.**

FIRST READING
Isa 62:1-5

About Zion I will not be silent,
about Jerusalem I will not grow weary,
until her integrity shines out like the dawn
and her salvation flames like a torch.
The nations then will see your integrity,
all the kings your glory,
and you will be called by a new name,
one which the mouth of the Lord will confer.
You are to be a crown of splendour in the
      hand of the Lord,
a princely diadem in the hand of your God;
no longer are you to be named 'Forsaken',
nor your land 'Abandoned',
but you shall be called 'My Delight'
and your land 'The Wedded';
for the Lord takes delight in you
and your land will have its wedding.
Like a young man marrying a virgin,
so will the one who built you wed you,
and as the bridegroom rejoices in his bride,
so will your God rejoice in you.

CATECHESIS

RESPONSORIAL PSALM
Ps 95:1-3, 7-10 (3)

℟. Proclaim the wonders of the Lord
   among all the peoples.

O sing a new song to the Lord,
sing to the Lord all the earth.
O sing to the Lord, bless his name.

℟. Proclaim the wonders of the Lord
   among all the peoples.

Proclaim his help day by day,
tell among the nations his glory
and his wonders among all the peoples.

℟. Proclaim the wonders of the Lord
   among all the peoples.

Give the Lord, you families of peoples,
give the Lord glory and power,
give the Lord the glory of his name.

℟. Proclaim the wonders of the Lord
   among all the peoples.

Worship the Lord in his temple.
O earth, tremble before him.
Proclaim to the nations: 'God is king.'
He will judge the peoples in fairness.

℟. Proclaim the wonders of the Lord
   among all the peoples.

SECOND READING
1 Cor 12:4-11

There is a variety of gifts but always the same Spirit; there are all sorts of service to be done, but always to the same Lord; working in all sorts of different ways in different people, it is the same God who is working in all of them. The particular way in which the Spirit is given to each person is for a good purpose. One may have the gift of preaching with wisdom given him by the Spirit; another may have the gift of preaching instruction given him by the same Spirit; and another the gift of faith given by the same Spirit; another again the gift of healing, through this one Spirit; one, the power of miracles; another, prophecy; another the gift of recognising spirits, another the gift of tongues and another the ability to interpret them. All these are the work of one and the same Spirit, who distributes different gifts to different people just as he chooses.

About Liturgy

What happened to the First Sunday in Ordinary Time?: You might have thought that last Sunday, the Baptism of the Lord, was the *First* Sunday in Ordinary Time. But the liturgical books are clear that the Baptism of the Lord is part of the Christmas season and that 'Ordinary Time begins on Monday after the Sunday following 6 January' (Lectionary 103).

This rubric isn't just a calendar instruction but also a theological statement. We call Sunday both the first and eighth day of the week. For Christians it is both the chronological and spiritual beginning and end of our week. When we talk about 'ordinary time', we aren't referring to a quality of being mundane but to something being ordered – put into right relationship. The weeks between the seasons of Advent/Christmas and Lent/Easter are ordered towards the 'ordinary' or normative mystery of Christ, a mystery that pervades every moment. Striving to be aware of Christ's enduring presence reminds us to live in constant right relationship. Thus, the Lord's Day on which we gather orders gives us the lens for how we are to see Christ's presence in the days that follow.

Since these last six days are rightly called the days of the first week of Ordinary Time, today, January 20, is rightly called the Second Sunday in Ordinary Time for it orders and directs us how to live this coming week aware of Christ's presence.

Epiphany, part three: In the ordinary event of a wedding feast, we encounter today the third traditional epiphany of Christ. God, who has sanctified all human life by the incarnation, shows us that holiness is not confined to the sacred space of the church or to the vocation of a few people but is readily poured out wherever people hear Jesus's words, believe, and follow him.

About Initiation

Preparation for Purification and Enlightenment: Not everyone who has become a catechumen this past year will be ready for baptism this coming Easter Vigil. Ideally, catechumens are given an entire liturgical year for encountering the mystery of Christ in the Sunday celebrations and feasts of the Lord and the saints. During these next seven Sundays of Ordinary Time pay special attention to the catechumens and look for markers of conversion as they are listed in RCIA 120. These behavioural and spiritual changes are required before one can celebrate the Rite of Election at the beginning of Lent. Those who need more time to develop these hallmarks of conversion continue through the liturgical year, encountering Christ and allowing him to change their hearts.

About Liturgical Music

Setting a musical environment: As we discussed at the beginning of Advent, music can also set a liturgical environment in the same way that liturgical colours and décor enhance the liturgical season. One way to begin doing this is to start with just three Mass settings a year. The first is a musical setting for Ordinary Time. This would be something that can be flexible enough to accommodate a variety of ensemble arrangements, from a single cantor to an SATB choir, but presents itself as simple yet substantial. One such example is 'The *Psallite* Mass: At the Table of the Lord', which employs both metred and chanted melodies. Normally winter Ordinary Time is relatively short, making it best to introduce new Mass settings over the summer and autumn weeks to give the assembly time to become familiar with a setting before it is changed with the season. This year, however, Easter is very late, giving a longer stretch of Ordinary Time.

Then select two other settings: one that complements the sobriety of the preparatory seasons of Advent and Lent, and one that expresses the exuberant festivity of Christmas and Easter.

SPIRITUALITY

GOSPEL ACCLAMATION
See Luke 4:18

R̸. Alleluia, alleluia.
The Lord has sent me to bring the good news to
    the poor,
to proclaim liberty to captives.
R̸. Alleluia, alleluia.

Gospel   Luke 1:1-4; 4:14-21

Seeing that many others have undertaken to draw up accounts of the events that have taken place among us, exactly as these were handed down to us by those who from the outset were eyewitnesses and ministers of the word, I in my turn, after carefully going over the whole story from the beginning, have decided to write an ordered account for you, Theophilus, so that your Excellency may learn how well founded the teaching is that you have received.

Jesus, with the power of the Spirit in him, returned to Galilee; and his reputation spread throughout the countryside. He taught in their synagogues and everyone praised him.

He came to Nazara, where he had been brought up, and went into the synagogue on the sabbath day as he usually did. He stood up to read, and they handed him the scroll of the prophet Isaiah. Unrolling the scroll he found the place where it is written:

**The spirit of the Lord has been given to me, for he has anointed me.
He has sent me to bring the good news to the poor,
to proclaim liberty to captives
and to the blind new sight,
to set the downtrodden free,
to proclaim the Lord's year of favour.
He then rolled up the scroll, gave it back to the assistant and sat down. And all eyes in the synagogue were fixed on him. Then he began to speak to them, 'This text is being fulfilled today even as you listen.'**

Reflecting on the Gospel

When embarking on an important work, task, or life choice, we often indicate so. A person proposes marriage to another in a meaningful way that is remembered. And special events like birthdays, baptisms, and anniversaries are marked by rituals. Afterwards, we settle into routine. Luke does something similar when he begins his gospel. He opens with a four-verse prologue that is one long sentence in Greek! And the Greek he writes is florid, high in style, and reminiscent of classical Greek. After these four verses he descends from that style to the more common (*koinē*) Greek.

There are many things to note in this brief opening to the gospel, but it is

significant that Luke says he is relying on the eyewitness of others, and thereby indicates that he was not an eyewitness himself. Otherwise, he might have said something like 'and my own eyewitness'. But it is clear that he is at least a second-generation Christian, who has looked into this story and told it so the believer Theophilus (the name means 'God-lover') might have surety. And in fact, the word 'surety' (*asphaleian* in Greek) concludes the first four-verse sentence in Greek, indicating its importance. By this emphasis on surety, even the modern reader recognises that the story of Jesus is no mere myth. As Luke says later in Acts, '[T]his was not done in a corner' (Acts 26:26; NABRE). The events of Jesus's life, death, and resurrection really and truly happened.

But the church is not content to give us only the first four verses of the gospel on this Sunday. The second significant item to note is that we also read about Jesus's preaching in the synagogue at Nazareth in chapter 4. Luke is intent to show that the Scriptures of old are fulfilled in Jesus. Jesus reads the prophet and proclaims that the message is fulfilled in their midst. The message will be Jesus's guiding light. He will refer to it again when John the Baptist's followers come to Jesus and ask if he is the one they should expect. Jesus causes the blind to see and proclaims glad tidings to the poor. In so doing, he is the fulfilment of the hopes and expectations of the prophets, for the Spirit of the Lord is upon him.

Living the Paschal Mystery

How do we imagine the ministry of Jesus? What was it that he did? We know it ultimately ended in his passion, death, and resurrection, but what about his work among the people? Today's gospel reading, with Jesus quoting the prophet, gives us an indication as to what occupied the mind and thoughts of Jesus as he performed his ministry. He brings glad tidings to the poor, liberty to captives, sight to the blind, and freedom for the oppressed. This was the message of the prophet and to use a modern term, it is the mission statement of Jesus's ministry. If we want to be his followers, it is up to us to take on this mission statement as well. This ministry is in conformity with the prophets. It animated Jesus himself, and it should animate his followers. Jesus does not talk here about prayer, or doing liturgy, or even going to church. The ministry of Jesus is action in the world. And this action, as indicated by the mission statement, upends the powerful and the privileged. It ultimately (and fairly quickly) leads to Jesus's death. Faced with such a leader, will we be followers as well, undergoing our own paschal mystery? Or are we content to read about his ministry rather than do it, hear about it rather than practise it?

Focusing the Gospel

Key words and phrases: This text is being fulfilled today even as you listen.

To the point: Following his baptism in the Jordan and time of temptation in the desert, Jesus returns to his hometown of Nazareth to worship in the synagogue. After reading from the scroll of Isaiah the people look at Jesus intently as he tells them, 'This text is being fulfilled today even as you listen'. When we read the Bible we remember the history of this great book. We think about the context in which these words were first written and proclaimed. But then we go further for we believe the *living* word has something to tell us today. How can these words of comfort and justice for the poor and oppressed be fulfilled in our time? What role do we have in making these words come alive here and now?

Connecting the Gospel

to the first reading: The prophet Nehemiah lived in a time of great upheaval for the people of Israel. Following the Babylonian exile the Israelites were gradually allowed to return to their homeland. They returned to find Jerusalem in ruins. The walls that protected the city are no longer standing. Hearing of the distress of his fellow Israelites, Nehemiah also returns to Jerusalem to lead the restoration efforts. Under Nehemiah's leadership the people repair the walls to the city so they might once again dwell in safety and begin the task of restoring their houses and the temple. The first thing Nehemiah does once the walls are repaired is to gather all of the people together and to have Ezra, the scribe, read to them from the Torah. This is the moment we hear about in today's first reading. In Ezra we can see a precursor to Jesus's proclamation of Scripture in Nazareth. Ezra reads the words to the people to remind them of who they are. They are the people of God, God's beloved. Because of this they are called from their desolation and mourning into joy, for through 'the joy of the Lord' they will regain their strength.

to experience: In today's first reading and gospel we see the people listening to the word of God. We are called to be formed by this word as well, to encounter it deeply and to invite it to change our lives.

Connecting the Responsorial Psalm

to the readings: Today's passage from Psalm 18 is a hymn to the beauty and value of the law. When the psalmist sings in praise of the law, it is not just the Ten Commandments that are being lauded. The 'law of the Lord' refers to the Torah, the first five books of the Bible and the most precious books to the Jewish people. These books form the Jewish people in their identity. In today's first reading Ezra reads to the people from 'early morning till noon . . . the Book of the Law'. Though the people have been in a time of desperation and mourning as they work to restore Jerusalem, they are reminded to rejoice, for their most precious possession, one that can never be taken away or destroyed, is the law of the Lord.

to psalmist preparation: Consider what it would be like to sing these words in the midst of difficult times – in grief, sorrow, or uncertainty. What does it mean to place your trust and hope in the law of the Lord and to count it as your greatest treasure?

PROMPTS FOR FAITH-SHARING

As it says in the book of Nehemiah, Ezra reads from the book of the law of Moses to the people from daybreak to midday and 'all the people listened attentively.' What helps you to listen attentively to the word of God?

St. Paul tells us, 'Now you together are Christ's body; but each of you is a different part of it'. How do you see this metaphor within your life? How does your family and/or community respect and encourage the gifts of all?

In the gospel, Jesus reads from the scroll of the prophet Isaiah what could be considered his mission statement, one that all of us as followers of Christ could also consider *our* mission statement. What is one action you could do this week to help bring about the liberty, justice, freedom, and healing that Isaiah talks about?

Jesus tells the people, 'This text is being fulfilled today even as you listen'. How have you experienced the word of God being fulfilled in your own life?

CELEBRATION

Model Penitential Act

Presider: In today's second reading the apostle Paul tells us we are all members of Christ's body. For the times we have not acted in a way befitting of the body of Christ, we ask for pardon and forgiveness . . . [*pause*]

Lord Jesus, you are the fulfilment of the law and the prophets: Lord, have mercy.

Christ Jesus, you are the anointed one: Christ, have mercy.

Lord Jesus, you proclaim liberty to captives and free the oppressed: Lord, have mercy.

Homily Points

• Jesus goes to the synagogue in Nazareth 'as he usually did'. Jesus prepares for his ministry, as all prophets must, by first listening to God and becoming immersed in God's word. Synagogues are places of worship as well as places of study. We, who have been anointed 'priest, prophet, and king', must also be immersed in the word of God. This is the only way we will be able to bring 'good news to the poor' and 'proclaim liberty to captives'.

• There is a beautiful prayer attributed to St. Teresa of Avila called 'Christ has no body'. She tells us, 'Christ has no body but yours, no hands, no feet on earth but yours'. In today's gospel we hear that Jesus is the fulfilment of the prophet Isaiah's words, 'The spirit of the Lord has been given to me, for he has anointed me. / He has sent me to bring the good news to the poor'. As the body of Christ we are called to fulfill this prophecy in our time.

• We cannot do this work on our own, however. One of the apostle Paul's themes in his letter to the Corinthians is unity. The Christian community at Corinth struggled with divisions as members clamored to claim superiority over one another. Today we hear Paul's analogy of the Christian community as the Body of Christ. Within a body all parts are necessary and no part is expendable. Only when we work together in concert and under the guidance of the Holy Spirit do we see the kingdom of God, a kingdom of justice and peace, break forth.

Model Universal Prayer (Prayer of the Faithful)

Presider: As members of the Body of Christ we lift up our prayers to God.

Response: Lord, hear our prayer.

That the church recognise and respect its diversity of members and the importance of all their gifts and talents . . .

That rulers of nations embrace a preferential option for the poor and oppressed . . .

That all those experiencing poverty, whether materially or spiritually, know the abundance of the Lord. . .

That all gathered here might, in gratitude and joy, use our gifts to build up the body of Christ . . .

Presider: Gracious God, you have called us, as members of the body of Christ, to bring glad tidings to the poor and to proclaim freedom to the captive and the oppressed. Hear our prayers that we might live into the fulness of this call. We ask this through Christ our Lord. Amen.

COLLECT

Let us pray.

Pause for silent prayer

Almighty ever-living God,
direct our actions according
    to your good pleasure,
that in the name of your beloved Son
we may abound in good works.
Through our Lord Jesus Christ, your Son,
who lives and reigns with you
    in the unity of the Holy Spirit,
one God, for ever and ever. **Amen.**

FIRST READING
Neh 8:2-6, 8-10

Ezra the priest brought the Law before the assembly, consisting of men, women, and children old enough to understand. This was the first day of the seventh month. On the square before the Water Gate, in the presence of the men and women, and children old enough to understand, he read from the book from early morning till noon; all the people listened attentively to the Book of the Law.

Ezra the scribe stood on a wooden dais erected for the purpose. In full view of all the people – since he stood higher than all the people – Ezra opened the book; and when he opened it all the people stood up. Then Ezra blessed the Lord, the great God, and all the people raised their hands and answered, 'Amen! Amen!'; then they bowed down and, face to the ground, prostrated themselves before the Lord. And Ezra read from the Law of God, translating and giving the sense, so that the people understood what was read.

Then Nehemiah – His Excellency – and Ezra, priest and scribe (and the Levites who were instructing the people) said to all the people, 'This day is sacred to the Lord your God. Do not be mournful, do not weep.' For the people were all in tears as they listened to the words of the Law.

He then said, 'Go, eat the fat, drink the sweet wine, and send a portion to the man who has nothing prepared ready. For this day is sacred to our Lord. Do not be sad: the joy of the Lord is your stronghold.'

CATECHESIS

RESPONSORIAL PSALM
Ps 18:8-10, 15 (John 6:63)

℟. Your words are spirit, Lord,
and they are life.

The law of the Lord is perfect,
it revives the soul.
The rule of the Lord is to be trusted,
it gives wisdom to the simple.

℟. Your words are spirit, Lord,
and they are life.

The precepts of the Lord are right,
they gladden the heart.
The command of the Lord is clear,
it gives light to the eyes.

℟. Your words are spirit, Lord,
and they are life.

The fear of the Lord is holy,
abiding for ever.
The decrees of the Lord are truth
and all of them just.

℟. Your words are spirit, Lord,
and they are life.

May the spoken words of my mouth,
the thoughts of my heart,
win favour in your sight, O Lord,
my rescuer, my rock!

℟. Your words are spirit, Lord,
and they are life.

SECOND READING
1 Cor 12:12-14, 17

Just as a human body, though it is made
up of many parts is a single unit because
all these parts, though many, make one
body, so it is with Christ. In the one Spirit
we were all baptised, Jews as well as
Greeks, slaves as well as citizens, and one
Spirit was given to us all to drink.

Nor is the body to be identified with any
one of its many parts.

Now you together are Christ's body; but
each of you is a different part of it.

or 1 Cor 12:12-30

See Appendix A, p. 274.

About Liturgy

Observing the liturgy: If you truly want to assess the quality of your Sunday liturgy, at some point you will need to be an objective observer. This can be difficult if you're also trying to pray and be part of the assembly. So these Sundays before Lent may be a good time to schedule two or three times when you will attend one of your parish Masses as an outside observer and just watch and take notes discreetly, looking for specific areas for improvement. Here are some points that will help you get started.

First, it may be easier to do this with a small group of people doing the observation. This group might be made up of other liturgical ministers, but also be sure to include other parishioners as well whose only Sunday role is in the assembly. Have each person sit in a different place of the church than they are used to sitting in order to get a better sense of the variety of perspectives your assembly has each Sunday. In addition, you might set up a couple of stationary video cameras, one focused towards the sanctuary and one focused towards the assembly. This is to help you observe the body language of the people and the ministers.

Second, use a worksheet to help you look for specific points. Immediately after the Mass is over gather with the team and share your notes while it is fresh. You might watch the video, too, while you do this. As you notice things in the video, write down the time marker and notate what you saw.

Third, be sure to let all the liturgical ministers and pastoral staff know that these observations will be taking place. Also let them know that follow-up gatherings will be scheduled where they will be able to hear about what you observed and view any specific parts of the videos you want to highlight. Assure everyone that these observations are to help everyone see where the parish is strong and where it can improve: it is not to critique any one person.

Finally, when you gather with all the liturgical ministers and staff set some ground rules for the discussion. Comments should begin with what went well, including what each person saw they themselves did well during the liturgy. Any criticisms of how someone did their ministry should be limited to the points on your worksheet and be given kindly. If you feel that the discussion might get too negative, try facilitating these discussions in smaller groups. Always end the gatherings with inviting everyone to share a few simple next steps each person can take to improve and what the entire liturgy team will commit to doing to continue improving.

In these next few Sundays we'll look at specific items to observe in each part of the liturgy.

About Liturgical Music

Helping the Body of Christ: 'If one part suffers, all the parts suffer with it; / if one part is honored, all the parts share its joy' (1 Cor 12:26; NABRE). One way ministers can help one another is to take some time to share in supportive feedback of one another. This can be done with cantors in a master class format in a rehearsal. Each cantor prepares a psalm and leads it while the choir members act as an assembly, facing the cantor. The 'assembly' pays attention not only to what they hear but also to gestures, body posture, and facial expression. Then they give the cantor constructive feedback, starting first with what the cantor did well, followed by one or two specific points for improvement.

SPIRITUALITY

GOSPEL ACCLAMATION
John 14:5

℟. Alleluia, alleluia.
I am the Way, the Truth and the Life, says
    the Lord;
no one can come to the Father
    except through me.
℟. Alleluia, alleluia.

Gospel

Luke 4:21-30

Jesus began to speak in the synagogue, 'This text is being fulfilled today even as you listen.' And he won the approval of all, and they were astonished by the gracious words that came from his lips.

They said, 'This is Joseph's son, surely?' But he replied, 'No doubt you will quote me the saying, "Physician, heal yourself" and tell me, "We have heard all that happened in Capernaum, do the same here in your own countryside."' And he went on, 'I tell you solemnly, no prophet is ever accepted in his own country.

'There were many widows in Israel, I can assure you, in Elijah's day, when heaven remained shut for three years and six months and a great famine raged throughout the land, but Elijah was not sent to any one of these: he was sent to a widow at Zarephath, a Sidonian town. And in the prophet Elisha's time there were many lepers in Israel, but none of these was cured, except the Syrian, Naaman.'

When they heard this everyone in the synagogue was enraged. They sprang to their feet and hustled him out of the town; and they took him up to the brow of the hill their town was built on, intending to throw him down the cliff, but he slipped through the crowd and walked away.

Reflecting on the Gospel

It can be difficult to be surprised by the familiar. We experience it regularly; it is customary. We follow routine and habit. Even people we encounter can become familiar to the point of predictability. We expect certain reactions from those we know. So when someone familiar does something unexpected or different we can be puzzled. The actions did not follow the script; the person did not meet my expectations. What follows can be problematic. In these cases, it's usually best for us to reassess our expectations and reexamine our habits.

Something similar happens in today's gospel when Jesus preaches in his hometown synagogue. The audience thought they knew him: 'This is Joseph's son, surely?' But what he preached, the fulfilment of the Scriptures, was shocking to the point of their attempting to silence him for good. In the face of such objection, Jesus does not change his message. On the contrary, he says that 'no prophet is ever accepted in his own country'. By this, Jesus refers to himself as a prophet in the manner of Elisha and Elijah.

The reference to Elijah going to the widow in Zarephath and Elisha to Naaman the Syrian prefigures Jesus's own ministry to those who are not Jewish. Luke is foreshadowing the eventual Gentile mission and demonstrating that it, too, is rooted in Scripture. Just as Elijah and Elisha went beyond the bounds of the Israelites, Jesus will too. Luke's story of Jesus is rooted in the prophets, especially the ministry of Elijah and Elisha who raised the dead, fed multitudes, and ministered to non-Israelites. For Luke more than any other evangelist, the prophets, John the Baptist, and Jesus himself in his ministry, passion, death, and subsequent entrance into glory follow 'God's plan' (Luke is the New Testament author who uses the term 'God's plan' more than any other New Testament author). Jesus behaves in a way wholly unexpected by those in his hometown who ostensibly knew him best. Rather than seek to silence him for good, they might have reassessed their own preconceptions. But as we know, such a task is difficult. It's much easier to believe what I already 'know' to be true.

On this Fourth Sunday in Ordinary Time may we be open to the unexpected, for it might simply be the plan of God.

Living the Paschal Mystery

Mark Twain once said, 'What gets us into trouble is not what we don't know. It's what we know for sure that just ain't so'. Our brains are wired to be comfortable with the familiar. We don't need to think about walking; we simply walk. We don't need to invest much mental energy in routine tasks simply because they are so familiar. The human brain spends minimal mental energy on the routine. And this is a good thing as the brain can then spend its mental energy on other more critical tasks.

But this can also be a problem in that the unexpected, by definition, does not conform to routine. So being open to the unexpected is probably a good habit for us to cultivate. Aware that we are hardwired for routine, it takes extra energy to be open to new things and new experiences, even new information that does not conform to what we already know or even 'know for sure that just ain't so'.

When we take in new information that causes a change in our way of thinking we experience a *metanoia*, to use a favourite term of Luke. We die to our old preconceived notions and allow something new to rise up. But sometimes our first reaction can be like the townspeople of Nazareth, and we can seek to destroy the messenger. Allowing new information to influence us and ultimately to shape or even change our minds is a difficult process. We let go of the past; we let go of our old ways of thinking. We let go of what 'just ain't so' and embrace something new. This is a kind of paschal mystery.

Focusing the Gospel

Key words and phrases: They said, 'This is Joseph's son, surely?'

To the point: It is often difficult to see something (or someone) that we know well with fresh eyes. Jesus returns to his hometown and the people there see him as they always have, as the son of Joseph the carpenter. Jesus tells them, 'no prophet is ever accepted in his own country'. Prophets, by their very nature, are called to shake people out of their complacency and to point out when something new is happening. Like the people of Nazareth, we might feel like we know Jesus. His words may not sound radical to us. As Christians we must continually strive to be open to the words of Jesus, the prophet, who would like to show us something new.

Connecting the Gospel

to the first reading: Jeremiah is also a prophet who finds no welcome in his hometown. He receives the call from God as a young man and is given the difficult task of prophesying the coming Babylonian exile to the king and temple court. It does not go well. At one point Jeremiah, unlike Jesus who is able to pass through the midst of those who wish to hurl him over a cliff, is actually tossed into a pit. Even though Jesus and Jeremiah both face resistance, God continues to be with them. As God tells Jeremiah, 'They will fight against you / but shall not overcome you, / for I am with you to deliver you'.

to experience: The prophet's life is not one of popularity and acclaim, but often includes derision and solitude. When it is difficult to follow the path of Jesus and to speak the word of God to others we, too, can hear God's instruction to Jeremiah, 'So now brace yourself for action. / Stand up and tell them / all I command you. / Do not be dismayed at their presence'.

Connecting the Responsorial Psalm

to the readings: Today's psalm reinforces the theme of reliance on God in difficult times. The psalmist proclaims, 'In you, O Lord, I take refuge; / let me never be put to shame'. This hope in the Lord has been founded on an experience of God's love even from infancy: 'On you I have leaned from my birth, / from my mother's womb you have been my help'. In the reading from Jeremiah we hear how God has known and dedicated the prophet even before he was 'formed . . . in the womb'. In the gospel Jesus's neighbours, who have witnessed his own growth from child to manhood, ask each other, 'This is Joseph's son, surely?' The psalm reminds us that no matter how intimately we might know a person or for how long a time, it is God alone who has accompanied this individual from the secret life of the womb.

to psalmist preparation: In the gospel Jesus encounters resistance to his ministry and even the threat of violence. In this passage we see the foreshadowing of the cross when Jesus will not '[slip] through the crowd and [walk] away' but will give himself up to be crucified. Today's psalm speaks of radical trust in God. When have you relied on the Lord to be a refuge in times of struggle?

PROMPTS FOR FAITH-SHARING

In the first reading God tells the prophet Jeremiah, '[B]efore you came to birth I consecrated you; / I have appointed you as prophet to the nations'. What work has God dedicated you for?

In the second reading St. Paul expounds on the true nature of love beginning, 'Love is always patient and kind'. In your family and/or parish community where is this love present? Where is it lacking?

Jesus's hometown crowd is shocked at the words he speaks to them. They ask, 'This is Joseph's son, surely?' Are there areas in your life where you feel stifled by people's preconceptions of you? How might you embrace the freedom of God to be who he is calling you to be?

At the end of today's gospel Jesus passes through the midst of the angry crowd and goes away. Are there areas of conflict in your life where you are being called to walk away?

CELEBRATION

Model Penitential Act

Presider: Today we read the beloved words of the apostle Paul, 'Love is always patient and kind'. We pause to reflect on the times we have not embodied this love that 'endures whatever comes' . . . [*pause*]

Lord Jesus, you are our rock of refuge: Lord, have mercy.

Christ Jesus, you call us to faith and hope: Christ, have mercy.

Lord Jesus, you show us the way of perfect love: Lord, have mercy.

Homily Points

• Today's first reading presents the call of the prophet Jeremiah. God tells Jeremiah, 'Before I formed you in the womb I knew you; / before you came to birth I consecrated you; / I have appointed you as prophet to the nations'. God has created each one of us with intentionality and gifts to use for the building of the kingdom of God.

• In the gospel we see Jesus at the beginning of the work for which he has been dedicated and already he is facing resistance and violence. In this first altercation he is able to pass through the midst of the angry mob. He has work to do and a mission to accomplish. At the end of his ministry in Jerusalem instead of passing through the crowd he will submit to it and give his life. In all that he does, Jesus is animated and led by love, the love that St. Paul talks about in his letter to the Corinthians.

• Often we hear the second reading from St. Paul at weddings. It might lead us to associate Paul's words with romantic love and, indeed, this is the kind of love necessary to sustain a lifelong covenant between two people. Far from exclusively romantic love, however, Paul is telling us of the love that must surround and infuse our entire lives as Christians. Without this love Paul says, 'I am nothing'. In our lives as Christians we are called to follow the examples of Jeremiah, Paul, and Jesus. To accept the work God has dedicated us to and to strive to meet all the circumstances of our lives with patient and enduring love.

Model Universal Prayer (Prayer of the Faithful)

Presider: Trusting in the all-encompassing love of God, which sustains and surrounds us, we offer up our prayers.

Response: Lord, hear our prayer.

That the church strive to be a living model of the love of God . . .

That leaders of nations listen to present-day prophets who point the way to hope, faith, and love . . .

That those who grieve the loss of a family member or friend be comforted . . .

That all gathered here might heed our baptismal call to be prophets of God's love . . .

Presider: Gracious God, hear the prayers we bring before you today and in your generous love, grant them. We ask this through Christ our Lord. Amen.

COLLECT

Let us pray.

Pause for silent prayer

Grant us, Lord our God,
that we may honour you
    with all our mind,
and love everyone in truth of heart.
Through our Lord Jesus Christ, your Son,
who lives and reigns with you
    in the unity of the Holy Spirit,
one God, for ever and ever. **Amen.**

FIRST READING

Jer 1:4-5, 17-19

In the days of Josiah, the word of the Lord
was addressed to me, saying,
   'Before I formed you in the womb I
      knew you;
   before you came to birth I
      consecrated you;
   I have appointed you as prophet to
      the nations.
   So now brace yourself for action.
   Stand up and tell them
   all I command you.
   Do not be dismayed at their presence,
   or in their presence I will make
      you dismayed.
   I, for my part, today will make you
   into a fortified city,
   a pillar of iron,
   and a wall of bronze
   to confront all this land:
   the kings of Judah, its princes,
   its priests and the country people.
   They will fight against you
   but shall not overcome you,
   for I am with you to deliver you –
   it is the Lord who speaks.'

RESPONSORIAL PSALM

Ps 70:1-6, 15, 17 (15)

℟. My lips will tell of your help.

In you, O Lord, I take refuge;
let me never be put to shame.
In your justice rescue me, free me:
pay heed to me and save me.

℟. My lips will tell of your help.

Be a rock where I can take refuge,
a mighty stronghold to save me;
for you are my rock, my stronghold.
Free me from the hand of the wicked.

℟. My lips will tell of your help.

It is you, O Lord, who are my hope,
my trust, O Lord, since my youth.
On you I have leaned from my birth,
from my mother's womb you have been
        my help.

R̷. My lips will tell of your help.

My lips will tell of your justice
and day by day of your help.
O God, you have taught me from my youth
and I proclaim your wonders still.

R̷. My lips will tell of your help.

SECOND READING
1 Cor 13:4-13

Love is always patient and kind; it is
never jealous; love is never boastful or
conceited; it is never rude or selfish; it
does not take offence, and is not resentful.
Love takes no pleasure in other people's
sins but delights in the truth; it is always
ready to excuse, to trust, to hope, and to
endure whatever comes.

Love does not come to an end. But if
there are gifts of prophecy, the time will
come when they must fail; or the gift of
languages, it will not continue for ever;
and knowledge – for this, too, the time will
come when it must fail. For our knowledge
is imperfect and our prophesying is
imperfect; but once perfection comes, all
imperfect things will disappear. When I
was a child, I used to talk like a child, and
think like a child, and argue like a child,
but now I am a man, all childish ways are
put behind me. Now we are seeing a dim
reflection in a mirror; but then we shall be
seeing face to face. The knowledge that
I have now is imperfect; but then I shall
know as fully as I am known.

In short, there are three things that last:
faith, hope and love; and the greatest of
these is love.

or 1 Cor 12:31-13:13

See Appendix A, p. 275.

CATECHESIS

About Liturgy

Observing the Introductory Rites: Here are a few points to notice and include in
your observation and evaluation worksheet for your community's introductory rites
(see previous Sunday). Although the Mass starts with the entrance chant, there are
many things before Mass, which you could also observe.

Hospitality: Were there greeters outside the church, at the church doors, and inside
the church welcoming people as they arrived? Did assembly members greet each other
in a friendly and genuine way as people gathered in and around their seats? Would
a visitor or newcomer feel welcomed? Would a visitor leave the Mass having been
personally greeted, welcomed, and invited to return by at least one other person? Are
the locations of lavatories clearly marked so that visitors know where to find them?
Is there 'code language' in your bulletin, such as 'RCIA'? Can visitors easily find the
parish phone number and a name of someone to talk to if they are new to the parish?
Do you have to be an insider to know where meeting rooms are? Are the parking lot,
gathering areas, and church space clean and inviting? Do those in wheelchairs have
easy access to all parts of the church grounds? Are worship aids or projected materials
printed clearly in type that is easily read? Do all who use the microphones use them
effectively so that all can hear well?

Silence: If there is a music rehearsal, announcements, or welcome before Mass, is
there some period of silence before the entrance chant begins? Was there an ample
amount of silence at the beginning of the penitential rite and after the invitation, 'Let
us pray', in the collect? Describe the quality of the silence, for example, uncomfortable,
deep, rushed, peaceful, etc.

Procession: Did the entrance procession look like a procession? Did the ministers
walk with dignity? Were the cross, book of the gospels, and other items carried and
placed with dignity? Did the ministers walk slowly or hurriedly? Did they all move
gracefully? Was the assembly instructed to 'greet Father' by singing the opening song,
or were there other ways that the procession focused on the celebrant rather than the
assembly?

Prayers: Was the sign of the cross done slowly with large dignified and deliberate
movements? Did the celebrant add extraneous words, such as a greeting before the
sign of the cross, or 'thank you' or 'good morning' after the assembly's response, 'And
with your spirit'? Was the opening prayer proclaimed clearly, slowly, and solemnly in a
way that felt like prayer?

About Liturgical Music

Liturgical music observation points for the Introductory Rites: If
someone rehearsed music with the assembly before Mass, did they do it respectfully,
encouraging and not scolding people? Are song numbers clearly marked? Are there
enough hymnals in every pew? Can visitors find books and song numbers easily?
Was the entrance chant familiar, known and sung by all, even those in the procession?
Did the entrance chant accomplish the task of gathering the assembly? Were enough
verses sung to do this, or did the opening song end once the ministers arrived at
their places? Did the assembly know and sing the Gloria? Did the presider, deacon,
and altar servers sing all the music? Did the accompaniment support and enable the
full participation of the assembly in sung prayer? Was the music and the way it was
played and sung joyful?

FOURTH SUNDAY IN ORDINARY TIME

SPIRITUALITY

GOSPEL ACCLAMATION
John 15:15

R̲⁊. Alleluia, alleluia.
I call you friends, says the Lord,
because I have made known to you
everything I have learnt from my Father.
R̲⁊. Alleluia, alleluia.

Gospel   Luke 5:1-11

Jesus was standing one day by the lake of Gennesaret, with the crowd pressing round him listening to the word of God, when he caught sight of two boats close to the bank. The fishermen had gone out of them and were washing their nets. He got into one of the boats – it was Simon's – and asked him to put out a little from the shore. Then he sat down and taught the crowds from the boat.

When he had finished speaking he said to Simon, 'Put out into deep water and pay out your nets for a catch.' 'Master,' Simon replied 'we worked hard all night long and caught nothing, but if you say so, I will pay out the nets.' And when they had done this they netted such a huge number of fish that their nets began to tear, so they signalled to their companions in the other boats to come and help them; when these came, they filled the two boats to sinking point.

When Simon Peter saw this he fell at the knees of Jesus saying 'Leave me, Lord; I am a sinful man.' For he and all his companions were completely overcome by the catch they had made; so also were James and John, sons of Zebedee, who were Simon's partners. But Jesus said to Simon, 'Do not be afraid; from now on it is men you will catch.' Then, bringing their boats back to land, they left everything and followed him.

Reflecting on the Gospel

Hometown monuments, markers, and memorials sometimes go by different names. For example, people who grew up in one era might recall an earlier name for a stadium or a building. In Chicago, the Sears Tower became the Willis Tower in 2009. Investors bought it several years later and were considering another name change. But many locals still refer to it as the Sears Tower. Many stadiums undergo name changes as well based on naming rights sold to the highest bidding corporation. These names are a reflection of our culture and

can be difficult for foreigners or others to follow. Just imagine some talking about the Willis Tower when others know it only as the Sears Tower. Are we speaking of the same thing? Where is the Willis Tower?

We see something like this happening in the Gospel of Luke today, when we hear about the Lake of Gennesaret, which is also known as the Sea of Tiberias and the Sea of Galilee! The New Testament uses three different names for the same body of water, which makes it challenging for those of us reading about this two thousand years later and far away.

Such is the setting for the call of Simon as Luke tells it. This story is different from that told in Mark, Matthew, or John. Here Luke has a focus on Simon, without his brother Andrew. In fact, Luke mentions Andrew only in the list of the twelve (Luke 6:12; Acts 1:13) where he calls him the brother of Simon. Otherwise we hear nothing of Andrew from Luke. Luke also tells us in this story that Simon was 'Simon Peter', prior to Jesus naming him 'Peter'. And we also hear about James and John, the sons of Zebedee, partners of Simon. According to Luke, this was not Simon's first encounter with Jesus. Immediately prior to the story in today's gospel, Jesus healed Simon's mother-in-law (Luke 4:38-39). So this provides more background to Simon's appeal to Jesus, 'Leave me, Lord; I am a sinful man'. Simon has encountered the power of Jesus in the healing of his mother-in-law and now in the miraculous catch of fish. Faced with this Simon is utterly aware of his own humanity and humility. Jesus responds with a line that has reverberated through the centuries, 'Do not be afraid; from now on it is men you will catch'. What a difference this story is in the hands of the master storyteller Luke. From Mark (1:16-20) he inherited a story about Jesus's call of Simon, Andrew, James, and John, all of whom immediately dropped their nets to follow him. Luke instead places the focus squarely on Simon *Peter* to the point that we lose Andrew and only hear of James and John in the closing verses. Furthermore, by preceding this story with the healing of the mother-in-law, Simon's leaving everything to follow Jesus becomes more plausible. We are in the hands of a remarkable theologian and evangelist. We would do well to read his story carefully and with attention to detail.

Living the Paschal Mystery

So often today's gospel story is read symbolically so that the tearing nets mean one thing and the great number of fish mean something else. The boat's near sinking is sometimes interpreted symbolically too. But it can be more fruitful simply to read Luke's story on its own terms, without fishing for meaning so to speak.

Jesus provides more than enough. There is bounty with Jesus who surpasses every expectation. When experience teaches Simon that there is no hope, or no use in trying, Jesus encourages him nonetheless and provides excess. This dramatic scene captures something of the initial excitement, humility, and genuineness that often accompanies the early stages of true discipleship. It is then that we die to our own preconceived notions and our own experience, and open ourselves up to the munificence of the divine. That is when our cup overflows with the good things God wants to provide. In the face of such generosity, we can only be humble. Simon knows he did not earn this miraculous catch, but it was a free gift. May we, too, die to our own self-importance and grandiosity and recognise that the good things we have are a gift of God.

Focusing the Gospel

Key words and phrases: Leave me, Lord; I am a sinful man.

To the point: After witnessing the miraculous catch of fish Peter begs Jesus to leave him. Knowing his own sinfulness, Peter believes he is not worthy to be in the presence of the Lord of life. Jesus has other ideas, however. Throughout salvation history we witness God's pattern of choosing the small and weak, and yes, even sinful, to fulfill God's plan. Jesus responds to Peter's plea by reassuring him, 'Do not be afraid'. Jesus knows our sinfulness, loves us, and calls us to follow him anyway.

Connecting the Gospel

to the first and second readings: In the first and second readings, both the prophet Isaiah and the apostle Paul echo Peter's words of self-reproach. When Isaiah receives a heavenly vision of seraphim surrounding God's throne he cries out, 'What a wretched state I am in! I am lost'. Isaiah cites his 'unclean lips' as a reason he cannot possibly be a prophet for the Lord of Hosts. In Paul's litany of the appearances of the risen Lord to the apostles he ends with Jesus's appearance to himself, but adds, 'I am the least of the apostles; in fact, since I persecuted the Church of God, I hardly deserve the name apostle'. Just as with Peter, the failings of Isaiah and Paul do not dissuade God from calling them to be of service.

to experience: As human beings we all possess flaws and weaknesses. Rather than being a cause for shame, these flaws might be a way that God is speaking to us. The musician Leonard Cohen says that cracks allow light to get in.

Connecting the Responsorial Psalm

to the readings: In the gospel and the first reading Peter and Isaiah encounter the living God and respond in awe and fear. While Isaiah experiences a mystical vision, Peter comes face to face with the Lord who can cause the very fish in the Sea of Galilee to flock to his net. Today's psalm is a hymn of gratitude and praise for the Lord of all. Often the most authentic prayer is one of wonder. Words can escape us upon witnessing the grandeur of God through nature or miraculous intervention. Even speechless, we can turn to the Lord in gratitude and simply be in the presence of God.

to psalmist preparation: Today's psalm is one of simple and exultant praise. Pope Francis tells us, 'Praise is the "breath" which gives us life, because it is intimacy with God, an intimacy that grows through daily praise' (address to Catholic Fraternity, Oct. 31, 2014). How do you praise God in your daily life?

PROMPTS FOR FAITH-SHARING

In the first reading we hear of the call of the prophet Isaiah. Isaiah responds, 'Here I am, send me'. Where in your life do you hear the call of God? What do you need in order to respond to this call as Isaiah did?

In the second reading, St. Paul reminds the Corinthians of the witness he has provided to them of Jesus's life, death, and resurrection. In your own life, who has been a witness of faith for you? How are you a witness for others?

In the life of faith we are called to persistence. Where might Jesus be calling you to try one more time to put out your nets for a catch?

In response to Peter's protestations of his own sinfulness, Jesus tells him, 'Do not be afraid.' Are there places in your own life where fear of failure keeps you from attempting something new? Can you hear Jesus telling you, 'Do not be afraid?'

CELEBRATION

Model Penitential Act

Presider: In today's gospel Jesus calls Peter, James, and John to be his first disciples. Peter responds by crying out, 'Leave me, Lord; I am a sinful man'. For the times we have let our own sinfulness prohibit us from following Jesus, we ask for mercy and forgiveness . . . [*pause*]

Lord Jesus, you call us to leave everything and follow you: Lord, have mercy.

Christ Jesus, you died for our sins: Christ, have mercy.

Lord Jesus, you invite us to be fishers of men: Lord, have mercy.

Homily Points

• Today Jesus urges Peter not to be afraid of his own sinfulness, his self-perceived unworthiness. We hear this phrase, 'Do not be afraid', again and again throughout the Scriptures. In the First Letter of St. John we are given a clue as to why. John tells us that 'perfect love drives out fear' (4:18; NABRE). God desires perfect love in his relationship with us, and in perfect love there is no room for fear.

• In the life of faith we are also called to persistence and perseverance. Sometimes things seem hopeless. We have tried again and again to repair a relationship or conquer a bad habit, but to no avail. Jesus tells Peter to put out his nets into the deep for a catch, and even though he has been fishing all night and caught nothing, he acquiesces to Jesus's request. His success is beyond his wildest imagining. He catches such an abundance of fish he must call other fishermen to partake.

• As seen in the gospel encounter between Peter and Jesus, Christianity is a religion passed on through relationships. The last part of St. Paul's first letter to the Corinthians is a discourse on the resurrection of Christ. Today we begin this discourse, which we will read for the next three Sundays. In building his case for the resurrection of Jesus, Paul cites the many people whom Jesus appeared to after his crucifixion. All of these people passed on what they had heard and seen to invite others to faith. Today, we believe because of what we have experienced, read, and most importantly, because of the testimony of others in our lives. Despite our own failings and weaknesses, we are called like Isaiah, Paul, and Simon Peter to witness to Jesus through our persistence, relationships, and a love that casts out fear.

Model Universal Prayer (Prayer of the Faithful)

Presider: In today's gospel Jesus reassures Peter, 'Do not be afraid'. With faith in the goodness of God, let us lift our prayers to the Lord.

Response: Lord, hear our prayer.

That the pope, the successor of Peter, might point the way to Jesus with fidelity . . .

That all the peoples of the world come to know the glory and majesty of God . . .

That all those who feel overwhelmed by sin receive the grace to live in righteousness . . .

That all gathered here might be renewed in our commitment to leave everything and follow Jesus . . .

Presider: Good and gracious God, throughout history you have called human beings to collaborate with you in your work of salvation. Hear our prayers, that we might be strengthened in your grace to continue to serve you. We ask this through Christ our Lord. Amen.

COLLECT

Let us pray.

Pause for silent prayer

Keep your family safe, O Lord,
    with unfailing care,
that, relying solely on the hope
    of heavenly grace,
they may be defended always
    by your protection.
Through our Lord Jesus Christ, your Son,
who lives and reigns with you
    in the unity of the Holy Spirit,
one God, for ever and ever. **Amen.**

FIRST READING

Isa 6:1-8

In the year of King Uzziah's death I saw the Lord seated on a high throne; his train filled the sanctuary; above him stood seraphs, each one with six wings.
    And they cried out one to another in
        this way,
    'Holy, holy, holy is the Lord of hosts.
    His glory fills the whole earth.'
The foundations of the threshold shook with the voice of the one who cried out, and the Temple was filled with smoke. I said:
    'What a wretched state I am in! I am lost,
    for I am a man of unclean lips
    and I live among a people of unclean lips,
    and my eyes have looked at the King,
        the Lord of hosts.'
Then one of the seraphs flew to me, holding in his hand a live coal which he had taken from the altar with a pair of tongs. With this he touched my mouth and said:
    'See now, this has touched your lips,
    your sin is taken away,
    your iniquity is purged.'
Then I heard the voice of the Lord saying:
    'Whom shall I send? Who will be
        our messenger?'
I answered, 'Here I am, send me.'

CATECHESIS

RESPONSORIAL PSALM

Ps 137:1-5, 7-8 (1)

R℣. Before the angels I will bless you,
  O Lord.

I thank you, Lord, with all my heart,
you have heard the words of my mouth.
Before the angels I will bless you.
I will adore before your holy temple.

R℣. Before the angels I will bless you,
  O Lord.

I thank you for your faithfulness and love
which excel all we ever knew of you.
On the day I called, you answered;
you increased the strength of my soul.

R℣. Before the angels I will bless you,
  O Lord.

All earth's kings shall thank you
when they hear the words of your mouth.
They shall sing of the Lord's ways:
'How great is the glory of the Lord!'

R℣. Before the angels I will bless you,
  O Lord.

You stretch out your right hand and
  save me.
Your hand will do all things for me.
Your love, O Lord, is eternal,
discard not the work of your hand.

R℣. Before the angels I will bless you,
  O Lord.

SECOND READING

1 Cor 15:3-8, 11

In the first place, I taught you what I had been taught myself, namely that Christ died for our sins, in accordance with the scriptures; that he was buried; and that he was raised to life on the third day, in accordance with the scriptures; that he appeared first to Cephas and secondly to the Twelve. Next he appeared to more than five hundred of the brothers at the same time, most of whom are still alive, though some have died; then he appeared to James, and then to all the apostles; and last of all he appeared to me too; it was as though I was born when no one expected it. But what matters is that I preach what they preach, and this is what you all believed.

or 1 Cor 15:1-11

See Appendix A, p. 275.

About Liturgy

Observing the Liturgy of the Word: Here are items to look for as you continue to observe and evaluate your Sunday Mass.

Silence: Was there an ample amount of silence before the first reading to allow people to be settled and ready to hear the Word? Was there a good amount of silence after the first and second readings? Was there silence after the homily?

Proclamation of the readings: Did the lector, deacon, or priest proclaim the reading clearly and confidently? Did they have good eye contact with the assembly? Did they project well, speaking so all could hear? Did they convey the emotion and meaning of the reading? Describe the pace of their reading. Was it too fast or too slow? Describe their posture at the ambo. Did they look attentive? Did they slouch? Describe their gestures. Did they do anything distracting? Was there a different reader for each reading? Did the readers use the microphone well? Are there areas in the church space where the proclamation sounds unclear?

Procession: Did the procession during the gospel acclamation look like a procession? Did the ministers walk with dignity? Was the book of the gospels carried with dignity in the procession?

Homily: Did the homily connect and interpret the people's lives with the Scriptures proclaimed at that liturgy? Did the homily strengthen people's faith to participate in Communion or whatever blessing or sacrament was being celebrated at that liturgy?

Prayers: Did the profession of faith feel like a 'profession' by the whole assembly? Did the universal prayer include prayers for the church, the world, the needs of the community, the needs of those suffering or oppressed? Were the prayers written thoughtfully? Did they include prayers for current important events in the neighbourhood, city, or world? Were they announced by the reader prayerfully and clearly? Did the presider seem confident in leading the prayer of the people? Did the presider engage the assembly in prayer?

Assembly: During the readings did the assembly read along in a missalette, or did they actively listen to the proclamations? During the songs did the assembly listen to the choir, or did they actively sing the responses and acclamations? Did the assembly seem engaged during the homily and the universal prayer?

About Liturgical Music

Evaluating the Liturgy of the Word: During the Liturgy of the Word, the music ministers serve in a role similar to that of the lectors in that one of their main liturgical actions is to proclaim the Scripture through music. Here are some points to watch for as you evaluate your music ministry this week:

Did the assembly sing the responsorial psalm well? Did the assembly sound as if they knew the music? Did the assembly know when to sing? Did the assembly sing confidently? Did a cantor lead the responsorial psalm from the ambo? Did the cantor communicate the meaning of the text through both their voice and body? Did the assembly sing the gospel acclamation well? Was the verse of the gospel acclamation sung or spoken? If the response of the universal prayer was sung, did the assembly sing it confidently?

SPIRITUALITY

GOSPEL ACCLAMATION
Cf. Mt 11:25

℟. Alleluia, alleluia.
Blessed are you, Father,
Lord of heaven and earth;
for revealing the mysteries of the kingdom.
to mere children.
℟. Alleluia, alleluia.

Gospel Luke 6:17, 20-26

Jesus came down with the Twelve and stopped at a piece of level ground where there was a large gathering of his disciples with a great crowd of people from all parts of Judaea and from Jerusalem and from the coastal region of Tyre and Sidon who had come to hear him and to be cured of their diseases.

Then fixing his eyes on his disciples he said:

'How happy are you who are poor: yours is the kingdom of God.

Happy you who are hungry now: you shall be satisfied.

Happy you who weep now: you shall laugh.

'Happy are you when people hate you, drive you out, abuse you, denounce your name as criminal, on account of the Son of Man. Rejoice when that day comes and dance for joy, for then your reward will be great in heaven. This was the way their ancestors treated the prophets.

'But alas for you who are rich: you are having your consolation now.

Alas for you who have your fill now: you shall go hungry.

Alas for you who laugh now: you shall mourn and weep.

'Alas for you when the world speaks well of you! This was the way their ancestors treated the false prophets.'

Reflecting on the Gospel

When parents leave children on their own for the first time it can be a big decision. Instructions are clear, often written down on a sheet of paper. Maybe a mobile phone or a house phone is available so the parties can stay in touch. And often the children remember or misremember instructions, reaching out to parents for additional clarity. Did the parents say no dessert? Or no dessert until after dinner? Did they say no TV/screen time, or limited TV/screen time? Some might remember the instructions differently.

Today in the Gospel of Luke we have Jesus's Sermon on the Plain as opposed to Matthew's Jesus who gives the Sermon on the Mount. Luke's Jesus preaches to a great crowd of disciples (indicating there were more than twelve) whereas Matthew's Jesus preaches to the disciples (and there were only twelve in the Gospel of Matthew).

But perhaps one of the greatest differences in the two versions of this story is not the setting or the audience but the message itself. Both Luke and Matthew begin with four beatitudes, but Matthew concludes with additional beatitudes. Luke, on the other hand, matches the four beatitudes with four woes that are frankly disturbing to the moderate, middle-class listener from the developed world.

We might ask what's wrong with being well off, having our fill of food and laughter, and being spoken well of? This might even be the goal of the so-called prosperity gospel we hear about so often in popular culture. But Luke sees it differently. Blessings are for those who are poor, hungry, weeping, and those hated. For whom is this good news? The rich and content? Hardly. Luke's Sermon on the Plain echoes themes introduced in Mary's *Magnificat* in the opening of the gospel. The hungry are fed while the rich are turned away empty. Jesus's values are not those of the world. To be countercultural means identifying with those who are blessed, not clawing our way to keep company with those who are destined for woe.

Luke has something to say to us today. This message is not limited to the time of Jesus. It is for us. Where do we find ourselves? In the four beatitudes or the four woes? This message is as much for us as it is for the disciples, if we dare to carry that name.

Living the Paschal Mystery

Sometimes it can be difficult to imagine why Jesus faced suffering and death. Often there is a popular idea that would have Jesus preaching only love, peace, kindness, and lilies of the field. The thinking goes that in the face of such preaching he was put to death by those who were against love, peace, and kindness. Such is too facile an explanation.

Jesus's preaching was certainly about love, but it was about much more. Somebody preaching love is no threat to the establishment, no threat to the powerful. Somebody preaching love can easily be dismissed as a dreamer and best left alone.

Today's gospel gives us some of Jesus's preaching that likely created enemies for himself. His preaching favoured the poor, hungry, weeping, and hated. He upended not only ancient cultural norms and values but modern ones too. Rather than simply give a verbal pat on the head to those on the bottom rungs of society, he also pulls down the mighty and issues woes that apply just as much to us as they did to those in power in antiquity. In so doing, Jesus creates enemies, not of the poor but of the powerful. It is they who will ultimately put him to death. But as we know, his suffering and death is not the end. God raises him up to glory, giving us the paschal mystery. His followers find themselves allied with those blessed by Jesus.

Focusing the Gospel

Key words and phrases: How happy are you who are poor: yours is the kingdom of God.

To the point: Jesus begins his famous Sermon on the Plain in Luke (a companion to Matthew's Sermon on the Mount) by turning the world on its head. In the kingdom of God the blessed are those who are marginalised and oppressed in our societies. And those who enjoy favour now will not find it in God's kingdom. Today Jesus gives us a choice. Do we glory in the richness of the kingdom of God or in what our world counts as riches? Do we stand with the hungry and grieving, or are we too busy feasting and laughing to notice their pain?

Connecting the Gospel

to the first reading: The cursed and the blessed are also mentioned in the first reading from the prophet Jeremiah. Here the distinguishing feature centres on trust. While the cursed trust in fallible humanity, the blessed trust in God. Jeremiah prophesied during a time of great peril in Israel's history. Instead of remaining faithful to the covenant, many of the people had begun to worship idols. Through Jeremiah, God invites the people to once more be faithful to the covenant of their ancestors and to trust in him alone.

to experience: At times it is difficult to trust in God, whom we do not see, when there are so many products and people assuring us that by turning ourselves over to their patented formula, three-step method, or unique programme, all will be well. Where in your own life might God be calling you to trust in him alone?

Connecting the Responsorial Psalm

to the readings: Today's psalm, the first in the book of Psalms, also contrasts the just with the wicked, the blessed with the cursed. Whereas Luke separates these groups by what they have and experience, and Jeremiah separates them by whom they trust, the psalmist makes a distinction in how they are rooted – in the law of the Lord or in the ways of the wicked. This psalm can be seen as an introduction to the entire book of Psalms and it states its thesis quite clearly: Happy is the one who is rooted in God. This person 'ponders his law day and night'. The 'law' in this case can be read as 'Torah', the first five books of the Old Testament, traditionally attributed to Moses by the people of Israel. In today's gospel we see allusions to Moses, the lawgiver, coming down from Mount Sinai. Jesus returns from the mountain where he has chosen twelve of his disciples to be apostles and preaches God's law to the great multitude of people who are gathered. As the psalmist proclaims, Happy is the one 'whose delight is the law of the Lord and who ponders his law day and night'.

to psalmist preparation: Like the gospel, this psalm clearly lays out two ways for us to choose from – the way of the just or the way of the wicked. This choice is before us always, in every decision and action that make up our daily lives. Let your love for God's law and desire to remain rooted in God shine through as you proclaim this psalm.

PROMPTS FOR FAITH-SHARING

In the reading from the prophet Jeremiah and in the psalm, there is a common image: the one who trusts in God and meditates on God's law is like a tree planted beside flowing water. Nourished deeply by the living water of God's love, the just one flourishes and bears fruit. Where do you find living water in your own life? How might God be inviting you to drink even more deeply?

In the Nicene Creed we state: 'I look forward to the resurrection of the dead.' How does belief in the resurrection of the dead affect your faith life?

In your daily life what are some actions you can take to align yourself with those Jesus proclaims as blessed: the poor, the hungry, the grieving, and the outcast?

In Luke's Sermon on the Plain Jesus includes statements of woe after the more familiar statements of blessing that are also included in Matthew's Sermon on the Mount. Why do you think these statements are included? How do they challenge you in your life of faith?

CELEBRATION

Model Penitential Act

Presider: Today, Jesus lays out for us the path to blessedness. For the times we have not followed this path by aligning ourselves with the poor and the hungry, we ask for pardon and forgiveness . . . [*pause*]

Lord Jesus, you show us the way to blessedness: Lord, have mercy.

Christ Jesus, you call us to identify with the poor and hungry: Christ, have mercy.

Lord Jesus, you are the risen one: Lord, have mercy.

Homily Points

• In today's readings we are offered a choice: trust in God or trust in humans (the first reading), the way of the just or the way of the wicked (the psalm), belief in or denial of Christ's resurrection, and blessing or woe (the gospel). There is no middle ground. Instead, our decisions will define the course of our lives.

• In the reading from the First Letter to the Corinthians, the apostle Paul continues to set down his arguments for the improbable occurrence of Jesus's resurrection from the dead. We, who have come to this mystery so long after the historical event, might find it difficult to conceptualise Jesus's resurrection. And yet, we choose to trust in God and believe that life is stronger than death in both Jesus of Nazareth and also in those who share his light land life.

• In three weeks we will be celebrating the First Sunday of Lent. Today's gospel and those for the next two weeks are taken from Jesus's Sermon on the Plain. Jesus's words emphasise the closeness of God to those who are poor, oppressed, and grieving. As we approach the season of Lent, a time of prayer, fasting, and almsgiving, we might begin to consider how we could use that holy time to align ourselves with those whom Jesus proclaims as blessed. In every decision and action that make up our daily lives we have an opportunity to encounter blessing or woe, justice or wickedness, trust in God or trust in the things of the world that are passing away. The choice is ours.

Model Universal Prayer (Prayer of the Faithful)

Presider: Today Jesus shows us the way of blessing and the way of woe. Let us pray for the strength to choose the way of blessing.

Response: Lord, hear our prayer.

That the church might be aligned with the poor and oppressed of society, and as such, show the way of blessing to all . . .

That leaders of nations not seek their own success but work tirelessly for the needs of all . . .

That those who hunger and grieve be fed and comforted by their neighbours . . .

That all of us here might align ourselves with the poor, hungry, grieving, and excluded within our families, our community, our nation, and our world . . .

Presider: Loving God, you sent your son to show us the way of holy living. Hear our prayers that we might become ever more people of your way. We ask this through Christ our Lord. Amen.

COLLECT

Let us pray.

Pause for silent prayer

O God, who teach us that you abide
in hearts that are just and true,
grant that we may be so fashioned by
      your grace
as to become a dwelling pleasing to you.
Through our Lord Jesus Christ, your Son,
who lives and reigns with you in the unity
      of the Holy Spirit,
one God, for ever and ever. **Amen.**

FIRST READING
Jer 17:5-8

The Lord says this:
'A curse on the man who puts his trust
      in man,
who relies on things of flesh,
whose heart turns from the Lord.
He is like dry scrub in the wastelands:
if good comes, he has no eyes for it,
he settles in the parched places of the
      wilderness,
a salt land, uninhabited.

'A blessing on the man who puts his
      trust in the Lord,
with the Lord for his hope.
He is like a tree by the waterside
that thrusts its roots to the stream:
when the heat comes it feels no alarm,
its foliage stays green;
it has no worries in a year of drought,
and never ceases to bear fruit.'

RESPONSORIAL PSALM
Ps 1:1-4, 6 (Ps 39:5)

R̸. Happy the man who has placed his
   trust in the Lord.

Happy indeed is the man
who follows not the counsel of the wicked;
nor lingers in the way of sinners
nor sits in the company of scorners,
but whose delight is the law of the Lord
and who ponders his law day and night.

R̸. Happy the man who has placed his
   trust in the Lord.

He is like a tree that is planted
beside the flowing waters,
that yields its fruit in due season
and whose leaves shall never fade;
and all that he does shall prosper.

R̸. Happy the man who has placed his
   trust in the Lord.

Not so are the wicked, not so!
For they like winnowed chaff
shall be driven away by the wind.
For the Lord guards the way of the just
but the way of the wicked leads to doom.

R̸. Happy the man who has placed his
   trust in the Lord.

SECOND READING
1 Cor 15:12, 16-20

If Christ raised from the dead is what has
been preached, how can some of you be
saying that there is no resurrection of the
dead? For if the dead are not raised, Christ
has not been raised, and if Christ has not
been raised, you are still in your sins. And
what is more serious, all who have died in
Christ have perished. If our hope in Christ
has been for this life only, we are the most
unfortunate of all people.

But Christ has in fact been raised from
the dead, the first-fruits of all who have
fallen asleep.

About Liturgy

Rare readings: Today and the next two Sundays give us the opportunity to hear a
set of readings we don't often hear because of the logistics of the liturgical year. The
last time we celebrated the Sixth Sunday of Ordinary Time, Year C, was in 2010; the
Seventh Sunday, Year C, in 2007; and the Eighth Sunday, Year C, in 2001! These are a
lovely set of readings from Luke, so be sure to alert your homilists and lectors to how
special these coming Sundays are.

Observing the Preparation of Gifts and the Eucharistic Prayer: We
continue our observation of the liturgy with these points to pay attention to in the
preparation of gifts and the Eucharistic Prayer.

Gifts: Were the gifts of bread and wine brought to the altar by assembly members
from the midst of the assembly, or were they simply retrieved from a side table by the
priest or assistant? Were the vessels used for the bread and wine of genuine, beautiful,
and dignified quality? Was enough bread and wine for the whole assembly brought to
the altar?

Procession: Did the procession of gifts look like a procession? Were the gifts of
bread, wine, and money processed to the altar with care and dignity? Was money
collected in a graceful, unhurried, efficient manner? Were additional gifts other than
bread, wine, and money brought forward? Why?

Eucharistic Prayer: Did the priest lead the Eucharistic Prayer clearly and
confidently? Did the priest engage the assembly in the Eucharistic Prayer through
graceful gestures and appropriate tone of voice and eye contact? Describe the pace of
the Eucharistic Prayer. Was it spoken too quickly or too slowly? Did the priest convey
a sense of praise and thanksgiving through his voice, posture, and gestures during the
Eucharistic Prayer? Did the priest chant or sing any parts of the Eucharistic Prayer? In
your opinion, what was the climax of the Eucharistic Prayer in this celebration? Why?
Overall, did it feel like the assembly '[joined] with Christ in confessing the great deeds
of God and in the offering of Sacrifice' (GIRM 78), or did it feel like just the priest's
prayer? What made it feel that way?

About Liturgical Music

Evaluating the Preparation of Gifts and the Eucharistic Prayer: The
preparation of gifts is a bridge between the Liturgy of the Word and the Liturgy of
the Eucharist. Though it is secondary to these two main parts of the Mass, it still
requires some careful preparation. Because the liturgical action during this time is
relatively simple with very little to no spoken audible text, the music often takes the
focal lead. This is an appropriate time for the choir to exercise its ministry by singing a
hymn or motet on its own. However, the music here still must serve the liturgical action
and cannot delay the flow of the Mass. The text should also relate to the celebration of
the day or liturgical season, reflecting back on the Liturgy of the Word.

The Eucharistic Prayer, on the other hand, is the 'centre and high point of the entire
celebration' (GIRM 78). The ritual music here is critical to the assembly's ritual action
of offering praise to the Father through Christ. Here are some points to observe as
you evaluate the liturgical music for the Eucharistic Prayer: Did the assembly sing all
three Eucharistic Prayer acclamations (Holy, Mystery of Faith, Great Amen)? Did the
assembly know the music? Did they sing confidently? Did the musical setting of the
acclamations match the feel of the liturgical season? Did the Great Amen feel 'Great'?

SPIRITUALITY

GOSPEL ACCLAMATION
Jn 13:34

℟. Alleluia, alleluia.
I give you a new commandment:
love one another,
just as I have loved you,
says the Lord.
℟. Alleluia, alleluia.

Gospel   Luke 6:27-38

Jesus said to his disciples: 'I say this to you who are listening: Love your enemies, do good to those who hate you, bless those who curse you, pray for those who treat you badly. To the man who slaps you on one cheek, present the other cheek too; to the man who takes your cloak from you, do not refuse your tunic. Give to everyone who asks you, and do not ask for your property back from the man who robs you. Treat others as you would like them to treat you. If you love those who love you, what thanks can you expect? Even sinners love those who love them. And if you do good to those who do good to you, what thanks can you expect? For even sinners do that much. And if you lend to those from whom you hope to receive, what thanks can you expect? Even sinners lend to sinners to get back the same amount. Instead, love your enemies and do good, and lend without any hope of return. You will have a great reward, and you will be sons of the Most High, for he himself is kind to the ungrateful and the wicked.

'Be compassionate as your Father is compassionate. Do not judge, and you will not be judged yourselves; do not condemn, and you will not be condemned yourselves; grant pardon, and you will be pardoned. Give, and there will be gifts for you: a full measure, pressed down, shaken together, and running over, will be poured into your lap; because the amount you measure out is the amount you will be given back.'

Reflecting on the Gospel

A classic device when children are called upon to share something is to have one divide it and the other choose which half is hers. This can happen with a piece of cake, cookie, pizza, or other food. But it can also happen with other items as well. Rarely does one child say to the other, 'You can have it all'. The purpose of the device is to share something in an equitable manner. And perhaps this works for children. It sometimes works for adults too!

The advice Jesus gives in today's gospel couldn't be more different. He is calling us to a higher standard. It's as though we are asked to divvy up the

treat and instead we say, 'You can have it all'. Even more, the way of sharing a cookie between children might assume they are friendly. But Jesus speaks here of 'enemies'. This is an entirely different category. Jesus assumes his ancient listeners have enemies, and that is something that transcends culture and time. Enemies are not limited to the ancient world!

Christians are to love their enemies, blessing them and praying for them. The Christian standard is one higher than what we could expect from the world with its transactional view of relationships. As Jesus himself notes, it's fairly easy to love those who love us, and to do good to those who do good to us. But it's another thing entirely to love those who are our enemies, to pray for them and to bless them.

We Christians are to be this way because God is this way. God is 'kind to the ungrateful and the wicked'. Should we be any different? We are to be merciful as the Father is merciful. And here we see in our own time the example of mercy given to us by Pope Francis. It is said that the word 'mercy' is the hermeneutical key to his papacy. It is the way to understand and make sense of his actions. Pope Francis chose mercy because mercy is of God, and acting in this way demonstrates that we are followers of his son, Jesus.

Living the Paschal Mystery

When faced with the extraordinary demands of the gospel outlined in today's reading, one person said, 'How can I do that? I'd end up with nothing'? Then we look to the example of Jesus who enfleshed the words he preached. Jesus himself loved his enemies and prayed for those who persecuted him. In the Gospel of Luke we will hear Jesus from the cross pray for their forgiveness. What did he end up with? Nothing: he died on a cross. But of course we know the rest of the story. God raised him from the dead. Only by Jesus giving himself completely and without reservation to the point of death is he ultimately raised up to glory with the Father. The words that form the conclusion of today's gospel are especially apropos. 'Forgive and you will be forgiven. . . . For the measure with which you measure / will in return be measured out to you'. We forgive others not so much for their sake but for our own.

Focusing the Gospel

Key words and phrases: [L]ove your enemies

To the point: In today's gospel Jesus tells us twice, '[L]ove your enemies'. This statement is nestled into a longer list of moral injunctions. We could say, however, that this phrase, 'love your enemies', encompasses all the others and also points the way to emulating God's love. God does not love only those who are worthy or good. God loves everyone simply because of their very existence. And so are we called to love as well. Our enemies could be one specific person with whom we have a feud, or it could be a group of people that we see (even if it is subconsciously) as 'other' than ourselves and therefore not worthy of our concern. No matter how we might encounter 'enemies' Jesus's command remains the same, love them with the mercy, forgiveness, and compassion of God.

Connecting the Gospel

to the first reading: In the first reading from First Samuel we have an example par excellence of one man loving his enemy. David is pursued by King Saul. In his jealousy, Saul fears that David wants the throne for himself. Bent on killing David, Saul takes three thousand of his best warriors into the wilderness area where he hears David is hiding. Through the work of the Lord it is David, not Saul, who comes upon his enemy unawares. David finds Saul asleep with a spear stuck into the ground at his head, while all of his warriors slumber around him. And yet, with a clear opportunity to end his life of hiding and running from Saul, he does the king no harm. Our reading ends with David (now safely separated from Saul by a hilltop) telling the king, 'The Lord repays everyone for his uprightness and loyalty'.

to experience: Is there a contentious relationship in your life where you can follow David's example and refuse to pick up the spear?

Connecting the Responsorial Psalm

to the readings: In the gospel Jesus tells us to be 'compassionate, as your Father is compassionate'. And how would we define God's mercy? Today's psalm paints a picture for us. Our God is 'slow to anger and rich in mercy'. No wrongdoing can put us beyond the reach of God, who 'forgives all your guilt', removing them '[a]s far as the east is from the west'. We cannot give to our brothers and sisters what we have not received ourselves. Let us immerse ourselves in the infinite mercy of our God – only then will we be able to offer it to others.

to psalmist preparation: It is only in acknowledging our sins that we experience the gracious mercy of God. As you prepare to proclaim this psalm, lauding God's abundant mercy, call to mind a time when you experienced forgiveness – either from a person in your life, or from God. What did it feel like to know your sin had been wiped away and your wrongdoing was forgotten?

PROMPTS FOR FAITH-SHARING

In the first reading, David refuses to do harm to his enemy when he comes upon Saul unprotected. Where in your own life are you being called to choose peace and mercy over bitterness and revenge?

In the second reading, St. Paul tells us that we will bear the image of the heavenly man, Jesus, just as we have born the image of the earthly man, Adam. How might we, as individuals and as a parish, conform ourselves more perfectly to the image of Christ, the one who loves without counting the cost?

How does your family and/or parish follow Jesus's command to 'bless those who curse you, pray for those who treat you badly?'

In the gospel we are told, 'Give, and there will be gifts for you'. When have you experienced in your own life generosity begetting abundance?

CELEBRATION

Model Penitential Act

Presider: In today's gospel we hear the Golden Rule, 'Treat others as you would like them to treat you'. We pause now to consider the times we have not lived up to this rule . . . [*pause*]

Lord Jesus, you call us to love our enemies: Lord, have mercy.

Christ Jesus, show us the way of mercy and compassion: Christ, have mercy.

Lord Jesus, you are the Son of the Most High: Lord, have mercy.

Homily Points

• As human beings we are often caught up in the question of fairness. We want to be fair to our children, our students, our employees, our neighbours. . . . And we want others to be fair to us. In the gospel today Jesus tells us to love without limit, to go beyond being fair, for 'if you love those who love you, what thanks can you expect'? As Christians we are called to radically trust in the power of love beyond what is fair.

• When we love the way Jesus loves we might be surprised at what happens. But then again we might not. People continue to be people no matter our actions. Is this reason to stop? No. St. Teresa of Calcutta inscribed a poem on the wall of her children's house called 'Paradoxical Commandments' by Dr. Kent M. Keith. It begins, 'People are illogical, unreasonable, and self-centred. Love them anyway'.

• As Christians we are tasked with being Christ-bearers in the world. To love as Jesus himself loves. We are to respond to hate with compassion, empathy, and mercy. We are to lend to others expecting nothing in return. We are to forgive others, even as the 'other' persecutes and tortures us. Adopting this way of living is not easy. Perhaps this week we might begin by taking one area in our lives where we have been focused on fairness, on loving others with the same amount of love they show us, and instead strive to personify the abundant, illogical, joyful love of Christ.

Model Universal Prayer (Prayer of the Faithful)

Presider: Confident in God's mercy and compassion, let us present our needs to the Lord.

Response: Lord, hear our prayer.

That the church be a sign of unity and reconciliation . . .

That the prosperous nations of the world share their resources and gifts with nations in need . . .

That those who are enslaved by bitterness and thoughts of revenge receive the grace to grant forgiveness . . .

That all of us here grow in our vocation to show the merciful, compassionate love of Christ to all we encounter . . .

Presider: Gracious God, you call us to emulate your way of love. Grant our prayers that we may trust in your grace as we travel this holy way. We ask this through Jesus Christ, our Lord. Amen.

COLLECT

Let us pray.

Pause for silent prayer

Grant, we pray, almighty God,
that, always pondering spiritual things,
we may carry out in both word and deed
that which is pleasing to you.
Through our Lord Jesus Christ, your Son,
who lives and reigns with you in the unity
    of the Holy Spirit,
one God, for ever and ever. **Amen.**

FIRST READING
1 Sam 26:2,7-9,12-13,22-23

Saul set off and went down to the wilderness of Ziph, accompanied by three thousand men chosen from Israel to search for David in the wilderness of Ziph.

So in the dark David and Abishai made their way towards the force, where they found Saul lying asleep inside the camp, his spear stuck in the ground beside his head, with Abner and the troops lying round him.

Then Abishai said to David, 'Today God has put your enemy in your power; so now let me pin him to the ground with his own spear. Just one stroke! I will not need to strike him twice.' David answered Abishai, 'Do not kill him, for who can lift his hand against the Lord's anointed and be without guilt?' David took the spear and the pitcher of water from beside Saul's head, and they made off. No one saw, no one knew, no one woke up; they were all asleep, for a deep sleep from the Lord had fallen on them.

David crossed to the other side and halted on the top of the mountain a long way off; there was a wide space between them. David then called out, 'Here is the king's spear. Let one of the soldiers come across and take it. The Lord repays everyone for his uprightness and loyalty. Today the Lord put you in my power, but I would not raise my hand against the Lord's anointed.'

CATECHESIS

RESPONSORIAL PSALM
Ps 102:1-4, 8, 10, 12-13 (8)

℟. The Lord is compassion and love.

My soul, give thanks to the Lord,
all my being, bless his holy name.
My soul, give thanks to the Lord
and never forget all his blessings.

℟. The Lord is compassion and love.

It is he who forgives all your guilt,
who heals every one of your ills,
who redeems your life from the grave,
who crowns you with love and
compassion.

℟. The Lord is compassion and love.

The Lord is compassion and love,
slow to anger and rich in mercy.
He does not treat us according to our sins
nor repay us according to our faults.

℟. The Lord is compassion and love.

As far as the east is from the west
so far does he remove our sins.
As a father has compassion on his sons,
the Lord has pity on those who fear him.

℟. The Lord is compassion and love.

SECOND READING
1 Cor 15:45-49

The first man, Adam, as scripture says,
became a living soul; but the last Adam
has become a life-giving spirit. That is,
first the one with the soul, not the spirit,
and after that, the one with the spirit.
The first man, being from the earth, is
earthly by nature; the second man is from
heaven. As this earthly man was, so are
we on earth; and as the heavenly man is,
so are we in heaven. And we, who have
been modelled on the earthly man, will be
modelled on the heavenly man.

About Liturgy

Observing the Communion Rite: The communion rite is often where the liturgical flow and logistics of a Mass may fall apart or lag. The communion rite begins with the Lord's Prayer and continues through the end of the prayer after Communion. Because there is so much movement of ministers and people during this time, you will want to plan the 'choreography' and placement of ministers with careful attention to your specific liturgical space. Then all liturgical ministers assisting during this time need to know and rehearse their movements and tasks. This includes not only the clergy who are assisting at the altar but also servers, extraordinary ministers of Holy Communion, ushers, sacristans, and choir members. Here are some specific points to observe during the communion rite as you continue to evaluate each part of your Sunday Mass:

Lord's Prayer: If the Lord's Prayer was sung, did the whole assembly sing it confidently? If it was spoken, was the pacing prayerful?

Sign of Peace: Did you feel that people shared the sign of peace with you genuinely? Did the gesture feel like a ritual sign of peacemaking, reconciliation, and commitment to the Body of Christ, or did it feel simply like a cordial handshake? Was the rite overly lengthened by the priest or other ministers sharing the sign of peace with many people? If so, did the assembly feel engaged during this time, or did the assembly become spectators?

Fraction Rite: Were hosts from the tabernacle used in the fraction rite? Why? Did the rite seem to take too long? If so, why? Did the rite look calm? Chaotic? Organised? Did the priest break the first piece of the Blessed Sacrament in a way that made it look like a dignified ritual for the whole assembly to see? Did the assembly sing the Lamb of God confidently? Did the singing of the Lamb of God begin as the priest broke the first host, and did the singing continue until all the communion vessels were ready?

Communion: After the assembly said, 'Lord, I am not worthy . . .', how long did the assembly have to wait before they began processing to the altar? Was the Precious Blood available for the whole assembly? Were there enough communion ministers for the whole assembly so that the procession did not take too long? Did communion ministers have good eye contact with you? Did communion ministers speak clearly and loudly? How did the consecrated host taste? How did the consecrated wine taste? Overall, did the assembly feel united as one body through posture, movement, and song during the entire communion procession, or did it feel like each person's own private time for prayer? Was there a good amount of silence after Communion?

About Liturgical Music

Evaluating the Communion Rite: Music during this time will help to unite the various parts and keep the flow of the ritual prayer moving. Here are a few points to assist in your evaluation of the musical elements of the communion rite:

If the Lord's Prayer was sung, did the whole assembly sing it confidently? After the assembly said, 'Lord, I am not worthy . . .', did the communion song begin immediately as the priest received the Sacrament (see GIRM 86)? Was the assembly able to sing the communion song(s) confidently? How many communion songs were sung? Was this the right amount of songs to use for the length of the communion procession? Did the song 'bring out more clearly the "communitarian" character of the procession to receive the Eucharist' (see GIRM 86)? Did the song reflect back on the Liturgy of the Word as a 'Gospel Communion,' as do the Songs for the Table in Psallite? If there was a song of praise after communion, did everyone sing it (see GIRM 88), or was it a song performed by one person or just the choir?

℟. Alleluia, alleluia!
If you make my word your home
you will indeed be my disciples,
and you will learn the truth, says the Lord.
℟. Alleluia, alleluia!

Gospel
Matt 5:13-19

Jesus said to his disciples: 'You are the salt of the earth. But if salt becomes tasteless, what can make it salty again? It is good for nothing, and can only be thrown out to be trampled underfoot by men.

'You are the light of the world. A city built on a hill-top can not be hidden. No one lights a lamp to put it under a tub; they put it on the lamp-stand where it shines for everyone in the house. In the same way your light must shine in the sight of men, so that, seeing your good works, they may give the praise to your Father in heaven.'

See Appendix, p. 276, for the other readings.

Reflecting on the Gospel

Grandparents and elders are often the source of wisdom, passing along bits of advice in pithy phrases or witty sayings. But kernels of wisdom come from many other sources as well. There is an entire book of the Old Testament (Proverbs) that is a collection of such sayings. Even today, we have books of quotations or inspirational adages. Bits of wisdom and sage advice can be easy to recall and handy to pass on to children, friends, and others.

On this feast of Saint David of Wales, the church gives us a reading from the Sermon on the Mount. How appropriate too that the selection is the four verses that make up some of the most memorable aphorisms of Jesus: 'You are the salt of the earth. . . . You are the light of the world'. In many ways, these sayings complement David's own maxim, 'Do the little things in life'. Indeed, the gospel reading today concludes with Jesus's exhortation to let your light shine before others. In saying so, Jesus means for the good deeds we do to be seen by others. This is not to be done in a kind of 'look at me' way, but so that our acts of mercy can be a witness to the love of God in the world.

It might be difficult to imagine being a saint. But the words of David and the words of Jesus give us hope. Sanctity is not beyond us, but is within our reach. Merely by doing the little things well, our good deeds will shine. In an environment when the culture tells us quicker is better, faster is cheaper, and time is money, we might slow down and be more mindful in our approach. Not content to be cogs in someone else's machine, we recognise that the quotidian events of our lives are imbued with sanctity and grace. How we treat one another matters. The kindness we impart to strangers, and especially friends, without taking them for granted, is doing the 'little things'.

As Christians, followers of Jesus, disciples of Christ, we are to be 'salt for the earth' and 'light for the world'. These words and images are steeped in the ancient world but quite rightly understood today. These are sayings worth passing on to friends and family, encapsulating some of the Christian wisdom by which we live our lives. In doing good deeds, including the little things in life, our light shines and gives glory to God.

Living the Paschal Mystery

Though there are no contemporaneous written records from David of Wales, his fame spread and lasted for centuries. Legends grew and stories accrued so that it can be difficult to separate fact from fiction. But the sayings attributed to him, especially that of 'do the little things in life', can be a meaningful way to engage this saint and his wisdom. Like David, Jesus did not leave us any contemporaneous written record. Jesus taught his disciples and entrusted his words and deeds to these same followers.

In the end, we can 'do the little things in life' entrusting our efforts to God's will. Even in the face of Jesus's own death, with little outwardly to show for his efforts, he trusted God, who raised him from the dead. The spirituality of the paschal mystery animates us as well, who trust not in our designs, but in the master designer, who raises from the dead. For our part, we 'do the little things in life' and leave the rest to God.

Focusing the Gospel

Key words and phrases: '[Y]our light must shine in the sight of men, so that, seeing your good works, they may give the praise to your Father in heaven'.

To the point: Jesus tells the gathered crowds that they are meant to be the salt of the earth and the light of the world. Both of these elements, salt and light, effect the world around them. Salt brings out the flavour in food, and light dispels darkness. Sometimes we might think that holiness is a private affair, something we strive to do in our own lives and that has nothing to do with the wider community. And yet, Jesus's call to us is to lead lives that bless others. We see this in the lives of the saints and people of faith throughout history. St. David's light continues to shine on us as we remember his life and ask for his intercession.

Model Penitential Act

Presider: On this feast day we look to St. David's simplicity of faith and love as a model for our own lives. For the times we have become distracted in the life of faith, let us ask for pardon and healing . . . *[pause]*

Lord Jesus, you are the strength of love within us: Lord, have mercy.
Christ Jesus, you are the way to everlasting life: Christ, have mercy.
Lord Jesus, you call us to be the salt of the earth and the light of the world:
Lord, have mercy.

Model Universal Prayer (Prayer of the Faithful)

Presider: Through the intercession of St. David, let us bring our needs and desires to our good and gracious God.

Response: Lord, hear our prayer.

That the church of God, inspired by the witness of St. David, might continue to go forth and bring the good news of Jesus Christ to all nations . . .

That leaders of nations might humbly employ their authority to safeguard the rights and dignity of workers . . .

That those who suffer religious persecution throughout the world might encounter safe havens to worship in peace . . .

That all gathered here might recommit our lives to performing small acts of kindness and charity with great love . . .

Presider: God of wisdom and compassion, through your son, Jesus Christ, you call us to be light for the world. Hear our prayers, that by emulating the life of St. David, we might be a light and blessing to all those we meet. We ask this through Christ our Lord. **Amen.**

About Liturgy

Among the many miracles attributed to St. David are the raising of a dead boy to life and restoring sight to the blind St. Paulinus. It could therefore be appropriate to consider a service of healing within Mass on this day. St. David is also reputed to have placed a handkerchief on the ground and transformed it into a hill on which he could stand so that his preaching would be more easily heard by the crowds. This could prompt an emphasis on the proclamation of the Word today. St. David's flag is a yellow cross on a black background. One symbol of St. David is the daffodil, also yellow. In addition to incorporating daffodils into the environment, they could be distributed at the end of Mass on this day.

COLLECT

Let us pray.

Pause for silent prayer

O God, who graciously bestowed on your
    Bishop Saint David of Wales
the virtue of wisdom and the gift of eloquence
and made him an example of prayer and
    pastoral zeal,
grant that, through his intercession
your Church may ever prosper and render you
    joyful praise.
Through our Lord Jesus Christ, your Son,
who lives and reigns with you in the unity of
    the Holy Spirit,
one God, for ever and ever. **Amen.**

FOR REFLECTION

• Following in the footsteps of St. David, what are the 'little things in life' God might be calling you to pay attention to right now?

• In today's gospel we hear the familiar Scripture passage where Jesus calls his disciples to be the light of the world and the salt of the earth. In your life of faith, who has been 'salt' and 'light' for you?

Homily Points

• In the life of St. David and in all the saints we find people who have truly been 'salt of the earth' and 'light of the world'. Which is to say, they made a difference in the lives of those around them. Jesus's words to the crowds in the Sermon on the Mount say plainly that being a disciple is a public as well as a private commitment.

• To be Christian one must be oriented towards the other. To be a light that shines in darkness and salt that offers flavour to those whose lives have been made bland through depression, despair, or hopelessness. St. David points out to us that this difference is made through the little things of life and faith. The small kindnesses we practise day in and day out are what make us a blessing to those who share our lives.

SPIRITUALITY

GOSPEL ACCLAMATION
Ph 2:15-16

R̸. Alleluia, alleluia.
You will shine in the world like bright stars
because you are offering it the word of life.
R̸. Alleluia, alleluia.

Gospel

Luke 6:39-45

Jesus told a parable to his disciples. 'Can one blind man guide another? Surely both will fall into a pit? The disciple is not superior to his teacher; the fully trained disciple will always be like his teacher. Why do you observe the splinter in your brother's eye and never notice the plank in your own? How can you say to your brother, "Brother, let me take out the splinter that is in your eye," when you cannot see the plank in your own? Hypocrite! Take the plank out of your own eye first, and then you will see clearly enough to take out the splinter that is in your brother's eye.

'There is no sound tree that produces rotten fruit, nor again a rotten tree that produces sound fruit. For every tree can be told by its own fruit; people do not pick figs from thorns, nor gather grapes from brambles. A good man draws what is good from the store of goodness in his heart; a bad man draws what is bad from the store of badness. For a man's words flow out of what fills his heart.'

Reflecting on the Gospel

We all have words to live by. Maybe they were told to us by parents or grandparents, or perhaps a teacher or a relative. But we can all recall maxims by which we live. Today's gospel gives us life lessons or words to live by. In fact, if read in isolation, this reading is broader than Christianity. It could readily be accepted by non-Christians too. And such is often the case with life lessons. They are not limited to one religious or denominational outlook.

The life lessons Jesus teaches in this gospel are akin to homespun wisdom rooted in daily life and experience. When we say a project at work is being performed like 'the blind leading the blind', we are echoing Jesus's teaching. Though we mean no disrespect to the blind, the metaphor is easily grasped and understood.

And how often have we experienced the nitpicking nag who quickly points out the fault in others while conveniently overlooking his or her own. Jesus's warning about noticing the splinter in another's eye while neglecting the wooden beam in our own captures that sentiment well. Even so, Jesus is more adamant about us removing the beam from our own eye than simply not noticing the splinter in another.

The concluding bit of wisdom is based on lived experience as well. Just as a good tree does not produce bad fruit, so it is with people. 'By their fruits you shall know them' is another way to sum this up; 'actions speak louder than words' is another. If a person is performing good works, it's likely they are a good person. On the other hand, if a person performs only selfish acts, that, too, is a window into their soul, for as Jesus puts it, '[F]rom the fulness of the heart the mouth speaks'. Here the basis on their fundamental goodness is not whether they believe in Jesus, or even God. It's not whether they go to church or synagogue. And given the time this was written, it's certainly not about praying the rosary or attending First Fridays. Instead, a person's heart is ultimately known by their words and actions. And actions speak louder than words. These are words to live by.

Living the Paschal Mystery

Churchy people can often and easily be caught up in churchy things. What colours are we displaying for the season? What song is most appropriate at this time? What is the second reading and how does it connect to the first? But today we are reminded by Jesus that there are many things broader and perhaps more important than church or even religious identity. We are told not to be hypocritical, finding fault in others while overlooking our own. We are reminded to consider how they act as an indication of their character.

Jesus's teaching and preaching was fundamental to his ministry. He was considered a sage and a prophet. His understanding of human beings moved the crowds. His insight into how we behave versus how we ought to behave, encapsulated in pithy and memorable sayings was profound. And certainly after his death and resurrection his teaching carried new meaning. In light of his undergoing the paschal mystery, he is the Son of God raised to new life. His words are more than homespun wisdom. They are light and life.

Focusing the Gospel

Key words and phrases: every tree is known by its own fruit

To the point: Jesus lived in an agrarian culture where people tilled the soil to provide for themselves and their families. In today's gospel he uses a metaphor that his audience would immediately have understood: 'A good tree does not bear rotten fruit, / nor does a rotten tree bear good fruit. / For every tree is known by its own fruit'. We might ask, what 'fruit' do we bear that marks us as Christians?

Connecting the Gospel

to the first reading: Just as 'every tree is known by its own fruit', the writer of Sirach counsels that the true test of a person's heart is in their speech and conversation. The book of Sirach belongs to the category of wisdom literature in the Bible. Uprightness of speech is an important theme in all of wisdom literature. In the book of Proverbs we hear, 'Dishonest mouth put away from you, / deceitful lips put far from you' (Prov 4:24; NABRE). Devious and crooked speech might include falsehoods, but gossip and slander are also condemned.

to experience: Survey your own conversation. What percentage of it might you categorise as righteous speech – words that uplift and inspire others? What percentage is crooked or devious – words that put others down or convey anger, hatred or enmity?

Connecting the Responsorial Psalm

to the readings: If slander, gossip, and lying are all speech that places a wedge between the speaker and his or her neighbours and God, what is godly speech? The psalms might be our best guide for speech that uplifts. In Psalm 91 we hear, 'It is good to give thanks to the Lord, / to make music to your name, O Most High'. Praise and thanksgiving are not only for the glory of God; these patterns of speech also change the person who is speaking. By focusing on gratitude and praise, his or her eyes are further opened to the countless gifts of God and the wonders of creation. Furthermore, the psalmist tells us that the one who is rooted in justice (right relationship with God and others) will 'flourish in the courts of our God, / still bearing fruit when they are old'.

to psalmist preparation: As a cantor, your words within the liturgy lead the people in prayer and praise of God. How might you bring all the other words you speak throughout the week into better alignment with the ones you proclaim in the liturgy?

PROMPTS FOR FAITH-SHARING

The first reading from Sirach warns, '[T]he test of a person is in conversation' (NABRE). What do your own patterns and habits of speech reveal about you and about 'the bent' of your heart?

St. Paul urges us to '[n]ever give in . . .; keep on working at the Lord's work always, . . .' Where is God calling you to be steadfast at this time?

In the gospel we hear, '[E]very tree is known by its own fruit.' In what areas of your life are good fruits being born? Where is your life less fruitful?

Sometimes we are most distressed by the faults of others that we also notice subconsciously in ourselves. Where have you become preoccupied with a 'splinter in your brother's eye?' What might this preoccupation tell you about 'the plank in your own?'

CELEBRATION

Model Penitential Act

Presider: Jesus tells us today, 'There is no sound tree that produces rotten fruit, / nor again a rotten tree that produces sound fruit. / For every tree can be told by its own fruit'. For the times we have failed to produce good fruit we ask for pardon and mercy . . . [*pause*]

Lord Jesus, you conquer sin and death: Lord, have mercy.
Christ Jesus, you are Son of the Most High: Christ, have mercy.
Lord Jesus, you lead us to wisdom: Lord, have mercy.

Homily Points

• On Wednesday we will enter into the season of Lent. As we think about what practice of penance we will embrace it is often easier to come up with penances for our spouse, children, colleagues, or friends than it is for ourselves. Jesus knew the human propensity to point out others' faults. He counsels, 'Take the plank out of your eye first, and then you will see clearly to take out the splinter that is in your brother's eye'. Perhaps this year you might invite a trusted friend or family member to help you in choosing a Lenten practice. Receive feedback with an open mind and then ask God to help you discern what will be the most fruitful practice for you this Lenten season.

• Speech is one of our most precious abilities as humans. Travelling in a foreign country or visiting a neighbourhood where one does not speak the language quickly shows us how much we miss out on when we cannot communicate with others. As with all precious gifts, however, there is the possibility of misusing this ability. This week take some time to reflect on how you use speech in your daily life. Perhaps your Lenten practice could include fasting from speech that tears others down, and bestowing words that uplift as a way of giving alms.

• Sometimes we grow weary in the spiritual life. These last few weeks Jesus has called to us through the gospels to do the seemingly impossible: 'Be compassionate as your Father is compassionate'; '[L]ove your enemies'; 'Give to everyone who asks you'. While we strive to fulfill these commandments, we will often fail. And yet, today St. Paul urges us, 'Never give in then, my dear brothers, never admit defeat; keep on working at the Lord's work always, knowing that, in the Lord, you cannot be labouring in vain'. Let us not become weary by our failures, but continue to trust in Jesus's call to bear good fruit.

Model Universal Prayer (Prayer of the Faithful)

Presider: Heeding Jesus's call to repentance, we humbly voice our petitions, trusting in God's never-ending mercy.

Response: Lord, hear our prayer.

That the church might bear good fruit for the glory of God . . .

That religious and civic leaders support conditions where all people might grow and flourish . . .

That those in need reap the good fruit of charity, love, and mercy . . .

That all members of our community use their talents and gifts to build up the kingdom of God . . .

Presider: Gracious God, all that we have is a gift from you. May we tend and cultivate these gifts so they might bear abundant fruit for the glory of your name. We ask this through Jesus Christ, our Lord. Amen.

COLLECT

Let us pray.

Pause for silent prayer
Grant us, O Lord, we pray,
that the course of our world
may be directed by your peaceful rule
and that your Church may rejoice,
untroubled in her devotion.
Through our Lord Jesus Christ, your Son,
who lives and reigns with you in the unity
     of the Holy Spirit,
one God, for ever and ever. **Amen.**

FIRST READING

Eccl 27:4-7

In a shaken sieve the rubbish is left behind,
so too the defects of a man appear in
     his talk.
The kiln tests the work of the potter,
the test of a man is in his conversation.
The orchard where the tree grows is
     judged on the quality of its fruit,
similarly a man's words betray what
     he feels.
Do not praise a man before he has spoken,
since this is the test of men.

RESPONSORIAL PSALM
Ps 91:2-3, 13-16 (2)

℞. It is good to give you thanks, O Lord.

It is good to give thanks to the Lord
to make music to your name, O Most High,
to proclaim your love in the morning
and your truth in the watches of the night.

℞. It is good to give you thanks, O Lord.

The just will flourish like the palm-tree
and grow like a Lebanon cedar.

℞. It is good to give you thanks, O Lord.

Planted in the house of the Lord
they will flourish in the courts of our God,
still bearing fruit when they are old,
still full of sap, still green,
to proclaim that the Lord is just.
In him, my rock, there is no wrong.

℞. It is good to give you thanks, O Lord.

SECOND READING
1 Cor 15:54-58

When this perishable nature has put on imperishability, and when this mortal nature has put on immortality, then the words of scripture will come true: Death is swallowed up in victory. Death, where is your victory? Death, where is your sting? Now the sting of death is sin, and sin gets its power from the Law. So let us thank God for giving us the victory through our Lord Jesus Christ.

Never give in then, my dear brothers, never admit defeat; keep on working at the Lord's work always, knowing that, in the Lord, you cannot be labouring in vain.

About Liturgy

Observing the Concluding Rites: We come to the last, and possibly most important, part of the Mass. The concluding rites give the Mass its name and, quite literally, its mission: 'Go and announce the Gospel of the Lord'. Here the faithful are commissioned to evangelise by doing what they have done in the Mass. Out in the world, we welcome the stranger, acknowledge our sins, and give glory for the Father's mercy we have encountered in Christ through the Spirit. Then we listen with the ear of our hearts to God's word, which gives us the lens for recognising Christ acting in the world and shapes us for mission. We confess our faith, lift up the needs of those who suffer, share our blessings, and, in union with all God's people, praise God and ask God to make us one in Christ. All we have rehearsed in the liturgy of the church we do in our daily lives in the liturgy of the world. This concluding part of the Mass is the beginning of our mission to glorify God by our lives. Here are some points to observe as you evaluate the concluding rites:

Did the announcements come after the prayer after Communion? Were they brief and included only those things that were necessary in order to assist the faithful in doing their mission in the world this week? Was there a second collection? Was it necessary, or is there a better way to ritually attend to the parish's financial stewardship and community's needs? For example, could the second collection have been collected during the preparation of gifts? Were there additional blessings or rituals that were scheduled appropriately so that no single Mass was overburdened with too many additional rites? On more solemn occasions, did the priest use an appropriate solemn (triple) blessing or prayer over the people? Were any part of the dialogues or blessings sung by the priest and people?

About Initiation

Rite of Sending: On this last Sunday before Lent it may be appropriate to celebrate the optional Rite of Sending for those catechumens who are ready to be elected for baptism at Easter. Note that this rite is similar to the Rite of Election, except it does not include the declaration or act of election. Those are the words spoken by the bishop that give your catechumens the promise of baptism at the next Easter Vigil. You will want to find out from your diocesan staff if the catechumens are expected to sign the Book of the Elect prior to coming to the Rite of Election, or if that signing takes place at the Rite of Election itself. Also, if you choose to celebrate the Rite of Sending the godparents typically offer testimony about the catechumen's readiness. However, the godparents do not officially begin their role until the Rite of Election. Therefore, if the godparents are not available for the Rite of Sending the catechumen's sponsor or other community members may give that testimony. Be sure, however, that the godparents are prepared to be present at next week's Rite of Election.

About Liturgical Music

Evaluating the Concluding Rites: There are not many musical elements in this section of the Mass, other than possibly having the ritual dialogues sung or chanted and the concluding song. A note about this song: there are no rubrics or instructions that refer to a concluding song. The expectation is simply that the ministers reverence the altar then leave. Therefore, there is much freedom as to what song, if any, is used at this time. Regardless, the song should still support and enhance the ritual action, even if it is instrumental or sung only by the choir.

SEASON OF LENT

GOSPEL ACCLAMATION
Cf. Ps 94:8

R̸. Praise to you, O Christ, king of eternal glory!
Harden not your hearts today,
but listen to the voice of the Lord.
R̸. Praise to you, O Christ, king of eternal glory!

Gospel

Matt 6:1-6, 16-18

Jesus said to his disciples:

'Be careful not to parade your good deeds before men to attract their notice; by doing this you will lose all reward from your Father in heaven. So when you give alms, do not have it trumpeted before you; this is what the hypocrites do in the synagogues and in the streets to win men's admiration. I tell you solemnly, they have had their reward. But when you give alms, your left hand must not know what your right is doing; your almsgiving must be secret, and your Father who sees all that is done in secret will reward you.

'And when you pray, do not imitate the hypocrites: they love to say their prayers standing up in the synagogues and at the street corners for people to see them. I tell you solemnly, they have had their reward. But when you pray go to your private room and, when you have shut your door, pray to your Father who is in that secret place, and your Father who sees all that is done in secret will reward you.

'When you fast do not put on a gloomy look as the hypocrites do: they pull long faces to let men know they are fasting. I tell you solemnly, they have had their reward. But when you fast, put oil on your head and wash your face, so that no one will know you are fasting except your Father who sees all that is done in secret; and your Father who sees all that is done in secret will reward you.'

See Appendix, p. 276, for the other readings.

Reflecting on the Gospel

Today, depending on where we live, we'll likely see people with ashes on their foreheads indicating that they've been to Mass. It might seem strange that we do what the gospel exhorts us not to do! When we fast we are not to look gloomy but to wash our faces! We are also told to perform righteous deeds in secret; give alms without letting the left hand know what the right is doing, and pray in an inner room with no audience.

The lesson of the gospel is that our deeds should be done for God the Father, not for anyone else. That is something to which we may aspire, but do our actions match our words? How many of our parishes use envelopes for weekly giving? How many annual funds print the names and amounts of donors, sometimes in categories ranked by the amount given? There are reasons for such things, but they seem to contradict a plain reading of today's gospel. How much has to be stripped away before we are doing deeds solely for the Father rather than to receive the reward of others' admiration? Much as we may hesitate to admit it, our acts of kindness, deeds of righteousness, and alms of sacrifice may be accompanied by a bit of pride.

The exhortation from Jesus today is a reminder that crowds, neighbours, friends, or fellow Christians are not the audience for our works. Indeed, if they are, we have already received a reward. Instead, God the Father is our 'audience' and it is He alone that we seek to impress, to put it in those terms.

There is a temptation among religious people to be seen or perceived as 'doing it right'. Many religious people take care to be seen at church. Perhaps they want others to know they've fulfilled their duty. That kind of attitude was prevalent in antiquity too. But that approach is not sufficient for a disciple of Christ. Our mission is to perform deeds of mercy for God the Father without seeking glory or attention from fellow human beings.

In the end, Jesus lived this mission as he faced death on a cross. What must that have looked like to those around him? Only those cursed by God were hanged on a tree (Deut 21:22-23). But to be true to his calling he fulfilled this mission, and received a reward from God the Father, which is life eternal.

Living the Paschal Mystery

Each year we begin Lent with Ash Wednesday. Though it is not a holy day of obligation, nonetheless, many people attend Mass on this weekday. That fact alone tells us that the day connects with something deep in Christians. The smearing of ashes on our forehead reminds us that we are dust animated by the breath of life, which is the spirit of Christ. When we pass on from this life our bodies will return to the dust from which they came, and we will have the hope of eternal life. Something so elemental, life and death, is the focal point of the liturgy today, especially with the sign of the ashes. We call to mind our ultimate destiny is not to be buried in this earth; rather, our destiny is life with God the Father, and his Son Jesus our Lord, in the Spirit. And perhaps this is why the church begins Lent each year with this elemental sign. It is a fundamental indication of our relationship with the paschal mystery.

Focusing the Gospel

Key words and phrases: 'Be careful not to parade your good deeds before men to attract their notice'.

To the point: In Lent we intentionally enter into the practices of prayer, fasting, and almsgiving, and every year as we begin this journey we hear this gospel. Jesus tells us that more is required of us than simply to pray, fast, and give alms. We must also be attentive to our motivation for these actions. Are we embracing righteous deeds so that others might see and laud our righteousness? If so, our actions are empty. They will not change us and they will not change the world. Instead, Jesus invites us to enter into Lent in the secrecy of our hearts. It is there that true transformation occurs – the transformation that will lead to Easter joy.

Model Universal Prayer (Prayer of the Faithful)

Presider: As we enter into this season of Lent, we lift up our prayers to God that our fasting, almsgiving, and prayer might bear abundant fruit.

Response: Lord, hear our prayer.

That the church be a welcome refuge to all who come to her seeking solace, peace, and healing . . .

That leaders throughout the world show sacrificial love and care for those under their leadership . . .

That those in need might benefit from the prayer, fasting and almsgiving of our Lenten practice . . .

That all gathered here encounter the Lord within the secrecy of our hearts this Lent and, transformed by his love, be brought to Easter joy . . .

Presider: Merciful and compassionate God, you call us to return to you with our whole hearts. Hear our prayers this day, that our Lenten prayer, fasting, and almsgiving might bring us ever closer to you. Through Christ our Lord. **Amen.**

About Liturgy

Keeping fonts full: Some churches make it a custom to empty baptismal fonts and holy water stoops during Lent as a way to emphasise a desert-like thirst for God. This may seem like a good idea, but it goes contrary to the nature of Lent: '[By] the recalling of Baptism or the preparation for it, and Penance . . . the church prepares the faithful for the celebration of Easter, while they listen more attentively to God's word and devote more time to prayer. Accordingly . . . more use is to be made of the baptismal features which are part of the Lenten liturgy' (Constitution on the Sacred Liturgy 109).

Instead of removing holy water from your church during this season, or covering up fonts with purple cloth, making the water inaccessible, or replacing the water with sand or rocks, keep your fonts filled with water. Let the constant visual reminder of our baptismal promises inspire greater penitence in the faithful and a deeper thirst for God in our catechumens.

COLLECT

Let us pray.

Pause for silent prayer

Grant, O Lord, that we may begin with holy fasting
this campaign of Christian service,
so that, as we take up battle against spiritual evils,
we may be armed with weapons of self-restraint.
Through our Lord Jesus Christ, your Son,
who lives and reigns with you in the unity of the Holy Spirit,
one God, for ever and ever. **Amen.**

FOR REFLECTION

• How would you live this Lent if you knew it were your last?

• What in your life causes division in your heart and your relationships?

• What actions can you take this Lent to pledge your whole heart to God?

Homily Points

• The apostle Paul assures us in the second reading that 'now is the favourable time; this is the day of salvation'. Each year we enter into Lent anew, realising that in each of our lives there is the need for penance and transformation. Even though Lent comes around every year, there is an urgency to the readings we hear today.

• 'Now, now . . . come back to me with all your heart', God pleads through the prophet Joel in the first reading. One way to think of sin is that which fragments us. Our Lenten practices of prayer, almsgiving, and fasting are not only acts of penitence, they are also disciplines aimed at bringing us into union with ourselves, our neighbours, and God. With hope, let us embrace the 'now' we hear of in the first and second reading. God is always ready to welcome us back to him. Now is the day of salvation.

SPIRITUALITY

GOSPEL ACCLAMATION
Matt 4:4

℟. Praise to you, O Christ, king of eternal glory!
Man does not live on bread alone,
but on every word that comes from the mouth
    of God.
℟. Praise to you, O Christ, king of eternal glory!

Gospel   Luke 4:1-13

**Filled with the Holy Spirit, Jesus
left the Jordan and was led by the
Spirit through the wilderness
being tempted there by the devil
for forty days. During that time he
ate nothing and at the end he was
hungry. Then the devil said to him,
'If you are the Son of God, tell this
stone to turn into a loaf.' But Jesus
replied 'Scripture says: Man does not
live on bread alone.'**

**Then leading him to a height, the devil
showed him in a moment of time all the
kingdoms of the world and said to him,
'I will give you all this power and the
glory of these kingdoms, for it has been
committed to me and I give it to anyone
I choose. Worship me, then, and it shall
all be yours.' But Jesus answered him,
'Scripture says:**

> **You must worship the Lord your God,
>   and serve him alone.'**

**Then he led him to Jerusalem and made
him stand on the parapet of the Temple.
'If you are the Son of God,' he said to
him 'throw yourself down from here, for
scripture says:**

> **He will put his angels in charge of you
>   to guard you,**

and again:

> **They will hold you up on their hands
>   in case you hurt your foot against
>   a stone.'**

But Jesus answered him, 'It has been said:

> **You must not put the Lord your God to
>   the test.'**

**Having exhausted all these ways of
tempting him, the devil left him, to return
at the appointed time.**

Reflecting on the Gospel

Even the devil can quote Scripture! This dismissive line is often declared when someone tries to 'one-up' another by quoting a familiar Scripture passage to make a point. Simply knowing Scripture does not guarantee someone's right relationship with God. One scholar said, 'Give me thirty minutes with the Bible and I'll make up any religion you want'. So merely citing Scripture does not win the argument. There is much more to it than that. Luke's version of the temptation of Jesus is more elaborate than the story we find in Mark, which Luke used as a source. In fact, Mark tells the story (if we can even call it that) of the temptation in two verses, whereas Luke uses thirteen (cf. Mark 1:12-13). Luke gives us a dialogue between Jesus and the devil that is completely absent in Mark. To each of the devil's temptations, some supported by Scripture, Jesus retorts with Scripture. The scene is almost one of a theological debating club. Luke expanded on the story he inherited from Mark to convey theological insights and truths rather than compose a journalist's description of 'what really happened'. Early church fathers recognised this immediately when they asked how the devil could take Jesus to a place where he could show him all the kingdoms of the world in an instant when no such place exists. The church fathers knew that this story was meant to convey theology, and it was meant to be read metaphorically rather than literally.

By this story Luke tells us a number of things, not least of which is that Jesus was tempted by the devil. And Luke's expansion of the story from what he inherited read more like debating societies than true temptations. They also indicate that even the devil can quote Scripture. In other words, it is not enough merely to know the Scriptures and have the ability to quote them.

As a master storyteller, Luke concludes the episode with three words that set the stage for later drama, namely, that the devil departed from him 'for a time'. We know that this was not to be the last encounter between the devil and Jesus. This first encounter with its triple temptations ultimately would lead to the Last Supper, the agony in the garden, the passion, and the cross.

Living the Paschal Mystery

Human beings are faced with temptations that concern our well-being (bread), our own power and glory (kingdoms of the world), or the limits of God's power (throwing oneself off the parapet of the temple). Jesus overcame each of these temptations with the power and knowledge of Scripture, and secure in his relationship with God as his son. As Jesus faced such fundamental temptations we shouldn't be surprised by temptation either. However, in Luke's telling there might be a slight disservice to the reader. For our temptations will likely not come in the physical personification of the devil. But we will be tempted, nonetheless, by appeals to our well-being, our own power and glory, and what we would consider the limits of God's power. If we, like Jesus, can be assured of our relationship with God, secure in our filial relationship with the divine, we can overcome temptation as well. Though the devil left Jesus for a time, he did return. And it was then that the ultimate temptation faced Jesus. Then he trusted in God to the point of death, only to be raised up to new life.

Focusing the Gospel

Key words and phrases: Filled with the Holy Spirit, Jesus left the Jordan and was led by the Spirit through the wilderness being tempted there by the devil for forty days.

To the point: Following his baptism, Jesus is led out into the desert. Though he is without both human company and food he is not lacking comfort and nourishment. Jesus is led by, and filled with, the Holy Spirit. We, too, are called into the desert of Lent. For forty days we embrace fasting, prayer, and almsgiving so as to empty ourselves in order to be filled anew with the abundance of God.

Connecting the Gospel

to the first reading: Today's first reading from Deuteronomy comes at the end of Moses' address to the Israelites before they enter the land of Israel. The people have wandered in the desert for forty years, being formed as the people of God, and now they are on the cusp of a new life. In today's reading Moses details a religious ceremony the people are to observe once they have celebrated the first harvest in the land they have been promised by God. Along with offering a basket of the first fruits of the harvest they are also to recall the history that has brought them to this point: from refugee, to slave, to free person, to landowner. And in this recounting it is clear that nothing has been earned or gained on its own; it is all pure gift from God. This is the same humility that Jesus embraces in the gospel today. Although he has been declared God's own 'beloved Son' at his baptism, he does not exploit this identity. When challenged by the devil to use his power to turn stone into bread or throw himself from the parapet of the temple Jesus refuses. The gifts he has been given by God are not meant to be used for his own gain or to prove his authority; instead they are to be given away for the good of God's people.

to experience: God, the gift-giver, has bestowed on us all that we have. How are we being called to offer the 'first-fruits' of these gifts back to God?

Connecting the Responsorial Psalm

to the readings: In the last verses of today's psalm God speaks and says, 'When he calls I shall answer: "I am with you". / I will save him in distress and give him glory'. In the gospel today Jesus undergoes his temptation in the desert. For forty days he stays in the desert alone and hungry, and then at the end – when we can imagine his hunger for both food and human contact has become intense – he is visited by the devil. And yet throughout this experience, Jesus isn't alone. Led by and filled with the Holy Spirit he is able to remain resolute in the face of every luring temptation offered by the devil.

to psalmist preparation: Throughout each of our lives there will be desert experiences where we undergo isolation and distress. In those times, the psalmist tells us, God is with us. How have you experienced God in times of distress?

CELEBRATION

Model Penitential Act

Presider: In today's gospel Jesus is led out into the desert filled with the Holy Spirit. He remains there for forty days and is tempted by the devil. As we begin these forty days of fasting and prayer we ask for God's grace to sustain us, and for the times we have given into temptation we ask for pardon and mercy . . . [*pause*]

    Confiteor: I confess . . .

Homily Points

• Following his baptism Jesus is led into the desert for forty days of fasting and prayer. Two other heroes of our faith underwent similar experiences. Before receiving the Ten Commandments on Mount Sinai, Moses went without food and water for forty days. The prophet Elijah also fasted for forty days before travelling to Mount Horeb (another name for Mount Sinai), where God came to him as a 'light silent sound' (1 Kgs 19:12; NABRE). Moses, Elijah, and Jesus all fast in preparation for an event – for Moses and Elijah it is a particular encounter with God, while for Jesus it is an encounter with temptation. In Lent we fast for both reasons, to prepare for an encounter with God on our holiest feast of the year – the feast of Easter – and also to strengthen us against temptation.

• When the devil tempts Jesus to turn stone into bread, Jesus responds, 'Scripture says: Man does not live on bread alone'. These words come from the book of Deuteronomy where Moses tells the people, '[God] let you be afflicted with hunger, and then fed you with manna . . . so you might know that it is not by bread alone that people live, but by all that comes forth from the mouth of the LORD' (8:3; NABRE). By taking up the spiritual practice of fasting during Lent we open up space and time within our lives for that which provides us true nourishment.

• Jesus's temptation in the desert reminds us that we are not alone when we face our own temptations. Let us invite God into our experience of temptation, so that filled with the Holy Spirit we might be strengthened to follow the path of holiness.

Model Universal Prayer (Prayer of the Faithful)

Presider: Our God is with us in times of need and so we place our petitions before him.

Response: Lord, hear our prayer.

That all members of the church enter into these forty days of fasting, penance, and almsgiving with fidelity and grace . . .

That leaders of nations resist the temptations of power and wealth . . .

That those overwhelmed by the temptation of addiction be filled with the grace of God and know they are not alone . . .

That all those here, in this time of fasting, might feast on the love and mercy of God . . .

Presider: God of infinite love, you accompany us through distress and anxiety and protect us from temptation and evil. Trusting in your mercy and compassion, we bring you our petitions asking that you hear and grant them through Christ our Lord. **Amen.**

COLLECT

Let us pray.

Pause for silent prayer

Grant, almighty God,
through the yearly observances of
    holy Lent,
that we may grow in understanding
of the riches hidden in Christ
and by worthy conduct pursue their effects.
Through our Lord Jesus Christ, your Son,
who lives and reigns with you in the unity
    of the Holy Spirit,
one God, for ever and ever. **Amen.**

FIRST READING
Deut 26:4-10

Moses said to the people: 'The priest shall take the pannier from your hand and lay it before the altar of the Lord your God. Then, in the sight of the Lord your God, you must make this pronouncement:
    "My father was a wandering Aramaean. He went down into Egypt to find refuge there, few in numbers; but there he became a nation, great, mighty, and strong. The Egyptians ill-treated us, they gave us no peace and inflicted harsh slavery on us. But we called on the Lord, the God of our fathers. The Lord heard our voice and saw our misery, our toil and our oppression; and the Lord brought us out of Egypt with mighty hand and outstretched arm, with great terror, and with signs and wonders. He brought us here and gave us this land, a land where milk and honey flow. Here then I bring the first-fruits of the produce of the soil that you, Lord, have given me." You must then lay them before the Lord your God, and bow down in the sight of the Lord your God.'

CATECHESIS

RESPONSORIAL PSALM
Ps 90:1-2, 10-15 (15)

℟. Be with me, O Lord, in my distress.

He who dwells in the shelter of the
    Most High
and abides in the shade of the Almighty
says to the Lord: 'My refuge,
my stronghold, my God in whom I trust!'

℟. Be with me, O Lord, in my distress.

Upon you no evil shall fall,
no plague approach where you dwell.
For you has he commanded his angels,
to keep you in all your ways.

℟. Be with me, O Lord, in my distress.

They shall bear you upon their hands
lest you strike your foot against a stone.
On the lion and the viper you will tread
and trample the young lion and
    the dragon.

℟. Be with me, O Lord, in my distress.

His love he set on me, so I will rescue him;
protect him for he knows my name.
When he calls I shall answer: 'I am
    with you.'
I will save him in distress and give
    him glory.

℟. Be with me, O Lord, in my distress.

SECOND READING
Rom 10:8-13

Scripture says: The word, that is the faith we proclaim, is very near to you, it is on your lips and in your heart. If your lips confess that Jesus is Lord and if you believe in your heart that God raised him from the dead, then you will be saved. By believing from the heart you are made righteous; by confessing with your lips you are saved. When scripture says: those who believe in him will have no cause for shame, it makes no distinction between Jew and Greek: all belong to the same Lord who is rich enough, however many ask his help, for everyone who calls on the name of the Lord will be saved.

About Liturgy

Paschale solemnitatis: A little-known but valuable liturgical document is the 1988 circular letter from the Vatican Congregation for Divine Worship and the Discipline of Sacraments entitled On Preparing and Celebrating the Paschal Feasts (*Paschale Solemnitatis*). This universal document has the same authority as an instruction. It gathers references on Lent, Triduum, and Easter from other liturgical documents and gives guidance and recommendations on how to implement current rubrics and directives. This season would be a good time to read and review this resource.

The section on Lent in this letter begins by quoting the *Ceremonial of Bishops*, an instruction manual for the liturgies celebrated by bishops: 'The annual observance of Lent is the special season for the ascent to the holy mountain of Easter' (PS 6; CB 249). This beautiful image recalls the high places we encounter throughout this Lectionary cycle for Lent: the high place where Jesus was tempted by the devil in today's gospel; the mountain where he was transfigured, which we will recall next Sunday; Mount Horeb where Moses encountered the burning bush on the Third Sunday of Lent; and the Mount of Olives where Jesus prayed before his arrest, which we proclaim this Palm Sunday.

Mountains are traditional places where we encounter God's glory. If we reframe the Lenten journey as a slow yet steady climb towards the hill of Golgotha where the ultimate glory of the Father will be revealed in the sacrifice of his Son, we can help our communities connect Lent to the fulness of the paschal mystery that always leads us to the resurrection.

About Initiation

Rite of Election: The period of purification and enlightenment coincides with the season of Lent. During these final weeks of preparation for baptism, the catechumens who will be initiated this Easter participate in 'intense spiritual preparation, consisting more in interior reflection than in catechetical instruction' (RCIA 139). For the catechumens, their godparents, and the entire community of the faithful, Lent should be like a five-week retreat. It is not a time for last-minute catechetical sessions to catch up on what they have missed during their catechumenate. Remember that this is an initiation: it is just the *beginning* of their lifelong formation in the Christian way of life. Instead of doing catechesis as usual, trust in the power of the liturgy to catechise and form us. Focus on the liturgies of Lent and on daily prayer, fasting, and works of charity.

About Liturgical Music

Litany of Saints: The circular letter, On Preparing and Celebrating the Paschal Feasts, recommends that on the First Sunday of Lent, 'there should be some distinctive elements that underline this important moment; e.g., the entrance procession with litanies of the saints' (PS 23). This is also referenced in the *Ceremonial of Bishops*, which further recommends that 'the names of the holy patron or founder and the saints of the local Church may be inserted at the proper places' (261). What a beautiful way not only to begin this holy season of Lent but also to bookend the paschal season by beginning these days in communion with the saints who will accompany the catechumens to the baptismal font at the Easter Vigil. With this in mind, if you choose to sing the Litany of Saints as the entrance chant on this Sunday, use the setting that is sung at the Easter Vigil.

SPIRITUALITY

GOSPEL ACCLAMATION

Matt 17:5

R̰. Glory and praise to you, O Christ!
From the bright cloud the Father's voice
    was heard:
'This is my Son, the Beloved. Listen
    to him.'
R̰. Glory and praise to you, O Christ!

Gospel   Luke 9:28-36

**Jesus took with him Peter and
John and James and went up the
mountain to pray. As he prayed,
the aspect of his face was changed
and his clothing became brilliant
as lightning. Suddenly there were
two men there talking to him; they
were Moses and Elijah appearing in
glory, and they were speaking of his
passing which he was to accomplish in
Jerusalem. Peter and his companions
were heavy with sleep, but they kept
awake and saw his glory and the two
men standing with him. As these
were leaving him, Peter said to Jesus,
'Master, it is wonderful for us to be
here; so let us make three tents, one for
you, one for Moses and one for Elijah.'
– He did not know what he was saying.
As he spoke, a cloud came and covered
them with shadow; and when they
went into the cloud the disciples were
afraid. And a voice came from the cloud
saying, 'This is my Son, the Chosen
One. Listen to him.' And after the voice
had spoken, Jesus was found alone. The
disciples kept silence and, at that time,
told no one what they had seen.**

Reflecting on the Gospel

For the Second Sunday of Lent the church gives us the reading of the transfiguration of Jesus, a story found in the Synoptics but not in the Gospel of John. Luke tells the story in a way similar to that of Mark, from whom he received it. Any differences are slight.

The presence of Elijah and Moses indicates Jesus as the fulfilment of the prophets (Elijah) and the law (Moses). Only the three disciples are there to witness this terrific encounter, and they, too, are enveloped in the cloud, which itself is another image from the Old Testament. In particular, during the wandering in the wilderness, the Lord preceded the Hebrew people by means of a column of cloud during the day, and a column of fire at night (Exod 13:21; cf. Num 9:16-23). There, too, the cloud covered the meeting tent, and in doing so the glory of the Lord filled the place (Exod 40:34-38). Even in the time of Solomon we hear about the presence of the Lord in a cloud filling the house of the Lord (1 Kgs 8:9-10). Suffice it to say there are many instances in the Old Testament where the presence of the Lord is indicated by a cloud, and that is the sense intended here by Luke as well. The cloud represents the Lord's glory; this is not a story about what happened one foggy day. Moreover, a voice from the cloud speaks, echoing the message heard at Jesus's baptism, 'This is my Son, the Chosen One. Listen to him'.

More symbolism is present in the face of Jesus changing in appearance and his clothing becoming 'brilliant as lightning'. There is so much that is symbolic and representative of Jesus's glory in this gospel reading that some scholars of Scripture refer to it as a 'displaced resurrection account'. In other words, this was originally a story of a resurrection appearance or a story about the risen Jesus that was transposed into the narrative of his earthly ministry by Mark (Matthew and Luke simply followed suit). Whether it is a displaced resurrection story or not, its Christology is profound, demonstrating that Jesus shares the glory of the Lord and fulfills the prophets and the law. He is on par with Elijah and Moses: He is called God's son, to whom we should listen.

Living the Paschal Mystery

As the term itself implies, peak experiences do not come often and they do not last. But they can become a touchstone, a marker to which we may return mentally and spiritually at various points in our lives. The birth of a child, falling in love, a special day, or an encounter in nature may all be peak experiences we want to preserve, remember, and cherish. Perhaps like Peter we want to 'make . . . tents', or otherwise make a memorial to the event and the person(s) with whom we shared it. But like the events in today's gospel, as soon as the incident happens, it seems to end. 'And after the voice had spoken, Jesus was found alone'. The encounter was over and those who had witnessed it were humbled into silence. The encounter of the transfiguration informs our own peak experiences. They are a taste of the life that is to come, an eternal peak experience that satisfies all longings.

Focusing the Gospel

Key words and phrases: This is my Son, the Chosen One. Listen to him.

To the point: For the second time in the Gospel of Luke the voice of God claims Jesus as God's son. The first moment was at his baptism when 'the holy Spirit descended upon him in bodily form' (Luke 3:22; NABRE). At that time the voice of God proclaimed, 'You are my beloved Son; with you I am well pleased' (NABRE). At the Jordan River the voice from heaven speaks directly to Jesus, but on the mountain where Jesus goes to pray with his closest companions the voice addresses those around Jesus – Peter, James, and John – telling them, 'This is my Son, the Chosen One. Listen to him'. These words are addressed to us when we encounter our Lord in the Word and the Eucharist, 'Behold, here is Jesus the chosen one, listen to him'.

Connecting the Gospel

to the second reading: In St. Paul's letter to the Philippians we hear the promise of what is to come, '[H]e will transfigure these wretched bodies of ours into copies of his glorious body. He will do that by the same power with which he can subdue the whole universe'. On the mountain Peter, James, and John see Jesus's 'glory' when 'the aspect of his face was changed and his clothing became brilliant as lightning'. We might wonder how this experience of encountering Jesus as he truly is, transfigured in glory, affected them in the life of faith.

to experience: As Christians our ultimate goal is to be Christ-like, to reflect the dazzling glory of Christ in all of our interactions and so to bring honour to God. In our pursuit of this goal the more clearly we see Jesus, the more clearly we see the way to our own transformation in Christ.

Connecting the Responsorial Psalm

to the readings: In Psalm 26 the psalmist yearns for God: 'Of you my heart has spoken: / "Seek his face"'. In the gospel, Peter, James, and John encounter God in a whole-body way. They see the face of Jesus transfigured before them, and then, entering into a cloud, they hear the voice of God. The cloud is reminiscent of Moses' meeting with God on Mount Sinai when he received the tablets of the law. As happened with Moses, God's presence envelops Peter, James, and John. Naturally we hear that 'when they went into the cloud the disciples were afraid'. Yearning for God's presence cannot prepare us for the unfathomable reality of experiencing the living God. And yet we continue to seek God knowing, as St. Augustine said, 'Our hearts are restless until they rest in you'.

to psalmist preparation: Today's psalm is one of trust and of desire. We know God and yet we yearn to know God more fully. We live in God's kingdom, and yet we long for the complete fulfilment of that kingdom. How do you experience the deep desire to see God's face in your own life?

PROMPTS FOR FAITH-SHARING

Today's psalm encourages us to '[h]ope in the Lord!' Where is God asking you to be hopeful and patient at this time in your life?

What does it mean to you that your 'homeland is in heaven?'

The voice from the cloud tells Peter, James, and John, 'This is my Son, the Chosen One. Listen to him'. How do you listen to Jesus in daily life?

In your life, which places of darkness are longing for the light of Christ? How might you lift these places up to the Light?

CELEBRATION

Model Penitential Act
Presider: In today's gospel, Peter, John, and James hear a voice from the cloud saying, 'This is my Son, the Chosen One. Listen to him'. For the times we have not listened to the voice of Jesus, our Good Shepherd, we ask for pardon and mercy . . . [*pause*]

   Confiteor: I confess . . .

Homily Points
• Today's readings are filled with imagery of the covenant relationship we have with God. In the first reading God enters into a covenant with Abram. The ritual that cements this covenant might sound odd to us, but was common in Abraham's time. When two parties entered into a treaty or serious agreement they would walk between the bodies of animals, which had been split in two. The animals were a cautionary sign, for if either party broke the treaty they could expect to share the animals' fate. In the covenant between Abram and God, however, only one party walks between the slain animals; the smoking fire pot and the flaming torch represent God, who enters into a covenant of unending fidelity to Abram and his descendants. Even when the human parties of this covenant fail, God remains faithful.

• In the gospel Moses and Elijah appear on the mountain with Jesus and speak 'of his passing [exodus] which he was to accomplish in Jerusalem'. With the first exodus, God saves the people of Israel from slavery, forms them as his people, and then delivers them into the Promised Land. With Jesus's exodus (his death and resurrection) we are freed from the slavery of sin, formed as the Body of Christ, and made citizens of the kingdom of God.

• In the second reading St. Paul also reminds us as of the Christian identity that defines us: '[O]ur homeland is in heaven'. As we continue on with our Lenten journey, let us consider how we might show in both word and deed that we are Christ's. Even when we fail, our merciful God invites us to continue living ever deeper into this covenant of love.

Model Universal Prayer (Prayer of the Faithful)
Presider: Like Abraham, our father in faith, we trust God's promises and so dare to voice our petitions.

Response: Lord, hear our prayer.

That the church might be a reflection of the dazzling face of Jesus . . .

That all the nations of the world would extend a welcome to refugees and immigrants within the lands they claim as their own . . .

That those who live in anxiety and fear might know the peace of God that surpasses understanding . . .

That all gathered here would be renewed in faith and filled with courage to go with joy where God calls us to go . . .

Presider: Faithful God, you honour the covenant you have made with your people throughout the world. Trusting in this covenant relationship we ask you to hear our prayers this day and always. Through Christ our Lord. **Amen.**

COLLECT
Let us pray.

Pause for silent prayer

O God, who have commanded us
to listen to your beloved Son,
be pleased, we pray,
to nourish us inwardly by your word,
that, with spiritual sight made pure,
we may rejoice to behold your glory.
Through our Lord Jesus Christ, your Son,
who lives and reigns with you in the unity
     of the Holy Spirit,
one God, for ever and ever. **Amen.**

FIRST READING
Gen 15:5-12, 17-18

Taking Abram outside the Lord said, 'Look up to heaven and count the stars if you can. Such will be your descendants' he told him. Abram put his faith in the Lord, who counted this as making him justified.

   'I am the Lord' he said to him 'who brought you out of Ur of the Chaldaeans to make you heir to this land.' 'My Lord, the Lord' Abram replied 'how am I to know that I shall inherit it?' He said to him, 'Get me a three-year-old heifer, a three-year-old goat, a three-year-old ram, a turtledove and a young pigeon.' He brought him all these, cut them in half and put half on one side and half facing it on the other; but the birds he did not cut in half. Birds of prey came down on the carcasses but Abram drove them off.

   Now as the sun was setting Abram fell into a deep sleep, and terror seized him. When the sun had set and darkness had fallen, there appeared a smoking furnace and a firebrand that went between the halves. That day the Lord made a Covenant with Abram in these terms:
   'To your descendants I give this land, from the wadi of Egypt to the Great River.'

RESPONSORIAL PSALM
Ps 26:1, 7-9, 13-14 (1)

R̰. The Lord is my light and my help.

The Lord is my light and my help;
whom shall I fear?
The Lord is the stronghold of my life;
before whom shall I shrink?

R̰. The Lord is my light and my help.

O Lord, hear my voice when I call;
have mercy and answer.
Of you my heart has spoken:
'Seek his face.'

R̰. The Lord is my light and my help.

It is your face, O Lord, that I seek;
hide not your face.
Dismiss not your servant in anger;
you have been my help.

R̰. The Lord is my light and my help.

I am sure I shall see the Lord's goodness
in the land of the living.
Hope in him, hold firm and take heart.
Hope in the Lord!

R̰. The Lord is my light and my help.

SECOND READING
Phil 3:17-4:1

My brothers, be united in following
my rule of life. Take as your models
everybody who is already doing this
and study them as you used to study
us. I have told you often, and I repeat it
today with tears, there are many who
are behaving as the enemies of the cross
of Christ. They are destined to be lost.
They make foods into their god and they
are proudest of something they ought
to think shameful; the things they think
important are earthly things. For us, our
homeland is in heaven, and from heaven
comes the saviour we are waiting for, the
Lord Jesus Christ, and he will transfigure
these wretched bodies of ours into copies
of his glorious body. He will do that by the
same power with which he can subdue the
whole universe.

So then, my brothers and dear friends,
do not give way but remain faithful in the
Lord. I miss you very much, dear friends;
you are my joy and my crown.

or Phil 3:20-4:1, see Appendix A, p. 277.

About Liturgy

Darkness and light: In today's readings we see the image of darkness as the place where God's shining glory is revealed. In Genesis, once the sun had set and it was dark, the smoking fire pot and the flaming torch represented God who made the covenant with Abram. In the gospel, the disciples were afraid to enter the cloud, which had cast a shadow over them, yet it was from this cloud where the voice was heard: 'This is my Son, the Chosen One'.

The circular letter, On Preparing and Celebrating the Paschal Feasts, recommends that 'catechesis on the paschal mystery and the sacraments should be given a special place in the Sunday homilies' (PS 12). Today's image of darkness leading to light gives homilists an opportunity to focus on baptism and on the mercy of God. For example, you can help the assembly understand better the purpose for the church's rubric that the Easter Vigil begin in darkness only after sundown, or the baptismal symbol of the Easter candle as the Light of Christ given to all of us at baptism.

In the liturgy, symbols and symbolic actions express our belief. Therefore, when we say that Christ dispels the darkness of our hearts and minds (Roman Missal, Easter Vigil, 14) as we light the paschal fire at the Easter Vigil, our Christian faith is more clearly visible when the fire we light actually dispels darkness – not a twilight darkness or a darkness we can control with a switch, but one that reflects our fear and confusion as well as our hope and faith in Christ. Like Moses and the disciples today, we are called to enter into the dark places of our human hearts in order to allow Christ's light to shine there. The abiding Light of Christ, present even in our darkest moments, is symbolised by the paschal candle, which we will light from the Easter fire lit in the dark of night. Thus the entire Lenten season, especially the Lenten liturgies for those preparing for baptism, is meant to uncover these dark places and then strengthen the grace that the Spirit has already poured into our hearts.

About Initiation

The role of the faithful: The faithful are the most important ministers of the RCIA because 'the initiation of adults is the responsibility of all the baptised' (RCIA 9). Find ways to help all your parishioners take a more active role in the formation and preparation of adults to be baptised.

During Lent, 'the faithful should take care to participate in the rites of the scrutinies and presentations and give the elect the example of their own renewal in the spirit of penance, faith, and charity' (RCIA 9.4). The faithful do this primarily through their own practice of prayer, fasting, works of charity, and penitential disciplines. They can also more directly support the elect by intentional prayer. One creative way to do this is to prepare a box for each of your elect with their name on it. Place these boxes in your vestibule, and invite parishioners to write notes of encouragement and prayer for each elect. In these Sundays before Easter, they can place these notes into the boxes. The elect can read these notes during the preparation rites on Holy Saturday.

About Liturgical Music

Use of instruments: GIRM 313 tells us: 'In Lent the playing of the organ and musical instruments is allowed only in order to support the singing. Exceptions, however, are Laetare Sunday (Fourth Sunday of Lent), Solemnities, and Feasts'. Many parishes have not followed this and previous similar directives, sometimes even banning the use of instruments during Lent altogether (which was obligatory up to 1958, but not subsequently). However, the church now recognises that some churches possess repertoires that simply do not work without instrumental accompaniment. Changing the mood of the season can equally well be done by the sensitive choice of music as by changing how it is accompanied.

ST. PATRICK, BISHOP, PATRON OF IRELAND

GOSPEL ACCLAMATION
Jm 1:21

℟. Glory to you, O Christ, you are the Word
    of God!
Accept and submit to the word which has been
    planted in you
and can save your souls.
℟. Glory to you, O Christ, you are the Word
    of God!

Gospel

Matt 13:24-32

Jesus put a parable before the crowds, 'The kingdom of heaven may be compared to a man who sowed good seed in his field. While everybody was asleep his enemy came, sowed darnel all among the wheat, and made off. When the new wheat sprouted and ripened, the darnel appeared as well. The owner's servants went to him and said, "Sir, was it not good seed that you sowed in your field? If so, where does the darnel come from?" "Some enemy has done this" he answered. And the servants said, "Do you want us to go and weed it out?" But he said, "No, because when you weed out the darnel you might pull up the wheat with it. Let them both grow till the harvest; and at harvest time I shall say to the reapers: First collect the darnel and tie it in bundles to be burnt, then gather the wheat into my barn."'

He put another parable before them, 'The kingdom of heaven is like a mustard seed which a man took and sowed in his field. It is the smallest of all the seeds, but when it has grown it is the biggest shrub of all and becomes a tree so that the birds of the air come and shelter in its branches.'

See Appendix, p. 277, for the other readings.

Reflecting on the Gospel

We celebrate the feast of St. Patrick today, when much of the rest of the church is celebrating the Second Sunday of Lent. This is because Ireland enjoys an indult to celebrate this important feast day, even when it falls on a Sunday in Lent. This special indult alone is a signal to the significance that this saint holds in Ireland, and frankly throughout the world.

The readings from the Gospel of Matthew are particularly appropriate as well. We hear two parables, the second much shorter than the first. Each has something profound to say to us. The first is a reminder for the early church, and for us as well, that there are weeds within the wheat. Even though the master sower sows only what he intends to harvest, there is another force at work sowing dissension and trouble. Yet, it is not merely a 'weed' that is planted but 'darnel', a mimic plant, sometimes called 'false wheat', which requires human care to survive. It bears such a similarity to wheat that it can be sown unintentionally, then it sprouts and grows among wheat, and is harvested as such, completing the life cycle. It does not require much imagination to apply this parable to church life. Too often there are 'false disciples' in the church, closely mimicking the true disciples. Jesus's advice in the parable is to let all grow together. In the end, God will make the proper distinctions. Such advice can be difficult to hear, when our sense of justice may call for the elimination or expulsion of such false disciples. In the face of a desire to uproot, we are reminded that this is God's role.

The second, brief parable speaks of the kingdom of heaven as a mustard seed, which is about the size of a sesame seed. This metaphor calls to mind the image of Patrick himself. What began with the paschal fire lit by Patrick on the Hill of Slane grew to enlighten the people of Ireland with the knowledge and love of Christ. One small action, one person, can alter the trajectory of history. The smallest seed grows to become a tree, providing shade and shelter.

In times of trial and tribulation, when it seems there are weeds among the wheat, we are assured that God knows the difference and we are promised that action will be taken. As for ourselves, we are reminded in the second parable that even small, seemingly insignificant things can turn out to grow into something substantial. With this knowledge we embark upon our daily routines with a sense of meaning and purpose. What is within our power to do, let us do. As for the rest, we grow amidst the weeds and the wheat.

Living the Paschal Mystery

On the feast of St. Patrick, falling as it does on a Sunday in Lent, we call to mind so many aspects of our faith. The celebration of this beloved saint who is recognised worldwide gives us a foretaste of the heavenly banquet, when festivity and merriment are the norm. And yet, we are immersed in the Lenten season; we celebrate St. Patrick by indult, fully aware of the grand themes of *metanoia* and baptism which so mark the penitential season.

The gospel readings which mark this feast give us stark reminders of both judgement (the wheat and the weeds) and the powerful effects of seemingly insignificant things or actions (the mustard seed which becomes a tree). In the midst of such profound and deep mysteries we settle into the one mystery par excellence: the paschal mystery. Our dying and rising with Christ animates this life we experience on earth, with all the trials, joys, failings, and feasting that punctuate our existence, giving it meaning.

Focusing the Gospel

Key words and phrases: The kingdom of heaven is like a mustard seed which a man took and sowed in his field.

To the point: In the parable of the mustard seed we see an image of collaboration between God and human beings. While a human being might be tasked with helping to sow the seeds of the kingdom of heaven, only through the power of God do these tiniest of seeds grow to become 'the biggest shrub of all', large enough to provide shelter and shade. Within the lives of the saints we see God's greatest collaborators who, with immense joy, have scattered and sown the seeds of the kingdom in the work of their lives. Centuries later, we continue to enjoy the shade and shelter their model of faith provides.

Model Penitential Act

Presider: On this feast of St. Patrick, and the Second Sunday of Lent, we turn our gaze to the mustard seed, the tiniest of all seeds that grows into a bush large enough to provide shade and protection. Through the intercession of St. Patrick let us implore the Lord to attune our eyes to his strength within all creation . . . *[pause]*

Lord Jesus, you call us to persistence and faithfulness as we follow you: Lord, have mercy.

Christ Jesus, your word brings us strength and peace: Christ, have mercy.

Lord Jesus, you teach us the ways of the kingdom of God: Lord, have mercy.

Model Universal Prayer (Prayer of the Faithful)

Presider: Confident in God's love and care for us, we bring our needs before him through the intercession of St. Patrick.

Response: Lord, hear our prayer.

That bishops, priests, and clergy within the church may be inspired and strengthened through the model of St. Patrick and his care for the people of Ireland . . .

That nations torn apart by conflict and oppression might follow the Lord of freedom and charity in building just societies where all are welcome . . .

That those who are floundering in the spiritual life, through the intercession of St. Patrick, may come to wisdom in Christ . . .

That all gathered here might be strengthened in our Lenten practices of prayer, fasting, and almsgiving, so as to arrive at the joy of Easter . . .

Presider: God of creation, in your servant, St. Patrick, we are given a model of faithful discipleship. Hear our prayers, that as we continue on our journey to Easter joy we might be renewed in fervor to follow you as he did. We ask this through Christ our Lord. **Amen.**

About Liturgy

In England, Wales, and Scotland, St. Patrick is celebrated as a feast. In 2019, the day gives way to the Second Sunday of Lent and is therefore not celebrated liturgically in those countries. In Ireland, however, St. Patrick is both a solemnity and a holy day of obligation. Although the colour green and the shamrock are traditionally associated with St. Patrick (and are often used to excess), his cross is a red saltire, or *X*, on a white background. St. Patrick is also associated with the ringing of bells. In fact, the Irish Gaelic word for bell, *clog*, is the ultimate origin of the English word 'clock' and the French word *cloche* (bell).

COLLECT
Let us pray.

Pause for silent prayer

Lord, through the work of Saint Patrick in Ireland
we have come to acknowledge the mystery of the one true God
and give thanks for our salvation in Christ;
grant by his prayers
that we who celebrate this festival
may keep alive the fire of faith he kindled.
Through our Lord Jesus Christ, your Son,
who lives and reigns with you in the unity of the Holy Spirit,
one God, for ever and ever. **Amen.**

FOR REFLECTION

• In the second reading, St. Paul urges Timothy, 'proclaim the message and, welcome or unwelcome, insist on it'. Where in your life are you in need of the virtue of persistence?

• The gospel offers us the image of the mustard seed as an illustration of the slow, silent growth of God's kingdom. How do you see this kingdom growing in your family, parish, or community?

Homily Points

• The first reading describes '[h]ow different the person who devotes himself / to the study of the law of the Most High!' (Eccl 39:1; NABRE). Without God's word, and God's revelation in the person of Jesus, our practices of prayer, almsgiving, and fasting would have no meaning. The second reading invites us to persistence, whether it is 'welcome or unwelcome'. And the gospel tells us that even when we cannot see it, the kingdom of God is continuing to grow and develop in our midst. Let us ask for the intercession of St. Patrick as we recommit ourselves with devotion, persistence, and patience to building up the kingdom of God within our families, parishes, communities, and world.

GOSPEL ACCLAMATION
Ps 83:5

℟. Glory and praise to you, O Christ.
They are happy who dwell in your house, O Lord,
for ever singing your praise.
℟. Glory and praise to you, O Christ.

Gospel   Luke 2:41-51

Every year the parents of Jesus used to go
to Jerusalem for the feast of the Passover.
When he was twelve years old, they went
up for the feast as usual. When they were
on their way home after the feast, the boy
Jesus stayed behind in Jerusalem without
his parents knowing it. They assumed
he was with the caravan, and it was only
after a day's journey that they went to
look for him among their relations and
acquaintances. When they failed to find him
they went back to Jerusalem looking for
him everywhere.

Three days later, they found him in the
Temple, sitting among the doctors, listening
to them, and asking them questions; and
all those who heard him were astounded
at his intelligence and his replies. They
were overcome when they saw him and his
mother said to him, 'My child, why have
you done this to us? See how worried your
father and I have been, looking for you.'
'Why were you looking for me?' he replied.
'Did you not know that I must be busy
with my Father's affairs?' But they did not
understand what he meant.

He then went down with them and came
to Nazareth and lived under their authority.

or Matt 1:16, 18-21, 24 in Appendix, p. 278.

See Appendix, p. 278, for the other readings.

Reflecting on the Gospel

Scandals of the political, gossipy, and celebrity type are often in the news.
We know from our own experience that our lives sometimes have scandals,
embarrassments, and fodder for gossip. How we love to talk about people who
are down on their luck, made a mistake, or are facing hard times. Maybe talking
about others makes us feel better about ourselves. The underlying attitude is
that at least we're not in their situation, facing their troubles.

We can also consider the 'holy family' and 'Joseph the Most Chaste Spouse' of
Mary to have had an idyllic home, a perfect family. But today's gospel reading
from Matthew tells us otherwise. Joseph and Mary were betrothed (engaged) and
Mary was found to be pregnant 'through the Holy Spirit'. Can we imagine the
talk of the town if such a thing happened today? Who would believe that kind
of story? Two thousand years and a major world religion later we do not stop to
think about the shame and scandal that would have been the reaction to Mary's
pregnancy. The shame was not only upon her but also Joseph and her family,
and certainly upon her child, Jesus. Even later anti-Christian legends tell of Mary
being impregnated by a Roman soldier, not the Holy Spirit. If those stories have
survived for so long, what must have been said at the time Mary was pregnant?

The gospel tells us that since Joseph was a 'a man of honour', meaning one
who stood upright in the eyes of God by following the law of Moses, he did not
want to expose Mary to shame. Exposing her to shame is a euphemistic way
of saying exposing her to the law, which required adulterers to be stoned (Deut
22:21-23). Joseph's solution was a quiet divorce. In other words, Joseph would
end the betrothal (engagement) before the wedding day.

At that point God intervened by communicating with Joseph in a dream via
an angel, assuring him that he should go forward with the marriage. Mary's
story was sincere and true. It was through the Holy Spirit that this child was
conceived. Joseph acts accordingly and takes Mary into his household as his wife.
After that we scarcely hear anything else about Joseph. He is righteous, never
speaking a word, but following God's will. His noble decision was likely seen as
anything but that in his time. We might look around our own world, nation, and
neighbourhood. Where are the Josephs today? Those noble, righteous, often silent
individuals sheltering those who would otherwise be exposed to shame.

Living the Paschal Mystery

Family life can sometimes seem like an endless onslaught of responsibilities
for caring for others and providing for them. And it doesn't necessarily end
when the children reach early (or later!) adulthood. In fact, some in the so-called
sandwich generation may find themselves caring for both children and parents.
Our celebration of St. Joseph today is a good reminder that family life is sacred.
Joseph welcomed Mary into his household and they lived together as a family.
They didn't live at a synagogue or temple, and certainly not a church (as there
were none then). They were in many ways a typical family with family issues.
Yet Joseph was rearing a child that was not his own. Mary's story of being
with child by the Holy Spirit was enough to drive Joseph to divorce, but he
was guided away from that by a dream. The Holy Family did not live a perfect
idyllic life. Quite likely they faced gossip, slander, and perhaps even insults.
They would not have been perceived in their time as a model family. And yet,
we celebrate them not because they lived without scandal, but precisely the
opposite. They lived through scandal and gossip in a righteous way. On this
feast of St. Joseph, let's imagine his life not reduced to a plastic holy card, but
one lived in the complexity and moral ambiguity of adulthood.

Focusing the Gospel

Key words and phrases: Her husband Joseph, being a man of honour . . .

To the point: Within the trio of the Holy Family, St. Joseph is the one most often overlooked, and so we pause today to celebrate the protection, support, and love with which he lived out his vocation as a righteous man and as husband to Mary and foster-father of Jesus. We see his righteousness as he listens to the angel's message with faith and then welcomes Mary and the miraculous baby she bears into his household. May we seek to follow the model of Joseph, the husband of Mary, in his fidelity, love, and trust.

Model Penitential Act

Presider: Today we honour St. Joseph, and remember his model of love and fidelity within the holy family. As we enter into this celebration let us pause to remember the times we have not embodied this same love . . . [*pause*]

Lord Jesus, you are the son of David: Lord, have mercy.

Christ Jesus, your kingdom endures forever: Christ, have mercy.

Lord Jesus, you teach us to call God 'Father': Lord, have mercy.

Model Universal Prayer (Prayer of the Faithful)

Presider: Along with St. Joseph, patron of the universal church, we lift up our prayers to God.

Response: Lord, hear our prayer.

That all members of the church strive to live with the perseverance, compassion, and fidelity of St. Joseph . . .

That workers throughout the world might have meaningful employment and a just wage . . .

That foster and adoptive parents find solace, strength and joy in the example of St. Joseph . . .

That each of us here encounter and welcome Christ within the people who share our households and workplaces . . .

Presider: Gracious God, you called St. Joseph to be the husband of Mary and the foster father of Jesus. Hear our prayers that we might emulate his model of love and faithfulness. Through Christ our Lord. **Amen.**

About Liturgy

A saint for dreamers and doers: Have you noticed that St. Joseph says nothing in Scripture? Rather, what he created with his hands as a carpenter and did with his feet as a protector of his family proclaimed his faith in God. Perhaps that is why much of our iconography for Joseph depicts him carrying, holding, moving, making, and building.

Yet Joseph is also the patron of dreamers, those who see visions others can't and hear God's voice in their dreams. Like Joseph, our work as liturgists, musicians, presiders, and liturgical ministers is both artistic and functional. It requires dreaming and doing, discernment and follow-through. Joseph does both and thus is more an artisan and craftsperson than an impractical daydreamer or detached worker. Let us rekindle our commitment to be dreamers *and* doers of the Gospel in the work and art of liturgy.

COLLECT

Let us pray.

Pause for silent prayer

Grant, we pray, almighty God,
that by Saint Joseph's intercession
your Church may constantly watch over
the unfolding of the mysteries of human
    salvation,
whose beginnings you entrusted to his
    faithful care.
Through our Lord Jesus Christ, your Son,
who lives and reigns with you in the unity
    of the Holy Spirit,
one God, for ever and ever. **Amen.**

FOR REFLECTION

• St. Paul tells us we are to follow the example of Abraham, 'father of all of us'. On this feast of St. Joseph, foster father of Jesus, who in your life has 'fathered' you in faith?

• As we seek to emulate St. Joseph, how do you offer Jesus a place to dwell in your own life?

Homily Points

• In the Gospel of Matthew, it is Joseph instead of Mary who is visited by an angel bringing the news of Jesus's conception by the Holy Spirit. It is Joseph who must give his *fiat*, his 'yes' to the wondrous plan of God. Unlike the annunciation to Mary, we don't hear Joseph's response to the angel. Instead of words, Joseph responds with actions by immediately doing 'what the angel of the Lord had told him to do'. Joseph shows us a model of love in action.

• In the first reading, the prophet Nathan speaks to Joseph's ancestor David, asking on God's behalf, 'Is it you who would build me a house to dwell in'? (NABRE). Instead, God proclaims that there is one who is to come who will 'build a house for my name'. In the gospel we see Joseph, the carpenter, welcoming Mary (and the baby in her womb) into his own house. He offers them a place to dwell in safety and comfort.

SPIRITUALITY

GOSPEL ACCLAMATION
Matt 4:17

℟. Glory to you, O Christ, you are the Word
  of God!
Repent, says the Lord,
for the kingdom of heaven is close at hand.
℟. Glory to you, O Christ, you are the
  Word of God!

Gospel

Luke 13:1-9

Some people arrived and told Jesus about the Galileans whose blood Pilate had mingled with that of their sacrifices. At this he said to them, 'Do you suppose these Galileans who suffered like that were greater sinners than any other Galileans? They were not, I tell you. No; but unless you repent you will all perish as they did. Or those eighteen on whom the tower at Siloam fell and killed them? Do you suppose that they were more guilty than all the other people living in Jerusalem? They were not, I tell you. No; but unless you repent you will all perish as they did.'

He told this parable: 'A man had a fig tree planted in his vineyard, and he came looking for fruit on it but found none. He said to the man who looked after the vineyard, "Look here, for three years now I have been coming to look for fruit on this fig tree and finding none. Cut it down: why should it be taking up the ground?" "Sir," the man replied "leave it one more year and give me time to dig round it and manure it: it may bear fruit next year; if not, then you can cut it down."'

Reflecting on the Gospel

Human beings have an innate drive to find causation, a reason for things and events happening. This generally works well and helps us devise systems and ways of doing things that are safer and more productive. For example, automobile accident rates have been going down for years, measured by deaths per million miles driven. We design cars and trucks to be safer, based on research and testing. Though there might be an accident, it is far more likely that a human being will survive due to better engineering, design, etc. And yet, when an accident happens we still look for reasons, for example, excessive speed of the vehicle, or perhaps the driver was impaired by alcohol, lack of sleep, or something else. We seek to explain reasons for events, especially accidents.

In the ancient world, and perhaps even our own, many accidents or tragic events were explained by appeal to the gods, or God. It was understood that bad things happened to bad people; in other words, if something bad happened to someone, it's because that someone did something bad. Good people lived lives that were blessed and filled with good things. A tragedy or accident nearly guaranteed that the victim was somehow at fault, had reaped the tragic remuneration for what he had sown. Much of the Old Testament, especially the Torah, provides the underpinnings for this view. But there are other books, for example, Job, that question it.

At the time of Jesus, when a tragic event happened at Siloam or when Pilate desecrated Jewish blood, the popular idea was that these people somehow had it coming. They must have done something bad for which they were punished. Jesus, however, interprets these events differently. He does not see this as a just punishment for some hidden sin. Instead, he tells those who are self-righteous in their smugness that the same will happen to them unless they repent. The period of time they have between witnessing the tragedy that befell others and the unknown time of their own death is a time for repentance. And the parable Jesus gives them underlines this point. The parable also subtly informs the audience that they have not been producing the fruit of good works. They have been given a limited amount of time to repent, but if that doesn't happen they, too, will be cut down like the barren fig tree, like those who suffered the tragedy at Siloam or desecration at the hands of Pilate. The message of today's gospel can be summarised in one simple word: Repent!

Living the Paschal Mystery

A tragic and untimely death has a way of focusing our attention. Unfortunately, when we lose someone dear suddenly we become painfully aware of how short our life is, how precious are the days that we have been given. Too often our lives are occupied with simple tasks rather than profound meaning. There are daily chores to do, people who rely on us to do our part. But today's gospel reminds us that the time we are given is short and may come to a conclusion quickly and without warning. The time we have on this earth is for repentance and subsequently for doing the will of God. When we see tragedy strike others it can be easy for some to explain away the circumstances to poor decision making on their part, or plain bad luck. We might even become a bit proud at our own more fortunate and prudent decision making, not recognising the many close calls we have certainly faced. But the time we are given is not for smugness or pride. Tragedy can befall any of us without warning. The gospel is a call for us to appreciate the limited time we have on earth, to respond generously to the needs of others, and to walk humbly.

Focusing the Gospel
Key words and phrases: unless you repent you will all perish

To the point: When Jesus tells the crowds that they must repent lest they perish, he is speaking of a spiritual death rather than a physical one. After all, the first part of the gospel is denying the all-too-human belief that bad things only happen to bad people. Instead, we are called to focus on the fruitfulness of our own fig trees. Have we been cultivating and fertilizing the soil of our lives so that we might bear good fruit in the kingdom of God?

Connecting the Gospel
to the second reading: A tone of warning continues in the second reading from St. Paul's first letter to the Corinthians. Paul warns the community at Corinth against the scourge of overconfidence: 'The man who thinks he is safe must be careful that he does not fall'. In the gospel reading we are not told whom Jesus is talking to. But we can assume that whatever the demographics of this particular crowd, Jesus is intent upon warning them against complacency and self-righteousness. The parable of the barren fig tree invited them – as it invites us today – to consider whether we are bearing good fruit or merely exhausting the soil.

to experience: Each year during the season of Lent we heed the gospel call to repent. This season helps to protect against the overconfidence that St. Paul warns of. Instead of spending our spiritual lives in a self-satisfied bubble, we are called to place them under a microscope and to see where we are in need of God's grace and forgiveness.

Connecting the Responsorial Psalm
to the readings: While the gospel and the second reading call us to repentance, the psalm reminds us of the response we can expect from God. The psalmist assures us that we have a God who 'forgives all your guilt, / who heals every one of your ills'. His compassion and mercy are infinite and unfathomable for '[a]s far as the east is from the west, / so far has he removed our sins from us' (NABRE). We can depend on the mercy of God because we have witnessed it throughout history. The psalmist reminds us, 'He made known his ways to Moses / and his deeds to Israel's sons'. In the first reading, God speaks to Moses from the burning bush and tells him, 'I have seen the miserable state of my people in Egypt. I have heard their appeal to be free of their slave-drivers. Yes, I am well aware of their sufferings'. Our God is a God of empathy. Just as God entered into the suffering of the Israelites in bondage in Egypt, he enters into the bondage and suffering we experience when our lives are touched by sin. The psalmist's message reminds us to heed the warnings of Jesus and St. Paul with complete trust in God's love, mercy, and forgiveness.

to psalmist preparation: In the readings for this Third Sunday of Lent it is your role to proclaim the good news of God's never-ending mercy and compassion. How have you experienced this mercy in your own life?

PROMPTS FOR FAITH-SHARING

God calls Moses by name and Moses answers, 'Here I am'. How have you experienced God's call in your own life? What has been your response?

God identifies himself to Moses as the 'the God of your ancestors' (NABRE). We know God throughout history and also within our own lives of faith. How does your family and/or community pass on faith to younger generations?

St. Paul admonishes us, 'You must never complain'. What situations in your life are met with complaining? How might you greet them a different way?

Jesus gives us the parable of the barren fig tree. Where in your life, family, or parish is there a lack of fruit being borne? How might you cultivate the ground to encourage fruitfulness?

CELEBRATION

Model Penitential Act

Presider: In our first reading, God appears to Moses from a burning bush and gives him a mission to lead his people to freedom. As we prepare to enter into this liturgy, let us pause to consider how God might be calling to us this day, and to ask for mercy and pardon for the times we have not responded to this call . . . [*pause*]

> *Confiteor:* I confess . . .

Homily Points

• In the second reading, St. Paul tells the Corinthians, 'I want to remind you, brothers, how our fathers were all guided by a cloud above them and how they all passed through the sea'. Paul raises a theme that is common throughout both the Bible and the liturgy. As Christians we are to consider ourselves as having participated in each of the great historical moments that we commemorate. Each time we come to the table of the Lord at Mass we are participating in the Last Supper, death, and resurrection of Jesus.

• Today when we read the familiar story of Moses at the burning bush we can place ourselves within that narrative. God calls from the bush, 'Moses, Moses'. There is a pattern in the Bible that whenever someone's name is called twice, his or her life is about to change forever. And Moses' life does change. He is called from being a shepherd in the wilderness of Egypt to shepherding the Hebrew people by leading them out of slavery and into the freedom of God.

• Just as with Moses, God also has a plan for each of our lives. Even if this plan is not as grand as challenging a powerful political figure to gain freedom for an entire nation, it is a call for us to collaborate in building the kingdom of God on earth – a kingdom where all are cared for and where peace, love, and hope prevail. Listen. Do you hear God calling your name?

Model Universal Prayer (Prayer of the Faithful)

Presider: Jesus calls us to repentance and conversion and so, trusting in the God of redemption, we bring our needs before the Lord.

Response: Lord, hear our prayer.

That the church bear abundant fruit throughout the world . . .

That all the nations of the world come together to end human trafficking and slavery . . .

That all those who experience calamities and trauma know the healing love of God and the support of a compassionate community . . .

That all those gathered in this place might hear God calling them by name and have the courage to answer, 'Here I am, Lord' . . .

Presider: God of compassion and mercy, no matter how far we wander from your love you are always ready to welcome us home. Hear these prayers that, as we continue this Lenten journey, we are brought ever closer to you. Through Christ our Lord. **Amen.**

COLLECT

Let us pray.

Pause for silent prayer

O God, author of every mercy and of all
    goodness,
who in fasting, prayer and almsgiving
have shown us a remedy for sin,
look graciously on this confession of our
    lowliness,
that we, who are bowed down by our
    conscience,
may always be lifted up by your mercy.
Through our Lord Jesus Christ, your Son,
who lives and reigns with you in the unity
    of the Holy Spirit,
one God, for ever and ever. **Amen.**

FIRST READING
Exod 3:1-8, 13-15

Moses was looking after the flock of Jethro, his father-in-law, priest of Midian. He led his flock to the far side of the wilderness and came to Horeb, the mountain of God. There the angel of the Lord appeared to him in the shape of a flame of fire, coming from the middle of a bush. Moses looked; there was the bush blazing but it was not being burnt up. 'I must go and look at this strange sight,' Moses said 'and see why the bush is not burnt.' Now the Lord saw him go forward to look, and God called to him from the middle of the bush. 'Moses, Moses!' he said. 'Here I am' he answered. 'Come no nearer' he said. 'Take off your shoes, for the place on which you stand is holy ground. I am the God of your father,' he said 'the God of Abraham, the God of Isaac and the God of Jacob.' At this Moses covered his face, afraid to look at God.

And the Lord said, 'I have seen the miserable state of my people in Egypt. I have heard their appeal to be free of their slave-drivers. Yes, I am well aware of their sufferings. I mean to deliver them out of the hands of the Egyptians and bring them up out of that land to a land rich and broad, a land where milk and honey flow.'

Then Moses said to God, 'I am to go, then, to the sons of Israel and say to them, "The God of your fathers has sent me to you". But if they ask me what his name is, what am I to tell them?' And God said to Moses, 'I Am who I Am. This' he added 'is what you must say to the sons of Israel: "The Lord, the God of your fathers, the God of Abraham, the God of Isaac, and the God of Jacob, has sent me to you." This is my name for all time; by this name I shall be invoked for all generations to come.'

RESPONSORIAL PSALM

Ps 102:1-4, 6-8, 11 (8)

R̸. The Lord is compassion and love.

My soul, give thanks to the Lord,
all my being, bless his holy name.
My soul give thanks to the Lord
and never forget all his blessings.

R̸. The Lord is compassion and love.

It is he who forgives all your guilt,
who heals every one of your ills,
who redeems your life from the grave,
who crowns you with love and
      compassion.

R̸. The Lord is compassion and love.

The Lord does deeds of justice,
gives judgement for all who are oppressed.
He made known his ways to Moses
and his deeds to Israel's sons.

R̸. The Lord is compassion and love.

The Lord is compassion and love,
slow to anger and rich in mercy.
For as the heavens are high above the earth
so strong is his love for those who fear him.

R̸. The Lord is kind and merciful.

SECOND READING

1 Cor 10:1-6, 10-12

I want to remind you, brothers, how our fathers were all guided by a cloud above them and how they all passed through the sea. They were all baptised into Moses in this cloud and in this sea; all ate the same spiritual food and all drank the same spiritual drink since they all drank from the spiritual rock that followed them as they went, and that rock was Christ. In spite of this, most of them failed to please God and their corpses littered the desert.

These things all happened as warnings for us, not to have the wicked lusts for forbidden things that they had. You must never complain: some of them did, and they were killed by the Destroyer.

All this happened to them as a warning, and it was written down to be a lesson for us who are living at the end of the age. The man who thinks he is safe must be careful that he does not fall.

About Liturgy

Repentance: Sometimes we might think that the suffering a person experiences is caused by God because of their sinfulness. Somehow, God is punishing them. Although the readings today at first might sound that way, a careful reading of them shows exactly the opposite. We hear the Lord say, 'I have seen the miserable state of my people in Egypt. I have heard their appeal to be free of their slave-drivers. Yes, I am well aware of their sufferings. I mean to deliver them' (Exod 3:7-8). God wants to save us from our suffering. The one who is the source of all goodness can never desire harm to come upon his own children.

Yet, suffering is a reality because it is the nature of being human. We who have been saved by Christ by baptism are not immune to human suffering. However, the difference that our baptism makes is that we are aware that we have been given the promise of God's mercy. Therefore, we live always in hope and in constant repentance for when we have doubted in God's merciful love.

Today is a good opportunity to reflect on the second form of the penitential act that may be unfamiliar to most assemblies. This second form is a brief dialogue between presider and people.

Priest: Lord, we have sinned against you; Lord, have mercy.
People: Lord, have mercy.
Priest: Lord, show us your mercy and love.
People: And grant us your salvation.

This dialogue is a succinct summary of what we believe about repentance and God's mercy. Forgiveness and mercy are not rewards for being repentant. Rather, God desires to forgive us and ever awaits that moment when we turn to God with hearts open to his mercy.

About Initiation

Scrutinies: Today and the next two Sundays call for the celebration of the scrutinies if you have elect present in your assembly. Remember three important points about these rituals. First, you must use the readings for Year A even though we are in Year C of the Lectionary. Second, all three scrutinies are required. If your elect miss one or two of these scrutinies for a serious reason, and they cannot be rescheduled, you must request dispensation from your bishop. See RCIA 20. Third, the scrutinies cannot be combined with the presentations of the Creed and the Lord's Prayer because each ritual has readings assigned specifically to it.

About Liturgical Music

Suggestions: Today should be filled with songs of God's mercy. Look especially for text that reflects the need for our repentance and turning (conversion) of our hearts to God, from whom we receive the fulness of mercy. One suggestion is 'Attende, Domine', which is a simple yet accessible chant. Although many resources have an English translation of this text, the Latin text and melody of the refrain are easy enough to be memorable. The verses can be sung by a schola or cantor. Another suggestion is *Psallite*'s 'Those Who Love me, I Will Deliver'. The refrain text is, 'Those who love me, I will deliver; those who know my name, I will protect. When you call me, I will answer you, I will be with you who know my name'. This connects to today's first reading in which God loves us so much as to reveal his own name to us. This is a God who is present to us and ready to save us as soon as we turn towards the one who has called us each by name.

GOSPEL ACCLAMATION
John 1:14

R⁊. Praise to you, O Christ. King of Eternal Glory.
The Word was made flesh,
he lived among us,
and we saw his glory.
R⁊. Praise to you, O Christ. King of Eternal Glory.

Gospel   Luke 1:26-38

The angel Gabriel was sent by God to a town in Galilee called Nazareth, to a virgin betrothed to a man named Joseph, of the house of David; and the virgin's name was Mary. He went in and said to her, "Rejoice, so highly favoured! The Lord is with you.' She was deeply disturbed by these words and asked herself what this greeting could mean, but the angel said to her, 'Mary, do not be afraid; you have won God's favour. Listen! You are to conceive and bear a son, and you must name him Jesus. He will be great and will be called Son of the Most High. The Lord God will give him the throne of his ancestor David; he will rule over the House of Jacob for ever and his reign will have no end.' Mary said to the angel, 'But how can this come about, since I am a virgin?' 'The Holy Spirit will come upon you, the angel answered, 'and the power of the Most High will cover you with its shadow. And so the child will be holy and will be called Son of God. Know this too: your kinswoman Elizabeth also, in her old age, herself conceived a son, and she whom people called barren is now in her sixth month, for nothing is impossible to God.' 'I am the handmaid of the Lord,' said Mary, 'let what you have said be done to me.' And the angel left her.

See Appendix, p. 279, for the other readings.

Reflecting on the Gospel

The story of the annunciation, set in Nazareth, with the angel Gabriel and his greeting that forms the basis of the first lines of the Hail Mary prayer, Mary's *fiat* ('let what you have said be done to me') and more are all packed into this short thirteen-verse story told by Luke. There is no other evangelist who relates this event. And no other New Testament author even references it. The later stories, artistic depictions, legends, and lore surrounding the annunciation ultimately find their source in today's gospel. The Gospel of Matthew, as we read earlier, has a different story about Joseph and Mary living separately as a betrothed couple, not in Nazareth but Bethlehem, when Joseph discovers that Mary is pregnant. In Matthew there is no annunciation, only Joseph's dream in which he is assured that he can take her as his wife. So even though we are in the liturgical year when we read Luke, we also read him today because he's the only evangelist to tell us the story of the annunciation. Liturgically, this feast is nine months prior to Christmas, the feast of the Nativity, when we celebrate the birth of Jesus.

It is significant that we hear about this event from Luke's pen as he is the evangelist who tells us more stories about women than any other evangelist. And here we have not only Mary, but Elizabeth, her cousin. Mary displays the attitude of a proper disciple. She listens to the word of God spoken through Gabriel. Her response is a simple but profound, '[L]et what you have said be done to me'. She knows that nothing is impossible for God. There were stories in the Scriptures about women becoming pregnant in older age, like Sarah, Abraham's wife. Mary learns that Elizabeth, thought to be barren, will also have a child. But Mary herself is young and betrothed to Joseph. She, too, will have a child. Here Luke and Matthew have in common the idea that Mary was a virgin when she conceived. And this is a theological point echoed even in the Qur'an (chap. 19). In this way Luke draws attention to Jesus's identity as 'Son of God', for he was born of a virgin. Ultimately, this is a theological, rather than a biological, truth. For the Gospel of Mark, the Gospel of John, the apostle Paul, and other New Testament authors also claim Jesus as 'Son of God' without saying anything about Mary's virginity. Today we focus on the theological significance of the annunciation because the story is more about theology than biology.

Living the Paschal Mystery

If an angel were to appear to us and tell us what to do, it would be much easier to follow God's will for our lives. But such an appearance is unlikely. Instead, we are left to meander through life making a series of choices, most if not all of which seem like a good idea at the time. But with reflection, some of our choices might not seem to have been all that good! How we wish for an angel to show us the way!

Adult Christianity demands that we are open to God and God's will for our lives. But our discernment of his will is especially important. To become attuned to the spirit of God at work in our lives we would do well to be aware of God's presence in the quotidian aspects of our routine. God breaks into our daily routine not according to our schedule, but his. When Gabriel broke into Mary's world it was with good news, an announcement of her bearing a child, the Son of God, and that his kingdom would be everlasting. We do not need to wait until Jesus returns to live in this kingdom. We can do it now, and by so doing we help usher in his everlasting reign.

Focusing the Gospel

Key words and phrases: Rejoice, so highly favoured! The Lord is with you.

To the point: These words are familiar to us as the opening line of the Hail Mary. Mary is not only a model of discipleship, she is also a model of what the Lord would like to do for each of us. Jesus longs to make his home in us as well. We, too, are called to be Christ-bearers in the world. On this day, we honour Mary and we also pray to be like her. Listen for these words in your own life, for the angel wants to tell each of us, 'Rejoice, so highly favoured! The Lord is with you'.

Model Penitential Act

Presider: On this feast of the Annunciation we celebrate Mary's response to the angel that made Jesus's birth possible: '[L]et what you have said be done to me'. For the times we have not lived up to the example of Mary's free and generous collaboration with God we ask for pardon and healing . . . [*pause*]

Lord Jesus, you were born of the Virgin Mary: Lord, have mercy.

Christ Jesus, you are Emmanuel, God with us: Christ, have mercy.

Lord Jesus, you are the Son of God: Lord, have mercy.

Model Universal Prayer (Prayer of the Faithful)

Presider: Through the intercession of Mary, the Mother of God, we offer our prayers to the Lord.

Response: Lord, hear our prayer.

That all members of the church might receive the gifts of God with the joy and humility of Mary . . .

That leaders in governments throughout the world do all within their power to protect life in the womb . . .

That all married couples who experience infertility, miscarriage, and stillbirth be comforted and their dreams of a family brought to fruition . . .

That all of us here follow the model of Mary, our Mother, and proclaim to God, '[L]et what you have said be done to me' . . .

Presider: Most High God, you sent your only son to be born of the Virgin Mary through the power of the Holy Spirit. Hear these prayers that we might emulate Mary's trust in your power and generous collaboration in your plan. We ask this through Christ our Lord. **Amen.**

About Liturgy

To Jesus through Mary: The phrase 'To Jesus through Mary' is often heard among those with great devotion to the Blessed Virgin Mary. This saying is attributed to St. Louis de Montfort, although many earlier saints and spiritual writers also expressed this deep connection between Jesus to Mary and Mary to us. More recently, St. John Paul II had promoted St. Louis's spirituality that focused on consecrating our entire life to Mary in order to be in closer union with Christ. (John Paul II's coat of arms used a motto inspired by St. Louis's own writings on true devotion to Mary.)

Today's solemnity is a good reminder that any true Christian devotion must always have as its goal and focus closer union to Christ. The incarnation of God through a human, no matter how holy or revered the human, is foremost Christocentric, and authentic Marian devotion must be as well.

Therefore, resist any urge to add Marian devotional practices or songs to the Mass today. The rosary or the Hail Mary find their rightful place as prayerful preparation for Mass so that the faithful may give their complete focus and praise to Christ alone.

COLLECT

Let us pray.

Pause for silent prayer

O God, who willed that your Word
should take on the reality of human flesh
in the womb of the Virgin Mary,
grant, we pray,
that we, who confess our Redeemer to be God
   and man,
may merit to become partakers even in his
   divine nature.
Who lives and reigns with you in the unity of
   the Holy Spirit,
one God, for ever and ever. **Amen.**

FOR REFLECTION

• The angel proclaims, '[N]othing is impossible to God'. Where in your life do you need this reminder of God's power?

• Our God is a great gift-giver. How might you follow the example of Mary in saying yes to the gifts God is offering to you?

Homily Points

• The secular definition of 'annunciation' is simply 'the announcement of something'. In today's gospel there are two announcements made. There is the announcement of the angel that Mary will conceive and bear a son, the Son of God; and also Mary's announcement, 'I am the handmaid of the Lord, . . . let what you have said be done to me'.

• These announcements are of equal importance because our God respects free will. He desires a relationship in love with us, his creatures, but love is not love if it is coerced. And so the annunciation to Mary requires Mary's announcement back in order to bear fruit. And Mary responds freely, '[L]et what you have said be done to me'.

SPIRITUALITY

GOSPEL ACCLAMATION
Luke 15:18

R̷. Praise and honour to you, Lord Jesus!
I will leave this place and go to my father
and say:
'Father, I have sinned against heaven and
against you.'
R̷. Praise and honour to you, Lord Jesus!

Gospel   Luke 15:1-3, 11-32

The tax collectors and the sinners were all seeking the company of Jesus to hear what he had to say, and the Pharisees and the scribes complained. 'This man' they said 'welcomes sinners and eats with them.' So he spoke this parable to them:

'A man had two sons. The younger said to his father, "Father, let me have the share of the estate that would come to me." So the father divided the property between them. A few days later, the younger son got together everything he had and left for a distant country where he squandered his money on a life of debauchery.

'When he had spent it all, that country experienced a severe famine, and now he began to feel the pinch, so he hired himself out to one of the local inhabitants who put him on his farm to feed the pigs. And he would willingly have filled his belly with the husks the pigs were eating but no one offered him anything. Then he came to his senses and said, "How many of my father's paid servants have more food than they want, and here am I dying of hunger! I will leave this place and go to my father and say: Father, I have sinned against heaven and against you; I no longer deserve to be called your son; treat me as one of your paid servants." So he left the place and went back to his father.

Continued in Appendix A, p. 279.

Reflecting on the Gospel

Often we hear today's gospel referred to as the story of the Prodigal Son. But this might be a bit of a misnomer. Even the New American Bible has a different title for this story, calling it the 'lost son'. The term 'prodigal' means 'wastefully extravagant', as in, 'My holiday spending this summer was especially prodigal, as I was having a good time after working so hard during the previous year'. The word has a different etymology from 'prodigy', which means 'one endowed with exceptional abilities', although sometimes preachers conflate the meaning of the two terms. So when we refer to the Prodigal Son it might be worth the time to clarify what we actually mean by the term prodigal!

But ultimately the story is not so much about the lost or prodigal son. It's not even so much about his brother, though we could call it the story of the two sons. In reality, the story is about the loving father, how the father is a personification of God, and the kind of love God has for us.

The story is sometimes interpreted so that the sons represent Gentile (lost) and Jewish (favoured) identities. In this, the Gentiles have lost their way and lived generally wanton lives of decadence, whereas Jews have followed the wishes of God. But in the end both sons, Gentile and Jew, receive the same reward.

In today's telling, the story is often interpreted more literally, or at least personally, as referring to a wayward person who has ultimately been redeemed. The story is particularly meaningful to many who have lived lives of regret or shame, only to feel the loving embrace of God, a community of hope, a family, or even church upon turning away from their wayward lifestyle.

One of the advantages of a story like this is that it has so many possible interpretations. And this story is told only by Luke. Without him we would know nothing of the Prodigal Son, and certainly nothing of the many works of art inspired by the parable, such as Rembrandt's 'Return of the Prodigal Son'. There is no sole or singular point to this story. The parable is polyvalent and ought to make us ponder it, as the church has done for centuries.

Living the Paschal Mystery

Redemption and forgiveness are powerful themes, and they are articulated in today's gospel in a particularly dramatic way. These themes are also favourites of Luke, who uses the term 'forgiveness [of sins]' more than any other New Testament author. The apostle Paul, for example, never says the word 'forgiveness'. (And perhaps he should have, as it's a much easier concept to grasp than 'justification'!) Luke is a master storyteller, he crafts a brief but memorable narrative here. The characters are stock: we probably know people like the sons in today's gospel. Do we know people like the father? Would *we* react like the father? *Do* we react like the father? Though we might or might not have lost wayward children, there are many opportunities to express mercy and loving kindness, and share reconciliation and forgiveness with another. When we behave in this way, we are acting like the father, acting in a way that God acts. Perhaps this is why Pope Francis chose the theme 'mercy' for his pontificate. As we learn in today's gospel, mercy is a fundamental expression of God and God's character. Mercy is not merely for God alone: mercy is worthy of emulation.

Focusing the Gospel

Key words and phrases: While he was still a long way off, his father saw him and was moved with pity.

To the point: In our gospel Jesus gives us a parable illustrating the abundant mercy of God. The father in the parable respects his son's freedom. He gives him the inheritance he requests and lets him go. But he never stops watching for this son to return home. And when he does catch sight of his wayward son, the father does not wait for the son to complete his journey or to speak the words of contrition he had so carefully practised. It's as if Jesus wants to tell us that we need only turn towards God for our merciful father to run out to meet us and usher us home.

Connecting the Gospel

to the second reading: The apostle Paul's words in his second letter to the Corinthians are a perfect partner to the gospel of the Prodigal Son and the forgiving father. St. Paul counsels us to 'be reconciled to God'. Not only are we called to personal reconciliation but also to become messengers of this reconciliation to the entire world. God waits and watches for each one of us individually, and also for the world as a whole to come to our senses just as the prodigal did and realise who we truly are, beloved daughters and sons of God.

to experience: We are halfway through with our Lenten journey. How have you experienced reconciliation so far with God and with others? What areas in your life are still in need of God's healing touch and redeeming embrace?

Connecting the Responsorial Psalm

to the readings: We might imagine Psalm 33 as the song of one who has been redeemed and saved. In fact, it could be the psalm of the prodigal returned to dignity and joy as a child of God. The psalmist sings, 'Look towards him and be radiant; / let your faces not be abashed'. Our God wants nothing more than to find the lost and to save the sinner. Just before the parable of the Prodigal Son in Luke's gospel, Jesus tells of the shepherd who searches for his lost sheep. He ends this parable by saying, '[T]here will be more joy in heaven over one sinner who repents than over ninety-nine righteous people who have no need of repentance' (NABRE). Sometimes this is a difficult teaching to accept, especially for those of us who identify more with the older brother in the parable of the Prodigal Son. The truth is, each and every one of us is in need of repentance. In experiencing our need for forgiveness, we can share in the joy of the prodigal returned fully to his father's embrace.

to psalmist preparation: In Psalm 33 we hear the line, 'Glorify the Lord with me. / Together let us praise his name'. Reflect on your ministry of leading the people of God in prayer. How do you invite the assembly to pray with you?

PROMPTS FOR FAITH-SHARING

The psalmist tells us, 'Look towards [God] and be radiant; / let your faces not be abashed'. Where do you feel shame or guilt over past transgressions? How might you give these emotions to the Lord?

St. Paul tells us we are entrusted with the 'news that they are reconciled'. How does your parish carry out the ministry of reconciliation within the wider community?

Which figure in the parable of the Prodigal Son do you identify with the most at this point in your faith journey: the prodigal, the older son, or forgiving father? Why?

At this halfway point in our Lenten journey, how have you been living the spiritual practices of prayer, fasting, and almsgiving? Is there anything you would like to do differently for the second half of Lent?

CELEBRATION

Model Penitential Act

Presider: In today's gospel we hear the familiar parable of the Prodigal Son. As we prepare to enter into this celebration, let us pause to consider the times we have wandered far from God and to ask for pardon and healing . . . [*pause*]

    Confiteor: I confess . . .

Homily Points

• In the parable from today's gospel it is easy to focus on the characters of the two sons. We can relate with the younger son, mired in sin, who realises his need for repentance, or with the older son who is so focused on comparing his behaviour with his brother's that he is unable to appreciate the love his father continues to gift him with. But what happens if we turn our attention instead to the father?

• Everything changes when we consider the father as the protagonist of the parable today. Instead of the shame of the younger son or the bitterness of the elder one taking centre stage, our attention is focused on the tender love of the father who yearns for his children to be close to him. In fact, it is the remembrance of his father's love and care for his servants, which leads the younger son to repentance. And hopefully it will be the father's gentle invitation to join the celebration that will induce the older son to be reconciled to father and brother alike.

• Pope Francis wrote in his apostolic exhortation, *Evangelii Gaudium,* 'God never tires of forgiving us; we are the ones who tire of seeking his mercy'. We are human and sinful. And it is disheartening when we fall into sin (sometimes the same one) again and again. And yet our God continues to watch and wait for us to 'come to ourselves', as the young son did, and return to him. Let us pray for perseverance in the way of repentance this Lent.

Model Universal Prayer (Prayer of the Faithful)

Presider: Trusting in the compassionate mercy of our heavenly Father we lift our prayers and needs to God.

Response: Lord, hear our prayer.

That the church be a beacon of mercy to all people, especially those on the margins of society . . .

That nations at war be reconciled . . .

That families experiencing conflict and division encounter the healing touch of God . . .

That all gathered here might receive the grace to emulate the love of the forgiving father who welcomes his son with open arms . . .

Presider: Merciful God, you constantly wait and watch for your children to return to you. Hear our prayers that we might be reconciled to you and to each other. We ask this through Christ our Lord. **Amen.**

About Liturgy

Examination of conscience: Today's familiar gospel reading of the Prodigal Son – though many would rightly rename it the 'Prodigal Father' for his abundant compassion – gives us an opportunity to look at how we examine our conscience. Many of us will recall from our childhood our preparations for making a good confession by going through some kind of list of questions that helped us see where we had failed to live up to our baptism. Such lists can be very useful when preparing for the sacrament of reconciliation. In fact, the church gives us several examples of an examination of

COLLECT

Let us pray.

Pause for silent prayer

O God, who through your Word
reconcile the human race to yourself in a
    wonderful way,
grant, we pray,
that with prompt devotion and eager faith
the Christian people may hasten
toward the solemn celebrations to come.
Through our Lord Jesus Christ, your Son,
who lives and reigns with you in the unity
    of the Holy Spirit,
one God, for ever and ever. **Amen.**

FIRST READING

Josh 5:9-12

The Lord said to Joshua, 'Today I have taken the shame of Egypt away from you.'
    The Israelites pitched their camp at Gilgal and kept the Passover there on the fourteenth day of the month, at evening in the plain of Jericho. On the morrow of the Passover they tasted the produce of that country, unleavened bread and roasted ears of corn, that same day. From that time, from their first eating of the produce of that country, the manna stopped falling. And having manna no longer, the Israelites fed from that year onwards on what the land of Canaan yielded.

CATECHESIS

RESPONSORIAL PSALM
Ps 33:2-7 (9)

R⁷. Taste and see that the Lord is good.

I will bless the Lord at all times,
his praise always on my lips;
in the Lord my soul shall make its boast.
The humble shall hear and be glad.

R⁷. Taste and see that the Lord is good.

Glorify the Lord with me.
Together let us praise his name.
I sought the Lord and he answered me;
from all my terrors he set me free.

R⁷. Taste and see that the Lord is good.

Look towards him and be radiant;
let your faces not be abashed.
This poor man called; the Lord heard him
and rescued him from all his distress.

R⁷. Taste and see that the Lord is good.

SECOND READING
2 Cor 5:17-21

For anyone who is in Christ, there is a new creation; the old creation has gone, and now the new one is here. It is all God's work. It was God who reconciled us to himself through Christ and gave us the work of handing on this reconciliation. In other words, God in Christ was reconciling the world to himself, not holding men's faults against them, and he has entrusted to us the news that they are reconciled. So we are ambassadors for Christ; it is as though God were appealing through us, and the appeal that we make in Christ's name is: be reconciled to God. For our sake God made the sinless one into sin, so that in him we might become the goodness of God.

conscience, which you can find in appendix III of the Rite of Penance. The purpose of these is to help us examine our life in the light of God's word.

However, the church also invites us to do a daily examination of conscience. We see this embedded in the liturgy of Compline, or Night Prayer, which is part of the Liturgy of the Hours. It is the final liturgy before sleeping that we pray either individually or communally.

At the beginning of Night Prayer we are invited to spend some moments examining our conscience. Some use the Ignatian discipline of the *examen*. A simple structure for this has five steps: 1) recall God's presence; 2) look back on the day and give thanks; 3) pay attention to your feelings, whether positive or negative; 4) reflect more deeply on one part of your day that God may be calling you to examine more closely; and 5) give thanks again to God in hope for more opportunities to encounter Christ in our daily lives.

Finally, every Eucharist we celebrate invites us into an examination of conscience. At the beginning of the penitential rite the presider calls us to acknowledge our sin in order to prepare ourselves for the sacred mysteries. Then follows a brief silence during which we examine our hearts.

When we practise a daily, weekly, and sacramental examination of our lives, we will be participating in Christ's ministry of reconciliation and will be ambassadors of his constant mercy.

About Initiation
Sacrament of Reconciliation: Baptised adults who are preparing for Reception into the Full Communion of the Catholic Church or for the celebration of confirmation and Eucharist are encouraged to celebrate the sacrament of reconciliation. This would take place at a time prior to and distinct from the celebrations of reception or confirmation and Eucharist. Whether or not they do partake of the sacrament of reconciliation, they should be strongly encouraged to participate in your parish's Lenten penitential liturgies.

Note that catechumens cannot celebrate the sacrament of reconciliation; however, they can certainly participate in your parish's penitential liturgies.

About Liturgical Music
Rejoice!: We come to the midway point of Lent and Laetare ('Rejoice') Sunday. We get the name for this Sunday from the entrance antiphon: 'Rejoice, Jerusalem, and all who love her. / Be joyful, all who were in mourning; / exult and be satisfied at her consoling breast' (Isa 66:10-11). Like Gaudete Sunday in Advent, today is a little break from the austerity of Lent. Therefore, GIRM 313 reminds us that 'the playing of the organ and musical instruments is allowed' not just to support the singing.

One delightful piece to consider as an entrance antiphon is *Psallite*'s 'Rejoice, Rejoice, All You Who Love Jerusalem'! The refrain melody borrows from Handel's *Messiah*, but one need not be a colouratura soprano to sing it! Another *Psallite* piece that would be excellent for Communion is 'Come, Come to the Banquet'. The text reflects the 'prodigal' father's plea to his older son, 'Come to the banquet: all that I have is yours'.

SPIRITUALITY

GOSPEL ACCLAMATION
Joel 2:12-13

℟. Praise to you, O Christ, king of eternal glory!
Now, now – it is the Lord who speaks –
come back to me with all your heart,
for I am all tenderness and compassion.
℟. Praise to you, O Christ, king of
    eternal glory!

Gospel   John 8:1-11

Jesus went to the Mount of Olives. At daybreak he appeared in the Temple again; and as all the people came to him, he sat down and began to teach them.

The scribes and Pharisees brought a woman along who had been caught committing adultery; and making her stand there in full view of everybody, they said to Jesus, 'Master, this woman was caught in the very act of committing adultery, and Moses has ordered us in the Law to condemn women like this to death by stoning. What have you to say?' They asked him this as a test, looking for something to use against him. But Jesus bent down and started writing on the ground with his finger. As they persisted with their question, he looked up and said, 'If there is one of you who has not sinned, let him be the first to throw a stone at her.' Then he bent down and wrote on the ground again. When they heard this they went away one by one, beginning with the eldest, until Jesus was left alone with the woman, who remained standing there. He looked up and said, 'Woman, where are they? Has no one condemned you?' 'No one, sir,' she replied. 'Neither do I condemn you,' said Jesus 'go away, and don't sin any more.'

Reflecting on the Gospel

Although liturgically we are reading from the Gospel of Luke, Cycle C, today we read from John. But interestingly, this story is not in the earliest or best manuscripts of the Gospel of John. In fact, many later manuscripts place this story in the Gospel of Luke, effectively between Luke 21:38 and 22:1, or after the last chapter of the gospel. And other manuscripts have this story not in John 8 (where we find it in the canon) but following John 7:36. Of course, none of this detracts from the story being canonical and inspired Scripture. But it's good to keep in mind the varied history and manuscript difficulties with the story. The notes in the New American Bible explain more.

Part of the reason we pay attention to the problematic background of the story is that it gives us an insight into the early church that produced the text. There was a time in church history, a few centuries after Jesus's death and resurrection, that some Christians did not believe in forgiveness of sin after baptism. As a result, many Christians were delaying baptism until well after their 'sinning years' were over, effectively delaying baptism until their deathbed! But that can be a difficult time to predict. Other Christians were proclaiming what was perceived to be a more libertine attitude, namely, that one could be forgiven for sins even after one was baptised. Recall that part of the difficulty was that the Letter to the Hebrews states quite clearly, 'If we sin deliberately after receiving knowledge of the truth, there no longer remains sacrifice for sins but a fearful prospect of judgement and a flaming fire that is going to consume the adversaries' (Heb 10:26-27; NABRE; cf. Heb 10:26-31). Further, Tertullian argued against any forgiveness of sins after baptism.

In the face of such internal church disputes comes this story about Jesus. That is to say, it was about the time that the church was engaging in the debate about forgiveness of sins that the story of Jesus forgiving the woman caught in adultery began to appear in early manuscripts. It's as though the church recalled an episode from Jesus's life, or told a story about how Jesus might approach the issue. And now, of course, we have the sacrament of reconciliation. The history of the sacrament of reconciliation is beyond the purview of this brief essay. But the story in today's gospel seems to have been a prominent post in the journey of how the church went from Jesus's personal ministry to the sacrament of reconciliation we have today.

Living the Paschal Mystery

Forgiveness is not an easy thing to express; it is not an easy thing to do. We see from Jesus's own ministry, from the experience of the early church, and probably our own past experiences how quickly we exclude others, setting apart and separating them. But Jesus's ministry, and by extension, the church's own ministry, is about inclusion through reconciliation. Jesus proclaims the forgiveness of sins, even undergoing a baptism of forgiveness. By his ministry those on the margins, those who have been condemned, are brought back and welcomed into the fold. The disciples of Jesus carry this ministry forwards into the world. And like the time of Jesus, this ministry moves forwards even when there are forces present who prefer exclusion. The question on the WWJD bracelet, 'What would Jesus do'? is particularly appropriate here. Jesus did not condemn. Neither should we. Jesus forgave. So should we.

Focusing the Gospel

Key words and phrases: If there is one of you who has not sinned, let him be the first to throw a stone at her.

To the point: It is so much easier to point out other people's sins than to confront our own. Jesus reminds us in the gospel today that when our focus shifts to another's sinfulness we need to refocus our attention. Following Jesus's challenge, 'If there is one of you who has not sinned, let him be the first to throw a stone at her', the crowd slowly dissipates. Finally the woman is left with the only one who *is* without sin, Jesus himself. But instead of hurling vicious words or any other projectiles intent on hurting, Jesus offers the woman forgiveness. As in all things, Jesus shows us the way. We are called to love our neighbours, not to condemn them.

Connecting the Gospel

to the first and second readings: In the first reading from the prophet Isaiah, God proclaims words of hope and redemption, saying, 'See, I am doing a new deed, / even now it comes to light; can you not see it?' In the second reading, St. Paul also emphasises the newness of his life in Christ: 'All I can say is that I forget the past and I strain ahead for what is still to come; I am racing for the finish, for the prize'. Our God is not rigid and predictable, but creative and uncontained. And this is how Jesus reveals him to be. In the gospel reading Jesus invites the adulterous woman to new life through forgiveness. Her sin is removed and she can look forward with hope, instead of remaining mired in her sin and forever marked by condemnation.

to experience: The God of newness offers each of us a fresh beginning as well. We are invited in every moment to step into the freedom of Christ and to leave our past sins behind.

Connecting the Responsorial Psalm

to the readings: Psalm 125 recalls the joy the people of Israel felt when their exile in Babylon ended and they were allowed to return to their homeland. After fifty years in captivity the people returned to Israel to begin the long difficult work of rebuilding their cities, temple, and lives as a free people. This is the time that Isaiah speaks of in the first reading. God is doing something new by delivering God's people from Babylon. Restoring the Babylonian captives is compared to God's action in saving the people from slavery in Egypt when God opened 'a way through the sea, / a path in the great waters'. The theme is clear. Our God longs to save the downcast, brokenhearted, enslaved, and marginalised, whether this is an entire people or a woman accused of adultery and threatened with capital punishment.

to psalmist preparation: Today's psalm is a powerful message of hope in despair. Consider a person in your life who needs this message. Proclaim this psalm as if you were singing directly to this person.

PROMPTS FOR FAITH-SHARING

In the reading from Isaiah, God proclaims, 'See, I am doing a new deed'. Where do you see God's action in your life, family, or parish bringing about something new?

St. Paul writes to the Philippians, 'For him I have accepted the loss of everything, and I look on everything as so much rubbish if only I can have Christ'. How has your practice of fasting been this Lent? How has it enriched or affected your relationship with God and others?

How does your parish extend forgiveness to those who have committed a public sin?

Jesus gives us a model of mercy in today's gospel. How have you experienced giving and receiving mercy in your own life of faith?

CELEBRATION

Model Penitential Act

Presider: In today's gospel Jesus tells the accusers of the adulterous woman, 'If there is one of you who has not sinned, let him be the first to throw a stone at her'. For the times we have cast stones of accusation and condemnation at our brothers and sisters let us ask for God's mercy and forgiveness . . . [*pause*]

    Confiteor: I confess . . .

Homily Points

• We are nearing the end of Lent. Next week will be Palm Sunday and together we will read the account of Jesus's passion and death. In his letter to the Philippians, St. Paul tells us that he counts everything else in his life as 'loss' compared to 'the supreme advantage of knowing Christ Jesus my Lord'. Throughout this time of Lenten fasting, our intention has been to loosen the hold material things have over us. By removing indulgences of food, drink, and possessions, we are able to focus on what gives our life direction and purpose, our relationship with Jesus.

• Now as we come closer to Palm Sunday and the beginning of Holy Week, instead of waning, our spiritual practices of prayer, fasting, and almsgiving become even more intense. Our desire in these holiest days of the year that will soon be upon us is to be 'reproducing the pattern of [Jesus'] death', as St. Paul urges us.

• In today's gospel Jesus takes a potential act of violence (the stoning of the adulterous woman) and turns it into a moment of encounter and forgiveness. Jesus's death is another transformational moment. Within the violence of the crucifixion, Jesus's infinite love transforms the violence into the ultimate reconciliation of humanity and divinity. In longing to be conformed to Jesus's death, we are asking for the grace to become the light that is stronger than darkness, the love that is stronger than hatred, the life that is stronger than death. Let us persevere in our Lenten practices confident that the God of life will bring us to Easter joy.

Model Universal Prayer (Prayer of the Faithful)

Presider: Let us raise our prayers up to the God of mercy and compassion.

Response: Lord, hear our prayer.

That the church be a beacon of forgiveness and redemption for those condemned by society . . .

That leaders of nations enact laws that balance mercy and justice . . .

That those who have been sentenced to death within our criminal justice systems might know the Lord of life and be spared capital punishment . . .

That all of us gathered here be given the grace to forgive those who have wronged us . . .

Presider: God of infinite kindness, who redeems sinners and restores captives, hear our prayers that we might be led to Easter joy. We ask this through Christ our Lord. **Amen.**

COLLECT

Let us pray.

Pause for silent prayer

By your help, we beseech you, Lord
    our God,
may we walk eagerly in that same charity
with which, out of love for the world,
your Son handed himself over to death.
Through our Lord Jesus Christ, your Son,
who lives and reigns with you in the unity
    of the Holy Spirit,
one God, for ever and ever. **Amen.**

FIRST READING
Isa 43:16-21

Thus says the Lord,
who made a way through the sea,
a path in the great waters;
who put chariots and horse in the field
and a powerful army,
which lay there never to rise again,
snuffed out, put out like a wick:
    No need to recall the past,
    no need to think about what was
        done before.
    See, I am doing a new deed,
    even now it comes to light; can you not
        see it?
    Yes, I am making a road in the
        wilderness,
    paths in the wilds.
    The wild beasts will honour me,
    jackals and ostriches,
    because I am putting water in
        the wilderness
    (rivers in the wild)
    to give my chosen people drink.
    The people I have formed for myself
    will sing my praises.

RESPONSORIAL PSALM
Ps 125 (3)

℟. What marvels the Lord worked for us!
Indeed we were glad.

When the Lord delivered Zion
    from bondage,
it seemed like a dream.
Then was our mouth filled with laughter,
on our lips there were songs.

℟. What marvels the Lord worked for us!
Indeed we were glad.

The heathens themselves said:
    'What marvels
the Lord worked for them!'
What marvels the Lord worked for us!
Indeed we were glad.

R̸. What marvels the Lord worked for us!
Indeed we were glad.

Deliver us, O Lord, from our bondage
as streams in dry land.
Those who are sowing in tears
will sing when they reap.

R̸. What marvels the Lord worked for us!
Indeed we were glad.

They go out, they go out, full of tears,
carrying seed for the sowing:
they come back, they come back, full
    of song,
carrying their sheaves.

R̸. What marvels the Lord worked for us!
Indeed we were glad.

SECOND READING
Phil 3:8-14

I believe nothing can happen that will outweigh the supreme advantage of knowing Christ Jesus my Lord. For him I have accepted the loss of everything, and I look on everything as so much rubbish if only I can have Christ and be given a place in him. I am no longer trying for perfection by my own efforts, the perfection that comes from the Law, but I want only the perfection that comes through faith in Christ, and is from God and based on faith. All I want is to know Christ and the power of his resurrection and to share his sufferings by reproducing the pattern of his death. That is the way I can hope to take my place in the resurrection of the dead. Not that I have become perfect yet: I have not yet won, but I am still running, trying to capture the prize for which Christ Jesus captured me. I can assure you my brothers, I am far from thinking that I have already won. All I can say is that I forget the past and I strain ahead for what is still to come; I am racing for the finish, for the prize to which God calls us upwards to receive in Christ Jesus.

About Liturgy

Misery and mercy meet: In his lecture on the Gospel of John, St. Augustine beautifully describes the moment in today's gospel story when the woman and Jesus were left alone. Augustine said, *Relicti sunt duo: misera et misericordia* (Two were left: misery and mercy) (Tract 33.5). When we hear this gospel passage we often focus on the woman's sin, which is certainly serious. Yet she is not the only sinner in this story. The scribes and Pharisees were guilty of pride and anger disguised as religious piety, directed not only towards the woman but also Jesus, whom they hoped to ensnare. Although one could say that Jesus did not condemn the scribes and Pharisees for their sin, neither did Jesus offer them a word of forgiveness as he gave to the woman. Perhaps this is because the scribes and Pharisees had not recognised their own misery in the face of mercy, whereas the woman, dragged half naked into the streets to endure public scrutiny, had no choice but to stand silently in her misery.

Every time we pray the Lord's Prayer, particularly when we say, 'Forgive us our trespasses as we forgive those who trespass against us', we are given the opportunity to bring our misery before the Father, whose name is mercy. How often though do we say these words without careful attention and intention, without hearing them as a call to offer mercy as much as a plea for it?

As we pray the Lord's Prayer this week let us be even more attentive to the meaning of the words we pray so that we too might learn to act with mercy when we encounter another's misery, and thus sin no longer.

About Initiation

Presentation of the Lord's Prayer: During the Fifth Week of Lent the community of the faithful present the Lord's Prayer to the elect who will be baptised this Easter. (See RCIA 178–84.) This presentation is celebrated outside of the Sunday Mass either at a liturgy of the word or a weekday Mass. This is because the presentation has assigned readings that must be used in place of the readings for the Mass of the day. In particular, the gospel reading comes from Matthew 6:9-13 in which Jesus teaches his disciples to pray and gives them the words we use today as the Our Father. Note that the presentation is oral. No scroll or piece of paper with the prayer is given to the elect during the presentation itself. Rather, the text is handed on orally and received orally.

If the elect are unable to participate in a parish weekday Mass schedule a gathering with a group from the parish that will already be meeting that week, or plan this for the weekly parish Lenten gathering, such as your Friday soup supper or Stations of the Cross. This presentation might even work as part of your parish communal reconciliation liturgy.

About Liturgical Music

Singing the Lord's Prayer: The Lord's Prayer is a communal prayer that all recite together. Some communities will remember the Gregory Murray 1966 English chant setting. Rather more will be able to sing the Latin text with its corresponding chant also found in the missal. Even more are familiar with the Rimsky Korsakov and *Psallite* settings, which can also be sung by the choir in harmony. Others use metrical settings: there are plenty published to choose from. However, the priority is always that the assembly be able to participate in this venerable prayer. If they or visitors to the parish are unfamiliar with the musical setting you have chosen, it is better that it be spoken so that all might participate.

SPIRITUALITY

GOSPEL ACCLAMATION
Phil 2:8-9

℟. Praise to you, O Christ, king of eternal glory.
Christ was humbler yet,
even to accepting death, death on a cross.
But God raised him high
and gave him the name which is above all names.
℟. Praise to you, O Christ, king of eternal glory.

Gospel at the Procession with Palms
Luke 19:28-40

Jesus went on ahead, going up
    to Jerusalem.
When he drew near to Bethphage
    and Bethany,
at the mount that is called Olivet,
he sent two disciples,
saying, 'Go into the village
    opposite,
where on entering you will find a
    colt tied,
on which no one has ever yet sat;
untie it and bring it here.
If any one asks you,
"Why are you untying it?"
you shall say this,
"The Lord has need of it."'
So those who were sent
went away and found it as he had
    told them.
And as they were untying the colt,
its owners said to them,
'Why are you untying the colt?'
And they said,
'The Lord has need of it.'
And they brought it to Jesus,
and throwing their garments on the colt
they set Jesus upon it.
And as he rode along,
they spread their garments on the road.

Continued in Appendix A, p. 280.

Gospel at Mass   Luke 22:14–23:56;
or Luke 23:1-49 *in Appendix A, pp. 280–282.*

Reflecting on the Gospel

We are fickle creatures. We can experience happiness to the point of being ecstatic one minute and sink to the depths of despair the next. We can sing the praises of somebody now that we will despise later. There are certainly reasons for the changes in our emotions and attitudes, but there can be no dispute that our emotions and attitudes change, and sometimes quickly so.

The church attempts to capture and express this fickleness in the liturgy today when we enter with palm branches singing songs of praise, only to cry out in unison moments later during the gospel, 'Crucify him! Crucify him'! Luke's version of the passion of Jesus has several unique characteristics when compared especially with his Marcan source. For example, Luke gives us the episode of the back-and-forth between Pilate and Herod that is absent in all other gospels. Some scholars see that Luke's Christology bears even on the relationship between these two rulers, who, unwittingly through their encounter with Christ, 'had been enemies before, they were reconciled that same day'. It's as though Christ has the power to bring friendship even among those who are seeking to have him executed.

The power of Christ is also on display in this gospel when Jesus prays from the cross, 'Father, forgive them'. The distinctly Lucan theme of forgiveness is on Jesus's lips at the moment before his death. And the mercy of Jesus extends even to a criminal, which Luke relates to us in an exchange between them. Again, no other evangelist tells this story. The other evangelists simply narrate that two criminals were crucified along with Jesus.

The profundity of these two chapters (or even only one if the parish reads the shorter reading) is something that we reflect upon year after year. We will not exhaust this story. It will exhaust us, and we shall return to it to gain insight, understanding, and strength. The grand themes that Luke employed in his gospel are on full display here: mercy and forgiveness.

Let's soak up the gospel today and try to keep our fickleness in check. Let's wave palm branches and sing songs of praise without losing ourselves in a call to 'Crucify him! Crucify him'! But even if, and perhaps when, we do, we know that forgiveness awaits from a merciful God.

Living the Paschal Mystery

Perhaps the liturgical expression of palm branches followed by shouts of crucifixion has something in common with our spiritual life. When are the moments we are ecstatic? When are our palm branch and singing moments? What causes those moments? Are we caught up with the crowd? Are we praising the Messiah, or the things we want the Messiah to do? Are we caught up in expectations, or ready to be a disciple, which literally means 'to follow'?

It's much easier to sing somebody's praise when we think that person will live up to our expectations. But what happens when they do not? What happens when there is another path to follow?

The moments in our spiritual life when we cry, 'Crucify him! Crucify him'! are not likely to be 'high praise' moments. Crucifixions happen by our negligence and our selfishness. We crucify when we destroy, uproot, tear down, or otherwise extinguish life and that which is life-giving. And often we don't realise it until it's too late. But we believe in a God who brings life from death, even when we cause the death. And that is the ultimate paschal mystery.

Focusing the Gospel

Key words and phrases: This is my body which will be given for you; do this as a memorial of me.

To the point: Before the pain and horror of Good Friday, Jesus gives his disciples the key to understand what will happen to him when he celebrates the Passover with them for one last time. Though it will take on the guise of a terrible act of violence, the crucifixion will be a gift of Jesus in his totality for the salvation of the world. It is the physical enacting of Jesus's words over the bread and wine, 'This is my body, [this is my blood,] which will be given for you'. As we read the passion today let us remember the mystery we are celebrating. Jesus died, but that is not the end of the story. The sorrow of Palm Sunday leads to the overflowing joy of Easter.

Connecting the Gospel

to the first reading: Isaiah also speaks of gift: 'The Lord has given me / a disciple's tongue'. And Isaiah uses this well-trained tongue to preach a word to the weary. The words of Isaiah continue to chasten and comfort us when world-weariness infects our souls. Isaiah also gives his 'back to those who struck [him], / [his] cheeks to those who tore at [his] beard'. Just as Jesus freely gives his body and blood in the crucifixion, Isaiah's gift of his back and cheeks to his tormentors free him from their tyranny.

to experience: We often feel that we have no control in our lives. When tragedy strikes in the form of illness, the death of a loved one, or being wronged, we can become bitter and fearful. But what would happen if we followed the example of Isaiah and Jesus? Can we make a gift of what is being demanded of us?

Connecting the Responsorial Psalm

to the readings: The psalm today is Psalm 21, which begins, 'My God, my God, why have you forsaken me?' Jesus speaks these words from the cross in both the gospels of Mark and Matthew. We can see from the verses we sing today, however, that the first line of the psalm does not dictate the rest. Though the psalmist begins with this cry of despair, soon he sings, 'You who fear the Lord give him praise; / all sons of Jacob, give him glory'. In the account of the passion that we read in Luke's gospel, Jesus does not become despondent. Instead, from the cross we hear him say, just before he takes his final breath, 'Father, into your hands I commit my spirit'.

to psalmist preparation: Despair and hope live side by side in Psalm 21. The first verses bespeak the most terrible suffering. But the last verses give glory to God who does not 'stay far off' when trouble comes (NABRE). To be a disciple, one must follow Jesus to Calvary. Are you ready?

PROMPTS FOR FAITH-SHARING

The prophet Isaiah tells us, 'The Lord has given me / a disciple's tongue. / So that I may know how to reply to the wearied / he provides me with speech'. Who are the weary in your parish or community? What word do they need to hear?

St. Paul records an early hymn to Christ in his letter to the Philippians, lauding the one who 'emptied himself.' What spiritual practice helps you to empty yourself so as to make room for Jesus?

At the beginning of today's gospel we hear Luke's account of the Last Supper, when Jesus gives his body and blood, his entire self, to us. How do you experience Jesus's presence in the Eucharist?

How will you set aside your regular routine these next eight days to enter into Holy Week?

CELEBRATION

Model Penitential Act

Presider: On this feast of Palm Sunday we read from St. Paul's letter to the Philippians the ancient hymn of Jesus's glory. The Son of God emptied himself and became obedient unto death, death on a cross. Let us pause now to empty ourselves so there might be room within us for the Lord of Life to dwell . . . [*pause*]

    Confiteor: I confess . . .

Homily Points

• In last week's second reading St. Paul urged us to be conformed to the death of Christ, and today we come face to face with that death. In it Jesus once again shows us the way. Jesus shows us the way of generosity. At the Last Supper Jesus tells his disciples (then and now) that his death will be a total and complete gift of self. For what more is body and blood than a way of saying 'all of me'. Jesus holds nothing back.

• Jesus shows us the way of nonviolence. When the crowd approaches to arrest Jesus, his followers react by drawing a sword and cutting off the ear of a servant of the high priest. Jesus's response is swift. He tells them unequivocally, 'Leave off! That will do!' and heals the servant's ear. Jesus does not meet violence with violence. He meets harm with healing and hatred with love. So must we, if wish to be called his disciples.

• Jesus shows us the way of compassion. Even as he is being nailed to the cross Jesus prays, 'Father, forgive them; they do not know what they are doing'. In his own physical pain and suffering, Jesus's concern is for the spiritual welfare of his executioners. No physical pain can compare to the spiritual agony of being far from God. In the Gospel of Luke, Jesus gives us the parables of the Lost Sheep, Lost Coin, and Lost (Prodigal) Son in quick succession. The common feature of these parables? God never stops seeking the lost. Neither does Jesus, and upon the cross he finds one more lost child, the thief who asks for forgiveness and is promised paradise. May we be conformed to the way of the cross, the way of generosity, nonviolence, and compassion.

Model Universal Prayer (Prayer of the Faithful)

Presider: Clinging to God, our shelter and strength, we make our needs known.

Response: Lord, hear our prayer.

That the pope, bishops, priests, deacons, and lay ministers of the church might recommit themselves to serving the poor and outcast within society . . .

That nations of the world embrace the nonviolence of Jesus who said, 'Leave off! That will do!' at the maiming of the high priest's servant . . .

That political prisoners and victims of torture be strengthened and comforted by the passion of Jesus, the Lord of life . . .

That all those gathered here might enter into this holiest of weeks with fidelity and love . . .

Presider: Life-giving God, you are the light in our darkness. Be our strength as we journey with Jesus through his passion and death into the glory of Easter. We ask this through Christ our Lord. **Amen.**

COLLECT

Let us pray

Pause for silent prayer

Almighty ever-living God,
who as an example of humility for the
    human race to follow
caused our Saviour to take flesh and
    submit to the Cross,
graciously grant that we may heed his
    lesson of patient suffering
and so merit a share in his Resurrection.
Who lives and reigns with you in the unity
    of the Holy Spirit,
one God, for ever and ever. **Amen.**

FIRST READING

Isa 50:4-7

The Lord has given me
a disciple's tongue.
So that I may know how to reply to
    the wearied
he provides me with speech.
Each morning he wakes me to hear,
to listen like a disciple.
The Lord has opened my ear.
For my part, I made no resistance,
neither did I turn away.
I offered my back to those who struck me,
my cheeks to those who tore at my beard;
I did not cover my face
against insult and spittle.
The Lord comes to my help,
so that I am untouched by the insults.
So, too, I set my face like flint,
I know I shall not be shamed.

RESPONSORIAL PSALM

21:8-9, 17-20, 23-24 (2)

R⁊. My God, my God, why have you
forsaken me?

All who see me deride me.
They curl their lips, they toss their heads.
'He trusted in the Lord, let him save him;
let him release him if this is his friend.'

R⁊. My God, my God, why have you
forsaken me?

Many dogs have surrounded me,
a band of the wicked beset me.
They tear holes in my hands and my feet.
I can count every one of my bones.

R⁊. My God, my God, why have you
forsaken me?

They divide my clothing among them.
They cast lots for my robe.
O Lord, do not leave me alone,
my strength, make haste to help me!

R⁊. My God, my God, why have you
forsaken me?

I will tell of your name to my brethren
and praise you where they are assembled.
'You who fear the Lord give him praise;
all sons of Jacob, give him glory.
Revere him, Israel's sons.'

R⁊. My God, my God, why have you
forsaken me?

SECOND READING

Phil 2:6-11

His state was divine,
yet Christ Jesus did not cling
to his equality with God
but emptied himself
to assume the condition of a slave,
and became as men are;
and being as all men are,
he was humbler yet,
even to accepting death,
death on a cross.
But God raised him high
and gave him the name
which is above all other names
so that all beings
in the heavens, on earth and in
the underworld,
should bend the knee at the name of Jesus
and that every tongue should acclaim
Jesus Christ as Lord,
to the glory of God the Father.

About Liturgy

Proclamation of the Passion: Holy Week is unlike any other week of the year for Christians. All our usual routines that attempt to satisfy our need for convenience and efficiency take a back seat to the lavish 'waste' of our rituals this week. The extravagance of these days has no other purpose than to immerse us fully into the meaning of paschal mystery, which is inexhaustible. In that light, let us look at the proclamation of the passion, which is proclaimed today and again on Good Friday.

The first clue that this proclamation is different from other Sundays is this rubric in the Roman Missal: 'The narrative of the Lord's Passion is read without candles and without incense, with no greeting or signing of the book' (Palm Sunday 21). The absence of the usual signs of honour we give to the gospel call our attention to what truly is required in order to reverence the presence of Christ in the gospel, that is, our full attention, heart, soul, and strength, to hearing and doing the Word in our lives.

Second, the normative posture for the assembly to hear the gospel is standing. This is no different even for longer readings. If we are to give our full attention, our bodies must also be *at* attention, which is standing. Those who are too weak to remain standing for the entirety of the gospel should be given the option to be seated if they find it necessary. However, that invitation to sit should be presented as the pastoral exception for those who need it and not the normative posture for all in the assembly.

Finally, the passion reading cuts to the heart of the paschal mystery: the cross. Those who offer this proclamation given only twice a year should be among the best lectors of the parish. Ideally, the deacon or priest who leads the proclamation has rehearsed this gospel carefully as well.

A caution about enacting the gospel reading: although it is popular to dramatize this reading, the primary ritual action is proclamation and listening. Acting out the scenes of the gospel tends to distract from the primary ritual action and runs the risk of historicizing text that is meant to be *anamnetic*, that is, a memorial of a past event whose reality is fully present now.

About Initiation

Preparation rites: On Holy Saturday the elect refrain from their usual routine and spend time in prayer and reflection. RCIA 185–205 gives a possible outline for this time of preparation. Be sure to remind your elect and their godparents of these preparation rites and the schedule for the liturgies this week.

About Liturgical Music

Suggestions: Instead of putting extra energy into a choral anthem or other special musical hymn for this Sunday, consider keeping the music simple and concentrating more effort into presenting the gospel proclamation of the passion as a sung proclamation. Any proclamation of the gospel can be sung using chant tones provided in the Roman Missal. But especially today and Good Friday that option should be considered in order to highlight the unique solemnity of the liturgies of Holy Week. GIA Publications has a collection of the four passion gospels set to the traditional Vatican chants.

For simple yet beautiful assembly antiphons, look to *Psallite*'s 'Hosanna, Hosanna, Hosanna in the Highest' and 'If I Must Drink the Cup' (*Sacred Song*). The latter would be perfect as a gospel refrain for Communion, recalling Jesus's own prayer in today's passion reading. Also, 'What Wondrous Love Is This' is an excellent hymn that should be used throughout the liturgies of this week.

EASTER
TRIDUUM

How many exclaim: What a joy it would be to behold his face; even his clothing, or merely his sandals! Yet, in the Eucharist, He is the one you see, He is the one your hands touch, He is the one who becomes one flesh with you.

– John Chrysostom, *Homily on Matthew* 80 (PG 58.743)

Reflecting on the Triduum

The 'Triduum', these three sacred days are unlike any other in the liturgical year for the Christian. They carry forward an echo of faith from centuries ago and then ripple through the year with their profound theological significance. The three days are not a reenactment of events from two thousand years ago, but they make the effects of that event present in our lives today. The Triduum is a touchstone of faith to which we return year after year.

On these three days we commemorate essential and everlasting elements of our incarnational spirituality, celebrating the death and resurrection of the author of life, the Word made flesh. This is too much for one liturgy or even one day. The movements of the sacred events take place over three days so that we may enter more fully into the mysteries we celebrate.

Holy Thursday commemorates the sign of service that Jesus gave us on that night of the Last Supper. He who came not to be served but to serve is our master who set an example for us. If the master served, we too must serve. Service is a constitutive element of following the one who served to the point of giving his life. Tragic themes of betrayal by a friend, a shared meal with the knowledge of betrayal, and the lure of money make this commemoration haunting in its near universal applicability.

On Good Friday we witness the cross; there is no eucharistic prayer, but only a significant Liturgy of the Word followed by Communion. As Christians have done for centuries, we pray for the world and for many other things. The prayers of intercession are accompanied by dramatic action and even movement. This day is unlike any other, and we leave the service in silence, alone with our thoughts.

After sunset on Saturday it's as though we cannot contain the Easter joy we know will be ours and we celebrate the resurrection. Readings of promise and salvation are punctuated by psalms of praise and exaltation. Easter lilies, lights, fire, bells, a Gloria – all signify that our Lord has risen, never to be subject to death again. Life has been transformed and will never be the same now that we have this existential promise of eternity with Christ.

The Triduum is too much for one liturgy or even one day. We are given three days to enter into this profound ancient mystery. Let's give ourselves the gift of not only preparing others for this experience, but undergoing it ourselves too.

Living the Paschal Mystery

The Triduum could be said to be the ultimate commemoration of the paschal mystery. In dramatic fashion, the Author of life is handed over to death by a friend for a few pieces of silver. Anyone who has been betrayed by another knows the hurt, pain, and loss of that experience, which is felt by the psalmist who says, 'Even my trusted friend / who ate my bread, / has raised his heel against me' (Ps 41:10; NABRE). This psalm is quoted in the Gospel of John (13:18), and is certainly apropos. In addition to betrayal, we experience a sham trial, rigged 'justice' that sends an innocent person to death. It is not too much of a leap to imagine those on death row today who have been exonerated because of DNA evidence. Unfortunately the condemnation of the innocent or not guilty is with us even today. The Triduum we celebrate is not only the paschal mystery that Jesus underwent, but it is being lived out in our midst today when people are betrayed and others sent to death. It's easy to look at Jesus as an unfortunate victim of betrayal and swift justice. But his experience should cause us to see all those who face similar action. When we do nothing, or cheer for vengeance, we are like those in the crowd on these days. The paschal mystery did not happen only once two millennia ago. It continues today. With eyes of faith we can see, and we have hope for an eternal future where God's justice truly reigns.

TRIDUUM

'Triduum' is an odd-sounding word that comes from the Latin term for 'three days.' These most sacred days begin Holy Thursday evening through Friday evening (day one), include Friday evening through Saturday evening (day two), and conclude with the Easter Vigil and Easter Sunday (day three). We recall that though the modern world (like the ancient Romans) starts a day at midnight, the Jewish day starts at sundown. (And a day for the ancient Greeks started at sunrise!)

These 'three days' are the most sacred of the year. And the pinnacle liturgical celebration of the Triduum is the Easter Vigil (General Norms for the Liturgical Year and the Calendar 19). Parishes sometimes begin this only an hour after sundown. It's as though the church can't wait to celebrate Easter.

SOLEMN PASCHAL FAST

Even though Lent officially ends with the Holy Thursday liturgy, that does not mean our Lenten fast ends too. Rather, the church keeps a solemn paschal fast on Good Friday and we are encouraged to keep it on Saturday as well, in anticipation of Communion at the Easter Vigil. Only then is our fast complete and the Easter season begun. 'But the paschal fast must be kept sacrosanct. It should be celebrated everywhere on Good Friday, and where possible should be prolonged through Holy Saturday so that the faithful may attain the joys of Easter Sunday with uplifted and receptive minds' (Constitution on the Sacred Liturgy 110).

GOSPEL ACCLAMATION
John 13:34

R̶. Praise and honour to you, Lord Jesus!
I give you a new commandment:
love one another just as I have loved you, says
the Lord.
R̶. Praise and honour to you, Lord Jesus!

Gospel

John 13:1-15

It was before the festival of the Passover, and Jesus knew that the hour had come for him to pass from this world to the Father. He had always loved those who were his in the world, but now he showed how perfect his love was.

They were at supper, and the devil had already put it into the mind of Judas Iscariot son of Simon, to betray him. Jesus knew that the Father had put everything into his hands, and that he had come from God and was returning to God, and he got up from table, removed his outer garment and, taking a towel, wrapped it round his waist; he then poured water into a basin and began to wash the disciples' feet and to wipe them with the towel he was wearing.

He came to Simon Peter, who said to him, 'Lord, are you going to wash my feet?' Jesus answered, 'At the moment you do not know what I am doing, but later you will understand.' 'Never!' said Peter 'You shall never wash my feet.' Jesus replied, 'If I do not wash you, you can have nothing in common with me.' 'Then, Lord,' said Simon Peter 'not only my feet, but my hands and my head as well!' Jesus said, 'No one who has taken a bath needs washing, he is clean all over. You too are clean, though not all of you are.' He knew who was going to betray him, that was why he said, 'though not all of you are.'

Continued in Appendix, p. 283.
See Appendix, p. 283, for the other readings.

Reflecting on the Gospel and Living the Paschal Mystery

Key words and phrases: washed their feet; as I have done for you, you should also do

To the point: This evening as we celebrate the institution of the Eucharist, we listen to the sole gospel that does not include that story! The Last Supper in the Gospel of John is not the story of the Passover meal, for John situates the Last Supper on the night before Passover, as the opening verses of this evening's gospel reading indicate. Recall that the Gospel of John gives us the eloquent and sophisticated bread of life discourse in chapter 6, which effectively theologizes about the Eucharist. No Passover meal is needed at the Last Supper, especially when we consider that for this gospel, Jesus is understood to be the Lamb of God. Upon seeing Jesus for the first time, John the Baptist cried out, 'Behold, the Lamb of God' (John 1:36; NABRE). And we shall see that the crucifixion takes place on the day of preparation, when the lambs are being slaughtered in *preparation* for Passover later that night.

So the Last Supper for the Gospel of John is not about Eucharist as much as service. Jesus the master becomes the servant of his disciples, thus giving them an example. Jesus overturns the role of master so that the master is the one who serves, not the one who is served. By so doing, Jesus exemplifies a core message of the gospel, and core message of his own identity. If we are to follow Jesus, we, too, must become servants. There will never be a time when we are content to sit back, relax, and be served. Instead, we are the ones who serve, in imitation of Jesus, our master, and the one true servant of God.

To ponder and pray: Service is a constitutive element of discipleship. Without service, it is nearly impossible to be a disciple of Jesus, for to be a disciple is to be a follower, which is what the term disciple means. And since Jesus the master became the servant of others we, too, have a duty and an obligation to do the same if we are to bear the name 'disciple'. Without service, we are mere admirers of Jesus.

Liturgically, the Eucharist is where we come to be fed so that we might continue this service in the name of Jesus. Bread broken and shared becomes an apt metaphor for our lives of service in which we, like the master, become broken and shared, food for others.

The sign Jesus instituted to represent this service was the washing of the feet. And according to early church fathers, this 'sacrament' of washing the feet was carried on for many decades, if not centuries, before the church officially declared there to be only seven sacraments, with a capital 'S'. But at the liturgy today we reenact this powerful sign. We only need to consider how powerful a sign it really is when we look to the reaction caused by Pope Francis washing the feet of inmates in 2013, some of whom were beyond the strict bounds of what the then rubrics (rules) permitted, including Muslims, nonbelievers, and women. The Holy Father officially changed the rubrics in 2016 to include the option of washing women's feet in this liturgy. The example of Jesus echoes down through the ages, giving us a clarion call to service.

Model Penitential Act

Presider: In the washing of his disciples' feet, Jesus has given us a model of humility and service. As he has done, so we are to do. Let us pause to ask forgiveness for the times we have failed to serve God and one another . . .[*pause*]

Lord Jesus, you are the Lamb of God: Lord, have mercy.

Christ Jesus, you give your body and blood for the life of the world: Christ, have mercy.

Lord Jesus, you show us the way of love: Lord, have mercy.

Model Universal Prayer (Prayer of the Faithful)

Presider: On this holy night we lift our prayers and petitions up to the Lord.

Response: Lord, hear our prayer.

That all members of the church might be strengthened and sanctified by this celebration of our most sacred feast: the Holy Triduum . . .

That all the peoples of the world might know the tender, compassionate, and saving love of Christ . . .

That those preparing for baptism, confirmation, and first communion might be ever more configured to the person of Christ and welcomed lovingly into his body, the church . . .

That all gathered here might follow the model of Jesus in washing the feet of our friends and enemies in humility and love . . .

Presider: Saving God, you have called us to yourself through the witness of Jesus, your son. Hear our prayers that we might celebrate these holy days with reverence and fidelity. Through Christ our Lord. **Amen.**

About Liturgy

Memorial: In the Triduum, we remember the past events of our salvation and keep memorial of the Lord crucified, buried, and risen. Memorial, however, is not the same as going back in time. Memorial is anamnetic. We recall the past event in our present reality so as to remember and reconnect to the future hope that is already here in Christ today.

In the liturgy, if we try to re-create the past or pretend to be characters from it, we step out of the *kairos* of the heavenly liturgy and into the *chronos* of human time. On this first day of the Triduum, we might be tempted to reconstruct the past by decorating the church as if it were the Upper Room, or by inviting twelve men to represent the twelve disciples in the washing of the feet, or by re-creating the garden of Gethsemane for the reposition of the Blessed Sacrament at the end of Mass.

Instead, focus on the primary symbols of assembly: word and altar. Imagine how you can help the assembly participate fully and encounter the mystery of Christ who is active and present today.

COLLECT

Let us pray.

Pause for silent prayer

O God, who have called us to participate in this most sacred Supper, in which your Only Begotten Son, when about to hand himself over to death, entrusted to the Church a sacrifice new for all eternity, the banquet of his love, grant, we pray, that we may draw from so great a mystery, the fulness of charity and of life. Through our Lord Jesus Christ, your Son, who lives and reigns with you in the unity of the Holy Spirit, one God, for ever and ever. **Amen.**

FOR REFLECTION

• In today's gospel Jesus tells Peter, 'If I do not wash you, you can have nothing in common with me'. How has serving or being served affected your understanding of being a Christian?

• We are told, 'He had always loved those who were his in the world, but now he showed how perfect his love was'. How do you experience Jesus's love in your life?

Homily Points

• In the first two readings today we hear about remembrance. The Hebrew people are to remember every year the Passover of the Lord when the angel of death passes over the houses marked by the blood of the lamb, and the people are led to freedom through the Red Sea. In celebrating the Passover, the Jewish people render the events of the past present so that each one of them can say, I was there when the angel of death passed over. I was there at the crossing of the Red Sea.

• And so it is with us. Two thousand years after the Last Supper we are also present there. In our churches as we gather for the Eucharist whenever it is celebrated, we are present with Jesus and his disciples at the table when Jesus first said these precious words, 'This is my body . . . [this is] my blood'. We can say, I was there.

GOSPEL ACCLAMATION
Phil 2:8-9

R∕. Glory and praise to you, O Christ!
Christ was humbler yet,
even accepting death, death on a cross.
But God raised him high
and gave him the name which is above all names.
R∕. Glory and praise to you, O Christ!

Gospel John 18:1–19:42

The symbols in the following passion narrative represent:

N Narrator
J Jesus
O Other single speaker
C Crowd, or more than one speaker

N Jesus left with his disciples and crossed the Kedron valley. There was a garden there, and he went into it with his disciples. Judas the traitor knew the place well, since Jesus had often met his disciples there, and he brought the cohort to this place together with a detachment of guards sent by the chief priests and the Pharisees, all with lanterns and torches and weapons. Knowing everything that was going to happen to him, Jesus then came forward and said,

J Who are you looking for?
N They answered,
C Jesus the Nazarene.
N He said,
J I am he.
N Now Judas the traitor was standing among them. When Jesus said, 'I am he', they moved back and fell to the ground. He asked them a second time,
J Who are you looking for?
N They said,
C Jesus the Nazarene.
N Jesus replied,
J I have told you that I am he. If I am the one you are looking for, let these others go.

Continued in Appendix, pp. 284–285.
See Appendix, p. 286, for the other readings.

Reflecting on the Gospel and Living the Paschal Mystery

Key words and phrases: I am he; Crucify him; Jesus the Nazarene, King of the Jews

To the point: On this day, the only one in the liturgical year without a Mass, we have two pivotal chapters from the Gospel of John. We feast on the Word before consuming Communion. And the feast is rich. The evangelist has been called simply, 'the theologian' and that is precisely because of his profound insight into the person of Jesus, and Jesus's relationship with the Father. In today's gospel we hear the dramatic story of the trial and ultimate crucifixion of Jesus, though even with the scourging and mockery it does not seem to be much of a 'passion'. In the Gospel of John, the moment of crucifixion is the ultimate 'lifting up', 'glorification', and 'exaltation' of Jesus that has been prefigured and predicted throughout the story. Jesus knew everything that was to happen to him. Even so, it is Pilate, rather than Jesus, who displays fear. The evangelist does not dwell on how physically painful was the experience for Jesus, and the preacher is advised to do the same. The story instead is imbued with theological and christological depth, posing questions about Jesus's identity ('Where do you come from?') and even the nature of truth itself, as Pilate infamously asks, 'Truth? What is that?' Yet the entire affair is a grand fulfilment of Scripture foreseen by Jesus himself, as well as the prophets.

Irony is replete in this gospel where the crowds claim they have no king but Caesar and thereby demand the death of the author of life. Pilate's inscription over the cross, written in mockery, is absolutely true. Jesus is a king; yet his kingdom is not of this world. Pilate claims to have power over life and death but does not know truth. The disciples who have been with Jesus throughout his ministry seek first to fight with a sword only to scatter moments later. Then, when Peter is faced with temptation, the simple yet profound question as to whether he knows Jesus, he melts like wax under a flame of inquisition. The public humiliation of Jesus on the cross is in reality his victory, as foretold by Scripture. The ways of the world are being upended.

To ponder and pray: Rather than a play to be reenacted, the Gospel of John gives us the eternal Word, sacred Scripture, on which to gnaw. It is good for us to ponder this lengthy reading and the profound insights it displays. Each Good Friday we read this passion narrative culminating in the death but ultimate exaltation of Jesus. Jesus is the eternal Word made flesh, because God so loved the world. And yet the world does not respond in kind. Instead, the world executes the Word made flesh. Perfect love made incarnate is killed on a cross by us who prefer a king like Caesar to the author of life who comes to serve. When faced with love we crush it underfoot claiming not to know, 'Truth? What is that?' But now we have the opportunity to reflect on this drama that happened not only two millennia ago, but each and every day. When we encounter the lowly and downtrodden, those who are trampled underfoot by the state, or religious authorities, or any system, what is our response? Do we argue away our responsibility, claiming like Peter not to know Jesus in our midst? Or are we like Pilate and engage in philosophical speculation and shuck responsibility? The death and exaltation of Jesus should cause us to reexamine our values. To follow the master, to be a disciple, is to follow the example of service. And that service pours itself out for another to the point of ultimate exhaustion and self-sacrifice, which is itself our glory.

About Liturgy

The Holy Cross: On this second day of the Triduum we turn our full gaze towards the Cross. Just as we adored the Blessed Sacrament the night before, on this night, we behold and adore the wood on which hung the Saviour of the world.

This showing of the cross at the liturgy of the passion of the Lord can take two forms. In the first form, the covered cross in the sanctuary is gradually unveiled by the priest as a deacon or the choir sings an acclamation. In the second form, the priest or deacon processes the veiled cross from the door of the church through the assembly to the sanctuary, stopping at various points to unveil a portion of the cross. The one carrying the cross leads the sung acclamation. Note that this second form parallels the stational procession with the paschal candle that will take place the following night at the Easter Vigil.

The Roman Missal directs that there be only one cross offered for adoration. Also, at the end of the liturgy the cross remains in the church with four lit candles so that people may stay to pray before it.

About Liturgical Music

Enlivening the Passion: If the passion is not sung, a considerable number of parishes insert sung interludes into the passion reading, acting as meditation points. A good hymn for this purpose is 'O Sacred Head' to the PASSION CHORALE: use one verse for each interlude.

A sense of progression: The mood of this service moves from passion and death to the triumph of the cross and resurrection. Although you might sing the Peter Jones *Reproaches* or the Iona Commnity's 'Lord Jesus Christ, shall I stand still / and stare at you hung on the tree' during the veneration of the Cross, during Communion consider a hymn such as 'Sing my tongue the glorious battle' (the other *Pange, lingua* text!) or 'What Wondrous Love Is This,' already mentioned above on Palm Sunday.

COLLECT
Let us pray.

Remember your mercies, O Lord,
and with your eternal protection sanctify your servants,
for whom Christ your Son,
by the shedding of his Blood,
established the Paschal Mystery.
Who lives and reigns for ever and ever.
Amen.

or:

O God, who by the Passion of Christ your Son, our Lord,
abolished the death inherited from ancient sin
by every succeeding generation,
grant that just as, being conformed to him,
we have borne by the law of nature
the image of the man of earth,
so by the sanctification of grace
we may bear the image of the Man of heaven.
Through Christ our Lord.
Amen.

FOR REFLECTION

• On Good Friday we pause at this moment when Jesus breathes his last and is placed in the tomb. How do you keep the stillness of Good Friday?

Homily Points

• A few days before his crucifixion Jesus gives his disciples a new and cryptic parable, '[U]nless a grain of wheat falls to the ground and dies, it remains just a grain of wheat; but if it dies, it produces much fruit' (John 12:24; NABRE). And now as we are gathered around the foot of the cross we look on as the grain falls to the ground and dies.

• There is a stillness to Good Friday. All the earth witnesses the death of the grain of wheat. And all the earth holds its breath in anticipation of the fruit it will bear.

Gospel   Luke 24:1-12

On the first day of week, at the first sign of dawn, the women went to the tomb with the spices they had prepared. They found that the stone had been rolled away from the tomb, but on entering discovered that the body of the Lord Jesus was not there. As they stood there not knowing what to think, two men in brilliant clothes suddenly appeared at their side. Terrified, the women lowered their eyes. But the two men said to them, 'Why look among the dead for someone who is alive? He is not here; he has risen. Remember what he told you when he was still in Galilee: that the Son of Man had to be handed over into the power of sinful men and be crucified, and rise again on the third day?' And they remembered his words.

When the women returned from the tomb they told all this to the Eleven and to all the others. The women were Mary of Magdala, Joanna, and Mary the mother of James. The other women with them also told the apostles, but this story of theirs seemed pure nonsense, and they did not believe them.

Peter, however, went running to the tomb. He bent down and saw the binding cloths, but nothing else; he then went back home, amazed at what had happened.

See Appendix A, pp. 287–291, for the other readings.

Reflecting on the Gospel and Living the Paschal Mystery

Key words and phrases: [Empty] tomb, first sign of dawn, women, Mary of Magdala

To the point: Easter morning was a time of confusion. The women who had come with Jesus from Galilee only a few days earlier were now prepared to anoint his crucified, dead body. But they would find instead an empty tomb and two men. Though Luke says they were in dazzling garments, and that has been understood to mean angels, he clearly calls them 'men'. Matthew, on the other hand, tells his readers that there was an angel who came down from heaven to roll away the stone and then speak to the women, for the guards were struck with fear (Matt 28:1-5). But this is one instance where Matthew has the better story, simply in terms of clearing up any perceived anomalies. Were the men really angels? How was the stone rolled away? Why were there no guards? These are all questions one might rightly ask after reading Luke's account. But in the end Luke's account was not written to convince an unbeliever, but to give 'certainty' to the faith of the believer (Luke 1:1-4; NABRE).

The confusion experienced by those early disciples is perhaps something of the confusion we might have upon reading the various narratives of Easter morning. Each evangelist tells the tale with certain differences. Ultimately, each is convinced that Jesus rose from the dead to eternal life.

Despite Jesus's having foretold this event, it seems to have taken the disciples and his friends by surprise. They were not expecting a resurrection after all. Interestingly too, the women are the first to find the empty tomb, and among them, Mary Magdalene. Luke, who is the one evangelist to tell us more stories about women than any other, is also the one to tell us the most about Mary Magdalene. In the first three verses of chapter 8, Luke related how the women from Galilee were providing for Jesus and his followers out of their resources. The women seem to have been wealthy, and this might explain how Jesus and the Twelve could have travelled throughout Galilee during his ministry seemingly without a way to make money. They were being supported by these rich women! Luke also tells us how the women witnessed the events of the crucifixion (Luke 23:49) and saw where his body was laid (Luke 23:55). It should be no surprise then that in Luke's telling it was the women (rather than the disciples) who came upon the empty tomb first. This is why church fathers referred to Mary Magdalene as *apostola apostolorum* (apostle to the apostles). Out of the confusion of Easter morning, Mary Magdalene and her female companions were the first to preach the good news.

To ponder and pray: The ways of God are not our ways. How often do we make plans, have expectations, and firm ideas only to have them dashed? With hindsight we can see more clearly that perhaps our understanding of a situation was not entirely complete. We lacked a critical piece of information or a crucial perspective. This might be something similar to what happened with the disciples and the women who followed Jesus from Galilee. The first to make sense of the empty tomb were the women, and it's likely because they had accompanied Jesus throughout this time. Not only that, they witnessed the crucifixion and the deposition of the body. They returned after Passover to perform a kind of ministry and their expectations were shattered. Soon they 'remembered his words' and ran to announce the good news to the eleven and the others. On this Easter morning let us sit before the empty tomb, ponder his words, then go out to announce the good news. In so doing, we will follow the example of the earliest apostles, the women followers of Jesus.

Model Universal Prayer (Prayer of the Faithful)

Presider: With Easter joy we lift up our prayers to the God of light and life.

Response: Lord, hear our prayer.

That the church embody the good news of the gospel that life is stronger than death, light is stronger than darkness, and love is stronger than hatred . . .

That all the peoples of the world be drawn together in peace and communion . . .

That those who have been baptised this night might know the light and love of Jesus alive within them, now and always . . .

That all gathered here, renewed in our baptismal promises, might go forwards to be light which brightens the darkness of our world . . .

Presider: God of everlasting life and light, throughout history you have led your people from darkness to light, from death to life, from despair to joy. Hear our prayers on this holy night that we might proclaim the good news of the resurrection with our lives. Through Christ our Lord. **Amen.**

About Liturgy

Why darkness matters: One of the most important directives to come from the restoration of the Triduum liturgies is that the entire Easter Vigil must take place after nightfall (Roman Missal, Easter Vigil 3). Prior to this, it was not uncommon for parishes to celebrate the Easter Vigil on Holy Saturday morning. Imagine lighting the paschal fire in the bright of day, proclaiming how the light of Christ has dispelled the darkness! No wonder so many parishes have become content with tiny paschal fires. When darkness doesn't matter, neither does the fire.

Today, most parishes wait until the evening. However many of these will still begin their vigil while daylight remains on the horizon. Though it may technically be nightfall, the intent of the lighting of the paschal fire is clear. We must show fully by our symbols how the light of Christ has dispelled not just partial darkness but the complete and overwhelming darkness of death, a darkness we cannot control.

The exact time for total darkness depends on your location. So check your local sunset timetables. Also turn off any unnecessary exterior lights near the place of your paschal fire.

COLLECT
Let us pray.

Pause for silent prayer

O God, who make this most sacred night radiant with the glory of the Lord's Resurrection, stir up in your Church a spirit of adoption, so that, renewed in body and mind, we may render you undivided service. Through our Lord Jesus Christ, your Son, who lives and reigns with you in the unity of the Holy Spirit, one God, for ever and ever. **Amen.**

FOR REFLECTION

• 'Why look among the dead for someone who is alive?' the men in dazzling garments ask. How is God calling you to new life and to embrace the good news of the resurrection?

• Lent is over and the Easter season of joy and celebration has begun. How will you keep this season?

Homily Points

• Tonight we gather to sit vigil and hear the story of salvation proclaimed anew. From the seven days of creation, to the crossing of the Red Sea, to the voices of the prophets, we listen to the greatest love story ever told. God, who created the world and proclaimed it good, continues to redeem and restore it when darkness, death, and despair threaten to destroy everything.

• The waters of baptism are blessed tonight after we hear St. Paul tell us, 'When we were baptised in Christ Jesus we were baptised in his death'. This hardly seems to be the triumphant proclamation of Easter, until we hear the words of the mysterious men at the empty tomb who ask the women, 'Why look among the dead for someone who is alive? He is not here; he has risen'. Death does not have the last word. We are baptised into the death of Christ and so rise with him in the light of the resurrection. Alleluia!

GOSPEL ACCLAMATION
1 Cor 5:7-8

R̶/. Alleluia, alleluia!
Christ, our passover, has been sacrificed;
let us celebrate the feast then, in the Lord.
R̶/. Alleluia!

Gospel

John 20:1-9

It was very early on the first day of the week and still dark, when Mary of Magdala came to the tomb. She saw that the stone had been moved away from the tomb and came running to Simon Peter and the other disciple, the one Jesus loved. 'They have taken the Lord out of the tomb' she said 'and we don't know where they have put him.'

So Peter set out with the other disciple to go to the tomb. They ran together, but the other disciple, running faster than Peter, reached the tomb first; he bent down and saw the linen cloths lying on the ground, but did not go in. Simon Peter who was following now came up, went right into the tomb, saw the linen cloths on the ground, and also the cloth that had been over his head; this was not with the linen cloths but rolled up in a place by itself. Then the other disciple who had reached the tomb first also went in; he saw and he believed. Till this moment they had failed to understand the teaching of scripture, that he must rise from the dead.

See Appendix, p. 292, for the other readings.

Reflecting on the Gospel and Living the Paschal Mystery
Key words and phrases: Mary of Magdala; rise from the dead; [empty] tomb; disciple, the one Jesus loved

To the point: The Fourth Gospel gives us many takes on the stories about the life and ministry of Jesus. Now with the story of the discovery of the empty tomb we have another story. Though Luke tells us that Mary Magdalene (in the Gospel of John: Mary of Magdala) and other women were the first to encounter the empty tomb, that story also had two men 'in brilliant clothes' speaking to the women. In John's account Mary seems to be alone, and upon finding the stone turned away, she runs to Simon Peter and the disciple whom Jesus loved. We need to read further in the gospel than what we hear in today's liturgy to find out more about Mary's role on that morning. The gospel reading for today is content to have Mary fetch Peter and the other disciple. We hear no more about her.

And though Luke tells us in one verse, which happens to be missing from many ancient manuscripts, that Peter found the tomb empty, John tells us that he was accompanied by the disciple whom Jesus loved. And it is he, this latter disciple, who is the first to believe, even though neither he nor Peter at that time understood the Scripture about rising from the dead.

So this becomes something of a model of faith. We, like the beloved disciple, believe before we understand completely. Upon believing, we spend the rest of our lives contemplating the mystery of faith. And like the Beloved Disciple we are led to faith by another, in this case Mary of Magdala. She is the one who indicates that the stone was rolled away. She points to something that needs to be explored, investigated. And once the Beloved Disciple has that encounter the response is faith.

To ponder and pray: How often do we say yes before completely understanding the ramifications of our assent? How often does something simply feel right and we dive in before we have a complete picture of what's at stake? That might happen upon falling in love, having a child, or making another sort of life commitment. Once made, these decisions and commitments alter the course of our lives.

In the case of the Beloved Disciple, once he encountered the empty tomb he believed even before he understood. It's quite likely that he spent the rest of his life pondering the events of Jesus's life, death, and ultimate resurrection, drawing connections between the Scriptures and what he had witnessed. The entirety of Jesus is something we can never fully comprehend or understand, much like we can never fully comprehend or understand any human being. At the centre of each is mystery.

On this Easter Day, let us sit with Simon Peter and the Beloved Disciple in the empty tomb, having been drawn there by Mary. Let us ponder the meaning of this extraordinary event and believe. We have the rest of our lives to unpack and better understand what that entails.

Model Penitential Act

Presider: Christ is risen, alleluia! We gather together on this feast of life that is stronger than death and ask the Lord to bring light to the darkness within us. . .[*pause*]

> Lord Jesus, you rose from the tomb, conquering death forever: Lord, have mercy.
> Christ Jesus, you call us to proclaim the Good News to everyone we meet: Christ, have mercy.
> Lord Jesus, you reign at the right hand of God: Lord, have mercy.

Model Universal Prayer (Prayer of the Faithful)

Presider: On this day of joy, we dare to bring our needs and petitions to the God of everlasting life.

Response: Lord, hear our prayer.

That the leaders of the church be examples of faith and hope for all those who doubt . . .

That the world be renewed by the light and life of Christ . . .

That all those who were baptised at the Easter Vigil experience the abundant life of the risen Lord . . .

That all gathered here be strengthened in our baptismal vocation to proclaim Christ to everyone we meet . . .

Presider: God of light and life, you called us by name and washed us clean in the waters of baptism. May we grow more Christlike with each day. We ask this through your son Jesus, our Lord. **Amen.**

About Liturgy

Endings and beginnings: Triduum doesn't end after the Easter Vigil or even after the Masses on Easter Sunday. The three days of the Triduum are counted from nightfall on Thursday to nightfall on Friday (day 1); nightfall Friday to nightfall Saturday (day 2); and nightfall Saturday to nightfall Sunday (day 3). Thus, the General Norms of the Liturgical Year and the Calendar says that the Triduum ends with evening prayer on Easter Sunday (19).

You will probably be exhausted by the time Easter Sunday comes, and having one more liturgy to prepare really isn't feasible. But consider giving your parishioners a simplified Evening Prayer outline to use at home on Sunday night to end the Triduum. This can be as simple as giving them the words of Psalm 117, a brief Scripture reading, and the text for the *Magnificat.* When people gather for Easter dinner at home on this day, they can use this to conclude the three days in a simple but prayerful way.

Easter Sunday also begins the Easter Octave, eight days of solemnities that extend the joy of Easter Sunday. Be sure to highlight the special nature of these daily Masses of the octave.

COLLECT
Let us pray.

Pause for silent prayer

O God, who on this day,
through your Only Begotten Son,
have conquered death
and unlocked for us the path to eternity,
grant, we pray, that we who keep
the solemnity of the Lord's Resurrection
may, through the renewal brought by your Spirit,
rise up in the light of life.
Through our Lord Jesus Christ, your Son,
who lives and reigns with you in the unity of
the Holy Spirit,
one God, for ever and ever. **Amen.**

FOR REFLECTION

• At the empty tomb the Beloved Disciple believes but does not yet understand. What mysteries of faith do you lack understanding of? How might God be calling you to strengthen your belief?

• How are you being called to live deeper into this mystery of life coming from death?

Homily Points

• Peter and the Beloved Disciple race to the tomb and once they arrive find it empty except for the burial cloths. These trappings of death lie in the tomb but the body they swaddled is nowhere to be found. These mysterious happenings hint that the story of Jesus's life is not over, but the disciples '[t]ill this moment . . . had failed to understand the teaching of scripture, that he must rise from the dead'. Today we gather with cries of 'Alleluia, he is risen'! But the question remains for us, do we, even now, nearly two thousand years after the event, understand the rising from the dead?

• Surely, it defies understanding. How can one who has been confirmed dead and lain within a tomb for three days be 'raised'? How can life return stronger than death? And yet, we are resurrection people, called to proclaim the death and resurrection of Christ in our words, actions, and very being. If we truly believe in this audacious event it changes everything.

SEASON OF EASTER

SPIRITUALITY

GOSPEL ACCLAMATION
John 20:29

R⒵. Alleluia, alleluia!
Jesus said: 'You believe because you can see me.
Happy are those who have not seen and
        yet believe.'
R⒵. Alleluia!

Gospel John 20:19-31

In the evening of that same day, the first day
of the week, the doors were closed in the
room where the disciples were, for fear of the
Jews. Jesus came and stood among them. He
said to them 'Peace be with you,' and showed
them his hands and his side. The disciples
were filled with joy when they saw the Lord,
and he said to them again, 'Peace be with you.

    'As the Father sent me,
    so am I sending you.'
After saying this he breathed on them
and said:
    'Receive the Holy Spirit.
    For those whose sins you forgive,
    they are forgiven;
    for those whose sins you retain,
    they are retained.'
Thomas, called the Twin, who was one of
the Twelve, was not with them when Jesus
came. When the disciples said, 'We have
seen the Lord,' he answered, 'Unless I see
the holes that the nails made in his hands
and can put my finger into the holes they
made, and unless I can put my hand into his
side, I refuse to believe.' Eight days later
the disciples were in the house again and
Thomas was with them. The doors were
closed, but Jesus came in and stood among
them. 'Peace be with you,' he said. Then he
spoke to Thomas, 'Put your finger here; look,
here are my hands. Give me your hand; put
it into my side. Doubt no longer but believe.'
Thomas replied, 'My Lord and my God!'
Jesus said to him:
    'You believe because you can see me.
    Happy are those who have not seen and
        yet believe.'
There were many other signs that Jesus
worked and the disciples saw, but they are
not recorded in this book. These are recorded
so that you may believe that Jesus is the
Christ, the Son of God, and that believing
this you may have life through his name.

Reflecting on the Gospel
The Second Sunday of Easter, which the church calls Divine Mercy Sunday, is
punctuated by a reading from John, the conclusion of that gospel. Of course,
if we open our Bibles we will see that there is another chapter (John 21) that
follows this conclusion (John 20:30-31), but that chapter is usually referred to as
an epilogue, as it was written later by another author. Indeed, simply reading
the closing verses of today's gospel gives one the sense that the story is over,
the gospel is complete. Thomas makes a christological claim *par excellence*,
addressing Jesus as, 'My Lord and my God'! With that, the gospel rightfully and

elegantly comes to a close. How strange
it is that there is yet another chapter! Yes,
that's the epilogue.

But in today's gospel reading Thomas
encounters the risen Christ the week
after the initial resurrection appearance.
He has been called 'doubting Thomas',
even though the word 'doubt' does not
appear in the story. Still, it's clear Thomas
was hesitant to believe. More than one
preacher has likened Thomas's attitude
to a 'show me' scepticism. His belief is
conditioned on physically inspecting
the risen Christ. And yet, the story does
not say that when given the opportunity
Thomas actually probed the nail marks
or put his hand in Jesus's side. Instead, upon encountering the risen Christ he
immediately proclaims, 'My Lord and my God'! What the reader has known from
the opening verses of the gospel – 'In the beginning was the Word, / and the
Word was with God, / and the Word was God. . . . And the Word became flesh'
(John 1:1, 14; NABRE) – is effectively proclaimed by a human being, Thomas.
Then Jesus appropriately has the last word, and the gospel concludes with two
verses from the author.

Moreover, it is significant that Roman historians tell us that the emperor
Domitian (r. 81–96) gave himself the title, 'Dominus et Deus' (Lord and God; cf.
Suetonius, Domitian 13.2). If the author of the Gospel of John knew about this
imperial claim, he would be effectively undermining it by showing that Jesus
is the true Lord and God. The Gospel of John has a profound Christology. The
closing verses of chapter 20 give us some indication as to why.

Living the Paschal Mystery
In the Fourth Gospel, knowledge of Jesus as the Son of God, the Word made
flesh, is fundamental to being a disciple. In some ways, belief is as important as
another commandment in the Gospel of John: love. This axis of belief and love
informs our identity as disciples as well. In many ways it is a fine summation
of the Christian life, bypassing other terms like 'righteousness', 'Trinity', and
other theologically sophisticated words. Once we believe in the Son of God
and love one another as he loves us, our life is complete. We then unfold this
relationship day after day, week after week, month after month, and year after
year. Neither 'belief' nor 'love' know fulfilment. There is always more, there is
always a frontier, a horizon we never reach. As human beings we can never
achieve perfect belief or perfect love. But the pursuit of both is lifelong. On

this Second Sunday of Easter when we encounter divine mercy, we recall the simplicity yet profundity of the gospel message: Believe and love.

Focusing the Gospel
Key words and phrases: Peace be with you.

To the point: In our gospel passage today Jesus speaks the words 'Peace be with you' three times. When we hear the word 'peace', we often think of it as the absence of war or conflict, but the meaning of *shalom* (the Hebrew word for peace) denotes the presence of something instead of an absence. To offer someone peace in Jesus's time meant to wish him or her a completeness and fulness of life. Earlier in John's gospel Jesus proclaims that he has come that we 'might have life and have it more abundantly' (10:10; NABRE). Despite the locks the disciples had placed upon the door, Jesus enters the room in which they are barricaded and says to them, 'Peace be with you'. Their fear cannot keep him away. Once again he stands before them, offering them abundant life.

Connecting the Gospel
to the first reading: Throughout the Easter season we read the Acts of the Apostles, the story of the early church. In today's first reading we hear of the fruitfulness of the apostle's evangelising mission in which many men and women are added to their number and people are cured, but also of the persecution they undergo when they are put in jail. But just as Jesus passes through locked doors unimpeded, the apostles cannot be contained by a jail cell. The angel of the Lord opens the prison doors and leads them out.

to experience: Fear, anger, and jealousy are no match for the love, peace, and mercy of God. God's spirit of love and peace breaks down barriers and calls us to true communion with one another.

Connecting the Responsorial Psalm
to the readings: As we did on Easter Sunday, again we hear the triumphant chant of Psalm 117. The psalm begins with a litany whose response is 'His love has no end'. In the gospel we see that God's mercy indeed endures forever, even beyond the grave and the end of earthly life. Jesus returns to his disciples and the first words he speaks to them are, 'Peace be with you'. This might not have been the greeting they expected. During Jesus's passion and crucifixion Peter had denied knowing him three times, and we only hear of one man, the unnamed Beloved Disciple who is present at the foot of the cross. But far from anger or bitterness, Jesus greets his closest followers with joy and love. 'Peace be with you'. And thus redeemed, Jesus invites them to become instruments of mercy, 'For those whose sins you forgive, / they are forgiven; / for those whose sins you retain, / they are retained'.

to psalmist preparation: Today is a day of exultation. In the death and resurrection of Jesus, the paschal mystery, we have been offered everlasting life and freedom from sin. The divine mercy of our God is the balm our broken world desperately craves. As you lead the assembly in prayer today, pray for mercy to cover the earth.

PROMPTS FOR FAITH-SHARING

In today's first reading the apostles carry on the work of Jesus, performing signs and wonders as the Holy Spirit enables them. We are also called to carry on Jesus's work. How do you proclaim the good news of the resurrection in your everyday life?

Jesus tells the disciples, 'Peace be with you', three times in today's gospel. Where in your life are you in need of the peace of the Lord?

How do you offer peace to others through your words and actions?

We are offered mercy and also instructed to offer it to others. Who is in need of mercy in your life? How might you offer them this gift?

CELEBRATION

Model Rite for the Blessing and Sprinkling of Water

Presider: In the waters of baptism we have been buried with Christ, the one who tells St. John in Apocalypse, '[I]t is I, the First and the Last; / I am the Living One'. May this water remind us of the life that conquers death . . . [*pause*]

   [*continue with* The Roman Missal, *Appendix II*]

Homily Points

• Today is not only the Second Sunday of Easter but also the completion of the octave of Easter and the feast of Divine Mercy. In the year 2000, St. Pope John Paul II established this feast. On the first anniversary of the founding of Divine Mercy Sunday, John Paul II recalled, 'Jesus said to St. Faustina one day: "Humanity will never find peace until it turns with trust to Divine Mercy".' Divine Mercy! This is the Easter gift that the Church receives from the risen Christ and offers to humanity'.

• Jesus enters the room where the apostles are hiding in fear and offers them peace, the peace of God that surpasses understanding (Phil 4:7). And then he gives them a commission, 'Receive the Holy Spirit. / For those whose sins you forgive, / they are forgiven; / for those whose sins you retain, / they are retained'. The apostles are not offered peace merely for themselves. In receiving this peace they are in turn to bear peace to others.

• In the spiritual life every action begins with God's initiative. God speaks and we listen. God gives a gift and we receive it. Only after God's action can we form a response. On Divine Mercy Sunday we must celebrate this twofold movement. God offers us Divine Mercy, which we are invited to receive and then pass on to others. Individually in our lives and collectively as the church, the Body of Christ, we experience mercy as a transformational gift from God. Now it's our job to offer it to humanity.

Model Universal Prayer (Prayer of the Faithful)

Presider: Jesus greets the disciples gathered in the upper room, 'Peace be with you'. In confidence we pray for the peace of the Lord.

Response: Lord, hear our prayer.

That the church might have the resources to deal with conflict in grace . . .

That leaders of the world band together to forge lasting peace . . .

That refugees from war-torn countries find welcome, shelter, and safety in their new homes . . .

That all of us gathered here know the peace of the Lord that banishes all fear . . .

Presider: God of mercy and love, you call us to live in harmony with one another. Show us the path of peace. We offer our prayers through Christ our Lord. **Amen.**

COLLECT

Let us pray.

Pause for silent prayer

God of everlasting mercy,
who in the very recurrence of the
      paschal feast
kindle the faith of the people you have
      made your own,
increase, we pray, the grace you
      have bestowed,
that all may grasp and rightly understand
in what font they have been washed,
by whose Spirit they have been reborn,
by whose Blood they have been redeemed.
Through our Lord Jesus Christ, your Son,
who lives and reigns with you in the unity
      of the Holy Spirit,
one God, for ever and ever. **Amen.**

FIRST READING

Acts 5:12-16

The faithful all used to meet by common consent in the Portico of Solomon. No one else even dared to join them, but the people were loud in their praise and the numbers of men and women who came to believe in the Lord increased steadily. So many signs and wonders were worked among the people at the hands of the apostles and the sick were even taken out into the streets and laid on beds and sleeping-mats in the hope that at least the shadow of Peter might fall across some of them as he went past. People even came crowding in from the towns round about Jerusalem, bringing with them their sick and those tormented by unclean spirits, and all of them were cured.

RESPONSORIAL PSALM

Ps 117:2-4, 15-18, 22-24 (1)

R̶. Give thanks to the Lord for he is good, for his love has no end.
   or:
R̶. Alleluia, alleluia, alleluia!

Let the sons of Israel say:
'His love has no end.'
Let the sons of Aaron say:
'His love has no end.'
Let those who fear the Lord say:
'His love has no end.'

R̶. Give thanks to the Lord for he is good, for his love has no end.
   or:
R̶. Alleluia, alleluia, alleluia!

The stone which the builders rejected
has become the corner stone.
This is the work of the Lord
a marvel in our eyes.
This day was made by the Lord;
we rejoice and are glad.

R̶/. Give thanks to the Lord for he is good,
for his love has no end.
  or:
R̶/. Alleluia, alleluia, alleluia!

O Lord, grant us salvation;
O Lord, grant success.
Blessed in the name of the Lord
is he who comes.
We bless you from the house of the Lord;
the Lord God is our light.

R̶/. Give thanks to the Lord for he is good,
for his love has no end.
  or:
R̶/. Alleluia, alleluia, alleluia!

SECOND READING
Apoc 1:9-11, 17-19

My name is John, and through our union
in Jesus I am your brother and share your
sufferings, your kingdom, and all you
endure. I was on the island of Patmos
for having preached God's word and
witnessed for Jesus; it was the Lord's day
and the Spirit possessed me, and I heard a
voice behind me, shouting like a trumpet,
'Write down all that you see in a book.' I
turned round to see who had spoken to
me, and when I turned I saw seven golden
lamp-stands and, surrounded by them, a
figure like a Son of man, dressed in a long
robe tied at the waist with a golden girdle.

When I saw him, I fell in a dead faint at
his feet, but he touched me with his right
hand and said, 'Do not be afraid; it is I, the
First and the Last; I am the Living One.
I was dead and now I am to live for ever
and ever, and I hold the keys of death and
of the underworld. Now write down all
that you see of present happenings and
things that are still to come.'

About Liturgy

Putting on our 'mystagoggles': In all three cycles of the Lectionary, the Second
Sunday of Easter presents to us this gospel passage from John that recalls Thomas's
conversion from sceptical doubter to professor of faith. I can think of no other non-
thematic Sunday that has the same gospel every year. What might this mean?

I think the key is Jesus's final statement: 'Happy are those who have not seen and yet
believe' (John 20:29). He's talking about *us*! This is a blessing specifically for *us*! None
of the disciples who walked with Jesus are as blessed as we who have never seen him
face to face. This is the blessing of faith – to believe not with our eyes but with our
heart. When you love a person completely and know that you are completely loved,
everything looks different. The sky is bluer, the daylight clearer, even the people you
meet on the street seem friendlier. Is it because the world has changed? No, you have
changed. You've been given a new way of seeing so that you see all creation as God
sees it – blessed. You've been given mystagoggles!

The church teaches that during the period of mystagogy, the newly baptised 'derive
a new perception of the faith, of the Church, and of the world' out of their experience
of the sacraments, and this new way of seeing 'increases as it is lived' (RCIA 245). The
neophytes, fresh from the font, can't help but see Christ everywhere, just as newlyweds
can see and think of only their beloved. But for us who may not be so fresh in our
faith, our 'mystagoggles' might have clouded, and we sound more like Thomas the
sceptic than Thomas the believer.

The Easter season is a time for all of us with the neophytes to train our eyes to see
the world sacramentally. When we put on our 'mystagoggles', every meal is the supper
of the Lord, every wound is the brand mark of Christ, and every moment of doubt is
an invitation to cry in faith, 'My Lord and my God'!

About Initiation

Postbaptismal catechesis: The catechesis that takes place during this period of
mystagogy is unlike the catechesis during the catechumenate in that 'its main setting
is the so-called Masses for neophytes, that is, the Sunday Masses of the Easter season'
(RCIA 247). Let the Sunday Masses this Easter season be the primary gathering for
your neophytes and their godparents, and be sure that these Masses are the best of the
year, for they are how the neophytes are catechised to live as new 'Christs' in the world.

About Liturgical Music

Easter's long tail: The first few weeks of the Easter season revel in the joy of the
Resurrection. These weeks are a bit like the temporary high you feel from a mountaintop experience. As the season progresses, that joy is transformed into a more constant
and steadfast call to witness and mission into the world driven by the Spirit. As you
prepare your music and music ministers, keep in mind that the Triduum was not the
final objective for all your liturgical efforts this year. Rather, it was the summit that
now propels us towards Pentecost and beyond. Help your music ministers keep their
focus towards that goal so that the energy you inspired from them in the Triduum
keeps building throughout the weeks of Easter.

A delightful antiphon to use for Communion today is *Psallite*'s 'Put Your Hand Here,
Thomas'. Pairing these words with the act of sharing in the Body and Blood of Christ
deepens our view of whom we are receiving and what we are called to do in faith.

ST. GEORGE, MARTYR, PATRON OF ENGLAND

GOSPEL ACCLAMATION
Jm 1:12

R̷. Alleluia, alleluia!
Happy the man who stands firm,
for he has proved himself,
and will win the crown of life.
R̷. Alleluia!

Gospel

John 15:18-21

Jesus said to his disciples:
'If the world hates you,
remember that it hated me
before you.
If you belonged to the world,
the world would love you as its own;
but because you do not belong to
the world,
because my choice withdrew you
from the world,
therefore the world hates you.
Remember the words I said to you:
A servant is not greater than
his master.
If they persecuted me,
they will persecute you too;
if they kept my word,
they will keep yours as well.
But it will be on my account that
they will do all this,
because they do not know the one
who sent me.'

or John 15:1-8 in Appendix, p. 293.

See Appendix, p. 293, for the other readings.

Reflecting on the Gospel

On this feast of St. George, we have some hard-hitting words from the Gospel of John. Generally, we teach our children to avoid words like 'hate', but today's gospel begins with that stark term. This portion of the gospel (chaps. 15–17) was likely written later than the rest of the work. One clue is that chapter 14 concludes with Jesus saying to his disciples, 'I will no longer speak much with you/for the ruler of the world is coming' (John 14:30; NABRE). But then he speaks for three more chapters! If chapters 15–17 were not there, chapter 14 would flow directly to John 18:1 which reads, 'When he had said this, Jesus went out with this disciples across the Kidron valley . . .' (John 18:1; NABRE). This is only one reason many scholars believe chapters 15–17 were added later, reflecting a time of persecution, or at least hostility vis-a-vis the world. Thus, this section includes the language of the world hating the disciples, or even more starkly, 'the world hates you' (John 15:19). The passage reminds the disciples that the world hated Jesus too, and he ultimately faced crucifixion.

Legends about St. George abound but there is little historical evidence that goes back to this figure. He is the patron saint not only of England but of many other countries and cities in Europe. There are various stories of this legendary figure and not all can be reconciled with one another neatly. It is said that he was a Roman soldier who faced martyrdom during the persecution of one or another emperor. One of the most oft cited tales of George comes from the medieval book *The Golden Legend*, which relates how George slew a dragon that had terrorised a kingdom. In this same story, the emperors Diocletian and Maximian were persecuting Christians when George renounced his knighthood, sold what he had, and gave his money to the poor. He was therefore singled out as a Christian and subsequently withstood many attempts to take his life, including being plunged into molten lead! But George survived all such attempts save the last when he finally succumbed and was beheaded. The medieval *Golden Legend* preserves such tales which surely must have delighted the audiences of the day.

In stories such as these, Christians are reminded that being a follower of Jesus may lead to derision, and even death. The words of Jesus, that the world hates you, find fulfilment in the martyrdom of the saints. But we do not need to look only to medieval legends or Christian Roman soldiers to find such stories. Unfortunately, even today Christians throughout the world (though not necessarily in the West) face persecution and death. It is then that the words of Jesus may have a new meaning.

Living the Paschal Mystery

On the feast of St. George, martyr, we are reminded that Jesus himself, as well as thousands of saints through the centuries, have gone to their death due to their faith. It is in the face of such persecution that the words of Jesus about the world hating his disciples may have a different ring. In domesticated Christianity, with parishes, regular meetings of service organisations, and parochial schools, we may unfortunately forget that some Christians throughout the world go to their death precisely because of their faith.

As Jesus too faced death, so God raised him from the dead. As disciples of Jesus, we too will be raised on the last day, when all violence will cease, and every tear will be wiped away. All the martyrs who have gone before us will participate in this paschal mystery as well, enjoying eternal life with the one who exalts the lowly.

126

Focusing the Gospel

Key words and phrases: 'you do not belong to the world'

To the point: Jesus's words to his disciples on the eve of his crucifixion seem to offer little comfort to those who followed him then or those who seek to follow him now. We are assured of persecution and resistance if we take on the name of Jesus. And yet, when we proclaim that we are Christian in word and deed, we reveal to whom we truly belong. Jesus, the crucified and raised, the one who has conquered death and sin, is our Lord and Saviour. Of whom shall we fear?

Model Penitential Act

Presider: In today's gospel, Jesus warns that his disciples will face persecution for the sake of his name. Let us pause to ask our Lord to strengthen and sustain us in every trial . . . *[pause]*

Lord Jesus, you are the Lamb of God who takes away the sins of the world: Lord, have mercy.

Christ Jesus, you stand with the persecuted and oppressed: Christ, have mercy.

Lord Jesus, you are the anointed one who has conquered sin and death: Lord, have mercy.

Model Universal Prayer (Prayer of the Faithful)

Presider: On this feast of St. George let us bring the needs of our families, country, and the world before our gracious Lord.

Response: Lord, hear our prayer.

That persecuted Christians throughout the world might worship in safety and be free of oppression . . .

That leaders of nations commit to safeguarding religious liberty for all their people while modeling respect for differences and encouraging interreligious dialogue . . .

That those who perpetuate religious persecution might experience a conversion to love and respect all people as brothers and sisters . . .

That all gathered here might be nourished by Christ's Body and Blood and so strengthened to meet every trial with peace of mind, body, and spirit . . .

Presider: God of power and might, you have gifted us with stories of St. George's courage and faithfulness. Hear our prayers that we might embrace our own strength of spirit to bring about your kingdom here on earth. We ask this through Christ, our Lord. **Amen.**

About Liturgy

The legend of St. George and the dragon does not lend itself very well to liturgical celebration, but fortunately there are some other things associated with him which could influence our liturgical environment on this day. The red cross on a white background is an obvious symbol of Christian martyrdom. The red rose is another symbol of St. George, although St. George's favourite colour is said to have been blue. Hence the insignia of the Order of the Garter, founded by Edward III, includes a blue garter, and it is traditional to wear something blue on this day. However, military symbols, such as swords, are best avoided.

COLLECT

Let us pray.

Pause for silent prayer

God of hosts,
who so kindled the fire of charity
in the heart of Saint George your martyr
that he bore witness to the risen Lord
both by his life and by his death,
grant us through his intercession, we pray,
the same faith and power of love,
that we who rejoice in his triumph
may be led to share with him
in the fullness of the resurrection.
Through our Lord Jesus Christ, your Son,
who lives and reigns with you in the unity of
      the Holy Spirit,
one God, for ever and ever. **Amen.**

FOR REFLECTION

• Do you have a favourite legend of St. George? How has this saint inspired you?

• Jesus tells his disciples, 'If they persecuted me, / they will persecute you too'. Where have you heard about or seen persecution taking place in your community, country, or the world?

Homily Points

• Before Christianity became the state religion of the Roman Empire in 380 AD there were many persecutions that the followers of Jesus faced. St. George is said to have died in one of these persecutions in 303 AD under the emperor Diocletian. In today's gospel passage, Jesus, looking forward to his own martyrdom on the cross the following day, tells his disciples, 'If they persecuted me, / they will persecute you too'.

• While Jesus's stark words might give us pause, this is not the only time in the gospels that Jesus lays out the demands of discipleship. He says that those who wish to follow him 'must deny himself, [and] take up his cross' (Matt 16:24; Luke 9:23; NABRE). What allows us to follow this command? The grace of God, and the models of the saints who witness to us that love is stronger than hatred, and life is stronger than death.

127

SPIRITUALITY

GOSPEL ACCLAMATION

℟. Alleluia, alleluia.
Christ has risen: he who created all things,
and has granted his mercy to men.
℟. Alleluia, alleluia.

Gospel   John 21:1-19

Jesus showed himself again to the disciples. It was by the Sea of Tiberias, and it happened like this: Simon Peter, Thomas called the Twin, Nathanael from Cana in Galilee, the sons of Zebedee and two more of his disciples were together. Simon Peter said, 'I'm going fishing.' They replied, 'We'll come with you.' They went out and got into the boat but caught nothing that night.

It was light by now and there stood Jesus on the shore, though the disciples did not realise that it was Jesus. Jesus called out, 'Have you caught anything, friends?' And when they answered, 'No,' he said, 'Throw the net out to starboard and you'll find something.' So they dropped the net, and there were so many fish that they could not haul it in. The disciple Jesus loved said to Peter, 'It is the Lord.' At these words 'It is the Lord', Simon Peter, who had practically nothing on, wrapped his cloak round him and jumped into the water. The other disciples came on in the boat, towing the net and the fish; they were only about a hundred yards from land.

As soon as they came ashore they saw that there was some bread there, and a charcoal fire with fish cooking on it. Jesus said, 'Bring some of the fish you have just caught.' Simon Peter went aboard and dragged the net to the shore, full of big fish, one hundred and fifty-three of them; and in spite of there being so many the net was not broken. Jesus said to them, 'Come and have breakfast.' None of the disciples was bold enough to ask, 'Who are you?'; they knew quite well it was the Lord. Jesus then stepped forward, took the bread and gave it to them, and the same with the fish. This was the third time that Jesus showed himself to the disciples after rising from the dead.

Continued in Appendix A, p. 294.

or John 21:1-14

Reflecting on the Gospel

Last week we read from the conclusion of John's gospel. Today we read from the epilogue, the chapter that follows the conclusion. Scholars refer to John 21 as the epilogue in part because it is markedly different from the preceding chapters in some vocabulary and in style. In fact, it is so different that it was likely written by a different author to address, in part, realities that had emerged in the decades following the initial composition of the gospel.

Today's reading incorporates two stories: one of the appearance on the seashore, followed by another of the rehabilitation of Peter. The Beloved

Disciple, who remains nameless, is the first to recognise Jesus with the proclamation, 'It is the Lord' (John 21:7). This is an echo of the discovery of the empty tomb when, even though Peter was the first to go into the empty tomb, the Beloved Disciple 'saw and believed' (John 20:8; NABRE). The Beloved Disciple is portrayed as the true model of discipleship. And he does not appear in any other gospel!

Another nod to earlier stories in the Gospel of John includes the mention of a 'charcoal fire', as that is the place where Peter denied Jesus three times (John 18:18; NABRE). The presence of a charcoal fire here sets the stage, narratively speaking, for his threefold rehabilitation. Three times Jesus asks Peter, 'Do you love me'? and three times Peter responds affirmatively. This three-time inquisition is quite obviously a retort to Peter's threefold denial during the passion. After the Beloved Disciple died, the Johannine community – for whom the Beloved Disciple was a model of discipleship – was coming to recognise their role in the greater Christian world, which was led (at least figuratively) by Peter. But the last story we heard about Peter was his denial of Christ. Thus, the epilogue, the additional chapter following the conclusion, tells the story of Peter's rehabilitation. Peter represents the larger Christian community. Though he denied Jesus, unlike the Beloved Disciple who was the ideal, Peter was effectively forgiven and placed in a leadership role. Thus in the Christian imagination, Peter represents the ideals and realities of discipleship. No Christian community is an island in itself. Even leaders can stumble; when they do they can be forgiven by Jesus himself. Such is the power of the risen Christ.

Living the Paschal Mystery

Sometimes it's easy to imagine the saints and disciples as those who had it all figured out. But today's gospel reminds us otherwise. Even now, a time after the resurrection, the disciples are fishing. They do not seem to be about the business of preaching or teaching. Instead, they have gone back to what they were doing before they met Jesus. One nameless disciple recognises Jesus and his proclamation causes Peter to jump into the water and swim to the seashore to meet Jesus. Jesus does not harangue or scold Peter for the weakness he showed during the passion. Instead, Jesus asks him three times whether he loves him. And three times Peter says yes, though clearly becoming a bit agitated. But in so doing, Jesus rehabilitates Peter and gives each subsequent Christian the hope and promise of rehabilitation when we fall short too. The saints and disciples were real human beings with faults and shortcomings. Jesus did not choose perfect human beings. Rather, he chose disciples, those who would follow him. And he chose us too. Our task is to follow. When we fall short Jesus will be there for us too.

Focusing the Gospel

Key words and phrases: Do you love me?; Feed my sheep

To the point: Jesus asks Peter three times, 'Do you love me'? Each time Peter answers him in the affirmative, Jesus gives him an action in which to show his love: feed my lambs, tend my sheep, feed my sheep. Next Sunday (commonly known as Good Shepherd Sunday) we will read from chapter 10 of John's gospel where Jesus proclaims, 'I am the good shepherd'. Now Jesus calls on Peter to continue his work. He might have denied Jesus three times during the passion, but now, in his proclamations of love, Peter is called to serve Jesus by serving those Jesus loved, by feeding and tending the lambs of the Good Shepherd.

Connecting the Gospel

to the first reading: Peter is true to his word. In the first reading from the Acts of the Apostles we hear yet another instance of his care and ministry to the early church. Peter feeds Jesus's 'sheep' by witnessing to them about the good news of Jesus of Nazareth who has been exalted at the right hand of God as 'leader and saviour, to give repentance and forgiveness of sins through him to Israel'. In his fear Peter might have denied Jesus three times during the passion, but now he gladly undergoes persecution, even flogging. He and his companions accept this treatment, 'glad to have had the honour of suffering humiliation for the sake of the name'.

to experience: Jesus asks us, 'Do you love me'? He invites us to continue his work of caring for and tending the flock of the Lord. How do you tend Jesus's lambs? How do you feed his sheep?

Connecting the Responsorial Psalm

to the readings: There is a temptation in the spiritual life to believe that if we do everything right we will escape hardship and suffering. And yet, we know from experience that this is simply not true. Through no fault of our own, calamity strikes. Today the psalmist reminds us to cling to God when we pass through these moments of despair and darkness: 'O Lord, you have raised my soul from the dead, / restored me to life from those who sink into the grave'. In the gospel we witness the journey from one state to another. The disciples go from catching nothing all night to filling their nets with such an abundance of fish they fear they might burst. And then, confronted by the Lord of life, Peter's threefold expression of love redeems him from his earlier three-fold denial and liberates him from the fear of following in the footsteps of the risen Lord.

to psalmist preparation: We believe in a God who journeys with us through darkness and despair and who will not abandon us in times of trial and suffering. How do you hold onto this hope in your own life?

PROMPTS FOR FAITH-SHARING

In the first reading the apostles, led by Peter, tell the authorities, 'Obedience to God comes before obedience to men'. Has there been a time in your life where you needed to take a stand for God's law? How did you find the strength to do so?

Today's psalm proclaims, 'O Lord, you have raised my soul from the dead, / restored me to life from those who sink into the grave'. What sustains your faith in times of despair?

What groups of people are missing in your parish community? How might the parish become more welcoming for all?

Who are the lambs that Jesus has given you to tend and feed? How do you serve them?

CELEBRATION

Model Rite for the Blessing and Sprinkling of Water

Presider: In today's gospel, Simon Peter recognises the risen Lord on the shores of the Sea of Galilee and immediately jumps from his boat into the water. May this sprinkling rite symbolise our own desire to be close to Jesus . . . [*pause*]

[*continue with* The Roman Missal, *Appendix II*]

Homily Points

• Much has been made of the number 153 in the gospel passage we read from today about the miraculous catch of fish that was so great the disciples were not able to haul the net in, instead dragging it to shore. And yet, the net held. Of all of the theories surrounding what this number might mean, the most popular is from St. Jerome who postulates that at the time of the gospel writing it was believed there were precisely 153 species of fish in the world.

• By including all 153 within the net we see the radical inclusivity of the new covenant. All the people of the world are invited into the net of the church. And even if it seems like this 'net' might burst, it will hold; we need not fear inviting everyone.

• There is a tremendous difference between ministering out of fear and ministering out of abundance. A community that ministers from fear will find excuses for why certain people (whether individuals or entire classes and races) cannot be included within its walls. They fear that such diversity will stress the 'net' beyond its limits. And yet today we hear that our fears have no place within the expansive vision of God. This net was meant to hold every kind of fish, every kind of person. Today let us pause to consider who is welcome and who is not in our community, in our family, our parish. As Christians, we are all called to carry on the ministry of Christ and today he shows us the way. Out of love, along with St. Peter, we are called to feed Jesus's lambs and to tend his sheep. All of his lambs. All of his sheep.

Model Universal Prayer (Prayer of the Faithful)

Presider: Confident that God provides for all our needs, we lift up our prayers to the Lord.

Response: Lord, hear our prayer.

That the church show her love for God by tenderly feeding and tending Jesus's flock . . .

That all peoples of the world know the love of God who calls them by name and invites them to abundant life . . .

That all those who are persecuted for their religious beliefs find sanctuary and protection . . .

That all gathered here have the strength to follow the law of God when it conflicts with human laws . . .

Presider: Gracious God, you sustain us in life and provide us with everything we need. Help us to trust in your loving care. We ask this through Christ our Lord. **Amen.**

COLLECT

Let us pray.

Pause for silent prayer

May your people exult for ever, O God,
in renewed youthfulness of spirit,
so that, rejoicing now in the restored glory
     of our adoption,
we may look forward in confident hope
to the rejoicing of the day of resurrection.
Through our Lord Jesus Christ, your Son,
who lives and reigns with you
     in the unity of the Holy Spirit,
one God, for ever and ever. **Amen.**

FIRST READING
Acts 5:27-32, 40-41

The high priest demanded an explanation of the apostles. 'We gave you a formal warning' he said 'not to preach in this name, and what have you done? You have filled Jerusalem with your teaching, and seem determined to fix the guilt of this man's death on us.' In reply Peter and the apostles said, 'Obedience to God comes before obedience to men; it was the God of our ancestors who raised up Jesus, but it was you who had him executed by hanging on a tree. By his own right hand God has now raised him up to be leader and saviour, to give repentance and forgiveness of sins through him to Israel. We are witnesses to all this, we and the Holy Spirit whom God has given to those who obey him.' They warned the apostles not to speak in the name of Jesus and released them. And so they left the presence of the Sanhedrin glad to have had the honour of suffering humiliation for the sake of the name.

RESPONSORIAL PSALM
Ps 29:2, 4-6, 11-13 (2)

R︎. I will praise you, Lord,
for you have rescued me.
or
R︎. Alleluia.

I will praise you, Lord, you have rescued me
and have not let my enemies rejoice
over me.
O Lord, you have raised my soul from
the dead,
restored me to life from those who sink
into the grave.

R︎. I will praise you, Lord,
for you have rescued me.
or
R︎. Alleluia.

Sing psalms to the Lord, you who love him,
give thanks to his holy name.
His anger lasts but a moment; his favour
through life.
At night there are tears, but joy comes
with dawn.

R︎. I will praise you, Lord,
for you have rescued me.
or
R︎. Alleluia.

The Lord listened and had pity.
The Lord came to my help.
For me you have changed my mourning
into dancing;
O Lord my God, I will thank you for ever.

R︎. I will praise you, Lord,
for you have rescued me.
or
R︎. Alleluia.

SECOND READING
Apoc 5:11-14

In my vision, I, John, heard the sound of an immense number of angels gathered round the throne and the animals and the elders; there were ten thousand times ten thousand of them and thousands upon thousands, shouting, 'The Lamb that was sacrificed is worthy to be given power, riches, wisdom, strength, honour, glory and blessing.' Then I heard all the living things in creation – everything that lives in the air, and on the ground, and under the ground, and in the sea, crying, 'To the One who is sitting on the throne and to the Lamb, be all praise, honour, glory and power, for ever and ever.' And the four animals said, 'Amen'; and the elders prostrated themselves to worship.

About Liturgy
Companions at table: How many of your most significant moments in life have taken place at a meal? There's something about sharing food and drink that enables us to share our innermost selves as well with the others at that table. In the same vein, how difficult it is to spend even one moment at a meal with someone who has hurt you.

How remarkable then is this breakfast at the seashore! Over a charcoal fire with a piece of fish and a bit of bread, the risen Christ reveals his true self to the one who betrayed him. Instead of resentful words that reprimand, Jesus gives to Peter words of mercy and trust: 'Feed my sheep'. Christ does not keep score; there is no logbook in heaven recording our every sin. There is only an empty seat at Jesus's table waiting for us to sit down and be fed, forgiven, and sent once again.

This is what we mean by being companions at the Lord's table. We are those who break bread with one another. Recognising that all of us are sinners before God, we share our brokenness and the brokenness of the world with Christ and with one another at the altar. In return Christ takes these broken pieces of our lives and mends them together, multiplying them into an abundance of blessing for those in need of mercy. In grateful response to this healing, we say 'Amen' to the cup of sacrifice and the new covenant, a sharing in the Blood of Christ that will lead us where we might not want to go. Yet we do not go alone. Our companions around the heavenly and earthly altars go with us.

Pope Francis said, 'All family life is a "shepherding" in mercy. Each of us, by our love and care, leaves a mark on the life of others' (*Amoris Laetitia* 322). In our households, there is a table where every day, over a bit of bread, we have the opportunity to shepherd and feed our companions in mercy, forgiveness, courage, and love.

About Initiation
Found worthy to suffer: In the period of the catechumenate, the RCIA says that the formation of catechumens in the discipline of living as part of the Christian community will lead them to 'experience divisions and separations' because 'the Lord in whom they believe is a sign of contradiction' (RCIA 75.2). As the neophytes continue on their mystagogical journey, today might be a good opportunity to help them reflect on how they may have been 'glad to have had the honour of suffering humiliation for the sake of the name' (Acts 5:41) and how their sharing in the Eucharist with the faithful strengthen and encourage them even in moments of discord.

About Liturgical Music
Singing during Communion: What is the best time for the musicians to receive? At the end of the distribution, when all are praying quietly. During Communion, the musicians' role is to support the prayer of the singing community, thus ensuring the that Communion procession does not become instead a queue with incidental music.

To help the assembly take their part, choose songs that have simple and memorable refrains, as with Taizé refrains (e.g. 'Eat This Bread'). One such refrain is *Psallite*'s 'If You Love Me, Feed My Lambs', which has two different textual versions for this Sunday.

SPIRITUALITY

GOSPEL ACCLAMATION
John 10:14

℞. Alleluia, alleluia.
I am the good shepherd, says the Lord;
I know my own sheep and my own know me.
℞. Alleluia, alleluia.

Gospel

John 10:27-30

Jesus said:
    'The sheep that belong to me listen
        to my voice;
    I know them and they follow me.
    I give them eternal life;
    they will never be lost
    and no one will ever steal them
        from me.
    The Father who gave them to me is
        greater than anyone,
    and no one can steal from
        the Father.
    The Father and I are one.'

Reflecting on the Gospel

Though we are in Cycle C (the Gospel of Luke), today we have another reading from the Gospel of John. Each week since Easter we have read from this gospel. Today we read not about a resurrection appearance but instead we hear about the familiar, comforting image of Jesus as the Good Shepherd. We are his sheep who hear his voice and respond by following him. Of course, to follow means to be a disciple, so the image of a shepherd and his sheep is especially apt.

Pope Francis seems to find this image instructive as well. He speaks of the role of bishops and priests to be shepherds (for that is the meaning of the Latin term *pastor*). Pope Francis says that the shepherd must have the 'smell of the sheep'. Such an image is certainly vivid, graphic, and leaves little to the imagination. It conjures up one who is uncomfortably close to the sheep. But that is essentially the model of the Good Shepherd, and one to be emulated by those who serve.

Not only do we follow the Good Shepherd upon hearing his voice, but we learn that the Good Shepherd gives eternal life.

The symbolism is profound and perhaps even more so because the snippet we read today is so short. The meaning of the words should not be lost in their brevity. The relationship of the sheep to the shepherd is dependent upon the Father and Jesus. The Father has given the sheep to Jesus. No one can take them from the Father or the Son, for the Father and the Son are one. Again, the theological sophistication and the high Christology are worthy of meditation.

Given the symbolism, the task of the sheep is pure and simple, to follow Jesus, to be a disciple. The task of the Father and the Son is not to lose the sheep, or perhaps not to give them up to those who might try to pry open their hands.

Our task, therefore, is no more difficult than following Jesus. To do that we must be attentive to his voice.

Living the Paschal Mystery

It would be easy to follow Jesus if he were physically present here upon the earth, healing the sick and curing the lame. Who wouldn't leave everything to do that? But it's much more difficult to be attentive to the voice of Jesus after the resurrection. And that is precisely what this gospel passage requires of us. We are to listen closely amidst the noise and sound of our world and discern the voice of the Good Shepherd. What is he calling us to do? Where does he want us to go? We would like to follow him, but how to hear his voice?

When we speak do we sound more like we are echoing the gospel or syndicated TV or radio shows? Are we following Christ, attuned to his voice in Scripture? Or are we more closely attuned to the culture, knowing the voice of the more popular media? How we speak and how we act may tell us more about who we are ultimately following. On this Fourth Sunday of Easter it is good to pause and reflect on our path. Whose voice do we follow?

Focusing the Gospel

Key words and phrases: no one will ever steal them from me.

To the point: John's gospel gives us the beloved image of Jesus, the Good Shepherd, who calls his sheep by name and leads them in safety along the pathways of life. In today's gospel passage we hear only a fraction of Jesus's discourse on the Good Shepherd, and yet we are told what is most essential, we are united to Jesus in an unbreakable bond of love. Jesus proclaims, '[N]o one will ever steal [my sheep] from me'. In the spiritual life we are called to attune our ears to the voice of our Good Shepherd showing us the way, and to fear not; nothing can separate us from the love of God.

Connecting the Gospel

to the second readings: In the second reading from Apocalypse we are given a vision of 'a huge number, impossible to count, of people from every nation, race, tribe and language'. It is revealed that this multitude is comprised of the ones who have 'been through the great persecution' and 'washed their robes white again in the blood of the Lamb'. The early church encountered grave persecution. From the martyrdom of nearly all of the apostles (tradition tells us only John died of old age on the island of Patmos) to the violent campaigns of the Roman government intent on ending the fledgling religion, many would have cause to doubt Jesus's statement that 'no one will ever steal them from me'. And yet, as the apostle Paul stated in his First Letter to the Corinthians, 'O death, where is your victory'? (15:55; NABRE). Our Good Shepherd gives us eternal life. Even death itself cannot separate us from him.

to experience: In joy and in despair we can rely on the voice of the Good Shepherd to lead us.

Connecting the Responsorial Psalm

to the readings: Psalm 99 is an invitation to come before the Lord with joy and thanksgiving knowing who we truly are, '[G]od's people, the sheep of his flock'. This simple psalm speaks to our self-understanding as a community dedicated to the Lord. We are not individuals intent on our own personal salvation, but a group of disciples that listens to the Lord in community and comes before him (together) with joy and thanksgiving. The beautiful diversity of the 'huge number' in Apocalypse reveals this to us. Among them are counted 'every nation, race, tribe and language', and yet they sing out in one voice to their God. So may we worship, in one voice, unified in our diversity.

to psalmist preparation: Your voice in song calls the community to come before the Lord with joy and to know they are the flock of God. How do you experience and rejoice in your parish community?

PROMPTS FOR FAITH-SHARING

Psalm 99 tells us we are '[G]od's people, the sheep of his flock'. How is your parish community a unified flock, led by the Good Shepherd? How can you strive to embrace even greater unity?

How do you listen for the voice of the Good Shepherd in your daily life?

How is Jesus, the Good Shepherd, calling you to follow him at this moment in your life?

Good Shepherd Sunday is a traditional time to pray for vocations to serve the church. What are some ways you can grow in your vocation, whether to marriage, holy orders, religious life, or single life, over the coming year?

CELEBRATION

Model Rite for the Blessing and Sprinkling of Water

Presider: In the waters of baptism we entered the church, the sheepfold of the Lord. May this water remind us of the joy of that day and strengthen us in our baptismal promises . . . [*pause*]

[*continue with* The Roman Missal, *Appendix II*]

Homily Points

• In the gospel today we are given a condensed model of the spiritual life. It involves listening and knowing and following. The sheep of the Good Shepherd listen to his voice. Unlike the voice of strangers, the sheep listen and respond to the voice of their shepherd. They are attuned to his tone and the rhythm of his speech. They find a home within his words. We who belong to the flock of the Lord might ask, how well do we know this voice? How much time do we spend listening to it with love each day? How might we build a home with the Word of God?

• Whether we recognise it or not we are deeply known by this Shepherd. Indeed, he knows us better than we know ourselves. In this knowing there is no shame. We are recognised for who we are as beloved children of God. And we are called to become even more authentically ourselves. The Good Shepherd knows us and calls us by name. Are there pieces of yourself you are still trying to hide from God? It is no use. The psalmist tells us, 'My very self you know' (Psalm 139:14; NABRE). Take time to experience yourself as deeply known (and deeply loved) by the Lord of life.

• Only after we have listened to the voice of the Good Shepherd and heard him call us by name can we then follow him. Theologian Sofia Cavalletti wrote, 'It is only in love, and not in fear, that one may have a moral life worthy of the name' (*The Religious Potential of the Child*). God does not crave our fearful submission but our loving and joyful collaboration in building the kingdom of God. May we listen, know, and follow.

Model Universal Prayer (Prayer of the Faithful)

Presider: We follow Jesus, the Good Shepherd, who calls us by name and cares for us tenderly, and so we lift up our needs with gratitude and confidence.

Response: Lord, hear our prayer.

That the church be sustained and buoyed through an increase in vocations to the religious life and holy orders . . .

That every nation of the world might hear the voice of the Good Shepherd calling in their native language, 'Come, follow me' . . .

That those who are spiritually lost and seeking meaning in life would encounter leaders and guides to show them the way . . .

That all gathered here be strengthened in our own vocation, whether to marriage, the single life, religious life, or holy orders . . .

Presider: Heavenly Father, we are your people, the flock that you shepherd. Hear our prayers that we might listen for your voice and follow you always. We ask in the name of Jesus, the Good Shepherd. **Amen.**

COLLECT

Let us pray.

Pause for silent prayer

Almighty ever-living God,
lead us to a share in the joys of heaven,
so that the humble flock may reach
where the brave Shepherd has gone before.
Who lives and reigns with you in the unity
of the Holy Spirit,
one God, for ever and ever. **Amen.**

FIRST READING
Acts 13:14, 43-52

Paul and Barnabas carried on from Perga till they reached Antioch in Pisidia. Here they went to synagogue on the Sabbath and took their seats.

When the meeting broke up, many Jews and devout converts joined Paul and Barnabas, and in their talks with them Paul and Barnabas urged them to remain faithful to the grace God had given them.

The next sabbath almost the whole town assembled to hear the word of God. When they saw the crowds, the Jews, prompted by jealousy, used blasphemies and contradicted everything Paul said. Then Paul and Barnabas spoke out boldly. 'We had to proclaim the word of God to you first, but since you have rejected it, since you do not think yourselves worthy of eternal life, we must turn to the pagans. For this is what the Lord commanded us to do when he said:

I have made you a light for the nations,
so that my salvation may reach the ends
of the earth.'

It made the pagans very happy to hear this and they thanked the Lord for his message; all who were destined for eternal life became believers. Thus the word of the Lord spread through the whole countryside.

But the Jews worked upon some of the devout women of the upper classes and the leading men of the city and persuaded them to turn against Paul and Barnabas and expel them from their territory. So they shook the dust from their feet in defiance and went off to Iconium; but the disciples were filled with joy and the Holy Spirit.

CATECHESIS

RESPONSORIAL PSALM
Ps 99:1-3, 5 (3)

R̸. We are his people, the sheep of his flock.
or
R̸. Alleluia.

Cry out with joy to the Lord, all the earth.
Serve the Lord with gladness.
Come before him, singing for joy.

R̸. We are his people, the sheep of his flock.
or
R̸. Alleluia.

Know that he, the Lord, is God.
He made us, we belong to him,
we are his people, the sheep of his flock.

R̸. We are his people, the sheep of his
    flock.
or
R̸. Alleluia.

Indeed, how good is the Lord,
eternal his merciful love.
He is faithful from age to age.

R̸. We are his people, the sheep of his flock.
or
R̸. Alleluia.

SECOND READING
Apoc 7:9, 14-17

I, John, saw a huge number, impossible to count, of people from every nation, race, tribe and language; they were standing in front of the throne and in front of the Lamb, dressed in white robes and holding palms in their hands. One of the elders said to me, 'These are the people who have been through the great persecution, and because they have washed their robes white again in the blood of the Lamb, they now stand in front of God's throne and serve him day and night in his sanctuary; and the One who sits on the throne will spread his tent over them. They will never hunger or thirst again; neither the sun nor scorching wind will ever plague them, because the Lamb who is at the throne will be their shepherd and will lead them to springs of living water; and God will wipe away all tears from their eyes.'

About Liturgy

Vocations: One layer of meaning that has been given to this Fourth Sunday of Easter is that of vocations, especially to ordained ministries and religious life. This is a laudable lens through which to see the image of Christ, the Good Shepherd. However, it is not the only way we should understand vocation.

Pope Benedict XVI described a broader understanding of vocation in a greeting he gave to a parish council at a church in Rome administered by the Vocationist Fathers: 'Every person carries within himself a project of God, a personal vocation, a personal idea of God on what he is required to do in history to build his Church. . . . And the priest's role is above all to reawaken this awareness, to help the individual discover his personal vocation, God's task for each one of us' (March 25, 2007).

As you prepare the liturgies for this day, certainly connect the image of the Good Shepherd to all who shepherd the church, and include prayers for vocations to the priesthood, diaconate, and religious life. But also help your assemblies understand that all of us are called to a vocation and have a specific role to play in the mission of Christ in whatever state of life we are in. Also include prayers for those called to the vocations of spouses, widows, and single persons.

We are God's people: In *Called to Participate: Theological, Ritual, and Social Perspectives* (Liturgical Press), liturgist and theologian Mark Searle wrote: 'The Church community is less a network of friends than it is, in Parker Palmer's striking phrase, "a company of strangers".' This "company of strangers" will often have little in common beyond our common humanity and the Spirit poured into our hearts in baptism' (75).

True parish communities in which evangelisation and radical hospitality are practised will be a mix of people who are different. If everyone we know in our parish looks and sounds and talks and acts the same way as we do, we might not be reflecting as clearly as we can the people of God who come 'from every nation, race, tribe and language' (Apoc 7:9). If that is the case, it is a call for us to seek out those who are missing from the flock. And you might not have to go to the ends of the earth to find them. They may even be sitting in another part of the church. All we have to do is make an effort to go and meet them.

About Liturgical Music

Singing in a language not our own: If the heavenly gathering of God's people includes those from every nation and tongue, it would be well for us to begin learning some music that reflects the diversity of God's people so that we'll be ready for the heavenly choir! In our increasingly diverse neighbourhoods, this would not be difficult to do. We simply have to seek out those who have different roots than we do and spend time listening to their story and their song. If your parish has a Mass in a different language from yours, make an effort to participate in it even if you don't understand the language. Simply being present in the other's community gatherings will speak more about your care for them than if you learned their language but never spent time with them.

Many English-language hymnals today include at least a few songs in other languages. One beautiful and simple song in Spanish that fits nicely with today's readings is '*Pues Si Vivimos* / When We Are Living' ('We Belong to God'). There are several versions in different hymn books, but by far the best is the one in John Bell's collection *One Is the Body.*

SPIRITUALITY

GOSPEL ACCLAMATION
John 13:34

R̸. Alleluia, alleluia.
Jesus said: 'I give you a new commandment:
love one another, just as I have loved you.'
R̸. Alleluia, alleluia.

Gospel

John 13:31-33a, 34-35

When Judas had gone Jesus said:
   'Now has the Son of Man been
      glorified,
   and in him God has been glorified.
   If God has been glorified in him,
   God will in turn glorify him
      in himself,
   and will glorify him very soon.
   My little children,
   I shall not be with you much longer.
   I give you a new commandment:
   love one another;
   just as I have loved you,
   you also must love one another.
   By this love you have for
      one another,
   everyone will know that you are
      my disciples.'

Reflecting on the Gospel

We continue reading from the Gospel of John during the Easter season. This evangelist has unique things to say about Jesus, and he relates stories about Jesus not found anywhere else. Our gospel reading for today is a case in point. Other gospels have Jesus saying, 'Love your neighbour' (Matt 19:19; Mark 12:31; Luke 10:27; NABRE), or even, 'Love your enemies' (Matt 5:44; Luke 6:27; NABRE). But today we hear the simple but profound command to 'love one another', which presumes that there are others in the community. In cases where semantics can open a debate about 'who is my neighbour'? or how precisely we 'love' an 'enemy', the command to love one another is straightforward and leaves little room for negotiation or explanation. Further, it is a command related to 'one another', which means those in the Christian community closest to us. In some senses it harkens to family, and the relationships we have with one another as family. It's nearly a plea for siblings to do more than 'get along' but to actually 'love one another'.

But Jesus goes further, pointing to the example he gave them as a model for love: '[J]ust as I have loved you, / you also must love one another'. In a few chapters, we will see that includes laying down his life for them. The disciples will be known by their love for one another. Our own displays of charity and acts of love will mark us as Christian.

To love one another is challenging. It can be easier and more convenient to go to church, or to sit in our room and pray. But love requires action and some doing. As is often said, 'Love is a verb'. The image of a family comes to mind again as it can be easier to love those on the outside or the margins. But what about those most familiar to us? We know their foibles, idiosyncrasies, annoying tics, and habits. We have a history with them. Yet, we are called, perhaps even reminded, to love one another.

For the Fourth Gospel, all ethical commands of Jesus may be summed up in this one command to love. Other than some references that seem to reflect the Ten Commandments (don't steal, lie, covet) the Gospel of John has one over-riding exhortation: Love.

Living the Paschal Mystery

Ghandi is reported to have said: 'I love your Christ, but your Christians are not like Christ'. From this we might be fairly sure that the Christians he encountered were not living up to the ideal reflected in today's gospel. That is certainly unfortunate. But what image of Christianity do we present by our actions? By our love? Do we love like Jesus did, to the point of laying down our life?

It can be easier to be consumed with external rituals or internal theological debates. But Jesus's command today is simply to love. In its simplicity, it is exceptionally difficult. Love knows no bounds. Love does not say, 'That's enough'. Love puts the needs of the other ahead of our own. And in our global society we see that vast numbers of people have more needs than we do. Where to begin? It is our life's calling as a disciple of Jesus to follow him in the way of love. It's been said that a great journey begins with a single step. So we love one another and in doing so we become more devoted disciples of Christ.

Focusing the Gospel

Key words and phrases: just as I have loved you, / you also must love one another

To the point: Jesus prefaces this new commandment to his disciples by telling them, 'I shall not be with you much longer'. Speaking at the Last Supper, Jesus prepares his disciples for what is to come. Soon Jesus will not be with them in the tangible way they are used to. They will no longer be able to walk with him in person or to ask him their questions and hear an answer with their ears. They are moving into a new time of discipleship, a time that will require more from them. In this time to come they are to love one another as Jesus has loved them. And soon, Jesus will show them just what that love looks like when he lays down his life.

Connecting the Gospel

to the first reading: Although in some places the Acts of the Apostles presents an idyllic picture of the early church, the first communities of Christians were not without their disagreements. One of the first of these was about how to admit Gentiles to the church, and whether they must first undergo a process of Jewish conversion, that is, be circumcised and follow Jewish dietary laws. In the first reading, Paul, the apostle to the Gentiles, shares with the Jewish Christian communities 'how [God] had opened the door of faith to the pagans'. This time of transition where the Jewish Christians welcomed Gentiles must have been difficult at times, and yet, the church survived and thrived by following the commandment Jesus gave to his closest friends on the night before he died, '[L]ove one another'.

to experience: Only in love are we able to form the Body of Christ. Only in love are we given the grace to find unity in our diversity and to worship God as one.

Connecting the Responsorial Psalm

to the readings: Just as modern authors and poets enjoy word play, so, too, did the psalmists of ancient Israel. Though it's hard to tell in English, in Hebrew, today's psalm is an acrostic in which the first word of each line begins with the letter of the alphabet in alphabetical order: *aleph, bet, gimel, dalet,* etc. There are about a dozen alphabetic acrostic psalms in the Bible. The verses we pray with today centre around the theme of God's mercy and goodness, as well as the glory of his reign. In the second reading from Apocalypse we see an image of God's kingdom where 'there will be no more death, and no more mourning or sadness'. Even as we await the fulfilment of this kingdom, we can continue to build it every day when we follow the new commandment Jesus gave, '[J]ust as I have loved you, / you also must love one another'.

to psalmist preparation: We belong to the glorious reign of God when we love with the self-giving love of Christ. How do you embody this love? Where in your life is God asking you to love with more intention?

In the first reading, Barnabas and Paul minister to the fledgling Christian communities through prayer, fasting, and proclaiming the Good News. How do you support others in faith?

Jesus gives us a new commandment: '[L]ove one another'. How do you show love for the people closest to you?

When in your life have you needed to make a conscious decision to act out of love? What helped you make this decision?

Jesus says we will be recognised as his disciples by how we love each other. How loving is your parish community? What issues are you currently dealing with that might require an extra outpouring of love and charity?

CELEBRATION

Model Rite for the Blessing and Sprinkling of Water

Presider: In the waters of baptism we are washed clean of original sin and filled with the grace and love of God. May this water renew our hearts and spirits to be signs of God's love and life on the earth . . . *[pause]*

    [continue with The Roman Missal, *Appendix II]*

Homily Points

• In today's gospel Jesus gets to the point very quickly: Love one another as I have loved you. In all things, Jesus leads by example and so when we ask ourselves, 'How did Jesus love'? many images come to mind. We see Jesus healing the blind and lame. We see him touching lepers and blessing children. We hear him telling the woman caught in adultery, 'Neither do I condemn you' (John 8:11; NABRE). And we see his arms stretched wide on the cross, submitting to a criminal's death.

• Jesus's entire life, not just his death, was a continual outpouring of self for others. Jesus loved with his presence, and he continues to love us this way. We experience his presence when we come to the Word of God, seek him out in prayer, and encounter his Body and Blood in the Eucharist.

• Jesus gives this new commandment at the Last Supper. His disciples have travelled with him for several years now. They have witnessed him loving everyone he has encountered. And hopefully these images of Jesus's love are seared into their memories because this new commandment asks them to continue the work of bringing Christ's love to the world. St. Teresa of Ávila wrote a famous prayer called 'Christ has no body'. In it she tells us, 'Christ has no body but yours, / no hands, no feet on earth but yours, / yours are the eyes with which he looks / compassion on the world'. The mantle has been passed to us. Now we are the ones who are given this mission: '[J]ust as I have loved you, / you also must love one another'.

Model Universal Prayer (Prayer of the Faithful)

Presider: Jesus gives us a new commandment, to love one another as he has loved us. Let us pray for the self-giving, compassionate love of Jesus to transform the world.

Response: Lord, hear our prayer.

That the church might stand with the persecuted throughout the world and be a voice of hope for the time when God 'will wipe every tear from their eyes' . . .

That people throughout the world, especially those in power, embrace Jesus's way of selfless giving and love . . .

That those in need of love, especially the orphaned, abandoned and imprisoned, experience Christ's care and compassion through the actions of those they encounter . . .

That all gathered here be strengthened to act as Christ's body on earth, to be 'the hands with which he blesses all the world' and 'the feet with which he walks to do good' . . .

Presider: God of unending love, you call us to be a people after your own heart. Hear our prayers that we might witness to your love throughout the earth. In the name of Jesus we pray. **Amen.**

COLLECT

Let us pray.

Pause for silent prayer

Almighty ever-living God,
constantly accomplish the Paschal
    Mystery within us,
that those you were pleased to make new
    in Holy Baptism
may, under your protective care, bear
    much fruit
and come to the joys of life eternal.
Through our Lord Jesus Christ, your Son,
who lives and reigns with you in the unity
    of the Holy Spirit,
one God, for ever and ever. **Amen.**

FIRST READING
Acts 14:21-27

Paul and Barnabas went back through Lystra and Iconium to Antioch. They put fresh heart into the disciples, encouraging them to persevere in the faith. 'We all have to experience many hardships' they said 'before we enter the kingdom of God.' In each of these churches they appointed elders, and with prayer and fasting they commended them to the Lord in whom they had come to believe.

They passed through Pisidia and reached Pamphylia. Then after proclaiming the word at Perga they went down to Attalia and from there sailed for Antioch, where they had originally been commended to the grace of God for the work they had now completed.

On their arrival they assembled the church and gave an account of all that God had done with them, and how he had opened the door of faith to the pagans. The word of the Lord.

CATECHESIS

RESPONSORIAL PSALM

Ps 144:8-13 (Cf. 1)

R̠. I will bless your name for ever, O God
  my King.
  or
R̠. Alleluia.

The Lord is kind and full of compassion,
slow to anger, abounding in love.
How good is the Lord to all,
compassionate to all his creatures.

R̠. I will bless your name for ever, O God
  my King.
  or
R̠. Alleluia.

All your creatures shall thank you, O
  Lord,
and your friends shall repeat their
  blessing.
They shall speak of the glory of your reign
and declare your might, O God,
to make known to men your mighty deeds
and the glorious splendour of your reign.

R̠. I will bless your name for ever, O God
  my King.
  or
R̠. Alleluia.

Yours is an everlasting kingdom;
your rule lasts from age to age.

R̠. I will bless your name for ever, O God
  my King.
  or
R̠. Alleluia.

SECOND READING

Apoc 21:1-5

I, John, saw a new heaven and a new earth;
the first heaven and the first earth had
disappeared now, and there was no longer
any sea. I saw the holy city, and the new
Jerusalem, coming down from God out of
heaven, as beautiful as a bride all dressed
for her husband. Then I heard a loud voice
call from the throne, 'You see this city?
Here God lives among men. He will make
his home among them; they shall be his
people, and he will be their God; his name
is God-with-them. He will wipe away all
tears from their eyes; there will be no more
death, and no more mourning or sadness.
The world of the past has gone.'

Then the One sitting on the throne
spoke: 'Now I am making the whole of
creation new.'

About Liturgy

Proof of discipleship: If you pay attention to Catholic websites, social media, or maybe even your diocesan newspaper, it probably doesn't take long for you to find mean-spirited comments about fellow Christians who hold different viewpoints than the writer's. Reading these articles and comments might lead us to believe that the proof of discipleship is measured by our level of orthodoxy, obedience, liberalism, or whatever measuring stick you like.

However, today's gospel reminds us that the proof of discipleship is not how right we are but how loving we are. If we are to follow Jesus's commandment to love one another as he has loved us, there can be no room in our language or in our hearts for such meanness.

How then should we prepare ourselves to be witnesses for the gospel when we encounter others who may disagree with us? Let us look at how Paul and Barnabas helped the earliest Christian disciples. They strengthened the spirits of the disciples. They encouraged them to persevere in faith. They recognised their hardships. They discerned good leaders to help them, and they all prayed and fasted. Did this guarantee harmony and agreement? Not really. But it did prove to all that they were followers of Christ.

When we encounter discord among our fellow Christians, let us remember that our primary objective is to love as Jesus loved us. That requires an ongoing, gradual relationship that recognises the dignity of each person and sees them as our brother or sister in Christ.

About Initiation

Glorifying God: Today's gospel reflects the final command we receive at every Eucharist: 'Go in peace, glorifying the Lord by your lives'. The neophytes had been training to be witnesses to Christ through their words and deeds all during their catechumenate. As they continue to be visible signs in our midst of the new life we receive in Christ, invite some of them who are comfortable to share their testimony of how Christ has loved them. They can do this either as a brief reflection during Mass, a written testimony included in the parish bulletin, or as a short video on the website.

About Liturgical Music

Suggestions: There are so many excellent songs that express today's gospel command to love. It is always good to return to those with solid texts taken from Scripture and our tradition. One example of this is the text of *Ubi caritas* from the Mass of the Lord's Supper. Settings of this include: 'Where Charity and Love Prevail' (Westendorf/Benoît) and 'Ubi Caritas' by Bob Hurd (OCP). James Quinn's 'This Is My Will, My One Command' and the traditional 'A New Commandment I Give Unto You' are both good options for the preparation of gifts. For Communion, look to *Psallite*'s 'A New Commandment I Give to You'. A recent song by Paul Inwood, 'Go In Peace to Love and Serve the Lord' (OCP), would work well for dismissal.

As you choose music for this Sunday, keep some of these selections in mind as well for the liturgies of matrimony in your parish. These texts give us a deeper understanding of Christian love and can enhance your wedding repertoire with songs that build upon spousal love to become a vocation of love for others.

SPIRITUALITY

GOSPEL ACCLAMATION
John 14:23

R̷. Alleluia, alleluia.
Jesus said: 'If anyone loves me he will keep
    my word,
and my Father will love him, and we shall come
    to him.'
R̷. Alleluia, alleluia.

Gospel

John 14:23-29

Jesus said to his disciples:
    'If anyone loves me he will keep
        my word,
    and my Father will love him,
    and we shall come to him
    and make our home with him.
    Those who do not love me do
        not keep my words.
    And my word is not my own:
    it is the word of the one who
        sent me.
    I have said these things to you
    while still with you;
    but the Advocate, the Holy Spirit,
    whom the Father will send in
        my name,
    will teach you everything
    and remind you of all I have said
        to you.
    Peace I bequeath to you,
    my own peace I give you,
    a peace the world cannot give, this
        is my gift to you.
    Do not let your hearts be troubled
        or afraid.
    You heard me say:
    I am going away, and shall return.
    If you loved me you would have
        been glad to know that I am
        going to
    the Father,
    for the Father is greater than I.
    I have told you this now before
        it happens,
    so that when it does happen you
        may believe.'

Reflecting on the Gospel

Our reading today continues to be from the Gospel of John, and interestingly it's from Jesus's Last Supper discourse. So even though we are in the Easter season, we hearken back to the Last Supper for words of wisdom from Jesus. And these words are appropriate as we approach the conclusion of the Easter season at Pentecost, the feast of the giving of the Holy Spirit, which we will celebrate in two weeks. But here Jesus tells the disciples forthrightly that the Father will send the Holy Spirit, the Advocate, in Jesus's name. The role of the Spirit is to teach the disciples, and to remind them of what Jesus said. The Spirit then is a

gift of the Father. This gift was given not only to that generation of Christians but to us too. We have that same Advocate to teach us and the other followers of Jesus. But that is not the only gift we receive.

A gift of Jesus given to the disciples is peace, but Jesus is quick to say that it's not the peace given by the world, but that given by Jesus. The world's peace can be understood as the absence of war, or a cessation of hostilities. Others interpret it as the peace gained by domination of subject peoples. And in Jesus's time and place we recall that the Romans were the occupying power. A generation after Jesus the city of Jerusalem with its temple would be destroyed by Rome. At the conclusion of that campaign the Romans would say they pacified Judea! The death, destruction, slaughter, fire, and pillaging of Jerusalem and its temple meant for the Romans that the land was at peace! So, no, Jesus's peace is not like that given by the world, given by the Romans.

The peace Jesus gives is an interior wholeness, to be at peace with oneself and the world around us. The inner disposition of a disciple is one of peace, not aggression; peace, rather than anger; peace, not hostility; peace, rather than anxiety; peace, not pursuit of ill-gotten gain. The life of a disciple is marked by the gift of peace given by Jesus.

Living the Paschal Mystery

How many of us live lives of peace? And by peace do we mean absence of strife? Or the peace that Christ gives? The peace that Christ gives is not only for those disciples in the New Testament, it is for us. The relationship we have with Christ means that we do not look to outside forces or external sources for validation. Our worth and sense of self is not measured by a job, position, house, children, family, retirement plan, or the praise of others. Instead, our peace and well-being come from Christ himself. That peace and security can never be taken away. We are no longer subject to the whims of others, the hazards of the world, or the vagaries of passing fancies. Regardless of our condition in life, we have something fundamental at our core that is a gift. Let us rest in the knowledge that we have been given the gift of peace that comes from Christ himself.

Focusing the Gospel

Key words and phrases: Peace I bequeath to you, / my own peace I give you

To the point: Just as we read on the Second Sunday of Easter, Jesus again offers the disciples peace. The gospel we hear today is actually taken from earlier in the Gospel of John, during the Last Supper discourse. These closest friends of Jesus are about to be shaken completely in faith. They will see the man they have come to know as the Lord die on a cross. But before these calamities take place Jesus gives them one final gift, peace, and not just a general feeling of peace, but the very peace of Christ. When he sees them for the first time after the resurrection in the Upper Room where they are huddled due to fear, Jesus offers this gift again, 'Peace be with you'. Jesus had told his friends, 'Do not let your hearts be troubled or afraid'. This is a difficult lesson to learn, but Jesus never tires of offering his peace to us.

Connecting the Gospel

to the first reading: In the Acts of the Apostles the early church continues to ponder and discern the process for Gentiles to join the new Christian faith. Paul and Barnabas go to Jerusalem to discuss with the apostles if circumcision should be required for Gentile Christians. Led by Peter and James, the council comes to a decision that circumcision will not be required and writes a letter to the Gentile churches. In it they express concern that these matters have disturbed the Gentiles' peace of mind and clarify that they do not want to place any undue burden upon them.

to experience: When our rules for worship or faith place burdens upon others we are called to step back and discern if this is truly the will of Jesus, the Prince of Peace.

Connecting the Responsorial Psalm

to the readings: In Psalm 66 we hear the cry, 'Let the peoples praise you, O God; / let all the peoples praise you'. And in the first and second reading we see this exclamation coming true. In the Acts of the Apostles, Gentiles receive the good news of Jesus's death and resurrection and are brought into the early church along with their Jewish brothers and sisters. In the second reading from Apocalypse we are given a vision of the holy city, Jerusalem, becoming a beacon for the world that all nations may 'walk by its light' (21:24). Our faith has never been a treasure to hoard and stow away. It is to be shared with all nations and peoples.

to psalmist preparation: This psalm begins, 'O God, be gracious and bless us / and let your face shed its light upon us'. After asking for blessing from the Lord it also expresses the desire that all the peoples of the world might bless the Lord in return. How do you experience blessing in your life? What or who blesses you? What or whom do you bless?

PROMPTS FOR FAITH-SHARING

In the Acts of the Apostles we see the Jewish leaders of the early church reaching out to the Gentile members of the community. Within your own church community are there groups that seem at odds with each other? How might they be invited to reach out to one another in peace?

In the reading from Apocalypse we hear of a city that needs no sun or moon for it is lit by the glory of the Lord. What are the places in your life that need to be touched by the Lord's light?

How do you experience the peace of Christ in your daily life?

Jesus tells us, 'Do not let your hearts be troubled or afraid'. What troubles your heart at this moment? How might you entrust this fear to God?

CELEBRATION

Model Rite for the Blessing and Sprinkling of Water

Presider: Through the waters of Baptism we are given new life in the Spirit of God. May this sprinkling rite renew us in joy, hope, and love . . . [*pause*]

[*continue with* The Roman Missal, *Appendix II*]

Homily Points

• In the Last Supper discourse of John's gospel Jesus carefully prepares the disciples for the time when he will no longer be with them in the way they are used to. His physical presence in the human body they are accustomed to might be gone, but he wants them to know in no uncertain terms that he will still dwell with them through his word, his peace, and the Holy Spirit.

• We live in the time of waiting – the time after Jesus's ascension to the Father but before the fulfilment of the kingdom of God where God will be 'all in all' (1 Cor 15:28; NABRE) and 'all tears' will be wiped away as we heard in last week's reading from Apocalypse. In this time of waiting and building the kingdom of God Jesus reassures us as well that he will dwell with us always, even when we can't see him.

• Our lives as disciples require that we cultivate these gifts of the Lord. That we love his word with our whole heart, mind, soul, and self. That we take time to experience and receive Jesus's peace so that we might share it with others. That we know the Holy Spirit through prayer and worship. The first Easter season when Jesus appeared to his disciples after his resurrection was a time of joy and a time of transition. Jesus knew his disciples would need time to integrate this new reality. And so it is with us. We have experienced the great fast of Lent, the solemnity of the Holy Triduum, and the overwhelming joy of Easter. Now we are given time to integrate these new spiritual insights into our own life before we return to the routine rhythm of Ordinary Time. How will your life be different after encountering Jesus in his word, peace, and Spirit anew?

Model Universal Prayer (Prayer of the Faithful)

Presider: Jesus tells us, 'Do not let your hearts be troubled or afraid' and so with confidence in God's love and care we bring our needs before the Lord.

Response: Lord, hear our prayer.

That the church may trust in the Advocate, the Holy Spirit, to lead her now and always . . .

That nations might walk in the light of the Lamb of God . . .

That those who are burdened by anxiety and depression know the peace of the Lord . . .

That all gathered here today be strengthened in our love of Jesus and our fidelity to his word . . .

Presider: God of peace, you sent your only son to dwell among us and to teach us your ways. Hear our prayers that we might become instruments of his peace. Through Christ our Lord. **Amen.**

COLLECT

Let us pray.

Pause for silent prayer

Grant, almighty God,
that we may celebrate with heartfelt
    devotion these days of joy,
which we keep in honour of the risen Lord,
and that what we relive in remembrance
we may always hold to in what we do.
Through our Lord Jesus Christ, your Son,
who lives and reigns with you in the unity
    of the Holy Spirit,
one God, for ever and ever. **Amen.**

FIRST READING
Acts 15:1-2, 22-29

Some men came down from Judaea and taught the brothers, 'Unless you have yourselves circumcised in the tradition of Moses you cannot be saved.' This led to disagreement, and after Paul and Barnabas had had a long argument with these men it was arranged that Paul and Barnabas and others of the church should go up to Jerusalem and discuss the problem with the apostles and elders.

Then the apostles and elders decided to choose delegates to send to Antioch with Paul and Barnabas; the whole church concurred with this. They chose Judas known as Barsabbas and Silas, both leading men in the brotherhood, and gave them this letter to take with them:

'The apostles and elders, your brothers, send greetings to the brothers of pagan birth in Antioch, Syria and Cilicia. We hear that some of our members have disturbed you with their demands and have unsettled your minds. They acted without any authority from us, and so we have decided unanimously to elect delegates and to send them to you with Barnabas and Paul, men we highly respect who have dedicated their lives to the name of our Lord Jesus Christ. Accordingly we are sending you Judas and Silas, who will confirm by word of mouth what we have written in this letter. It has been decided by the Holy Spirit and by ourselves not to saddle you with any burden beyond these essentials: you are to abstain from food sacrificed to idols, from blood, from the meat of strangled animals and from fornication. Avoid these, and you will do what is right. Farewell.'

CATECHESIS

RESPONSORIAL PSALM
Ps 66:2-3, 5, 6, 8 (4)

R̸. Let the peoples praise you, O God;
let all the peoples praise you.
or
R̸. Alleluia.

O God, be gracious and bless us
and let your face shed its light upon us.
So will your ways be known upon earth
and all nations learn your saving help.

R̸. Let the peoples praise you, O God;
let all the peoples praise you.
or
R̸. Alleluia.

Let the nations be glad and exult
for you rule the world with justice.
With fairness you rule the peoples,
you guide the nations on earth.

R̸. Let the peoples praise you, O God;
let all the peoples praise you.
or
R̸. Alleluia.

Let the peoples praise you, O God;
let all the peoples praise you.
May God still give us his blessing
till the ends of the earth revere him.

R̸. Let the peoples praise you, O God;
let all the peoples praise you.
or
R̸. Alleluia.

SECOND READING
Apoc 21:10-14, 22-23

In the spirit, the angel took me to the
top of an enormous high mountain and
showed me Jerusalem, the holy city,
coming down from God out of heaven.
It had all the radiant glory of God and
glittered like some precious jewel of
crystal-clear diamond. The walls of it were
of a great height, and had twelve gates;
at each of the twelve gates there was an
angel, and over the gates were written the
names of the twelve tribes of Israel; on the
east there were three gates, on the north
three gates, on the south three gates, and
on the west three gates. The city walls
stood on twelve foundation stones, each
one of which bore the name of one of the
twelve apostles of the Lamb.

I saw that there was no temple in the
city since the Lord God Almighty and the
Lamb were themselves the temple, and the
city did not need the sun or the moon for
light, since it was lit by the radiant glory
of God and the Lamb was a lighted torch
for it.

About Liturgy
The temple where the Spirit dwells: Today's reading from Apocalypse gives us
an opportunity to contemplate the symbol of the parish church as a sign of Christ's
presence. For this we look to the Rite of Dedication of a Church:

'Christ became the true and perfect temple of the New Covenant and gathered
together a people to be his own. This holy people . . . is the Church, that is, the temple
of God built of living stones, where the Father is worshiped in spirit and in truth.
Rightly, then, from early times "church" has also been the name given to the building
in which the Christian community gathers' (1). Here we see that the church is first the
people assembled to give praise to God. Second, it is the building in which the people
gather. *Ekklesia* is the Greek word for the Hebrew *qahal:* it describes a group of people
who are summoned or convoked, set apart for a purpose.

What is the purpose of this gathering of the people called the church? Again, we
look to the Rite of Dedication: 'May we open our hearts and minds to receive his word
with faith; may our fellowship born in the one font of baptism and sustained at the one
table of the Lord, become the one temple of his Spirit, as we gather round his altar in
love' (30). By hearing and receiving God's word and in unity through font and table, we
become the temple of the Spirit made visible around the altar. What makes the church
building holy is not so much the prayers and anointings over the stone and wood but
the love and unity that is visible and shared among its members, most especially with
those who have been left out.

This week look deeper into the history of your parish church. When was it
dedicated? Why was it given the name it bears? Look also to the neighbourhood. Who
is missing from the neighbourhood among your Sunday assemblies? What are some
ways to help them know this building called the church belongs to them?

About Initiation
No greater burden: Today's reading from Acts gives us this line: 'It has been
decided by the Holy Spirit and by ourselves not to saddle you with any burden beyond
these essentials' (Acts 15:28). This is echoed in the introductory notes for the Rite of
Reception of Baptised Christians into the Full Communion of the Catholic Church:
'The rite is so arranged that no greater burden than necessary is required for the
establishment of communion and unity' (RCIA 473). This means that those who have
been baptised in another ecclesial community whose baptism is recognised as valid are
to be treated with the dignity of God's chosen ones. What is primary is their baptism
in Christ; secondary is their ecclesial affiliation. Therefore, those who are ready to
renew their baptismal promises and make a profession of faith in the Catholic Church
should do so as soon as possible (see RCIA 476). We need not wait until the next Easter
Vigil to establish their full communion with the Catholic Church.

About Liturgical Music
Singing us home: Theologian Timothy Matovina has said: 'The church is holy not
just because all are welcome. The church is holy because all belong'. Two songs that
express clearly that church is first the people of God called to be a home for all God's
children are 'All Are Welcome' by Marty Haugen and 'A Place Called Home' with text
by Michael Joncas set to FINLANDIA, both from GIA. This latter was written as a
response to the need to welcome immigrants and refugees into our communities.

SPIRITUALITY

GOSPEL ACCLAMATION
Matt 28:19, 20

R/. Alleluia, alleluia!
Go, make disciples of all nations;
I am with you always; yes, to the end of time.
R/. Alleluia!

Gospel

Luke 24:46-53

**Jesus said to his disciples:
'You see how it is written that
the Christ would suffer and
on the third day rise from the
dead, and that, in his name,
repentance for the forgiveness
of sins would be preached to
all the nations, beginning from
Jerusalem. You are witnesses
to this.**

**'And now I am sending
down to you what the Father
has promised. Stay in the
city then, until you are clothed with
the power from on high.' Then he
took them out as far as the outskirts
of Bethany, and lifting up his hands
he blessed them. Now as he blessed
them, he withdrew from them and was
carried up to heaven. They worshipped
him and then went back to Jerusalem
full of joy; and they were continually in
the Temple praising God.**

Reflecting on the Gospel

Beginnings and endings are important. Sometimes we even ritualise those events, such as with baptism and funerals. But there are other important beginnings and endings throughout our lives too. Today's reading is from the end of the Gospel of Luke. It ends where it began, in the Jerusalem temple. It's as though Luke is telling us that all has come full circle. And immediately prior to the disciples being in the temple, they had been brought out to Bethany, a village on the slope of the Mount of Olives, about a mile and a half from ancient Jerusalem. There at Bethany they witnessed for the final time the

visible, risen Christ. And that is the fundamental definition of the ascension, the going up to the heavens; it is the final leave-taking of Jesus before his assembled followers. After this, the risen Lord will no longer appear as he did.

Importantly, we are reading today from the Gospel of Luke, where the ascension of Jesus takes place on Easter Sunday evening. Later, when Luke writes the Acts of the Apostles, he says that the ascension took place forty days after Easter (Acts 1:9-11). But in the Acts of the Apostles Luke is also telling us the story of Pentecost, a Jewish feast celebrated fifty days after Passover, which we do not hear about in the gospel. So that might be part of the reason Luke gives us the extended time frame in Acts, because it brings the narrative forwards to Pentecost.

Luke is keen to indicate both in the gospel and in Acts that there was a time when the resurrection appearances to the disciples came to an end. After that time Jesus would be known in the 'breaking of the bread' (Luke 24:35; NABRE).

So, according the Gospel of Luke, the story has come full circle. What began in the temple with the appearance to Zechariah (Luke 1:9) has now been completed. The disciples are left praising God in the temple for the wondrous works God has done in and through Jesus. No longer will they witness the risen Christ, but from now on, they know him in the breaking of the bread.

Living the Paschal Mystery

So many of us Christians long to have witnessed Christ. Why does he not appear anymore? Where is he now? These are questions the ascension is meant to answer. Jesus has ascended to his glory with the Father. The time of his appearance has been completed. And now, as we will learn in Acts, the gift of the Spirit has been given to us. Moreover, as we learn in the last chapter of Luke, we now come to know Jesus in the breaking of the bread.

The ascension, then, is not so much about a physically present Jesus floating up and up into the clouds as it is a theologically sophisticated concept proclaiming his eternal presence with the Father in glory. When we take this image too literally we miss the theological truth it attempts to convey. As we live the paschal mystery we are reminded that rising with Christ is rising to new life, no longer to be subject to death. Rising with Christ is rising to glory with the Father. This is much more profound and sophisticated than flying through the sky without wings.

Focusing the Gospel

Key words and phrases: You are witnesses to this.

To the point: Before ascending to his Father, Jesus commissions the disciples to take the seed of faith that has been planted in Israel and to bring it to the whole world. They are to proclaim the good news that God became man, was crucified, died, and then rose again on the third day and now offers his very light and life to us. This light and life comes to us through 'repentance for the forgiveness of sins'. Let us pause to consider for a moment where this good news has spread in the two thousand years since the disciples saw the risen Lord ascend into heaven. Where has the good news found you?

Connecting the Gospel

to the first reading: The first reading and the gospel for today tell the same story by the same author, but with slightly different details. Both contain the central theme of witness. Jesus tells the disciples in the Gospel of Luke, 'You are witnesses to this'. In the Acts of the Apostles he instructs them, '[Y]ou will be my witnesses not only in Jerusalem but throughout Judaea and Samaria, and indeed to the ends of the earth'. A witness is someone who has seen an event and gives testimony about it. For the disciples it is not enough that they have been the firsthand witnesses to the ministry, death, and resurrection of Jesus. They need one more thing to carry out their mission: 'power from on high'.

to experience: Only through the grace of God are we able to accomplish the tasks we are given. In the Holy Spirit the disciples of today are also able to witness to the risen Lord, even without the firsthand experiences of the original disciples.

Connecting the Responsorial Psalm

to the readings: Once again the psalm for today calls for all the peoples of the world to 'clap your hands, / cry to God with shouts of joy'! For the Lord is not Lord of Israel alone, but of 'all the earth'. Today's readings from the New Testament confirm this as well. Jesus wishes for the redemption of the cross to spread to 'the ends of the earth'. The saving action that has taken place in a particular time and place is actually meant for all times, all places, and all peoples.

to psalmist preparation: In the psalm today we are given the image, 'God goes up with shouts of joy; / the Lord goes up with trumpet blast'. Today's feast of the Ascension calls for joy, even though it marks a transition from Christ's earthly ministry to his reign at the right hand of God. This transition ushers in a new time when Jesus, no longer limited in time and space, is present to us always and everywhere. How do you experience the risen Lord in your life? Can you cultivate even more joy in this relationship?

PROMPTS FOR FAITH-SHARING

In the Acts of the Apostles, the two men in white ask the disciples, 'Why are you . . . standing here looking into the sky?' Where have you been looking for Jesus in your life?

Jesus calls his disciples to witness 'to the ends of the earth'. What places are 'the ends of the earth' for you? What people are the most difficult for you to contemplate witnessing the love of Jesus to?

In what areas of your life are you in need of 'power from on high' in order to persevere and be successful?

The Gospel of Luke ends where it began, in the temple in Jerusalem. Often our lives seem cyclical. Where and when did your spiritual journey begin? Where is the journey taking you now?

CELEBRATION

Model Rite for the Blessing and Sprinkling of Water

Presider: Jesus tells us today, '[Y]ou will be my witnesses not only in Jerusalem but throughout Judaea and Samaria, and indeed to the ends of the earth'. May this water sprinkled over us strengthen our resolve to witness to the love of Jesus in all aspects of our lives . . . [*pause*]

[*continue with* The Roman Missal, *Appendix II*]

Homily Points

• In today's reading from the Acts of the Apostles we hear many phrases that echo to us from the women's experience at the empty tomb in Luke's gospel. In both instances we have two men in white who show up to ask the onlookers questions. The women, who are staring in disbelief at the place where they expected to find Jesus's body, are asked, 'Why look among the dead for someone who is alive?' At the scene of the ascension, we hear these men asking the disciples, who are still looking at the place where Jesus disappeared, 'Why are you men from Galilee standing here looking into the sky?'

• In both cases the women at the tomb and the disciples who have just witnessed the ascension are looking in the wrong place for Jesus. Their attention is turned in the wrong direction. For the women it is in the direction of death and grief. They were certain they would find the body of their Lord and friend within the tomb and would be able to minister to him and prepare his body for burial. But he is not to be found among the dead. He is alive! The disciples are also looking in the wrong direction. Jesus is not in the sky. He is with them in a different way. Now they will meet him in the breaking of the bread. They will meet him when they minister to each other. They will meet him in prayer.

• And so in our lives we might ask the same question. Where are we looking for Jesus? Do we look for him only within the confines of our parish church? Or do we look for him among the poor and lonely, in the Eucharist, and all those we meet?

Model Universal Prayer (Prayer of the Faithful)

Presider: Jesus calls us to be witnesses to the ends of the earth. Let us pray for the wisdom, knowledge, and fidelity to fulfill this call.

Response: Lord, hear our prayer.

That the church faithfully pass on all that she has been taught by Christ . . .

That the good news of Jesus's life, death, and resurrection be known throughout all the nations of the earth . . .

That those in desperate need of the hope, love, and peace of Christ encounter preachers of the good news . . .

That all gathered here be enlightened and strengthened by the Holy Spirit to carry out the work given to us by Jesus . . .

Presider: Good and gracious God, you sent us your Son so that we might know and love you. Grant our prayers that we would continue to spread the good news of Jesus Christ to the ends of the earth, through the power of the Holy Spirit. We ask this through Jesus, our Lord. **Amen.**

COLLECT

(from the Mass during the Day)
Let us pray

Pause for silent prayer

Gladden us with holy joys, almighty God,
and make us rejoice with devout
     thanksgiving,
for the Ascension of Christ your Son
is our exaltation,
and, where the Head has gone before
     in glory,
the Body is called to follow in hope.
Through our Lord Jesus Christ, your Son,
who lives and reigns with you in the unity
     of the Holy Spirit,
one God, for ever and ever. **Amen.**

FIRST READING
Acts 1:1-11

In my earlier work, Theophilus, I dealt with everything Jesus had done and taught from the beginning until the day he gave his instructions to the apostles he had chosen through the Holy Spirit, and was taken up to heaven. He had shown himself alive to them after his Passion by many demonstrations: for forty days he had continued to appear to them and tell them about the kingdom of God. When he had been at table with them, he had told them not to leave Jerusalem, but to wait there for what the Father had promised. 'It is', he had said, 'what you have heard me speak about: John baptised with water but you, not many days from now, will be baptised with the Holy Spirit.'

Now having met together, they asked him, 'Lord, has the time come? Are you going to restore the kingdom to Israel?' He replied, 'It is not for you to know times or dates that the Father has decided by his own authority, but you will receive power when the Holy Spirit comes on you, and then you will be my witnesses not only in Jerusalem but throughout Judaea and Samaria, and indeed to the ends of the earth.'

As he said this he was lifted up while they looked on, and a cloud took him from their sight. They were still staring into the sky when suddenly two men in white were standing near them and they said, 'Why are you men from Galilee standing here looking into the sky? Jesus who has been taken up from you into heaven, this same Jesus will come back in the same way as you have seen him go there.'

CATECHESIS

RESPONSORIAL PSALM

Ps 46:2-3, 6-9 (6)

R̹. God goes up with shouts of joy;
the Lord goes up with trumpet blast.
   or:
R̹. Alleluia!

All peoples, clap your hands,
cry to God with shouts of joy!
For the Lord, the Most High, we must fear,
great king over all the earth.

R̹. God goes up with shouts of joy;
the Lord goes up with trumpet blast.
   or:
R̹. Alleluia!

God goes up with shouts of joy;
the Lord goes up with trumpet blast.
Sing praise for God, sing praise,
sing praise to our king, sing praise.

R̹. God goes up with shouts of joy;
the Lord goes up with trumpet blast.
   or:
R̹. Alleluia!

God is king of all the earth.
Sing praise with all your skill.
God is king over the nations;
God reigns on his holy throne.

R̹. God goes up with shouts of joy;
the Lord goes up with trumpet blast.
   or:
R̹. Alleluia!

SECOND READING

Heb 9:24-28; 10:19-23

or Eph 1:17-23

See Appendix A, p. 295.

About Liturgy

Commissioned to go: One unique aspect of Luke's gospel account of the ascension is that Jesus 'lifting up his hands he blessed them' (Luke 24:50), that is, he blessed the disciples. Every Sunday the same gesture is made over us at the end of the Mass when the priest raises his hands over the assembly, blesses us, and he or the deacon dismisses us to '[g]o and announce the Gospel of the Lord'. The word 'mass' is taken from this very ritual of sending in which, at one point, the words of dismissal were *Ite, missa est*, meaning 'Go, she [the church] has been sent'.

In the ascension, what is primary is not so much *where* Jesus went but where Jesus sends *us*. We are sent to 'be [Christ's] witnesses not only in Jerusalem but throughout Judaea and Samaria, and indeed to the ends of the earth' (Acts 1:8). Imagine that! Every time we celebrate the Mass, we are given a mission to go as far as we can beyond our neighbourhoods and familiar places, beyond our comfort zones and our own preferences, needs, and biases, to announce what we have seen, heard, touched, tasted, and known – that Jesus has conquered death by death, so we need not be afraid any longer to lay down our lives for one another.

Yet, sometimes the dismissal is seen as a welcome end to what might have been a less than life-giving ritual and our final 'Thanks be to God' takes on a sense of relief rather than readiness for the work that continues in the world. If we find that our assembly is lacking in its sense of mission, let us look to the other parts of the Mass to see where we can better emphasise the liturgical rhythm of gathering and sending.

As we begin the days awaiting the memorial of the coming of the Spirit upon the disciples, let us pray that the Spirit will also rekindle the flame of Christ's mission in our hearts this day.

About Initiation

Dismissing catechumens: Once unbaptised adults have entered the order of catechumens, they are 'kindly dismissed before the liturgy of the eucharist begins' whenever they are present at Mass (RCIA 75.3). Some RCIA teams avoid dismissing catechumens from the Eucharist for fear of seeming inhospitable. This negative feeling may come from a misunderstanding of the meaning of the dismissal.

Each member of the church is given a mission. Those in the order of the faithful are sent at the end of Mass to '[g]o and announce the Gospel of the Lord'. Those in the order of catechumens are sent at the end of the Liturgy of the Word to 'share their joy and spiritual experiences' (RCIA 67).

The reason catechumens are dismissed before the Liturgy of the Eucharist is not because they cannot yet share in Communion but because their 'order' has a specific mission – to share what they have heard in the Word. Once they enter the order of the baptised, their mission will include the priestly duty to pray the prayers of the faithful (the Creed, universal prayer, and the eucharistic prayer), to share in the Body and Blood of Christ, and to go be that presence of Christ in the world.

About Liturgical Music

Songs of sending: Two beautiful hymns will help put the mission of the church on the lips of the assembly today: first, Paul Inwood's 'Take Christ to the World'; second, 'The Church of Christ in Every Age' with text by Fred Pratt Green, set to WAREHAM. An alternative to a dismissal song could be a simple song sung after Communion that anticipates the coming of the Spirit, such as Ginny Vissing's 'Abba, Father, send your Spirit'.

SEVENTH SUNDAY OF EASTER

SPIRITUALITY

GOSPEL ACCLAMATION
Cf. John 14:18

℞. Alleluia, alleluia.
I will not leave you orphans, says the Lord;
I will come back to you, and your hearts will be
    full of joy.
℞. Alleluia, alleluia.

Gospel   John 17:20-26

Jesus raised his eyes to heaven
and said:
  'Holy Father,
  I pray not only for these,
  but for those also
  who through their words will
      believe in me.
  May they all be one.
  Father, may they be one in us
  as you are in me and I am in you,
  so that the world may believe it
      was you who sent me.
  I have given them the glory you
      gave to me,
  that they may be one as we are one.
  With me in them and you in me,
  may they be so completely one
  that the world will realise that it was
      you who sent me
  and that I have loved them as much as
      you love me.
  Father,
  I want those you have given me
  to be with me where I am,
  so that they may always see the glory
  you have given me
  because you loved me
  before the foundation of the world.
  Father, Righteous One,
  the world has not known you,
  but I have known you,
  and these have known
  that you have sent me.
  I have made your name known to them
  and will continue to make it known,
  so that the love with which you loved
      me may be in them,
  and so that I may be in them.'

Reflecting on the Gospel

There is a joke among Scripture scholars that if you ask Jesus in the Gospel of John how he's doing, he'll take three chapters to say that he and the Father are just fine. That's certainly a stretch, but today's gospel reading from John gives us an insight into where that joke comes from.

All joking aside, the Christology conveyed in this gospel is essentially theology, for Jesus and the Father are one, as is repeated several times in these few verses. But the image of unity does not stop with the Father and Son. For in Jesus's prayer he is sure to include his followers, not only his living, breathing disciples at the time, but all those who 'through their words will believe in me'. That is, he is praying for us today. And he is praying for us that we all might be one. Unfortunately, we only need to look out on the street corners of our towns, villages, and cities to see that we are not one in Christ. There are many, many denominations split by creedal statements, theological beliefs, doctrinal beliefs, ethical practices, treatment and role of women, gender differences, sexual orientation, care for the earth, and more. Sadly, Jesus's prayer has not yet been realised. And we know from the Johannine literature (Gospel of John, 1 John, 2 John, and 3 John) that the early community faced ruptures and schisms too. So that reality is not new to us, or new to the Reformation in the sixteenth century. As long as there have been Christians there has been disunity.

Still, Jesus prays for our unity just the same. A critical theme, then, in these few verses is unity: unity of the Father and Son, and of the Son in believers.

There is a juxtaposition, too, between the believers who know Jesus and the world that does not know him. One goal is that when believers – Christians – are one, the world will know that the Father sent Jesus. So if we Christians want the world to believe, we might start with reconciling ourselves to one another. According to the words of Jesus in this gospel, Christian unity will cause the world to know Christ.

Living the Paschal Mystery

It's so easy for us to spot differences. Our brains are made to do just that. Rather than know every possible way to make a counterfeit banknote, we instead know the true note. Then, when we find a note with something amiss we can label it a counterfeit. Spotting differences saves our mental energy for more important things. But it's good to be aware that sometimes our snap judgements or inclination to find the difference is not always required. In fact, sometimes it is better (and it takes more energy) to find what's common. And perhaps if we did that with our Christian brothers and sisters we'd be more apt to find occasions of agreement, or reconciliation. In so doing, we would be working towards Christian unity. And unity does not mean sameness or even similarity. There can be differences in unity. Jesus does not pray for us to be the same. He prays for us to be one, as he and the Father are one. Today, let's be more mindful about finding common ground than finding difference. By doing so, we just might be realising the prayer of Jesus.

Focusing the Gospel

Key words and phrases: may they be so completely one

To the point: We are not saved on our own, but as the community of the Body of Christ. Jesus prays for the unity of his followers. Not only the ones immediately in front of him but for the followers that will stretch throughout the centuries as one unbroken family of the people of God. It seems that in this prayer Jesus asks for the impossible. As humans, our sinfulness keeps us both from perfection and from complete unity with one another. Luckily, Jesus is not asking that we be perfect or unified through our own efforts alone. Instead he prays to God for that which makes all things possible, 'so that the love with which you loved me may be in them, / and so that I may be in them'.

Connecting the Gospel

to the first and second readings: In the Acts of the Apostles we see a scene dominated by division and enmity. Stephen becomes the first martyr to follow in the footsteps of Jesus. He is brought before the Sanhedrin and is ultimately stoned. Before he dies, however, Stephen's last words echo those of Jesus on the cross, 'Lord, do not hold this sin against them'. Only through the perfect love of God is Stephen able to hope for unity with his assailants. Despite their mortal violence against him, his words of forgiveness leave the door open for reconciliation. Today we also come to the end of the book of Apocalypse, which we have been reading throughout the Easter season. Within this reading we receive a clue about what will bring us to the fulfilment of God's kingdom and Jesus's hope for unity: our own desire. Jesus invites us, 'Then let all who are thirsty come; all who want it may have the water of life, and have it free'.

to experience: How much do we long for the unity that Jesus prays for in the gospel? Do we long for it so much we are willing to follow the example of Stephen and pray for the forgiveness of those who wound, hurt, and persecute us?

Connecting the Responsorial Psalm

to the readings: Psalm 96 presents a picture of Israel worshipping among other nations who serve other gods. In this day and age idols are not foreign gods, but whatever we let rule our lives in place of the God of love. Chaos and division reign when our primary devotion is to money, power, fame, drugs, alcohol, or any other *thing*. The unity that Jesus prays for can only come about when these addictions and desires are submitted to God. When our primary devotion is to the 'most high above all the earth' we will find peace and unity.

to psalmist preparation: Where are false idols disturbing the peace and unity of your own life? How might you reject these idols in favour of the God of 'justice and right'?

PROMPTS FOR FAITH-SHARING

In the Acts of the Apostles Stephen prays for his executioners shortly before dying. Jesus has instructed us to pray for our enemies (see Matt 5:44). Who are you being called to pray for?

In today's gospel Jesus prays for those who will become followers through the word of the disciples. In your life of faith, whose 'word' helped lead you to belief?

Jesus also prays for unity among his followers. Where do you see division in your local Christian community? How might you work for unity?

When have you experienced unity with other Christian denominations? How did this experience come about?

CELEBRATION

Model Rite for the Blessing and Sprinkling of Water

Presider: In baptism we are born into the universal church, the Body of Christ. May the sprinkling of this water strengthen us in unity with one another and with Christians throughout the world . . . [*pause*]

    [*continue with* The Roman Missal, *Appendix II*]

Homily Points

• Jesus begins his prayer in today's gospel by praying not only for the disciples who are with him, but also for 'for those also / who through their words will believe in me. / May they all be one'. Let us pause together to consider the web of connections that have led from that moment in time to this one. How many people in how many different places and times have continued to pass on the word of Jesus so that it might come to us today? And when did our specific family first hear the word of Jesus? Was it in a foreign country, many centuries ago, or just recently within the very community you find yourself now sitting?

• We might also consider the many people who underwent persecutions in order for this word to come to us today. In the Acts of the Apostles we hear of the first martyr, St. Stephen. Even today, people continue to give their lives as a consequence of sharing the word of Jesus. And yet, in the book of Apocalypse we are given hope. The Jesus who prayed for his disciples in the Upper Room in Jerusalem is also 'the Alpha and the Omega, the First and the Last, the Beginning and the End'.

• And this Jesus continues to pray for us and for all of the people in the future who will hear his word through our lips. We are now threads on the web of good news reaching out to cover all space and all time. Who will God bring to us to preach the Word? We are given a part to play in bringing about the full unity and breadth of the kingdom of God.

Model Universal Prayer (Prayer of the Faithful)

Presider: Jesus prays in today's gospel that his followers might be unified as he and the Father are unified. Let us join our voices to Jesus's as we offer up our petitions.

Response: Lord, hear our prayer.

That the church reach out in love and fraternity to other Christian denominations and work for the unity of all Christians . . .

That leaders of nations join together to work for the well-being of all the world's people . . .

That those who are housebound find comfort in the love of their community who are unified with them in prayer . . .

That all gathered here might take on the work of peacemaking and conflict resolution as we seek to build up the unity of the people of God . . .

Presider: God of all creation, you call us to live in harmony and love. Hear our prayers that we might be signs of your unity throughout the earth. In the name of Jesus Christ our Lord. **Amen.**

COLLECT

Let us pray.

Pause for silent prayer

Graciously hear our supplications, O Lord,
so that we, who believe that the Saviour of
    the human race
is with you in your glory,
may experience, as he promised,
until the end of the world,
his abiding presence among us.
Who lives and reigns with you in the unity
    of the Holy Spirit,
one God, for ever and ever. **Amen.**

FIRST READING
Acts 7:55-60

Stephen, filled with the Holy Spirit, gazed into heaven and saw the glory of God, and Jesus standing at God's right hand. 'I can see heaven thrown open' he said 'and the Son of Man standing at the right hand of God.' At this all the members of the council shouted out and stopped their ears with their hands; then they all rushed at him, sent him out of the city and stoned him. The witnesses put down their clothes at the feet of a young man called Saul. As they were stoning him, Stephen said in invocation, 'Lord Jesus, receive my spirit.' Then he knelt down and said aloud, 'Lord, do not hold this sin against them'; and with these words he fell asleep.

CATECHESIS

RESPONSORIAL PSALM
Ps 96:1-2, 6-7, 9 (1-9)

R̝. The Lord is king, most high above all
    the earth.
    or
R̝. Alleluia.

The Lord is king, let earth rejoice,
the many coastlands be glad.
His throne is justice and right.

R̝. The Lord is king, most high above all
    the earth.
    or
R̝. Alleluia.

The skies proclaim his justice;
all peoples see his glory.
All you spirits, worship him.

R̝. The Lord is king, most high above all
    the earth.
    or
R̝. Alleluia.

For you indeed are the Lord
most high above all the earth
exalted far above all spirits.

R̝. The Lord is king, most high above all
    the earth.
    or
R̝. Alleluia.

SECOND READING
Apoc 22:12-14, 16-17, 20

I, John, heard a voice speaking to me:
'Very soon now, I shall be with you again,
bringing the reward to be given to every
man according to what he deserves. I
am the Alpha and the Omega, the First
and the Last, the Beginning and the End.
Happy are those who will have washed
their robes clean, so that they will have
the right to feed on the tree of life and can
come through the gates into the city.'

I, Jesus, have sent my angel to make
these revelations to you for the sake of the
churches. I am of David's line, the root of
David and the bright star of the morning.

The Spirit and the Bride say, 'Come.' Let
everyone who listens answer, 'Come.' Then
let all who are thirsty come; all who want it
may have the water of life, and have it free.

The one who guarantees these
revelations repeats his promise: I shall
indeed be with you soon. Amen; come,
Lord Jesus.

About Liturgy

Hearing as the beginning of prayer: Notice how in the account of Stephen's martyrdom, those who were about to stone him 'stopped their ears' (Acts 7:57). What agitated this mob to kill Stephen was his long discourse before the Sanhedrin and the high priest recounting how God's people time and time again refused to hear the voice of God. Stephen's testimony before his accusers ends with this charge: 'You stiff-necked people, uncircumcised in heart and ears, you always oppose the holy Spirit; you are just like your ancestors' (Acts 7:51; NABRE). His murderers would hear no more of this, and rushed upon him in anger.

Hearing in Judeo-Christian tradition is closely tied to obedience. The great *Shema* prayer from Deuteronomy 6, 'Hear, O Israel! . . . you shall love the LORD, your God . . . Take to heart these words' (NABRE), is an example of the close connection between 'hearing' and 'obeying'. *Shema* connotes more than simply perceiving sounds; it implies hearing the meaning behind the words so deeply that it changes our hearts and moves us to respond in obedience. Recall how often Jesus referred to hearing as the beginning of conversion, especially after a parable or teaching, for example, 'Whoever has ears ought to hear', concluding the parable of the Sower (Matt 13:9; NABRE).

Those who do the word of God are those who have first heard it and allowed it into their hearts. The mob that killed Stephen closed their ears and their hearts to the word.

As we pray this week, in common in the liturgy and in our own private prayers, let us commit to first *hearing* what God has to say so that when we open our lips, our words may become a response to the Spirit we have heard in our hearts that leads us to embody that same Word by our lives.

About Liturgical Music

Singing our unity: The very act of singing itself is a lesson in unity. Specifically, it teaches us three things. First, we cannot sing together unless we breathe together. We must, in a literal sense, *conspire* with one another in order to make the song a reality. Second, we cannot make music together unless we submit our individual preferences to the common good of singing the song. Communal singing is a group effort, not an individual action done in the same room with others. Finally, we cannot make something beautiful unless we give up something of ourselves for the sake of the other. We open our mouths to give up our breath. We allow ourselves to be vulnerable by offering our voice, as imperfect as it might be. We humble ourselves by remembering the song is not about me but about us and who God has called us to be – one voice singing with the breath of the Spirit.

This week let us listen to one another as we sing that we may breathe together and sacrifice ourselves for the sake of becoming one body in Christ.

Suggestions: Good choices for today include 'We gather together as brothers and sisters', 'We come to share our story' (Song of the Body of Christ) and 'O thou, who at thy Eucharist didst pray'.

SPIRITUALITY

GOSPEL ACCLAMATION

R. Alleluia, alleluia.
Come, Holy Spirit, fill the hearts of your faithful
and kindle in them the fire of your love.
R. Alleluia, alleluia.

Gospel (Mass during the Day)

John 14:15-16, 23-26

Jesus said to his disciples:
　'If you love me you will keep my
　　　　commandments.
　I shall ask the Father,
　and he will give you another
　　　　Advocate
　to be with you for ever.
　'If anyone loves me he will keep
　　　　my word,
　and my Father will love him,
　and we shall come to him
　and make our home with him.
　Those who do not love me do
　　　　not keep my words.
　And my word is not my own;
　it is the word of the one who
　　　　sent me.
　I have said these things to you
　while still with you;
　but the Advocate, the Holy Spirit,
　whom the Father will send in
　　　　my name,
　will teach you everything
　and remind you of all I have said
　　　　to you.'

Reflecting on the Gospel

We are now about fifty days, or seven weeks, from Easter. To be clear, Pentecost was a Jewish feast of the springtime, also known as the Feast of Weeks, or the Feast of the New Harvest or even the Feast of New Wine. Because it comes about fifty days (Lev 23:16) after the feast of Passover it was also called Pentecost (which means 'fifty' in Greek). The Acts of the Apostles tell us that it was on the Jewish Feast of Pentecost that the apostles were emboldened by the Spirit to preach to Israel, assembled in Jerusalem for the feast. Thus, Luke precedes the story of Peter (as representing the Twelve) and his preaching, with the outpouring of the Spirit, thereby emboldening the Twelve so.

But today we read from the Gospel of John, which seems not to know anything about the feast of Pentecost and the emboldened Peter preaching. Instead, the story we have in John takes place on Easter Sunday when the risen Christ appears to the disciples (save Thomas, which we shall learn later) to give them the Spirit and the gift of peace. Upon receiving the gift of the Spirit, the disciples are emboldened not to preach (as Luke would have it) but to forgive sins. Though Jesus conquered the cosmic power of sin on the cross, it is the role of the disciples to forgive individual sins, almost as a clean-up operation after the major victory has been won.

Though this power to forgive sins has been traditionally understood to be the sacrament of reconciliation, this should not stop modern followers of Jesus (disciples) from forgiving others. In other words, forgiveness is not limited to sacramental ritual. Forgiveness has a power to unleash one held by some wrongdoing. We need think only about our own friends and families. How often do we forgive someone who has wronged us? How often do we seek forgiveness when we've wronged another? Those tasks belong to the disciples of Jesus per his handing on of the Spirit after Easter. We can certainly forgive and seek forgiveness without taking anything away from the sacrament of reconciliation.

Living the Paschal Mystery

The paschal mystery calls us to die to ourselves so we might be lifted up by and with Christ. One way we die to ourselves is to seek forgiveness when we do something wrong. Simply asking for forgiveness is a sign of humility, and it is something not often done. Not only are we to ask for forgiveness, but we are to forgive when someone wrongs us. Rather than hold a grudge our role as disciples is to forgive, in imitation of Jesus who set the example for us. If he can forgive those who wronged him, how much more must we forgive those who wrong us. To be a disciple requires nothing less. An admirer will certainly respect and praise the forgiveness Jesus effects, but a follower will seek to do the same, and forgive. As disciples, followers of Jesus, let us forgive as he forgave.

Focusing the Gospel

Key words and phrases: As the Father sent me, / so am I sending you.

To the point: We come to the end of the Easter season and we are given a mission. After being formed anew in the life and light of Jesus's death and resurrection we are to go forth as Jesus did in his ministry. Jesus sends us out into the world to be with people. To feed the hungry, comfort the outcast, touch the sick and lame, and everywhere proclaim the redemptive love of God.

Connecting the Gospel

to the first and second readings: In the gospel, Jesus gives the gift of the Holy Spirit by breathing on the disciples. In the first and second readings we see the effects of this gift. In the first reading, the apostles proclaim 'the marvels of God' to Jews 'from every nation under heaven', and yet, through the power of the Holy Spirit each person hears the message in their own native language. In the second reading we hear a listing of the many different gifts the Holy Spirit confers upon us. From these two readings we see that the Spirit's work is universal and also particular. The Spirit works within the community to draw people from every nation together in praising God. But the Spirit also works within us individually by giving gifts that are to be used to build up the kingdom of God. The action of the Holy Spirit enables the followers of Jesus to carry on Jesus's mission, 'As the Father sent me, / so am I sending you.'.

to experience: It is difficult not to compare the gifts we recognise in ourselves with the gifts we see in others. St. Paul reminds us that all gifts come from the same source, God. Instead of comparing our abilities and talents to those around us, let us focus on how we can use our gifts for the good of all.

Connecting the Responsorial Psalm

to the readings: In the readings today there are many allusions to the first two chapters of Genesis and the creation of the world. The 'powerful wind' that fills the Upper Room where the apostles are gathered is reminiscent of the 'mighty wind' that swept over the waters on the first day of creation. And Jesus breathing on the disciples parallels the action of God who 'blew into [Adam's] nostrils the breath of life' (Gen 2:7; NABRE). It is no surprise then that our psalm today speaks of creation too: 'You send forth your spirit, they are created; / and you renew the face of the earth'. The God of creation continues to create. By ushering in the time of our redemption through his death and resurrection, Jesus's breath imparts new life that is stronger than death upon his followers.

to psalmist preparation: Where do you notice the creative and renewing work of God in your own life? Where is the Spirit at work within you?

PROMPTS FOR FAITH-SHARING

In the Acts of the Apostles the gift of the Holy Spirit allows the apostles to communicate to people from many different countries. Have you ever experienced the Mass in a foreign language? What was this experience like?

In the psalm we pray for the Holy Spirit to renew the face of the earth. In your community where is there the need of renewal? How might you be a part of the renewing work of the Spirit?

In the First Letter to the Corinthians St. Paul lists the gifts of the Holy Spirit: wisdom, knowledge, faith, healing, mighty deeds, prophecy, discernment, tongues, interpretation of tongues. Which gift do you feel the most comfortable with? Which gift discomforts or challenges you?

In the gospel reading we find one of the scriptural sources for the sacrament of reconciliation. What was your first experience of reconciliation like? Was it positive or negative? Have you celebrated reconciliation recently? If not, what is holding you back?

CELEBRATION

Model Rite for the Blessing and Sprinkling of Water

Presider: On the Third Sunday of Advent we heard John the Baptist proclaim that the one who was to come would baptise with the Holy Spirit and with fire. And now on the Feast of Pentecost we see this come true. In baptism we are baptised into the life of the Holy Spirit. May this water rekindle the fire of the Holy Spirit within us . . . [*pause*]
   [*continue with* The Roman Missal, *Appendix II*]

Homily Points

• In the second chapter of Genesis God creates man from the dust of the earth and brings him to life by blowing into his nostrils. And so Adam comes alive with the very breath of God. God's breath is all that distinguishes Adam from the lifeless clay. In today's psalm we hear, 'You take back your spirit, they die, / returning to the dust from which they came'. The breath of God is an apt metaphor for the spiritual life. Without breath we die within minutes, and yet how often are we actually aware of this essential bodily function?

• In today's gospel Jesus appears to the disciples on the evening of Easter Sunday and breathes on them. In the four gospels we hear about breathing four times. Each of the synoptic gospels records how Jesus 'breathed his last' upon the cross (see Matt 27:50, Mark 15:37, Luke 23:46). The Gospel of John, instead of recording the last breath of Jesus before death, records the first breath the disciples receive of resurrected life. Within this breath we witness a kind of new creation. Jesus confers the life that cannot be overcome.

• Today concludes our paschal feast that began fifty days ago on Easter Sunday. Our liturgical calendar invites us to enter into times of fasting and feasting and also into Ordinary Time, where we live and grow in our faith. Perhaps this Ordinary Time will be a good opportunity to heighten our awareness of the breath of God sustaining us in every moment. On this feast of Pentecost we pray for the Spirit of God, the breath of life, to renew the face of the earth and to renew us.

Model Universal Prayer (Prayer of the Faithful)

Presider: Emboldened by the Holy Spirit we bring our prayers before the Lord.

Response: Lord, hear our prayer.

That the church proclaim the joy of the gospel to people of every language . . .

That the earth be protected and renewed by our constant care and tending . . .

That all those who are confirmed on this feast of Pentecost be filled with the breath of Christ . . .

That all those gathered here might receive an abundance of spiritual gifts and be led by the Holy Spirit to use them for the building of the Kingdom of God . . .

Presider: God of creation, you sent your Holy Spirit upon the apostles as tongues of fire. Hear our prayers that our hearts may be set on fire by this same Spirit so that we might spread your love throughout the earth. We ask this through Jesus's name. **Amen.**

COLLECT

Let us pray.

Pause for silent prayer

O God, who by the mystery of today's
      great feast
sanctify your whole Church in every
      people and nation,
pour out, we pray, the gifts of the
      Holy Spirit
across the face of the earth
and, with the divine grace that was at work
when the Gospel was first proclaimed,
fill now once more the hearts of believers.
Through our Lord Jesus Christ, your Son,
who lives and reigns with you in the unity
      of the Holy Spirit,
one God, for ever and ever. **Amen.**

FIRST READING
Acts 2:1-11

When Pentecost day came round, the apostles had all met in one room, when suddenly they heard what sounded like a powerful wind from heaven, the noise of which filled the entire house in which they were sitting; and something appeared to them that seemed like tongues of fire; these separated and came to rest on the head of each of them. They were all filled with the Holy Spirit, and began to speak foreign languages as the Spirit gave them the gift of speech.

   Now there were devout men living in Jerusalem from every nation under heaven, and at this sound they all assembled, each one bewildered to hear these men speaking his own language. They were amazed and astonished. 'Surely' they said 'all these men speaking are Galileans? How does it happen that each of us hears them in his own native language? Parthians, Medes and Elamites; people from Mesopotamia, Judaea and Cappadocia, Pontus and Asia, Phrygia and Pamphylia, Egypt and the parts of Libya round Cyrene; as well as visitors from Rome – Jews and proselytes alike – Cretans and Arabs; we hear them preaching in our own language about the marvels of God.'

CATECHESIS

RESPONSORIAL PSALM
Ps 103:1, 24, 29-31, 34 (30)

Ry. Send forth your Spirit, O Lord,
and renew the face of the earth.
or:
Ry. Alleluia.

Bless the Lord, my soul!
Lord God, how great you are.
How many are your works, O Lord!
The earth is full of your riches.

Ry. Send forth your Spirit, O Lord,
and renew the face of the earth.
or:
Ry. Alleluia.

You take back your spirit, they die,
returning to the dust from which
　　they came.
You send forth your spirit, they
　　are created;
and you renew the face of the earth.

Ry. Send forth your Spirit, O Lord,
and renew the face of the earth.
or:
Ry. Alleluia.

May the glory of the Lord last for ever!
May the Lord rejoice in his works!
May my thoughts be pleasing to him.
I find my joy in the Lord.

Ry. Send forth your Spirit, O Lord,
and renew the face of the earth.
or:
Ry. Alleluia.

SECOND READING
Rom 8:8-17

SEQUENCE

See Appendix A, p. 295.

About Liturgy

A second wind: Hopefully, by the time we get to Pentecost we have not exhausted ourselves so much during the seven weeks plus one day of the Easter season. But even if you're feeling relief more than rejuvenation on this day, you can still find simple ways to catch a second wind of the Spirit from Easter. Here are some ideas:

Wear red: If you're the presider, that's easy. But even beyond liturgical vestments, find a way to add a touch of red to your clothing – in a pendant, or socks, with a tie, or shoes. As you go about your day, you will be a walking reminder to yourself and others that the Spirit dwells among us.

Remember and give thanks for your godparents: If your baptismal or confirmation godparents are still around, contact them and thank them for the gift of their faith. If you are a godparent, connect with your companion and let them know you are praying for them.

Make every breath count: A beautiful image from today's reading from the Gospel of John is Jesus breathing on his disciples and blessing them with his words. Pay special attention to the words you share with others today. Make every word you give a blessing upon them.

Remember the neophytes: Invite the neophytes of your parish to be part of the entrance procession, and, if possible, have them wear their baptismal garments. This reminds us that the fulness of the Spirit's presence is found in these 'new plants' who have been brought to new life by the saving breath of God.

About Initiation

Celebrating with the neophytes: Easter Vigil seemed so long ago, fifty days, to be exact. Are your neophytes still front and centre in the focus of the parish as we all continue to deepen our grasp of the paschal mystery in our lives (see RCIA 244)? Even if the neophytes have been overshadowed by the many other celebrations and important occasions of this time of year, you can still rekindle your parish's care and concern for them during these days near Pentecost. A simple way to do this is just to plan a party. RCIA 249 says, '[S]ome sort of celebration should be held at the end of the Easter season near Pentecost Sunday'. It might even be as easy as hosting coffee and donuts after Sunday Mass and making sure the neophytes and their godparents are present and greeted by the parishioners. Also invite those who were baptised at last year's Easter Vigil to be part of this celebration, too.

About Liturgical Music

Suggestions: There is an abundance of music that refers to the Holy Spirit that you can find in any of your liturgical music resources. Other kinds of texts to seek out include those that speak of mission, baptism, and forgiveness. One such example is 'Church of God, Elect and Glorious' with text by J. E. Seddon. This text works well set to either NETTLETON, HYFRYDOL, or BLAENWERN. Also look for ways to reprise the music from the entire Easter season. For example, including the Litany of the Saints in some way at today's Mass provides a beautiful thread from First Sunday of Lent (when you might have used the Litany of the Saints as an entrance chant), to the Easter Vigil when we sang the litany as the elect processed to the font, to this last day of the paschal feasts.

Finally, don't forget to plan for the Pentecost sequence. This is a hymn that precedes the gospel acclamation Alleluia. Several settings of the text can be found in your hymnals, including a beautiful Psallite setting. Consider using one that all the assembly can sing together.

ORDINARY TIME II

SPIRITUALITY

GOSPEL ACCLAMATION
Cf. Apoc 1:8

℞. Alleluia, alleluia.
Glory be to the Father, and to the Son,
and to the Holy Spirit,
the God who is, who was, and who is to come.
℞. Alleluia, alleluia.

Gospel

John 16:12-15

Jesus said to his disciples:
'I still have many things to say to you
but they would be too much for
you now.
But when the Spirit of truth comes
he will lead you to the complete truth,
since he will not be speaking as
from himself
but will say only what he has learnt;
and he will tell you of the things
to come.
He will glorify me,
since all he tells you
will be taken from what is mine.
Everything the Father has is mine;
that is why I said:
All he tells you
will be taken from what is mine.'

Reflecting on the Gospel

On this feast of the Most Holy Trinity we read from the Gospel of John. Some modern readers of the New Testament are often surprised that the word 'Trinity' does not appear in the Bible at all, not in the New Testament and certainly not in the Old Testament. The term 'Trinity' is a Latin-based word from *trinitas*, meaning the number three or a triad. It can also mean the state of being threefold, or triple. It's a term that later Christian theologians, particularly in the patristic era, coined to talk about God, and the relationship of Father, Son, and Spirit. So, though the New Testament has many texts that speak of God the Father, the Son, and the Spirit, it never refers to them as Trinity.

Today's reading is one such where Jesus the Son is speaking, making reference to the Spirit of truth and to the Father. As such, this is one of many texts that church fathers used to develop the theology of the Trinity. And that theology developed over centuries with many roadblocks, hurdles, and missteps, but also many advances, developments, and clarifications along the way. One conclusion from the theological developments is that the doctrine of the Trinity is sophisticated, subtle, and worthy of reflection. There is a dynamic relationship between the three 'persons' of the Trinity that is expressed in a variety of ways in different scriptural passages. Today's passage from John gives us some of the subtlety of the relationship among the three that will be explored for centuries.

In this passage, we have the 'Spirit of truth' rather than the more standard or classical, Holy Spirit. And the Spirit of truth has a particular role, which is to guide the disciples to truth, speaking what is heard from the Father and the Son. The Spirit of truth also glorifies the Son. He takes from the Son, who has everything the Father has, and declares it to the disciples.

This is only a four-verse passage! Consider how much more there is in the New Testament about the relationship between Father, Son, and Spirit! Rather than a mathematical formula to be explained and known, the Trinity is a shorthand expression for the dynamic relationship between Father, Son, and Spirit. We ponder this relationship and we will never exhaust it. We drink from the wellsprings of Scripture, which never run dry.

Living the Paschal Mystery

One challenge we have in discussing the Trinity is that we've been given so many images and metaphors for it. For example, it's been said that St. Patrick used the shamrock, a three-leafed clover, to teach the natives about Trinity. But of course God is more than three leaves, and each 'person of the Trinity' has a more dynamic relationship than leaves on a shamrock. Some church fathers used the image of the sun for the Trinity, saying that the Father was like the sun itself, the Son the light, and the Spirit the heat. All three are in dynamic relation, but the sun itself is primary. This is a better image than a shamrock, but expresses the three persons as inanimate objects. Something similar happens when modern thinkers imagine the Trinity as the three modes of water in a liquid, solid, and gaseous state, but all at once!

The many images of Trinity and each of them incomplete in one way or another contribute to a fundamental challenge in discussing Trinity. Ultimately, it is best to go back to Scripture itself, and let that inform our understanding, which we do today by reading from the Gospel of John.

Focusing the Gospel

Key words and phrases: Everything the Father has is mine; / that is why I said: / All he tells you / will be taken from what is mine.

To the point: In this one verse from today's gospel we see the interplay of the three persons of the Trinity. The Son has received everything from the Father, and the Spirit communicates the fulness of Father and Son. Within God there is a relationship among Father, Son, and Holy Spirit that can be seen as a complete outpouring from one to the other. We, who have been created in the image and likeness of God, are invited into this community of complete gift of self. In emptying ourselves, we are filled with the love of Father, Son, and Holy Spirit.

Connecting the Gospel

to the first and second readings: In the book of Proverbs we are introduced to the figure of 'Lady Wisdom'. In our first reading, Wisdom sings a hymn of self-revelation. Over the centuries theologians have seen this figure as both Jesus and the Holy Spirit. In this hymn we see the beginning of understanding that even before creation God lived in relationship. Wisdom tells us, 'The Lord created me when his purpose first unfolded, / before the oldest of his works'. The relationship between God, the creator, and Wisdom is one of joy: 'I was by his side, a master craftsman, / delighting in him day after day, / ever at play in his presence'. In the gospel passage for today Jesus explains the relationship of Father, Son, and Holy Spirit as a complete knowing. In Proverbs we see it as complete joy. In the second reading from St. Paul's letter to the Romans we hear how we are connected to this dynamic. The love of Father and Son are poured into one another, but also 'poured into our hearts by the Holy Spirit which has been given us'.

to experience: To receive more fully the love of the triune God we make space by taking on the work of spiritual housekeeping. Greed, anger, hatred, apathy – what can be removed from our lives to make more room for God's love?

Connecting the Responsorial Psalm

to the readings: Delving into the mystery of the Trinity increases our wonder in life. Mysteries, such as that of the Trinity, are not problems to be solved or questions with one clear distinct answer that our human minds can grasp as they might a number. Rather, theological mysteries invite us into a deeper relationship with the One who calls us into being. In today's psalm we see this wonder in God's mysterious ways. After witnessing the beauty of creation the psalmist asks, '[W]hat is man that you should keep him in mind, / mortal man that you care for him?'

to psalmist preparation: God invites us into the outpouring of love between Father, Son, and Holy Spirit. Such an invitation inspires wonder, awe, and even incredulity at times. What in your life fills you with wonder and awe in the presence of God?

PROMPTS FOR FAITH-SHARING

In the psalm we hear the psalmist marvel at the works of creation. When have you experienced wonder and awe in nature?

St. Paul tells us today that we can boast in our sufferings because 'sufferings bring patience'. When have you experienced suffering in your life that, looking back on, you can see made you stronger?

In your prayer, which member of the Trinity do you address the most often? Why do you think this is?

How has your understanding of the Trinity grown throughout your life?

CELEBRATION

Model Penitential Act

Presider: As we prepare to celebrate this feast of the Holy Trinity, let us pray for the grace to always listen to the call and counsel of God the Father, God the Son, and God the Holy Spirit . . . [*pause*]

 Lord Jesus, you are the wisdom of God: Lord, have mercy.

 Christ Jesus, you are the second person of the Holy Trinity: Christ, have mercy.

 Lord Jesus, you call us to listen to the Spirit of Truth: Lord, have mercy.

Homily Points

• God, within God's own nature, is relationship. We believe in one God of three persons, the Father, the Son, and the Holy Spirit. Is it any surprise then that we, who are created in the image and likeness of God, are so hardwired for relationship? After birth, a baby who is given food and shelter but does not receive loving human interaction will fail to develop normally. From the very beginning of our lives, our relationships are our greatest joy and also can cause us the deepest sorrow.

• In the readings for today we hear how God lives out this triune relationship. In Proverbs, Wisdom is personified – identified later with both Jesus and the Holy Spirit – and brings joy to God, the creator. Wisdom is God's companion and delight. In the second reading, the Holy Spirit conveys the love between Father and Son, just as in the gospel the Spirit gives truth. Could this combination of joy, love, and truth serve as a blueprint for our own relationships?

• All relationships require celebration. In our world where so much revolves around transactions, we need time in relationships where we simply enjoy the other. We know, too, that all relationships require love, whether it is the relationship between spouses, parents and children, friends, or coworkers. Within the Trinity, love is dynamic and constantly outpouring. Relationships also demand truth, especially an authentic sharing of oneself with the other. From the very beginning of our lives within the womb we have experienced relationship – the relationship with God and the relationship with other humans. On this feast of the Holy Trinity let us rededicate ourselves to living out these relationships in joy, love, and truth.

Model Universal Prayer (Prayer of the Faithful)

Presider: In the gospel, Jesus tells the disciples of the Spirit of truth who will 'lead you to the complete truth'. Confident in the Spirit's guidance we lift up our prayers for ourselves and for our world.

Response: Lord, hear our prayer.

That those entrusted with leadership in the church diligently seek for and proclaim the truth . . .

That the world might know the self-giving love of the Father, Son, and Holy Spirit that is constantly poured out on all . . .

That those who suffer from broken relationships experience God's healing . . .

That all of us gathered here would follow the Spirit of truth in our daily decisions . . .

Presider: Triune God, you give us everything we need. Hear our prayers that we might be signs of your generous and gracious care in our world. Through Christ our Lord. Amen.

COLLECT

Let us pray.

Pause for silent prayer

God our Father, who by sending into
 the world
the Word of truth and the Spirit of
 sanctification
made known to the human race your
 wondrous mystery,
grant us, we pray, that in professing the
 true faith,
we may acknowledge the Trinity of
 eternal glory
and adore your Unity, powerful in majesty.
Through our Lord Jesus Christ, your Son,
who lives and reigns with you in the unity
 of the Holy Spirit,
one God, for ever and ever. **Amen.**

FIRST READING
Prov 8:22-31

The Wisdom of God cries aloud:
 The Lord created me when his purpose
  first unfolded,
 before the oldest of his works.
 From everlasting I was firmly set,
 from the beginning, before earth came
  into being.
 The deep was not, when I was born,
 there were no Springs to gush
  with water.
 Before the mountains were settled,
 before the hills, I came to birth;
 before he made the earth, the
  countryside,
 or the first grains of the world's dust.
 When he fixed the heavens firm, I
  was there,
 when he drew ring on the surface of
  the deep,
 when he thickened the cloud above,
 when he fixed fast the springs of
  the deep,
 when he assigned the sea its boundaries
 – and the waters will not invade
  the shore –
 when he laid down the foundations of
  the earth,
 I was by his side, a master craftsman,
 delighting in him day after day,
 ever at play in his presence,
 at play everywhere in the world,
 delighting to be with the sons of men.

CATECHESIS

RESPONSORIAL PSALM
Ps 8:4-9 (2)

R̸. How great is your name, O Lord our God, through all the earth!

When I see the heavens, the work of
    your hands,
the moon and the stars which you arranged,
what is man that you should keep him
    in mind,
mortal man that you care for him?

R̸. How great is your name, O Lord our God, through all the earth!

Yet you have made him little less than
    a god;
with glory and honour you crowned him,
gave him power over the works of
    your hand,
put all things under his feet.

R̸. How great is your name, O Lord our God, through all the earth!

All of them, sheep and cattle,
yes, even the savage beasts,
birds of the air, and fish
that make their way through the waters.

R̸. How great is your name, O Lord our God, through all the earth!

SECOND READING
Rom 5:1-5

Through our Lord Jesus Christ, by faith we are judged righteous and at peace with God, since it is by faith and through Jesus that we have entered this state of grace in which we can boast about looking forward to God's glory. But that is not all we can boast about; we can boast about our sufferings. These sufferings bring patience, as we know, and patience brings perseverance, and perseverance brings hope, and this hope is not deceptive, because the love of God has been poured into our hearts by the Holy Spirit which has been given us.

About Liturgy

Join in the dance: In the fourth century, the Cappadocian Fathers developed a systematic theological connection between the Father, Son, and Holy Spirit. Their focus on the dynamic relationship among the divine persons led them to a description of the Trinity that was more an action than a definition. The interdependency and ongoing mutual self-giving in love of the divine persons not only made the Trinity One but also clarified each person as individuals. Their intimate relationship is a permeation of self, one with the other, but without any kind of confusion or blurring of self.

All this sounds quite complex! Perhaps a better image inspired by the Cappadocian Fathers to describe the dynamism of this divine relationship is a group dance. One word used to describe this dynamic communion of persons is *perichoresis*, translated by some as a circle dance. Each person contributes to a part of the dance and has a specific role in the choreography, but the entire group together and what they do together make up the dance. The partners pull and push against one another, not in resistance or by force but in support and unity. The dance is in constant motion, and the dancers are always focused on the other and not themselves. Moreover, the circle is never closed; the joy and unity of the dance and the dancers draw others into the circle to become part of the dance too.

Our celebration of the Trinity today gives us a moment to look at how we embody the open and intimate dynamism of the Trinity in our relationships with one another, especially in the ritual steps of the liturgy. Do our processions look like a joyful movement of gathering and sending? Can people feel connected to one another in the liturgy, or are there physical, psychological, or spiritual barriers that keep people inwardly focused on themselves or separated by status, distance, or disability? Do outsiders feel drawn in, and do they find a space ready and waiting for them so they can feel at home and part of the dance of the Trinity?

About Liturgical Music

Suggestions: Today's first reading, especially, reflects the dynamic movement of the Trinity as our vibrant, joyful source of life. How can one not delight in the image of the wisdom of God playing on the surface of the earth? Highlight this animated, life-giving aspect of the Trinity, and don't limit yourself to just using doctrinal statements set to music.

Consider settings such as 'Father in heaven, grant to your children', set to a charming Filipino melody, or John Bell's 'God to enfold you' which would work well as a dismissal song. Another vigorous closing song would be Ernest Sands's 'Sing of the Lord's Goodness'.

Whatever songs you choose for today, look carefully at the text. Many hymns written with the three persons of the Trinity in mind will focus one stanza on the Father, another on the Son, and a third on the Spirit. Be sure that you sing all the necessary stanzas so as to keep the Trinity's union intact!

SPIRITUALITY

GOSPEL ACCLAMATION
John 6:51

R̥. Alleluia, alleluia.
I am the living bread which has come down
    from heaven,
says the Lord;
Anyone who eats this bread will live for ever.
R̥. Alleluia, alleluia.

Gospel

Luke 9:11-17

**Jesus made the crowds welcome
and talked to them about the
kingdom of God; and he cured
those who were in need of healing.**

It was late afternoon when the
Twelve came to him and said,
'Send the people away, and they
can go to the villages and farms
round about to find lodging and
food; for we are in a lonely place here.'
He replied, 'Give them something to eat
yourselves.' But they said, 'We have
no more than five loaves and two fish,
unless we are to go ourselves and buy
food for all these people.' For there
were about five thousand men. But he
said to his disciples, 'Get them to sit
down in parties of about fifty.' They did
so and made them all sit down. Then
he took the five loaves and the two fish,
raised his eyes to heaven, and said the
blessing over them; then he broke them
and handed them to his disciples to
distribute among the crowd. They all
ate as much as they wanted, and when
the scraps remaining were collected
they filled twelve baskets.

Reflecting on the Gospel

'Mange, mange'! the Italian grandmother said to her grandchild. The plate of homemade pasta was too good to simply sit there untouched. The grandmother encouraged the child to 'eat, eat'! And so the grandchild did and soon there was nothing left but some stray noodles. It brought a smile to both faces.

The feast of the Most Holy Body and Blood of Christ has its historical roots in thirteenth-century Belgium but it is celebrated worldwide today. Our reading comes from the Gospel of Luke. Though we might expect Luke's account of the institution of the Eucharist at the Last Supper, we have, instead, the multiplication of the loaves. But of course, this episode is laden with eucharistic overtones, especially in the verbs used: taking, blessed, broke, and gave. These are the verbs used at the Last Supper, and the verbs we use today in our eucharistic liturgy. So even though we are not reading from the Last Supper, eucharistic theology is baked into the story of the multiplication of the loaves.

Recall that the evangelist Luke portrayed Jesus as an infant lying in a manger. The word manger is often misunderstood as a cozy, comfy place to set a sleeping baby. But a manger is actually a 'feed-trough', as the root word, *mange*, indicates. It's the place from which the animals eat. Narratively speaking, Luke is showing that from infancy Jesus, placed in the feed-trough, is food for the world. In the concluding chapter of the Gospel of Luke, on the road to Emmaus the disciples will learn that after the resurrection they come to know Jesus in the breaking of the bread. And in the Acts of the Apostles, too, the apostle Paul is shown celebrating a meal with the breaking of the bread (Acts 27:35). So this eucharistic theology is not limited to the Last Supper. It permeates the Gospel of Luke and his Acts of the Apostles. How appropriate that we read from his gospel today, on the feast of the Body and Blood of Christ. We feast on the body of Jesus, food for the world. *Mange, mange*!

Living the Paschal Mystery

It's said by Christians that Jesus is food for the world. This reflects the eucharistic theology that is the core of Christian spirituality. Jesus himself is the bread broken and shared. This is prefigured by Luke when the infant Jesus lies in the manger. Though we consider often the paschal mystery, the Eucharist itself is the food for our journey to the paschal mystery. Jesus himself comes to us as the Bread of Life, food for the world, and satisfaction for the hungry. Now, after the resurrection, after his many appearances to his disciples, we come to know him in the breaking of the bread. The breaking implies, and even foreshadows, the paschal mystery. The bread is not merely admired, but it is broken as Jesus himself is broken for us during the passion and death. In so doing, he becomes food for us, life-giving sustenance as we embark on the path to follow him.

Focusing the Gospel

Key words and phrases: Give them something to eat yourselves.

To the point: Jesus commands the bewildered disciples to feed the crowd of over five thousand. They reply, 'We have no more than five loaves and two fish'. The disciples are forgetting something, however. They also have the Bread of Life within their midst. The feeding of the five thousand comes immediately after the Twelve have returned from their first apostolic mission to proclaim the kingdom of God and heal the sick (Luke 9:1-6). Entrusted with a share in Jesus's saving work, the Twelve still do not comprehend the breadth of their mission. With Jesus there is no need to fear scarcity. The five loaves and two fish are enough to feed the hungry crowd with twelve baskets left over.

Connecting the Gospel

to the first and second readings: On this feast of Corpus Christi, it almost seems as if the first and second readings relate more readily to the Eucharist than the gospel reading from Luke. In Genesis, Abram is blessed by Melchizedek, 'priest of God Most High', who 'brought bread and wine' as part of the ceremony. In Paul's first letter to the Corinthians we have the earliest reference to Christian Eucharist! In all three of today's readings we see a similar pattern. Food – bread and wine, loaves and fishes – are taken, a blessing is said, and something is given. Abram gives a tenth of all he has to Melchizedek; the disciples distribute the five loaves and two fish to the crowd; and Jesus gives his own Body and Blood to his friends.

to experience: Jesus calls us each to the eucharistic feast where the bread and wine are taken, blessed, and shared. In this same way we, as the Body of Christ, are to experience ourselves as chosen, blessed, and shared.

Connecting the Responsorial Psalm

to the readings: 'You are a priest for ever, / a priest like Melchizedek of old'. When this psalm was first composed, hundreds of years before Jesus was born, it proclaimed the priesthood of the king of Israel. As Christians, we recognise in these words a prefiguring of Christ. When this psalm refrain is chanted we see the image of Christ, our high priest, presiding over the first Eucharist at the Last Supper and presiding still at every altar throughout the world where the words are said, 'This is my Body. This is my Blood'.

to psalmist preparation: Within our eucharistic celebration Christ is present in the bread and wine, in the Word, in the gathered assembly and in the priest who acts *in persona Christi* as he consecrates the bread and the wine to become the Body and Blood of our Lord. As a cantor you serve the priesthood of the people of God by leading them in prayer and song. As you prepare this week, consider how you exercise your own priesthood. How are you called to bless others and share with them the Body of Christ?

PROMPTS FOR FAITH-SHARING

Jesus tells the disciples, 'Give them something to eat yourselves', when they ask him to dismiss the hungry crowd. How does Jesus call you to feed those who experience hunger, whether physical or spiritual?

How do you see the eucharistic pattern of taking, blessing, breaking, and giving in your own life? How have you been chosen, blessed, and shared with others?

At first, in the feeding of the five thousand, the disciples react out of fear of scarcity, but Jesus abundantly provides. What resource in your life provokes this fear of scarcity? Is there a way you might see Jesus's abundant care in this experience?

In the Eucharist we experience Jesus present in the bread and wine, the Word of God, the priest who acts *in persona Christi* in the consecration of the Eucharist, and the gathered assembly singing and praying. Which of these communicates Christ's presence to you most strongly? Why?

CELEBRATION

Model Penitential Act

Presider: On this feast of Corpus Christi, we recall in a particular way Jesus's gift of his whole self to us in the Eucharist. As we begin this celebration let us pause to prepare ourselves to receive the Body and Blood of our Lord . . . [*pause*]

Lord Jesus, you are the bread of life: Lord, have mercy.

Christ Jesus, you are the wine of salvation: Christ, have mercy.

Lord Jesus, you are high priest forever: Lord, have mercy.

Homily Points

• Today we honour the gift of Christ's Body and Blood. In the second reading we hear the earliest account of the Last Supper in the New Testament. The words that Jesus speaks are the same words we hear spoken over the bread and the wine at every eucharistic celebration: 'This is my Body . . . [This is] my Blood . . . Do this in memory of me'.

• Our remembering is not a passive action recalling an event, which took place many centuries ago. Instead, it is a dynamic living of this past event in the present moment. Here, in this church, Jesus is present to us once more in the bread and the wine, his Body and Blood. Jesus gives himself to us completely. We might pause to ask ourselves, how present are we to Jesus? How willing are we to completely give ourselves to him?

• Unlike baptism and confirmation, the Eucharist isn't a sacrament we experience only once. Again and again we are called to this table to be with Jesus who desperately wants to be with us, to nourish us and strengthen us on this journey of faith. In a sermon given to catechumens on the feast of Pentecost, St. Augustine said of the Eucharist, 'Become what you see, and receive what you are'. The Body and Blood of Christ are not only to be adored, they are to be received with love and with the fervent prayer that we might become what we receive, the Body and Blood of Christ completely poured out for others.

Model Universal Prayer (Prayer of the Faithful)

Presider: Christ, our high priest, offers us his Body and Blood in the eucharistic feast. In thanksgiving for this great gift, we, in turn, offer up all that we are to God as we pray for our needs and the needs of our world.

Response: Lord, hear our prayer.

That all members of the church would heed the words of Jesus, 'Give them something to eat yourselves' and seek to alleviate spiritual and physical hunger throughout the world . . .

That Christian denominations around the world be led into unity by Jesus, our high priest . . .

That all those who experience hunger, especially children and vulnerable adults, be provided for out of the earth's abundant resources . . .

That all of us gathered here might be strengthened and nourished by the Body and Blood of Christ . . .

Presider: God of infinite love, you sent your only Son to dwell among us and to give us the gift of his very self in bread and wine. Hear our prayers, that in receiving him we might become his healing presence to all those we meet. We ask this through Christ, our Lord. Amen.

COLLECT

Let us pray.

Pause for silent prayer

O God, who in this wonderful Sacrament have left us a memorial of your Passion, grant us, we pray,
so to revere the sacred mysteries of your
    Body and Blood
that we may always experience in ourselves the fruits of your redemption.
Who live and reign with God the Father in the unity of the Holy Spirit,
one God, for ever and ever. **Amen.**

FIRST READING
Gen 14:18-20

Melchizedek king of Salem brought bread and wine; he was a priest of God Most High. He pronounced this blessing:
    'Blessed be Abraham by God Most
        High, creator of heaven and earth,
    and blessed be God Most High for
        handing over your enemies to you.'
And Abraham gave him a tithe of everything.

CATECHESIS

RESPONSORIAL PSALM
Ps 109:1-4 (4)

R℣. You are a priest for ever,
a priest like Melchizedek of old.

The Lord's revelation to my Master:
'Sit on my right:
I will put your foes beneath your feet.'

R℣. You are a priest for ever,
a priest like Melchizedek of old.

The Lord will send from Zion
your sceptre of power:
rule in the midst of all your foes.

R℣. You are a priest for ever,
a priest like Melchizedek of old.

A prince from the day of your birth
on the holy mountains;
from the womb before the dawn I
    begot you.

R℣. You are a priest for ever,
a priest like Melchizedek of old.

The Lord has sworn an oath he will
    not change.
'You are a priest for ever,
a priest like Melchizedek of old.'

R℣. You are a priest for ever,
a priest like Melchizedek of old.

SECOND READING
1 Cor 11:23-26

This is what I received from the Lord, and in turn passed on to you: that on the same night that he was betrayed, the Lord Jesus took some bread, and thanked God for it and broke it, and he said, 'This is my body, which is for you; do this as a memorial of me.' In the same way he took the cup after supper, and said, 'This cup is the new covenant in my blood. Whenever you drink it, do this as a memorial of me.' Until the Lord comes, therefore, every time you eat this bread and drink this cup, you are proclaiming his death.

OPTIONAL SEQUENCE

See Appendix A, p. 296.

About Liturgy

Hosts from the tabernacle at Mass: One of the least-followed instructions of the Roman Missal is this: 'It is most desirable that the faithful, just as the Priest himself is bound to do, receive the Lord's Body from hosts consecrated at the same Mass . . . so that even by means of the signs Communion may stand out more clearly as a participation in the sacrifice actually being celebrated' (General Instruction of the Roman Missal 85). This directive was first stated in the Constitution on the Sacred Liturgy (55), promulgated in 1963, and has been present in the Roman Missal ever since.

Yet, go to almost any Mass and you will see someone approach the tabernacle to retrieve hosts to be distributed to the assembly. The reasons they give for doing this have nothing to do with running out of hosts consecrated at that Mass. The practice is simply done because of old habits from preconciliar days, ignorance, or in some cases, because that's what they were taught to do.

Some proponents argue that the hosts at the altar and those in the tabernacle are one and the same Lord. That is certainly true, although it is not the primary issue.

First, the hosts reserved in the tabernacle are for the purpose of adoration and Communion to the dying and the sick unable to be present at Mass. There is no provision in any current liturgical document that allows for the assembly to normatively receive Communion from the hosts in the tabernacle during Mass.

Second and more importantly, the assembly's participation in the sacrifice of Christ stands out more clearly when they receive the hosts consecrated by the Holy Spirit through the Eucharistic Prayer they just prayed together with the priest. Sharing in the Eucharist at Mass is not simply about receiving the Body of Christ but about participating in what Christ did, that is, his sacrifice of praise to the Father through the giving of his life.

About Initiation

The Eucharistic Prayer: Although they are not yet able to share in Communion, the baptised who are preparing to be received or to celebrate the sacraments of confirmation and Eucharist are not dismissed from the Mass as are the catechumens. This is because their participation in Christ's sacrifice is embodied in their praying of the Eucharistic Prayer. The General Instruction of the Roman Missal says that 'the meaning of this Prayer is that the whole congregation of the faithful joins with Christ in confessing the great deeds of God and in the offering of Sacrifice' (78). The baptised are full members of the faithful by their baptism. Thus, they are called to pray the prayers reserved for the faithful, of which the Eucharistic Prayer is primary.

About Liturgical Music

Ostinato refrains: Ideally, the assembly should be able to sing the communion song fully even as they are processing to the altar to share in the Body and Blood of Christ. A hymnal or even projected music on a screen can still be difficult to manage while one is walking. Here, short, memorable ostinato refrains that are repeated like a mantra can be helpful.

One common song used for Communion is Taizé's 'Eat This Bread'. Another song that is similar in style is *Psallite*'s 'This Is My Body'. The repeated antiphon is, 'This is my body, given for you. This is my blood, poured out for you. Do this and remember me; do this and remember me'. The choir, cantor, or schola has verses using the words from Psalm 23 that can be sung in alternation with the refrain or as a countermelody.

23 JUNE 2019

THE MOST HOLY BODY AND BLOOD OF CHRIST (CORPUS CHRISTI)

THE NATIVITY OF SAINT JOHN THE BAPTIST

GOSPEL ACCLAMATION
Cf. Luke 1:76

℟. Alleluia, alleluia.
As for you, little child, you shall be called
a prophet of God, the Most High.
You shall go ahead of the Lord
to prepare his ways before him.
℟. Alleluia, alleluia.

Gospel   Luke 1:57-66, 80

The time came for Elizabeth to have her child, and she gave birth to a son; and when her neighbours and relations heard that the Lord had shown her so great a kindness, they shared her joy.

Now on the eighth day they came to circumcise the child; they were going to call him Zechariah after his father, but his mother spoke up. 'No,' she said 'he is to be called John.' They said to her, 'But no one in your family has that name', and made signs to his father to find out what he wanted him called. The father asked for a writing-tablet and wrote, 'His name is John.' And they were all astonished. At that instant his power of speech returned and he spoke and praised God. All their neighbours were filled with awe and the whole affair was talked about throughout the hill country of Judaea. All those who heard of it treasured it in their hearts. 'What will this child turn out to be?' they wondered. And indeed the hand of the Lord was with him. Meanwhile, the child grew up and his spirit matured. And he lived out in the wilderness until the day he appeared openly to Israel.

See Appendix A, p. 297, for the other readings.

Reflecting on the Gospel

Luke is the only evangelist to give us the story of John the Baptist's birth. And the way Luke tells it, John the Baptist and Jesus were cousins: their mothers were sisters. No other evangelist or New Testament author makes that connection. For Luke, other signs accompany the birth of John, demonstrating that the 'hand of the Lord was with him'. We recall how Zechariah, his father, doubted that Elizabeth would become pregnant, and he was subsequently struck dumb. That condition remained until he had the chance to ratify the name Elizabeth had chosen for the infant. Only then is Zechariah's 'power of speech returned' and he immediately blesses God.

These wondrous signs demonstrate clearly for Luke's audience that John will be something spectacular. Born six months prior to his cousin Jesus, John will prepare the way for the Son of God.

Luke has a particular concern for women as many of his stories throughout the gospel and the Acts of the Apostles demonstrate. The fact that Elizabeth is the one to name him John, when others wanted to name him Zechariah after his father, is significant. Not following Elizabeth's direction, her neighbours and relatives turn to Zechariah to get his input. He, of course, confirms Elizabeth's decision and the boy is named John, a heretofore-unknown family name. As Elizabeth plays a major role in the naming of John, so Mary will play a similar role for Jesus when he is born. In her case the angel tells her that 'you shall name him Jesus's (Luke 1:31; NABRE). Thus the mothers are instrumental in each case, demonstrating how critical women are in Luke's gospel.

The role of women in the lives of John the Baptist and Jesus should come as no surprise. Though not the focus of our attention in many cases, it's clear that Luke is sure to draw our eyes to these critical female relationships throughout his gospel. To borrow a phrase, Mary and Elizabeth were each the hand that rocked the cradle. Their input and influence made John and Jesus the men they became, standing up to injustice and preaching the reign of God. On this celebration of the birth of John the Baptist it is appropriate to look to Elizabeth and her relative Mary to ponder the role and importance of women in the life of this great saint, the forerunner of Christ.

Living the Paschal Mystery

The birth of a child is the cause for joy. New life springing into the world gives hope. There is possibility and tremendous potential when each person is born. We might ponder who or what she will become, how her life will influence others. Will this child be a leader or more of a follower? What are the exhilarations or sad events she will experience? How will he deal with success or disappointment?

It's likely that Elizabeth wondered about her child in a similar way, especially given the extraordinary events that surrounded his birth. Not only Elizabeth's child, but each new human life is special and to be treasured, as we know. New life is an expression of the paschal mystery, giving meaning and joy to our lives. We seek to create a loving, caring environment for each human being so every person can grow into their full potential.

Focusing the Gospel

Key words and phrases: indeed the hand of the Lord was with him

To the point: From the moment of his conception John was given a role in salvation history: point to Jesus. Even in the womb he witnessed to Christ's presence by leaping when Mary, bearing Jesus, drew near. After his birth we are told, '[T]he child grew up and his spirit matured. And he lived out in the wilderness until the day he appeared openly to Israel'. John's ministry throughout his life can be a model for us. Whether working actively, or in quiet recollection, John's whole life heralded the presence of Jesus to all those around him.

Model Penitential Act

Presider: On this feast of the Nativity of John the Baptist we celebrate this saint's complete and total devotion to God. For the times that our devotion has faltered we ask for pardon and forgiveness . . . [*pause*]

Lord Jesus, you are the saviour of the world: Lord, have mercy.
Christ Jesus, you call us to repentance: Christ, have mercy.
Lord Jesus, you are the light of the nations: Lord, have mercy.

Model Universal Prayer (Prayer of the Faithful)

Presider: Through the intercession of John the Baptist we lift up our prayers to the Lord.

Response: Lord, hear our prayer.

That the church, following the example of John the Baptist, constantly point to Jesus, the light of the world . . .

That leaders of nations embrace humble servant leadership . . .

That pregnant women and their unborn children receive necessary healthcare and support . . .

That this church community might help all of its young people discern God's call in their life . . .

Presider: God of salvation, you called John the Baptist to herald the coming of your Son. Hear our prayers that we might continue to proclaim the good news in everything we do. We ask this through Christ our Lord. Amen.

About Liturgy

A sacredness of a person's name: Today's readings give us an opportunity to reflect on our names. Many older Catholics grew up during a time when children's names looked like the litany of saints. Today, however, parents are more open to a greater variety of names for their children, so that many popular names today have no historical Christian connection to a saint or virtue.

Some may lament this trend in giving non-Christian-specific names to children. Although church teaching praises the practice of giving a child the name of a saint, the actual law does not require it for baptism or confirmation. Canon 855 of the Code of Canon Law simply states that the name should not be 'foreign to Christian sensibility'. The *Catechism of the Catholic Church* goes further and describes the holiness of a person's given name this way: 'Everyone's name is sacred. The name is the icon of the person. It demands respect as a sign of the dignity of the one who bears it' (2158).

In all our rites and interactions with one another, let us honour each person's given name with respect and reverence.

Let us pray.

Pause for silent prayer

O God, who raised up Saint John the Baptist
to make ready a nation fit for Christ
    the Lord,
give your people, we pray,
the grace of spiritual joys
and direct the hearts of all the faithful
into the way of salvation and peace.
Through our Lord Jesus Christ, your Son,
who lives and reigns with you in the unity
    of the Holy Spirit,
one God, for ever and ever. **Amen**.

FOR REFLECTION

• At John's birth the people gathered wonder, 'What will this child turn out to be?' How have you experienced God's evolving call in your own life?

• As John grew he was 'in the wilderness'. How do you experience 'wilderness times' of reflection and contemplation in your own life?

Homily Points

• In the Gospel of Luke we are given two birth stories in close succession, the birth of John the Baptist and six months later, the birth of Jesus. Though both are born to the same extended Jewish family these births are quite different.

• Elizabeth births John surrounded by her family and community. As a priest, John's father, Zechariah, has standing in the religious community, and so his circumcision and naming carry some import as evidenced by the discussion over John's name.

• Jesus's birth takes place far from family, community, and even human company as he is born in a place where animals are kept.

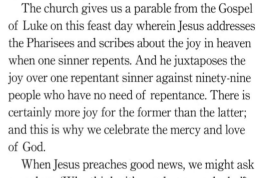

℟. Alleluia, alleluia.
Shoulder my yoke and learn from me,
for I am gentle and humble in heart.
℟. Alleluia, alleluia.

or

John 10:14

℟. Alleluia, alleluia.
I am the good shepherd, says
the Lord;
I know my own sheep and my
own know me.
℟. Alleluia, alleluia.

Gospel

Luke 15:3-7

**Jesus spoke this parable to
the scribes and Pharisees:**
**'What man among you
with a hundred sheep,
losing one, would not
leave the ninety-nine in
the wilderness and go
after the missing one till
he found it? And when
he found it, would he not
joyfully take it on his shoulders and
then, when he got home, call together
his friends and neighbours? "Rejoice
with me," he would say "I have found
my sheep that was lost." In the same
way, I tell you, there will be more
rejoicing in heaven over one repentant
sinner than over ninety-nine virtuous
men who have no need of repentance.'**

See Appendix A, p. 298, for the other readings.

Reflecting on the Gospel

On this feast of the Most Sacred Heart of Jesus we might encounter artwork that represents graphically a heart, sometimes wrapped in thorns or topped by a cross. Younger people might wince at such a depiction, wondering what precisely we are celebrating. Historically, this feast has been one of the most popular devotions in Catholicism, with roots deep into the eleventh century. A devotion to the heart of Jesus is meant to express a devotion to the love of God, or the mercy of Christ. The graphic portrayal of a physical heart might not capture that sense today, but it is what we celebrate nonetheless.

The church gives us a parable from the Gospel of Luke on this feast day wherein Jesus addresses the Pharisees and scribes about the joy in heaven when one sinner repents. And he juxtaposes the joy over one repentant sinner against ninety-nine people who have no need of repentance. There is certainly more joy for the former than the latter; and this is why we celebrate the mercy and love of God.

When Jesus preaches good news, we might ask ourselves, 'Who thinks it's good news and why'? This parable gives us one answer. The news of salvation is good for the repentant sinner. There is forgiveness, mercy, and redemption. And once that offer is accepted, all heaven rejoices mightily. On the other hand, for those who consider themselves righteous and do not repent there is not the same joy in heaven. These people do not seek forgiveness, mercy, or redemption because they do not sense that they need to repent of anything.

So the good news is 'good' precisely for those who repent and experience the mercy of God. Redemption is a possibility, and God is ready to welcome the lost. For this quality of the divine, we celebrate the 'Sacred Heart', the mercy and tenderness of our God.

So where do we find ourselves today? With the ninety-nine? Or are we the lost sheep? When lost, we know that mercy awaits, and for that, there is great rejoicing.

Living the Paschal Mystery

How many of us have it all figured out? How many of us have a plan and execute it flawlessly? Or, how do we present ourselves to friends and family? There is a natural human tendency to put the best face on things, to present a pleasant disposition, to act as though all is fine. But in reality each of us has been lost at some point and perhaps even now. When we experience that sensation of being lost, it is then that we are invited to undergo a death of sorts so that we might rise to new life. Not every plan is executed flawlessly. Ultimately we are not in control. By following our own designs it is likely that we will end up at a dead end, or walking in circles. It's then that we can turn matters over to the divine, recognising that God will raise us up to new life. When we repent of our own self-righteousness and embrace the role of lost sheep, there we will find rejoicing in heaven for we will have died to ourselves to live with the eternal one. It is then that we experience the mercy of God, the Sacred Heart.

Focusing the Gospel

Key words and phrases: What man among you . . .

To the point: Jesus offers the parable of the Lost Sheep in response to the grumbling of the Pharisees and scribes over his hospitality to sinners. Jesus begins with a question, 'What man among you with a hundred sheep, losing one, would not leave the ninety-nine in the wilderness and go after the missing one till he found it?' The scribes and Pharisees are invited to put themselves in the shoes of the shepherd. If the shepherd would so labour for one lost sheep, how much more does God labour and rejoice to find one who is lost?

Model Penitential Act

Presider: Today we celebrate the love and compassion of Jesus's Sacred Heart. Let us acknowledge our sins before the Lord and so prepare to receive his infinite mercy . . . [*pause*]

Lord Jesus, you are the Good Shepherd who seeks the lost: Lord, have mercy.
Christ Jesus, you came to show sinners the way: Christ, have mercy.
Lord Jesus, you invite us to live within your Sacred Heart: Lord, have mercy.

Model Universal Prayer (Prayer of the Faithful)

Presider: Confident in God's mercy, we lift up our prayers through the intercession of the Sacred Heart of Jesus.

Response: Lord, hear our prayer.

That the church be a welcome refuge for sinners and a place of healing and joy . . .

That all people of the world might know the compassionate and merciful love of God who never ceases to seek the lost . . .

That those who experience crushing grief, despair, anxiety, and depression find comfort and strength within the Sacred Heart of Jesus . . .

That all gathered here might follow the example of Jesus, our Good Shepherd, and offer fellowship, hospitality, and welcome to those on the outskirts of society . . .

Presider: Merciful Father, you sent your Son to reveal to all people the depths of your love for us. Hear our prayers that we might find shelter within this merciful love and become shelter for others. We ask this in the name of Jesus, Our Lord. Amen.

About Liturgy

Creed: When asked what Christians believe, we tend to think of the Creed. As we pray the Creed today on this solemnity, let us remember that faith is a relationship with the person of Christ, through whose heart we are called to love one another. As the post-communion prayer for this day says so well, 'make us fervent with the fire of holy love, / so that, drawn always to your Son, / we may learn to see him in our neighbour'.

COLLECT

Let us pray.

Grant, we pray, almighty God,
that we, who glory in the Heart of your
   beloved Son
and recall the wonders of his love for us,
may be made worthy to receive
an overflowing measure of grace
from that fount of heavenly gifts.
Through our Lord Jesus Christ, your Son,
who lives and reigns with you in the unity of
   the Holy Spirit,
one God, for ever and ever. **Amen.**

or:

O God, who in the Heart of your Son,
wounded by our sins,
bestow on us in mercy
the boundless treasures of your love,
grant, we pray,
that, in paying him the homage of our devotion,
we may also offer worthy reparation.
Through our Lord Jesus Christ, your Son,
who lives and reigns with you in the unity of
   the Holy Spirit,
one God, for ever and ever. **Amen.**

FOR REFLECTION

• On the feast of the Sacred Heart of Jesus we remember the Lord's infinite mercy. How have you experienced this mercy in your own life?

• Our gospel reading today is the familiar parable of the Lost Sheep. Who are the 'lost' in your community? How might you be called to embody Jesus's Sacred Heart to them?

Homily Points

• There are many images we use to relate to God: Father, Mother, Creator, Redeemer, King. . . . None, of course, is perfect or complete, but each may help us to draw closer to the mystery of God. In the passages we read today, it is revealed that God is an attentive, loving, shepherd. In the prophecy from Ezekiel, God proclaims, 'I shall look for the lost one, bring back the stray, bandage the wounded and make the weak strong'.

GOSPEL ACCLAMATION
Matt 16:18

R̸. Alleluia, alleluia.
You are Peter and on this rock I will build
   my Church.
And the gates of the underworld can never hold
   out against it.
R̸. Alleluia, alleluia.

Gospel

Matt 16:13-19

When Jesus came to the region of Caesarea Philippi he put this question to his disciples, 'Who do people say the Son of Man is?' And they said, 'Some say he is John the Baptist, some Elijah, and others Jeremiah or one of the prophets.' 'But you,' he said 'who do you say I am?' Then Simon Peter spoke up, 'You are the Christ,' he said 'the Son of the living God.' Jesus replied, 'Simon son of Jonah, you are a happy man! Because it was not flesh and blood that revealed this to you but my Father in heaven. So I now say to you: You are Peter and on this rock I will build my Church. And the gates of the underworld can never hold out against it. I will give you the keys of the kingdom of heaven: whatever you bind on earth shall be considered bound in heaven; whatever you loose on earth shall be considered loosed in heaven.'

See Appendix A, p. 299, for the other readings.

Reflecting on the Gospel

Peter and Paul were quite different people. Depending on which gospel we read, Peter was with Jesus from nearly the beginning of his ministry while Paul never knew or witnessed the historical Jesus. Peter denied knowing Jesus three times before being rehabilitated in a resurrection appearance when Jesus asked him three times, 'Do you love me'? Paul never denied Jesus, but certainly persecuted him by persecuting the disciples and encountered the risen Christ only once in 'a vision' on the road to Damascus. Peter evangelised the Jews and seemed content to stay with many of the other apostles in Jerusalem for several years after the resurrection. Paul saw the wider implications of the Christ-event and began evangelising Gentiles, referring to himself as an 'apostle' even though he was not one of the Twelve. After coming to an agreement at the Council of Jerusalem (Acts 15), Peter and Paul sparred with one another in Antioch as each had understood the ramifications of the council differently. Their parting ways in that important ancient city, where the disciples were first called Christians, is the last time the New Testament says they were together. All in all they might have spent less than three weeks of their lives together, and yet in martyrdom they are linked as founders of the church in Rome, even though neither was the first Christian in the Eternal City. This is a good reminder that there is more than one way to be a saint, or even live out a relationship with Christ.

In today's gospel we hear Peter's proclamation par excellence: 'You are the Christ,' . . . 'the Son of the living God'. And Jesus in reply refers to Peter – or perhaps his confession – as the rock on which he will build the church. Thus Peter becomes the de facto leader of the Twelve, though Paul will step in after the resurrection to play a critical role as well. As Peter and Paul had different but authentic responses to Christ we, too, will have our own response to what Christ calls us to be and to do. Peter was not Paul; Paul was not Peter. Each lived their response in their own way, and not even agreeing with each other all or perhaps even much of the time. Such is the life of the Christian disciple. United by Christ, we live our own response to his call, sometimes bumping heads along the way, but always united by something stronger.

Living the Paschal Mystery

On this feast of the saints Peter and Paul we might step back to consider our own response to Christ's call. Peter's confession of Jesus as the Messiah, Son of the Living God, became the cornerstone of the church. Paul's response on the road to Damascus turned him from a persecutor to a disciple, and ultimately, apostle to the Gentiles. Each died to a past way of life and opened themselves to new possibilities by their faith in Christ. Peter overcame his denial of Jesus and Paul overcame his persecution, but both did so only with the grace of God. Though neither could likely foresee their eventual martyrdom in Rome, the capital of the empire, each pursued what they knew to be true to the end. May we like Peter and Paul find the grace to pursue our own path of discipleship, remaining true to the end, no matter where that might lead.

Focusing the Gospel

Key words and phrases: who do you say I am?

To the point: Jesus's line of questioning goes from the general to the personal. After asking the disciples, 'Who do people say the Son of Man is?' he asks them directly, '[W]ho do you say I am?' The Christian faith requires from us both a communal and an individual response. Today we celebrate the witnesses of two foundational Christian saints, Peter and Paul. Their relationship to Jesus, response to his call, and mission in the early church were each different from the other's, and yet, in concert they helped to establish the universal church that we know today. Just as we celebrate the differences of Peter and Paul we are called to foster our own unique relationships with the Lord. Jesus calls us by name and asks us in this moment in our lives, '[W]ho do *you* say I am?'

Model Penitential Act

Presider: On this feast of Saints Peter and Paul we remember these two who gave everything for the Lord and his people. As we enter into this celebration let us call to mind the times we have not lived up to their example . . . [*pause*]

Lord Jesus, you are the Messiah, the Son of the Living God: Lord, have mercy.
Christ Jesus, you redeem sinners and offer salvation to all: Christ, have mercy.
Lord Jesus, you called Saints Peter and Paul to proclaim the good news to the Jews and the Gentiles: Lord, have mercy.

Model Universal Prayer (Prayer of the Faithful)

Presider: In their lives and in their deaths Saints Peter and Paul dedicated themselves to Jesus Christ and his people. Together with them, we offer our prayers to God.

Response: Lord, hear our prayer.

That, through the intercession of St. Peter and St. Paul, the church continue to bring the good news of Jesus Christ to all corners of the world . . .

That all nations ensure freedom of religion for their people . . .

That those who experience religious persecution be strengthened, comforted, and protected . . .

That all gathered here follow in the footsteps of St. Peter and St. Paul by serving Jesus with love and fidelity . . .

Presider: God of faithfulness, through your saints Peter and Paul you give us an example of lives poured out as a libation for others. Hear our prayers that we might give of ourselves with the same generosity and abandon. We pray through Jesus Christ our Lord. Amen.

About Liturgy

True Christian community: Parker Palmer, noted educator and author, says that true community is committing to sit down at dinner next to the person you dislike the most. And when they get up to leave, someone worse takes their place.

We can't know for sure what Peter and Paul's relationship was like, but we know that it wasn't always pleasant, and it got downright nasty at times. Yet, Christian iconography rarely shows one without the other. Although they may have spent no more than a few weeks together, their commitment to the gospel became a crucial element upon which the church was built.

COLLECT

Let us pray.

Pause for silent prayer

O God, who on the Solemnity of the Apostles Peter and Paul
give us the noble and holy joy of this day,
grant, we pray, that your Church
may in all things follow the teaching
of those through whom she received
the beginnings of right religion.
Through our Lord Jesus Christ, your Son,
who lives and reigns with you in the unity of the Holy Spirit,
one God, for ever and ever. **Amen.**

FOR REFLECTION

• St. Peter and St. Paul answered Jesus's call to mission through their own unique gifts and talents. Which God-given gifts are you being called to use for the good of Jesus and his church?

• In his second letter to Timothy St. Paul says, 'I have fought the good fight to the end; I have run the race to the finish'. Which aspects of the spiritual life require the most effort from you?

• At this point in your journey of faith how do you answer the question of Jesus, '[W]ho do you say I am?'

Homily Points

• Sts. Peter and Paul are spiritual giants in our faith. Together they continued the work of Jesus in establishing his church throughout the Eastern Mediterranean. The successor of St. Peter continues to lead and shape our Catholic Church whereas the epistles of St. Paul form nearly one quarter of the New Testament.

• And yet, both of these men were also sinners. Today on their feast day, let us not only stand back in awe at the good work they were able to accomplish, but let us also rejoice in the God who works with sinful humanity to bring life to the world.

SPIRITUALITY

Gospel Luke 10:1-12, 17-20

The Lord appointed seventy-two others and sent them out ahead of him, in pairs, to all the towns and places he himself was to visit. He said to them, 'The harvest is rich but the labourers are few, so ask the Lord of the harvest to send labourers to his harvest. Start off now, but remember, I am sending you out like lambs among wolves. Carry no purse, no haversack, no sandals. Salute no one on the road. Whatever house you go into, let your first words be, "Peace to this house!" And if a man of peace lives there, your peace will go and rest on him; if not, it will come back to you. Stay in the same house, taking what food and drink they have to offer, for the labourer deserves his wages; do not move from house to house. Whenever you go into a town where they make you welcome, eat what is set before you. Cure those in it who are sick, and say, "The kingdom of God is very near to you." But whenever you enter a town and they do not make you welcome, go out into its streets and say, "We wipe off the very dust of your town that clings to our feet, and leave it with you. Yet be sure of this: the kingdom of God is very near." I tell you, that on that day it will not go as hard with Sodom as with that town.'

Continued in Appendix A, p. 299,

or Luke 10:1-9, in Appendix A, p. 299.

Reflecting on the Gospel

How many people can play on a team? Many sports have, in addition to the particular number of players on the pitch at one time (eleven for football, or fifteen for rugby), a larger number of players in 'the squad,' some or all of whom may play part of a match, to replace a tired or an injured player or as a substitute because of their particular skills. They form a pool of players from whom a coach or manager can choose the team for a specific game.

During the ministry of Jesus there were many on the team as well: crowds, disciples, apostles, and a special few. In the Gospel of Matthew, there are only twelve disciples, and they were also the twelve apostles (Matt 10:1-2). But Luke has a much more expansive view of discipleship. In fact, in Acts, he invents a feminine form of the word to mention Tabitha, a female disciple (9:36). And in today's gospel we have the mission of the seventy-two! In Luke there were many, many disciples. Nearly anyone could be on the team!

And this simple lesson gives us great hope today. According to Luke, men, women, the Twelve, the seventy-two, and many more were in a special relationship with Jesus, chosen to follow him and chosen also to be sent by him. In this gospel there were not such tight boundaries around who could or could not be a disciple. Instead, the situation seems to have been more fluid or dynamic. And that's likely a more accurate reflection of the situation around Jesus's earthly ministry. It would also seem to reflect our lives more accurately too, with dynamic, fluid relationships.

Aside from this story in Luke we never hear about the seventy-two again. But surely these people were likely some of the early evangelisers after the resurrection. It all gives us a brief inkling into the situation of the early church. Though it might be easier to imagine the Twelve with Peter at the head, knowing who is 'on the team' and who isn't, today's gospel reading invites us to consider a much more complex picture.

Living the Paschal Mystery

Many of us like to draw boundaries, establishing membership and determining limits. But life is not often like that. Our lived realities are much more complex, and perhaps that's part of the reason we seek to create order! The mission of the seventy-two gives us a peek into the greater apostolic ministry of Jesus. He was content to *send* (the word 'apostle' means 'one sent') more than the twelve on mission. And the seventy-two are not specifically called disciples or apostles, though they are certainly sent. They go to the places Jesus intends to visit. We might ask ourselves who are the 'seventy-two' today? And are we part of that large group sent to places where Jesus intends to visit? Just because we are not part of the Twelve does not mean we don't have a mission. These seventy-two were critical to the ministry of Jesus. They prepared the way for him. In looking to a New Testament example of our call in life, there is something worthy of emulation here.

Focusing the Gospel

Key words and phrases: The Lord appointed seventy-two others and sent them out ahead of him, in pairs

To the point: Jesus continues on the road to Jerusalem by sending missionaries ahead of him to prepare the way. Much like John the Baptist at the beginning of Luke's gospel, these seventy-two disciples are to proclaim, 'The kingdom of God is very near to you'. and to call the people, communally and individually, to repentance. This account of the mission of the seventy-two reveals to us Jesus's method in ministry. He calls others to help him in spreading the good news of God's kingdom and he sends them to minister in pairs. The Christian mission is not to be undertaken as a solitary endeavour. If Jesus continually called on others to help him establish the kingdom of God, how much more do we, modern-day disciples, need to rely on co-labourers in ministry?

Connecting the Gospel

to the first reading: In last week's gospel we heard of a Samaritan village that would not welcome Jesus because his final destination was Jerusalem. This week as well, Jesus's disciples are sent on ahead of Jesus to 'all the towns and places he himself was to visit'. Jesus acknowledges that they might find welcome or they might not, but everywhere they venture they are first to say, 'Peace to this house!' The first reading from Isaiah is a hymn to Jerusalem, Jesus's final destination and the place of his death and resurrection. The prophet Isaiah, speaking after the exile into Babylon, reassures the people that Jerusalem will again be their 'comfort'. This sacred ground, which has seen such ruin and such glory, will once again nurture the people of God.

to experience: In Jerusalem throughout history and in the life of Jesus we see the paschal mystery made manifest. Death leads to new life. Are there broken places in your own life that are ready to be reborn?

Connecting the Responsorial Psalm

to the readings: In the gospel Jesus sends his disciples out on mission with a list of what they are not to take: 'no purse, no haversack, no sandals'. In fact they will be 'like lambs among wolves'. But this is no reason for distress. The psalmist sings a hymn to God's strength and deliverance: 'Come and see the works of God, / tremendous his deeds among men'. Though the disciples are sent without material possessions, they go with the love of God whose 'enemies cringe' before his 'great strength' (NABRE).

to psalmist preparation: In the life of faith we are at times asked to do the seemingly impossible. To love people who do not show love for us. To continue working on a task that seems doomed to failure. To wake up every morning and recommit ourselves to our own ongoing conversion in the ways of Christ. No matter how daunting our daily mission may be, we are not alone. The God of all love, compassion, and strength is with us. How do you proclaim this good news with your life?

The seventy-two are sent out to proclaim, 'The kingdom of God is very near to you'. What do these words mean to you?

Jesus sends the disciples out in pairs. Do you have a companion on the journey of faith? How does it change ministry when it is done in a team setting?

The disciples are to greet each house they enter by saying, 'Peace to this house!' How do you offer peace to those you visit?

Jesus tells the disciples, 'The harvest is rich but the labourers are few'. How do we experience this lack of labourers in our own time?

CELEBRATION

Model Penitential Act

Presider: As modern day disciples Jesus sends us out, like the seventy-two, to proclaim the good news of God's kingdom. Let us pause for a moment to pray for the strength, humility, and grace needed to fulfill this mission . . . [*pause*]

 Lord Jesus, you invite us to labour in building the kingdom of God: Lord, have mercy.
 Christ Jesus, you are the source of peace: Christ, have mercy.
 Lord Jesus, you call all people to yourself: Lord, have mercy.

Homily Points

• Seventy-two disciples are sent out along the road to Jerusalem, to all the places Jesus intends to visit on this last journey of his earthly life. The disciples are given a message to proclaim and they are to proclaim it whether the communities they enter are receptive to them or not: 'The kingdom of God is very near to you'. There is an urgency to their task and because of this Jesus tells them to not be encumbered by material things. They are to bring 'no purse, no haversack, no sandals' and even more than that they are to '[s]alute no one on the road'. Nothing must dissuade them from this mission, the mission of announcing the kingdom of God.

• The people of that time (much like the people of this time) were caught up in waiting for the kingdom of God to arrive. They longed for the time when there would be no more war, illness, hunger, oppression, hatred, or enmity, and all would live in peace and abundance. The message to them and to us is that this kingdom is already here. All it requires is for us to claim our places as citizens of the kingdom of God.

• What would the world be like if we all truly believed the bold proclamation of Jesus that the kingdom of God is at hand? We are kingdom people and when we act as kingdom people, just as the saints throughout history have shown us, the kingdom breaks out all around us. The hungry are fed, the grieving are comforted, and building lasting peace becomes more important than preparing for war. This urgent message proclaimed by the disciples on the road to Jerusalem is passed on to us today. The kingdom of God is at hand.

Model Universal Prayer (Prayer of the Faithful)

Presider: In today's gospel, Jesus sends out the seventy-two to proclaim, 'The kingdom of God is very near to you'. Let us pray for the seed of God's kingdom to continue to take root in the world.

Response: Lord, hear our prayer.

That missionaries of the church proclaim the kingdom of God to all they meet while also listening to, learning from, and growing alongside the people they serve . . .

That God's kingdom of justice, peace, and mercy continue to grow throughout the world . . .

That those who live in the darkness of sin might hear the good news that the kingdom of God is at hand and receive the grace to labour for this kingdom . . .

That all gathered here proclaim in our words and actions the joy inherent in the kingdom of God . . .

Presider: God of abundance, you sent your son Jesus to reveal to us the fulness of life in your kingdom. Hear our prayers that we might labour to build up the kingdom of God in all that we say and do. Through Jesus Christ, our Lord. Amen.

COLLECT

Let us pray.

Pause for silent prayer

O God, who in the abasement of your Son
have raised up a fallen world,
fill your faithful with holy joy,
for on those you have rescued from
  slavery to sin
you bestow eternal gladness.
Through our Lord Jesus Christ, your Son,
who lives and reigns with you in the unity
  of the Holy Spirit,
one God, for ever and ever. **Amen.**

FIRST READING
Isa 66:10-14

Rejoice, Jerusalem,
be glad for her, all you who love her!
Rejoice, rejoice for her,
all you who mourned her!

That you may be suckled, filled,
from her consoling breast,
that you may savour with delight
her glorious breasts.

For thus says the Lord:
Now towards her I send flowing
peace, like a river,
and like a stream in spate
the glory of the nations.

At her breast will her nurslings be carried
and fondled in her lap.
Like a son comforted by his mother
will I comfort you.
And by Jerusalem you will be comforted.

At the sight your heart will rejoice,
and your bones flourish like the grass.
To his servants the Lord will reveal
  his hand.

CATECHESIS

RESPONSORIAL PSALM
Ps 65:1-7, 16, 20 (1)

R̸. Cry out with joy to God all the earth.

Cry out with joy to God all the earth,
O sing to the glory of his name.
O render him glorious praise.
Say to God: 'How tremendous your deeds!

R̸. Cry out with joy to God all the earth.

'Before you all the earth shall bow;
shall sing to you, sing to your name!'
Come and see the works of God,
tremendous his deeds among men.

R̸. Cry out with joy to God all the earth.

He turned the sea into dry land,
they passed through the river dry-shod.
Let our joy then be in him;
he rules for ever by his might.

R̸. Cry out with joy to God all the earth.

Come and hear, all who fear God.
I will tell what he did for my soul.
Blessed be God who did not reject
     my prayer
nor withhold his love from me.

R̸. Cry out with joy to God all the earth.

SECOND READING
Gal 6:14-18

The only thing I can boast about is the
cross of our Lord Jesus Christ, through
whom the world is crucified to me, and I
to the world. It does not matter if a person
is circumcised or not; what matters is for
him to become an altogether new creature.
Peace and mercy to all who follow this
rule, who form the Israel of God. I want
no more trouble from anybody after this;
the marks on my body are those of Jesus.
The grace of our Lord Jesus Christ be
with your spirit, my brothers. Amen.

About Liturgy

Go, you are sent: Last week we looked at the opening of the Mass and the ritual
action of gathering. This week, let us examine the very last part of the Mass and what
some may call the most important part of the Mass itself: the dismissal.

Our word 'Mass' comes from the Latin text of the Mass's final dialogue, *Ite, missa
est*. Some liturgical scholars have translated this as, 'Go forth, the Mass is completed'.
Others have interpreted it as, 'Go forth, the assembly is dismissed'. No matter the exact
definition of *missa*, the meaning is clear. The grace we have received and shared in the
eucharistic action cannot remain here. It must go forth, and it can only do so through
us and our actions in our daily lives. The General Instruction of the Roman Missal
says the purpose of the dismissal is 'so that each may go back to doing good works,
praising and blessing God' (90).

Next the GIRM says that the priest and deacon kiss the altar. Then all the ministers
make a profound bow to the altar. There is no mention of a concluding procession nor
of a song to accompany that procession. It is simply presumed that there is some kind
of leave-taking by the ministers.

The abrupt quality of the instructions and rubrics here give us a sense of the
urgency of the dismissal. Go, now! You are sent. Take only what you have been given
here, and give it away freely to all you meet this week. Then come back next Sunday
rejoicing and giving thanks for all God has done.

About Initiation

Dismissal of catechumens: Although the catechumens are not present for
the assembly's dismissal at the end of Mass, they, too, are sent on mission. The
catechumens' dismissal takes place at every Mass after the homily and before the
Creed. The Rite of Christian Initiation of Adults provides a brief ritual dialogue
for this dismissal at number 67. More importantly, the rubrics found just before the
dialogue give us the purpose for the catechumens' dismissal. They are sent to 'share
their joy and spiritual experience'. Like the baptised who remain in the Mass and are
dismissed at the end of it, the catechumens also are sent to proclaim what they have
heard and to share what they have been given.

About Liturgical Music

How to choose a dismissal song: You may be surprised to discover that there are
no instructions or directives regarding singing a closing song at Mass. In contrast to
the lengthy description it provides for the entrance song, the General Instruction of the
Roman Missal mentions no such song for the end of Mass. This gives music ministers
much freedom in choice, but one that still requires forethought.

The bishops of England and Wales say this (*Celebrating the Mass* 225): 'The
practice of a final song or hymn is foreign to the Roman Rite, which is notably brief
in its concluding rites. The use of a final hymn at Mass which keeps ministers and
assembly in their place after the dismissal detracts somewhat from the dimension of
missionary imperative present in the dismissal texts. The use of instrumental music,
particularly an organ voluntary, is more appropriate to this moment'.

It might also be an opportunity for the choir to sing on their own as the assembly
departs. During Lent and other simpler liturgies, you might consider having the
assembly leave in silence.

SPIRITUALITY

GOSPEL ACCLAMATION
Cf. John 6:63, 68

R̰. Alleluia, alleluia.
Your words are spirit, Lord,
and they are life:
you have the message of eternal life.
R̰. Alleluia, alleluia.

Gospel   Luke 10:25-37

There was a lawyer who, to disconcert Jesus, stood up and said to him, 'Master, what must I do to inherit eternal life?' He said to him, 'What is written in the law? What do you read there?' He replied, 'You must love the Lord your God with all your heart, with all your soul, with all your strength, and with all your mind, and your neighbour as yourself.' 'You have answered right,' said Jesus 'do this and life is yours.'

But the man was anxious to justify himself and said to Jesus, 'And who is my neighbour?' Jesus replied, 'A man was once on his way down from Jerusalem to Jericho and fell into the hands of brigands; they took all he had, beat him and then made off, leaving him half dead. Now a priest happened to be travelling down the same road, but when he saw the man, he passed by on the other side. In the same way a Levite who came to the place saw him, and passed by on the other side. But a Samaritan traveller who came upon him was moved with compassion when he saw him. He went up and bandaged his wounds, pouring oil and wine on them. He then lifted him on to his own mount, carried him to the inn and looked after him. Next day, he took out two denarii and handed them to the innkeeper. "Look after him," he said "and on my way back I will make good any extra expense you have." Which of these three, do you think, proved himself a neighbour to the man who fell into the brigands' hands?' 'The one who took pity on him' he replied. Jesus said to him, 'Go, and do the same yourself.'

Reflecting on the Gospel

Luke introduces the parable of the Good Samaritan with a story found in Matthew and Mark, namely, a scholar of the law correctly summing up the law as loving God and loving our neighbour. In the other gospels the story effectively ends and another teaching is introduced. But Luke tells us that the scholar wanted 'to justify himself' and so to clarify who is his neighbour. Rather than answer straightforwardly, Jesus poses a story with which we are familiar. The priest and the Levite, both upright privileged people considered favoured by God, leave the unfortunate man in the ditch. Only the Samaritan, one of a group of people generally despised by many Jewish people of the time, offered any assistance. And it was no mere prayer or well-wish. He went out of his way, cared for the victim, bandaged him, carried him, and paid for his stay at the equivalent of a hotel. With that, Jesus asks the scholar which of the three was the neighbour to the man in the ditch? The scholar of the law in reply does not even use the word Samaritan, but says, 'The one who took pity on him'.

Though the question is about 'neighbour', mercy is the keyword in this gospel. The scholar was likely predisposed to believe that the priest or the Levite would be a neighbour, by acting mercifully. But it was the person the scholar did not expect who acted in that way.

When the scholar asks, 'And who is my neighbour?' the answer could rightfully be said, 'The one who took pity on him'. When one is in the ditch needing help, who is neighbour? More important than role or station, privilege or power, is the capacity and the willingness to be merciful and to receive mercy. Without mercy, the person in the ditch dies. One reading of Jesus's story might be that we are the person in the ditch. We should be open to receive acts of mercy no matter where they come from, or who performs them. Those who act in this way are neighbour, much more so than those we might otherwise expect. As Jesus continues to do, he creates upheaval in our worldview by a simple story that causes us to reconsider our priorities and prejudices.

Living the Paschal Mystery

Sometimes those who need to be helped want help on their own terms. But today's gospel is a reminder that to those in the ditch, help may come from the most unforeseen or even unimaginable people. When we place limitations on even such things as who might lend us help or assistance, we might not be open to the mercy of God, which is extended in a variety of ways. Though this parable of the Good Samaritan is often read to mean we should be neighbourly and act mercifully, it can also be read in a way so that we are open to receive mercy and kindness from others, no matter who they might be. Jesus invites us to move beyond ourselves in moments of crisis and to be open to mercy from wherever it might come. In doing so, we die to our own preconceived notions and live anew with an openness broader than we had before. For if we in the ditch are not willing to see the Samaritan as a neighbour, and accept his act of mercy, we will surely die in that same ditch.

Focusing the Gospel

Key words and phrases: 'You must love the Lord your God with all your heart, with all your soul, with all your strength, and with all your mind, and your neighbour as yourself'.

To the point: Everything in Judaism and Christianity can be reduced to this one essential statement: Love God and love your neighbour. And yet, the life-changing nature of this teaching to love God and love your neighbour as yourself is only discovered in the interpretation. In the parable of the Good Samaritan, the priest and the Levite pass by the man left for dead. Obviously, they did not recognise him as 'neighbour'. The Samaritan, acting with mercy, interprets this ancient Jewish commandment with the full abundance of the God of love.

Connecting the Gospel

to the first reading: The reading from Deuteronomy confirms the model of discipleship Jesus gives us in the parable of the Good Samaritan. The writer tells us that you can only keep the commandments and statutes of God when 'you shall return to the Lord your God with all your heart and soul'. The Samaritan gives not only of his time and energy but also of his material resources to care for the stranger he finds on the side of the road half-dead. His response begins when, seeing the robbers' victim, he is 'moved with compassion'. Unlike the Levite and the priest, the Samaritan allows himself to fully encounter the person in front of him in need.

to experience: Sometimes our lives become compartmentalized. In some ways this is good. We want our work to stay at work and our family life to take priority at home. But spirituality is not meant to be one of many facets of life that sits apart from the others. Instead of Christianity being something we do on Sunday morning, it is a way of *being*. As the first reading and the gospel show us, it is a way of being fully for God.

Connecting the Responsorial Psalm

to the readings: In the responsorial psalm we can hear the plea of the robbers' victim on the side of the road: 'As for me in my poverty and pain / let your help, O God, lift me up'. And if this was the prayer of the man left for dead, it is answered. But perhaps not in the way he expected.

to psalmist preparation: We are not told if the victim in the parable of the Good Samaritan is conscious, but if he was we can imagine his hope and excitement on seeing first a priest and then a Levite coming towards him on the road. We can also imagine his crushing disappointment as these men turned away from him. Being neglected by his own people, what must the victim's thoughts have been when he spied the Samaritan coming towards him? Did he still have hope or was he fearful? How would you feel if you saw your enemy coming towards you while you lay helplessly in a ditch? Jesus tells a parable to expand our vision of 'neighbour'. Both the Samaritan and the robbers' victim must look past external labels to recognise the neighbour within each other.

PROMPTS FOR FAITH-SHARING

Jesus confronts his Jewish audience by making a Samaritan the hero of his story. What groups within your life do you have a hard time believing well of? What happens if you imagine a member of this group as taking the place of the Samaritan in this parable?

The scholar of the law tries to get out of the commandment of God on a technicality. Love my neighbour, but who is my neighbour? Are there places in the life of faith where you are tempted to limit God and God's mercy? Are there some people you believe are outside the realm of God's mercy?

Jesus tells the scholar of the law, 'Go, and do the same yourself', after relaying the parable of the Samaritan's care for the robbers' victim. Who are the people in your community who are left on the side of the road isolated, wounded, and alone. How might you begin to be a neighbour to these people?

The man in the ditch must accept the help of the Samaritan in order to find relief. When have you received help from unexpected or even shocking sources?

CELEBRATION

Model Penitential Act

Presider: In today's gospel Jesus lifts up the example of the Samaritan who acts with mercy and commands us to 'Go, and do the same yourself'. Let us pause to remember the times we have not treated others as neighbour . . . [*pause*]

Lord Jesus, you welcome outcasts and sinners: Lord, have mercy.

Christ Jesus, you lift up outsiders as models of discipleship: Christ, have mercy.

Lord Jesus, you show us the way of love: Lord, have mercy.

Homily Points

• Today we hear the central teaching of Judaism and Christianity encapsulated in one sentence: Love God and love neighbour. As Rabbi Hillel stated shortly before the time of Jesus, 'What is hateful to yourself, do not do to your fellow man. That is the whole Torah; the rest is just commentary'. We are called to be a people rooted and grounded in the love of God who also extend that love to all we meet. The scholar of the law in today's gospel who asks Jesus, 'And who is my neighbour?' does not yet understand this teaching. His faithfulness to God has penetrated his mind, for he can recite the teachings of his faith, but they have not transformed his heart.

• In St. Paul's letter to the Colossians we find the source of the Samaritan's compassion in an early Christian hymn: 'God wanted all perfection / to be found in him / and all things to be reconciled through him and for him'. In Christ there is no division between races, religions, genders, or political parties. Instead, Christ, encompassing the fulness of creation, brings all together in unity. The Samaritan knows this. Instead of seeing only a Jewish man, the Samaritan sees a fellow human being. He sees his neighbour.

• Within our communities it is much easier to see the divisions rather than the similarities. This is because our human minds are primed to sort and identify. And the way we do this is by finding that which is different from the rest. Jesus invites us into a new worldview, one where we look for commonalities and celebrate unity. In this worldview we are all beloved children of God, and we are all neighbours.

Model Universal Prayer (Prayer of the Faithful)

Presider: Jesus calls us to recognise each person we encounter as our neighbour. With compassion we lift up our needs and the needs of others to the Lord.

Response: Lord, hear our prayer.

That the church recognise and lift up the loving deeds of all people of good will . . .

That wars and divisions cease as people look on each other with empathy . . .

That victims of crimes and all those who feel forgotten and abandoned experience the love of God and the care of their fellow human beings . . .

That all gathered here might know the law of God written on our hearts and live it with integrity . . .

Presider: God of all people, you call us to live your law by loving you and loving others. Hear our prayers that we might embody your compassion in the world. We ask this through Jesus Christ, our brother. Amen.

COLLECT

Let us pray.

Pause for silent prayer

O God, who show the light of your truth
to those who go astray,
so that they may return to the right path,
give all who for the faith they profess
are accounted Christians
the grace to reject whatever is contrary to
    the name of Christ
and to strive after all that does it honour.
Through our Lord Jesus Christ, your Son,
who lives and reigns with you in the unity
    of the Holy Spirit,
one God, for ever and ever. **Amen.**

FIRST READING
Deut 30:10-14

Moses said to the people: 'Obey the voice of the Lord your God, keeping those commandments and laws of his that are written in the Book of this Law, and you shall return to the Lord your God with all your heart and soul.

'For this Law that I enjoin on you today is not beyond your strength or beyond your reach. It is not in heaven, so that you need to wonder, "Who will go up to heaven for us and bring it down to us, so that we may hear it and keep it?" Nor is it beyond the seas, so that you need to wonder, "Who will cross the seas for us and bring it back to us, so that we may hear it and keep it?" No, the Word is very near to you, it is in your mouth and in your heart for your observance.'

RESPONSORIAL PSALM
Ps 68:14, 17, 30-31, 33-34, 36, 37 (Cf. 33)

R̸. Seek the Lord, you who are poor,
and your hearts will revive.

This is my prayer to you,
my prayer for your favour.
In your great love, answer me, O God,
with your help that never fails:
Lord, answer, for your love is kind;
in your compassion, turn towards me.

R̸. Seek the Lord, you who are poor,
and your hearts will revive.

As for me in my poverty and pain
let your help, O God, lift me up.
I will praise God's name with a song;
I will glorify him with thanksgiving.

R̸. Seek the Lord, you who are poor,
and your hearts will revive.

The poor when they see it will be glad
and God-seeking hearts will revive;
for the Lord listens to the needy
and does not spurn his servants in
    their chains.

R̸. Seek the Lord, you who are poor,
and your hearts will revive.

For God will bring help to Zion
and rebuild the cities of Judah.
The sons of his servants shall inherit it;
those who love his name shall dwell there.

R̸. Seek the Lord, you who are poor,
and your hearts will revive.

or

RESPONSORIAL PSALM
Ps 18:8-11 (9)

See Appendix A, p. 300.

SECOND READING
Col 1:15-20

Christ Jesus is the image of the unseen God
and the first-born of all creation,
for in him were created
all things in heaven and on earth:
everything visible and everything invisible,
Thrones, Dominations, Sovereignties,
    Powers –
all things were created through him and
    for him.
Before anything was created, he existed,
and he holds all things in unity.
Now the Church is his body,
he is its head.
As he is the Beginning,
he was first to be born from the dead,
so that he should be first in every way;
because God wanted all perfection
to be found in him
and all things to be reconciled through
    him and for him,
everything in heaven and everything
    on earth,
when he made peace
by his death on the cross.

About Liturgy

Effective strategies for hospitality: In today's gospel, the question posed by the scholar, 'And who is my neighbour?' gives us an opportunity to look at how we might answer this question based on our practice of hospitality at the Mass.

Like many good intentions, hospitality can become relegated to a committee or group of people who become responsible for hospitality on behalf of the parish. Thus we get hospitality committees, or we have announcements that go something like, 'Hospitality is provided after Mass today by the Knights of St. Columba'. Can you hear how strange that might sound to a visitor, as if being welcoming is a scheduled event or fulfilled by a specific group?

When we approach hospitality this way, we can often get the notion that we have 'done hospitality' if the priest asks all the visitors to stand up at some point during Mass 'so we can welcome them'. That may convey a sense of welcome to the visitors. However, if that were all they experienced as hospitality, and no one actually spoke to them or engaged them in personal conversation, one would doubt they would actually feel they belonged.

Hospitality is not a task we can check off a to-do list. It's not something that is scheduled. Hospitality is the attitude we take when we are going about our ordinary routine and we come across a stranger along the roadside who needs our attention. Hospitality is not welcoming people into *our* home but treating them as though this place is *their* home and they belong here and have a voice here. Hospitality then is everyone's responsibility, offered at all times, for the sake of acknowledging that the stranger is actually our neighbour. Here are some simple actions that you can encourage parishioners to take to cultivate an attitude of hospitality.

Ask parishioners to sit in the middle of the pew so that people who arrive after them have a place ready and waiting. When a person sits by you, say hello, shake their hand, and introduce yourself to them. Don't wait to be prompted to welcome them. Be sure greeters and other ministers standing in the vestibule before or after Mass are not clustered in groups of people they know. They should be searching out the newcomer and actively looking to talk to people they don't know.

About Liturgical Music

How to choose a psalm setting: Today's assigned readings give us the unusual occurrence in Ordinary Time of having two different responsorial psalms to choose from – Psalm 68 or Psalm 18. Although *Living Liturgy* is focusing on Psalm 68, this gives us an opportunity to explore how to select an appropriate psalm setting for an assembly.

The responsorial psalm is meant to help the assembly 'perceive the word of God speaking in the psalms and to turn these psalms into the prayer of the Church' (*Lectionary for Mass* 19). The Lectionary and GIRM (61) provides two ways to sing the psalms, with preference given to the first: 1) antiphonally as a dialogue between cantor and people; or 2) straight through like a hymn sung by cantor alone or by all the people.

Emphasizing the importance of the people's participation in singing the psalm, the Lectionary encourages us to use every means available to foster the people's singing of the psalms. To this end, select the setting that your assembly knows best and can almost sing by heart. When no such setting is available for your assembly, the Lectionary also provides seasonal psalms and refrains (Lectionary, pp. 949–63) that may be used if the assembly is more familiar with a setting of a different psalm than the one assigned for the day.

SPIRITUALITY

GOSPEL ACCLAMATION
cf. Luke 8:15

℟. Alleluia, alleluia.
Blessed are those who,
with a noble and generous heart,
take the word of God to themselves
and yield a harvest through their perseverance.
℟. Alleluia, alleluia.

Gospel

Luke 10:38-42

Jesus came to a village, and a woman named Martha welcomed him into her house. She had a sister called Mary, who sat down at the Lord's feet and listened to him speaking. Now Martha who was distracted with all the serving said, 'Lord, do you not care that my sister is leaving me to do the serving all by myself? Please tell her to help me.' But the Lord answered 'Martha, Martha,' he said 'you worry and fret about so many things, and yet few are needed, indeed only one. It is Mary who has chosen the better part; it is not to be taken from her.'

Reflecting on the Gospel

The Martha and Mary story in Luke is so familiar many people refer to themselves as either a 'Martha', meaning they are good at or even prefer working in the kitchen, or a 'Mary', meaning they do not worry about such things. Indeed this gospel has been quoted so often and used to support so many various understandings of ministry, household chores, the role of women, and more, that it is good to simply step back and read the words, or listen carefully when they are proclaimed.

Ultimately, it is the last verse that causes many to perk up or question their own priorities. Is it really the better part to sit and visit, leaving others to do the serving? What if the Marthas of the world stopped working in the kitchen, leaving the Marys and even Jesus himself without a meal!

At its worst, some use this passage to reinforce traditional domestic roles of women and men, with women doing the serving and men doing the reclining, visiting, and eating. Sometimes the reading is also used to claim that religious life (priesthood/sisterhood) is 'better' than the lay state. But such facile readings do not do justice to the short story in Luke. In fact, they turn the moral of the story on its head.

Primarily, it is significant that Jesus is interacting with two women. One, Mary, is seated at his feet, listening to his instruction as a disciple, though she is not called that here. The other, Martha, is 'distracted with all the serving' in attempting to prepare a meal for Jesus. Jesus tells Martha in effect that the proper service for a disciple in this situation is to listen to Jesus. It is not to fret about serving meals.

Luke will make this point again in Acts of the Apostles, when the apostles are too busy serving at table to be attentive to God's word and to prayer. To free themselves up for prayer and reading the word, the apostles appoint seven to serve at table, as 'deacons'. The deacons then do just that. They see to the needs of the Hebrew-speaking and Greek-speaking Christians, so that the apostles can devote themselves entirely to their ministry.

The gospel reading today is not about the role of women, or the clerical/religious state versus the laity. Instead, the story demonstrates that the proper role of a disciple is attentiveness to Jesus and his word.

Living the Paschal Mystery

It is so easy for us to be consumed by activities, checking boxes, crossing items off lists. There can be a great satisfaction in acting this way and a tremendous sense of accomplishment. But we hear a different message with other priorities today. Rather than busy ourselves or stir ourselves into a frenzy, it is the proper role of a disciple to listen to Jesus's instruction. And this does not mean become a priest or sister. Instead, it can mean to spend time in prayer, or with Scripture, coming to know the person of Jesus in a better way. This activity is critical for any disciple. And the example we have today is that of a woman. Luke is clear in presenting Jesus as giving pride of place to the disciple who listens to his instruction. Let us go and do the same.

Focusing the Gospel

Key words and phrases: Martha, Martha, . . . you worry and fret about so many things, and yet few are needed, indeed only one.

To the point: In the Bible we hear of seven people who are called by name twice: Abraham, Jacob, Moses, Samuel, Martha, Simon, and Saul. Some of these calls come in extraordinary circumstances. An angel stops Abraham's hand just as he is about to offer his son Isaac in sacrifice. Moses hears God's voice from a burning bush. Saul is thrown down on the road to Damascus in search of Christians to persecute. Martha's calling, however, takes place within the confines of everyday life as she and her sister Mary offer hospitality to an itinerant preacher, Jesus of Nazareth. Just as Moses is called away from shepherding his father-in-law's flock and hiding in the desert, and Saul is turned back from his pursuit of Christians, Martha is called from her anxieties and worries. Only without these burdens clouding her vision can she see the man who sits before her. He is the Word of God. The only hospitality he desires is for people to sit at his feet and listen.

Connecting the Gospel

to the first reading: Abraham and Sarah also offer hospitality to three mysterious visitors. Christians see these men as representing the triune God, though the Old Testament text says, 'The Lord appeared to Abraham'. Abraham's response seems much like Martha's. He eagerly invites the men to pause in their travel and rest awhile with him. He rushes about asking for Sarah to make bread and choosing a calf for one of his servants to butcher and prepare. Finally, he joins the men under the tree and waits on them while they eat. Abraham, like Martha, focuses on taking care of the physical needs of his guests. Unlike Martha, Abraham doesn't seem upset or worried about it – but then, he also has Sarah and his servant helping him with the work!

to experience: Hospitality was a revered part of the ancient culture of Abraham and even Jesus's time. It was important to offer food, drink, and rest in a desert or wilderness region, lest a traveller perish. As Christians we are invited into this hospitality, not for fear of death, but because we recognise Jesus within each and every person we welcome.

Connecting the Responsorial Psalm

to the readings: Our verses from Psalm 14 for today are in response to a question: 'LORD, who may abide in your tent? / Who may dwell on your holy mountain'? (15:1; NABRE). In the first reading and the gospel, Abraham, Sarah, Mary, and Martha all have an intimate encounter with God where they offer hospitality to the Lord. In a way they are 'abiding in God's tent'. The psalmist tells us that those who are upright, truthful, and just are the ones who will dwell with the Lord.

to psalmist preparation: We, also, are invited to abide with God. How do you put the traits of uprightness, truthfulness, justice into practice in your own life?

PROMPTS FOR FAITH-SHARING

In our readings we see Abraham and Sarah, Mary and Martha caring for the needs of a visitor. How do you practise hospitality in your own life?

If Jesus were speaking to you, what burdens and anxieties would he tell you to let go of?

When someone's name is called twice in the Bible his/her life is about to change forever. Have you experienced a moment in your life where you felt God calling you to something new?

How might you find more time in your daily life to sit at Jesus's feet and listen?

CELEBRATION

Model Penitential Act

Presider: In today's gospel Jesus gently calls Martha away from her many burdens and anxieties to encounter him with the peace and devotion of her sister Mary. For the times our burdens and anxieties have clouded us to the presence of the Lord we pause to ask for forgiveness . . . [*pause*]

Lord Jesus, you are the source of peace: Lord, have mercy.
Christ Jesus, you are the Word of God: Christ, have mercy.
Lord Jesus, you call us to everlasting life: Lord, have mercy.

Homily Points

• Jesus, the Word of God, is invited into the house of Mary and Martha. While Martha bustles about, preoccupied with the demands of hosting, Mary sits at Jesus's feet and listens. Martha is concerned with Jesus's human needs for comfort, food, and hospitality. And these are important, but they are not Jesus's only needs, nor his most important. As the Word of God, Jesus desires to be heard. In John's gospel, Jesus tells the bewildered disciples, 'My food is to do the will of the one who sent me and to finish his work' (4:34; NABRE). Jesus came into the world to proclaim the kingdom of God and Mary sits and listens.

• Martha also serves the Word of God. But instead of finding the peace of Mary, she is overcome by her work. She cannot hear the voice of Jesus when her mind is overflowing with recriminations and complaints against Mary! Jesus tells her, 'Martha, Martha, . . . you worry and fret about so many things, and yet few are needed, indeed only one'. And what is this one thing? Jesus, himself. The Word of God, spoken aloud, desperately desiring to be heard.

• In our lives there will always be much to do. We have tasks that demand our time and attention: houses to clean, children to feed and clothe, work to do. And yet, present among us is the Word of God, calling out to us amidst all the chaos. Like Martha, Jesus invites us to put down our burdens and choose the one thing – to know the peace and joy of Mary, sitting at the feet of the Lord and listening to the Word of God.

Model Universal Prayer (Prayer of the Faithful)

Presider: Through the intercession of St. Mary and St. Martha let us bring our needs before the Lord.

Response: Lord, hear our prayer.

That the church embrace the charisms of Mary and Martha in contemplation and in active service . . .

That societies all over the world support education opportunities for all of their people regardless of gender, race, or class . . .

That those who are overcome by burdens and anxieties hear the voice of the Lord inviting them to rest in his love . . .

That all gathered here might find time everyday to listen in contemplative silence to Jesus and his life-giving Word . . .

Presider: God of all, you rejoiced when Mary sat at the feet of your Son, Jesus, and listened to him. Hear our prayers that we might follow her example of devotion and contemplation. We ask this through Christ our Lord. Amen.

COLLECT

Let us pray.

Pause for silent prayer

Show favour, O Lord, to your servants
and mercifully increase the gifts of
    your grace,
that, made fervent in hope, faith and
    charity,
they may be ever watchful in keeping your
    commands.
Through our Lord Jesus Christ, your Son,
who lives and reigns with you in the unity
    of the Holy Spirit,
one God, for ever and ever. **Amen.**

FIRST READING
Gen 18:1-10

The Lord appeared to Abraham at the Oak of Mamre while he was sitting by the entrance of the tent during the hottest part of the day. He looked up, and there he saw three men standing near him. As soon as he saw them he ran from the entrance of the tent to meet them, and bowed to the ground. 'My Lord,' he said 'I beg you, if I find favour with you, kindly do not pass your servant by. A little water shall be brought; you shall wash your feet and lie down under the tree. Let me fetch a little bread and you shall refresh yourselves before going further. That is why you have come in your servant's direction.' They replied, 'Do as you say.'

Abraham hastened to the tent to find Sarah. 'Hurry,' he said 'knead three bushels of flour and make loaves.' Then running to the cattle Abraham took a fine and tender calf and gave it to the servant, who hurried to prepare it. Then taking cream, milk and the calf he had prepared, he laid all before them, and they ate while he remained standing near them under the tree.

'Where is your wife Sarah?' they asked him. 'She is in the tent' he replied. Then his guest said, 'I shall visit you again next year without fail and your wife will then have a son.'

CATECHESIS

RESPONSORIAL PSALM
Ps 14:2-5 (1)

℟. The just will live in the presence of
the Lord.

Lord, who shall dwell on your holy
        mountain?
He who walks without fault;
he who acts with justice
and speaks the truth from his heart;
he who does not slander with his tongue.

℟. The just will live in the presence of
the Lord.

He who does no wrong to his brother,
who casts no slur on his neighbour,
who holds the godless in disdain,
but honours those who fear the Lord.

℟. The just will live in the presence of
the Lord.

He who keeps his pledge, come what may;
who takes no interest on a loan
and accepts no bribes against the innocent.
Such a man will stand firm for ever.

℟. The just will live in the presence of
the Lord.

SECOND READING
Col 1:24-28

It makes me happy to suffer for you, as I
am suffering now, and in my own body
to do what I can to make up all that has
still to be undergone by Christ for the
sake of his body, the Church. I became the
servant of the Church when God made me
responsible for delivering God's message
to you, the message which was a mystery
hidden for generations and centuries and
has now been revealed to his saints. It was
God's purpose to reveal it to them and to
show all the rich glory of this mystery
to pagans. The mystery is Christ among
you, your hope of glory: this is the Christ
we proclaim, this is the wisdom in which
we thoroughly train everyone and instruct
everyone, to make them all perfect in Christ.

About Liturgy
Praying through the details: A question that many liturgists and liturgical ministers have is how to pray at Mass when they have so many things to worry about in doing their ministry. Presiders and liturgists, especially, have a tough job being in charge of the entire liturgical flow of a Mass while still appearing, as some of the old liturgical rubrics said, 'as if to pray'. Surely, Martha must be the patron saint of liturgists!

Unfortunately, Martha often gets placed in a bad light for her attention to detail and focus on the tasks at hand. Yet if we didn't have any Marthas, what would become of the liturgy, much less dinner?

Even as we might try to avoid being overly focused on small things and sustaining an unhealthy anxiety over things we cannot control, we can also revel in remembering that it was Martha, not Mary, who made the highest statement of faith in Jesus at the side of her brother's tomb: 'Yes, Lord. I have come to believe that you are the Messiah, the Son of God, the one who is coming into the world' (John 11:27; NABRE). When faced with ultimate crisis, Martha was prepared to place her faith in Jesus. If you worry about worrying as you do your ministry, here are some ideas that might help.

Be prepared as much as you can be before Mass. Use the days before Mass to prepare, rehearse, check, and double-check every small detail you are responsible for. On the day of Mass, take some time for yourself to pray. As you arrive at church, commit to giving your attention to the person right in front of you, for in them, you are entertaining angels. Then once the Mass begins, become the Martha not of the table but of the tomb, putting all your trust in Jesus.

About Initiation
Your parish is your RCIA team: Most RCIA coordinators wish they had a bigger team, more sponsors, or more people to help with catechesis and other tasks for RCIA gatherings. We certainly need to continually invite more people to participate directly in the work of initiation. However, we also need to recall that the responsibility of the initiation of adults belongs to all the faithful, not just the pastor or the RCIA team. Your parishioners, by their ordinary encounters with the catechumens and candidates at Mass and at other parish gatherings, will be your most effective team members. Don't wait for your parishioners to get involved with RCIA. Bring your catechumens and candidates to where your parishioners are already so all the faithful can exercise their role of being members of the RCIA team.

About Liturgical Music
How to choose a preparation of gifts song: The Liturgy of the Eucharist begins with the preparation of gifts. The song that is sung during this time is meant to accompany the ritual action of processing the gifts of bread and wine to the altar and of collecting other gifts for the poor and the church. Therefore, the length of the song you choose needs to match the logistics of your particular church and local custom.

The norms for the text follow the same guidelines given for the entrance song (see GIRM 48). However, you have more freedom in terms of the song's themes.

Although this part of the Mass is important, it is secondary to the ritual action that follows it, namely, the Eucharistic Prayer and the Communion Rite. Whatever music you select here, whether sung by the assembly or choir or instrumental, should not overshadow the highpoint of the Mass.

21 JULY 2019
SIXTEENTH SUNDAY
IN ORDINARY TIME

SPIRITUALITY

GOSPEL ACCLAMATION
Rom 8:15

℟. Alleluia, alleluia.
The spirit you received is the spirit of sons,
and it makes us cry out, 'Abba Father!'
℟. Alleluia, alleluia.

Gospel

Luke 11:1-13

Once Jesus was in a certain place praying, and when he had finished, one of his disciples said, 'Lord, teach us to pray, just as John taught his disciples.' He said to them, 'Say this when you pray:
"Father, may your name be held holy,
your kingdom come;
give us each day our daily bread,
and forgive us our sins,
for we ourselves forgive each one who is in debt to us.
And do not put us to the test."'
He also said to them, 'Suppose one of you has a friend and goes to him in the middle of the night to say, "My friend, lend me three loaves, because a friend of mine on his travels has just arrived at my house and I have nothing to offer him"; and the man answers from inside the house, "Do not bother me. The door is bolted now, and my children and I are in bed; I cannot get up to give it to you." I tell you, if the man does not get up and give it him for friendship's sake, persistence will be enough to make him get up and give his friend all he wants.

Continued in Appendix A, p. 300.

Reflecting on the Gospel

The Our Father prayer is something we likely learned as children, perhaps one of the first memorised or rote prayers we acquired. So, today's gospel and its version of the prayer might strike us as a bit odd. It's not the version we find in Matthew, which is much closer to the version we have memorised and recite at Mass. Instead, Luke's version has some elements that might be closer to the words uttered by Jesus himself. The Lukan version is certainly shorter and does not seem to have undergone the Matthean expansion from apparent liturgical use. Luke's version also begins dramatically with the direct address, 'Father', rather than the more communal, '*Our* Father'. The two petitions about the Father (three in Matthew) are shorter in Luke too, 'may *your* name be held holy, / *your* kingdom come'. But there are elements in Matthew that point to the words of Jesus too. For it seems a favourite Lukan theme, 'forgive us our sins' overcame the original, 'forgive us our debts' that Matthew preserves.

In the end, this short prayer of Jesus addressed directly to the Father likely offended sensibilities of the time. This was not the mere recitation of a psalm; this was not a lengthy sacrifice of praise and thanksgiving; this was not rooted in prophets, Moses, or the Law. This was the prayer of Jesus given to his disciples. And in just one generation the curt address was expanded as we find in Matthew. And some of the imagery, 'forgive debts' was changed by Luke to conform more closely to his theological outlook of 'forgive sins'. And yet, this prayer is not found in Mark, John, or anywhere else in the New Testament. Only Luke and Matthew give us their respective versions. Still, they are so similar – their differences can be understood and explained – that scholars believe we have here something very close to the words of the historical Jesus when he taught his disciples this prayer.

Next time we rush through this memorised prayer at Mass or another occasion, it might be good to set ourselves in the context of Jesus and his disciples, imagining receiving this prayer and his instruction. Let's consider the words we are praying and the worldview they depict. Ultimately, the prayer constitutes a way of life and disposition much deeper than mere prattle.

Living the Paschal Mystery

Jesus was no mere myth as were the ancient Greek and Roman gods and goddesses. He was a human being who walked the face of the earth, as even pagan historians relate. The Christian claim is not merely that Jesus existed, but that he was the Son of God, the Incarnate Word of God. But his existence as a human being on this earth is something that nearly every single noteworthy scholar admits.

Part of his time on earth consisted of prayer and teaching, and this prayer known as the Our Father or the Lord's Prayer is something that scholars can attribute to the Jesus of history with great certainty. As Luke has it, the prayer includes an injunction to keep us from the final test. The astute reader immediately thinks of Jesus and his coming passion. Later in the gospel, Jesus will pray that the cup pass him by, for such a passion and death is the desire of no one, not even Jesus. But his prayer has strengthened him for such a moment. After this final test he will be raised to new life in paradise eternally. Such a future awaits us too when we will ultimately live the paschal mystery *par excellence*.

Focusing the Gospel
Key words and phrases: Lord, teach us to pray.

To the point: In Luke's gospel we see Jesus at prayer many times. He prays at his baptism, after healing people, before choosing the twelve disciples, and before feeding the five thousand, to name only a few. Those closest to him in the gospel have witnessed his life of prayer, and you can sense their desire to have what Jesus has in the request, 'Lord, teach us to pray'. Jesus's response is the beloved words of the Our Father and several teachings on prayer: pray persistently and constantly and trust God to give you what you need. In our life of faith we are called to pray at all times. Sometimes these prayers are the traditional words passed down through generations of faith, but other times they are our own unique communication. Just like the disciples in today's gospel, let us trustingly request of Jesus, 'Lord, teach us to pray'.

Connecting the Gospel
to the first reading: In the first reading from Genesis we see Abraham at prayer with God. Far from how we might imagine conversing with God (kneeling, head bowed, alone) Abraham stands before the Lord, draws near, and begins a frank discussion over the requisite number of righteous people who must be in Sodom and Gomorrah for God to agree not to destroy the city. As Jesus instructs in today's gospel, Abraham's prayer is certainly persistent. He questions God six times, slowly moving the number of righteous people required from fifty to ten. At one point Abraham exclaims, 'I am bold indeed to speak like this to my Lord, I who am dust and ashes'. Jesus wants us to have this same boldness in approaching God the Father in prayer.

to experience: In prayer we give God thanks and praise, but we are also invited to converse with God freely about our needs, anxieties, frustrations, and even our anger. Nothing is out of bounds when it comes to prayer. All that is required is that, like Abraham, we show up, draw near, and share what's in our heart.

Connecting the Responsorial Psalm
to the readings: The psalmist sings, '[D]iscard not the work of your hands'. In prayer we demonstrate our belief in God's faithfulness. We reach out, asking for what we need, giving thanks and praise, because we believe in a God who loves us and desires only our good. Even in times when our faith is shaken or when we are struggling in the spiritual life, we enter into prayer relying on the God who 'is with me to the end'. The psalms themselves show us that we can come to God in every circumstance. Whether we approach him in hope or despair, joy or grief, love or anger, God is there.

to psalmist preparation: As a cantor, your ministry draws the people of God to pray through song. How do you experience your role as being a prayer leader in your community? As a prayer leader, how would you like to nourish and deepen your own prayer life?

PROMPTS FOR FAITH-SHARING

In today's gospel we are given the beginnings of the Our Father, our most treasured prayer. Say the Our Father slowly. Which line stands out to you? Why?

Jesus tells us, 'Ask, and it will be given to you'. How have you experienced God answering prayer?

In the film, *Shadowlands,* about Christian author C. S. Lewis, there is a well-known quote about prayer: 'It doesn't change God – it changes me.' How have you been changed by prayer?

How do you pray at this time in your faith journey? Alone or with others? Spontaneously or by reciting the prayers of the church? How is Jesus calling you to deepen your prayer life?

CELEBRATION

Model Penitential Act

Presider: In today's gospel the disciples approach Jesus with a simple request, 'Lord, teach us to pray'. Let us pause to prepare ourselves to be present to God in prayer . . . [*pause*]

Lord Jesus, you teach us to call God, "Father": Lord, have mercy.

Christ Jesus, you intercede for us at God's right hand: Christ, have mercy.

Lord Jesus, you show us how to pray without ceasing: Lord, have mercy.

Homily Points

• The disciples ask Jesus, '[T]each us to pray'. And Jesus complies with the words of the Our Father and instructions on prayer. But the real school of prayer is observing the place prayer held in Jesus's earthly life. Throughout the gospels Jesus prays publicly and privately, in front of crowds and in the intimate group of his closest disciples. He prays from the very beginning of his public ministry, marked with his baptism by John in the Jordan (Luke 3:21-22), to his last breath on the cross when he commends his spirit to his Father (23:46). And it is with a prayer that he ascends into heaven after his resurrection (Luke 24:50-53).

• What do we learn from Jesus's prayer? More than an action, prayer is a way of being, a way of living out a relationship with his Father. Because of this, Jesus can pray in all situations – in thanksgiving, blessing, or even deep grief as he prays in Gethsemane for the cup to pass him by. Jesus tells us, 'Ask, and it will be given to you', and yet it seems as though this Gethsemane prayer wasn't answered. Jesus did undergo 'the test' even as he taught his disciples to pray for God to deliver them from it.

• We have all known the experience of feeling as though our prayers have gone unanswered. In the film *Shadowlands*, about Christian author C. S. Lewis, there is a line spoken by Lewis's character: 'I pray because the need flows out of me all the time – waking and sleeping. . . . It doesn't change God – it changes me'. Seen this way, prayer is a tool of our own transformation. God didn't stop the crucifixion, and yet, through his complete love of God and gift of himself, Jesus could not remain dead. He rose. In prayer we enter into the paschal mystery. May it lead us to new life, too.

Model Universal Prayer (Prayer of the Faithful)

Presider: Jesus tells us, 'Ask, and it will be given to you'. With confidence and trust we bring our prayers before the Lord.

Response: Lord, hear our prayer.

That all members of the church grow and deepen in their relationship with God through prayer . . .

That the world might continue to be transformed into the kingdom of God where love, peace, and hope reign . . .

That those who suffer from hunger and poverty have their daily needs provided for . . .

That all gathered here might persistently intercede for those on the outskirts and margins of our community . . .

Presider: God of mercy, you sent your Son Jesus to teach us to pray. Hear these petitions that we might learn how to pray without ceasing. We ask this through Christ, our Lord. Amen.

COLLECT

Let us pray.

Pause for silent prayer

O God, protector of those who hope in you,
without whom nothing has firm
     foundation, nothing is holy,
bestow in abundance your mercy upon us
and grant that, with you as our ruler
     and guide,
we may use the good things that pass
in such a way as to hold fast even now
to those that ever endure.
Through our Lord Jesus Christ, your Son,
who lives and reigns with you in the unity
     of the Holy Spirit,
one God, for ever and ever. **Amen.**

FIRST READING
Gen 18:20-32

The Lord said, 'How great an outcry there is against Sodom and Gomorrah! How grievous is their sin! I propose to go down and see whether or not they have done all that is alleged in the outcry against them that has come up to me. I am determined to know.'

The men left there and went to Sodom while Abraham remained standing before the Lord. Approaching him he said, 'Are you really going to destroy the just man with the sinner? Perhaps there are fifty just men in the town. Will you really overwhelm them, will you not spare the place for the fifty just men in it? Do not think of doing such a thing: to kill the just man with the sinner, treating just and sinner alike! Do not think of it! Will the judge of the whole earth not administer justice?' The Lord replied, 'If at Sodom I find fifty just men in the town, I will spare the whole place because of them.'

Abraham replied, 'I am bold indeed to speak like this to my Lord, I who am dust and ashes. But perhaps the fifty just men lack five: will you destroy the whole city for five?' 'No,' he replied, 'I will not destroy it if I find forty-five just men there.' Again Abraham said to him, 'Perhaps there will only be forty there.' 'I will not do it' he replied 'for the sake of the forty.'

Abraham said, 'I trust my Lord will not be angry, but give me leave to speak: perhaps there will only be thirty there.' 'I will not do it' he replied 'if I find thirty there.' He said, 'I am bold indeed to speak like this, but perhaps there will only be twenty there.' 'I will not destroy it' he replied 'for the sake of the twenty.' He said, 'I trust my Lord will not be angry if I speak once more: perhaps there will only be ten.' 'I will not destroy it' he replied 'for the sake of the ten.'

CATECHESIS

RESPONSORIAL PSALM
Ps 137:1-3, 6-8 (3)

℟. On the day I called,
you answered me, O Lord.

I thank you, Lord, with all my heart,
you have heard the words of my mouth.
In the presence of the angels I will bless you.
I will adore before your holy temple.

℟. On the day I called,
you answered me, O Lord.

I thank you for your faithfulness and love
which excel all we ever knew of you.
On the day I called, you answered;
you increased the strength of my soul.

℟. On the day I called,
you answered me, O Lord.

The Lord is high yet he looks on the lowly
and the haughty he knows from afar.
Though I walk in the midst of affliction
you give me life and frustrate my foes.

℟. On the day I called,
you answered me, O Lord.

You stretch out your hand and save me,
your hand will do all things for me.
Your love, O Lord, is eternal,
discard not the work of your hands.

℟. On the day I called,
you answered me, O Lord.

SECOND READING
Col 2:12-14

You have been buried with Christ, when
you were baptised; and by baptism, too,
you have been raised up with him through
your belief in the power of God who
raised him from the dead. You were dead,
because you were sinners and had not been
circumcised: he has brought you to life
with him, he has forgiven us all our sins.

He has overridden the Law, and
cancelled every record of the debt that we
had to pay; he has done away with it by
nailing it to the cross.

About Liturgy

The Lord's Prayer: In the years leading up to the 2011 promulgation of the new English translation of the Mass, one thing was a common concern: that the words of the Lord's Prayer not be changed. Although the words remain the same, how we pray this prayer varies greatly from parish to parish, and even from Mass to Mass.

One variation is in the gestures of the assembly during the prayer. The rubrics in the Roman Missal say that the priest extends his hands as he leads the prayer. However, the ritual text gives no prescribed gesture for the people to make as they pray the Lord's Prayer. The United States bishops have determined that they would give no specific directive regarding this issue. Thus, in some communities, the custom is to hold their neighbours' hands during this prayer. Others have chosen to extend their hands as the priest does. Still others keep their hands lowered or folded.

Should there be uniformity in gesture in this prayer that expresses our unity? The answer is unclear. However, where unity can certainly be fostered, beyond gestures, is the way in which the prayer is prayed. The preferred form is singing by the entire assembly. The communal praying of the Lord's Prayer can never be replaced by a solo performance of it, no matter how stirring the rendition. Nor should a musical setting known only by a portion of the assembly be used. If the prayer is to be sung, then the best option for most assemblies will be the chant setting found in the Roman Missal.

About Initiation

Knocking on doors at the Rite of Acceptance: In some places, parishes have incorporated a custom of asking inquirers to knock on the doors of the church at the beginning of the Rite of Acceptance, explaining that it signifies the inquirers' desire to enter the church. However, this action is nowhere in the official rite, and it distorts the meaning of the rite itself. Forcing inquirers to knock on the church doors actually shows the church as passive, waiting for inquirers to come to them instead of going out to draw others to Christ through the work of evangelisation.

The rite's intention is to show the dual action of God's call through Christian witness and the inquirers' response to that call by following the gospel. Thus, the rubrics state that a group of the faithful go outside to meet the inquirers and their sponsors (RCIA 48) in order to bring them over the threshold of the church doors to hear the word of God.

About Liturgical Music

Repeating music: As music ministers, our primary job is to assist and enhance the assembly's voice as it sings the acclamations, responses, and hymns of the Mass. To do our job well, we need to rehearse the music ahead of time. In the course of the week we might sing through a particular song five or six times: several times during rehearsal, once before Mass, and once during Mass. The assembly, however, typically only gets one chance to sing that song that week. Thus, music ministers will get bored with a piece of music five times quicker than the assembly. Let us remember that repeating the same song over several weeks helps us do our job well because it helps the assembly learn that song. Recall that the community's unrehearsed singing 'is the primary song of the liturgy' (US Bishops, *Sing to the Lord* 28).

SPIRITUALITY

GOSPEL ACCLAMATION
Matt 5:3

R͟. Alleluia, alleluia.
How happy are the poor in spirit;
theirs is the kingdom of heaven.
R͟. Alleluia, alleluia.

Gospel

Luke 12:13-21

A man in the crowd said to Jesus, 'Master, tell my brother to give me a share of our inheritance.' 'My friend,' he replied, 'who appointed me your judge, or the arbitrator of your claims?' Then he said to them, 'Watch, and be on your guard against avarice of any kind, for a man's life is not made secure by what he owns, even when he has more than he needs.'

Then he told them a parable: 'There was once a rich man who, having had a good harvest from his land, thought to himself, "What am I to do? I have not enough room to store my crops." Then he said, "This is what I will do: I will pull down my barns and build bigger ones, and store all my grain and my goods in them, and I will say to my soul: My soul, you have plenty of good things laid by for many years to come; take things easy, eat, drink, have a good time." But God said to him, "Fool! This very night the demand will be made for your soul; and this hoard of yours, whose will it be then?" So it is when a man stores up treasure for himself in place of making himself rich in the sight of God.'

Reflecting on the Gospel

Many of us know and are familiar with Jesus's teachings. But what would we consider to be among the most popular topics that Jesus addressed? Or another question we might ask is, what are the most popular topics we hear about today in churches? Are the two related? Do the priorities of Jesus and his preaching align with preaching we hear at the parish? Interestingly, some of the issues Jesus addressed more than others were about money and the right use of it. Rarely did he address issues concerning buildings of worship, parish schools, sexuality, LGBT, or even contraception. Jesus preached often about how people use their money. And today's gospel is a case, or rather two cases, in point.

The first story is about someone who wants his share of the inheritance. Rather than get in the middle of that quagmire (Jesus seems to have been wise not to step into that battle!), he gives a quick aphorism that's appropriate for Christian and non-Christian alike, '[A] man's life is not made secure by what he owns'. In fact, this teaching reflects certain schools of Greek philosophy, and even modern common sense.

The second story is called the parable of the rich fool. Indeed, God himself addresses the rich man as 'Fool!', for he spent his time on earth acquiring a bountiful harvest, a 'treasure for himself'. But that very night he will die, not 'rich in the sight of God'. Here it is clear that bountiful harvests, storehouses, and great material blessings are not what matters to God. Other gospel passages from Luke will make clear what does matter to God. In this reading we learn *via negativa*, by a negative way, what does not.

The parable calls us to reconsider our own harvests and storehouses. What are we acquiring and for what purpose? '[A] man's life is not made secure by what he owns'. It's a lesson so clear and fundamental that we need to be reminded of it again and again.

Parish preaching would do well to echo themes introduced by Jesus himself. All other ancillary but related issues will then naturally fall in line. But how we spend our money says a great deal about us as human beings. Our values, priorities, and interests are all expressed by the way we spend money.

Living the Paschal Mystery

The reading from Luke invites us to take stock of our lives from a different perspective. When God calls us from this life, what will we have left? The old adage, 'you can't take it with you', comes to mind. No matter what physical things or possessions we acquire here on earth we take nothing with us after we die. Put another way, our lives are not our possessions. A monthly bank account statement or credit card statement can become a moment of prayer. Our spending reflects our priorities.

It behooves us to step back from a desire to acquire and ask ourselves why. What is the purpose of our possessions? Rather than become rich in the eyes of the world, it is better to become rich in what matters to God. When we lift up the lowly, feed the hungry, and forgive sins of others we acquire riches in what matters to God. We have no ledger sheet or bank account to track this behaviour. Instead, it flows from our identity as Christians, living a spirituality of the paschal mystery.

Focusing the Gospel

Key words and phrases: Watch, and be on your guard against avarice of any kind

To the point: Merriam-Webster's dictionary defines greed as 'a selfish and excessive desire for more of something than is needed'. We see this greed played out in today's gospel with the rich man who finds himself with such a bountiful harvest he cannot possibly use it all. Instead of sharing this bounty with others or putting it to some good use, he decides to tear down his current barn to build an even bigger one to hold the excess. If we are not careful, the desire for more can take over every aspect of our lives, because no *thing* will satisfy our deepest hunger. Only God can do that. As St. Augustine said, 'Our hearts are restless until they can find rest in you'.

Connecting the Gospel

to the first reading: In the reading from Ecclesiastes, Qoheleth laments, '[F]or what does he gain for all the toil and strain that he has undergone under the sun?' For the wise and knowledgeable face the same fate as the foolish (2:16), so what point is there in life? Reading through Ecclesiastes, we might ask ourselves, where is the good news here? If all is vanity, where is our sure foundation and a treasure that will last? The answer comes to us in the gospel. Our lives are meaningful when they belong to God. When we are rich in God we have all we need.

to experience: As Qoheleth tells us and as the rich fool in the gospel discovers, human lives are unpredictable. All things fade away, including those that we cling to like a life preserver: health, beauty, money . . . . Instead of placing our hope and trust in what is transitory, our lives become secure only when we turn to the one who is truly unchanging: our triune God.

Connecting the Responsorial Psalm

to the readings: Following Qoheleth's line of thought, the psalmist too reflects on the transitory nature of life. We are the creatures who will turn 'back into dust', our lives as fragile and as fleeting as the grass: 'In the morning it springs up and flowers: / by evening it withers and fades'. When considered in light of human limitations, it indeed seems to be vanity to toil for that which will pass away. Saint Paul urges us to put away 'the things that are on the earth' in order to enter into the life of Christ. We are mortals, made in the image and likeness of God, the eternal one, called by Jesus to become 'rich in the sight of God'.

to psalmist preparation: The final verse of today's psalm points to this true richness when we are bathed in the kindness, joy, and gladness of a life steeped in God's gracious care. Where do you find this richness in your life?

PROMPTS FOR FAITH-SHARING

Which activities in your life fall into the category of '[v]anity of vanities?' How might you exchange some of these meaningless pursuits for more fulfilling work?

Our finances can tell us a lot about our priorities in life. When you look at your monthly expenses is your spending in line with what is most important to you? What about what is most important to Jesus?

Where in your life are you 'rich in the sight of God?'

Where is there excess in your life? How might God be calling you to share that excess with others?

CELEBRATION

Model Penitential Act

Presider: In today's gospel Jesus counsels, 'Watch, and be on your guard against avarice of any kind, for a man's life is not made secure by what he owns, even when he has more than he needs'. For the times we have prioritised wealth, power, and possessions over the kingdom of God, let us pause to ask for pardon and mercy . . . [*pause*]

Lord Jesus, you fulfill the deepest longings of our hearts: Lord, have mercy.

Christ Jesus, you invite us to store up treasure in heaven: Christ, have mercy.

Lord Jesus, you shepherd us to everlasting life: Lord, have mercy.

Homily Points

• Today's gospel challenges us to consider one central question, what (or where) is our treasure? For the rich man in the parable the answer is obvious. His treasure is the stability provided by a bounteous harvest. He even builds a storehouse for this treasure (new and larger barns), and once it is safely tucked away tells himself, 'My soul, you have plenty of good things laid by for many years to come; take things easy, eat, drink, have a good time'. The stability he thinks he has found is an illusion, however, because life is fragile and uncertain.

• It is natural for human beings to seek stability and control. We want to know that we have enough to provide for our needs and the needs of our families. But at what point do we begin to place all of our faith and hope in material goods, instead of in God, the only true constant in life? And when can we truly say, enough is enough? Greed is a sickness of the spirit that constantly goads us to acquire more and more. The things we seek will never fill the deepest longings of our hearts, and, as long as wealth or power, fame, or beauty is our aim, we will never be satisfied.

• Jesus offers us another way. A few verses after this gospel reading he tells the disciples to focus on the 'inexhaustible treasure in heaven that no thief can reach nor moth destroy. For where your treasure is, there also will your heart be' (12:33-34; NABRE). Where do you store your treasure? Where do you keep your heart?

Model Universal Prayer (Prayer of the Faithful)

Presider: Jesus calls us to become rich in what matters to God. Humbly, we turn to God in prayer and lift up our needs and the needs of our world.

Response: Lord, hear our prayer.

That the church might be transparent in matters of finance and dedicate resources to caring for the poor . . .

That those who control a disproportionate amount of the world's resources might use their leadership and power for justice so that all may have what they need . . .

That those who have devoted themselves to the empty pursuit of wealth and power know the fulfilment found in Jesus's path of service and generosity . . .

That all gathered here listen for the voice of our Good Shepherd calling us to become rich in what matters to God . . .

Presider: God of life, you sent your son to lead us to you, our true treasure and source of all peace. Hear our prayers that we might be freed from the desire to always have more, and instead invest our time and resources in building the kingdom of God. We ask this through Christ, our Lord. Amen.

COLLECT

Let us pray.

Pause for silent prayer

Draw near to your servants, O Lord,
and answer their prayers with unceasing
    kindness,
that, for those who glory in you as their
    Creator and guide,
you may restore what you have created
and keep safe what you have restored.
Through our Lord Jesus Christ, your Son,
who lives and reigns with you in the unity
    of the Holy Spirit,
one God, for ever and ever. **Amen.**

FIRST READING
Eccl 1:2; 2:21-23

Vanity of vanities, the Preacher says. Vanity of vanities. All is vanity!

For so it is that a man who has laboured wisely, skilfully and successfully must leave what is his own to someone who has not toiled for it at all. This, too, is vanity and great injustice; for what does he gain for all the toil and strain that he has undergone under the sun? What of all his laborious days, his cares of office, his restless nights? This, too, is vanity.

RESPONSORIAL PSALM
Ps 89:3-6, 12-14, 17 (1)

℟. O Lord, you have been our refuge
from one generation to the next.

You turn men back into dust
and say: 'Go back, sons of men.'
To your eyes a thousand years
are like yesterday, come and gone,
no more than a watch in the night.

℟. O Lord, you have been our refuge
from one generation to the next.

You sweep men away like a dream,
like grass which springs up in the morning.
In the morning it springs up and flowers:
by evening it withers and fades.

℟. O Lord, you have been our refuge
from one generation to the next.

CATECHESIS

Make us know the shortness of our life
that we may gain wisdom of heart.
Lord, relent! Is your anger for ever?
Show pity to your servants.

R̂. O Lord, you have been our refuge
from one generation to the next.

In the morning, fill us with your love;
we shall exult and rejoice all our days.
Let the favour of the Lord be upon us:
give success to the work of our hands.

R̂. O Lord, you have been our refuge
from one generation to the next.

or

RESPONSORIAL PSALM
Ps 94:1-2,6-9 (7-8)

See Appendix A, p. 300.

SECOND READING
Col 3:1-5, 9-11

Since you have been brought back to true
life with Christ, you must look for the
things that are in heaven, where Christ
is, sitting at God's right hand. Let your
thoughts be on heavenly things, not on
the things that are on the earth, because
you have died, and now the life you have
is hidden with Christ in God. But when
Christ is revealed – and he is your life –
you too will be revealed in all your glory
with him.

That is why you must kill everything
in you that belongs only to earthly life:
fornication, impurity, guilty passion, evil
desires and especially greed, which is
the same thing as worshipping a false
god; and never tell each other lies. You
have stripped off your old behaviour
with your old self, and you have put on
a new self which will progress towards
true knowledge the more it is renewed
in the image of its creator; and in that
image there is no room for distinction
between Greek and Jew, between the
circumcised or the uncircumcised, or
between barbarian and Scythians, slave
and free man. There is only Christ: he is
everything and he is in everything.

About Liturgy

The collection at Mass: The collection taken up during Mass is an ancient tradition with its roots in the early church. Originally, the people brought forward bread and wine from their own households to be used for the Eucharist. They also presented goods from their possessions – foods they harvested, livestock from their farms, household items from their own storeroom. These would be distributed by the deacons to those in need in the community as well as given for the material needs of the church.

Today, the people still ritually present bread and wine, though not usually from their own household. Also, the gifts for the poor and the church are now given in the form of money.

Taking up a collection has significant meaning for what we do at the Eucharist. Giving money at Mass is not, as some might treat it, a measure of our satisfaction with the liturgy or with the church in general. Our Christian sacrifice cannot be some vague theoretical idea. We have to give something of ourselves that is a real sacrifice – something we would rather not give up. For most of us today, that's money. Beyond simply being a way to help the parish pay its bills, the collection is one way we bring ourselves – 'the work of human hands' along with the 'fruit of the earth' – to the altar. That's why the collection is brought forward with the bread and wine we use at Mass. The money we put in the basket helps the church do the mission of Christ not only by keeping the lights on but also by funding the activities and people of the church who help the poor, teach the faith, prepare the liturgy, visit the sick, and more.

Finally, giving money at Mass is also a way we express our trust in God. We give the fruit of our own labour back to God, acknowledging that every good gift we have been given comes first from God.

The most appropriate time to take up a collection is at the preparation of gifts. If a second collection must be taken, do this during this time as well instead of after Communion where it can disrupt the ritual flow of the communion rite. Once the collection has been brought forward, it is placed in another suitable and secure location away from the altar (see GIRM 73). Another option that works well is to invite the assembly to come forward to the altar to place their gifts at baskets located there. Once all have come forward, the baskets are gathered and the bread and wine are brought to the altar.

About Liturgical Music

Music suggestions: Today's readings are powerful challenges for us to trust completely in God's care. Three songs help express this call. First, *Psallite*'s 'Do Not Store Up Earthly Treasures' is a creative adaptation of J. S. Bach's hymn tune WACHET AUF (commonly found in hymnals as 'Wake, O Wake'). The *Psallite* version is intended to be sung a cappella but can also be accompanied by any familiar arrangement of the hymn tune. Two others would be 'Be thou my vision' and 'Seek ye first'. Finally, any setting of St. Ignatius of Loyola's *Suscipe* prayer fits well, including John Foley's 'Take, Lord, Receive' (OCP).

SPIRITUALITY

GOSPEL ACCLAMATION
Matt 24:42, 44

℟. Alleluia, alleluia.
Stay awake and stand ready,
because you do not know the hour
when the Son of Man is coming.
℟. Alleluia, alleluia.

Gospel   Luke 12:32-48

Jesus said to his disciples: 'There is no
need to be afraid, little flock, for it has
pleased your Father to give you the
kingdom.

'Sell your possessions and give
alms. Get yourselves purses that do
not wear out, treasure that will not
fail you, in heaven where no thief
can reach it and no moth destroy it.
For where your treasure is, there will
your heart be also.

'See that you are dressed for action
and have your lamps lit. Be like men
waiting for their master to return
from the wedding feast, ready to
open the door as soon as he comes and
knocks. Happy those servants whom
the master finds awake when he comes.
I tell you solemnly, he will put on an
apron, sit them down at table and wait
on them. It may be in the second watch
he comes, or in the third, but happy
those servants if he finds them ready.
You may be quite sure of this, that if
the householder had known at what
hour the burglar would come, he would
not have let anyone break through
the wall of his house. You too must
stand ready, because the Son of Man is
coming at an hour you do not expect.'

Continued in Appendix A, p. 301,

or Luke 12:35-40 in Appendix A, p. 301.

Reflecting on the Gospel

As we continue our Ordinary Time journey with Jesus to Jerusalem we hear
more parables and teachings, laden with ancient imagery. The images of
'dressed for action', 'have your lamps lit', 'like men waiting for their master to
return', and even 'sit them down at table' tell us we are in the ancient world,
in a culture quite removed from our own. But despite these images and the
imaginary cultural bridge we must cross, we can certainly gain a sense of what
is meant by these teachings. Some simply prefer to focus on the line 'stand
ready, because the Son of Man is coming at
an hour you do not expect', shedding all
ancient and other imagery.

When we reduce the teaching to
this essential element, it becomes
easier to grasp the message,
which is not solely about the end
times. Instead, the exhortation to be
prepared applies to each of us as we
do not know the time, place, or date
of our personal end. In other words,
we don't know when we will die.

It might be more exciting to
ponder the end of the world, but
it is far more likely that we will
not be around for that event. We
can be assured that will be around
for the end of *our own* world. And
for that we should be prepared
spiritually.

This might not be such a happy or pleasant
message at an August weekend in the midst of Ordinary Time. But perhaps
this is a good time to hear it. When summer plans are winding down and
attention is turning to the start of the school year, we ask ourselves if we
are ready for the coming of the Son of Man. Or, are we deluding ourselves in
thinking that day will never come? When it does, it comes like a thief in the
night. '[S]tand ready'!

Living the Paschal Mystery

There will come a time for each of us to pass on from this life. In all likelihood
it's not a topic we discuss much. Most of us live our lives in anticipation of
future events, making plans, and carrying on our way. Especially now in the
modern world when the science of medicine and the pace of technology has
improved day-to-day life a great deal, it seems there is nothing we cannot solve.
And yet, tragedy still strikes. Death and loss come. There is the pain of losing
someone we love. And at that point we might imagine all we wish we had said
or expressed.

The gospel passage today reminds us that we all will ultimately face our
own end. But the paschal mystery tells us that after death there is new life. It
is not the same, but it will be transformed. Even so, our current life can end in
a moment, coming 'like a thief in the night'. We are advised to be on guard, to
watch, to act in a way that we will be ready for that day. Where is our treasure?
There too is our heart.

Focusing the Gospel

Key words and phrases: You too must stand ready, because the Son of Man is coming at an hour you do not expect.

To the point: In our church year we have two great seasons of preparation: Advent and Lent. In these times we prepare our hearts and minds, as well as our households and families, to celebrate the feasts of Christmas and Easter. Though preparation can take on a penitential overtone, it is also filled with joy as a foretaste of the celebration to come. In our gospel today, Jesus counsels his disciples to be vigilant in preparation for the coming of the Son of Man. Whether we meet Jesus at the end of time or at the end of our earthly lives, we do not know the hour or the day when this will occur. May our preparation be intentional and constant, but also joyful as we look forward to an eternity with God.

Connecting the Gospel

to the second reading: The second reading from the Letter to the Hebrews focuses on the person of Abraham. Not knowing what lay ahead of him, Abraham followed God's call to leave his home and family to enter into a new land, which God would show him. Even when it seemed as if God's promises of a land of his own and descendants could not be fulfilled Abraham remained steadfast, for he 'believed that he who had made the promise would be faithful to it'. Jesus has promised that he will return for us, that he is preparing a place for us. Do we also hold the one who has made this promise to be trustworthy?

to experience: We can take Abraham as our model in faith as we wait for the fulfilment of God's promises. For a time when there will be no more war, sickness, death, or grief, for the time when God will be 'all in all' (1 Cor 15:28; NABRE).

Connecting the Responsorial Psalm

to the readings: To be like the servants in today's gospel requires not only vigilance but also extreme patience. The servants do not know when their master will return. If he is delayed will they grow tired of watching for him? Will they begin to lose hope that he is returning at all? The psalmist lifts up today the necessity of 'waiting for the Lord'. We know that God's ways are not our ways, nor God's thoughts our thoughts (Isa 55:8). And yet it is difficult to have patience when we feel like it is time for the Lord to show up and intervene. The psalmist reassures us, 'The Lord looks on those who revere him, / on those who hope in his love'. As we live in this time of waiting and preparation for the fulness of the kingdom of God, it might be easy to grow weary and to give up hope. But we come from generations upon generations of God's people who despite hardship and persecution continued to '[wait] for the Lord'. We are called to do the same.

to psalmist preparation: Patience is a muscle that grows stronger with use. Where is God calling on you to wait upon him?

PROMPTS FOR FAITH-SHARING

St. Paul lifts up for us Abraham, our father in faith, as a role model for our own trust in God. Who are the spiritual ancestors who have built up your faith?

Abraham goes forth from his homeland and family to a new land God will reveal to him. Has there been a time in your life when you left all that you knew to embark on a different path? What sustained you through that experience?

We do not know the hour or the day when the Son of Man will come or when we will go to meet the Son of Man. How are you exercising vigilance in preparation for this moment?

Jesus tells us, 'See that you are dressed for action and have your lamps lit'. How might we spiritually respond to these commands?

CELEBRATION

Model Penitential Act

Presider: Jesus counsels us, 'stand ready, because the Son of Man is coming at an hour you do not expect'. Let us pause to prepare our hearts and minds to welcome Jesus . . . [*pause*]

Lord Jesus, you are Son of God and Son of Man: Lord, have mercy.

Christ Jesus, you have gone on ahead to prepare a place for us: Christ, have mercy.

Lord Jesus, you point the way to everlasting life: Lord, have mercy.

Homily Points

• The themes of preparation, waiting, and hope are woven throughout today's readings. The first reading from the book of Wisdom hearkens back to the first Passover when the people of God, enslaved in Egypt, ate their meal of lamb and unleavened bread with hope in God's power to save them. The psalmist tells us to '[wait] for the Lord'. In the gospel Jesus admonishes the disciples, 'You too must stand ready'. And in the second reading from the Letter to the Hebrews we hear of how it all began with the covenant God established with Abraham.

• In the figure of Abraham we can see both where we have been and where we are going. God promised Abraham land and descendants, and Abraham lived to see both promises brought to fulfilment, though perhaps on a smaller scale than he might have wished. Near the end of his life Abraham acquires a field and a cave in the land of Canaan as a burial plot for his wife Sarah. He also lives to see his son Isaac married to Rebekah. Through the many ups and downs of his life, Abraham does not lose hope in God's promises for, the Letter to the Hebrews tells us, '[H]e looked forward to a city founded, designed and built by God'. Abraham trusted in the vision of God, even when he himself could not see how it could possibly come about.

• St. Paul reminds us that from Abraham came 'more descendants than could be counted, as many as the stars of heaven or the grains of sand on the seashore'. From one wandering nomad in the land of Israel has come forth the people of God spread throughout the world and throughout generations. We count ourselves as members of this family. Like Abraham, we look to the future when God's kingdom of peace and justice will come to fulfilment. We might not know when this will come about but we will continue preparing for it, because we believe that the one who has made this promise is trustworthy.

Model Universal Prayer (Prayer of the Faithful)

Presider: Let us bring our prayers to the Lord that we might always vigilantly be about the work of building the kingdom of God.

Response: Lord, hear our prayer.

That the church be a shining light, constantly in service to God and people . . .

That leaders of the world see themselves as servants of their people . . .

That those who are nearing death be consoled and supported in their transition from earthly life . . .

That those gathered here might joyfully prepare our hearts and minds for the day we meet the Son of Man face to face . . .

Presider: God of salvation, we joyfully await the fulfilment of your kingdom. Hear our prayers that we might never tire of the work you have given us to do. We ask this through Christ, our Lord. Amen.

COLLECT

Let us pray.

Pause for silent prayer

Almighty ever-living God,
whom, taught by the Holy Spirit,
we dare to call our Father,
bring, we pray, to perfection in our hearts
the spirit of adoption as your sons and
daughters,
that we may merit to enter into the
inheritance
which you have promised.
Through our Lord Jesus Christ, your Son,
who lives and reigns with you in the unity
of the Holy Spirit,
one God, for ever and ever. **Amen.**

FIRST READING

Wis 18:6-9

That night had been foretold to our
ancestors, so that,
once they saw what kind of oaths they had
put their trust in
they would joyfully take courage.
This was the expectation of your people,
the saving of the virtuous and the ruin of
their enemies;
for by the same act with which you took
vengeance on our foes
you made us glorious by calling us to you.
The devout children of worthy men
offered sacrifice in secret
and this divine pact they struck with
one accord:
that the saints would share the same
blessings and dangers alike;
and forthwith they had begun to chant the
hymns of the fathers.

RESPONSORIAL PSALM

Ps 32:1, 12, 18-22 (12)

R̰. Happy the people the Lord has chosen
as his own.

Ring out your joy to the Lord, O you just;
for praise is fitting for loyal hearts.
They are happy, whose God is the Lord,
the people he has chosen as his own.

R̰. Happy the people the Lord has chosen
as his own.

The Lord looks on those who revere him,
on those who hope in his love,
to rescue their souls from death,
to keep them alive in famine.

R̰. Happy the people the Lord has chosen
as his own.

Our soul is waiting for the Lord.
The Lord is our help and our shield.
May your love be upon us, O Lord,
as we place all our hope in you.

℟. Happy the people the Lord has chosen
as his own.

SECOND READING
Heb 11:1-2, 8-19

Only faith can guarantee the blessings
that we hope for, or prove the existence of
the realities that at present remain unseen.
It was for faith that our ancestors were
commended.

It was by faith that Abraham obeyed
the call to set out for a country that was
the inheritance given to him and his
descendants, and that he set out without
knowing where he was going. By faith he
arrived, as a foreigner, in the Promised
Land, and lived there as if in a strange
country, with Isaac and Jacob, who were
heirs with him of the same promise.
They lived there in tents while he looked
forward to a city founded, designed and
built by God.

It was equally by faith that Sarah, in
spite of being past the age, was made
able to conceive, because she believed
that he who had made the promise would
be faithful to it. Because of this, there
came from one man, and one who was
already as good as dead himself, more
descendants than could be counted, as
many as the stars of heaven or the grains
of sand on the seashore.

All these died in faith, before receiving
any of the things that had been promised,
but they saw them in the far distance and
welcomed them, recognising that they
were only strangers and nomads on earth.
People who use such terms about themselves make it quite plain that they are in
search of their real homeland. They can
hardly have meant the country they came
from, since they had the opportunity to go
back to it; but in fact they were longing for
a better homeland, their heavenly homeland. That is why God is not ashamed to
be called their God, since he has founded
the city for them.

Continued in Appendix A, p. 301,

or Heb 11:1-2, 8-12.

CATECHESIS

About Liturgy
Children's Liturgy of the Word: This is a good time to read or reread the
Directory for Masses with Children, issued by the then-called Congregation for Divine
Worship in 1973. The document explores principles for children who have not yet
reached preadolescence, generally considered the pre-teen years. Chapter 2 looks
specifically at Masses for adults at which children are present. A parish's Sunday
Masses will typically fall under the norms listed in that chapter.

In chapter 2, the document emphasises the importance of the witness of adult
believers upon the faith life of children. The presence of children in the assembly,
in turn, also benefits the faith life of adults. This is why the directory foresees that,
within such Masses where most are adults, the norm is for children to remain within
the assembly to participate in the Mass alongside adults. Paragraph 17 states that we
should take great care to ensure that children can participate fully even with adults.
Thus, the presider can speak to the children directly during the introduction to the
Mass or at the end and within the homily itself. The children may also participate in
some of the ministries and tasks of the Mass.

It might be surprising to learn that paragraph 17 envisions that the dismissal
of children to celebrate a separate Liturgy of the Word just for them should be an
occasional occurrence and not one celebrated every Sunday at the parish Masses.

Children learn how to pray and participate in the Mass by imitating what they see and
hear adults do. It would actually be detrimental to children if most of their experience of
the Sunday Mass is only with other children. If you are currently celebrating a separate
Liturgy of the Word for children every Sunday at the parish Mass, you might review
your reasons for doing so and consider if there are more benefits to the children and the
adults if all celebrated the Liturgy of the Word together on a regular basis.

About Initiation
Everyone has a year-round RCIA: If you have Sunday Mass at your parish
every week, you have a year-round RCIA. The process for preparing adults for
initiation is not a programme for a small group of people with a start and end date. It
is initiation into Christ by incorporation into the Christian community. Therefore, if
your community gathers on a regular basis to do what Christians do, such as Sunday
Mass, you have something right now that will help form a seeker to live the Christian
way of life. So stop telling inquirers to 'come back in September when RCIA classes
begin'. Just invite them to your next Sunday Mass.

About Liturgical Music
Being ritual ready: Music ministers have a huge influence on the ritual flow of a
liturgy. That is, they contribute to the pace of the liturgical action and can drag it, rush
it, or make it just right at each moment of the liturgy.

A primary place where this happens is in acclamations and responses preceded by
an invitation, for example, the Eucharistic Prayer acclamations. The presider's words
lead directly into the people's sung response. Any kind of delay in beginning the music
at these moments clouds the dialogic nature of this prayer. Consider shortening, or
even omitting altogether, lengthy musical introductions for these acclamations.

Another place is when an acclamation accompanies a ritual action, such as the
Lamb of God or the Communion of the priest. In all these cases, music ministers need
to be aware and ready so that the assembly is singing at just the right time.

R̟. Alleluia, alleluia!
Mary has been taken up into heaven;
all the choirs of angels are rejoicing.
R̟. Alleluia!

Gospel (Mass during the Day)

Luke 1:39-56

Mary set out and went as quickly as she could to a town in the hill country of Judah. She went into Zechariah's house and greeted Elizabeth. Now as soon as Elizabeth heard Mary's greeting, the child leapt in her womb and Elizabeth was filled with the Holy Spirit. She gave a loud cry and said, 'Of all women you are the most blessed, and blessed is the fruit of your womb. Why should I be honoured with a visit from the mother of my Lord? For the moment your greeting reached my ears, the child in my womb leapt for joy. Yes, blessed is she who believed that the promise made her by the Lord would be fulfilled.'

And Mary said:

'My soul proclaims the greatness of
    the Lord
and my spirit exults in God
    my saviour;
because he has looked upon his lowly
    handmaid.
Yes, from this day forward all
    generations will call me blessed,
for the Almighty has done great things
    for me.
Holy is his name,
and his mercy reaches from age to age
    for those who fear him.
He has shown the power of his arm,
he has routed the proud of heart.
He has pulled down princes from their
    thrones and exalted the lowly.
The hungry he has filled with good
    things, the rich sent empty away.
He has come to the help of Israel his
    servant, mindful of his mercy
– according to the promise he made to
    our ancestors –
of his mercy to Abraham and to his
    descendants for ever.'

Mary stayed with Elizabeth about three months and then went back home.

See Appendix, p. 302, for the other readings.

Reflecting on the Gospel

The feast of the Assumption, like all Marian feasts, says more about Jesus than it does about Mary. Marian feasts are fundamentally christological, expressing something foundational about Christ and the power of the incarnation and resurrection. With respect to the assumption, the church has long maintained, at least since the fourth century, a belief that Mary was taken up to heaven after her earthly life. The Eastern Church typically refers to this as the *dormition* (or sleeping) of Mary, expressing the belief that she did not die but slept, and then was taken up to heaven. The Roman Catholic Church refers to this as the *assumption*. Whether or not Mary actually died has never been dogmatically defined. However, in an act of papal infallibility, Pope Pius XII dogmatically proclaimed the assumption as a matter of faith in 1950.

It might seem odd that nineteen hundred years after the assumption it was proclaimed dogmatically, but again, it says more about Christ than about Mary. Ultimately, it is the power of Christ and his resurrection that prevented Mary's body from seeing decay.

Some believe that this dogma was proclaimed in 1950, shortly after World War II as so many millions had been killed in that war and in World War I that had shortly preceded it. With the value of human life apparently so cheapened, this dogma would underscore its sanctity, especially that of the body.

The reading that the church uses to celebrate this feast is Mary's *Magnificat*. She proclaims this upon meeting her relative Elizabeth. The *Magnificat* is a canticle that sets the stage for the gospel's themes. It sounds notes that will be reverberating throughout the gospel and in Acts. God lifts up the lowly and throws down the mighty. He fills the hungry with good things and turns the rich away empty. A great reversal is underway and the social order will be overturned. If this was Mary's theological outlook before Jesus was born, imagine the lessons he learned from her as a mother. Mary is no shrinking violet. She has been called the first disciple for good reason. The power of Christ's resurrection extended to her in life and death.

Living the Paschal Mystery

As we consider the life and death (or dormition) of Mary we recall that she witnessed the paschal mystery and lived it in her own way. She who said yes at the annunciation, who proclaimed her canticle to Elizabeth, and who gave birth to Jesus also witnessed his passion, death, resurrection, and the handing on of the Spirit at Pentecost according to Luke. We are reminded that as her life was full of grace, so are our lives. The power of the resurrection is celebrated in Mary's life but it is also present in our own. The pain, loss, grief, and even death that we experience will be brought to new life by Christ. As Mary listened to the word of God and gave birth to it, may we too listen attentively and bring to bear the word of God in our own world. When we raise up the lowly, fill the hungry with good things, we are bringing about the kingdom of God imagined by Mary, the first disciple. Her destiny is our own, which is a cause of celebration.

Focusing the Gospel
Key words and phrases: he has looked upon his lowly handmaid

To the point: Mary begins her hymn to God by identifying herself with the lowly. She knows the God of Israel and how he has a habit of choosing the small and unassuming to do his greatest work. So it is no surprise that he chose a young woman from Nazareth to be to the Mother of God. On this feast of the Assumption we celebrate Mary's entrance into heaven following her death. God honours Mary in death as he did in life by preserving her body, the first tabernacle of the Lord.

Model Penitential Act
Presider: On this feast of the Assumption we celebrate the life and death of Mary, the Mother of God, and her assumption, body and soul, into heaven. Let us pause to ask that we might also completely give our lives to God . . . [*pause*]

Lord Jesus, you are Son of God and son of Mary: Lord, have mercy.
Christ Jesus, you are the Messiah, the anointed one: Christ, have mercy.
Lord Jesus, you are the resurrection and the life: Lord, have mercy.

Model Universal Prayer (Prayer of the Faithful)
Presider: We offer our prayers to God through the intercession of the Blessed Virgin Mary who identified herself with the lowly.

Response: Lord, hear our prayer.

That the leaders of the church follow the example of Mary and be a prophetic voice for the poor . . .

That people all over the world know the compassionate love of the Mother of God . . .

That those who hunger might be filled . . .

That all gathered here might lead lives that proclaim the greatness of God . . .

Presider: God of justice, you chose Mary to be the mother of your Son. Hear our prayers that we might meditate on the precious words of her *Magnificat* and bring them to fruition in our own lives. We ask this through Christ, our Lord. Amen.

About Liturgy
The **Magnificat**: Preparing the liturgy for Marian feasts can always be a bit challenging. How do you appropriately give honour to the Blessed Virgin Mary while rightfully keeping the focus on Christ? Today's gospel text gives us a good model to follow.

In Luke's account of the visitation between Elizabeth and Mary, we hear two familiar canticles: Elizabeth's blessing from which developed the Hail Mary; and Mary's *Magnificat*. Mary's own focus in her song is on God's faithfulness and on what God has done.

The *Magnificat* holds a special place in the liturgical life of the church. It is the gospel canticle that is typically sung at Evening Prayer for the Liturgy of the Hours every day. It is also the prayer that we, too, hope to embody in our life of praise and trust in God's will for us.

Use a familiar setting of the *Magnificat* today. It would be very appropriate as a song of praise after Communion or as an entrance song. Also reflect on the canticle's text as part of the homily for this day.

COLLECT
Let us pray.

Pause for silent prayer

Almighty ever-living God,
who assumed the Immaculate Virgin Mary,
 the Mother of your Son,
body and soul into heavenly glory,
grant, we pray,
that, always attentive to the things that are above,
we may merit to be sharers of her glory.
Through our Lord Jesus Christ, your Son,
who lives and reigns with you in the unity of
 the Holy Spirit,
one God, for ever and ever. **Amen.**

FOR REFLECTION

• In St. Paul's first letter to the Corinthians we are told that Jesus will destroy all enemies, even death. How does it change your life, knowing death is not the end?

• When Mary and Elizabeth meet, Elizabeth recognises Jesus present within Mary. What relationships in your life foster your understanding of Jesus present within you?

• Mary's canticle of praise to God reads as a manifesto on justice. How are you called to serve the God of Mary who fills the hungry and lifts up the lowly?

Homily Points
• In our gospel today, Elizabeth proclaims who Mary is: Mother of the Lord, and blessed among all people. Mary's words to the angel, '[L]et what you have said be done to me'. at the annunciation changed her entire life. Elizabeth's greeting confirms what has occurred. She recognises the mystery of the incarnation in their midst.

• Mary's words, her canticle of praise, proclaim who God is: the merciful One who disperses the arrogant and lifts up the lowly. Mary doesn't know the end of the story when she meets with Elizabeth. But she trusts the God she loves. This is a God who keeps his promises. This is a God worthy of all honour and praise.

SPIRITUALITY

GOSPEL ACCLAMATION
John 10:27

℟. Alleluia, alleluia.
The sheep that belong to me listen to my voice,
says the Lord,
I know them and they follow me.
℟. Alleluia, alleluia.

Gospel

Luke 12:49-53

Jesus said to his disciples: 'I have come to bring fire to the earth, and how I wish it were blazing already! There is a baptism I must still receive, and how great is my distress till it is over!

'Do you suppose that I am here to bring peace on earth? No, I tell you, but rather division. For from now on a household of five will be divided: three against two and two against three; the father divided against the son, son against father, mother against daughter, daughter against mother, mother-in-law against daughter-in-law, daughter-in-law against mother-in-law.'

Reflecting on the Gospel

Christians are so familiar with 'peace on earth' as a tagline of Christianity that today's gospel can be something of a shock to the system. The angels sang, '[P]eace to those on whom his favour rests' (Luke 2:14; NABRE), and the cry of the crowds upon Jesus's entry into Jerusalem will be 'Blessed is the king who comes in the name of the Lord. / Peace in heaven and glory in the highest' (Luke 19:38; NABRE). So it sounds strange today to hear Jesus saying that he is *not* bringing peace but division.

But then, upon a closer reading of the Gospel of Luke we do hear inklings of this theme. As an infant, Jesus is said by Simeon to be 'destined for the fall and rise of many in Israel' (Luke 2:34; NABRE). Simeon continues by saying that Mary will be pierced with a sword (Luke 2:35). Moreover, early Christianity was perceived by the Romans and others as we would consider a cult today. No self-respecting Roman wanted their children to be caught up in this Judaean 'superstition' as they called it. And those who became Christian often pulled away from their families, forming new bonds with other Christians, whom they considered a new family. So given that background, the idea that Jesus brought division might be seen in a different light. The peace that the Christians experienced was with one another, not the peace the world gives. And that peace might have come at the price of family divisions who did not understand this new way of life.

Of course, Christianity has been so domesticated today, with the culture empowering it and supporting it, that we have little experiential sense of what the early Christians encountered simply to be Christian. Any perceived impingement of religious freedom in the Western world today can scarcely be compared to what the first generations of Christians experienced, or Christians in the Middle East or Africa today, when some were and are being executed for their faith.

Though we share many common elements of our faith with those who have gone before us, the divisions they experienced in the early years seem distant. Still, when we take seriously the gospel message and live it boldly, we may be shunned or avoided by those we considered friends or family.

Living the Paschal Mystery

Paradoxically, the peace that Jesus brings comes served with division. It's as though the poison is within the antidote. Living as a disciple of Jesus means that we will lose company with some, perhaps even family and friends. Disciples are no mere 'go along to get along' kind of people. Faith in Christ, service of the poor, and working for justice are essential elements of discipleship. Others may have a vested interest in the status quo, and do not want things overturned or upended. But for a serious follower of Christ, for a disciple who follows in the footsteps of Jesus, opposition can be expected. Jesus himself lost his life in a confrontation with evil. Many of his followers down to the present day have lost their lives as well, or faced imprisonment, persecution, and hostility. 'Good news' preached to the poor, the outcast, and the downtrodden, can sound eerily like sedition or revolution. When we stand on the side of the persecuted and marginalised we should not be surprised to face persecution and marginalization ourselves.

Focusing the Gospel

Key words and phrases: Do you suppose that I am here to bring peace on earth? No, I tell you, but rather division.

To the point: How do we reconcile today's gospel with Jesus, the Prince of Peace? Human beings, with our God-given free will, are able to accept or reject peace in whatever form it comes to us. We see this in the time of Jesus and throughout the past two thousand years. Jesus's proclamation of the kingdom of God where the poor and the humble are blessed and the rich and powerful are turned away has often been rejected and met with resistance. Jesus proclaimed the reign of God and this reign challenged people, especially those in power. However, when Jesus himself met with resistance, even resistance up to death on a cross, he responded with nonviolence, forgiveness, and love. On our journey of faith we will meet resistance too when we challenge the status quo. May our response be that of Jesus, the Prince of Peace.

Connecting the Gospel

to the first and second readings: The prophet Jeremiah also caused division in his own day. Speaking to the king and the temple elite in Jerusalem, Jeremiah urged the people to surrender to the Babylonian army attacking Judea. This was not a popular message. Jeremiah's fidelity to God's message landed him in prison and then in the pit of mud we hear of today. What gave Jeremiah and Jesus the strength to continue on in the face of imprisonment, torture, and even death? In the Letter to the Hebrews we hear, '[F]or the sake of the joy which was still in the future, he endured the cross, disregarding the shamefulness of it'.

to experience: What gives us the strength to carry on in times of struggle? It is the belief that life is stronger than death, light is stronger than darkness, and love is stronger than hatred.

Connecting the Responsorial Psalm

to the readings: The psalmist appears to have physically or metaphorically shared the experience of Jeremiah, sinking into the mud at the bottom of a cistern. And just as Jeremiah is drawn out of the cistern before perishing, the psalmist has also experienced God's saving action, for this is the Lord who 'drew me from the deadly pit, / from the miry clay'. In all three of today's readings and within the psalm we see that the spiritual life is not easy. One must undergo the cross in order to arrive at the resurrection.

to psalmist preparation: In the psalms we see extremes of emotion, from despair to joy and everything in between. And in the midst of our human volatility, we can say that our God is the rock that 'made my footsteps firm. / He put a new song into my mouth'. Where, in your life, are you in need of the steady foundation of God? When you look with the eyes of faith, can you see God, the bedrock of life, supporting you?

PROMPTS FOR FAITH-SHARING

Like Jeremiah, when in life have you taken an unpopular position because you felt it was the right thing to do? Where did you find the fortitude and perseverance to remain firm in your conviction?

The Letter to the Hebrews speaks of the 'witnesses in a great cloud' that surrounds us. How do you experience this cloud of witnesses in the life of faith?

Similar to the words of Jesus in the gospel, St. Catherine of Siena is quoted as saying, 'Be who God meant you to be and you will set the world on fire.' How is God calling you right now to be more faithful to who you are truly meant to be?

Where do you see division within your family, parish, or community? Where is Jesus within this division?

CELEBRATION

Model Penitential Act

Presider: Today Jesus proclaims, 'I have come to bring fire to the earth, and how I wish it were blazing already!' For the times we have failed to burn with the brilliance of God's love, let us ask for pardon and mercy . . . [*pause*]

Lord Jesus, you stand with the persecuted and outcast: Lord, have mercy.

Christ Jesus, you baptise with fire and the Holy Spirit: Christ, have mercy.

Lord Jesus, you are the Prince of Peace: Lord, have mercy.

Homily Points

• In today's gospel Jesus exclaims, 'I have come to bring fire to the earth, and how I wish it were blazing already!' We see fire in so many of the signs and symbols of our church: the candles that we light at the altar and ambo, the sanctuary lamp lit whenever Jesus is present in the tabernacle, the Easter fire that lights the paschal candle, which in turn lights our own individual candles and the candle of each newly baptised member of our church. Flame marks all of the significant moments in our life of faith, and often the everyday moments too, as we light a candle to pray at home, to enjoy a family meal, or to blow out on a birthday cake.

• And this makes sense. Jesus tells us in John's gospel, 'I am the light of the world' (8:12; NABRE), and in Matthew's gospel he commissions us to act as people of flame, saying: 'You are the light of the world' (5:14; NABRE). Why does Jesus use fire imagery so much? What does fire do? Fire transforms: what is cold becomes hot, what is hard becomes soft, what is dirty is purified, what is hidden in darkness becomes illuminated for all to see.

• In Jesus's life we see these moments of transformation taking place as he ministers to the people he meets on the dusty roads of ancient Israel. And now it is our turn. We are called into this mission of Jesus to set the world on fire. But how? At World Youth Day 2000, Pope John Paul II paraphrased a famous quote of St. Catherine of Siena, 'If you are what you should be, you will set the whole world ablaze'! Nothing more, nothing less: Be who God dreams you to be.

Model Universal Prayer (Prayer of the Faithful)

Presider: With trust in God's mercy and belief in his faithfulness, we bring our prayers before the Lord.

Response: Lord, hear our prayer.

That Christians throughout the world come together in unity to serve the Lord of life and to care for the human family . . .

That leaders of nations be endowed with skills to peacefully resolve conflicts within their societies . . .

That those who experience persecution due to religious belief might dwell in safety and in freedom to practise their faith . . .

That all gathered here be strengthened to stand firmly in faith in the face of division . . .

Presider: God of creation, you call us to yourself and invite us to be prophets of peace and justice. Hear our prayers that we might serve you in righteousness and truth. We ask this through Jesus Christ, our Lord. Amen.

COLLECT

Let us pray.

Pause for silent prayer

O God, who have prepared for those who love you
good things which no eye can see,
fill our hearts, we pray, with the warmth of your love,
so that, loving you in all things and above all things,
we may attain your promises,
which surpass every human desire.
Through our Lord Jesus Christ, your Son,
who lives and reigns with you in the unity of the Holy Spirit,
one God, for ever and ever. **Amen.**

FIRST READING
Jer 38:4-6, 8-10

The king's leading men spoke to the king. 'Let Jeremiah be put to death: he is unquestionably disheartening the remaining soldiers in the city, and all the people too, by talking like this. The fellow does not have the welfare of this people at heart so much as its ruin.' 'He is in your hands, as you know,' King Zedekiah answered 'for the king is powerless against you.' So they took Jeremiah and threw him into the well of Prince Malchiah in the Court of the Guard, letting him down with ropes. There was no water in the well, only mud, and into the mud Jeremiah sank.

Ebed-melech came out from the palace and spoke to the king. 'My lord king,' he said 'these men have done a wicked thing by treating the prophet Jeremiah like this: they have thrown him into the well where he will die.' At this the king gave Ebed-melech the Cushite the following order: 'Take three men with you from here and pull the prophet Jeremiah out of the well before he dies.'

CATECHESIS

RESPONSORIAL PSALM
Ps 39:2-4, 18 (14)

R̸. Lord, come to my aid!

I waited, I waited for the Lord
and he stooped down to me;
he heard my cry.

R̸. Lord, come to my aid!

He drew me from the deadly pit,
from the miry clay.
He set my feet upon a rock
and made my footsteps firm.

R̸. Lord, come to my aid!

He put a new song into my mouth,
praise of our God.
Many shall see and fear
and shall trust in the Lord.

R̸. Lord, come to my aid!

As for me, wretched and poor,
the Lord thinks of me.
You are my rescuer, my help,
O God, do not delay.

R̸. Lord, come to my aid!

SECOND READING
Heb 12:1-4

With so many witnesses in a great cloud on every side of us, we too, then, should throw off everything that hinders us, especially the sin that clings so easily, and keep running steadily in the race we have started. Let us not lose sight of Jesus, who leads us in our faith and brings it to perfection: for the sake of the joy which was still in the future, he endured the cross, disregarding the shamefulness of it, and from now on has taken his place at the right of God's throne. Think of the way he stood such opposition from sinners and then you will not give up for want of courage. In the fight against sin, you have not yet had to keep fighting to the point of death.

About Liturgy

The Sign of Peace: Who doesn't like the good feeling that comes with being part of a community? However, Christian community must go deeper than good feelings. The heart of our faith, Jesus, requires that we lay down our lives even for those who would hate us – even for those whom we do not love or like. For God does not save individuals one by one: God saves a people. What we express in the sharing of the Body and Blood of Christ is not a 'me-and-Jesus's relationship, for we cannot be a eucharistic people without dying to our own needs, preferences, likes, and dislikes. And our faith cannot be swayed by our ever-changing feelings towards others. Only a faith that is grounded in the faith of Christ will be able to transcend our selfish need for what feels good in order to seek the good of others, even if it means our own suffering.

In the sign of peace, we rehearse having this mind of Christ and showing that sacrificial kind of love. The rubrics of the Roman Missal say that this sign 'expresses peace, communion, and charity' (128). For it to be an authentic sign, we must seek daily to share peace with those with whom we have not been peaceful. If we are to show that our sharing in Communion is credible, then we must seek the ones we have harmed, the ones we have judged, and the ones whom we think are unworthy of God's love, and offer a sign of reconciliation with them. If we cannot see the stranger, the foreigner, the outcast, and sinner as one with us and in need of God's mercy just as we are, then our sign of peace is not a sign of charity but an empty sign.

On this day when the gospel discomforts the comfortable, help the assembly remember the meaning of the sign of peace and how it prepares our hearts to authentically share in the Eucharist.

About Initiation

RCIA is not a small faith community: RCIA teams often note how close-knit the RCIA community becomes. As the catechumens and candidates with their sponsors gather each week with the RCIA team to break open the word and deepen their faith, there truly is a sense of community that is rarely found in other parish groups. This is both a blessing and a curse, for the purpose of RCIA is not to create community but to initiate people into Christ. The people Christ gathers often will not be people we get along with. Yet to be Christian means to see them as our sister and brother anyway and to love them as Christ loves them. How will your RCIA process form seekers into this kind of community?

About Liturgical Music

Mass by musical style: What does it say about the unity of the church if we separate and promote each Mass by its unique musical and liturgical style? Saturday night is cantor-only; mid-morning Sunday is the family Mass; late-morning is the traditional organ Mass; Sunday night is the youth praise Mass; and early Sunday morning is the quiet Mass. Here we have commodified Sunday Mass and encouraged parishioners to find the style that fits their comfort level.

Sunday must train us to be the household of God in which we gather with a wide variety of people with their own preferences. Let us 'keep in mind that to live and worship in community often demands a personal sacrifice. All must be willing to share likes and dislikes with others whose ideas and experiences may be quite unlike [our] own' (*Music in Catholic Worship* 17).

SPIRITUALITY

℟. Alleluia, alleluia.
I am the Way, the Truth and the Life, says
the Lord;
no one can come to the Father except through me.
no one comes to the Father, except through me.
℟. Alleluia, alleluia.

Gospel

Luke 13:22-30

Through towns and villages Jesus went teaching, making his way to Jerusalem. Someone said to him, 'Sir, will there be only a few saved?' He said to them, 'Try your best to enter by the narrow door, because, I tell you, many will try to enter and will not succeed.

'Once the master of the house has got up and locked the door, you may find yourself knocking on the door, saying, "Lord, open to us" but he will answer, "I do not know where you come from." Then you will find yourself saying, "We once ate and drank in your company; you taught in our streets" but he will reply, "I do not know where you come from. Away from me, all you wicked men!"

'Then there will be weeping and grinding of teeth, when you see Abraham and Isaac and Jacob and all the prophets in the kingdom of God, and yourselves turned outside. And men from east and west, from north and south, will come to take their places at the feast in the kingdom of God.

'Yes, there are those now last who will be first, and those now first who will be last.'

Reflecting on the Gospel

Nobody likes disappointment. Dealing with it can be a difficult lesson that many of us learn in childhood, and some still struggle to learn as adults! We can avoid disappointment in a number of ways including being prepared, having proper expectations, and knowing a given situation. When we employ these strategies our chances for disappointment diminish. For example, we don't expect a friend who is chronically late to be punctual. It's a matter of managing expectations.

Today's gospel gives us a somewhat troubling story of those who were undoubtedly disappointed. Can we imagine standing, knocking on the door to the house only to be told by the master, 'I do not know where you come from'? or even more, 'Away from me, all you wicked men!' Yet this is precisely the story Jesus tells someone who asks whether only a few will be saved. Matthew (7:21-23; 25:31-46) tells a similar story and we are thereby reminded that simply knowing the Lord is not enough to be saved. Jesus exhorts the man to enter through the narrow door. And what is more, he is advised not to wait too late, for there will come a time when the master will lock the door.

This passage and others in the gospels like it remind us of an uncomfortable, and perhaps even disappointing, truth. The effective answer to the man's question about salvation is that many will attempt it but not be able. And some of those who know the Lord, who ate and drank in his company, are those who will be shut out. Such a message is far from the feel good, open wide, broad path to salvation that we might imagine. And the warning to those who know the Lord should fall squarely on us.

Still, those who will be saved may not be those who expect it, for in an echo of Mary's canticle and earlier Lucan themes, there will be a reversal of fortune. '[T]here are those now last who will be first, and those now first who will be last'. Moreover, salvation is not limited to a particular group of people as they will come from all directions to recline at table in the kingdom of God.

Are we open to disappointment? Or do we need to be prepared, manage our expectations, and know the given situation? Salvation is for all; many attempt to enter but are not strong enough. Even those who know the Lord are not guaranteed salvation.

Living the Paschal Mystery

A relationship with Christ is not an insurance policy whereby we pay our premiums and expect to receive a settlement when needed. This relationship with the Son of God is not so transactional that we do x, y, and z and Jesus in return grants salvation. If such were the case we would be effectively earning our own salvation by our works. But salvation is a free gift, undeserved, no matter how much we might feel we deserve it.

The master locks the door on the evildoers, barring entry to them. The frightening thing is that some of those locked out know the Lord. Would they consider themselves evildoers? Not likely.

Where are we in this story? Are we striving to enter through the narrow door? Are we waiting until later before we make up our minds? When will the door be shut, not in some apocalyptic sense, but when we come to the end of our own personal life? There will be a reversal of fortune. Let us be prepared and manage our expectations lest we be disappointed.

Focusing the Gospel

Key words and phrases: And men from east and west, from north and south, will come to take their places at the feast in the kingdom of God.

To the point: In today's gospel we hear a paradox. Jesus urges his followers to 'enter by the narrow door', but this constricted entrance leads to an abundant gathering that includes people from the four corners of the world. All people are welcome in the kingdom of God. Not because of their lineage, race, gender, or ancestors, but because they have followed the narrow way of peace and love: the way of Christ.

Connecting the Gospel

to the first reading: The first reading comes from the end of the book of the prophet Isaiah. In the gospel Jesus is travelling to Jerusalem to offer himself on the cross as a complete self-gift to humanity and to God. Isaiah shares a vision of others coming to Jerusalem as well. God is gathering 'nations of every language' to see God's glory. In Jerusalem, at the house of the Lord they will present their grain, and also themselves as 'an offering to the Lord'.

to experience: Jesus and Isaiah paint a picture of God's kingdom where all of creation is at home. These words would have challenged the people who originally heard them, and should challenge us today. We are not necessarily members of this kingdom because of the religion we identify with or our observance of the sacraments. Jesus points to the 'narrow door' that leads to this kingdom. Perhaps it is narrow because of all of the things that can bar our entry like fear, hatred, and pride. To enter into this kingdom that welcomes all people, we must also know radical hospitality. We can enter into the kingdom of God only if we can delight in the others who are also welcome there.

Connecting the Responsorial Psalm

to the readings: The paradox we saw in the gospel reading is also present in the psalm. This shortest of all psalms calls for nothing less than every nation and person to extol and praise the Lord. Even as a young nation, Israel knew their God was not only theirs alone, but also desired to gather all nations, all people together in unity. Jesus shares this vision, reminding the people of his own ancestry, and reminding us today that the kingdom is not ours alone. It does not belong to just one nation, one religion, or one race. The kingdom of God is as expansive as God's mercy and faithfulness.

to psalmist preparation: As you prepare to sing this Sunday's psalm, pause to consider how your community welcomes in those who are outside of its familiar borders. How do you show hospitality in your ministry and in your life as a Christian?

PROMPTS FOR FAITH-SHARING

The prophet Isaiah shares a vision of peoples of all nations and tongues converging on Jerusalem as an offering to the Lord. What place does Jerusalem hold in your journey of faith?

The Letter to the Hebrews says, '[W]hen the Lord corrects you, do not treat it lightly'. How have you experienced the Lord's correction or discipline? What place does discipline have in your spiritual life?

Jesus tells the people, 'Try your best to enter by the narrow door'. What do you think he is referring to? Where in your life do you find the 'narrow door?'

How does your family or parish welcome the stranger in your midst? How do you make room in your life for those that are different from you?

CELEBRATION

Model Penitential Act

Presider: In today's gospel, Jesus urges us to '[t]ry your best to enter by the narrow door'. For the times we have chosen what is easy instead of what is right let us pause to ask for pardon and mercy . . . [*pause*]

Lord Jesus, you show us the narrow way of righteousness: Lord, have mercy.

Christ Jesus, you gather all nations and all peoples to yourself: Christ, have mercy.

Lord Jesus, you lead the humble to the kingdom of God: Lord, have mercy.

Homily Points

• In the gospel Jesus continues on the road to Jerusalem. He is now about halfway through the journey that he began in chapter 9 of Luke's gospel. Along the way Jesus meets Samaritans, women, men, children, Pharisees, scholars, people who are lame, people who suffer from leprosy, people who are blind, a rich official, and tax collectors. To each of these diverse groups, Jesus proclaims the same message: the kingdom of God is at hand. In all that he does Jesus speaks the kingdom and lives the kingdom.

• Today's gospel gives us another vision of what this kingdom is about. The way to enter is 'narrow', but inside the kingdom we will find people from every race, nation, and tongue. We might be surprised about who we don't find, however. Jesus issues the warning that some of those who knock on the door and tell the Lord, 'We once ate and drank in your company; you taught in our streets', will not find welcome inside the kingdom of God. Instead the master of the kingdom will say, 'I do not know where you come from'.

• Entry to the kingdom does not depend on physical proximity to Jesus. Even those who spend their lives in the church, eating and drinking at the table of the Lord, cannot stop there, passively living a faith that demands much more from us, our very selves. In order to enter the kingdom we must be *from* the kingdom. Our words and actions must proclaim this kingdom as Jesus's did. Can we be found among the poor, vulnerable, and lost? Do we offer welcome and hospitality to all that we meet? We are called to be kingdom people. Where are you from?

Model Universal Prayer (Prayer of the Faithful)

Presider: With faith in God's mercy and fidelity, we bring our prayers before the Lord.

Response: Lord, hear our prayer.

That the church be a sign and symbol of the inclusivity of the kingdom of God . . .

That nations of the world come together to provide for the needs of refugees and those who are displaced from their homes by natural disasters . . .

That those who experience racism, prejudice, and bias in daily life have their inherent dignity and worth as children of God recognised by all they encounter . . .

That all gathered here would have the strength to embrace the radical hospitality of the kingdom of God and to live as kingdom people . . .

Presider: Faithful and merciful God, you call all people to yourself. Hear our prayers that we might build communities of welcome and refuge. We ask this in the name of Jesus, our Lord. Amen.

COLLECT

Let us pray.

Pause for silent prayer

O God, who cause the minds of the faithful
to unite in a single purpose,
grant your people to love what you
    command
and to desire what you promise,
that, amid the uncertainties of this world,
our hearts may be fixed on that place
where true gladness is found.
Through our Lord Jesus Christ, your Son,
who lives and reigns with youin the unity
    of the Holy Spirit,
one God, for ever and ever. **Amen.**

FIRST READING

Isa 66:18-21

The Lord says this: I am coming to gather the nations of every language. They shall come to witness my glory. I will give them a sign and send some of their survivors to the nations: to Tarshish, Put, Lud, Moshech, Rosh, Tubal, and Javan, to the distant islands that have never heard of me or seen my glory. They will proclaim my glory to the nations. As an offering to the Lord they will bring all your brothers, in horses, in chariots, in litters, on mules, on dromedaries, from all the nations to my holy mountain in Jerusalem, says the Lord, like Israelites bringing oblations in clean vessels to the Temple of the Lord. And of some of them I will make priests and Levites, says the Lord.

CATECHESIS

RESPONSORIAL PSALM
Ps 116 (Mark 16:15)

R℣. Go out to the whole world;
proclaim the Good News.
  or
R℣. Alleluia.

O praise the Lord, all you nations,
acclaim him all you peoples!

R℣. Go out to the whole world;
proclaim the Good News.
  or
R℣. Alleluia.

Strong is his love for us;
he is faithful for ever.

R℣. Go out to the whole world;
proclaim the Good News.
  or
R℣. Alleluia.

SECOND READING
Heb 12:5-7, 11-13

Have you forgotten that encouraging text in which you are addressed as sons? My son, when the Lord corrects you, do not treat it lightly; but do not get discouraged when he reprimands you. For the Lord trains the ones that he loves and he punishes all those that he acknowledges as his sons. Suffering is part of your training; God is treating you as his sons. Has there ever been any son whose father did not train him? Of course, any punishment is most painful at the time, and far from pleasant; but later, in those on whom it has been used, it bears fruit in peace and goodness. So hold up your limp arms and steady your trembling knees and smooth out the path you tread; there the injured limb will not be wrenched, it will grow strong again.

About Liturgy

Communion procession: What would happen if, in Communion, we took literally Jesus's prophecy in today's gospel that the last will be first and the first will be last? That's just what Roger Cardinal Mahony wanted to do in his own envisioning of what Sunday Mass might be like in the Archdiocese of Los Angeles if the entirety of the assembly made the sharing of Communion more than just lining up to receive the Body and Blood of Christ.

In his pastoral letter on the liturgy, 'Gather Faithfully Together' (1997), Cardinal Mahony described a community that desired to understand and reflect better what it meant for the Body of Christ, the church, to receive the Body of Christ in the Eucharist. That need led to exploring a practice that would replace an individualistic approach to sharing Communion with one in which the communal procession helped foster unity among the people and restore a sense of wonder and thanksgiving in the Eucharist.

The cardinal described a communion procession in which the first to come forward down the aisle towards the altar were not those seated in the front pews but those in the very back of the church. Imagine everyone in the assembly surrounded by the members of the Body of Christ singing together as they come forward to share in the Body of Christ. Imagine being aware not just of the people sitting by you but those who stay in the back whom you might never see, who may feel too self-conscious or unworthy, or who, for whatever reason, had a difficult time choosing to be at Mass that day but made it nonetheless. Can we deepen our understanding of the mystery of the Eucharist even more if we make one simple change to the way we come forward to the altar at Communion?

About Initiation

Rite of Acceptance: Today would be an appropriate time to celebrate the Rite of Acceptance, especially in light of the first reading's image of the gathering of all the nations to the holy mountain of God. Even if you do not have any possible persons to celebrate this rite, mark the day in your parish's calendar and schedule a possible rite for one of the main Masses so that you and all your parish will be prepared just in case the Spirit sends you a seeker who is ready to begin learning the gospel way of life.

About Liturgical Music

Intercultural liturgy: Every parish will find within its neighbourhood a diversity of cultures. This is simply a reality, if not today, then within the next few years. In liturgical music, we can describe this as a spectrum. On one end we have what can be called a 'diversity' phase, expressed in the use of multilingual music and reflecting an understanding of community from the head, focusing solely on language. In the middle of this spectrum, we have an 'inclusion' phase expressed by multicultural music reflecting a desire to understand with the heart. In addition to language, here we begin to incorporate the cultural rhythms, instruments, and musical styles of different cultures within our common repertoire. The other end of the spectrum is a 'communion' phase expressed by intercultural liturgy reflecting a desire for unity through our shared culture. Here we long for a spiritual communion that recognises one another as family members, equal in leadership and say in the good of the community and how it prays together.

Wherever your parish is on this spectrum, you will be heeding the psalm's message of going out to the world to tell the Good News if you continue to attend to the needs of those who are different from you.

SPIRITUALITY

GOSPEL ACCLAMATION
Matt 11:29

R̸. Alleluia, alleluia.
Shoulder my yoke and learn from me,
for I am gentle and humble in heart.
R̸. Alleluia, alleluia.

Gospel   Luke 14:1, 7-14

On a sabbath day Jesus had gone for a meal to the house of one of the leading Pharisees; and they watched him closely. He then told the guests a parable, because he had noticed how they picked the places of honour. He said this, 'When someone invites you to a wedding feast, do not take your seat in the place of honour. A more distinguished person than you may have been invited, and the person who invited you both may come and say, "Give up your place to this man." And then, to your embarrassment, you would have to go and take the lowest place. No; when you are a guest, make your way to the lowest place and sit there, so that, when your host comes, he may say, "My friend, move up higher." In that way, everyone with you at the table will see you honoured. For everyone who exalts himself will be humbled, and the man who humbles himself will be exalted.'

Then he said to his host, 'When you give a lunch or a dinner, do not ask your friends, brothers, relations or rich neighbours, for fear they repay your courtesy by inviting you in return. No; when you have a party, invite the poor, the crippled, the lame, the blind; that they cannot pay you back means that you are fortunate, because repayment will be made to you when the virtuous rise again.'

Reflecting on the Gospel

Who doesn't love a good dinner party?! Great food, excellent company, good wine, and lively conversation. Jesus certainly enjoyed himself at such events and was considered by some to be a glutton and a drunkard (Matt 11:19)!

In today's gospel Jesus is being hosted by a leading Pharisee. This was likely an extravagant event and certainly wasn't Jesus's first or last such dinner.

The first piece of advice Jesus gives is hardly unique to Christianity or even rooted in his identity as Son of God. Instead, it's practical advice reminiscent of Greek philosophers and good Jewish etiquette. In fact, it sounds much like modern-day Miss Manners! The aphorism, '[E]veryone who exalts himself will be humbled, and the man who humbles himself will be exalted', will be repeated later in the gospel (Luke 18:14).

The second piece of advice culminating in a promise to be repaid 'when the virtuous rise again' is rooted more in religious identity and a belief that there would even be a resurrection of the righteous. To receive such an invitation, Jesus implores his host to invite 'the poor, the crippled, the lame, the blind'. In other words, invite those people who cannot reciprocate. By so doing, God himself will reciprocate on their behalf!

So we have two lessons from today's reading: humble oneself and serve those who cannot reciprocate. There is certainly more to the entire gospel message than that, but it is an excellent place to start. Moreover, both can be done in imitation of Jesus himself, who truly humbled himself and served us, we who cannot truly reciprocate.

Living the Paschal Mystery

Our liturgies, prayers, Catholic culture, and more do much to promote a high Christology and rightly so. But a gospel reading like the one we have today reminds us that Jesus was a human being who attended dinner parties, told stories at such parties, and even offered sage advice. One modern teacher made the point that in the Gospel of Luke there are so many meals that Jesus attends that you can eat your way through the story! Is it no wonder then, that by the conclusion of this gospel the disciples come to know Jesus through the breaking of the bread? And this is the way the risen Christ is made known to believers ever since. Each meal, and even the liturgical Eucharist, is a foreshadowing of the heavenly banquet. Let's tap into this aspect of Christ, the one who enjoyed a good dinner party, to learn from him about the life that awaits us.

Focusing the Gospel

Key words and phrases: For everyone who exalts himself will be humbled, and the man who humbles himself will be exalted.

To the point: We are told in the gospel today that Jesus tells a parable. It's actually less of a parable and more of a saying, one that has become very famous but not necessarily very well followed: '[E]veryone who exalts himself will be humbled, and the man who humbles himself will be exalted'. The key is not what one does, but who one is. A humble person naturally chooses the lowest position, not wishing to draw attention to herself. Sometimes this leads to acclaim. Sometimes it just means that the humble are not as visible as those who would like to be exalted. Even if the world does not notice the humble, we know that God's eye is trained upon them, as ours should be.

Connecting the Gospel

to the first reading: In some ways Jesus is echoing the words of the writer of Sirach (Ben Sira) from two hundred years before Jesus's birth: 'The greater you are, the more you should behave humbly'. Both Jesus and Ben Sira seem to offer this advice in a pragmatic way. By embracing humility you will be exalted. By making yourself small you will be great. Merriam-Webster's dictionary defines humility as 'freedom from pride or arrogance'. Whereas pride and arrogance are shackles that imprison and weigh one down, humility allows a person to be filled with something other than himself, to be filled with God.

to experience: In the gospel reading Jesus speaks as a wisdom teacher, offering sage advice for living well. As Christians we take as our example Jesus, the Son of God, who humbled himself to become human and even die on a cross. Jesus shows us the way of humility. May we follow him.

Connecting the Responsorial Psalm

to the readings: In the gospel Jesus describes a banquet that might have been very different from the dinner he is attending at the house of one of the most prominent Pharisees. The banquet he envisions is populated not with the distinguished and honoured but with those who are too often invisible in society: 'the poor, the crippled, the lame, the blind'. Could this be an image of the heavenly banquet table? The psalmist sings of a God who is 'Father of the orphan, defender of the widow', who 'gives the lonely a home to live in; / he leads the prisoners forth into freedom'.

to psalmist preparation: The words of Jesus in the gospel and the psalmist are ones that challenge us to rethink our priorities and beliefs. In God's eyes, the people who are pushed to the margins of society like the homeless, those addicted to drugs and alcohol, prisoners are loved, precious, and worthy of the kingdom of God. Do we invite them to our banquet tables?

PROMPTS FOR FAITH-SHARING

The first reading comes from the Wisdom book, Sirach, whose author is intent on lifting up the Jewish wisdom tradition in a world increasingly influenced by Greek philosophy. What sources of wisdom do you turn to in your life?

Today's psalm encourages, 'The just shall rejoice at the presence of God . . . O sing to the Lord, make music to his name'. What place does joy and rejoicing hold in your spiritual life?

How have you experienced Jesus's saying, '[E]veryone who exalts himself will be humbled, and the man who humbles himself will be exalted', to be true?

In your parish community how are you following Jesus's command, '[W]hen you have a party, invite the poor, the crippled, the lame, the blind?' How are you being called to live into this more?

CELEBRATION

Model Penitential Act

Presider: In today's gospel Jesus cautions, 'everyone who exalts himself will be humbled, and the man who humbles himself will be exalted'. Let us pause to remember the times we have sought favour in the eyes of the world and shunned the path of humility . . . [*pause*]

Lord Jesus, you are the host of the heavenly banquet: Lord, have mercy.

Christ Jesus, you save the outcast and the lost: Christ, have mercy.

Lord Jesus, you show us the way of humility: Lord, have mercy.

Homily Points

• The first reading from Sirach ends with the line, '[A]n attentive ear is the sage's dream'. In today's gospel Jesus offers us two pieces of wisdom to incorporate into our lives: Be humble. Be hospitable.

• Being humble requires trust and contentment. When we are fearful of being overlooked or anxious about how we are perceived, we begin to grasp at 'exaltation'. We want people to recognise us and laud our accomplishments. And if they don't, we try to force them to. Jesus knows that when we strive after the world's approval it will never satisfy us. But when we let go of this desire – when we are free from the prisons of pride and arrogance, when we stop grasping at acceptance and recognition – we can finally know the peace of God.

• Jesus's second teaching is on hospitality, but not the hospitality of offering welcome to friends and family. The radical hospitality of Jesus is being open to 'the other', the ones who are not regularly seen at our tables. This is a difficult teaching. To break bread together requires a certain level of trust and comfort. Jesus is not asking us to be unsafe, but he is challenging us to do more than donate to charitable causes. We are called to personal contact with those on the outskirts of society, to sit down and eat a meal with the patrons of a homeless shelter instead of remaining in the kitchen preparing food. When we follow the paths of humility and hospitality, not only do we serve others, we are changed by our actions. Be humble. Be hospitable. As in all things, Jesus offers us these maxims as the way to 'life in the full' (see John 10:10). Sirach tells us, '[A]n attentive ear is the sage's dream'. Are we listening?

Model Universal Prayer (Prayer of the Faithful)

Presider: With humility and trust we bring our prayers before the Lord.

Response: Lord, hear our prayer.

That the church be in alignment with the humble, vulnerable, and needy of the world . . .

That all the people of the world might yearn for the wisdom of God and seek the path of humility . . .

That the poor, crippled, lame, and blind, whom Jesus speaks of in today's gospel, be met with a banquet of love, dignity, and welcome wherever they go . . .

That all gathered here might find ways to offer radical hospitality to those on the margins of society, especially the homeless, those who suffer from drug and alcohol addiction, and prisoners . . .

Presider: God of the humble and the outcast, you call us to build your kingdom here on earth. Hear our prayers that we might be living signs of your love and care to all we meet. We ask this through Christ, our Lord. Amen.

COLLECT

Let us pray.

Pause for silent prayer

God of might, giver of every good gift,
put into our hearts the love of your name,
so that, by deepening our sense of
     reverence,
you may nurture in us what is good
and, by your watchful care,
keep safe what you have nurtured.
Through our Lord Jesus Christ, your Son,
who lives and reigns with you in the unity
     of the Holy Spirit,
one God, for ever and ever. **Amen.**

FIRST READING
Eccl 3:17-20, 28-29

My son, be gentle in carrying out
     your business,
and you will be better loved than a
     lavish giver.
The greater you are, the more you should
     behave humbly,
and then you will find favour with the Lord;
for great though the power of the Lord is,
he accepts the homage of the humble.
There is no cure for the proud
     man's malady,
since an evil growth has taken root in him.
The heart of a sensible man will reflect on
     parables,
an attentive ear is the sage's dream.

RESPONSORIAL PSALM
Ps 67:4-7, 10-11 (Cf. 11)

R⁊. In your goodness, O God, you prepared
   a home for the poor.

The just shall rejoice at the presence of God,
they shall exult and dance for joy.
O sing to the Lord, make music to his name;
rejoice in the Lord, exult at his presence.

R⁊. In your goodness, O God, you prepared
   a home for the poor.

Father of the orphan, defender of the widow,
such is God in his holy place.
God gives the lonely a home to live in;
he leads the prisoners forth into freedom.

R⁊. In your goodness, O God, you prepared
   a home for the poor.

You poured down, O God, a generous rain:
when your people were starved you gave
   them new life.
It was there that your people found a home,
prepared in your goodness, O God, for
   the poor.

R⁊. In your goodness, O God, you prepared
   a home for the poor.

SECOND READING
Heb 12:18-19, 22-24

What you have come to is nothing known
to the senses: not a blazing fire, or a gloom
turning to total darkness, or a storm; or
trumpeting thunder or the great voice
speaking which made everyone that
heard it beg that no more should be said
to them. But what you have come to is
Mount Zion and the city of the living
God, the heavenly Jerusalem where the
millions of angels have gathered for the
festival, with the whole Church in which
everyone is a 'first-born son' and a citizen
of heaven. You have come to God himself,
the supreme Judge, and been placed with
spirits of the saints who have been made
perfect; and to Jesus, the mediator who
brings a new covenant.

About Liturgy
Making the church a home for the poor: There is a Catholic parish in the
poorest neighbourhood of San Francisco that opens its doors every weekday at 6:00
a.m. to welcome about 150 of its unhoused neighbours who have spent the night on
the streets and give them a secure place for a few hours of rest. They call it 'sacred
sleep'. A neighbouring Episcopal church does the same for about 75 of its unhoused
community members.

These women and men – some with mental health issues, others addicted to
drugs, all of them rejected in one way or another by family, friends, and our society
– sleep on the pews in the back two-thirds of the churches. At the Catholic church,
the parishioners gather for Mass at 12:15 p.m. each weekday and they celebrate the
Eucharist in the front part of the church as their neighbours sleep behind them. After
Mass, some parishioners stay to share a meal with their unhoused neighbours and offer
them material and spiritual support.

This work, called the Gubbio Project, strives to provide a beautiful and safe place
for people to rest, cultivate true community and shared responsibility between people
of the gospel and the least among them, and attend to the real and immediate needs of
their unhoused neighbours.

Not every church can open its doors every day to the same radical extent as these two
communities. But every parish can do something to bring beauty, safety, support, and
care to the poorest of its own neighbourhoods. For what we proclaim in liturgy must be
lived out in our daily lives if our Sunday Eucharist is to be authentic and credible.

About Initiation
Reserved places of honour: The only liturgical document to prescribe places
of honour for members of the assembly is the Rite of Christian Initiation of Adults
when it refers to the neophytes and their godparents during the period of mystagogy
and post-baptismal catechesis. The RCIA gives no mention of where catechumens,
candidates, and their sponsors should be seated during the periods of preparation and
formation. They could sit wherever they desire. Ideally, they would not be clustered
all together but seated throughout the church so that they can interact with more
members of the community.

About Liturgical Music
Who is the principle music minister? Music ministers might imagine that the
music director, the cantor, or the organist is the principle minister of music. Some choir
members may see themselves as the ones who provide music for the liturgy. In many
ways these are true. But two references in our liturgical documents give us a different
way of understanding who the primary music ministers in our assemblies are.

First, the US Bishops' *Liturgical Music Today* says, 'The entire worshiping assembly
exercises a ministry of music' (63). Second, their *Sing to the Lord* states that the
congregation's unrehearsed community singing 'is the primary song of the Liturgy' (28).

When music ministers remember that the people are the primary music makers,
they can begin to understand better their role in supporting and enhancing the primary
song of the liturgy.

One very easy way to remind everyone of this is to pay attention to how you invite
the assembly to take on its role as primary music minister. For example, instead of
saying to the assembly, 'Join us in singing the opening song', say instead, 'Let us sing
together . . .'

I SEPTEMBER 2019
TWENTY-SECOND SUNDAY
IN ORDINARY TIME

SPIRITUALITY

GOSPEL ACCLAMATION
Ps 118:135

℟. Alleluia, alleluia.
Let your face shine on your servant,
and teach me your decrees.
℟. Alleluia, alleluia.

Gospel

Luke 14:25-33

Great crowds accompanied Jesus on his way and he turned and spoke to them. 'If any man comes to me without hating his father, mother, wife, children, brothers, sisters, yes and his own life too, he cannot be my disciple. Anyone who does not carry his cross and come after me cannot be my disciple.

'And indeed, which of you here, intending to build a tower, would not first sit down and work out the cost to see if he had enough to complete it? Otherwise, if he laid the foundation and then found himself unable to finish the work, the onlookers would all start making fun of him and saying, "Here is a man who started to build and was unable to finish." Or again, what king marching to war against another king would not first sit down and consider whether with ten thousand men he could stand up to the other who advanced against him with twenty thousand? If not, then while the other king was still a long way off, he would send envoys to sue for peace. So in the same way, none of you can be my disciple unless he gives up all his possessions.'

Reflecting on the Gospel

Hyperbole and exaggeration can be effective rhetorical tools. They are used by almost everyone at some point. Even the fictitious news announcer Kent Brockman from the Simpsons said, 'Ladies and gentlemen, I've been to Vietnam, Iraq, and Afghanistan, and I can say without hyperbole that this is a million times worse than all of them put together'.

Of course, it's easy to spot hyperbole and we don't take it literally. But sometimes it's easy to miss this rhetorical tool when it's on the lips of Jesus in the Scriptures. A good rule of thumb is to see how the early Christians understood a passage in question. For example, Jesus advises his listeners in another story that 'if your eye causes you to sin, tear it out' (Matt 18:9; NABRE)! But early, as well as later Christians, did not take that literally. The passage is rhetorical hyperbole. Something similar is at work in today's gospel passage when Jesus says that no one coming to him 'without hating his father, mother, wife, children, brothers, sisters, yes and his own life too' can be a disciple. Rather than try to twist ourselves into knots over that quote, it's best to recognise it for what it is: rhetorical hyperbole. Even one of the concluding thoughts about renouncing all possessions is hyperbolic. Part of the reason we know this is by reading other passages in Luke in which Jesus's women followers provide for Jesus and the disciples from their means (Luke 8:1-3). So even Jesus did not expect his own followers to take this advice about renouncing all possessions literally. If they had, he would not have had such a widespread support network in Judea and Galilee.

Jesus is an effective preacher: he used the rhetorical tools of hyperbole and exaggeration to make his point. This can be a challenge for us if we want to take literally each and every saying of his in the New Testament. But gratefully we are part of a long line of believers, a large family of faith. And we can look to ancient Christians to see that they recognised this as hyperbole too.

In the end, what Jesus demands is a wholehearted, complete commitment, without distraction. And that's no exaggeration.

Living the Paschal Mystery

Discipleship is a lifelong process, often called a journey. We learn things along the way, likely starting out resolutely as Jesus does on his own journey to Jerusalem. During this lifelong process we encounter different ways of looking at reality, new insights, challenging statements, and more. The metaphor of a journey is especially apt as we never stay still, nor does our environment or the people around us. We are all growing in knowledge, understanding, and experience with former ways of understanding giving way to the new.

Developmentally, human beings tend to grow from a place of literalism to understanding the broader picture. Children can be told not to touch the cooker, but as they mature they internalise the lesson and take care around a hot cooker.

Discipleship follows a similar path. We tend to be more literal in the early stages of a relationship with Christ, but as we mature we see the deeper meaning of his injunctions and exhortations. Let us continue on this path to an adult relationship with Christ.

Focusing the Gospel

Key words and phrases: Anyone who does not carry his cross and come after me cannot be my disciple.

To the point: This phrase appears in all three of the Synoptic Gospels: Matthew (10:38, 16:24) and Luke (9:23, 14:27) repeat it twice, and Mark once (8:34). It's hard to imagine the pre-crucifixion Jesus uttering these words. What would they have meant to the crowd that was following him? Looking back from two thousand years after the event, we know Jesus is on his way to Jerusalem where he will literally carry his own cross and then be crucified upon it. The spiritual life requires struggle and sacrifice. But we also know the end of the story: life everlasting.

Connecting the Gospel

to the first and second readings: The sayings in today's gospel are demanding. Following Jesus requires single-minded dedication. The book of Wisdom reminds us how difficult it can be to follow the dictates of God. The author asks, 'Who can divine the will of the Lord?' Interpreting biblical texts requires an expansive mind. We cannot focus on one line in the Bible to the exclusion of everything else. Otherwise, lines like, 'If any man comes to me without hating his father, mother, wife, children, brothers, sisters, yes and his own life too, he cannot be my disciple' could lead us to renounce the wisdom of Jesus completely. In the second reading St. Paul writes to Philemon requesting that Philemon receive back his former (possibly runaway) slave with love and equality, 'so that you could have him back for ever, not as a slave any more, but something much better than a slave, a dear brother; especially dear to me, but how much more to you, as a blood-brother as well as a brother in the Lord'.

to experience: We know that the basis of Christianity is love: love of God and love of others. Interpreted through this lens today's shocking gospel helps us to put our lives in perspective. Jesus, the source of love and peace, must be at the centre of all that we do.

Connecting the Responsorial Psalm

to the readings: Today's psalm also reminds us to put our lives in perspective. To us, our days and years upon the earth might stretch out, but in the vast expanse of the history of salvation they are less than the blink of an eye. The psalmist prays, 'Make us know the shortness of our life / that we may gain wisdom of heart'. Though fleeting, our earthly lives are not futile. We are given a work to do. Jesus urges us to take up our cross and follow him, while the psalmist asks God to 'give success to the work of our hands'.

to psalmist preparation: In the assembly of the faithful, your work of leading the community in song and prayer is service to the people of God. How might you pray this week for God to 'give success to' your ministry and to bless the work of your hands?

PROMPTS FOR FAITH-SHARING

The writer of the book of Wisdom asks, 'Who can divine the will of the Lord?' If you could ask God one question, what would it be?

The psalmist prays '[G]ive success to the work of our hands'. Of the many things you do, what work or labour would you like to ask God's blessing on?

What cross are you being asked to carry right now? Are there crosses you have been struggling with that are not yours to carry?

The last line of today's gospel asks us to renounce our possessions in order to be Jesus's disciples. Is there a possession that does not lead to fulness of life that God might be calling for you to renounce?

CELEBRATION

Model Penitential Act

Presider: Today's gospel challenges us to be faithful disciples of Jesus. For the times we have put other things before our commitment to Christ let us pause to ask for pardon and mercy . . . [*pause*]

Lord Jesus, you call us to fidelity in discipleship: Lord, have mercy.

Christ Jesus, you gift us with your Holy Spirit so we might know your ways: Christ, have mercy.

Lord Jesus, you are the Wisdom of God: Lord, have mercy.

Homily Points

• This is the second time in Luke's gospel that Jesus has told his would-be followers that if they wish to be his disciples they must take up their crosses and follow him. We, who wear crosses around our necks and place them in prominent places in our churches and households, are probably not shocked by this statement. How might Jesus's original audience have felt when these words came out of his mouth? In Jesus's day the cross was a tool of torture and execution used by the Roman Empire to punish and make examples of those who would dare to defy its might. To carry your cross would be to constantly bear the weight of that which would ultimately kill you. And this is just what Jesus does. Knowing that his current path is leading him to Jerusalem and the crucifixion, he takes it anyway.

• What does this saying mean for us today? Fortunately, many of us will never face martyrdom for our beliefs. However, there are many ways of pouring out our lives for others. In *The Sound of Music*, the mother superior counsels Maria, the wayward postulant, to discern which path in life, marriage or sisterhood, 'will need / all the love you can give / every day of your life / for as long as you live'.

• For us today, the cross is not so much a symbol of violence or brutality, but of the complete and total gift of self that Jesus completes on Calvary. On the cross, just as he did with every moment of his life, Jesus pours out all the love he can give. He invites us to do the same, 'Take up your cross and follow me'.

Model Universal Prayer (Prayer of the Faithful)

Presider: Trusting in God's wisdom and love, let us bring our prayers before the Lord.

Response: Lord, hear our prayer.

That those in church leadership renew their commitment to complete fidelity to Christ and, with the help of the Holy Spirit, guide their communities with love . . .

That all peoples of the world might have meaningful work and adequate resources of food, water, and shelter . . .

That those who are victims of human trafficking be freed from their captors and receive support in healing and rebuilding their lives . . .

That all gathered here be strengthened to answer Jesus's call to take up our crosses and follow him . . .

Presider: God of wisdom, your ways are beyond our comprehension. Hear our prayers, that we might place our trust in you and dedicate our lives to building your kingdom. We ask this through Christ our Lord. Amen.

COLLECT

Let us pray.

Pause for silent prayer

O God, by whom we are redeemed and
 receive adoption,
look graciously upon your beloved sons
 and daughters,
that those who believe in Christ
may receive true freedom
and an everlasting inheritance.
Through our Lord Jesus Christ, your Son,
who lives and reigns with you in the unity
 of the Holy Spirit,
one God, for ever and ever. **Amen.**

FIRST READING
Wis 9:13-18

What man can know the intentions of God?
Who can divine the will of the Lord?
The reasonings of mortals are unsure
and our intentions unstable;
for a perishable body presses down the soul,
and this tent of clay weighs down the
 teeming mind.
It is hard enough for us to work out what
 is on earth,
laborious to know what lies within
 our reach;
who, then, can discover what is in the
 heavens?
As for your intention, who could have
 learnt it, had you not granted Wisdom
and sent your holy spirit from above?
Thus have the paths of those on earth
 been straightened
and men been taught what pleases you,
and saved, by Wisdom.

RESPONSORIAL PSALM
Ps 89:3-6, 12-14, 17 (1)

R̸. O Lord, you have been our refuge
from one generation to the next.

You turn men back into dust
and say 'Go back, sons of men.'
To your eyes a thousand years
are like yesterday, come and gone,
no more than a watch in the night.

R̸. O Lord, you have been our refuge
from one generation to the next.

You sweep men away like a dream,
like grass which springs up in the morning.
In the morning it springs up and flowers:
by evening it withers and fades.

Ry. O Lord, you have been our refuge
from one generation to the next.

Make us know the shortness of our life
that we may gain wisdom of heart.
Lord, relent! Is your anger for ever?
Show pity to your servants.

Ry. O Lord, you have been our refuge
from one generation to the next.

In the morning, fill us with your love;
we shall exult and rejoice all our days.
Let the favour of the Lord be upon us:
give success to the work of our hands.

Ry. O Lord, you have been our refuge
from one generation to the next.

SECOND READING
Phlm 9-10, 12-17

This is Paul writing, an old man now and,
what is more, still a prisoner of Christ
Jesus. I am appealing to you for a child
of mine, whose father I became while
wearing these chains: I mean Onesimus.
I am sending him back to you, and with
him – I could say – a part of my own self.
I should have liked to keep him with me;
he could have been a substitute for you,
to help me while I am in the chains that
the Good News has brought me. However,
I did not want to do anything without
your consent; it would have been forcing
your act of kindness, which should be
spontaneous. I know you have been
deprived of Onesimus for a time, but
it was only so that you could have him
back for ever, not as a slave any more,
but something much better than a slave,
a dear brother; especially dear to me, but
how much more to you, as a blood-brother
as well as a brother in the Lord. So if all
that we have in common means anything
to you, welcome him as you would me.

About Liturgy

Evaluating liturgical ministers: Ministry is a call that comes with great
responsibility. One should not treat ministry as a right but as a duty if given the
privilege of being called.

Yet, how often do we allow liturgical ministers to serve in a ministry although they
have not shown the necessary competence, desire to improve, or commitment to fulfil
the requirements of their ministry? Why are we content with poor or only passable
liturgical ministers? Shouldn't we desire excellence in the work we each do for the
benefit of the assembly? Contrary to common practice, it is perfectly appropriate – and
sometimes necessary – to ask a volunteer to step down from a ministry if she has not
committed herself to the disciplines of growing into excellence in ministry.

However, before we do that, we need to ensure that we have put into place processes
for fostering excellence in those who answer the call to serve. This requires good
discernment throughout the process of recruiting, training, forming, and evaluating
liturgical ministers.

A good process informs volunteers up front of the specific characteristics, talents,
disciplines, and attitudes necessary for each liturgical ministry. Better yet, instead of
making ministry an open invitation, have your best current liturgical ministers seek
out possible new ministers in your community whom they recognise as having the
gifts needed for that ministry. Then ask them to discern with those persons if they
might have a genuine call to serve.

A good process also includes ongoing training, even for veteran ministers, and
regular evaluations throughout the year. Think of these as opportunities for mutual
discernment with the ministers. Help them reflect on how well they are serving the
assembly, where their strengths are, where they need improvement, or where else they
might serve the assembly better.

About Initiation

Rite of Acceptance or Rite of Welcome: Because of the gospel's focus on
discipleship, today is a good day to celebrate a Rite of Acceptance into the Order of
Catechumens or a Rite of Welcoming Candidates.

About Liturgical Music

Introducing new music: Introducing new music to the assembly takes a bit of
strategic planning if your assembly is to embrace it as its own. This is especially true
if the music is for a critical moment of assembly singing, such as the entrance song,
eucharistic prayer acclamations, or communion song.

Several weeks before you want the assembly to sing the new piece in the Mass,
play the song as an instrumental for the prelude, preparation of gifts, or postlude.
The next week, sing the song with the choir alone as a prelude or, if appropriate, at
the preparation of gifts. The following week, invite the assembly to listen to the song
before Mass and start to teach it to them, but do not include it within the Mass yet.
If needed, teach the song again to the assembly before Mass the next week. Once the
assembly has heard the song over several weeks and has rehearsed singing it a few
more weeks, then schedule the song for use with the Mass.

This process works well if you plan to introduce a new Mass setting or seasonal
song for Advent later this year.

SPIRITUALITY

GOSPEL ACCLAMATION
2 Cor 5:19

℟. Alleluia, alleluia.
God in Christ was reconciling the world
    to himself,
and he has entrusted to us the news that they
    are reconciled.
℟. Alleluia, alleluia.

Gospel   Luke 15:1-32

The tax collectors and the sinners were all seeking the company of Jesus to hear what he had to say, and the Pharisees and the scribes complained. 'This man' they said 'welcomes sinners and eats with them.' So he spoke this parable to them:

'What man among you with a hundred sheep, losing one, would not leave the ninety-nine in the wilderness and go after the missing one till he found it? And when he found it, would he not joyfully take it on his shoulders and then, when he got home, call together his friends, and neighbours? "Rejoice with me," he would say "I have found my sheep that was lost." In the same way, I tell you, there will be more rejoicing in heaven over one repentant sinner than over ninety-nine virtuous men who have no need of repentance.

'Or again, what woman with ten drachmas would not, if she lost one, light a lamp and sweep out the house and search thoroughly till she found it? And then, when she had found it, call together her friends and neighbours? "Rejoice with me," she would say "I have found the drachma I lost." In the same way, I tell you, there is rejoicing among the angels of God over one repentant sinner.'

Continued in Appendix A, p. 303,

or Luke 15:1-10.

Reflecting on the Gospel

Our reading today is one of the most memorable of Jesus's parables and it's told only in the Gospel of Luke. It is the parable of the Prodigal Son, or the two sons, or perhaps more appropriately, the story of the mercy of the father. This short story has been the subject matter of innumerable artistic works, including paintings by some of the world's masters.

Since the story is a parable, it has many possible meanings. Each listener may have something different that speaks to them in the parable. But one meaning which would have been clear to the early Christians is that the two sons can represent Gentiles and Jews. The younger son, the one who spends his share of the inheritance on wanton living, is certainly representative of the Gentiles for it reflects the attitudes that many Jews had of the Gentiles of the day. The Gentiles, not having the Mosaic Law, had a different moral code than Jews. Because there was not a monolithic moral code among non-Jews, Gentiles were perceived by Jews as more libertine.

On the other hand, the Jews had Mosaic Law, which, in the parable, could be said to be the wishes of the father or God the Father. They kept the Mosaic Law and served God for many years without disobeying, as the parable indicates. But God rejoices when the hedonistic Gentile repents while offering nothing for the observant Jews? So although the story on its face is about two sons and their father, there is a deeper meaning with respect to the Gentiles and Jews of the apostolic era.

The moral of the story, the mercy of the father, is echoed throughout the gospel in other parables such as the payment of day labourers, who all receive the same wage even though some worked all day and others only an hour. These parables tell us about God's mercy, which does not follow strict justice. The love, care, and concern that our Father shows for his creation is superabundant. How do we react when faced with this overwhelming generosity? Are we repentant, ready to be received by this mercy? Or are we despondent, questioning why mercy is given so freely to others, thinking we might not have received our 'rightful' share?

Living the Paschal Mystery

Mercy is a keyword in the gospel today even though it does not appear in the text. But mercy is the motivating force behind the father's actions, and the experience of the younger son who has been forgiven. Only when the younger son has 'hit bottom', so to speak, does he awaken to the notion of returning to his father's house, where he hopes to be a hired hand. And that part of the story is an accurate reflection of human nature. Often, before we seek repentance and ask forgiveness we must hit bottom. The younger son was not interested in repentance when he had plenty of money and resources! Only when he was feeding the pigs and desirous of their food did the realisation strike him.

And so it may be with us. We must die to our own pride, self-assurance, and resources, recognising that all is a gift of the Father. The son did not earn this money on his own. Perhaps it is only when we hit bottom with the recognition that all is the Father's, not our own, will we be ready to return to the embrace of mercy, and live a new life of reconciliation.

Focusing the Gospel

Key words and phrases: [W]e should celebrate and rejoice, because your brother here was dead and has come to life; he was lost and is found.

To the point: Jesus tells the grumbling Pharisees and scribes three parables and each follows a similar pattern. There is loss, search, finding, and finally rejoicing. In our human condition it is easy to focus on the first few moments. Whether it's our keys, an overdue library book, or a child in the supermarket, we lose, search, and hopefully find on a daily basis. How often do we celebrate these findings though? This seems to be an important point that Jesus tries to convey to the self-righteous religious leaders of his day who were not pleased with Jesus's association with sinners. The lost being found demands a public celebration because their straying hurt not only them but also the entire community. In rejoicing the community is rebuilt and healed.

Connecting the Gospel

to the second reading: In the first letter to Timothy, St. Paul describes himself as 'the foremost' of sinners, given an abundance of mercy and grace so that 'Jesus Christ meant to make me the greatest evidence of his inexhaustible patience for all the other people who would later have to trust in him to come to eternal life'. If the parables from today's gospel illustrate God's mercy, Paul's conversion-story concretizes it. Stopped in his tracks on the way to Damascus where he is intending to arrest followers of the Way, and 'bring them back to Jerusalem in chains' (Acts 9:2; NABRE), Paul hears a voice that changes his life forever. Instead of condemning this man who is bent on violently destroying his followers, the risen Lord invites Paul to become a pillar of the early church.

to experience: We see the parables of mercy lived out in the lives of men and women who have had their lives changed by an experience of the living God. Although, like the apostle Paul's, some conversions are flashy and life altering, more often than not they are slow and subtle. Throughout our lives, Jesus continually calls us to return to him, to follow him more closely, to be found.

Connecting the Responsorial Psalm

to the readings: Psalm 50 is a fitting response to the first reading from Exodus where the people, having grown weary of waiting for Moses to return from Mount Sinai, construct a golden calf to worship. God laments to Moses, 'They have been quick to leave the way I marked out for them'. Such is life. We, inconstant creatures who are easily distracted and wearied, stumble and fall. And yet, like the psalmist, we are surrounded by the 'merciful love' and 'abundant compassion' of a God who never ceases to seek the lost and restore the sinner (v. 3; NABRE).

to psalmist preparation: This week consider how you have experienced God's 'merciful love' and 'abundant compassion' in your own life. Where do you most need God's renewing touch right now?

PROMPTS FOR FAITH-SHARING

Today's psalm reminds us of Lent, especially in the line, 'O wash me more and more from my guilt / and cleanse me from my sin'. How do you attend to repentance and reconciliation in Ordinary Time?

In the second reading we hear, 'Here is a saying that you can rely on and nobody should doubt: that Christ Jesus came into the world to save sinners'. Is this statement a cornerstone of your own faith? How does it affect your ministry and mission as a disciple?

In the parable of the Prodigal Son, which character do you empathize with the most: the younger son who returns, the father who waits, or the older son outside the celebration? What is the message for you today in this parable?

Who are the lost in your family and/or faith community? How is God calling you to seek them?

215

CELEBRATION

Model Penitential Act

Presider: In today's gospel, Jesus tells three parables of the lost being found. Let us pause to remember the times we have strayed far from God . . . [*pause*]

Lord Jesus, you search tirelessly for the lost: Lord, have mercy.
Christ Jesus, you came into the world to save sinners: Christ, have mercy.
Lord Jesus, you reveal the infinite compassion of God: Lord, have mercy.

Homily Points

• The scribes and the Pharisees are not happy. He whom the crowds follow, who multiplies loaves and fishes, and who heals those with infirmities also eats with tax collectors and sinners. In response to their grumblings, Jesus tells three parables of three things lost and found: a sheep, a coin, a son. In each parable the joy of finding is so great it must be shared with others. The shepherd and the woman invite their friends and neighbours to rejoice with them, while the father of the prodigal son slaughters the fattened calf and puts on a banquet with music and dancing.

• There are many layers to these parables to be explored, but one of them is certainly the joy of finding. The shepherd wastes no time scolding his sheep, and the father of the prodigal won't even let his son complete his apology before he clothes him in a fine robe and new sandals. Jesus answers the scribes' and the Pharisees' self-righteous stinginess with abundant welcome. The tax collectors and sinners are not to be turned away from Jesus's table; they are the very reason he is here. St. Paul says in today's second reading, 'Here is a saying that you can rely on and nobody should doubt: that Christ Jesus came into the world to save sinners'.

• There is a lesson here for us, especially those of us who find our place in the pews every Sunday and holy day. Are we prone to grumbling too when we see those who drop in once or twice a year join us at the table of the Lord? Does our community practise the hospitality of Jesus who welcomed all with joy, love, and compassion? If we call ourselves Christian we must take on the path of Jesus: seek the lost and welcome the sinner.

Model Universal Prayer (Prayer of the Faithful)

Presider: Confident in God's mercy to the lost and the sinful we bring our needs before the Lord.

Response: Lord, hear our prayer.

That the church embrace its mission to serve as a field hospital for wounded and weary souls . . .

That nations come together in peace and fellowship to provide for the needs of the poor, the powerless, and the vulnerable . . .

That those who have wandered far from the loving hand of God come to know the Lord who constantly seeks them . . .

That all gathered here might create a community of hospitality where sinners find welcome and the lost are called home . . .

Presider: God of compassion and mercy, you never cease to search for your wayward children or tire of gathering them to yourself. Hear our prayers that we might join you in seeking the lost and rejoicing when they are found. We ask this through Jesus Christ our Lord. Amen.

COLLECT

Let us pray.

Pause for silent prayer

Look upon us, O God,
Creator and ruler of all things,
and, that we may feel the working of
    your mercy,
grant that we may serve you
with all our heart.
Through our Lord Jesus Christ, your Son,
who lives and reigns with you in the unity
    of the Holy Spirit,
one God, for ever and ever. **Amen.**

FIRST READING
Exod 32:7-11, 13-14

The Lord spoke to Moses, 'Go down now, because your people whom you brought out of Egypt have apostasised. They have been quick to leave the way I marked out for them; they have made themselves a calf of molten metal and have worshipped it and offered it sacrifice. "Here is your God, Israel," they have cried "who brought you up from the land of Egypt!" I can see how headstrong these people are! Leave me, now, my wrath shall blaze out against them and devour them; of you, however, I will make a great nation.'

But Moses pleaded with the Lord his God. 'Lord,' he said, 'why should your wrath blaze out against this people of yours whom you brought out of the land of Egypt with arm outstretched and mighty hand? Remember Abraham, Isaac and Jacob, your servants to whom by your own self you swore and made this promise: I will make your offspring as many as the stars of heaven, and all this land which I promised I will give to your descendants, and it shall be their heritage for ever.' So the Lord relented and did not bring on his people the disaster he had threatened.

CATECHESIS

RESPONSORIAL PSALM
Ps 50:3-4, 12-13, 17, 19 (Luke 15:18)

R̸. I will leave this place and go to my father.

Have mercy on me, God, in your kindness.
In your compassion blot out my offence.
O wash me more and more from my guilt
and cleanse me from my sin.

R̸. I will leave this place and go to my father.

A pure heart create for me, O God,
put a steadfast spirit within me.
Do not cast me away from your presence,
nor deprive me of your holy spirit.

R̸. I will leave this place and go to my father.

O Lord, open my lips
and my mouth shall declare your praise.
My sacrifice is a contrite spirit;
a humbled, contrite heart you will not spurn.

R̸. I will leave this place and go to my father.

SECOND READING
1 Tim 1:12-17

I thank Christ Jesus our Lord, who has given me strength, and who judged me faithful enough to call me into his service even though I used to be a blasphemer and did all I could to injure and discredit the faith. Mercy, however, was shown me, because until I became a believer I had been acting in ignorance; and the grace of our Lord filled me with faith and with the love that is in Christ Jesus. Here is a saying that you can rely on and nobody should doubt: that Christ Jesus came into the world to save sinners. I myself am the greatest of them; and if mercy has been shown to me, it is because Jesus Christ meant to make me the greatest evidence of his inexhaustible patience for all the other people who would later have to trust in him to come to eternal life. To the eternal King, the undying, invisible and only God, be honour and glory for ever and ever. Amen.

About Liturgy

Penitential Act invocations: The third form of the penitential act gives us the opportunity to choose from a variety of invocations for the threefold litany: 'Lord/Christ, have mercy' or 'Kyrie/Christe, eleison'. Appendix VI of the Roman Missal includes several sample invocations. On occasion, you might want to compose your own invocations incorporating some of the images from the day's Scriptures.

A main principle to keep in mind when writing invocations for the penitential act is that the focus here is always on God's mercy in Christ and not on our sinfulness. The priest's invitation that opens the penitential act indicates that the acknowledgement of our sin, and not its forgiveness, is what makes us ready to celebrate the sacred mysteries. We place ourselves in right relationship before God by acknowledging that before the glory of God, none of us is without need of mercy.

Therefore, the invocations in the third form of the penitential act are invocations to Christ, not petitions for forgiveness. Look at the samples given in the Roman Missal. All of these have Christ as the subject, and the emphasis is on what Christ has done.

If you decide to write your own invocations, avoid wording such as, 'For the times we have sinned, Lord, have mercy'. Instead, keep Christ as the subject. Here are some examples using images from today's gospel: 'You are the Good Shepherd who sought out the lost sheep. Lord, have mercy'. 'You prepare a feast, rejoicing over the sinner who repents. Christ, have mercy'. 'You will run to meet us when we return home to you. Lord, have mercy'.

About Initiation

Reconciliation for baptised candidates: In the Rite of Christian Initiation of Adults, baptised but uncatechised candidates are to be prepared during their formation to celebrate the sacrament of penance (see RCIA 408). Ideally, they would participate in penitential celebrations with the rest of the faithful, doing an examination of conscience and discerning their need for the sacrament. Especially during penitential times of the liturgical year, such as Advent or Lent, they should be prepared and encouraged to celebrate reconciliation along with the rest of the parish.

Catechumens cannot yet celebrate penance until after their baptism. However, they can join the faithful in participating in other penitential disciplines.

About Liturgical Music

Lamb of God: In addition to the third form of the penitential act, the Lamb of God is another litany of praise for God's mercy in Christ. Unlike the penitential act, the singing or recitation of the Lamb of God does not stand as a ritual by itself but rather accompanies the ritual action of breaking the eucharistic bread for Communion.

Because it accompanies this ritual, the singing of the Lamb of God should begin as the priest breaks the first host. This requires music directors to be attentive during the sign of peace and accompanists to be flexible with the musical introduction, shortening or lengthening it as needed, so that the singing of the cantor's first invocation begins at the appropriate moment. (Remember that in the third edition of the Roman Missal, the only invocation allowed is 'Lamb of God'.)

Although neither the rubrics nor the General Instruction of the Roman Missal indicate the exact number of times the litany should be repeated, it is traditionally repeated at least three times. The rubrics do indicate that the litany should be repeated as many times as necessary to accompany the fractioning, with the final response always being 'Grant us peace' (GIRM 83; Roman Missal 130).

15 SEPTEMBER 2019
TWENTY-FOURTH SUNDAY IN ORDINARY TIME

SPIRITUALITY

GOSPEL ACCLAMATION
2 Cor 8:9

R̰. Alleluia, alleluia.
Jesus Christ was rich,
but he became poor for your sake,
to make you rich out of his poverty.
R̰. Alleluia, alleluia.

Gospel

Luke 16:1-13

Jesus said to his disciples: 'There was a rich man and he had a steward who was denounced to him for being wasteful with his property. He called for the man and said, "What is this I hear about you? Draw me up an account of your stewardship because you are not to be my steward any longer." Then the steward said to himself, "Now that my master is taking the stewardship from m e, what am I to do? Dig? I am not strong enough. Go begging? I should be too ashamed. Ah, I know what I will do to make sure that when I am dismissed from office there will be some to welcome me into their homes."

'Then he called his master's debtors one by one. To the first he said, "How much do you owe my master?" "One hundred measures of oil" was the reply. The steward said, "Here, take your bond; sit down straight away and write fifty." To another he said, "And you, sir, how much do you owe?" "One hundred measures of wheat" was the reply. The steward said, "Here, take your bond and write eighty."

'The master praised the dishonest steward for his astuteness. For the children of this world are more astute in dealing with their own kind than are the children of light.

Continued in Appendix A, p. 304,

or Luke 16:10-13.

Reflecting on the Gospel

Have you ever heard a story and wondered what exactly was its point? It's almost like not quite understanding a joke, and then asking for an explanation. Sometimes our wondering about the point of a story can happen listening to children, but it can also happen in a boardroom! Few times will a brave soul step up and ask, 'How does that apply'? or 'And what does that mean'?

Today's parable is a case in point. It has puzzled interpreters for centuries. Part of the problem is that Luke appends to the parable a number of other sayings that attempt to explain it, but which create more difficulties. At least as the Jerusalem Bible presents it, the parable ends with this phrase, 'The master praised the dishonest steward for his astuteness'. What follows is Jesus's commentary, which some misunderstand as somehow encouraging dishonest behaviour! But there is more going on than a facile reading might indicate.

In antiquity, a steward functioned as the agent of the master or lord of the estate with the power to hire, fire, enter into contracts, etc. The steward kept the books and received some payment for himself by charging interest. The loan note indicated the amount to be paid back, not the amount borrowed. In essence, the amount to be paid back included the interest, and that extra money was for the steward.

So in the parable, when the steward writes down the note, he is effectively giving up *his own share* of the money owed, 25 percent in one case, 50 percent in the other. The rich man will still receive what is his due in full. So the parable is not about encouraging dishonesty, but rather, the right use of money and resources, which itself is a favourite Lukan theme. It is certainly true that the steward is dishonest, as we learn at the opening verse. And it is for this reason that he is being released. But his writing down of the debt is a crafty way for him to use his own resources (the money owed to him) to curry favour with others.

In fact, this chapter of the Gospel of Luke will have a number of stories reflecting this theme of money. We will read another next week. The right use of wealth was foreshadowed even in last week's story of the prodigal son.

Luke is the only evangelist to tell this parable of the Dishonest Steward. It is rooted firmly in the ancient world; discerning the likely meaning is much like deciphering a puzzle. Rather than a quick, easy read it's important to understand something of the context of the ancient world so as to more appropriately apply its lesson.

Living the Paschal Mystery

Jesus has more to say about money and how we use it than nearly any other ethical or moral matter in the gospels. And Luke the evangelist gives us more of these sayings, parables, and teachings than any other evangelist. Though the steward is being released from his position due to some dishonesty, he now acts in a shrewd way to leverage his remaining resources. He understands quickly that the money in the ledger due to him is better utilized currying favour than being handed over to the master. The master, upon realising this, does not condemn him for stealing, for after all he was not stealing. Instead, the master admires him.

We are advised to be as cunning and creative as this steward. It would be a misreading and a sure misunderstanding to imagine Jesus is encouraging dishonesty. Instead, with our own resources we are to be creative, using wealth for a greater good.

Focusing the Gospel

Key words and phrases: No servant can be the slave of two masters

To the point: Today's gospel reading includes the parable of the Dishonest Steward as well as collected sayings of Jesus related to prudence, trustworthiness, and wealth. The passage concludes, 'You cannot be the slave both of God and of money'. As in all things, Jesus points to the true source of riches and wealth, the only one completely worthy of trust, the eternal God.

Connecting the Gospel

to the first reading: The sixteenth chapter of the Gospel of Luke, which we read from this Sunday and the next, is focused on the proper use of wealth and the unjust distribution of goods between the very rich and the very poor. This chapter is complemented perfectly by the prophet Amos who was called from the southern kingdom of Judah to prophesy against the northern kingdom of Israel. And what was Israel's most prominent offence? The callous mistreatment of the poor by the rich. In today's reading, Amos lists off the crimes of the wealthy Israelites who cheat the poor and then proclaims, 'The Lord swears it by the pride of Jacob, / "Never will I forget a single thing you have done".'

to experience: This Sunday we are given the warning that we cannot serve both God and earthly riches. We must choose one or the other. Are we willing to use our wealth and resources wisely and prudently in service of others?

Connecting the Responsorial Psalm

to the readings: Amos's emphasis on care of the poor is echoed in Psalm 112. Not only is God 'High above all nations', but he also 'lifts up the lowly, / from the dungheap he raises the poor / to set him in the company of princes, / yes, with the princes of his people'. Though today's gospel reading does not focus specifically on the plight of the poor, as next Sunday's will, we can see within it the roots of economic prudence. Wealth and riches can enslave a person who entrusts himself entirely to them. Instead, with God as the true master, wealth can take up its proper post, as a gift to be shared with others, especially those most in need.

to psalmist preparation: Today's psalm is good news for all who identify with, befriend, or care for the poor. To proclaim this psalm well, you must live it. How do you relate to the poor within your community?

CELEBRATION

Model Penitential Act

Presider: In today's gospel Jesus exhorts us, 'No servant can be the slave of two masters'. For the times we have placed other interests above God let us pause to ask forgiveness . . . [*pause*]

Lord Jesus, you call us to be trustworthy and honest in all matters large and small: Lord, have mercy.

Christ Jesus, you mediate for us at the right hand of God: Christ, have mercy.

Lord Jesus, you gave yourself as a ransom for all: Lord, have mercy.

Homily Points

• This week and next our gospel readings come from the sixteenth chapter of Luke. The bulk of this chapter is taken up with two parables: the parable of the Dishonest Steward and the parable of the Rich Man and Lazarus. Both of these parables begin with the character of a 'rich man'. In between the parables we hear a reason for this focus on wealth, 'The Pharisees, who loved money, heard all these things and sneered at him' (16:14; NABRE). Just as with the parables of the Lost Sheep, Lost Coin, and Prodigal Son from last Sunday's gospel, Jesus has an audience in mind for these parables about riches.

• The final verse of today's gospel is the most searing indictment of these Pharisees in his audience, 'No servant can be the slave of two masters: he will either hate the first and love the second, or treat the first with respect and the second with scorn. You cannot be the slave both of God and of money'. What do these words mean for us? Within our culture it is considered an acceptable goal to amass wealth for yourself and your family. In some ways it can be seen as foolhardy *not* to take as much as you can for yourself. Jesus shows us another way.

• We are to be devoted to only one master, God. Through the self-revelation of Jesus we begin to know what this master asks of us. Over and over again in his actions and his words we see Jesus place the highest value on communion between people and God. Jesus restores the sinner, seeks the lost, and shares table fellowship with people from all walks of life. Far from being interested in amassing things, Jesus preaches for us to store up treasure in heaven where neither moth nor decay destroy. This is the only treasure that lasts. This is the only treasure that satisfies.

Model Universal Prayer (Prayer of the Faithful)

Presider: With thanksgiving and trust we hand over to God all of our needs and petitions.

Response: Lord, hear our prayer.

That the church be a wise and prudent steward of financial and spiritual wealth in service to all God's people . . .

That all people of the world commit themselves to faithful stewardship of the earth's natural resources . . .

That those who are enslaved to the pursuit of money and power find freedom and peace in the one whose 'yoke is easy and burden light' . . .

That everyone gathered here strive for honesty and trustworthiness in all matters, large and small . . .

Presider: God of Creation, you are the giver of all good gifts. Hear our prayers that we might be good and faithful stewards to the resources you have entrusted to us. We ask this through Christ our Lord. Amen.

COLLECT

Let us pray.

Pause for silent prayer

O God, who founded all the commands of
    your sacred Law
upon love of you and of our neighbour,
grant that, by keeping your precepts,
we may merit to attain eternal life.
Through our Lord Jesus Christ, your Son,
who lives and reigns with you in the unity
    of the Holy Spirit,
one God, for ever and ever. **Amen.**

FIRST READING
Amos 8:4-7

Listen to this, you who trample on the needy
and try to suppress the poor people of
    the country,
you who say, 'When will the New Moon
    be over
so that we can sell our corn,
and sabbath, so that we can market
    our wheat?
Then by lowering the bushel, raising
    the shekel,
by swindling and tampering with
    the scales,
we can buy up the poor for money,
and the needy for a pair of sandals,
and get a price even for the sweepings of
    the wheat.'
The Lord swears it by the pride of Jacob,
'Never will I forget a single thing you
    have done.'

CATECHESIS

RESPONSORIAL PSALM
Ps 112:1-2, 4-8 (1, 7)

℟. Praise the Lord, who raises the poor.
or
℟. Alleluia.

Praise, O servants of the Lord,
praise the name of the Lord!
May the name of the Lord be blessed
both now and for evermore!

℟. Praise the Lord, who raises the poor.
or
℟. Alleluia.

High above all nations is the Lord,
above the heavens his glory.
Who is like the Lord, our God,
who has risen on high to his throne
yet stoops from the heights to look down,
to look down upon heaven and earth?

℟. Praise the Lord, who raises the poor.
or
℟. Alleluia.

From the dust he lifts up the lowly,
from the dungheap he raises the poor
to set him in the company of princes,
yes, with the princes of his people.

℟. Praise the Lord, who raises the poor.
or
℟. Alleluia.

SECOND READING
1 Tim 2:1-8

My advice is that, first of all, there should be prayers offered for everyone – petitions, intercessions and thanksgiving – and especially for kings and others in authority, so that we may be able to live religious and reverent lives in peace and quiet. To do this is right, and will please God our saviour: he wants everyone to be saved and reach full knowledge of the truth. For there is only one God, and there is only one mediator between God and mankind, himself a man, Christ Jesus, who sacrificed himself as a ransom for them all. He is the evidence of this, sent at the appointed time, and I have been named a herald and apostle of it and – I am telling the truth and no lie – a teacher of the faith and the truth to the pagans.

In every place, then, I want the men to lift their hands up reverently in prayer, with no anger or argument.

About Liturgy

Can a person serve multiple ministries?: Within the same Mass, can a lector also serve as a communion minister or a choir member proclaim one of the readings? According to a liturgical principle from the Constitution on the Sacred Liturgy, not really. That principle states: 'In liturgical celebrations each person, minister, or layman who has an office to perform, should carry out all and only those parts which pertain to his office by the nature of the rite and the norms of the liturgy' (28).

Many parishes do not really think of the roles of liturgical ministers, other than the priest or deacon, as 'offices'. Thus, many parishes allow people to serve in more than one ministry during a liturgy.

However, a central goal of the Second Vatican Council was to distribute the liturgical roles as widely as possible among the assembly to show more clearly the various members of the Body of Christ working together to do the action of the liturgy. This shows the hierarchical nature of the liturgy. In other words, each member of the body has a role to play. Thus, each member of the body is necessary. It also shows dignity to each member when we allow each person to do their proper role and we don't let others usurp it.

There will be times when this cannot be avoided because not enough trained persons are available. But those emergencies should not become our normative practice.

About Initiation

Apostolic witness: We often think that catechesis for initiation consists of learning only the doctrines and teachings of the church. However, a complete catechesis requires that catechumens live the Word they have heard by the witness of their lives. Thus, part of discerning the readiness of catechumens for baptism is knowing if they have learned 'how to work actively with others to spread the Gospel and build up the Church by the witness of their lives and by professing their faith' (RCIA 75.4). Or as the bishop will inquire of their godparents in the Rite of Election, 'Have they responded to [God's] word and begun to walk in God's presence'? Even before their baptism, they must show themselves to be credible witnesses to the Gospel.

About Liturgical Music

Copyright laws: Part of being just and honest as a music minister is to follow the copyright laws of your country. When we ignore these laws, we are essentially stealing. These regulations are in place to protect the rights of composers, performers and publishers and to give them just compensation for the work they have produced.

Before you make a photocopy of a song, share an electronic file of sheet music, or upload a recording from the internet to your own website, know first whether you have the right to do so. Unless a piece of music and its arrangement are specifically labelled 'public domain', you must typically purchase a licence from the copyright holder to make or share copies of that song.

You cannot make copies of music for your choir members even if your parish has legally purchased a copy of the octavo or accompaniment books. You must purchase a copy for each choir member. Even if you have a reprint licence for assembly editions of the music (melody and/or text of a song), making copies of sheet music with chords, harmonies, or keyboard accompaniment falls under a separate licence. Calamus are very helpful in this regard. Printed orders of service, music or text projected on a screen, and digital or physical recordings of music your choir performs also require a copyright licence from the copyright holder or licence scheme. Always check if you are unsure of your permission for using the music. Not doing so can legally jeopardize not only your parish but the entire diocese!

SPIRITUALITY

GOSPEL ACCLAMATION
2 Cor 8:9

℟. Alleluia, alleluia.
Jesus Christ was rich,
but he became poor for your sake,
to make you rich out of his poverty.
℟. Alleluia, alleluia.

Gospel Luke 16:19-31

Jesus said to the Pharisees: 'There was a rich man who used to dress in purple and fine linen and feast magnificently everyday. And at his gate there lay a poor man called Lazarus, covered with sores, who longed to fill himself with the scraps that fell from the rich man's table. Dogs even came and licked his sores. Now the poor man died and was carried away by the angels to the bosom of Abraham. The rich man also died and was buried.

'In his torment in Hades he looked up and saw Abraham a long way off with Lazarus in his bosom. So he cried out, "Father Abraham, pity me and send Lazarus to dip the tip of his finger in water and cool my tongue, for I am in agony in these flames." "My son," Abraham replied "remember that during your life good things came your way, just as bad things came the way of Lazarus. Now he is being comforted here while you are in agony. But that is not all: between us and you a great gulf has been fixed, to stop anyone, if he wanted to, crossing from our side to yours, and to stop any crossing from your side to ours."

'The rich man replied, "Father, I beg you then to send Lazarus to my father's house, since I have five brothers, to give them warning so that they do not come to this place of torment too." "They have Moses and the prophets," said Abraham "let them listen to them." "Ah no, father Abraham," said the rich man "but if someone comes to them from the dead, they will repent." Then Abraham said to him, "If they will not listen either to Moses or to the prophets, they will not be convinced even if someone should rise from the dead."'

Reflecting on the Gospel

As we continue to journey with Jesus to Jerusalem we hear another parable unique to Luke: the story of the Rich Man and Lazarus. This parable develops many themes in the gospel, including the right use of money from last week, and also the reversal of the social order that has been foretold in Mary's canticle: he has lifted up the lowly and sent the rich away empty.

We should find this story troubling for a number of reasons, not least of which is that those of us in the developed world are likely the rich man, dressed in fine clothes and eating well while there is a Lazarus effectively at our doorstep who needs our help. When examined from a global perspective, most human beings live on meager amounts each day. Most of the wealth in the world has been localized, and even if we are not part of the infamous '1 percent' we are likely among the top 25 percent globally. Indeed the annual median wage globally is about $10,000. So if we are looking to place ourselves in this parable, the person of the rich man is likely where we belong, generally enjoying the good things of this world while others go without, or go with less. The line on Abraham's lips sounds the toll of doom: 'My son, . . . remember that during your life good things came your way, just as bad things came the way of Lazarus. Now he is being comforted here while you are in agony'. A reversal is in order!

The message that Jesus preached was good news for those on the outside of power, privilege, and wealth. Those who enjoyed such things put him to death!

In the nether world, the rich man cries out for someone to warn his brothers. But the message of caring for your neighbour is spread liberally throughout the Law and Prophets. In a telling sign, which foreshadows the situation of the early Christians, Abraham says ominously that people will not learn even if someone rises from the dead.

The lesson is difficult and likely hits home now that globalization means someone an ocean away is our neighbour. While we may no longer see a poor Lazarus literally at our doorstep, he is there nonetheless, and can be seen with television, radio, internet, and other modern means of communication. But it would be a mistake to believe that the only Lazaruses are an ocean away. There may be a Lazarus picking vegetables for meager wages and no health care nearby. There may be a Lazarus working in unsafe conditions creating the latest technological device. And there is certainly a Lazarus overlooked by systems, institutions, and even churches. What is our response? We have been told by the Law, the Prophets, and even by someone who rose from the dead to care for them.

Living the Paschal Mystery

For many, Christianity has become a comfortable societal institution. Parishioners and church members attend Mass regularly, build community with others in their geographical boundary, and might even send their children to the parish school. Today's gospel is a reminder that Jesus did not found parishes. The basis of our salvation is not parish membership, but how we treat the poor and disenfranchised among us. And now that our world has become flat, we are so interconnected that nearly the entire globe is our neighbour. Our responsibility to one another has increased exponentially. No longer are we concerned merely with our neighbourhood, parish, or school, but we are concerned with a much broader spectrum. The moral life includes decisions we make while shopping, hiring labour, or disposing of waste. With today's reading, we are called to let go of any narrow vision we might have of 'neighbour' and see the Lazarus figures before us both locally and worldwide.

Focusing the Gospel

Key words and phrases: There was a rich man . . . And at his gate there lay a poor man called Lazarus

To the point: Where most parables deal with everyday objects and stock characters like farmers, travellers, or a woman baking bread, today's parable, the Rich Man and Lazarus, is distinctive in that it contains two first names. The rich man could be any person enjoying an extravagant lifestyle while others suffer but the poor man is *Lazarus* and when he dies he is carried to the bosom of *Abraham*. We're not given many details about Lazarus's life other than his poverty, his hunger, and his illness (sores). We don't know if Lazarus lived an upright life, how he came to his current state in life, or if he had any friends or family. But we are given a name. This man, lying at the rich man's door, is not just a poor person, a person in need, he is Lazarus. Perhaps if the rich man had crossed the chasm of social class that separated him and Lazarus in their earthly life he wouldn't have found himself staring across an even greater chasm in eternity. Who are the ones in need at your door? Do you know their names?

Connecting the Gospel

to the first and second readings: As in last Sunday's first reading, the prophet Amos condemns the rich who show no care and compassion for their neighbours in need. The ones that Amos berates are not only rich but one could say, obscenely wealthy, lying on 'ivory beds', and drinking 'wine by the bowlful'. The rich man who ignores Lazarus would be at home in their company with his 'sumptuous' dining and fine linen clothing. In many ways the role of the prophet is to point out the nature of God, especially when the behaviour of people is not in line with the Creator in whose image and likeness they were made.

to experience: In all three readings today, Amos, Jesus, and St. Paul challenge us to think not merely as humans, intent upon our own comfort, but with the compassion and love of God. Jesus tells us, '[L]ove your neighbour as yourself' (Mark 12:31; NABRE). When we love this way we cannot be content to simply enjoy the riches we have, because when others are poor and suffering, so are we.

Connecting the Responsorial Psalm

to the readings: Psalm 145 reads almost like a litany recounting the deeds of the Lord. These actions on God's part turn the world upside down: prisoners are freed, the blind can see, the lowly are raised up, and the most vulnerable are protected. In the first reading and the gospel, Amos and Jesus condemn those who profit from the status quo – the ones who lounge on ivory couches and dine at sumptuous feasts while their neighbours suffer in poverty.

to psalmist preparation: As God's children we are called to act as God acts. How does your lifestyle oppress others, especially in ways you don't intend? How might you become more like the God of today's psalm, intent upon caring for the vulnerable?

PROMPTS FOR FAITH-SHARING

Psalm 145 recounts the actions God takes in response to suffering and injustice. In the face of these situations God gives, frees, raises up, loves, and protects. What place does social action have in your faith life?

St. Paul exhorts Timothy to 'aim to be saintly and religious, filled with faith and love, patient and gentle'. Which of these traits do you find most difficult to embrace? How might you focus on building up that trait this week?

In his apostolic exhortation, *Evangelii Gaudium,* Pope Francis states we must allow ourselves to be 'evangelised' by the poor. Have you experienced this type of evangelisation in your own life? How might you open yourself up to this experience?

Today's parable is unique in that it includes the first name of Lazarus. What is the importance of knowing someone by name? Within your community how might you build relationships with people in need?

CELEBRATION

Model Penitential Act

Presider: Today Jesus tells us the parable of the rich man and Lazarus. For the times we have ignored the hungry and destitute at our door, let us pause to ask for mercy and forgiveness . . . [*pause*]

Lord Jesus, you call us to love our neighbour as ourselves: Lord, have mercy.

Christ Jesus, you show us the way of light and life: Christ, have mercy.

Lord Jesus, you embody the compassion and love of God: Lord, have mercy.

Homily Points

• We can find a companion for today's gospel of the Rich Man and Lazarus in Pope Francis's apostolic exhortation, *Evangelii Gaudium*. In it, Pope Francis states, 'there is an inseparable bond between our faith and the poor' (48). Just as Pope Francis minces no words, neither does Jesus. As followers of Christ, we cannot ignore the poor on our doorstep. When we build a chasm to separate ourselves from their suffering, this chasm in turn separates us from God. In our life of faith, concern for the poor needs to be just as central as prayers before meals and Sunday Mass.

• And yet, for those of us who live in the developed world, enjoying an outsized proportion of the world's resources, concern for the poor can be easily pushed to the side. Pope Francis writes, 'Almost without being aware of it, we end up being incapable of feeling compassion at the outcry of the poor . . . the culture of prosperity deadens us' (54).

• And so, the question becomes, how do we come back alive to the needs of others? Perhaps one of the places to start is through the example of today's gospel. The poor man has a name, Lazarus. We care for people when we know them. Do you know the names of the people in need in your community, in your neighbourhood? When you visit other countries do you take the time to see the places hidden away from tourists' eyes? Let us take up Pope Francis's challenge not only to know the poor but to learn from them: 'This is why I want a Church which is poor and for the poor. They have much to teach us . . . in their difficulties they know the suffering of Christ. We need to let ourselves be evangelised by them' (198).

Model Universal Prayer (Prayer of the Faithful)

Presider: Knowing the God of infinite justice and mercy, we offer up our prayers to the Lord.

Response: Lord, hear our prayer.

That parishes and dioceses around the world use their resources to care for the poor and neglected . . .

That nations that are rich in resources generously share with those in need . . .

That all people experiencing devastating poverty might find comfort and support within their communities . . .

That all gathered here might see their brothers and sisters in need with the eyes of God and in compassion and care reach out with love and kindness . . .

Presider: God of the poor and the outcast, you sustain and care for every human life. Hear our prayers that we might reach out from our abundance to share with all those in need. We ask this through Christ our Lord. Amen.

COLLECT

Let us pray.

Pause for silent prayer

O God, who manifest your almighty power
above all by pardoning and showing mercy,
bestow, we pray, your grace abundantly
    upon us
and make those hastening to attain
    your promises
heirs to the treasures of heaven.
Through our Lord Jesus Christ, your Son,
who lives and reigns with you in the unity
    of the Holy Spirit,
one God, for ever and ever. **Amen.**

FIRST READING
Amos 6:1, 4-7

The almighty Lord says this:
  Woe to those ensconced so snugly in Zion
  and to those who feel so safe on the
      mountain of Samaria.
  Lying on ivory beds
  and sprawling on their divans,
  they dine on lambs from the flock,
  and stall-fattened veal;
  they bawl to the sound of the harp,
  they invent new instruments of music
      like David,
  they drink wine by the bowlful,
  and use the finest oil for anointing
      themselves,
  but about the ruin of Joseph they do not
      care at all.
  That is why they will be the first to
      be exiled;
  the sprawlers' revelry is over.

CATECHESIS

RESPONSORIAL PSALM
Ps 145:6-10 (2)

℞. (1b) My soul, give praise to the Lord.
or
℞. Alleluia.

It is the Lord who keeps faith for ever,
who is just to those who are oppressed.
It is he who gives bread to the hungry,
the Lord, who sets prisoners free.

℞. My soul, give praise to the Lord.
or
℞. Alleluia.

It is the Lord who gives sight to the blind,
who raises up those who are bowed down.
It is the Lord who loves the just,
the Lord, who protects the stranger.

℞. My soul, give praise to the Lord.
or
℞. Alleluia.

He upholds the widow and orphan
but thwarts the path of the wicked.
The Lord will reign for ever,
Zion's God, from age to age.

℞. My soul, give praise to the Lord.
or
℞. Alleluia.

SECOND READING
1 Tim 6:11-16

As a man dedicated to God, you must
aim to be saintly and religious, filled with
faith and love, patient and gentle. Fight
the good fight of the faith and win for
yourself the eternal life to which you were
called when you made your profession and
spoke up for the truth in front of many
witnesses. Now, before God the source of
all life and before Jesus Christ, who spoke
up as a witness for the truth in front of
Pontius Pilate, I put to you the duty of
doing all that you have been told, with no
faults or failures, until the Appearing of
our Lord Jesus Christ,

who at the due time will be revealed
by God, the blessed and only Ruler of all,
the King of kings and the Lord of lords,
who alone is immortal,
whose home is in inaccessible light,
whom no man has seen and no man is
able to see:
to him be honour and everlasting
power. Amen.

About Liturgy

Does liturgy have anything to with justice?: Today's readings are a clear reminder that the way we treat those in need will be the criterion by which we will be judged on the last day. Yet, some will still claim that the celebration of the Eucharist is disconnected from our works of justice. They will say that the Mass is their one-hour retreat from the world and its concerns. Or they will complain if the homily mentions too much of the current events and issues of the day, wondering why we have to 'politicize' the Mass.

Our Christian faith is certainly not partisan in its politics, but it *is* political in that the gospel critiques the *polis*, that is, the structures we uphold in our society. So much Scripture focuses not on spiritual, mystical realms but on the concrete ways we operate as a society and use our resources in this world for the good of those who are poor.

We cannot separate praising God and doing justice. We praise God *by* doing justice: 'Go in peace, glorifying the Lord by your life'. We do justice *by* praising God: 'Lift up your hearts. . . . It is right and just'. On this Sunday, let us remember the words of St. John Paul II and of the Catechism:

'We cannot delude ourselves: by our mutual love and, in particular, by our concern for those in need we will be recognised as true followers of Christ. This will be the criterion by which the authenticity of our Eucharistic celebrations is judged (*Mane Nobiscum Domine* 28).

'The Eucharist commits us to the poor. To receive in truth the Body and Blood of Christ given up for us, we must recognise Christ in the poorest, his brethren' (*Catechism of the Catholic Church* 1397).

About Liturgical Music

Song of Farewell and **In paradisum***:* The final commendation of a funeral is the ritual in which the gathered assembly says its final farewell before the body is brought to the place for burial or cremation. In the final commendation, there are two important musical rituals that connect to today's gospel reading.

The first significant musical moment is singing the Song of Farewell. One option for this song includes the line, 'May angels lead you to the bosom of Abraham', quoting directly from verse 22 of today's Gospel of Luke.

The Song of Farewell is a stand-alone ritual, meaning that the singing itself, like the Gloria, is the primary liturgical action and does not accompany any other ritual action, although there is the option that the body to be sprinkled with holy water and incensed during the song. The Order of Christian Funerals calls this song, 'the climax of the rite of final commendation' (156). Therefore, it should be sung by the entire assembly.

The second significant musical moment comes at the procession to the place of committal. Although the funeral rite allows for any suitable song, the traditional Latin text that accompanies this procession is the *In paradisum*. One of the short refrains based on this antiphon found in the Order of Christian Funerals is: 'May choirs of angels welcome you / and lead you to the bosom of Abraham; / and where Lazarus is poor no longer / may you find eternal rest' (187B).

As we recall Lazarus and the rich man today, let us also remember that at the end of our lives as Christians, we hope that our compassion for those in need in this life will make us worthy to be with Lazarus at Abraham's side.

SPIRITUALITY

GOSPEL ACCLAMATION
1 Pet 1:25

℟. Alleluia, alleluia.
The word of the Lord remains for ever:
What is this word?
It is the Good News that has been brought to you.
℟. Alleluia, alleluia.

Gospel

Luke 17:5-10

The apostles said to the Lord, 'Increase our faith.' The Lord replied, 'Were your faith the size of a mustard seed you could say to this mulberry tree, "Be uprooted and planted in the sea," and it would obey you.

'Which of you, with a servant ploughing or minding sheep, would say to him when he returned from the fields, "Come and have your meal immediately"? Would he not be more likely to say, "Get my supper laid; make yourself tidy and wait on me while I eat and drink. You can eat and drink yourself afterwards"? Must he be grateful to the servant for doing what he was told? So with you: when you have done all you have been told to do, say, "We are merely servants: we have done no more than our duty."'

Reflecting on the Gospel

Philosophers and thinkers debate the meaning of justice and charity. Justice is often considered the doing or giving what is owed to another, for example, money, labour, or some other arrangement. On the other hand, charity is the gift one gives expecting nothing in return. A philosophical parlour game centres around the definition of charity. Can an act be considered charity if the doer expects a thank you? Or does the expectation of an expression of gratitude annul the act of charity, which is given expecting *nothing* in return?

The disciples have a simple request of Jesus today: 'Increase our faith'. How many of us have made the same request? But what did the disciples mean by it? And what would we mean by it? Further, what is the point of the request?

In another example of hyperbole, Jesus responds by saying that if their faith was the size of a mustard seed (about the size of a sesame seed) they would be able to move trees. Now, nobody, not even Jesus, moved trees. Significantly, there are other gospels where the claim is that they could with faith the size of a mustard seed move *mountains* (Mark 11:23; Matt 17:20). But apparently Luke thought that was hyperbole taken too far. For in this gospel the extent of faith is moving only trees. Mountains are not mentioned. Nevertheless, the point is simply that they have little faith, not even that the size of a mustard seed.

Jesus continues his lesson with a demonstration of the proper attitude of a servant who does what he is told expecting nothing, not even gratitude, in return. That attitude, striking for us today, is proper for discipleship.

So the disciples' query about increasing their faith brings a mild rebuke from Jesus, stating that their faith is smaller than the size of a mustard seed. Even so, they should simply carry out their mission without expecting even a thank you.

This 'tough love' approach to discipleship may seem at odds with the Jesus that has been portrayed in much of the gospel. It's as though he is sure to put the disciples in their place so they turn their attention away from their own wants, desires, and requests, and on to carrying out the mission of Jesus. This is the true call of discipleship, to serve the master rather than oneself. And upon offering and completing that service, to have no expectations at all, not even a thank you.

This is a tall order. How many of us, upon performing an act of kindness, no matter how small, appreciate a word of gratitude. In fact, many of us likely expect that. But the story we have today presents a different standard. It would be good for us to reevaluate our role in this relationship. We are mere servants, carrying out the wishes of the Lord. When complete, we are happy simply to have done his bidding.

Living the Paschal Mystery

Today's gospel reminds us of the place disciples have before the Lord. Jesus uses an image from the ancient world about servants and a master. Such an image can be problematic today, but it reflects the worldview of antiquity. We, as disciples, are advised to do what we are told, follow directions, and carry out what we are obliged to do. Such an image does not leave much room for self-agency, or self-determination, other than to align oneself with the Lord. And this is why the image has some challenges as we bring it to the modern world. And yet, doing the will of the Father is precisely the role of the disciple, the follower. Our task is to discern that will in our world and to carry it out, expecting nothing in return. We die to our own wants, needs, and desires, noble as they might be, such as an increase in faith. Instead, we follow the direction set for us, using our gifts, talents, and abilities in such a way that there is not even the expectation of a thank you.

Focusing the Gospel
Key words and phrases: Increase our faith.

To the point: What is faith? The Letter to the Hebrews defines it as, 'the realisation of what is hoped for and evidence of things not seen' (11:1; NABRE). The disciples continue to follow Jesus on the road to Jerusalem, the path that will end in his death and resurrection. We might wonder what are the disciples hoping for at this moment when they ask Jesus, 'Increase our faith'? Do they harbour a desire for Jesus to be the kind of Messiah who will lead them in a military revolt that will free Israel from the oppression of the Romans? Are they expecting a triumphant continuation of Jesus's life and ministry that might include earthly power and authority? Jesus has already chided the disciples once, calling them, 'you of little faith' (Luke 12:28; NABRE). Their request for Jesus to increase their faith seems reasonable. Perhaps Jesus's abrupt response points to the disciples' need to reevaluate what they are hoping for.

Connecting the Gospel
to the first reading: The book of Habakkuk contains a dialogue between God and the prophet. The prophet, frustrated with violence and injustice, cries out to God in reproach, 'How long, Lord, am I to cry for help / while you will not listen'. God responds with reassurance, urging patience and trust in God's help, 'if it comes slowly, wait, / for come it will, without fail'.

to experience: Faith requires perseverance, especially in times of distress and suffering. In these moments, we believe in the God of justice who does not will that which is evil, but continues to work for the good of all.

Connecting the Responsorial Psalm
to the readings: Today's gospel, and the gospels of the following two Sundays all touch on the concept of faith. While the disciples' request for the Lord to increase their faith meets with a harsh response, next Sunday the leper who returns to thank Jesus will have his faith upheld as the reason for his salvation. Jesus also praises the faith of the persistent widow in the gospel the week following. In Psalm 94 we are given a metaphor for faith, '[F]or he is our God and we / the people who belong to his pasture, / the flock that is led by his hand'. Sheep are known for their complete and total trust in their shepherd.

to psalmist preparation: Sheep follow their shepherd because they know him or her. While their sight and depth perception is a bit limited, sheep have excellent hearing and the sound of their voice is the primary way they recognise their shepherd. A stranger using the same words or sounds will not be able to effectively call a herd of sheep, only their shepherd's voice will be successful. How do you hone your ear to be attentive to the voice of the Lord?

PROMPTS FOR FAITH-SHARING

The prophet Habakkuk, living in a time of violence and injustice, cries out to God, 'How long, Lord, am I to cry for help / while you will not listen'. In the world today, what are the dire situations that cause you to cry out to God?

In Psalm 94 we are given the image of our relationship with God as that of a shepherd and sheep. Sheep recognise and follow their shepherd by listening to his or her voice. How do you cultivate deep listening to the voice of the Good Shepherd?

St. Paul urges Timothy, '[F]an into a flame the gift that God gave you when I laid my hands on you'. What are the spiritual practices that help you to keep the flame of faith alive?

The disciples implore Jesus, 'Increase our faith'. If faith is 'the realisation of what is hoped for and evidence of things not seen' (Heb 11:1), what is it that you are hoping for? What unseen realities are you convinced of being true?

CELEBRATION

Model Penitential Act

Presider: In today's gospel the disciples come to Jesus with a request, 'Increase our faith'. Let us echo this prayer of the disciples as we pause to remember the times our faith has failed us . . . [*pause*]

Lord Jesus, you are the Son of God: Lord, have mercy.

Christ Jesus, you show us the way of service and humility: Christ, have mercy.

Lord Jesus, you have given us your Spirit of love, power, and self-control: Lord, have mercy.

Homily Points

• In today's second reading Paul exhorts Timothy, '[F]an into a flame the gift that God gave you when I laid my hands on you'. Another biblical translation renders this verse, 'Rekindle the gift of God within you'. Paul reminds Timothy of who he is called to be, a disciple filled with the powerful spirit of love and self-control, one who testifies to Jesus, the Son of God, and who is ready to bear his share of hardship for the gospel. And how will Timothy become this? He must enkindle or stir into flame the gift of God within.

• Fires need constant tending: the coals must be stirred when the flames die out, new wood must be placed in a way that allows air to pass through, and sometimes our very own breath is required to urge a reluctant fire to spring to life. And so it is with the gift of God within. This flame must be stirred, nurtured, protected from rain and draughts, and also relished and enjoyed. The gift of God within, the spirit of power, love, and self-control animates our living to allow us to be a place of welcome, safety, and warmth for others.

• There are times that it might seem like the flame has gone out, when we are tired, grief-stricken, lost, and confused. In those times, maybe we can think of God blowing on the coals to bring the flame to life again, just as God blew life into the lungs of Adam. As Paul reminds Timothy, may we also remember who we are called to be – flames of God's love bringing light and warmth to the world.

Model Universal Prayer (Prayer of the Faithful)

Presider: With faith in the infinite mercy and complete justice of our God we lift up our prayers.

Response: Lord, hear our prayer.

That the church might remain faithful to the will of God in the spirit of the humble and unworthy servant . . .

That leaders of the world come together to remedy injustices and work for peace . . .

That those suffering from a crisis of faith come to know and trust in the voice of the Good Shepherd . . .

That all gathered here might rekindle the flame of faith in order to live our lives with courage and love . . .

Presider: Faithful God, in you we live and move and have our being. Hear our prayers that with increased faith we might humbly serve you and our neighbour. We ask this through Jesus our Lord. Amen.

COLLECT

Let us pray.

Pause for silent prayer

Almighty ever-living God,
who in the abundance of your kindness
surpass the merits and the desires of those
    who entreat you,
pour out your mercy upon us
to pardon what conscience dreads
and to give what prayer does not dare
    to ask.
Through our Lord Jesus Christ, your Son,
who lives and reigns with you in the unity
    of the Holy Spirit,
one God, for ever and ever. **Amen.**

FIRST READING
Hab 1:2-3; 2:2-4

How long, Lord, am I to cry for help
while you will not listen;
to cry 'Oppression!' in your ear
and you will not save?
Why do you set injustice before me,
why do you look on where there is
    tyranny?
Outrage and violence, this is all I see,
all is contention, and discord flourishes.
Then the Lord answered and said,
    'Write the vision down,
    inscribe it on tablets
    to be easily read,
    since this vision is for its own time only:
    eager for its own fulfilment, it does not
        deceive;
    if it comes slowly, wait,
    for come it will, without fail.
    See how he flags, he whose soul is not
        at rights,
    but the upright man will live by his
        faithfulness.'

RESPONSORIAL PSALM
Ps 94:1-2, 6-9 (8)

R℣. O that today you would listen to
his voice!
Harden not your hearts.

Come, ring out our joy to the Lord;
hail the rock who saves us.
Let us come before him, giving thanks,
with songs let us hail the Lord.

R℣. O that today you would listen to
his voice!
Harden not your hearts.

Come in; let us bow and bend low;
let us kneel before the God who made us
for he is our God and we
the people who belong to his pasture,
the flock that is led by his hand.

R℣. O that today you would listen to
his voice!
Harden not your hearts.

O that today you would listen to his voice!
'Harden not your hearts as at Meribah,
as on that day at Massah in the desert
when your fathers put me to the test;.
when they tried me, though they saw
my work.'

R℣. O that today you would listen to
his voice!
Harden not your hearts.

SECOND READING
2 Tim 1:6-8, 13-14

I am reminding you to fan into a flame
the gift that God gave you when I laid my
hands on you. God's gift was not a spirit
of timidity, but the Spirit of power, and
love, and self-control. So you are never to
be ashamed of witnessing to the Lord, or
ashamed of me for being his prisoner; but
with me, bear the hardships for the sake
of the Good News, relying on the power
of God.

Keep as your pattern the sound
teaching you have heard from me, in the
faith and love that are in Christ Jesus. You
have been trusted to look after something
precious; guard it with the help of the
Holy Spirit who lives in us.

About Liturgy

Commissioning liturgical ministers: We live as disciples not for recognition but simply because it is what our faith in Christ demands. The gift of faith is all we need in order to accomplish what we are obliged to do as followers of Christ. It does not mean discipleship will be easy; it simply means that we are not alone. We have the Word to guide us, the sacraments to nourish us, and one another to be companions in service.

Today may be an appropriate day to acknowledge, bless, and commission liturgical ministers who have been preparing for service to the worshipping assembly. The Book of Blessings has a rite in chapter 61 for blessing readers (lectors), and in chapter 62, a rite for blessing altar servers, sacristans, musicians, and ushers. The structure of these blessings is quite simple. After the homily, suggested intercessions are incorporated into the usual intercessions of the Mass. In place of the concluding prayer of the intercessions, the pastor or another priest (or a deacon outside of Mass) prays the blessing over the liturgical ministers. The texts for these prayers are different enough that the blessing of readers should take place at a separate liturgy from the blessing of the other ministers.

Extraordinary ministers of Holy Communion have a completely different and more complex ritual for their blessing. Those who serve in this ministry must be authorised and commissioned by the local bishop or his delegate, who is usually the parish pastor, since the bishop must give faculties to extraordinary ministers in order to assist the church's ordinary ministers of Communion, that is, priests, deacons, and instituted acolytes.

After the homily, the candidates for this ministry are presented to the assembly. The pastor questions them regarding their resolve to undertake the duties of this office. Next, all stand as the pastor prays the blessing over the candidates. The ritual ends with the intercessions and a concluding prayer. At the preparation of gifts, the newly commissioned extraordinary ministers bring forward the bread and wine.

About Liturgical Music

Applause at the end of Mass: Often, the assembly is so moved by a Mass that they applaud at the end of the closing song, or, perhaps, after a particularly inspiring homily or other piece of music. Although we don't want to encourage adulation of anyone other than God, we can understand how the Holy Spirit can move hearts so deeply that we naturally want to express our thanksgiving and gratitude. In Western culture, we often show this through applause.

We can never anticipate when the Spirit will touch people's hearts deeply, and we certainly don't want to stifle the movement of the Spirit. In those moments of true communal praise for the work of the Spirit in the liturgy, we can let our thanksgiving rise in whatever way is natural for the assembly to express it.

Where this response can become problematic is when the assembly applauds at the end of Mass out of habit, regardless of how moving the liturgy was. In this case, your pastoral staff might discern how to address this with some gentle catechesis. The goal is not to chastise but to help parishioners understand that the work of the liturgy is a common work shared by all the members of the assembly.

When the assembly applauds at the end of Mass, one nonverbal way music ministers can help with catechesis is simply to applaud the assembly right back, clearly indicating that the gratitude is shared by all and is rightly credited to the goodness of God at work in the assembly.

SPIRITUALITY

GOSPEL ACCLAMATION
1 Thess 5:18

R̶̷. Alleluia, alleluia.
For all things give thanks,
because this is what God expects you to do in
        Jesus Christ.
R̶̷. Alleluia, alleluia.

Gospel

Luke 17:11-19

On the way to Jerusalem Jesus travelled along the border between Samaria and Galilee. As he entered one of the villages, ten lepers came to meet him. They stood some way off and called to him, 'Jesus! Master! Take pity on us.' When he saw them he said, 'Go and show yourselves to the priests.' Now as they were going away they were cleansed. Finding himself cured, one of them turned back praising God at the top of his voice and threw himself at the feet of Jesus and thanked him. The man was a Samaritan. This made Jesus say, 'Were not all ten made clean? The other nine, where are they? It seems that no one has come back to give praise to God, except this foreigner.' And he said to the man, 'Stand up and go on your way. Your faith has saved you.'

Reflecting on the Gospel

Expressing gratitude is essential for positive, healthy relationships. Many of the Psalms are prayers of gratitude. And of course the word 'Eucharist' means 'thanksgiving', essentially giving gratitude. A pithy rhyme sums it up best in exhorting us to cultivate an 'attitude of gratitude'.

Today Luke reminds us that Jesus is continuing his long journey to Jerusalem, now through Samaria and Galilee. We recall that Jesus is a Galilean for whom the Samaritans were considered foreigners. The most famous Samaritan is probably the character in one of Jesus's parables known as the Good Samaritan, who offers care and comfort to the man left for dead in the ditch. That such mercy and kindness were performed by a foreigner rather than a priest or Levite would have been shocking. Today we have not a fictional Samaritan but a Samaritan leper who interacted with Jesus, along with nine other lepers.

Of course, the challenge is that the Samaritan was the only one of the ten who, upon being healed, went back to thank Jesus. Jesus himself seems to be surprised that no one but the foreigner, the Samaritan, expressed gratitude. Even Jesus could be surprised. And even Jesus appreciated a word of thanks.

Then, the Samaritan is sent on his way with the knowledge that his faith saved him.

Among many lessons we learn in this short story is the power and importance of saying thank you, as well as the fact that salvation is extended even to the foreigner. We try to instil an 'attitude of gratitude' in children, when we teach them to write thank-you notes after birthday parties, graduations, and even weddings. The lack of a thank you says much about the one who received the gift.

An expression of gratitude comes from a place in the heart that recognises the kindness done for another and acknowledges it, not because it's required, but because it is an authentic expression of someone's thoughts and feelings. Though we instil this lesson in children, we hope it becomes internalised by the time they grow to adulthood. When it's not internalised it can be a bit surprising, as Jesus himself expresses: 'Were not all ten made clean? The other nine, where are they?'

Today let's make a point to express thanks to someone, cultivating an 'attitude of gratitude'.

Living the Paschal Mystery

Saying thank you is much more than polite manners. When we express thanks we are forging and strengthening personal bonds. Whether it be a phone call, a handwritten note, or even a text, acknowledging an action or gift with a word of thanks does as much if not more for the receiver of the gift as the giver. There are so many occasions in our daily life to express gratitude that it can become something of a prayer, punctuating our day. Our ancient forebears in faith knew this quite well. The Psalms give voice to much of this attitude, as does the eucharistic prayer itself, 'Let us give thanks to the Lord our God'.

This week, let's consider the opportunities we have to say thank you. In so doing, we echo our forebears in faith and our eternal Eucharist; and we likewise spread gratitude throughout the world.

Focusing the Gospel

Key words and phrases: Jesus! Master!

To the point: On the road to Jerusalem, Jesus meets ten lepers who call out to him, 'Jesus! Master'! At the time of Jesus, people afflicted with skin diseases were quarantined from others to ensure that their disease would not spread. While keeping their distance the lepers attract Jesus's attention with their shouts. They call him, 'Master!' Jesus's reputation as a healer must have preceded him. These lepers recognise Jesus's mastery over disease, which flees at the touch of his hand or even at a word from his mouth. In this healing, Jesus does more than restore the lepers' bodies to health, he also restores them back to their families, friends, and communities, whom they may now approach, touch, and share life with again.

Connecting the Gospel

to the first and second readings: In today's readings we have two healings from leprosy. The prophet Elisha heals Namaan the Aramean in the first reading. In the gospel, Jesus restores ten lepers to health, but only one, a Samaritan, returns to express gratitude and to glorify God. In both instances the one who is 'other' and foreign is held to us as an example of faith. In his second letter to Timothy, St. Paul alludes to his imprisonment by saying, 'I have my own hardships to bear, even to being chained like a criminal'. He continues, 'but they cannot chain up God's news'. We witness the freedom of the word of God – spoken by Elisha, enfleshed in Jesus – in the first reading and the gospel.

to experience: God's abounding kindness cannot be controlled. At times, we may be tempted to define who is inside or outside of the kingdom of God, but this is not our place. God's unchained word offers healing and wholeness to all.

Connecting the Responsorial Psalm

to the readings: The opening phrase of Psalm 97 expresses the joy of Namaan and the Samaritan leper freed from their illnesses, 'Sing a new song to the Lord / for he has worked wonders'. For both of these men, their skin diseases defined their lives for a time. Now that they have been 'made clean' a new life can begin and, not only a new life of health, but also a new life in covenant with the God of Israel, the God of Jesus.

to psalmist preparation: We believe in and proclaim a God who is always ready to heal, forgive, and redeem. When we experience this healing and redemption in our own lives we are thrust into a new way of being, which requires new behaviours from us. To sing 'a new song' to the Lord we must step out from what is familiar into a new creativity in our relationship with God. Where is God calling you to newness of life?

PROMPTS FOR FAITH-SHARING

Today's psalm enjoins us to '[s]ing a new song to the Lord'. If you were to choose one song that symbolises your spiritual journey at this point in your life, what would it be?

Speaking from prison St. Paul tells Timothy, '[T]hey cannot chain up God's news'. How have you experienced the word of God, alive and free, in your life? How do you bring this word to others?

In today's gospel one of the ten lepers returns to 'give praise to God' for being healed. How do you give thanks to God for blessings received?

How do you practise an 'attitude of gratitude' in your daily life?

CELEBRATION

Model Penitential Act

Presider: In today's gospel ten lepers cry out to Jesus, 'Jesus! Master! Take pity on us'. Let us pause for a moment to bring our own brokenness before the Lord and to ask for mercy and healing . . . [*pause*]

>   Lord Jesus, you restore the sick to health and the broken to wholeness: Lord, have mercy.

>   Christ Jesus, you are the Word of God unchained: Christ, have mercy.

>   Lord Jesus, your faithfulness extends to every generation: Lord, have mercy.

Homily Points

• In the opening chapters of the Gospel of Luke we are told again and again that this child that is being born is a gift for the entire world, not just for one particular family, religion, or nation. The angel proclaims to the shepherds in the fields of Bethlehem, 'I proclaim to you good news of great joy that will be for all the people' (2:10; NABRE). In the temple Simeon prophesies that this child is 'a light for revelation to the Gentiles, / and glory for your people Israel' (2:32; NABRE). This is not a new theme for the people of Israel. Today's psalm speaks of 'the ends of the earth' seeing 'the salvation of our God', and in the first reading Namaan the Aramean is healed of leprosy and vows to 'no longer offer holocaust or sacrifice to any god except the Lord'.

• In the gospel, it is the Samaritan among the ten lepers who returns to give thanks and glory to God. Jesus continually stretches his followers' understanding of who is included within the kingdom of God. He eats with sinners and tax collectors. He heals the daughter of the Syrophoenician woman and the servant of the Roman centurion. He upholds a Samaritan as the hero within a parable about how to love our neighbours, and today he tells the man who returns to give thanks, 'Your faith has saved you'.

• In our lives of faith, how do we interact with people of differing nationalities, races, and religious beliefs? In the Second Vatican Council document, *Nostra Aetate*, we hear, 'The Catholic Church rejects nothing of what is true and holy' in other religions. Can we look with the eyes of Christ and recognise the holy and the true in those who are different from us? Jesus certainly does.

Model Universal Prayer (Prayer of the Faithful)

Presider: With hearts full of thanksgiving we bring our prayers before the Lord.

Response: Lord, hear our prayer.

That the church throughout the world might continually offer praise and thanksgiving to God, the giver of all good gifts . . .

That leaders of the world extend welcome to refugees, immigrants, and visitors from foreign lands . . .

That those who are isolated from family, friends, and community due to illness or disease be surrounded by care and compassion . . .

That all gathered here might bring our brokenness to the Lord and experience healing and mercy . . .

Presider: God of healing, you desire for each of your children to have fulness of life. Hear our prayers that we might be signs of your love and compassion to all people. We ask this through Jesus, our Lord. Amen.

COLLECT

Let us pray.

Pause for silent prayer

May your grace, O Lord, we pray,
at all times go before us and follow after
and make us always determined
to carry out good works.
Through our Lord Jesus Christ, your Son,
who lives and reigns with you in the unity
        of the Holy Spirit,
one God, for ever and ever. **Amen.**

FIRST READING
2 Kgs 5:14-17

Naaman the leper went down and immersed himself seven times in the Jordan, as Elisha had told him to do. And his flesh became clean once more like the flesh of a little child.

Returning to Elisha with his whole escort, he went in and stood before him. 'Now I know' he said 'that there is no God in all the earth except in Israel. Now, please, accept a present from your servant.' But Elisha replied, 'As the Lord lives, whom I serve, I will accept nothing.' Naaman pressed him to accept, but he refused. Then Naaman said, 'Since your answer is "No," allow your servant to be given as much earth as two mules may carry, because your servant will no longer offer holocaust or sacrifice to any god except the Lord.'

RESPONSORIAL PSALM

Ps 97:1-4 (Cf. 2)

R̃. The Lord has shown his salvation to
the nations.

Sing a new song to the Lord
for he has worked wonders.
His right hand and his holy arm
have brought salvation.

R̃. The Lord has shown his salvation to
the nations.

The Lord has made known his salvation;
has shown his justice to the nations.
He has remembered his truth and love
for the house of Israel.

R̃. The Lord has shown his salvation to
the nations.

All the ends of the earth have seen
the salvation of our God.
Shout to the Lord all the earth,
ring out your joy.

R̃. The Lord has shown his salvation to
the nations.

SECOND READING

2 Tim 2:8-13

Remember the Good News that I carry,
'Jesus Christ risen from the dead, sprung
from the race of David'; it is on account
of this that I have my own hardships to
bear, even to being chained like a criminal
– but they cannot chain up God's news. So
I bear it all for the sake of those who are
chosen, so that in the end they may have
the salvation that is in Christ Jesus and the
eternal glory that comes with it.

Here is a saying that you can rely on:

If we have died with him, then we shall
live with him.
If we hold firm, then we shall reign
with him.
If we disown him, then he will
disown us.
We may be unfaithful, but he is always
faithful,
for he cannot disown his own self.

About Liturgy

Pastoral care of the sick: Today's readings about the miraculous curing of those
who are sick can be a good opportunity for the homilist to reflect on the mystery of
illness and healing. If appropriate and the assembly has been prepared for it, you might
also consider celebrating the sacrament of anointing of the sick within the Mass today.

In all of the prayers and liturgical texts concerning the pastoral care of the sick, the
church stresses the importance of those who suffer from illness. Unlike our society that
measures the worth of a person by their power or by what they can achieve, those who
are sick, by their very weakness, are visible signs of the mystery of Christ's suffering
and resurrection. In their very bodies, they carry both the wounds of Christ and the
promise of salvation.

As we pray for the sick and for their recovery, we understand that the Christian
approach to healing is not primarily about bodily restoration – although that is always
our hope. The healing that Christ gives is a restoration of the one who is sick back
into the assembly of the faithful. Illness, no matter how minor, isolates us in some
way from our family, friends, and the community. We are unable to do the things we
normally do when we are well. Especially when we are very sick, we cannot join with
the assembly to give thanks in the celebration of the Eucharist.

When the church remembers the sick, and especially when it gathers with them in
prayer, the sick are spiritually reconnected to the assembly. When they are gathered
in the midst of the assembly, their very presence gives praise to God even before their
bodies are healed. For Christians, the very purpose of healing – whether or not the
body recovers – is always thanksgiving to God, for that is the primary work of the
body of Christ.

About Initiation

Eucharistic prayer: Unlike catechumens, baptised candidates preparing for
confirmation and Eucharist or for reception into the communion of the Catholic
Church stay for the entire Mass, even though they cannot yet share in Communion. By
their baptism, they are members of the order of the faithful. This means, they have the
right and duty to pray the prayers of the faithful, which are the Creed, the universal
prayer (general intercessions), and the eucharistic prayer. In response to the gift of
their baptism, they, with all the baptised, are called to offer with Christ their sacrifice
of praise and thanksgiving. The eucharistic prayer, embodied by a life of sacrifice, is
the premier way all the baptised offer their thanksgiving to God.

About Liturgical Music

Song of praise: One of the most misunderstood moments in the Mass is the time
after Communion. The General Instruction of the Roman Missal says that when the
distribution of Communion has ended, there may be silence, or 'if desired, a psalm or
other canticle of praise or a hymn may also be sung by the whole congregation' (88).

The time after Communion is not meant for a meditation song sung by a soloist or
the choir alone. It's not the time to feature a performance by the school children. If a
song is sung after Communion, it is a song praising God sung by the entire assembly
together. Having been healed by the Body and Blood of Christ, we must together give
our thanks to God for so great a gift.

SPIRITUALITY

GOSPEL ACCLAMATION
Heb 4:12

R⁷. Alleluia, alleluia.
The word of God is something alive and active;
it can judge secret emotions and thoughts.
R⁷. Alleluia, alleluia.

Gospel

Luke 18:1-8

Jesus told his disciples a parable about the need to pray continually and never lose heart. 'There was a judge in a certain town' he said 'who had neither fear of God nor respect for man. In the same town there was a widow who kept on coming to him and saying, "I want justice from you against my enemy!" For a long time he refused, but at last he said to himself, "Maybe I have neither fear of God nor respect for man, but since she keeps pestering me I must give this widow her just rights, or she will persist in coming and worry me to death."'

And the Lord said, 'You notice what the unjust judge has to say? Now will not God see justice done to his chosen who cry to him day and night even when he delays to help them? I promise you, he will see justice done to them, and done speedily. But when the Son of Man comes, will he find any faith on earth?'

Reflecting on the Gospel

'Are we there yet? Are we there yet'? Persistent questioning bordering on bothering behaviour is something with which we are all too familiar. Children have a knack for this, especially at an inquisitive age. But office drama can bring it out too, as well as adult family relationships. This is something Jesus was familiar with as well, as today's parable demonstrates.

In the parable, the judge is named 'unjust'. He is willing to (and likely has) perverted justice in cases before him, which is a clear violation of Mosaic Law. The point of naming him as an unjust judge is to make clear that his decision is for sale, whether to the widow (who likely has little money) or to her adversary. The judge is willing to make a decision in her favour simply to get rid of her, regardless of the merits of the case.

If an unjust judge is willing to do what is right simply to get rid of a persistent nag, how much more will a loving Father in heaven do what is right? This simple but profound insight forms the core of the message today.

Then, the gospel ends on a puzzling note, 'But when the Son of Man comes, will he find any faith on earth?' The story opens with the necessity to pray always, but concludes with a question about faith. It's as though the song started in a major key but ends on a minor. This is no mere 'throwaway' line, but is something significant and even vital to interpreting the parable.

Luke writes at a time when Jesus's expected return has been delayed, thus the injunction 'to pray continually and never lose heart'. Perhaps Luke himself is aware of some in his own generation who have given up on this expected return of Jesus, and gone back to a former way of life. This might be the reason, too, for the explanation of the parable on Jesus's lips: 'I promise you, he will see justice done to them, and done speedily'. The ceaseless praying is about justice, not necessarily Christ's return. And then the story ends on a wistful note, wondering whether, when the Son of Man ultimately does return, he will find faith. Or will it be that the disciples have effectively abandoned the injunction to pray always and thereby lost their faith? This question, pertinent as it was nearly two thousand years ago, is applicable still.

Living the Paschal Mystery

It can be so difficult to be patient. Lessons we learned or attempted to learn in childhood are still with us as adults. Opportunities to learn patience abound! One clever prayer, inspired by St. Francis of Assisi, reads: 'Lord, grant me patience . . . NOW'!

Early Christians, and maybe even modern, grew impatient with the delayed Parousia, the promised coming of Christ. Some Christians eventually abandoned this hope and therefore abandoned their discipleship. Luke's gospel is a reminder that disciples are 'to pray continually'. And not only that, but to do so 'and never lose heart'. That may seem like a tall order, equivalent to telling a child on a long drive to 'sit patiently; we'll be there soon enough'. Yet, that's the exhortation we receive, along with a final question wondering whether the Son of Man will find faith when he returns. This, too, in a nod to the children in the car, might be the equivalent of, 'I wonder if there will be ice cream for children who were quiet the entire way'? The issues that concerned the early church concern us. When will Jesus return? How long will this be? Is he slow to answer? The response is that we continue praying, doing justice, and God will act when he does.

Focusing the Gospel

Key words and phrases: Jesus told his disciples a parable about the need to pray continually and never lose heart.

To the point: What does it mean to pray and particularly to 'pray continually'? The widow in today's gospel continues to bring her petition to the judge, even when she has no reason to believe he will hear and answer her. Jesus presupposes that this relationship in prayer will require effort and persistence when he warns the disciples against 'los[ing] heart'. As in all relationships, sometimes communication is easy and at other times it might seem nearly impossible. In our relationship with God we are called to persevere even when it seems like our prayers are not being heard, much less answered. Unlike the widow, our Judge cares for us deeply and constantly works for our good.

Connecting the Gospel

to the first reading: In the book of Exodus Moses stands on the top of a hill with hands raised as Joshua engages the Amalekites in battle below. Throughout the day, as his arms grow weak, he is supported by Aaron and Hur. At this time in the story of the Exodus, the people have been delivered from slavery in Egypt into the freedom and desolation of the desert. Here they face new challenges. Where will they find water? What about food? In each instance God provides, first sweetening the bitter water at Marah and then providing quail and manna for the people every morning. Now the people face a new threat from the attacking Amalekites and once again they are assured that God is with them. Each answer to prayer builds up the relationship between God and God's people.

to experience: We no longer subscribe to the belief that God gives us power to vanquish our enemies in battle. Prayer is not a tool that we use to bend God's will to our own. Rather it is the other way around. Through prayer, we are changed, and change is often painful and tiring. Prayer demands spiritual perseverance. As Moses requires the support of Aaron and Hur to keep his hands upright, we also need the support of our community of faith to carry us in prayer when our strength is depleted.

Connecting the Responsorial Psalm

to the readings: There is only one reason to bring our needs, desires, and cares to the Lord in prayer: we believe in God's goodness and mercy. Indeed, the one we cry out to in prayer 'sleeps not nor slumbers', but 'will guard [our] going and coming / both now and for ever'. From our ancestors in faith like Moses, Aaron, Hur, the disciples, St. Paul, and Timothy, we can learn to walk in the way of prayerful trust.

to psalmist preparation: Today's psalm is indeed good news. Our God is faithful. His protective love surrounds us at all times. How does this knowledge of God's care for you affect your daily life? What areas of struggle is God calling you to place in his hands?

PROMPTS FOR FAITH-SHARING

Aaron and Hur hold up Moses' arms as he prays for Joshua. Who supports your prayer life?

How do you understand the line from today's psalm, 'The Lord will guard your going and coming'?

In today's second reading St. Paul urges Timothy to 'proclaim the message and, welcome or unwelcome, insist on it'. Where is God calling you to persistence right now in your spiritual life?

The gospel writer tells us the moral being illustrated in today's parable: we are to 'pray continually and never lose heart'. How do you follow Jesus's command to pray continually?

CELEBRATION

Model Penitential Act

Presider: In today's gospel Jesus calls us to persevere in prayer. Confident in God's mercy, let us lift up the broken places in our lives and ask for forgiveness and healing . . . [*pause*]

Lord Jesus, you call us to constant prayer: Lord, have mercy.

Christ Jesus, you are our help in times of trouble: Christ, have mercy.

Lord Jesus, you are the just One who will judge the living and the dead: Lord, have mercy.

Homily Points

• Some biblical scholars have viewed the second letter of St. Paul to Timothy as a farewell letter from the imprisoned apostle to his dearest and closest collaborator. In it, Paul encourages and exhorts Timothy to continue on with the mission of preaching the good news of Jesus Christ. In today's second reading Paul is clear: '[P]roclaim the message and, welcome or unwelcome, insist on it'. We see examples of this very persistence in today's first reading and gospel: Moses, with the help of Aaron and Hur, keeps his hands raised throughout the daylong battle with Amalek; the widow in Jesus's parable continues to pester the unfeeling judge to render justice for her.

• In a life of faith persistence is an important virtue to foster. Often we are called to be faithful even when we cannot see that our efforts are making any difference. We might embrace a new practice of prayer and continue on for weeks without seeing fruits in the way we interact with others or go about our day. We might take on a new ministry and devote time and energy to it only to become discouraged when it doesn't seem to be successful.

• In these times when we are tempted to give up it is helpful to 'step back and take a long view', as Bishop Ken Untener wrote in his well-known prayer inspired by Archbishop Oscar Romero. He counsels, 'We accomplish in our lifetime only a tiny fraction of the magnificent enterprise that is God's work. Nothing we do is complete, which is a way of saying that the Kingdom always lies beyond us'. Let us pray always for the persistence to continue building this magnificent kingdom, even when the reality of it lies beyond us.

Model Universal Prayer (Prayer of the Faithful)

Presider: In today's gospel Jesus tells a parable to illustrate the necessity to pray always. With persistence and faith let us bring our needs before the Lord.

Response: Lord, hear our prayer.

That the leaders of the church might dedicate themselves to constant prayer . . .

That Christians throughout the world follow the widow's example in today's parable and persist in praying for the needs of the poor and the persecuted . . .

That those who are vulnerable within society receive the support necessary to live lives of purpose and meaning . . .

That all gathered here might help each other in leading lives devoted to prayer and worship . . .

Presider: God of love, you hear the cries of your people. You know our needs before we even voice them. Hear our intercessions this day that we might never cease to come to you in prayer, knowing you hear and answer us through Jesus Christ, our Lord. Amen.

COLLECT
Let us pray.

Pause for silent prayer

Almighty ever-living God,
grant that we may always conform our
    will to yours
and serve your majesty in sincerity
    of heart.
Through our Lord Jesus Christ, your Son,
who lives and reigns with you in the unity
    of the Holy Spirit,
one God, for ever and ever. **Amen.**

FIRST READING
Exod 17:8-13

The Amalekites came and attacked Israel at Rephidim. Moses said to Joshua, 'Pick out men for yourself, and tomorrow morning march out to engage Amalek. I, meanwhile, will stand on the hilltop, the staff of God in my hand.' Joshua did as Moses told him and marched out to engage Amalek, while Moses and Aaron and Hur went up to the top of the hill. As long as Moses kept his arms raised, Israel had the advantage; when he let his arms fall, the advantage went to Amalek. But Moses's arms grew heavy, so they took a stone and put it under him and on this he sat, Aaron and Hur supporting his arms, one on one side, one on the other; and his arms remained firm till sunset. With the edge of the sword Joshua cut down Amalek and his people.

CATECHESIS

RESPONSORIAL PSALM
Ps 120 (2)

R̰. Our help is in the name of the Lord who made heaven and earth.

I lift up my eyes to the mountains:
from where shall come my help?
My help shall come from the Lord
who made heaven and earth.

R̰. Our help is in the name of the Lord who made heaven and earth.

May he never allow you to stumble!
Let him sleep not, your guard.
No, he sleeps not nor slumbers,
Israel's guard.

R̰. Our help is in the name of the Lord who made heaven and earth.

The Lord is your guard and your shade;
at your right side he stands.
By day the sun shall not smite you
nor the moon in the night.

R̰. Our help is in the name of the Lord who made heaven and earth.

The Lord will guard you from evil,
he will guard your soul.
The Lord will guard your going and
        coming
both now and for ever.

R̰. Our help is in the name of the Lord who made heaven and earth.

SECOND READING
2 Tim 3:14–4:2

You must keep to what you have been taught and know to be true; remember who your teachers were, and how, ever since you were a child, you have known the holy scriptures – from these you can learn the wisdom that leads to salvation through faith in Christ Jesus. All scripture is inspired by God and can profitably be used for teaching, for refuting error, for guiding people's lives and teaching them to be holy. This is how the man who is dedicated to God becomes fully equipped and ready for any good work.

Before God and before Christ Jesus who is to be judge of the living and dead, I put this duty to you, in the name of his Appearing and of his kingdom: proclaim the message and, welcome or unwelcome, insist on it. Refute falsehood, correct error, call to obedience – but do all with patience and with the intention of teaching.

About Liturgy

The Liturgy of the Hours: The rhythm of the church's liturgical cycle is one way we learn perseverance in prayer and how to pray always. Sunday is the heart of our week, with the Easter Triduum being the heart and highpoint of the liturgical year. This rhythm of prayer of the church is actually the constant prayer of Christ, who 'continues his priestly work through his Church. The Church, by celebrating the Eucharist and by other means, especially the celebration of the divine office, is ceaselessly engaged in praising the Lord and interceding for the salvation of the entire world' (Constitution on the Sacred Liturgy 83). The main scriptural texts for the Divine Office are the Psalms, which were also the daily prayers of Jesus himself.

The Divine Office, also called the Liturgy of the Hours, is the official daily prayer of the church. The schedule of prayer for the Liturgy of the Hours pervades the entire day and night in order to sanctify the entire day to God. However, the two principal hours are Morning and Evening Prayer. The daily Office turns on the hinges of these two liturgies (89).

In Morning Prayer, the church gives thanks to God for the rising sun symbolizing the promise of Christ's resurrection. In Evening Prayer, we place the work we have done into the merciful hands of God and give thanks for all the blessings God has done for us through the course of our day.

Although daily Mass is a venerable tradition, the practice of consecrating the day to God through the celebration of the Liturgy of the Hours deepens our encounter with Christ, with whom we sing the psalms and canticles in ceaseless praise of God's blessings.

About Initiation

How long does RCIA take?: That's a common question many seekers might have when they come to us asking for baptism, reception, or the other sacraments of initiation. We might be tempted to show them the schedule of gatherings and to ease their anxiety by promising them initiation by a specific date on the calendar. But this is a disservice not only to the process of initiation but also to the good of the seeker.

The work of initiation belongs to the Holy Spirit. And the goal of the Spirit is not a person's completion of a course of study but their complete conversion of heart to the Father through Christ. Ultimately, this is about falling in love, and how long that takes cannot be predetermined.

About Liturgical Music

Song suggestions: Today's responsorial psalm (Psalm 120) gives us an opportunity to explore various settings that could be used not only as the psalm response but also for other parts of the Mass. Two in particular could be considered.

First, *Psallite*'s 'Our Help Shall Come from the Lord' has a delightful and lilting refrain for the assembly that can be sung as a round. The verses are unmetred chant; however, the refrain alone might be very appropriate as a song of praise after Communion or even as a sending-forth song at the end of Mass leading into an instrumental improvisation.

For those who are able to sing Anglican chant with the wording of the Book of Common Prayer, the classic and beautiful setting is the one by Walford Davies (available at http://www.angelfire.com/ny3/vaguebrit/music/Psalm121.pdf).

SPIRITUALITY

GOSPEL ACCLAMATION
2 Cor 5:19

℟. Alleluia, alleluia.
God was in Christ was reconciling the world
    to himself,
and he has entrusted to us the news
    that they are reconciled.
℟. Alleluia, alleluia.

Gospel

Luke 18:9-14

Jesus spoke the following parable to some people who prided themselves on being virtuous and despised everyone else: 'Two men went up to the Temple to pray, one a Pharisee, the other a tax collector. The Pharisee stood there and said this prayer to himself, "I thank you, God, that I am not grasping, unjust, adulterous like the rest of mankind, and particularly that I am not like this tax collector here. I fast twice a week; I pay tithes on all I get." The tax collector stood some distance away, not daring even to raise his eyes to heaven; but he beat his breast and said, "God, be merciful to me, a sinner." This man, I tell you, went home again at rights with God; the other did not. For everyone who exalts himself will be humbled, but the man who humbles himself will be exalted.'

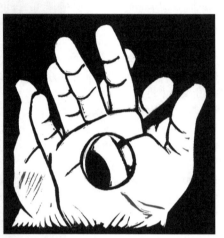

Reflecting on the Gospel

On this Thirtieth Sunday in Ordinary Time, the last Sunday of October, we come to the conclusion of the Lukan material on the journey to Jerusalem, also known as the 'major insertion' from Luke 9:51 through 18:14. We began reading from this section in June, on the Thirteenth Sunday in Ordinary Time! So we've been with Luke's special material for some time and we remain on the journey to Jerusalem with Jesus even after this week.

The parable today strikes our conscience with the desire most if not all Christians have to 'be right with God'. This desire animated the Jewish people of Jesus's time too, and it continues to be a goal of many religious people regardless of faith or denomination. But Jesus's parable penetrates deeply into the attitudes that often lie below the surface. And for the Pharisee in the parable, his attitudes were on full display. He prays in thanksgiving that he is not like 'the rest of mankind' (quite a broad stroke!) or 'like this tax collector.' The Pharisee has justified himself before God by following the rules, obeying Mosaic Law, doing 'what God wants' as he understands it. On the other hand, the tax collector approaches God with sincere humility, admitting his sinfulness. For that, he, rather than the Pharisee, is justified, or 'right with God'.

We are not the authors of our own salvation. Nothing we do or accomplish will achieve a right relationship with God other than admitting we are sinners and asking for God's mercy. A fundamental temptation for religious people the world over is to fall into the false notion that by our actions we make ourselves pleasing to God. The good deeds we do, attending Mass, keeping holy days, praying the rosary or other special prayers, being active at the parish are all well and good. But none by itself or in combination with the others will put us in a right relationship with God. Only by acknowledging our own shortfalls without excuse and by simply relying on the mercy of God will we be placed upright before God. There is a reversal at work as the concluding line of the gospel indicates: 'everyone who exalts himself will be humbled, but the man who humbles himself will be exalted'.

Living the Paschal Mystery

The Christian life and the entire paschal mystery is a reversal of the norms, standards, and structures of the world. We do not need to look far in our world to see those who seek to exalt themselves. We too are likely part of that group from time to time if we are honest with ourselves. Each of us has a bit of the Pharisee's attitude. Today's parable tells us that we are to identify with the tax collector, the one who comes humbly before God confessing himself to be a sinner. Only by humbling oneself will exaltation come. And those who seek exaltation will be humbled. This echoes a theme announced by Mary's canticle in the opening chapter of the gospel. 'He has thrown down the rulers from their thrones / but lifted up the lowly' (Luke 1:52).

Jesus, too, will be humbled to the point of death on the cross, and subsequently exalted to heaven. This fundamental reversal is an essential Christian message, and it can be difficult to absorb. In our modern world (and in the ancient) the proud are exalted, the humble are brought low. But we proclaim the Good News. The lowly will be exalted and the proud will be brought low. It is the paschal mystery.

Focusing the Gospel

Key words and phrases: God, be merciful to me, a sinner.

To the point: The words of the Pharisee and the tax collector provide an interesting contrast in prayer. The Pharisee is intent upon listing off his many attributes and even though he does this under the guise of giving God thanks for his many virtues, we get the sense that his prayer is about *him*, not about God. The tax collector's prayer is simple. He calls God 'merciful' and identifies himself as a 'sinner'. Despite his lowly standing in the religious community, this tax collector, whose job requires him to collude with the Roman oppressors, has a relationship with the living God, the Merciful One. This is what sends him home justified, while the Pharisee, too full of himself to have room for God's mercy, leaves empty.

Connecting the Gospel

to the second reading: St. Paul's words to Timothy in some ways could be likened to the prayer of the Pharisee in the gospel parable. St. Paul writes, 'I have fought the good fight to the end; I have run the race to the finish'. But whereas the Pharisee is self-satisfied and content with his own righteousness, Paul is focused on the larger picture that all might come to salvation in Jesus. He gives credit to Jesus for the strength afforded him in his ministry to the Gentiles. Paul even prays that the failure of some to stand by him when he was arrested 'not be held accountable for it'.

to experience: It is not the Pharisee's recognition of his own good works like fasting and tithing, and abstention from bad ones like greed, dishonesty, and adultery, that leads him to be the villain in this parable. Instead, it is the way his pride separates him from his fellow human being and from God that makes him the villain. Prayer should be an act of unity, not of exclusion.

Connecting the Responsorial Psalm

to the readings: The psalmist sings, 'The Lord is close to the broken-hearted; / those whose spirit is crushed he will save'. We see this illustrated in Jesus's parable. The tax collector, who knows his sin, beats his breast, and stands 'some distance away', is restored to right relationship with God. Despite this we should not whitewash the tax collector's sins. As Jewish New Testament scholar Amy-Jill Levine writes, this tax collector 'is probably rich, an agent of Rome, and, as a tax collector, has likely shown no mercy to others' (*Short Stories by Jesus*). We can assume he is in very real need of the mercy he asks for in the temple. And it is granted to him, for, as the psalmist knows, 'The Lord ransoms the souls of his servants. / Those who hide in him shall not be condemned'.

to psalmist preparation: We believe in a God of perfect justice and perfect mercy. Where in your life are you in need of God's justice? Where do you experience God's mercy?

PROMPTS FOR FAITH-SHARING

The author of Sirach tells us, 'Give to the Most High as he has given to you' (35:12; NABRE). What are the most precious gifts you have received from the Lord? How are you using these gifts to build God's kingdom?

The psalmist sings, 'The Lord is close to the broken-hearted; / those whose spirit is crushed he will save'. How have you experienced God's presence in times of extreme grief and sorrow?

Nearing the end of his letter to Timothy, St. Paul writes, 'I have fought the good fight to the end; I have run the race to the finish'. Does this metaphor of the spiritual life as a race speak to you? Why or why not?

If Jesus were to tell the parable of the Pharisee and the Tax Collector in your community, which characters would he use to illustrate his point about the humble and the proud? Who is given spiritual status in your community and who is looked down on?

Model Penitential Act

Presider: In the gospel parable of the Pharisee and the tax collector, the Pharisee is too focused on his own merits to accept God's mercy. For the times that pride has separated us from the love of God let us pause to ask for pardon and forgiveness . . . [*pause*]

Lord Jesus, you exalt the humble and humble the exalted: Lord, have mercy.

Christ Jesus, you call us to repentance: Christ, have mercy.

Lord Jesus, you redeem the souls of sinners and heal the brokenhearted: Lord, have mercy.

Homily Points

• There is a famous Zen Buddhist story about a man of import who goes to visit a spiritual master asking to be taught. The master suggests they begin by sharing a cup of tea. He fills his visitor's cup, but continues to pour even as the tea spills over the top and onto the table. When his visitor protests, the master tells him, 'You are like this cup. You are so full of your own ideas and opinions there is no room for teaching. Come back when your cup is empty'.

• And so it is with the Pharisee within our parable today. As he takes his position in the temple we are told he 'said this prayer to himself'. Even though he begins with the words, 'I thank you, God', it does seem indeed that he is mostly talking to himself. With self-satisfied contentment he lists off his own merits. The only mention of anyone other than himself is to draw a comparison between his own righteousness and the depravity of the tax collector. In the words of Jesus from Matthew's gospel, it seems that this Pharisee has already received his reward (6:1-18), the reward of feeling superior to others. The tax collector's prayer is a perfect foil for the Pharisee's bragging. His words are simple and direct, 'God, be merciful to me, a sinner'. He has a single focus on the mercy of God.

• Today's parable presents a challenge to us. Do we dare to place ourselves in the company of the tax collector, the public sinner? There is a temptation to mask our own sinfulness and to hide it under layers of propriety and self-righteousness. This is not what Jesus would have us do. He longs to be with us – wounds and warts and all. Can we empty our cups and invite him in?

Model Universal Prayer (Prayer of the Faithful)

Presider: With humble hearts let us bring our prayers before the Lord.

Response: Lord, hear our prayer.

That the church throughout the world be a sanctuary and spiritual home for repentant sinners and those in search of mercy . . .

That leaders of nations humbly seek to serve their people without care for political and personal gain . . .

That those who are nearing the end of life receive the compassionate care and spiritual support they need . . .

That all gathered here embrace a life of humble prayer and self-less service . . .

Presider: God of compassion, you are near to the brokenhearted and those whose spirits are crushed. Hear our prayers that we might bring your love to all those in need. We ask this through Jesus Christ, our Lord. Amen.

COLLECT

Let us pray.

Pause for silent prayer

Almighty ever-living God,
increase our faith, hope and charity,
and make us love what you command,
so that we may merit what you promise.
Through our Lord Jesus Christ, your Son,
who lives and reigns with you in the unity
    of the Holy Spirit,
one God, for ever and ever. **Amen.**

FIRST READING
Eccl 35:12-14, 16-19

The Lord is a judge
who is no respecter of personages.
He shows no respect of personages to the
    detriment of a poor man,
he listens to the plea of the injured party.
He does not ignore the orphan's
    supplication,
nor the widow's as she pours out her story.

The man who with his whole heart serves
    God will be accepted,
his petitions will carry to the clouds.
The humble man's prayer pierces the
    clouds,
until it arrives he is inconsolable,
nor will he desist until the Most High
    takes notice of him,
acquits the virtuous and delivers
    judgement.
And the Lord will not be slow,
nor will he be dilatory on their behalf.

RESPONSORIAL PSALM
Ps 32:2-3, 17-19, 23 (7)

R̸. This poor man called; the Lord
    heard him.

I will bless the Lord at all times,
his praise always on my lips;
in the Lord my soul shall make its boast.
The humble shall hear and be glad.

R̸. This poor man called; the Lord
    heard him.

The Lord turns his face against the wicked
to destroy their remembrance from
    the earth.
The just call and the Lord hears
and rescues them in all their distress.

R̸. This poor man called; the Lord
    heard him.

The Lord is close to the broken-hearted;
those whose spirit is crushed he will save.
The Lord ransoms the souls of
    his servants.
Those who hide in him shall not
    be condemned.

R̸. This poor man called; the Lord
    heard him.

SECOND READING
2 Tim 4:6-8, 16-18

My life is already being poured away as
a libation, and the time has come for me
to be gone. I have fought the good fight
to the end; I have run the race to the
finish; I have kept the faith; all there is to
come now is the crown of righteousness
reserved for me, which the Lord, the
righteous judge, will give to me on that
Day; and not only to me but to all those
who have longed for his Appearing.

The first time I had to present my
defence, there was not a single witness to
support me. Every one of them deserted
me – may they not be held accountable
for it. But the Lord stood by me and gave
me power, so that through me the whole
message might be proclaimed for all the
pagans to hear; and so I was rescued from
the lion's mouth. The Lord will rescue me
from all evil attempts on me, and bring me
safely to his heavenly kingdom. To him be
glory for ever and ever. Amen.

About Liturgy
That kind of liturgist: Shortly after I started my first job as a liturgist, I was
invited by one of the parish groups to give a talk on liturgy at their monthly meeting.
They wanted to begin the meeting with an adapted Morning Prayer from the Liturgy
of the Hours, which they would prepare, and asked if I would lead the singing. I was
more than happy to and looked forward to speaking with them. Fresh out of graduate
school, this would be my first chance to put my shiny new liturgy degree to work
helping people know how to do liturgy well.

The day of the talk came and I arrived early. The group leader gave me a copy of
the script for the prayer they prepared, and I was horrified! Everything was wrong.
The psalm was in the wrong place, the dialogues weren't right, and they had chosen a
gospel reading instead of one from the Old Testament or the epistles.

I couldn't have them go through with this, not on my watch! I stormed right up to the
leaders and demanded that they revise the script. They could see how upset I was and
graciously indulged me. It was a flurry of activity in the sacristy during that half hour
before prayer as they looked for a different reading and informed the nervous lector,
crossed out lines and drew arrows in the script for the presider showing the new order
of prayers, and rewrote dialogues to my satisfaction. I was pleased knowing I had saved
the liturgy that day. What would they have done if I had not corrected them?

They would have prayed just fine, in fact. The Spirit would have been just as present
and powerful without my intervention. Most importantly, they would have felt loved
and respected and not scolded like children. I would have learned humility and felt awe
and wonder at the goodness and passion of God's people. Instead, that day, I just felt
smug and loved the liturgy more than I loved the people called to do the liturgy.

It would be years later before I truly understood what I had done that day, and the
realisation gave me the gift of remorse, which has helped me try to be more humble.
Every day since I have done penance for being *that* kind of liturgist. Each day I pray,
'God, be merciful to me, a sinner'.

About Liturgical Music
Transparent ministry: Most music ministers really want to support and assist the
assembly. They get that their job is to enhance the singing and not overpower the song
of the assembly. Yet sometimes, our habits get the best of us, and our efforts actually
impede our goal. Here are some things to watch for as you strive to make yourselves
transparent and humble music ministers.

Use the microphone only when the assembly needs you to: if you're the cantor or
song leader, during songs, acclamations, and psalm refrains that the assembly knows
well, back off of the microphone. Better yet, let the assembly sing them without you.

Louder isn't always more supportive: if the assembly is tentative in their singing,
your singing or playing louder won't always help them. When cantors, choirs, and
musicians sing or play louder, especially through amplification, to try to get the
assembly singing more confidently, the assembly will often just sit back and let you do
the singing for them. When the assembly can hear themselves, then they will actually
sing better. Teach music *a cappella* and, on occasion, sing refrains or even entire songs
without accompaniment.

GOSPEL ACCLAMATION
Matt 11:28

R℣. Alleluia, alleluia!
Come to me, all of you who labour
and are overburdened,
and I will give you rest, says the Lord.
R℣. Alleluia!

Gospel

Matt 5:1-12

**Seeing the crowds, Jesus went
up the hill. There he sat down
and was joined by his disciples.
Then he began to speak. This is
what he taught them:**
    **'How happy are the poor
       in spirit;
    theirs is the kingdom
       of heaven.
**Happy the gentle:
    they shall have the earth for
       their heritage.
Happy those who mourn:
    they shall be comforted.
Happy those who hunger and thirst
       for what is right:
    they shall be satisfied.
Happy the merciful:
    they shall have mercy shown them.
Happy the pure in heart:
    they shall see God.
Happy the peacemakers:
    they shall be called sons of God.
Happy those who are persecuted in
       the cause of right:
    theirs is the kingdom of heaven.
'Happy are you when people abuse you
and persecute you and speak all kinds
of calumny against you on my account.
Rejoice and be glad, for your reward
will be great in heaven.'**

See Appendix, p. 304, for the other readings.

Reflecting on the Gospel

On this feast of All Saints the church gives us the Beatitudes of the Gospel of Matthew, sometimes called a 'self-portrait' of Jesus. We sometimes wonder what a life of Christ would look like in a different age or culture, or from different perspectives. For this we have the saints. Each saint takes as a keynote the life and mission of Jesus, then plays this song in his or her own time and place as one expression of the Christian life. St. Francis of Assisi shows how this is done in thirteenth-century Italy. St. Ignatius of Loyola shows how this is done in Reformation Spain. Mother Teresa shows how this is done in the late twentieth century. Our task is to play this song as well in our own time and place.

The gospel begins with Jesus ascending a mountain, taking his seat, and issuing these Beatitudes in a clear echo of the Sinai covenant when God himself issued the Law to Moses. It's as though Matthew is saying this teaching of Jesus is the (new) law. It enjoys pride of place.

In fact, chapters 5 through 7 are referred to as the Sermon on the Mount, opened by the Beatitudes. But it is the entire three chapters that might be considered the new 'law' for the disciples.

The nine Beatitudes that Matthew gives us are translated into English as 'Happy', but they could just as easily be translated as 'Blessed' as in 'Blessed are the poor in spirit'. These Beatitudes express a different way of approaching the world. The poor in spirit in Jesus's day were certainly not considered 'blessed' or 'happy', but for Jesus theirs was the kingdom of heaven. For Jesus, those mourning would be comforted and the meek would inherit the earth. A reversal was in order to be brought about by God himself. The kingdoms of this world do not alleviate all poverty and mourning. But God will! This doesn't mean we don't work to alleviate suffering, poverty, and the like, but it will happen once and for all with God himself as king.

The example of the saints shows us what the Christian life, the self-portrait of Jesus, looks like throughout history. We have many examples. Now let's go do this ourselves, live the Beatitudes in our time and place.

Living the Paschal Mystery

As the Beatitudes are often considered a self-portrait of Jesus, we might apply them to ourselves as disciples too. The disciples, like Jesus himself, are those who hunger and thirst for righteousness; they are merciful, clean of heart, and peacemakers. In a sense, the Beatitudes are our mission statement. Though God will bring about his kingdom in the end, that does not excuse us from doing the work of justice or bringing about peace. Paul VI showed the close link between the two when he said, 'If you want peace, work for justice' (World Day of Peace, 1972). We believe in both the 'already' and the 'not yet' of salvation. There will be a time when justice and peace rule, but we are not there yet. So we, like the many disciples and saints who have come before us, work towards it, knowing that only God can ultimately bring it about to completion.

Focusing the Gospel
Key words and phrases: Happy [Blessed]

To the point: Merriam-Webster's dictionary has two definitions for blessed. If used as an adjective 'blessed' means 'made holy, consecrated'. If used as a noun the definition is 'those who live with God in heaven'. For today's feast both definitions fit. The saints lived consecrated lives that gave glory to God. From heaven they continue to illumine the way for their fellow human beings. May we look to their blessedness as we embrace our own.

Model Rite for the Blessing and Sprinkling of Water
Presider: In the waters of Baptism we have been washed clean and sealed as Christ's own. May this water remind us of our blessedness and inspire us to follow in the footsteps of the saints . . . [*pause*]
[*continue with* The Roman Missal, *Appendix II*]

Model Universal Prayer (Prayer of the Faithful)
Presider: Together with all holy men and women throughout the ages we lift up our needs and the needs of our world to our loving God.

Response: Lord, hear our prayer.

That the church be a beacon of blessing within the darkness and chaos of the world . . .

That all people come to know the blessedness, happiness, and beauty of living a life faithful to the beatitudes . . .

That all those oppressed by grief and persecution might find hope and comfort . . .

That all gathered here, inspired by the lives of the saints, might persevere in the life of faith . . .

Presider: Holy God, throughout the ages you have called holy men, women, and children to live lives of peace, beauty, and blessing. Hear our prayers that we might answer your call to holiness within our own lives. We ask this through Christ our Lord. Amen.

About Liturgy
Saints among us: Our church walls are filled with images of the saints, and almost every parish has statues, icons, murals, banners, or windows depicting their stories. The saints are all around us! Use your parish church and the surrounding grounds to help people get to know the holy women and men of our faith.

Highlight these places with flowers, fabrics, or extra candles. Point them out in the homily, and tell the stories behind them. Focus especially on your parish's or diocese's patron saint. If your parish is preparing an altar of the dead (see 'About Liturgy' for November 2), consider also preparing an altar of the saints where parishioners can bring in holy cards, small statues, icons, or other images of their favourite saint.

Today is an appropriate day to sing the Litany of the Saints, especially as the entrance song or during the preparation of gifts. Another place to consider using the Litany is in place of the intercessions. In the appendix of the Rite of Baptism, there is a Litany of the Saints that is used for solemn intercessions. Be sure to include your parish's saint and other saints important to your local area.

COLLECT
Let us pray.

Pause for silent prayer

Almighty ever-living God,
by whose gift we venerate in one celebration
the merits of all the Saints,
bestow on us, we pray,
through the prayers of so many intercessors,
an abundance of the reconciliation with you
for which we earnestly long.
Through our Lord Jesus Christ, your Son,
who lives and reigns with you in the unity of
    the Holy Spirit,
one God, for ever and ever. **Amen.**

FOR REFLECTION
• In the second reading from the first letter of St. John we read, 'My dear people, we are already the children of God'. What implication does this have for your spirituality?

• Today we read from the Beatitudes, one of the most famous passages in all Scripture. Which Beatitude do you find most challenging? How might you seek to live this Beatitude in your own life?

• On this feast of All Saints, what saint have you found particularly inspiring in your journey of faith?

Homily Points
• The Beatitudes are often translated using the words 'blessed' or 'happy'. Dominican sister Carla Mae Streeter proposes another word we could substitute: 'beautiful'. She says, 'What moves us is the beauty of someone's life' (*Foundations of Spirituality*, 2012). This is particularly true when we look at the stories of the saints. Each contains beauty that calls to us.

• Within this beauty we see the face of God revealed in new ways. Each saint's life could be considered one facet of an infinite diamond. As we celebrate the saints we remember that this is what we are called to as well. To lead lives of beauty, happiness, blessedness and to show the face of God to all those we meet.

GOSPEL ACCLAMATION
See John 6:39

℟. Alleluia, alleluia!
It is my Father's will, says the Lord,
that I should lose nothing
of all that he has given to me,
and that I should raise it up on the last day.
℟. Alleluia!

Gospel

Luke 7:11-17

Jesus went to a town called Nain, accompanied by his disciples and a great number of people. When he was near the gate of the town it happened that a dead man was being carried out for burial, the only son of his mother, and she was a widow. And a considerable number of the townspeople were with her. When the Lord saw her he felt sorry for her. 'Do not cry,' he said. Then he went up and put his hand on the bier and the bearers stood still, and he said, 'Young man, I tell you to get up'. And the dead man sat up and began to talk, and Jesus gave him to his mother. Everyone was filled with awe and praised God saying, 'A great prophet has appeared among us; God has visited his people'. And this opinion of him spread throughout Judaea and all over the countryside.

See Appendix A., p. 305, for the other readings.

Reflecting on the Gospel

Yesterday we celebrated the feast of All Saints, those heroes of the faith who have gone before us as exemplars, and there are thousands! These are the ones who have been 'officially' proclaimed by the church as saints. But we know there are many more saints than those. Even the apostle Paul (himself a saint) addressed his letters to the 'saints' in the various locales to which he wrote. The term does not mean a 'holy roller', but instead it means one who is set apart for service to God. Those who did this exceptionally well are recognised by the church, but as noted above there are many who live lives of service to God but are not given the formal title of 'saint'.

In this latter category are likely those members of our family who have gone before us in faith: all our parents, grandparents, and even great-grandparents with all of their siblings and extended families as well may fall into this category. Christianity is a faith that is passed down through storytelling, one person telling another about what God has done in Christ. Many of these stories are in the Bible, but after two thousand years we have many more stories of heroic figures of faith to tell. And these heroes of faith extend to those we have known and loved.

One group, however, missing from the list given above of those who have died in faith, are our children. Yes, children, toddlers, even infants who never got the opportunity to experience life as we have. But God does not forget these little ones. God has compassion on them and their parents. Jesus, in his humanity, 'felt sorry' for the widow who lost her only son and in this heartfelt sorrow tells the young man, '[G]et up'. This 'get up' is the gift of new life promised to all who have died in faith. And, yes, even our children will hear these words on that last day.

On this day of commemoration of all the faithful departed, let us celebrate all those who have gone before us, never failing to share their stories which enkindle in us that Christian hope which inspires.

Living the Paschal Mystery

As the weather is turning colder and we approach the winter season, it seems an apt time to recall those who have gone before us. All lived lives of Christian hope built on the promise of Jesus to raise them up on the last day. This is our hope too, inspired by that same promise. And there will be Christians who come after us who might be remembering us too. We are in a long line of disciples who believe in Jesus, the one sent by the Father. And with that belief comes eternal life. Our own personal death is not the end, and Jesus's own death was not the end for him. Resurrection and new life await. This is not a restoration of the old, but something new and transformative when we will all be united in him, generations past and those still to come. This is the paschal mystery where dying leads to new life. One end leads to a beginning, and the tomb opens to the resurrection. At this time of year, when darkness and cold increase, our Christian hope in eternal life remains resilient.

Focusing the Gospel

Key words and phrases: When the Lord saw her he felt sorry for her.

To the point: Our gospel reading today is about the love and sympathy God has for all God's people. In it, the humanity of God is on full display. The Scriptures say God, in the person of Christ Jesus, 'saw her' and 'felt sorry for her'. Remember that God is *Emmanuel*, that is, God is with us. We serve an ever-present God, one who shares in our joy just as much as in our grief. May we rest in this knowledge that God sees us, God feels with us.

Model Penitential Act

Presider: As we gather together to commemorate the souls of all the faithful departed, let us pause to remember the times our own faith has wavered and to ask for pardon and healing . . . [*pause*]

Lord Jesus, you came to do the will of the Father: Lord, have mercy.
Christ Jesus, you welcome all who come to you: Christ, have mercy.
Lord Jesus, you are the Lord of everlasting life: Lord, have mercy.

Model Universal Prayer (Prayer of the Faithful)

Presider: United with our brothers and sisters who have fallen asleep in the hope of the resurrection, let us lift up our prayers to the Lord.

Response: Lord, hear our prayer.

That, strengthened by the faith of countless disciples throughout the ages, the church might grow in holiness and fidelity to the Lord's will . . .

That nations throughout the world be guided by the wisdom of their ancestors in caring for the earth . . .

That those grieving the loss of a loved one may be comforted by the Lord of everlasting life . . .

That all gathered here might extend the radical hospitality of Jesus to all those we meet . . .

Presider: God of eternal life, you desire to raise all souls to the abundance of heaven. Hear our prayers that we, and all people, might lead lives of holiness and peace. We ask this through Christ our Lord. Amen.

About Liturgy

Altar of the dead: On November 1st and 2nd in Mexico, families remember their beloved dead by preparing an *altarcito de los muertos* (little altar of the dead) in their households. There they place photos of their deceased loved ones and decorate the table with candles, crosses, marigolds, and other flowers. Often, they include some of their loved ones' favourite foods and drinks. They also add colourful fabrics, paper cutouts, and sugar candies in the shape of skulls and skeletons. These are not meant to be macabre images but are ways to say, 'O Death, where is your sting'? Thus, these days of *Dia de los Muertos* are joyful times for spending with family and friends, telling the stories of our loved ones, and once again making space for their memory.

Some Catholic churches help their Mexican communities continue this tradition by building *altarcitos* in a church or parish hall alcove. Throughout November, they invite parishioners to add the photos of their loved ones to the altar. Sometimes they begin and end the month with some kind of prayer at the *altarcito* in memory of the dead.

COLLECT (from the first Mass)
Let us pray.

Pause for silent prayer

Listen kindly to our prayers, O Lord, and, as our faith in your Son, raised from the dead, is deepened, so may our hope of resurrection for your departed servants also find new strength. Through our Lord Jesus Christ, your Son, who lives and reigns with you in the unity of the Holy Spirit, one God, for ever and ever. **Amen.**

FOR REFLECTION

• What is a treasured story of faith within your family?

• What cultural, family, or religious traditions shape your celebration of the feast of All Souls' Day?

• Even in the event of the death of a loved one, how do you experience the God of abundant life?

Homily Points

• Today's gospel sets the humanity of God on full display. God is not some distant, abstract idea. No, God is *Emmanuel*, God with us. God sees us. God journeys with us. Gods feels with us. These are all signs and proof of how much God *loves* us.

• On All Souls' Day we celebrate the relationship we continue to have with past generations. They form links on a chain leading back to the time of Christ, even back to the people who stood there with Christ at the city gates of Nain. These are the ones who saw God's compassion and heard God's words, saying, '[G]et up'. May we be strengthened in our journey as Christian believers, striving always to form our link on the chain of faith until we, too, hear those blessed words, '[G]et up'. Get up, rise, come into the place prepared for you for all eternity.

SPIRITUALITY

GOSPEL ACCLAMATION
John 3:16

R̸. Alleluia, alleluia.
God loved the world so much
that he gave his only Son,
so that everyone who believes in him
may have eternal life.
R̸. Alleluia, alleluia.

Gospel   Luke 19:1-10

Jesus entered Jericho and was going through the town when a man whose name was Zacchaeus made his appearance; he was one of the senior tax collectors and a wealthy man. He was anxious to see what kind of man Jesus was, but he was too short and could not see him for the crowd; so he ran ahead and climbed a sycamore tree to catch a glimpse of Jesus who was to pass that way. When Jesus reached the spot he looked up and spoke to him: 'Zacchaeus, come down. Hurry, because I must stay at your house today.' And he hurried down and welcomed him joyfully. They all complained when they saw what was happening. 'He has gone to stay at a sinner's house' they said. But Zacchaeus stood his ground and said to the Lord, 'Look, sir, I am going to give half my property to the poor, and if I have cheated anybody I will pay him back four times the amount.' And Jesus said to him, 'Today salvation has come to this house, because this man too is a son of Abraham; for the Son of Man has come to seek out and save what was lost.'

Reflecting on the Gospel

Crowds are difficult places to be for many of us, especially those of short stature! Even at relatively tame events like a city parade, the hustle and bustle and bumps and jolts can be challenging, and that's before we see anything. With our example of a parade, sometimes parents will raise children up on their shoulders to give them a better glimpse. Zacchaeus seems to have had a similar idea when he decided to climb a sycamore tree to have a better view. Though a tax collector and a very wealthy man, Jesus chose to stay with him.

What follows develops a major Lukan theme: the right use of wealth. We recall the many other stories in Luke's gospel that touch on this theme as well: the Prodigal Son, the Rich Man and Lazarus, and the Dishonest Steward, to name a few. These were parables. The story of Zacchaeus is about Jesus and his interaction with the wealthy tax collector. Interestingly, he does not tell him to sell his possessions and give them all to the poor. That commandment is reserved for only one person, a lover of money whose sole love prevented him from following Jesus (Luke 18:18-23). No, Zacchaeus does not receive that command. He tells Jesus that he will give half of his possessions to the poor. Moreover, any extortion will be paid back four times over. With that, he is right with the Lord. So the story is about the right use of wealth, in this case, up to half of his money for the poor, making amends for any unsavory activity in his business, and paying four times anything he might have extorted.

The question naturally comes to us, how do we use our wealth? How have we gained it? Are we willing to make amends if some of our resources were ill-gotten? Such amends are much more than merely paying a fine as a part of doing business. Zacchaeus offers up to four times the amount extorted if such a thing happened.

In the end, this 'sinner', for he is a tax collector, is willing to use his money rightly, and for that he has salvation. We too can examine how we use our money, resources, and wealth. Is it for the building up of other people or for our own self-hording or indulgence? Our own salvation may hang in the balance.

Living the Paschal Mystery

The right use of money has been a perennial challenge for Christians and many others. We are not in the 'rat race' to enrich ourselves but we undoubtedly want to provide for our families and give them the care and concern that leads to a healthy, productive life. Yet we hear injunctions to give to the poor, in one case to sell everything and give it to the poor! Luke's admonition in today's story is not that every Christian disciple sell everything and give it to the poor. That command was for one person, for whom wealth had become a true obstacle to following Jesus. Rather, each disciple is required to use wealth and money rightly. What that looks like will be as different as each person. But ultimately, we are not disciples of money. We are disciples of Christ. And nobody can serve two masters. Perhaps one question we might ask ourselves today is: Do we serve money, or does our money serve us? In Zacchaeus's case, his wealth served him. He was master over his wealth and was willing to give away a substantial portion. What are we willing to give away to serve the Lord. Is there anything we serve rather than him?

Focusing the Gospel

Key words and phrases: Zacchaeus . . . was anxious to see what kind of man Jesus was

To the point: In the gospel we hear that both Zacchaeus and Jesus share something in common. They are both 'seekers'. In the beginning of this gospel passage we are told that Zacchaeus is 'anxious [seeking] to see what kind of man Jesus was' and at the end Jesus discloses that he is in fact the one who has 'come to seek out and save what was lost'. To seek requires effort and an ability to be open to what one might find. Jesus and Zacchaeus are both rewarded in their seeking. Their search ends with joy and communion.

Connecting the Gospel

to the first reading: When Jesus enters Jericho his plan is to pass 'through the town'. Upon seeing Zacchaeus perched in the sycamore, however, this plan changes, and Jesus tells this man who is a wealthy, chief tax collector, '[C]ome down. Hurry, because I must stay at your house today.' The crowd surrounding Jesus is surprised and dismayed. Why would this man who has profited from his collaboration with a foreign, oppressive government be rewarded with a personal invitation from Jesus? Who is this God who seeks the lost? The author of the book of Wisdom names him the 'Ruler and Lover of souls'. This divine ruler and lover can 'loathe nothing' he has made, and 'overlook[s] sins for the sake of repentance' (NABRE).

to experience: As with the parable of the Prodigal Son we are left with the question, can we be happy at the repentance and forgiveness of a sinner? If not, we are not fit for the kingdom of God as revealed by our first reading and gospel today.

Connecting the Responsorial Psalm

to the readings: Psalm 144 is written as an acrostic, with each verse beginning with a successive letter of the Hebrew alphabet. Its theme covers the 'greatness and goodness of God'. How fitting, therefore, that it uses every letter available to praise that which is limitless and infinite. As first-century Jews, both Jesus and Zacchaeus would have grown up with the words of the psalms citing God's grandeur and mercy. While the crowd surrounding Jesus is aghast at his decision to stay with such a well-known sinner, it makes sense when we remember that this is the Lord who is 'kind and full of compassion, / slow to anger, abounding in love', who is 'faithful in all his words / and loving in all his deeds'.

to psalmist preparation: Sometimes it seems that we are at a loss for words when we think about God. This week, take some time to try and write your own acrostic of praise. Beginning with each letter of the alphabet write a statement about the God who has been with you even from your mother's womb, the one who seeks the lost, and shows sinners the way.

PROMPTS FOR FAITH-SHARING

The book of Wisdom names God the 'Ruler and Lover of souls'. Other than Father, Son, and Holy Spirit, what name for God are you most drawn to at this point in your spiritual journey?

St. Paul tells the Thessalonians, 'We pray continually that our God will make you worthy of his call, and by his power fulfil all your desires for goodness and complete all that you have been doing through faith'. How does your family and/or parish practice intercessory prayer?

In the gospel, Zacchaeus climbs a sycamore tree because he is seeking to see Jesus. What helps you to see Jesus clearly?

How would you answer the question, Do I serve money or does my money serve me?

247

CELEBRATION

Model Penitential Act

Presider: In today's gospel, Zacchaeus, a tax collector and a sinner, climbs a sycamore tree so he can see Jesus. Let us pause to prepare ourselves to encounter the Lord in Word and sacrament today . . . [*pause*]

Lord Jesus, you came to seek and save the lost: Lord, have mercy.

Christ Jesus, you are Son of Man and Son of God: Christ, have mercy.

Lord Jesus, you are trustworthy in all your words and loving in all your works: Lord, have mercy.

Homily Points

• In today's gospel you could say that there are three distinct characters: Zacchaeus, Jesus, and the crowd. Seeking to see Jesus, Zacchaeus runs ahead of the crowd to perch on the limb of a sycamore tree. Instead of a stationary group of bystanders watching Jesus make his way through the streets of Jericho, this is a mobile crowd following Jesus on his journey to Jerusalem. Even though they are walking with Jesus and surrounding him they don't seem to know who he is. But they think they know. When Jesus looks up and sees Zacchaeus perched on a limb, he stops, and calls the man by name and tells him, 'I must stay at your house today', and the crowd is outraged.

• Zacchaeus climbs down from the tree and receives Jesus with joy. But the others, the ones who have been travelling with Jesus, grumble. Somewhere along their journey they've stopped seeking to see who Jesus is, and they've started expecting him to be who they want him to be. And that isn't someone who calls sinners by name and goes to dine with them.

• This moment in Jericho with Zacchaeus and the crowd is the last occurrence in Luke's gospel before Jesus enters Jerusalem on the eve of his passion, death, and resurrection, and so the revelation he offers to Zacchaeus and the crowd is all the more striking. He tells them that 'the Son of Man has come to seek out and save what was lost'. And this is indeed good news, but only for those who are willing to identify with 'the lost'. And so today, we might ask ourselves, where do we stand? Are we most comfortable among the crowd surrounding Jesus, shrouded in our false confidence that we know the identity of the Son of Man and who he would welcome into his company? Or do we dare to go out on the limb of the sycamore tree with Zacchaeus and seek to see who Jesus really is?

Model Universal Prayer (Prayer of the Faithful)

Presider: With humble spirits and contrite hearts let us bring our prayers before the Lord.

Response: Lord, hear our prayer.

That leaders of the church seek to use resources and wealth for the good of those in need . . .

That the world be filled with the grace of God bringing all of creation to the fulfilment of God's plan of salvation . . .

That those who are weighed down by sin would come to know Jesus, the compassionate One, who came to seek the lost . . .

That all gathered here might continue to seek to see Jesus and to follow him in all we do . . .

Presider: God of creation, lover and ruler of souls, you never cease to seek the lost and sinful. Hear our prayers that we might give our burdens to you so as to live in the joy and peace of your friendship. We ask this through Jesus Christ our Lord. Amen.

COLLECT

Let us pray.

Pause for silent prayer

Almighty and merciful God,
by whose gift your faithful offer you
right and praiseworthy service,
grant, we pray,
that we may hasten without stumbling
to receive the things you have promised.
Through our Lord Jesus Christ, your Son,
who lives and reigns with you in the unity
of the Holy Spirit,
one God, for ever and ever. **Amen.**

FIRST READING

Wis 11:22–12:2

In your sight, Lord the whole world is like
a grain of dust that tips the scales,
like a drop of morning dew falling on
the ground.
Yet you are merciful to all, because you
can do all things
and overlook men's sins so that they
can repent.
Yes, you love all that exists, you hold
nothing of what you have made
in abhorrence,
for had you hated anything, you would not
have formed it.
And how, had you not willed it, could a
thing persist,
how be conserved if not called forth
by you?
You spare all things because all things are
yours, Lord, lover of life,
you whose imperishable spirit is in all.
Little by little, therefore, you correct those
who offend,
you admonish and remind them of how
they have sinned,
so that they may abstain from evil and
trust in you, Lord.

CATECHESIS

RESPONSORIAL PSALM
Ps 144:1-2, 8-11, 13-14 (Cf. 1)

R̮. I will bless your name for ever,
O God my King.

O God my King.
I will give you glory, O God my King,
I will bless your name for ever.
I will bless you day after day
and praise your name for ever.

R̮. I will bless your name for ever,
O God my King.

The Lord is kind and full of compassion,
slow to anger, abounding in love.
How good is the Lord to all,
compassionate to all his creatures.

R̮. I will bless your name for ever,
O God my King.

All your creatures shall thank you,
    O Lord,
and your friends shall repeat their
    blessing.
They shall speak of the glory of your reign
and declare your might, O God.

R̮. I will bless your name for ever,
O God my King.

The Lord is faithful in all his words
and loving in all his deeds.
The Lord supports all who fall
and raises all who are bowed down.

R̮. I will bless your name for ever,
O God my King.

SECOND READING
2 Thess 1:11–2:2

We pray continually that our God will
make you worthy of his call, and by his
power fulfil all your desires for goodness
and complete all that you have been doing
through faith; because in this way the name
of our Lord Jesus Christ will be glorified
in you and you in him, by the grace of our
God and the Lord Jesus Christ.

To turn now, brothers, to the coming
of our Lord Jesus Christ and how we
shall all be gathered round him: please
do not get excited too soon or alarmed
by any prediction or rumour or any letter
claiming to come from us, implying that
the Day of the Lord has already arrived.

About Liturgy

Your collection is an act of justice: If it is true that where your treasure lies, there also your heart will be, then how we disburse money from the weekly collection can be seen as an act of justice. We discussed the history and ritual meaning of the collection in the section on liturgy for the Eighteenth Sunday in Ordinary Time, but what might today's gospel tell us about how to use the collection to show our own conversion of heart?

Churches depend greatly on the weekly collection to cover internal costs. They need to pay just wages to its employees, take care of bills, purchase equipment and supplies, and invest in programmes that help parishioners grow in their faith.

Many churches also depend on collections to help them directly serve those in need. Daily, people come to its doors looking for food, clothing, housing, or some other assistance, and parishes have many programmes designed specifically for works of service. How can the ritual action of the collection be more clearly connected to a parish's ministry to those in need?

Some parishes have prepared a list of charitable organisations, both local and abroad, to whom they will give a percentage of each week's collection. Before the preparation of gifts begins, the presider or another commentator makes an announcement, such as, 'Ten percent of this week's collection will go to the Downtown Women's Shelter, a local organisation where abused women and their children can find a place of safety and long-term help. Thank you for your generosity'. A similar statement can be included in the bulletin and parish website.

This is not a second collection but an intentional way a parish can include monetary support for those in need into both their parish budget and ritual practice.

About Initiation

Should catechumens pay?: Should catechumens pay to go through the RCIA process, just as some parishes require registration fees for infant baptism classes? It seems completely against the intent of the church's call to evangelise to make people pay to hear and learn to follow the gospel. Therefore, there should not be fees associated with RCIA. However, part of formation for living the Christian way of life is learning to sacrifice, especially on behalf of those in need. Although catechumens are dismissed at Mass before the collection is taken up, you might consider asking them to contribute to the parish's ministry to the poor as part of their formation. They could prepare their donation ahead of time and give it to their sponsor at Mass to be placed into the collection basket for them.

About Liturgical Music

Suggestions: There aren't many songs about Zacchaeus that aren't more appropriate for a children's liturgy. But *Psallite* provides us with one beautiful setting that identifies the main point of today's gospel: today salvation has come to this house. In 'Salvation Has Come to This House', the assembly is given a stately refrain with verses that employ Psalm 16. This would be a perfect processional song for Communion.

Another appropriate *Psallite* setting for Communion is 'Listen, I stand at the door and knock'.

3 NOVEMBER 2019
**THIRTY-FIRST SUNDAY
IN ORDINARY TIME**

SPIRITUALITY

GOSPEL ACCLAMATION
Apoc 1:5, 6

R̸. Alleluia, alleluia.
Jesus Christ is the First-born from
  the dead;
to him be glory and power for ever
  and ever.
R̸. Alleluia, alleluia.

Gospel   Luke 20:27-38

Some Sadducees – those who say that there is no resurrection – approached Jesus and they put this question to him, 'Master, we have it from Moses in writing, that if a man's married brother dies childless, the man must marry the widow to raise up children for his brother. Well, then, there were seven brothers. The first, having married a wife, died childless. The second and then the third married the widow. And the same with all seven, they died leaving no children. Finally the woman herself died. Now, at the resurrection, to which of them will she be wife since she had been married to all seven?'

Jesus replied, 'The children of this world take wives and husbands, but those who are judged worthy of a place in the other world and in the resurrection from the dead do not marry because they can no longer die, for they are the same as the angels, and being children of the resurrection they are sons of God. And Moses himself implies that the dead rise again, in the passage about the bush where he calls the Lord the God of Abraham, the God of Isaac and the God of Jacob. Now he is God, not of the dead, but of the living; for to him all men are in fact alive.'

or Luke 20:27, 34-38 in Appendix A, p. 305.

Reflecting on the Gospel

Theological sophistication is on display today when Jesus responds to the derogatory question about resurrection. While Jesus is in the Jerusalem temple after making his lengthy journey, he faces a question from a powerful party of religious leaders. The Sadducees did not accept resurrection, as they focused squarely on Mosaic Law, the first five books of the Bible. And in those books the word resurrection is not mentioned. Instead, it's a term more closely associated with the book of Daniel or even 2 Maccabees, which were not accepted by the Sadducees as authoritative. So the question the Sadducees pose to Jesus is meant to illustrate how ridiculous the concept of resurrection is. This is a good reminder that not all Jews of Jesus's day had similar beliefs. There were differences in understanding and applying Jewish faith, much as there are differences among Jews today. And for that matter, there are doctrinal differences between Christians today too!

But this question allows Jesus the chance to correct their misunderstanding, using Mosaic Law, something they would have accepted as authoritative. Jesus's words indicate that there is no marriage in the afterlife, thereby undercutting the foundation of their question. His response also indicates that resurrection was not for all, but only those who are deemed worthy. This, too, reflects a common understanding at that time by those who believed in resurrection. They held that only the just were raised as a reward for their right conduct. In later centuries Christians wondered whether the unjust would be raised too, if only to be punished eternally. But that is not the question Jesus faced. For him, the question was a literal understanding of resurrection to such a degree that it involved marriage in the afterlife. Jesus continues his counterargument by citing Mosaic Law and the words of Moses, who spoke of the God of Abraham, Isaac, and Jacob, all of whom died centuries before Moses.

As God is the God of the living, Abraham, Isaac, and Jacob must be alive. This is a clever twist on a familiar passage, and it demonstrates the theological sophistication of this Jew from the backwaters of Galilee. He was in Jerusalem now, arguing with the learned in the temple. His audience was likely growing, and after this encounter so too was the opposition he faced.

Living the Paschal Mystery

Today's gospel is one of the few stories where we hear Jesus's thoughts on the question of resurrection. Of course, one of the reasons it's so interesting is that we know he will experience resurrection after a humiliating public death less than a week later. Though resurrection is a central element of Christian faith, it continues to be debated through the centuries. Even the apostle Paul had issues with preaching the resurrection, as the longest chapter in any of his letters (1 Cor 15) deals entirely with the topic, while some of the Pastoral Letters indicate that other Christians continued to misunderstand resurrection. And the Apostolic Fathers also address the issue, as do many others in every century including our own.

What do we believe about resurrection? How does this central element of our belief animate our daily life? How is our life different because of this promise? We proclaim the paschal mystery: suffering and death ultimately lead to joy and new life.

Focusing the Gospel

Key words and phrases: [H]e is God, not of the dead, but of the living; for to him all men are in fact alive.

To the point: The Sadducees pose a ridiculous scenario to Jesus in the hopes it will trip him up. But Jesus cuts through to the heart of their question about the resurrection of the dead. Do we really believe that God has authority over life and death and the ability to bring life *from* death? Jesus is about to live his certainty in the resurrection by submitting to death. He knows, as he tells the Sadducees, that God is God of the living – there is no death in him.

Connecting the Gospel

to the first reading: Jesus is not alone in believing in the resurrection of the dead. In the first reading from the second book of Maccabees we hear of the martyrdom of a mother and her seven sons. Rather than profane their ancestral beliefs, the brothers willingly submit to execution, each first stating complete trust that 'the King of the world will raise us up . . . to live again for ever'. The question of resurrection is one that divided the two main Jewish religious groups of Jesus's day, the Sadducees and the Pharisees. In his teaching and his preaching Jesus seems to offer a challenge and an invitation to everyone he meets. He calls the tax collectors to repentance, the self-righteous to humility, and the complacent to continue to delve into the mystery of God.

to experience: In a sermon St. Augustine famously said, 'We are talking about God. What wonder is it that you do not understand? If you do understand, then it is not God'. Our faith in God is not about perfect understanding or knowledge, but about radical trust in the king of the universe, the God of the living.

Connecting the Responsorial Psalm

to the readings: The first and the second readings present communities facing distress and persecution. At the time of the Maccabees, the second century BC, the Israelites were under the rule of the Seleucid Empire, whose brutal leader, Antiochus, plays a role in the torture and execution of the seven brothers and their mother from today's first reading. In his second letter to the Thessalonians, St. Paul mentions the persecutions and trials this community has undergone. He also alludes to his own safety when he asks the Thessalonians to pray 'that we may be preserved from the interference of bigoted and evil people'. Sandwiched in the middle of these two readings, today's psalm is fittingly a prayer for rescue from persecution. While the psalmist implores the Lord, 'Lord, hear a cause that is just, / pay heed to my cry', this plea is balanced by deep trust. The psalm ends, 'in my justice I shall see your face / and be filled, when I awake, with the sight of your glory'.

to psalmist preparation: When have you most needed the Lord's strength and faithfulness to continue on in the face of life's trials?

PROMPTS FOR FAITH-SHARING

The second book of Maccabees lifts up the seven sons and their mother as models of faith and trust in God's authority over life and death. Which saints have inspired you with their belief (even unto death) in God's power to bring life from death?

Psalm 16 is a prayer for deliverance from persecution. How have you experienced persecution in your life? What gave you the strength to continue on?

In the second letter to the Thessalonians St. Paul prays, 'May our Lord Jesus Christ . . . comfort you and strengthen you in everything good that you do or say'. What kind of encouragement is your heart in need of at this time?

Jesus tells us in the gospel that God is 'not of the dead, but of the living; for to him all men are in fact alive'. How do you experience this in your own life of faith?

CELEBRATION

Model Penitential Act

Presider: In today's gospel some Sadducees question Jesus about the resurrection. Jesus tells them God is 'not of the dead, but of the living; for to him all men are in fact alive'. In thanksgiving for this gift of everlasting life, let us pause to prepare ourselves to enter into these sacred mysteries . . . [*pause*]

Lord Jesus, you lay down your life to take it up again: Lord, have mercy.

Christ Jesus, you are the King of the universe: Christ, have mercy.

Lord Jesus, you strengthen and guard us: Lord, have mercy.

Homily Points

• The Sadducees and the Pharisees were the major sects in Judaism at the time of Jesus. In Luke's gospel we've heard a lot about the Pharisees and most of it hasn't been positive. They accuse Jesus of blasphemy, complain when he eats with sinners, and reproach him for breaking the law when he heals on the Sabbath. Jesus in turn paints the Pharisees as hypocrites and lovers of money. By contrast, we read about the Sadducees only once. With this inequality of attention, it may come as a surprise that the Pharisees enjoyed the support of common people, like the fishermen and townspeople that Jesus spent most of his time with, while the aristocratic Sadducees weren't very popular.

• The Sadducees don't seem to take any notice of Jesus until the very end of his life when he is in Jerusalem where they are. They begin to worry he will start a revolt against their own authority and against the Roman Empire. In the gospel passage today, the Sadducees aren't concerned about the implications of marriage and the resurrection. Their intent is to undermine Jesus's message. They want to expose the improbably absurd notion of life after death.

• But Jesus will not be deterred. Throughout his ministry Jesus calls people away from the boxes in which they have placed God. He preaches and reveals a God beyond human comprehension. In the Sadducees and the Pharisees, Jesus is talking to the religious people of his day, the ones who faithfully visited the temple and studied in the synagogue. The ones who felt they had the most claim on Judaism of the time. There is a lesson here for us. Like the Sadducees do we try to control God, or to claim that we understand who God is and what God can do? If so, Jesus tells us, 'Look again'.

Model Universal Prayer (Prayer of the Faithful)

Presider: With trust in the God of life let us offer our prayers to the Lord.

Response: Lord, hear our prayer.

That persecuted Christians throughout the world find safe harbour and be granted the grace to forgive their persecutors . . .

That leaders of nations come together to advance the right of religious freedom for all people . . .

That those who grieve might be comforted by the Lord of everlasting life . . .

That all gathered might be renewed in our commitment to follow Jesus with fidelity, trust, and joy . . .

Presider: God of abundance, you desire to gift all people with life everlasting. Hear our prayers that we might proclaim your love to all the world. We ask this through Christ our Lord. Amen.

COLLECT

Let us pray.

Pause for silent prayer

Almighty and merciful God,
graciously keep from us all adversity,
so that, unhindered in mind and body alike,
we may pursue in freedom of heart
the things that are yours.
Through our Lord Jesus Christ, your Son,
who lives and reigns with you in the unity
    of the Holy Spirit,
one God, for ever and ever. **Amen.**

FIRST READING
2 Macc 7:1-2, 9-14

There were seven brothers who were arrested with their mother. The king tried to force them to taste pig's flesh, which the Law forbids, by torturing them with whips and scourges. One of them, acting as spokesman for the others, said, 'What are you trying to find out from us? We are prepared to die rather then break the Law of our ancestors.'

With his last breath the second brother exclaimed, 'Inhuman fiend, you may discharge us from this present life, but the King of the world will raise us up, since it is for his laws that we die, to live again for ever.'

After him, they amused themselves with the third, who on being asked for his tongue promptly thrust it out and boldly held out his hands, with these honourable words, 'It was heaven that gave me these limbs; for the sake of his laws I disdain them; from him I hope to receive them again.' The king and his attendants were astounded at the young man's courage and his utter indifference to suffering.

When this one was dead they subjected the fourth to the same savage torture. When he neared his end he cried, 'Ours is the better choice, to meet death at men's hands, yet relying on God's promise that we shall be raised up by him; whereas for you there can be no resurrection, no new life.'

CATECHESIS

RESPONSORIAL PSALM

Ps 16:1, 5-6, 8, 15 (15)

R̂. I shall be filled, when I awake,
with the sight of your glory, O Lord.

Lord, hear a cause that is just,
pay heed to my cry
Turn your ear to my prayer:
no deceit is on my lips.

R̂. I shall be filled, when I awake,
with the sight of your glory, O Lord.

I kept my feet firmly in your paths;
there was no faltering in my steps.
I am here and I call, you will hear me,
    O God.
Turn your ear to me; hear my words.

R̂. I shall be filled, when I awake,
with the sight of your glory, O Lord.

Guard me as the apple of your eye.
Hide me in the shadow of your wings.
As for me, in my justice I shall see
    your face
and be filled, when I awake, with the sight
    of your glory.

R̂. I shall be filled, when I awake,
with the sight of your glory, O Lord.

SECOND READING

2 Thess 2:16–3:5

May our Lord Jesus Christ himself, and
God our Father who has given us his love
and, through his grace, such inexhaustible
comfort and such sure hope, comfort you
and strengthen you in everything good
that you do or say.

Finally, brothers, pray for us; pray that
the Lord's message may spread quickly,
and be received with honour as it was
among you; and pray that we may be
preserved from the interference of bigoted
and evil people, for faith is not given to
everyone. But the Lord is faithful, and he
will give you strength and guard you from
the evil one, and we, in the Lord, have
every confidence that you are doing and
will go on doing all that we tell you. May
the Lord turn your hearts towards the love
of God and the fortitude of Christ.

About Liturgy

Liturgical gymnastics: The hypothetical and hyperbolic situation posed by the
Sadducees in today's gospel reminds me of some people who take liturgical rubrics a
bit too far. Like the Sadducees, they focus on the letter of the law and miss the spirit of
it entirely.

We see this quite often in concerns about the Eucharist and the consecrated host
and wine. For example, in training sessions for extraordinary ministers of Holy
Communion, I often hear questions like, 'What if I drop the host'? or, 'What if the
communicant spills some of the wine'? Those who are overly focused on the letter
of the law respond with an answer that attends solely to the Body of Christ in the
eucharistic species while ignoring completely the Body of Christ in the person of
the minister or the communicant. They will give detailed instructions on how to
cleanse then purify the spot of carpet where the Precious Blood was spilled, advising
communion ministers to create some kind of barrier to ensure that people don't walk
over the spot. Or they will recommend that the communion minister pick up the fallen
host then take it directly and solemnly to the sacristy where it could be disposed of
properly, while leaving the person in the queue who dropped the host feeling guilty of
the gravest of sins.

We absolutely must take care of the sacred gifts of the Eucharist in these kinds of
situations. But the very reason we show so much reverence to the Body and Blood of
Christ is because Christ was one of us, and through the Eucharist in which we share
his Body and Blood, we become one with him. If we bend over backward to follow
the letter of the law in order to honour the Body of Christ in the Eucharist while
disregarding the spirit of the law that calls us to care for the Body of Christ in the
person before us, we have missed the point of the law altogether.

About Initiation

Marriage issues: One of the most painful aspects of the initiation process for some
can be helping catechumens and candidates understand the church's teachings on
divorce and remarriage. Especially if they may be in need of an annulment, we have
a great responsibility to inform them of the canonical requirements early on and to
assist them as much as possible in the annulment process.

Just as important is our responsibility to help catechumens and candidates know and
see the grace and dignity of the church's teaching on marriage. We cannot focus only on
the details of policy and canon law. We must first and foremost express the beauty of
what the church teaches about marriage and why it matters to us in our own faith.

About Liturgical Music

Suggestions: Many songs about resurrection and eternal life would be very
appropriate today. One song that highlights the image of God as a God of the living
and not of the dead is *Psallite*'s 'God of Life, God of Hope'. A soloist sings verses from
Psalm 104 superimposed over an *ostinato* refrain sung by the assembly. This could
work very well as a communion song.

Another song comes from the OCP collection *Search for the Lord*. Bill Tamblyn's
'God of the Living' is also available separately from Chiswick Music.

10 NOVEMBER 2019
THIRTY-SECOND SUNDAY IN ORDINARY TIME

SPIRITUALITY

GOSPEL ACCLAMATION
Luke 21:28

R7. Alleluia, alleluia.
Stand erect, hold your heads high,
because your liberation is near at hand.
R7. Alleluia, alleluia.

Gospel

Luke 21:5-19

When some were talking about the Temple, remarking how it was adorned with fine stonework and votive offerings, Jesus said, 'All these things you are staring at now – the time will come when not a single stone will be left on another: everything will be destroyed.' And they put to him this question: 'Master,' they said 'when will this happen, then, and what sign will there be that this is about to take place?'

'Take care not to be deceived,' he said 'because many will come using my name and saying, "I am he" and, "The time is near at hand." Refuse to join them. And when you hear of wars and revolutions, do not be frightened, for this is something that must happen but the end is not so soon.' Then he said to them, 'Nation will fight against nation, and kingdom against kingdom. There will be great earthquakes and plagues and famines here and there; there will be fearful sights and great signs from heaven.

Continued in Appendix A, p. 306.

Reflecting on the Gospel

The end of the world is a popular topic among some religious people. Apocalyptic doom, fire and brimstone, death and destruction are hallmarks of the violent end of this earth by these preachers. But as we can see from today's gospel, eschatological fervor has been with us from the time of Jesus and even before. In the decades after Jesus, many claimed to be the Messiah. Some even led certain Jews into rebellion against Rome. But Rome was decisive about striking back. Roman troops led by General Vespasian swept into Judea and Galilee to put down the rebellion. There was a brief pause in the action when the Roman Emperor Nero committed suicide. The year AD 69 saw four emperors, the first three of whom died by suicide or assassination. The fourth was General Vespasian himself, who upon becoming emperor empowered his son Titus as general in his place. Roman troops under his command quickly got back to work and destroyed Jerusalem and its temple.

Many Christians of the time considered these unfolding events a sure sign of the end-times. And yet Christ's return was delayed. Luke wrote his gospel in about the 80s in part to deal with dampened and disappointed apocalyptic fervor. Christians were looking for signs that the end was near, as it had seemed to be so clear. Today's gospel story is Luke's way of addressing this topic. Even though many will come claiming to be a Messiah, and there will be wars and insurrections, it will not be the end.

Perhaps the lesson in all of this is that looking for such signs, discerning the events of our day seeking clues to the end of the world is essentially misguided. After nearly two thousand years of such expectation, we are better off concerning ourselves with helping our neighbours, caring for the sick, and comforting the afflicted. There will always be nation rising against nation and kingdom against kingdom. That is unfortunately the experience of our world. The kingdoms of this age tend to promote war. But Jesus preached a kingdom of God, when God himself will rule, putting an end once and for all to unjust systems, practices, and war itself. Then we will experience an age of peace. This is good news indeed.

Living the Paschal Mystery

The *examen* is a Jesuit practice at the end of the day, when we review the day's activities discerning God's presence and looking for his direction in our lives. It can help place our emotions and experiences in a different perspective, sometimes seeing a bigger picture. Events in daily life may take on new meaning with reflection. What seemed to be a critically important encounter may not have been so critical, whereas a small gesture might become more profound upon reflection.

In today's gospel, the disciples want to know when the end of the world is coming. What signs will they be able to read to discern this important time? Jesus responds with a number of various elements that each generation since has interpreted to be fulfilled in their own time and place.

But perhaps we might experience something of the *examen* and reflect on the events in our own lives to see a bigger picture. Perhaps there is more meaning and more of God's activity in our daily coming and going than we imagine. While it could be more exciting to be on the hunt for clues to Jesus's return, in actuality, nobody knows when that will be! But God is present with us here and now, not only in the apocalyptic future. Let us discern his presence in the quotidian mystery of daily activity, the ebb and flow of our emotions, our existence, and our dying and rising to newness of life.

Focusing the Gospel

Key words and phrases: [D]o not be frightened

To the point: We began the church year with a gospel much like this one speaking of wars and calamities but with the reassurance also that 'when these signs begin to happen, stand erect and raise your heads because your redemption is at hand' (Luke 21:28; NABRE). Again, Jesus gives us comfort in the middle of prophecies of wars, insurrections, earthquakes, famines, and plagues when, in today's gospel, he tells the disciples, '[D]o not be frightened'. Although the material world may be passing away, there is a firm foundation underfoot, the compassionate care of God the Father, Son, and Holy Spirit.

Connecting the Gospel

to the first reading: The verses from Malachi in the first reading are among the last of the Old Testament canon. The book of Malachi closes out the prophetic books. Written in the dark times of destruction and exile in the history of Israel, the prophets point to the enduring faithfulness of God. Today's verses reveal God's perfect justice where evil is destroyed through purifying fire and the just are strengthened in the rays of the sun. Light is shed on both, but the results are remarkably different. Today Jesus, in the prophetic tradition, proclaims the light in the darkness. The disciples will undergo persecutions. They will witness nation rising against nation and kingdom against kingdom. But in their persecutions they will be given wisdom to refute their adversaries. And even if they are put to death not a hair on their head will be destroyed.

to experience: At times in the life of faith we will need to remember the words of the prophets. In our broken world nations continue to war with each other, and each year brings its share of natural and manmade disasters. However, as people of faith, we look for the light shining in the darkness, the light that will purify our world from evil and heal us in justice.

Connecting the Responsorial Psalm

to the readings: The psalmist proclaims the justice of God who 'comes to rule the earth'. We are reminded that the earth is the Lord's from the rivers to the mountains, from the seas to the dry land. Jesus tells the disciples not to fear even when it seems that their world is being shaken at its foundations. God, Creator of the universe, continues to hold them in love even as they experience persecutions, wars, and earthquakes. Even death cannot ultimately touch them, for God is powerful over even death.

to psalmist preparation: Experiencing the beauty and grandeur of creation is a revelation of the Creator. Walking by a river, climbing to the top of a mountain, or witnessing the beauty of a sunset all speak to us of the love of God. This week, find some time to experience God in nature. What do the mountains and rivers, the seas and dry lands tell you about your God?

PROMPTS FOR FAITH-SHARING

Today's psalm calls on creation itself – rivers, mountains, seas, land – to rejoice in God. How have you experienced God in the natural world?

In the second letter to the Thessalonians, St. Paul calls upon the community to imitate his actions. Who has inspired you to imitation in the life of faith: a friend, relative, saint?

The gospel reading ends with Jesus calling the disciples to perseverance. Where in your life are you in need of perseverance at this moment?

Where do you notice God's presence, direction, and activity in your daily life?

CELEBRATION

Model Penitential Act

Presider: As we near the end of our church year let us pause to remember the Lord's faithfulness in times of joy and times of sorrow . . . [*pause*]

Lord Jesus, you are the source of wisdom and the font of salvation: Lord, have mercy.

Christ Jesus, you are the Prince of Peace: Christ, have mercy.

Lord Jesus, you comfort the afflicted and protect the persecuted: Lord, have mercy.

Homily Points

• As corporal beings, it is easy for us to get caught up in *stuff*. We take comfort in things we can see, touch, hear, and smell. Today's gospel begins with people around Jesus appreciating the beauty of the temple. In architecture we can see what is really important to a community. Just as Europeans in the Middle Ages spent decades and precious resources on their great cathedrals, the people of Jesus's time spent forty-six years constructing the temple, a privileged place to be with God.

• As we look to our own lives, we can name the places that we rely on and appreciate for their beauty and comfort: our houses, churches, schools, government buildings, and national monuments. These structures are good, but not permanent. They can be destroyed by any number of forces, many beyond our control. And yet, Jesus tells us, '[D]o not be frightened'. The firm foundation under our feet is not one of wood, concrete, brick, or stone. It is the Lord in which 'we live and move and have our being' (Acts 17:28; NABRE).

• As we come to the end of our church year, we can take this time to think about where we place our hope, our time, and our resources. Is there architecture within your interior life that could use some building up? Is God calling you to create more space for prayer, community, and love? Jesus reminds us that these structures alone can never be destroyed.

Model Universal Prayer (Prayer of the Faithful)

Presider: With confidence in God's faithfulness and mercy let us bring our prayers before the Lord.

Response: Lord, hear our prayer.

That the church might be a sign of hope and healing within the chaos of the world . . .

That warring nations turn their attention and care to working for lasting peace . . .

That those who experience terror and fear due to natural and manmade disasters receive physical and spiritual comfort and healing . . .

That all gathered here might lead lives of justice and peace that proclaim the love of God to all we meet . . .

Presider: God of creation, your mercy and justice is revealed in the life, death, and resurrection of your son Jesus Christ. Hear our prayers that we might follow his example in all that we do. We ask this through Christ our Lord. Amen.

COLLECT
Let us pray.

Pause for silent prayer

Grant us, we pray, O Lord our God,
the constant gladness of being devoted
     to you,
for it is full and lasting happiness
to serve with constancy
the author of all that is good.
Through our Lord Jesus Christ, your Son,
who lives and reigns with you in the unity
     of the Holy Spirit,
one God, for ever and ever. **Amen.**

FIRST READING
Mal 3:19-20

The day is coming now, burning like a furnace, and all the arrogant and the evil-doers will be like stubble. The day that is coming is going to burn them up, says the Lord of hosts, leaving them neither root nor stalk. But for you who fear my name, the sun of righteousness will shine out with healing in its rays.

CATECHESIS

RESPONSORIAL PSALM
Ps 97:5-9 (9)

R̊. The Lord comes to rule the peoples
with fairness.

Sing psalms to the Lord with the harp,
with the sound of music.
With trumpets and the sound of the horn
acclaim the King, the Lord.

R̊. The Lord comes to rule the peoples
with fairness.

Let the sea and all within it, thunder;
the world, and all its peoples.
Let the rivers clap their hands
and the hills ring out their joy
at the presence of the Lord.

R̊. The Lord comes to rule the peoples
with fairness.

For the Lord comes,
he comes to rule the earth.
He will rule the world with justice
and the peoples with fairness.

R̊. The Lord comes to rule the peoples
with fairness.

SECOND READING
2 Thess 3:7-12

You know how you are supposed to imitate us: now we were not idle when we were with you, nor did we ever have our meals at anyone's table without paying for them; no, we worked night and day, slaving and straining, so as not to be a burden on any of you. This was not because we had no right to be, but in order make ourselves an example for you to follow.

We gave you a rule when we were with you: not to let anyone have any food if he refused to do any work. Now we hear that there are some of you who are living in idleness, doing no work themselves but interfering with everyone else's. In the Lord Jesus Christ, we order and call on people of this kind to go on quietly working and earning the food that they eat.

About Liturgy

Prophets of doom: Pope Francis famously included in his apostolic exhortation, the Joy of the Gospel (*Evangelii Gaudium*), the term 'sourpuss', cautioning that pessimism and defeatism cannot help us proclaim the enduring joy the gospel gives us. As liturgical ministers, we have to take this seriously. When people come to church on Sunday, especially visitors, newcomers, and those seeking a relationship with Christ, we will be the closest thing to the face of God they might see that day. And if our faces look like we just sucked on a lemon, what will that communicate about the joy of our faith?

Jesus gives his listeners the same kind of admonishment in today's gospel when he speaks of pessimism, worry, or fear in the face of persecution, wars, and chaos. Just listening to the news today can make any person feel like sucking a lemon. But for us who proclaim a gospel of life and hope, we must testify by our lives – especially by our words, actions, and faces – that God is not finished with us yet.

As liturgical ministers and leaders, we rehearse this by embodying joy especially when we celebrate the Eucharist. This is not to say that we need to spend the entire Mass with a Pollyanna-ish smile plastered on our face. But it does mean that we should not let nervousness or worry about the things of the liturgy prevent us from showing compassion to the person in front of us who needs our attention.

Boredom and routine can also give us a sourpuss look. So each time you prepare to exercise your ministry on behalf of the assembly, pray for the Spirit to warm your heart with the sun of justice and to kindle the fire of love again in you. Then heed the gospel acclamation verse today: 'Stand erect, hold your heads high, / because your liberation is near at hand' (Luke 21:28).

About Initiation

Daily discernment: Catechumens must learn to keep their hopes set on Christ and follow 'supernatural inspiration in their deeds' (RCIA 75.2). Essentially this means learning how to do a daily discernment of where they have seen God in their lives and what God is asking them to do. This is the purpose of the Ignatian daily *examen*, a way of praying at the end of each day to learn to follow supernatural inspiration.

There are many ways to do an *examen*, but the five basic parts are 1) be aware of God's presence right now; 2) review the day's events; 3) listen to your feelings; 4) focus on one specific moment from the day, good or bad, and pray about it; 5) ask God to lead you in your actions for tomorrow.

About Liturgical Music

Music minister's examination of conscience: As we come to the end of another liturgical year, we might take this time to do an examination of conscience, reflecting on how well, individually and together, we have served our community as music ministers. Here are some questions that might stir up personal and group reflection, leading to conversion of heart for the following year.

How well have I prepared myself spiritually each week to hear the gospel and participate fully in the Mass with the assembly?

Do I understand the meaning behind the words I sing, and do I strive to believe what I am singing?

How have I grown in faith this past year? Where has my faith become stagnant or weak?

Beyond being part of the choir, will people recognise me as a disciple of Christ by my words and actions?

SPIRITUALITY

GOSPEL ACCLAMATION
Mark 11:9, 10

R̖. Alleluia, alleluia.
Blessings on him who comes in the name of
    the Lord!
Blessings on the coming kingdom of our
    father David!
R̖. Alleluia, alleluia.

Gospel

Luke 23:35-43

The people stayed there before the cross watching Jesus. As for the leaders, they jeered at him. 'He saved others,' they said 'let him save himself if he is the Christ of God, the Chosen One.' The soldiers mocked him too, and when they approached to offer him vinegar they said, 'If you are the king of the Jews, save yourself.' Above him there was an inscription: 'This is the King of the Jews.'

One of the criminals hanging there abused him. 'Are you not the Christ?' he said. 'Save yourself and us as well.' But the other spoke up and rebuked him. 'Have you no fear of God at all?' he said. 'You got the same sentence as he did, but in our case we deserved it: we are paying for what we did. But this man has done nothing wrong. Jesus,' he said 'remember me when you come into your kingdom.' 'Indeed, I promise you,' he replied 'today you will be with me in paradise.'

Reflecting on the Gospel

Though we repeat it at church often without thinking, it can be odd to call Jesus, 'King'. There are not many kings or queens today and those that do exist are usually figureheads. Perhaps the most famous is Queen Elizabeth II. When we call Jesus a king are we equating him in some ways with a figure like Queen Elizabeth II? Or is the queen in some ways equivalent to Jesus? Jesus has many titles in Scripture, one of which is Christ (Messiah, the Anointed), others are Lamb of God, the Alpha and the Omega, Lion of David, Saviour, Lord, Son of

God, Son of Man, and King. Of course, today's reading tells us that he was given the title 'King' by Pilate, or at least by the Romans who crucified him, as they were the ones who would have had the authority and responsibility for placing any sign above the cross.

What is a Christian response to the Romans calling him 'king' in such a mocking, derisive way? Christians embraced it and said he was king in a way unlike earthly kings, for his kingdom was not of this world. Even the thieves crucified alongside him encouraged him to save himself if he really is the Anointed One (Christ, Messiah). But again, his kingdom is not of this world. What he does have he offers the repentant thief, '[T]oday you will be with me in paradise'. The true king of a kingdom not of this world offers repentance, forgiveness, and paradise to those who seek it. The suffering encountered in this world will be reversed and overcome in the next. The one dying on a cross is destined for paradise. The authorities of this world are putting to death the king of the kingdom of God. But this king will upend the ways of the world.

We proclaim Jesus as king, but he is no mere figurehead. He rules a kingdom of God where justice reigns, the lowly are raised up, and the mighty brought low. Those who hunger and thirst are satisfied whereas the rich are sent away empty. Is this our king? Are we subjects in this kingdom? Or are we more content being subjects of the kingdoms of this age? Jesus is our king, the crucified, humiliated one whose destiny is paradise. Let us align ourselves with him and all the poor and lowly in the world.

Living the Paschal Mystery

The two thieves on either side of Jesus have remarkably different attitudes towards Jesus. One reviled Jesus, prodding him into saving himself and them. The mockery from the bystanders wasn't enough. Jesus faced mockery from one of his fellow condemned criminals. The other placed faith in Jesus with a simple request to 'remember me when you come into your kingdom'. That request belies a faith statement that Jesus is a king. What was said in mockery on the cross is true, and the thief knows it. Not only will Jesus remember him, but he promises to be with him in paradise that day. There seems to be no 'descent into hell' in Luke's understanding. That very day Jesus and the thief will be in paradise.

Our call is to recognise Jesus's kingship as well, though knowing it is a kingdom not of this world. The paschal mystery gives us hope that upon death

Jesus is in paradise without a pit stop along the way. Death leads to new life. And Jesus will bring others with him as they too experience the paschal mystery.

Focusing the Gospel

Key words and phrases: Jesus, . . . remember me when you come into your kingdom.

To the point: In Jesus's final moments on the cross he is surrounded by people calling out, 'Save yourself'. The rulers, soldiers, and even one of the criminals being crucified at his side repeat this taunt. In their words we might hear an echo of the temptation Jesus underwent at the very beginning of his ministry, when the devil asks him to change rock into bread to sate his hunger, or to throw himself from the parapet of the temple and be saved by angels. Jesus refuses, of course. Our king is not interested in saving himself. Throughout his ministry Jesus multiplies bread and fish to satisfy the needs of others. He heals physical and spiritual maladies. The second criminal understands and makes a request Jesus immediately grants, 'Jesus, . . . remember me when you come into your kingdom'. Jesus lives a life poured out for others from the very beginning to the very end. Even now our king stands ready, not to save himself, but to save us.

Connecting the Gospel

to the second reading: Today's second reading is taken from St. Paul's letter to the Colossians. In a hymn about the person of Jesus, Paul writes, 'God wanted all perfection / to be found in him / and all things to be reconciled through him and for him, / everything in heaven and everything on earth, / when he made peace / by his death on the cross'. In our world of divisions and categorizations, Paul invites us into a vision of Jesus as whole: the one in whom all the fulness was pleased to dwell. The one who takes all into himself and transforms it, reconciles it through the blood of his cross.

to experience: When we proclaim Jesus as king of the entire universe, we proclaim him king in fulness – king of the vulnerable harshness of the cross just as much as he is king in the transcendence of the resurrection.

Connecting the Responsorial Psalm

to the readings: In the first reading David is crowned king of Israel. The people claim him a family member, shepherd, and ruler. David will govern his people and also lead them spiritually. His home is Jerusalem, the seat of the king, and it becomes the place to be close to God when David's son Solomon builds a temple there. In today's psalm Jerusalem is praised as the centre of pilgrimage to draw near the Lord. The temple is 'God's house', a place of justice, and a place of thanksgiving.

to psalmist preparation: Unlike the Israelites before the destruction of the temple in the first century, we don't claim a geographical place as the centre of our worship. Jesus, the king of the universe, is found in creation, in community, in the Eucharist, in our hearts. Where do you go to draw close to the Lord? Where do you meet your king?

PROMPTS FOR FAITH-SHARING

David is called by God to be a 'shepherd' and a 'leader'. How do you balance authority with service and compassion, as a shepherd might lead his sheep?

Psalm 121 begins 'I rejoiced when I heard them say: / "Let us go to God's house." ' How is your worship of the Lord joyful?

Read the hymn from Colossians (1:15-20) slowly. Which phrase about Jesus speaks to you the loudest at this moment in your life of faith?

On this feast of Christ the King of the Universe, why do you think the church would choose for us to read and meditate on Jesus's crucifixion?

CELEBRATION

Model Penitential Act

Presider: On this final Sunday of our liturgical year we celebrate the feast of Christ, the King of the Universe. Let us pause to revel in the glory of our God, and the privilege of being one of his children . . . [*pause*]

Lord Jesus, you are the chosen one, the Messiah, the anointed: Lord, have mercy.

Christ Jesus, you are the King of heaven and earth: Christ, have mercy.

Lord Jesus, you desire to reconcile all things and people to yourself: Lord, have mercy.

Homily Points

• On this triumphant feast of Christ, King of the Universe we might be surprised by our gospel reading. While Jesus dies on the cross, the rulers and soldiers shout and taunt, 'Save yourself' if you are really the Christ of God. But that is not the kingship of Jesus. Not because he couldn't. Surely the one who healed lepers and fed the five thousand was perfectly capable of climbing down off the cross and walking unharmed through the angry crowd just as he did in Nazareth when his neighbours wanted to throw him off of a cliff. But he doesn't. Jesus's kingship is not about his own glory or power. His kingship is not about saving himself. Instead, in Jesus we witness a life poured out completely, to the last breath, for others.

• As we come to the end of the year in the Northern Hemisphere we see the seasons change. The light grows shorter and the weather colder. Our life follows the patterns of the seasons, and the patterns of the liturgical year. On this feast we proclaim Christ the King, who entered into creation, even to the ultimate brokenness of death. And in Christ, death is transformed. Theologian Sofia Cavalletti writes, 'Calvary is not only a brutal, violent act; above all else, it is a tremendous act of love. A tremendous act of violence becomes a tremendous act of love' (*Ways to Nurture the Relationship with God*).

• We end our church year by recalling this tremendous act of love. Jesus, King of the Universe, gives himself completely on the wood of the cross. As we enter into a new year of living and growing in faith, may we keep this paradox of kingship always ahead of us, for at the very beginning of our Christian lives we, too, were anointed priest, prophet, and king. May we come to embrace the kingship of Jesus, a kingship completely poured out for others, transforming death into life, and violence into love.

Model Universal Prayer (Prayer of the Faithful)

Presider: Grateful for our many blessings and confident in God's goodness and mercy, let us bring our prayers before the Lord.

Response: Lord, hear our prayer.

That the church emulate the kingship of Jesus in mercy, charity, and compassion . . .

That the justice and peace of Jesus the King would be known throughout the world . . .

That those who suffer from mental illness, depression, and anxiety be comforted by the love of God, which surpasses understanding . . .

That all gathered here might be strengthened in our resolve to follow and serve Jesus, the King of the Universe . . .

Presider: Saving God, you desire to redeem and consecrate all that you have created. Hear our prayers that we might use our gifts and talents to build your kingdom. We ask this through Christ our Lord. Amen.

COLLECT

Let us pray.

Pause for silent prayer

Almighty ever-living God,
whose will is to restore all things
in your beloved Son, the King of
    the universe,
grant, we pray,
that the whole creation, set free
    from slavery,
may render your majesty service
and ceaselessly proclaim your praise.
Through our Lord Jesus Christ, your Son,
who lives and reigns with you in the unity
    of the Holy Spirit,
one God, for ever and ever. **Amen.**

FIRST READING
2 Sam 5:1-3

All the tribes of Israel came to David at Hebron. 'Look' they said 'we are your own flesh and blood. In days past when Saul was our king, it was you who led Israel in all their exploits; and the Lord said to you, "You are the man who shall be shepherd of my people Israel, you shall be the leader of Israel."' So all the elders of Israel came to the king at Hebron, and King David made a pact with them at Hebron in the presence of the Lord, and they anointed David king of Israel.

RESPONSORIAL PSALM

Ps 121:1-5 (Cf. 2)

R̸. I rejoiced when I heard them say:
'Let us go to God's house.'

I rejoiced when I heard them say:
'Let us go to God's house.'
And now our feet are standing
within your gates, O Jerusalem.

R̸. I rejoiced when I heard them say:
'Let us go to God's house.'

Jerusalem is built as a city
strongly compact.
It is there that the tribes go up,
the tribes of the Lord.

R̸. I rejoiced when I heard them say:
'Let us go to God's house.'

For Israel's law it is,
there to praise the Lord's name.
There were set the thrones of judgement
of the house of David.

R̸. I rejoiced when I heard them say:
'Let us go to God's house.'

SECOND READING

Col 1:12-20

We give thanks to the Father who has
made it possible for you to join the saints
and with them to inherit the light.
   Because that is what he has done: he has
taken us out of the power of darkness and
created a place for us in the kingdom of
the Son that he loves, and in him, we gain
our freedom, the forgiveness of our sins.
   He is the image of the unseen God
   and the first-born of all creation,
   for in him were created
   all things in heaven and on earth:
   everything visible and everything
         invisible,
   Thrones, Dominations, Sovereignties,
         Powers –
   all things were created through him and
         for him.
   Before anything was created, he existed,
   and he holds all things in unity.
   Now the Church is his body,
   he is its head.
   As he is the Beginning,
   he was first to be born from the dead,
   so that he should be first in every way;
   because God wanted all perfection
   to be found in him
   and all things to be reconciled through
         him and for him,
   everything in heaven and everything
         on earth,
   when he made peace
   by his death on the cross.

About Liturgy

Triumphalism: Our rich liturgical tradition is filled with grandeur. Our worship spaces should rightfully elicit feelings of wonder and awe, and our rituals should reflect the best of our gifts we have to offer to our God.

However, there is a great difference between earthly extravagance and divine glory. We can proclaim the victory and triumph of God over death without triumphalism, pomposity, or ostentation. The key to knowing the difference may lie in today's gospel reading.

The kind of king we have in Christ is one who is quite human, suffering the injustices of other humans, and succumbing to the one human trait we all share – death. What made his cross a throne was his compassion for those just as broken – the crowd that reviled him, the mother who wept before him, and the criminals who died with him a criminal's death.

To express the glory and triumph that is rightly Christ's is to take what is broken and to reveal in it that which is royal, holy, and sacred. Our liturgies need not be magnificent in their splendor, erudite and polished to perfection, but they do need to be human and authentic, revealing the best of ourselves in our brokenness.

There is another aspect to the temptation of triumphalism that is even more insidious and can go unnoticed. We can fall into the trap of holding a bias towards one culture, language, style of praying, or genre of music as superior, judging other cultures, languages, styles, and forms as unrefined and less appropriate for worship. The cross, Christ's throne, reminds us that all that is human has been redeemed. Therefore, let us all approach the throne of mercy to receive grace, for the Father has 'made it possible for [us] to join the saints and with them to inherit the light' (Col 1:12).

About Initiation

The liturgical year as teacher: The Rite of Christian Initiation of Adults advises that the duration of the catechumenate 'should be long enough – several years if necessary – for the conversion and faith of the catechumens to become strong' (RCIA 76). The RCIA does not recommend this simply to give you more time for catechesis with the catechumens. Rather, the RCIA intends that the catechumens' encounter with Christ through the celebration of the liturgical year is how 'the Church completes [their] education' (Universal Norms on the Liturgical Year and the Calendar 1). Through the gradual observance of all the Sundays, holy days, feasts, and seasons of the liturgical year, the church 'unfolds the whole mystery of Christ' (Constitution on the Sacred Liturgy 102), for it is Christ who teaches us and initiates the catechumens into the mystery of salvation.

About Liturgical Music

Suggestions: A beautiful antiphon for today comes from *Psallite*'s 'Christ Laid Down His Life for Us', which says, 'Christ laid down his life for us; so we should do for each other'. The verses incorporate parts of the well-known Philippians canticle about Christ emptying himself, taking the form of a slave.

Another piece for this day is the well-known hymn, 'Let All Mortal Flesh Keep Silence', set to PICARDY and found in many hymnals. This would be a lovely song for the preparation of gifts.

Because this is the last Sunday before Advent, be sure to enhance the Gloria on this day, using a setting the assembly already knows and loves, but adding more to the instrumentation. Today is also a good day to sing a song of praise with the assembly after Communion. Consider just the refrain of Suzanne Toolan's 'Jesus Christ, Yesterday, Today, and Forever' (OCP). Complement this stately hymn with a spirited instrumental for the closing procession.

24 NOVEMBER 2019
OUR LORD JESUS CHRIST, KING OF THE UNIVERSE

GOSPEL ACCLAMATION
2 Chr 7:16

℟. Alleluia, alleluia!
Follow me, says the Lord,
and I will make you fishers of men.
℟. Alleluia!

Gospel

Matt 4:18-22

As Jesus was walking by the Sea of Galilee he saw two brothers, Simon, who was called Peter, and his brother Andrew; they were making a cast in the lake with their net, for they were fishermen. And he said to them, 'Follow me and I will make you fishers of men'. And they left their nets at once and followed him.

Going on from there he saw another pair of brothers, James son of Zebedee and his brother John; they were in their boat with their father Zebedee, mending their nets, and he called them. At once, leaving the boat and their father, they followed him.

See Appendix, p. 306, for the other readings.

Reflecting on the Gospel

We celebrate the feast of St. Andrew, brother of Simon Peter, today; and, the story of Jesus's call of these brothers is the gospel reading. Matthew tightens up the story he inherited from Mark and makes minor changes. But one significant change is that he refers to 'Peter' rather than 'Simon', as the Gospel of Mark has it. By doing so, the Gospel of Matthew looks forward to Jesus's naming him 'Peter' after his famous confession of Jesus as Son of the living God (Matt 16:16). But today is not about Peter; it's about his brother Andrew.

There is not much in the gospels about Andrew and even less in the Acts of the Apostles, where he's mentioned only once (Acts 1:13) and that in a list of the apostles. When there is a paucity of information, legends and lore abound! One of the most popular legends about Andrew is that he was crucified on an *X* cross. The image of the *X* cross is often referred to as 'the saltire'. It was this shape in the clouds that Oengus II, ninth century king of the Picts, is said to have seen as he led his army into battle. The victory he thus attributed to St. Andrew. Perhaps this legend seems far from the call of Andrew we hear about in today's reading. Or perhaps it reflects an ingenious way to link the Picts with Andrew, brother of Peter, and thus make relevant a gospel character for the ninth century, removed by geography and time from the New Testament.

By the gospel story, we are reminded of our own personal call to discipleship, as Andrew himself was called. Andrew and his brother responded immediately, dropping their nets to follow Jesus. Our own response may not be as forthright and immediate, but we follow Jesus nonetheless. We may ask ourselves how we make the gospel story relevant to our own time and place. Most likely it is not visions of clouds in the heavens, but something more mundane, more quotidian. As Jesus called Andrew, he calls us too. What has been, what will be, our response?

Living the Paschal Mystery

The saltire reminds us of Andrew, who according to legend was crucified on an *X* cross. Peter, the brother of Andrew, is said to have been crucified too, only upside down. And of course we know the story of Good Friday, how Jesus himself faced crucifixion. A disciple of Jesus should be prepared to face rejection and even death as Jesus himself did. But the story does not end with Good Friday. We celebrate Easter Sunday as death leads to resurrection. Just as Peter and Andrew followed Jesus to the cross (literally), they will follow him in being raised to new life. Just as we follow Jesus throughout our lives up to and including our own personal death, we will likewise follow him into new life. This is the paschal mystery, lived not only by Jesus and his disciples, but also by us.

Focusing the Gospel

Key words and phrases: And they left their nets at once and followed him.

To the point: We might imagine the scene on the beach that day. An unknown, itinerant preacher approaches four fishermen and calls to them saying, 'Follow me and I will make you fishers of men'. If this weren't surprising enough, even more astonishing is that all four men follow him without hesitation. Jesus's very presence must have been compelling. We see throughout the gospels that the people who encounter Jesus often react strongly, whether it is to join him, chastise him, or condemn him. There is a danger in our own time in history to try and domesticate Jesus and his message. And yet, if we allow him to, his call to follow him will change the course of our lives, just as it did for Simon, Andrew, James, and John that day on the shore of the Sea of Galilee.

Model Penitential Act

Presider: In today's gospel, Jesus calls two pairs of brothers to leave behind family and livelihood to follow him. Simon and Andrew, James and John respond without hesitation to this invitation to become 'fishers of men'. Let us pause to ask for pardon and healing so that we might also give our lives completely to the Lord . . . *[pause]*

Lord Jesus, you chose lowly fishermen as your first disciples: Lord, have mercy.

Christ Jesus, you send forth your disciples to preach to every nation: Christ, have mercy.

Lord Jesus, you save all those who call upon your name: Lord, have mercy.

Model Universal Prayer (Prayer of the Faithful)

Presider: Through the intercession of St. Andrew, apostle and martyr, we place our needs before the Lord who hears and answers us.

Response: Lord, hear our prayer.

That all members of the church might follow in the footsteps of St. Andrew in single hearted devotion to the Lord . . .

That leaders of nations be granted the wisdom to discern policies and statutes which support the freedom of all people and enhance the common good . . .

That those who lack shelter, food, and water, in our country and in all countries of the world, might be cared for with compassion and empathy . . .

That all gathered here might deeply listen for the voice of the Lord calling to us and have the courage to answer and follow wherever he leads . . .

Presider: God of mercy and love, you called St. Andrew to leave his family and livelihood and become a 'fisher of men'. Hear our prayers, that we might be strengthened by St. Andrew's example to devote our lives to you and to building your kingdom. We ask this through Christ our Lord. **Amen.**

About Liturgy

In some countries branches from bushes and trees are gathered on the eve of St. Andrew's feast. The saint is sometimes associated with fisheries and very frequently with marriage. Consider incorporating a renewal of commitment for married couples into the liturgy on this day. (NB: this does not mean repeating your marriage vows verbatim – these can only be made once! – but rather praying for the strength and blessing to continue to work towards a good and happy marriage.) Since St. Andrew's day is close to, or even at, the beginning of Advent, such a renewal of commitment would be an appropriate start to a new liturgical year. St. Andrew's cross is a white saltire, or *X*, on a blue background.

COLLECT
Let us pray.

Pause for silent prayer

We humbly implore your majesty, O Lord, that, just as the blessed Apostle Andrew was for your Church a preacher and pastor, so he may be for us a constant intercessor before you.
Through our Lord Jesus Christ, your Son, who lives and reigns with you in the unity of the Holy Spirit,
one God, for ever and ever. **Amen**.

FOR REFLECTION

• The first reading from Wisdom talks of God 'prov[ing]' the souls of the righteous as 'gold in a furnace'. What have you discovered about yourself from times of trial?

• In today's gospel passage Jesus calls his first disciples by the Sea of Galilee. What does it mean for Christians living in our world today to hear the call?

Homily Points

• Jesus's first act upon beginning his public ministry is to call others to join him. Obviously, Jesus does not desire to be a 'one man show'. Just as God has invited human collaboration throughout the history of salvation, Jesus invites Simon, Andrew, James, and John to leave their nets and boats and become 'fishers of men'. By answering this call, these first disciples start on a trajectory that will lead them to their own passion, deaths, and newness of life through Jesus's resurrection.

• In our own time, Jesus continues to issue the call, searching for human collaborators to help bring about the kingdom of God where peace and justice reign and sorrowing and death cease to exist. The invitation we read of today, 'Follow me and I will make you fishers of men', is issued to us as well. What will our response be?

The Immaculate Conception of the Blessed Virgin Mary, *8 December 2018*

Gospel (cont.)
Luke 1:26-38

Mary said to the angel, 'But how can this come about, since I am a virgin?' 'The Holy Spirit will come upon you' the angel answered, 'and the power of the Most High will cover you with its shadow. And so the child will be holy and will be called Son of God. Know this too: your kinswoman Elizabeth has, in her old age, herself conceived a son, and she whom people called barren is now in her sixth month, for nothing is impossible to God.' 'I am the handmaid of the Lord,' said Mary, 'let what you have said be done to me.' And the angel left her.

FIRST READING
Gen 3:9-15, 20

After Adam had eaten of the tree, the Lord God called to him, 'Where are you?' he asked. 'I heard the sound of you in the garden,' he replied. 'I was afraid because I was naked, so I hid.' 'Who told you that you were naked?' he asked. 'Have you been eating of the tree I forbade you to eat?' The man replied, 'It was the woman you put with me; she gave me the fruit, and I ate it.' Then the Lord God asked the woman, 'What is this you have done?' The woman replied, 'The serpent tempted me and I ate.'

Then the Lord God said to the serpent,
    'Because you have done this,
'Be accursed beyond all cattle,
all wild beasts.
You shall crawl on your belly and eat dust
every day of your life.
I will make you enemies of each other:
you and the woman,
your offspring and her offspring.
It will crush your head
and you will strike its heel.'

The man named his wife 'Eve' because she was the mother of all those who live.

RESPONSORIAL PSALM
Ps 97:1-4 (1)

R̸. Sing a new song to the Lord
for he has worked wonders.

Sing a new song to the Lord
for he has worked wonders.
His right hand and his holy arm
have brought salvation.

R̸. Sing a new song to the Lord
for he has worked wonders.

The Lord has made known his salvation;
has shown his justice to the nations.
He has remembered his truth and love
for the house of Israel.

R̸. Sing a new song to the Lord
for he has worked wonders.

All the ends of the earth have seen
the salvation of our God.
Shout to the Lord all the earth,
ring out your joy.

R̸. Sing a new song to the Lord
for he has worked wonders.

SECOND READING
Eph 1:3-6, 11-12

Blessed be God the Father of our Lord
    Jesus Christ,
who has blessed us with all the spiritual
    blessings of heaven in Christ.
Before the world was made, he chose us,
    chose us in Christ,
to be holy and spotless, and to live through
    love in his presence,
determining that we should become his
    adopted sons,
through Jesus Christ
for his own kind purposes,
to make us praise the glory of his grace,
his free gift to us in the Beloved.
And it is in him that we were claimed as
    God's own,
chosen from the beginning,
under the predetermined plan of the one who
    guides all things
as he decides by his own will;
chosen to be,
for his greater glory,
the people who would put their hopes in
    Christ before he came.

Gospel (cont.)
Matt 1:1-25

Asa was the father of Jehoshaphat,
Jehoshaphat the father of Joram,
Joram the father of Azariah,
Azariah was the father of Jotham,
Jotham the father of Ahaz,
Ahaz the father of Hezekiah,
Hezekiah was the father of Manasseh,
Manasseh the father of Amon,
Amon the father of Josiah;
and Josiah was the father of Jechoniah and his brothers.
Then the deportation to Babylon took place.

After the deportation to Babylon:
Jechoniah was the father of Shealtiel,
Shealtiel the father of Zerubbabel,
Zerubbabel was the father of Abiud,
Abiud the father of Eliakim,
Eliakim the father of Azor,
Azor was the father of Zadok,
Zadok the father of Achim,
Achim the father of Eliud,
Eliud was the father of Eleazar,
Eleazar the father of Matthan,
Matthan the father of Jacob,
and Jacob was the father of Joseph the husband of Mary; of her
     was born
Jesus who is called Christ.
   The sum of generations is therefore: fourteen from Abraham
to David; fourteen from David to the Babylonian deportation; and
fourteen from the Babylonian deportation to Christ.
   This is how Jesus Christ came to be born. His mother Mary was
betrothed to Joseph; but before they came to live together she was
found to be with child through the Holy Spirit. Her husband Joseph,
being a man of honour and wanting to spare her publicity, decided to
divorce her informally. He had made up his mind to do this when the
angel of the Lord appeared to him in a dream and said, 'Joseph son of
David, do not be afraid to take Mary home as your wife, because she
has conceived what is in her by the Holy Spirit. She will give birth to a
son and you must name him Jesus, because he is the one who is to save
his people from their sins.' Now all this took place to fulfil the words
spoken by the Lord through the prophet:
   The Virgin will conceive and give birth to a son
   and they will call him Emmanuel,
a name which means 'God-is-with-us'. When Joseph woke up he did
what the angel of the Lord had told him to do: he took his wife to his
home and, though he had not had intercourse with her, she gave birth
to a son; and he named him Jesus.

or Matt 1:18-25

This is how Jesus Christ came to be born. His mother Mary was
betrothed to Joseph; but before they came to live together she was
found to be with child through the Holy Spirit. Her husband Joseph,
being a man of honour and wanting to spare her publicity, decided to
divorce her informally. He had made up his mind to do this when the
angel of the Lord appeared to him in a dream and said, 'Joseph son of
David, do not be afraid to take Mary home as your wife, because she
has conceived what is in her by the Holy Spirit. She will give birth to a
son and you must name him Jesus, because he is the one who is to save
his people from their sins.' Now all this took place to fulfil the words
spoken by the Lord through the prophet:
   The Virgin will conceive and give birth to a son
   and they will call him Emmanuel,
a name which means 'God-is-with-us'. When Joseph woke up he did
what the angel of the Lord had told him to do: he took his wife to his
home and, though he had not had intercourse with her, she gave birth
to a son; and he named him Jesus.

FIRST READING
Isa 62:1-5

About Zion I will not be silent,
about Jerusalem I will not grow weary,
until her integrity shines out like the dawn
and her salvation flames like a torch.
The nations then will see your integrity,
all the kings your glory,
and you will be called by a new name,
one which the mouth of the Lord will confer.
You are to be a crown of splendour in the
     hand of the Lord,
a princely diadem in the hand of your God;
no longer are you to be named 'Forsaken'
nor your land 'Abandoned',
but you shall be called 'My Delight'
and your land 'The Wedded';
for the Lord takes delight in you
and your land will have its wedding.
Like a young man marrying a virgin,
so will the one who built you wed you,
and as the bridegroom rejoices in his bride,
so will your God rejoice in you.

RESPONSORIAL PSALM
Ps 88:4-5, 16-17, 27, 29 (2)

R̪. I will sing for ever of your love, O Lord.

'I have made a covenant with my chosen one;
I have sworn to David my servant:
I will establish your dynasty for ever
and set up your throne through all ages.'

R̪. I will sing for ever of your love, O Lord.

Happy the people who acclaim such a king,
who walk, O Lord, in the light of your face,
who find their joy every day in your name,
who make your justice the source of
     their bliss.

R̪. I will sing for ever of your love, O Lord.

'He will say to me: "You are my father,
my God, the rock who saves me."
I will keep my love for him always;
for him my covenant shall endure.'

R̪. I will sing for ever of your love, O Lord.

SECOND READING
Acts 13:16-17, 22-25

When Paul reached Antioch in Pisidia, he
stood up in the synagogue, held up a hand for
silence and began to speak:
   'Men of Israel, and fearers of God, listen!
The God of our nation Israel chose our
ancestors, and made our people great when
they were living as foreigners in Egypt; then
by divine power he led them out.
   'Then he made David their king, of whom
he approved in these words, "I have selected
David son of Jesse, a man after my own heart,
who will carry out my whole purpose." To
keep his promise, God has raised up for Israel
one of David's descendants, Jesus, as Saviour,
whose coming was heralded by John when he
proclaimed a baptism of repentance for the
whole people of Israel. Before John ended his
career he said, "I am not the one you imagine
me to be; that one is coming after me and I am
not fit to undo his sandal."'

Gospel (cont.)
Luke 2:1-14

In the countryside close by there were shepherds who lived in the fields and took it in turns to watch their flocks during the night. The angel of the Lord appeared to them and the glory of the Lord shone round them. They were terrified, but the angel said, 'Do not be afraid. Listen, I bring you news of great joy, a joy to be shared by the whole people. Today in the town of David a saviour has been born to you; he is Christ the Lord. And here is a sign for you: you will find a baby wrapped in swaddling clothes and lying in a manger.' And suddenly with the angel there was a great throng of the heavenly host, praising God and singing:

'Glory to God in the highest heaven,
and peace to men who enjoy his favour'.

FIRST READING
Isa 9:1-7

The people that walked in darkness
has seen a great light;
on those who live in a land of deep shadow
a light has shone.
You have made their gladness greater,
you have made their joy increase;
they rejoice in your presence
as men rejoice at harvest time,
as men are happy when they are dividing
        the spoils.
For the yoke that was weighing on him,
the bar across his shoulders,
the rod of his oppressor,
these you break as on the day of Midian.

For all the footgear of battle,
every cloak rolled in blood,
is burnt,
and consumed by fire.
For there is a child born for us,
a son given to us
and dominion is laid on his shoulders;
and this is the name they give him:
Wonder-Counsellor, Mighty-God,
Eternal-Father, Prince-of-Peace.
Wide is his dominion
in a peace that has no end,
for the throne of David
and for his royal power,
which he establishes and makes secure
in justice and integrity.
From this time onwards and for ever,
the jealous love of the Lord of hosts will
        do this.

RESPONSORIAL PSALM
Ps 95:1-3, 11-13 (Luke 2:11)

R̸. Today a saviour has been born to us;
he is Christ the Lord.

O sing a new song to the Lord,
sing to the Lord all the earth.
O sing to the Lord, bless his name.

R̸. Today a saviour has been born to us;
he is Christ the Lord.

Proclaim his help day by day,
tell among the nations his glory
and his wonders among all the peoples.

R̸. Today a saviour has been born to us;
he is Christ the Lord.

Let the heavens rejoice and earth be glad,
let the sea and all within it thunder praise,
let the land and all it bears rejoice,
all the trees of the wood shout for joy
at the presence of the Lord for he comes,
he comes to rule the earth.

R̸. Today a saviour has been born to us;
he is Christ the Lord.

SECOND READING
Titus 2:11-14

God's grace has been revealed, and it has made salvation possible for the whole human race and taught us that what we have to do is to give up everything that does not lead to God, and all our worldly ambitions; we must be self-restrained and live good and religious lives here in this present world, while we are waiting in hope for the blessing which will come with the Appearing of the glory of our great God and saviour Christ Jesus. He sacrificed himself for us in order to set us free from all wickedness and to purify a people so that it could be his very own and would have no ambition except to do good.

The Nativity of the Lord, *25 December 2018 (Mass at Dawn)*

FIRST READING
Isa 62:11-12

This the Lord proclaims
to the ends of the earth:
   Say to the daughter of Zion, 'Look,
   your saviour comes,
   the prize of his victory with him,
   his trophies before him.'
   They shall be called 'The Holy People',
   'The Lord's Redeemed'.
   And you shall be called 'The-sought-after',
   'City-not-forsaken'.

RESPONSORIAL PSALM
Ps 96:1, 6, 11-12

R̸. This day new light will shine upon
   the earth:
the Lord is born for us.

The Lord is king, let earth rejoice,
the many coastlands be glad.
The skies proclaim his justice;
all peoples see his glory.

R̸. This day new light will shine upon
   the earth:
the Lord is born for us.

Light shines forth for the just
and joy for the upright of heart.
Rejoice, you just, in the Lord;
give glory to his holy name.

R̸. This day new light will shine upon
   the earth:
the Lord is born for us.

SECOND READING
Titus 3:4-7

When the kindness and love of God our
saviour for mankind were revealed, it was not
because he was concerned with any righteous
actions we might have done ourselves; it was
for no reason except his own compassion that
he saved us, by means of the cleansing water
of rebirth and by renewing us with the Holy
Spirit which he has so generously poured
over us through Jesus Christ our saviour. He
did this so that we should be justified by his
grace, to become heirs looking forward to
inheriting eternal life.

The Nativity of the Lord, *25 December 2018 (Mass During the Day)*

Gospel (cont.)
John 1:1-18
The Word was made flesh,
he lived among us,
and we saw his glory,
the glory that is his as the only Son of the Father,
full of grace and truth.

John appears as his witness. He proclaims:
'This is the one of whom I said:
He who comes after me
ranks before me
because he existed before me.'
Indeed, from his fulness we have, all of us, received –
yes, grace in return for grace,
since, though the Law was given through Moses,
grace and truth have come through Jesus Christ.
No one has ever seen God,
it is the only Son, who is nearest to the Father's heart,
who has made him known.

or John 1:1-5, 9-14

In the beginning was the Word:
the Word was with God
and the Word was God.
He was with God in the beginning.
Through him all things came to be,
not one thing had its being but through him.
All that came to be had life in him
and that life was the light of men,
a light that shines in the dark,
a light that darkness could not overpower.

The Word was the true light
that enlightens all men;
and he was coming into the world.
He was in the world
that had its being through him,
and the world did not know him.
He came to his own domain
and his own people did not accept him.
But to all who did accept him
he gave power to become children of God,
to all who believe in the name of him
who was born not out of human stock
or urge of the flesh
or will of man
but of God himself.
The Word was made flesh,
he lived among us,
and we saw his glory,
the glory that is his as the only Son of the Father,
full of grace and truth.

The Nativity of the Lord, *25 December 2018 (Mass During the Day)*

FIRST READING
Isa 52:7-10

How beautiful on the mountains,
are the feet of one who brings good news,
who heralds peace, brings happiness,
proclaims salvation,
and tells Zion,
'Your God is king!'
Listen! Your watchmen raise their voices,
they shout for joy together,
for they see the Lord face to face,
as he returns to Zion.
Break into shouts of joy together,
you ruins of Jerusalem;
for the Lord is consoling his people,
redeeming Jerusalem.
The Lord bares his holy arm
in the sight of all the nations,
and all the ends of the earth shall see
the salvation of our God.

RESPONSORIAL PSALM
Ps 97:1-6 (3)

R̸. All the ends of the earth have seen
the salvation of our God.

Sing a new song to the Lord
for he has worked wonders.
His right hand and his holy arm
have brought salvation.

R̸. All the ends of the earth have seen
the salvation of our God.

The Lord has made known his salvation;
has shown his justice to the nations.
He has remembered his truth and love
for the house of Israel.

R̸. All the ends of the earth have seen
the salvation of our God.

All the ends of the earth have seen
the salvation of our God.
Shout to the Lord all the earth,
ring out your joy.

R̸. All the ends of the earth have seen
the salvation of our God.

Sing psalms to the Lord with the harp,
with the sound of music.
With trumpets and the sound of the horn
acclaim the King, the Lord.

R̸. All the ends of the earth have seen
the salvation of our God.

SECOND READING
Heb 1:1-6

At various times in the past and in various
different ways, God spoke to our ancestors
through the prophets; but in our own time,
the last days, he has spoken to us through
his Son, the Son that he has appointed to
inherit everything and through whom he
made everything there is. He is the radiant
light of God's glory and the perfect copy of
his nature, sustaining the universe by his
powerful command; and now that he has
destroyed the defilement of sin, he has gone to
take his place in heaven at the right hand of
divine Majesty. So he is now as far above the
angels as the title which he has inherited is
higher than their own name.

   God has never said to any angel: You are
my Son, today I have become your father; or:
I will be a father to him and he a son to me.
Again, when he brings the First-born into
the world, he says: Let all the angels of God
worship him.

Solemnity of Mary, the Holy Mother of God, *1 January 2019*

FIRST READING
Num 6:22-27

The Lord spoke to Moses and said, 'Say this
to Aaron and his sons: "This is how you are to
bless the sons of Israel. You shall say to them:

May the Lord bless you and keep you.
May the Lord let his face shine on you and be
     gracious to you.
May the Lord uncover his face to you and
     bring you peace."

This is how they are to call down my name on
the sons of Israel, and I will bless them.'

RESPONSORIAL PSALM
Ps 66:2-3, 5, 6, 8 (2)

R̸. O God, be gracious and bless us.

God, be gracious and bless us
and let your face shed its light upon us.
So will your ways be known upon earth
and all nations learn your saving help.

R̸. O God, be gracious and bless us.

Let the nations be glad and exult
for you rule the world with justice.
With fairness you rule the peoples,
you guide the nations on earth.

R̸. O God, be gracious and bless us.

Let the peoples praise you, O God;
let all the peoples praise you.
May God still give us his blessing
till the ends of the earth revere him.

R̸. O God, be gracious and bless us.

SECOND READING
Gal 4:4-7

When the appointed time came, God sent
his Son, born of a woman, born a subject
of the Law, to redeem the subjects of the
Law and to enable us to be adopted as sons.
The proof that you are sons is that God has
sent the Spirit of his Son into our hearts: the
Spirit that cries, 'Abba, Father', and it is this
that makes you a son, you are not a slave any
more; and if God has made you son, then he
has made you heir.

Gospel (cont.)
Matt 2:1-12

Then Herod summoned the wise men to see him privately. He asked them the exact date on which the star had appeared, and sent them on to Bethlehem. 'Go and find out all about the child,' he said 'and when you have found him, let me know, so that I too may go and do him homage.' Having listened to what the king had to say, they set out. And there in front of them was the star they had seen rising; it went forward and halted over the place where the child was. The sight of the star filled them with delight, and going into the house they saw the child with his mother Mary, and falling to their knees they did him homage. Then, opening their treasures, they offered him gifts of gold and frankincense and myrrh. But they were warned in a dream not to go back to Herod, and returned to their own country by a different way.

Third Sunday in Ordinary Time, *27 January 2019*

SECOND READING
1 Cor 12:12-30

Just as a human body, though it is made up of many parts is a single unit because all these parts, though many, make one body, so it is with Christ. In the one Spirit we were all baptised, Jews as well as Greeks, slaves as well as citizens, and one Spirit was given to us all to drink.

Nor is the body to be identified with any one of its many parts. If the foot were to say, 'I am not a hand and so I do not belong to the body,' would that mean that it stopped being part of the body? If the ear were to say, 'I am not an eye, and so I do not belong to the body,' would that mean that it is not a part of the body? If your whole body was just one eye, how would you hear anything? If it was just one ear, how would you smell anything?

Instead of that, God put all the separate parts into the body on purpose. If all the parts were the same, how could it be a body? As it is, the parts are many but the body is one. The eye cannot say to the hand, 'I do not need you,' nor can the head say to the feet, 'I do not need you.'

What is more, it is precisely the parts of the body that seem to be the weakest which are the indispensable ones; and it is the least honourable parts of the body that we clothe with the greatest care. So our more improper parts get decorated in a way that our more proper parts do not need. God has arranged the body so that more dignity is given to the parts which are without it, and so that there may not be disagreements inside the body, but that each part may be equally concerned for all the others. If one part is hurt, all parts are hurt with it. If one part is given special honour, all parts enjoy it.

Now you together are Christ's body; but each of you is a different part of it. In the Church, God has given the first place to apostles, the second to prophets, the third to teachers; after them, miracles, and after them the gift of healing; helpers, good leaders, those with many languages. Are all of them apostles, or all of them prophets, or all of them teachers? Do they all have the gift of miracles, or all have the gift of healing? Do all speak strange languages, and all interpret them?

Fourth Sunday in Ordinary Time, *3 February 2019*

SECOND READING
1 Cor 12:31-13:13

Be ambitious for the higher gifts. And I am going to show you a way that is better than any of them.

If I have all the eloquence of men or of angels, but speak without love, I am simply a gong booming or a cymbal clashing. If I have the gift of prophecy, understanding all the mysteries there are, and knowing everything, and if I have faith in all its fulness, to move mountains, but without love, then I am nothing at all. If I give away all that I possess, piece by piece, and if I even let them take my body to burn it, but am without love, it will do me no good whatever.

Love is always patient and kind; it is never jealous; love is never boastful or conceited; it is never rude or selfish; it does not take offence, and is not resentful. Love takes no pleasure in other people's sins but delights in the truth; it is always ready to excuse, to trust, to hope, and to endure whatever comes.

Love does not come to an end. But if there are gifts of prophecy, the time will come when they must fail; or the gift of languages, it will not continue for ever; and knowledge – for this, too, the time will come when it must fail. For our knowledge is imperfect and our prophesying is imperfect; but once perfection comes, all imperfect things will disappear. When I was a child, I used to talk like a child, and think like a child, and argue like a child, but now I am a man, all childish ways are put behind me. Now we are seeing a dim reflection in a mirror; but then we shall be seeing face to face. The knowledge that I have now is imperfect; but then I shall know as fully as I am known.

In short, there are three things that last: faith, hope and love; and the greatest of these is love.

Fifth Sunday in Ordinary Time, *10 February 2019*

SECOND READING
1 Cor 15:1-11

Brothers, I want to remind you of the gospel I preached to you, the gospel that you received and in which you are firmly established; because the gospel will save you only if you keep believing exactly what I preached to you – believing anything else will not lead to anything.

Well then, in the first place, I taught you what I had been taught myself, namely that Christ died for our sins, in accordance with the scriptures; that he was buried; and that he was raised to life on the third day, in accordance with the scriptures; that he appeared first to Cephas and secondly to the Twelve. Next he appeared to more than five hundred of the brothers at the same time, most of whom are still alive, though some have died; then he appeared to James, and then to all the apostles; and last of all he appeared to me too; it was as though I was born when no one expected it.

I am the least of the apostles; in fact, since I persecuted the Church of God, I hardly deserve the name apostle; but by God's grace that is what I am, and the grace that he gave me has not been fruitless. On the contrary, I, or rather the grace of God that is with me, have worked harder than any of the others; but what matters is that I preach what they preach, and this is what you all believed.

St. David, Bishop, Patron of Wales, 1 March 2019

FIRST READING
Gen 12:1-4

The Lord said to Abram, 'Leave your country, your family and your father's house, for the land I will show you. I will make you a great nation; I will bless you and make your name so famous that it will be used as a blessing.
    'I will bless those who bless you:
    I will curse those who slight you.
    All the tribes of the earth
    shall bless themselves by you.'
So Abram went as the Lord told him.

RESPONSORIAL PSALM
Ps 1:14, 6 (39:5)

R℣. Happy the man who has placed
his trust in the Lord.

Happy indeed is the man
who follows not the counsel of the wicked;
nor lingers in the way of sinners
nor sits in the company of scorners,
but whose delight is the law of the Lord
and who ponders his law day and night.

R℣. Happy the man who has placed
his trust in the Lord.

He is like a tree that is planted
beside the flowing waters,
that yields its fruit in due season
and whose leaves shall never fade;
and all that he does shall prosper.

R℣. Happy the man who has placed
his trust in the Lord.

Not so are the wicked, not so!
For they like winnowed chaff
shall be driven away by the wind;
for the Lord guards the way of the just
but the way of the wicked leads to doom.

R℣. Happy the man who has placed
his trust in the Lord.

SECOND READING
Phil 3:8-14

I believe nothing can happen that will outweigh the supreme advantage of knowing Christ Jesus my Lord. For him I have accepted the loss of everything, and I look on everything as so much rubbish if only I can have Christ and be given a place in him. I am no longer trying for perfection by my own efforts, the perfection that comes from the Law, but I want only the perfection that comes through faith in Christ, and is from God and based on faith. All I want is to know Christ and the power of his resurrection and to share his sufferings by reproducing the pattern of his death. That is the way I can hope to take my place in the resurrection of the dead. Not that I have become perfect yet: I have not yet won, but I am still running, trying to capture the prize for which Christ Jesus captured me. I can assure you my brothers, I am far from thinking that I have already won. All I can say is that I forget the past and I strain ahead for what is still to come; I am racing for the finish, for the prize to which God calls us upwards to receive in Christ Jesus.

Ash Wednesday, 6 March 2019

FIRST READING
Joel 2:12-18

'Now, now – it is the Lord who speaks –
come back to me with all your heart,
fasting, weeping, mourning.'
Let your hearts be broken not your
        garments torn,
turn to the Lord your God again,
for he is all tenderness and compassion,
slow to anger, rich in graciousness,
and ready to relent.
Who knows if he will not turn again, will
        not relent,
will not leave a blessing as he passes,
oblation and libation
for the Lord your God?
Sound the trumpet in Zion!
Order a fast,
proclaim a solemn assembly,
call the people together,
summon the community,
assemble the elders,
gather the children,
even the infants at the breast.
Let the bridegroom leave his bedroom
and the bride her alcove.
Between vestibule and altar let the priests,
the ministers of the Lord, lament.

Let them say,
'Spare your people, Lord!
Do not make your heritage a thing of shame,
a byword for the nations.
Why should it be said among the nations,
"Where is their God?"'
Then the Lord, jealous on behalf of his land,
took pity on his people.

RESPONSORIAL PSALM
Ps 50:3-6, 12-14, 17 (3)

R℣. Have mercy on us, O Lord, for we
        have sinned.

Have mercy on me, God, in your kindness.
In your compassion blot out my offence.
O wash me more and more from my guilt
and cleanse me from my sin.

R℣. Have mercy on us, O Lord, for we
        have sinned.

My offences truly I know them;
my sin is always before me.
Against you, you alone, have I sinned:
what is evil in your sight I have done.

R℣. Have mercy on us, O Lord, for we
        have sinned.

A pure heart create for me, O God,
put a steadfast spirit within me.
Do not cast me away from your presence,
nor deprive me of your holy spirit.

R℣. Have mercy on us, O Lord, for we
        have sinned.

Give me again the joy of your help;
with a spirit of fervour sustain me.
O Lord, open my lips
and my mouth shall declare your praise.

R℣. Have mercy on us, O Lord, for we
        have sinned.

SECOND READING
2 Cor 5:20–6:2

We are ambassadors for Christ; it is as though God were appealing through us, and the appeal that we make in Christ's name is: be reconciled to God. For our sake God made the sinless one into sin, so that in him we might become the goodness of God. As his fellow workers, we beg you once again not to neglect the grace of God that you have received. For he says: At the favourable time, I have listened to you, on the day of salvation I came to your help. Well, now is the favourable time; this is the day of salvation.

Second Sunday of Lent, *17 March 2019*

SECOND READING
Phil 3:20-4:1

For us, our homeland is in heaven, and from heaven comes the saviour we are waiting for, the Lord Jesus Christ, and he will transfigure these wretched bodies of ours into copies of his glorious body. He will do that by the same power with which he can subdue the whole universe.

So then, my brothers and dear friends, do not give way but remain faithful in the Lord. I miss you very much, dear friends; you are my joy and my crown.

St. Patrick, Bishop, Patron of Ireland, *17 March 2019*

FIRST READING
Eccl 39:6-10

If it is the will of the great Lord,
the scholar will be filled with the spirit of
    understanding,
he will shower forth words of wisdom,
and in prayer give thanks to the Lord.
He will grow upright in purpose and learning,
he will ponder the Lord's hidden mysteries.
He will display the instruction he has
    received,
taking his pride in the Law of the Lord's
    covenant.
Many will praise his understanding,
and it will never be forgotten.
His memory will not disappear,
generation after generation his name will live.
Nations will proclaim his wisdom,
the assembly will celebrate his praises.

RESPONSORIAL PSALM
Ps 115:12-19 (12)

R⒎. How can I repay the Lord for his goodness
    to me?

How can I repay the Lord
for his goodness to me?
The cup of salvation I will raise;
I will call on the Lord's name.

R⒎. How can I repay the Lord for his goodness
    to me?

My vows to the Lord I will fulfil
before all his people.
O precious in the eyes of the Lord
is the death of his faithful.

R⒎. How can I repay the Lord for his goodness
    to me?

Your servant, O Lord, your servant am I;
you have loosened my bonds.
A thanksgiving sacrifice I make;
I will call on the Lord's name.

R⒎. How can I repay the Lord for his goodness
    to me?

My vows to the Lord I will fulfil
before all his people,
in the courts of the house of the Lord,
in your midst, O Jerusalem.

R⒎. How can I repay the Lord for his goodness
    to me?

SECOND READING
2 Tim 4:1-8

Before God and before Christ Jesus who is to be judge of the living and the dead, I put this duty to you, in the name of his Appearing and of his kingdom: proclaim the message and, welcome or unwelcome, insist on it. Refute falsehood, correct error, call to obedience – but do all with patience and with the intention of teaching. The time is sure to come when, far from being content with sound teaching, people will be avid for the latest novelty and collect themselves a whole series of teachers according to their own tastes; and then, instead of listening to the truth, they will turn to myths. Be careful always to choose the right course; be brave under trials; make the preaching of the Good News your life's work, in thoroughgoing service.

As for me, my life is already being poured away as a libation, and the time has come for me to be gone. I have fought the good fight to the end; I have run the race to the finish; I have kept the faith; all there is to come now is the crown of righteousness reserved for me, which the Lord, the righteous judge, will give me on that Day; and not only to me but to all those who have longed for his Appearing.

Gospel
Matt 1:16, 18-21, 24

Jacob was the father of Joseph the husband of Mary; of her was born Jesus who is called Christ.

This is how Jesus Christ came to be born. His mother Mary was betrothed to Joseph; but before they came to live together she was found to be with child through the Holy Spirit. Her husband Joseph, being a man of honour and wanting to spare her publicity, decided to divorce her informally. He had made up his mind to do this when the angel of the Lord appeared to him in a dream and said, 'Joseph son of David, do not be afraid to take Mary home as your wife, because she has conceived what is in her by the Holy Spirit. She will give birth to a son and you must name him Jesus, because he is the one who is to save his people from their sins.' When Joseph woke up he did what the angel of the Lord had told him to do.

FIRST READING
2 Sam 7:4-5, 12-14, 16

The word of the Lord came to Nathan:

'Go and tell my servant David, "Thus the Lord speaks: When your days are ended and you are laid to rest with your ancestors, I will preserve the offspring of your body after you and make his sovereignty secure. (It is he who shall build a house for my name and I will make his royal throne secure for ever.) I will be a father to him and he a son to me. Your House and your sovereignty will always stand secure before me and your throne be established for ever."'

RESPONSORIAL PSALM
Ps 88:2-5, 27, 29 (37)

R. His dynasty shall last for ever.

I will sing for ever of your love, O Lord;
through all ages my mouth will proclaim
    your truth.
Of this I am sure, that your love lasts for ever,
that your truth is firmly established as
    the heavens.

R. His dynasty shall last for ever.

'I have made a covenant with my chosen one;
I have sworn to David my servant:
I will establish your dynasty for ever
and set up your throne through all ages.'

R. His dynasty shall last for ever.

He will say to me: 'You are my father,
my God, the rock who saves me.'
I will keep my love for him always;
for him my covenant shall endure.

R. His dynasty shall last for ever.

SECOND READING
Rom 4:13, 16-18, 22

The promise of inheriting the world was not made to Abraham and his descendants on account of any law but on account of the righteousness which consists in faith. That is why what fulfils the promise depends on faith, so that it may be a free gift and be available to all of Abraham's descendants, not only those who belong to the Law but also to those who belong to the faith of Abraham who is the father of all of us. As scripture says: I have made you the ancestor of many nations – Abraham is our father in the eyes of God, in whom he put his faith, and who brings the dead to life and calls into being what does not exist.

Though it seemed Abraham's hope could not be fulfilled, he hoped and he believed, and through doing so he did become the father of many nations exactly as he had been promised: Your descendants will be as many as the stars. This is the faith that was 'considered as justifying him'.

The Annunciation of the Lord, 25 March 2019

FIRST READING
Isa 7:10-14; 8:10

The Lord spoke to Ahaz and said, 'Ask the Lord your God for a sign for yourself coming either from the depths of Sheol or from the heights above.' 'No,' Ahaz answered, 'I will not put the Lord to the test.'

Then Isaiah said:

Listen now, House of David:
are you not satisfied with trying the
    patience of men
without trying the patience of my God, too?
The Lord himself, therefore,
will give you a sign.
It is this: the maiden is with child
and will soon give birth to a son
whom she will call Emmanuel,
a name which means 'God-is-with-us'.

RESPONSORIAL PSALM
Ps 39:7-11 (8, 9)

℟. Here I am, Lord!
I come to do your will.

You do not ask for sacrifice and offerings,
but an open ear.
You do not ask for holocaust and victim.
Instead, here am I.

℟. Here I am, Lord!
I come to do your will.

In the scroll of the book it stands written
that I should do your will.
My God, I delight in your law
in the depth of my heart.

℟. Here I am, Lord!
I come to do your will.

Your justice I have proclaimed
in the great assembly.
My lips I have not sealed;
you know it, O Lord.

℟. Here I am, Lord!
I come to do your will.

I have not hidden your justice in my heart
but declared your faithful help.
I have not hidden your love and your truth
from the great assembly.

℟. Here I am, Lord!
I come to do your will.

SECOND READING
Heb 10:4-10

Bulls' blood and goats' blood are useless for taking away sins, and this is what Christ said, on coming into the world:

You who wanted no sacrifice or oblation,
    prepared a body for me.
you took no pleasure in holocausts or
    sacrifices for sin;
then I said,
just as I was commanded in the scroll of
    the book,
'God, here I am! I am coming to obey
    your will.'

Notice that he says first: You did not want what the Law lays down as the things to be offered, that is: the sacrifices, the oblations, the holocausts and the sacrifices for sin, and you took no pleasure in them; and then he says: Here I am! I am coming to obey your will. He is abolishing the first sort to replace it with the second. And this will was for us to be made holy by the offering of his body made once and for all by Jesus Christ.

Fouth Sunday of Lent, 31 March 2019

Gospel (cont.)
Luke 15:1-3, 11-32

'While he was still a long way off, his father saw him and was moved with pity. He ran to the boy, clasped him in his arms and kissed him tenderly. Then his son said, "Father, I have sinned against heaven and against you. I no longer deserve to be called your son." But the father said to his servants, "Quick! Bring out the best robe and put it on him; put a ring on his finger and sandals on his feet. Bring the calf we have been fattening, and kill it; we are going to have a feast, a celebration, because this son of mine was dead and has come back to life; he was lost and is found." And they began to celebrate.

'Now the elder son was out in the fields, and on his way back, as he drew near the house, he could hear music and dancing. Calling one of the servants he asked what it was all about. "Your brother has come" replied the servant "and your father has killed the calf we had fattened because he has got him back safe and sound." He was angry then and refused to go in, and his father came out to plead with him; but he answered his father, "Look, all these years I have slaved for you and never once disobeyed your orders, yet you never offered me so much as a kid for me to celebrate with my friends. But, for this son of yours, when he comes back after swallowing up your property – he and his women – you kill the calf we had been fattening."

'The father said, "My son, you are with me always and all I have is yours. But it is only right we should celebrate and rejoice, because your brother here was dead and has come to life; he was lost and is found."'

Gospel (cont.) at the procession with palms

As he was drawing near,
at the descent of the Mount of Olives,
the whole multitude of the disciples
began to rejoice and praise God with a loud voice
for all the mighty works that they had seen,
saying,
'Blessed is the King who comes in the name of the Lord!
Peace in heaven and glory in the highest!'
And some of the Pharisees in the multitude said to him,
'Teacher, rebuke your disciples.'
He answered,
'I tell you, if these were silent,
the very stones would cry out.'

Gospel at Mass
Luke 22:14–23:56

The symbols in the following passion narrative represent:

N   Narrator
J   Jesus
O   Other single speaker
C   Crowd, or more than one speaker

N   When the hour came Jesus took his place at table, and the apostles with him. And he said to them,
J   I have longed to eat this Passover with you before I suffer; because, I tell you, I shall not eat it again until it is fulfilled in the kingdom of God.
N   Then, taking a cup, he gave thanks and said,
J   Take this and share it among you, because from now on, I tell you, I shall not drink wine until the kingdom of God comes.
N   Then he took some bread, and when he had given thanks, broke it and gave it to them, saying,
J   This is my body which will be given for you; do this as a memorial of me.
N   He did the same with the cup after supper, and said,
J   This cup is the new covenant in my blood which will be poured out for you.
    And yet, here with me on the table is the hand of the man who betrays me. The Son of Man does indeed go to his fate even as it has been decreed, but alas for that man by whom he is betrayed!
N   And they began to ask one another which of them it could be who was to do this thing.
    A dispute arose also between them about which should be reckoned the greatest, but he said to them,
J   Among pagans it is the kings who lord it over them, and those who have authority over them are given the title Benefactor. This must not happen with you. No; the greatest among you must behave as if he were the youngest, the leader as if he were the one who serves. For who is the greater: the one at table or the one who serves? The one at table, surely? Yet here I am among you as one who serves!
    You are the men who have stood by me faithfully in my trials; and now I confer a kingdom on you, just as my Father conferred one on me: you will eat and drink at my table in my kingdom, and you will sit on thrones to judge the twelve tribes of Israel.
    Simon, Simon! Satan, you must know, has got his wish to sift you all like wheat; but I have prayed for you, Simon, that your faith may not fail, and once you have recovered, you in your turn must strengthen your brothers.

N   He answered,
O   Lord, I would be ready to go to prison with you, and to death.
N   Jesus replied,
J   I tell you, Peter, by the time the cock crows today you will have denied three times that you know me.
N   He said to them,
J   When I sent you out without purse or haversack or sandals, were you short of anything?
N   They answered,
C   No.
N   He said to them,
J   But now if you have a purse, take it: if you have a haversack, do the same; if you have no sword, sell your cloak and buy one, because I tell you these words of scripture have to be fulfilled in me: He let himself be taken for a criminal. Yes, what scripture says about me is even now reaching its fulfilment.
N   They said,
C   Lord, there are two swords here now.
N   He said to them,
J   That is enough!
N   He then left the upper room to make his way as usual to the Mount of Olives, with the disciples following. When they reached the place he said to them,
J   Pray not to be put to the test.
N   Then he withdrew from them, about a stone's throw away, and knelt down and prayed, saying,
J   Father, if you are willing, take this cup away from me. Nevertheless, let your will be done, not mine.
N   Then an angel appeared to him coming from heaven to give him strength. In his anguish he prayed even more earnestly and his sweat fell to the ground like great drops of blood.
    When he rose from prayer he went to the disciples and found them sleeping for sheer grief. He said to them,
J   Why are you asleep? Get up and pray not to be put to the test.
N   He was still speaking when a number of men appeared, and at the head of them the man called Judas, one of the Twelve, who went up to Jesus to kiss him. Jesus said,
J   Judas, are you betraying the Son of Man with a kiss?
N   His followers, seeing what was happening, said,
C   Lord, shall we use our swords?
N   And one of them struck out at the high priest's servant, and cut off his right ear. But at this Jesus spoke,
J   Leave off! That will do!
N   And touching the man's ear he healed him.
    Then Jesus spoke to the chief priests and captains of the Temple guard and elders who had come for him. He said,
J   Am I a brigand that you had to set out with swords and clubs? When I was among you in the Temple day after day you never moved to lay hands on me. But this is your hour; this is the reign of darkness.
N   They seized him then and led him away, and they took him to the high priest's house. Peter followed at a distance. They had lit a fire in the middle of the courtyard and Peter sat down among them, and as he was sitting there by the blaze a servant-girl saw him, peered at him and said,
O   This person was with him too.
N   But he denied it, saying,
O   Woman, I do not know him.
N   Shortly afterwards, someone else saw him and said,
O   You are another of them.
N   But Peter replied,

O I am not, my friend.

N About an hour later, another man insisted, saying,

O This fellow was certainly with him. Why, he is a Galilean.

N Peter said,

O My friend, I do not know what you are talking about.

N At that instant, while he was still speaking, the cock crew, and the Lord turned and looked straight at Peter, and Peter remembered what the Lord had said to him, 'Before the cock crows today, you will have disowned me three times.' And he went outside and wept bitterly.

Meanwhile the men who guarded Jesus were mocking and beating him. They blindfolded him and questioned him, saying,

C Play the prophet. Who hit you then?

N And they continued heaping insults on him.

When day broke there was a meeting of the elders of the people, attended by the chief priests and scribes. He was brought before their council, and they said to him,

C If you are the Christ, tell us.

N He replied,

J If I tell you, you will not believe me, and if I question you, you will not answer. But from now on, the Son of Man will be seated at the right hand of the Power of God.

N Then they all said,

C So you are the Son of God then?

N He answered,

J It is you who say I am.

N They said,

C What need of witnesses have we now? We have heard it for ourselves from his own lips.

N The whole assembly then rose, and they brought him before Pilate.

They began their accusation by saying,

C We found this man inciting our people to revolt, opposing payment of the tribute to Caesar, and claiming to be Christ, a king.

N Pilate put to him this question,

O Are you the king of the Jews?

N He replied,

J It is you who say it.

N Pilate then said to the chief priests and the crowd,

O I find no case against this man.

N But they persisted,

C He is inflaming the people with his teaching all over Judaea; it has come all the way from Galilee, where he started, down to here.

N When Pilate heard this, he asked if the man were a Galilean; and finding that he came under Herod's jurisdiction he passed him over to Herod who was also in Jerusalem at that time.

Herod was delighted to see Jesus; he had heard about him and had been wanting for a long time to set eyes on him; moreover, he was hoping to see some miracle worked by him. So he questioned him at some length; but without getting any reply. Meanwhile the chief priests and the scribes were there, violently pressing their accusations. Then Herod, together with his guards, treated him with contempt and made fun of him; he put a rich cloak on him and sent him back to Pilate. And though Herod and Pilate had been enemies before, they were reconciled that same day.

Pilate then summoned the chief priests and the leading men and the people. He said,

O You brought this man before me as a political agitator. Now I have gone into the matter myself in your presence and found no case against the man in respect of all the charges you bring against him. Nor has Herod either, since he has sent him back to us. As you can see, the man has done nothing that deserves death, so I shall have him flogged and then let him go.

N But as one man they howled,

C Away with him! Give us Barabbas!

N This man had been thrown into prison for causing a riot in the city and for murder.

Pilate was anxious to set Jesus free and addressed them again, but they shouted back,

C Crucify him! Crucify him!

N And for the third time he spoke to them,

O Why? What harm has this man done? I have found no case against him that deserves death, so I shall have him punished and let him go.

N But they kept on shouting at the top of their voices, demanding that he should be crucified, and their shouts were growing louder.

Pilate then gave his verdict: their demand was to be granted. He released the man they asked for, who had been imprisoned for rioting and murder, and handed Jesus over to them to deal with as they pleased.

As they were leading him away they seized on a man, Simon from Cyrene, who was coming in from the country, and made him shoulder the cross and carry it behind Jesus. Large numbers of people followed him, and of women too who mourned and lamented for him. But Jesus turned to them and said,

J Daughters of Jerusalem, do not weep for me; weep rather for yourselves and for your children. For the days will surely come when people will say, 'Happy are those who are barren, the wombs that have never borne, the breasts that have never suckled!' Then they will begin to say to the mountains, 'Fall on us!'; to the hills, 'Cover us!' For if men use the green wood like this, what will happen when it is dry?

N Now with him they were also leading out two other criminals to be executed.

When they reached the place called The Skull, they crucified him there and the criminals also, one on the right, the other on the left. Jesus said,

J Father, forgive them; they do not know what they are doing.

N Then they cast lots to share out his clothing. The people stayed there watching him. As for the leaders, they jeered at him, saying,

C He saved others; let him save himself if he is the Christ of God, the Chosen One.

N The soldiers mocked him too, and when they approached to offer him vinegar they said,

C If you are the king of the Jews, save yourself.

N Above him there was an inscription: 'This is the King of the Jews.'

One of the criminals hanging there abused him, saying,

O Are you not the Christ? Save yourself and us as well.

N But the other spoke up and rebuked him,

O Have you no fear of God at all? You got the same sentence as he did, but in our case we deserved it: we are paying for what we did. But this man has done nothing wrong. Jesus, remember me when you come into your kingdom.

N He replied,

J Indeed, I promise you, today you will be with me in paradise.

N It was now about the sixth hour and, with the sun eclipsed, a darkness came over the whole land until the ninth hour. The veil of the Temple was torn right down the middle; and when Jesus had cried out in a loud voice, he said,

J Father, into your hands I commit my spirit.

N With these words he breathed his last.

All kneel and pause a moment.

When the centurion saw what had taken place, he gave praise to God and said,

O This was a great and good man.

N And when all the people who had gathered for the spectacle saw what had happened, they went home beating their breasts.

All his friends stood at a distance; so also did the women who had accompanied him from Galilee, and they saw all this happen.]

Then a member of the council arrived, an upright and virtuous man named Joseph. He had not consented to what the others had planned and carried out. He came from Arimathaea, a Jewish town, and he lived in the hope of seeing the kingdom of God. This man went to Pilate and asked for the body of Jesus. He then took it down, wrapped it in a shroud and put him in a tomb which was hewn in stone in which no one had yet been laid. It was Preparation Day and the sabbath was imminent.

Meanwhile the women who had come from Galilee with Jesus were following behind. They took note of the tomb and of the position of the body.

Then they returned and prepared spices and ointments. And on the sabbath day they rested, as the law required.

or Luke 23:1-49

N The whole assembly then rose, and they brought him before Pilate. They began their accusation by saying,

C We found this man inciting our people to revolt, opposing payment of the tribute to Caesar, and claiming to be Christ, a king.

N Pilate put to him this question,

O Are you the king of the Jews?

N He replied,

J It is you who say it.

N Pilate then said to the chief priests and the crowd,

O I find no case against this man.

N But they persisted,

C He is inflaming the people with his teaching all over Judaea; it has come all the way from Galilee, where he started, down to here.

N When Pilate heard this, he asked if the man were a Galilean; and finding that he came under Herod's jurisdiction he passed him over to Herod who was also in Jerusalem at that time.

Herod was delighted to see Jesus; he had heard about him and had been wanting for a long time to set eyes on him; moreover, he was hoping to see some miracle worked by him. So he questioned him at some length; but without getting any reply. Meanwhile the chief priests and the scribes were there, violently pressing their accusations. Then Herod, together with his guards, treated him with contempt and made fun of him; he put a rich cloak on him and sent him back to Pilate. And though Herod and Pilate had been enemies before, they were reconciled that same day.

Pilate then summoned the chief priests and the leading men and the people. He said,

O You brought this man before me as a political agitator. Now I have gone into the matter myself in your presence and found no case against the man in respect of all the charges you bring against him. Nor has Herod either, since he has sent him back to us. As you can see, the man has done nothing that deserves death, so I shall have him flogged and then let him go.

N But as one man they howled,

C Away with him! Give us Barabbas!

N This man had been thrown into prison for causing a riot in the city and for murder.

Pilate was anxious to set Jesus free and addressed them again, but they shouted back,

C Crucify him! Crucify him!

N And for the third time he spoke to them,

O Why? What harm has this man done? I have found no case against him that deserves death, so I shall have him punished and let him go.

N But they kept on shouting at the top of their voices, demanding that he should be crucified, and their shouts were growing louder.

Pilate then gave his verdict: their demand was to be granted. He released the man they asked for, who had been imprisoned for rioting and murder, and handed Jesus over to them to deal with as they pleased.

As they were leading him away they seized on a man, Simon from Cyrene, who was coming in from the country, and made him shoulder the cross and carry it behind Jesus. Large numbers of people followed him, and of women too who mourned and lamented for him. But Jesus turned to them and said,

J Daughters of Jerusalem, do not weep for me; weep rather for yourselves and for your children. For the days will surely come when people will say, 'Happy are those who are barren, the wombs that have never borne, the breasts that have never suckled!' Then they will begin to say to the mountains, 'Fall on us!'; to the hills, 'Cover us!' For if men use the green wood like this, what will happen when it is dry?

N Now with him they were also leading out two other criminals to be executed.

When they reached the place called The Skull, they crucified him there and the criminals also, one on the right, the other on the left. Jesus said,

J Father, forgive them; they do not know what they are doing.

N Then they cast lots to share out his clothing. The people stayed there watching him. As for the leaders, they jeered at him, saying,

C He saved others; let him save himself if he is the Christ of God, the Chosen One.

N The soldiers mocked him too, and when they approached to offer him vinegar they said,

C If you are the king of the Jews, save yourself.

N Above him there was an inscription: 'This is the King of the Jews.'
One of the criminals hanging there abused him, saying,

O Are you not the Christ? Save yourself and us as well.

N But the other spoke up and rebuked him,

O Have you no fear of God at all? You got the same sentence as he did, but in our case we deserved it: we are paying for what we did. But this man has done nothing wrong. Jesus, remember me when you come into your kingdom.

N He replied,

J Indeed, I promise you, today you will be with me in paradise.

N It was now about the sixth hour and, with the sun eclipsed, a darkness came over the whole land until the ninth hour. The veil of the Temple was torn right down the middle; and when Jesus had cried out in a loud voice, he said,

J Father, into your hands I commit my spirit.

N With these words he breathed his last.

All kneel and pause a moment.

When the centurion saw what had taken place, he gave praise to God and said,

O This was a great and good man.

N And when all the people who had gathered for the spectacle saw what had happened, they went home beating their breasts.

All his friends stood at a distance; so also did the women who had accompanied him from Galilee, and they saw all this happen.

Gospel (cont.)
John 13:1-15

When he had washed their feet and put on his clothes again he went back to the table. 'Do you understand' he said 'what I have done to you? You call me Master and Lord, and rightly; so I am. If I, then, the Lord and Master, have washed your feet, you should wash each other's feet. I have given you an example so that you may copy what I have done to you.'

FIRST READING
Exodus 12:1-8, 11-14

The Lord said to Moses and Aaron in the land of Egypt, 'This month is to be the first of all the others for you, the first month of your year. Speak to the whole community of Israel and say, "On the tenth day of this month each man must take an animal from the flock, one for each family: one animal for each household. If the household is too small to eat the animal, a man must join with his neighbour, the nearest to his house, as the number of persons requires. You must take into account what each can eat in deciding the number for the animal. It must be an animal without blemish, a male one year old; you may take it from either sheep or goats. You must keep it till the fourteenth day of the month when the whole assembly of the community of Israel shall slaughter it between the two evenings. Some of the blood must then be taken and put on the two doorposts and the lintel of the houses where it is eaten. That night, the flesh is to be eaten, roasted over the fire; it must be eaten with unleavened bread and bitter herbs. You shall eat it like this: with a girdle round your waist, sandals on your feet, a staff in your hand. You shall eat it hastily; it is a passover in honour of the Lord. That night, I will go through the land of Egypt and strike down all the first-born in the land of Egypt, man and beast alike, and I shall deal out punishment to all the gods of Egypt, I am the Lord. The blood shall serve to mark the houses that you live in. When I see the blood I will pass over you and you shall escape the destroying plague when I strike the land of Egypt. This day is to be a day of remembrance for you, and you must celebrate it as a feast in the Lord's honour. For all generations you are to declare it a day of festival, for ever."'

RESPONSORIAL PSALM
Ps 115:12-13, 15-18 (Cf. 1 Cor 10:16)

R̦. The blessing-cup that we bless is a communion with the blood of Christ.

How can I repay the Lord
for his goodness to me?
The cup of salvation I will raise;
I will call on the Lord's name.

R̦. The blessing-cup that we bless is a communion with the blood of Christ.

O precious in the eyes of the Lord
is the death of his faithful.
Your servant, Lord, your servant am I;
you have loosened my bonds.

R̦. The blessing-cup that we bless is a communion with the blood of Christ.

A thanksgiving sacrifice I make:
I will call on the Lord's name.
My vows to the Lord I will fulfil
before all his people.

R̦. The blessing-cup that we bless is a communion with the blood of Christ.

SECOND READING
1 Cor 11:23-26

This is what I received from the Lord, and in turn passed on to you: that on the same night that he was betrayed, the Lord Jesus took some bread, and thanked God for it and broke it, and he said, 'This is my body, which is for you; do this as a memorial of me.' In the same way he took the cup after supper, and said, 'This cup is the new covenant in my blood. Whenever you drink it, do this as a memorial of me.' Until the Lord comes, therefore, every time you eat this bread and drink this cup, you are proclaiming his death.

Gospel (cont.)
John 18:1–19:42

N   This was to fulfil the words he has spoken: 'Not one of those you gave me have I lost.'

Simon Peter, who carried a sword, drew it and wounded the high priest's servant, cutting off his right ear. The servant's name was Malchus. Jesus said to Peter,

J   Put your sword back in its scabbard; am I not to drink the cup that the Father has given me?

N   The cohort and its captain and the Jewish guards seized Jesus and bound him. They took him first to Annas, because Annas was the father-in-law of Caiaphas, who was high priest that year. It was Caiaphas who had suggested to the Jews, 'It is better for one man to die for the people.'

Simon Peter, with another disciple, followed Jesus. This disciple, who was known to the high priest, went with Jesus into the high priest's palace, but Peter stayed outside the door. So the other disciple, the one known to the high priest, went out, spoke to the woman who was keeping the door and brought Peter in. The maid on duty at the door said to Peter,

O   Aren't you another of that man's disciples?

N   He answered,

O   I am not.

N   Now it was cold, and the servants and guards had lit a charcoal fire and were standing there warming themselves; so Peter stood there too, warming himself with the others.

The high priest questioned Jesus about his disciples and his teaching. Jesus answered,

J   I have spoken openly for all the world to hear; I have always taught in the synagogue and in the Temple where all the Jews meet together: I have said nothing in secret. But why ask me? Ask my hearers what I taught: they know what I said.

N   At these words, one of the guards standing by gave Jesus a slap in the face, saying,

O   Is that the way to answer the high priest?

N   Jesus replied,

J   If there is something wrong in what I said, point it out; but if there is no offence in it, why do you strike me?

N   Then Annas sent him, still bound, to Caiaphas, the high priest. As Simon Peter stood there warming himself, someone said to him,

O   Aren't you another of his disciples?

N   He denied it saying,

O   I am not.

N   One of the high priest's servants, a relation of the man whose ear Peter had cut off, said,

O   Didn't I see you in the garden with him?

N   Again Peter denied it, and at once a cock crew.

They then led Jesus from the house of Caiaphas to the Praetorium. It was now morning. They did not go into the Praetorium themselves or they would be defiled and unable to eat the passover. So Pilate came outside to them and said,

O   What charge do you bring against this man?

N   They replied,

C   If he were not a criminal, we should not be handing him over to you.

N   Pilate said,

O   Take him yourselves, and try him by your own Law.

N   The Jews answered,

C   We are not allowed to put a man to death.

N   This was to fulfil the words Jesus had spoken indicating the way he was going to die.

So Pilate went back into the Praetorium and called Jesus to him and asked,

O   Are you the king of Jews?

N   Jesus replied,

J   Do you ask this of your own accord, or have others spoken to you about me?

N   Pilate answered,

O   Am I a Jew? It is your own people and the chief priests who have handed you over to me: what have you done?

N   Jesus replied,

J   Mine is not a kingdom of this world; if my kingdom were of this world, my men would have fought to prevent me being surrendered to the Jews. But my kingdom is not of this kind.

N   Pilate said,

O   So you are the king then?

N   Jesus answered,

J   It is you who say it. Yes, I am a king. I was born for this; I came into the world for this; to bear witness to the truth, and all who are on the side of truth listen to my voice.

N   Pilate said,

O   Truth? What is that?

N   And with that he went out again to the Jews and said,

O   I find no case against him. But according to a custom of yours I should release one prisoner at the Passover; would you like me, then, to release the king of Jews?

N   At this they shouted:

C   Not this man, but Barabbas.

N   Barabbas was a brigand.

Pilate then had Jesus taken away and scourged; and after this, the soldiers twisted some thorns into a crown and put it on his head, and dressed him in a purple robe. They kept coming up to him and saying,

C   Hail, king of the Jews!

N   and they slapped him in the face.

Pilate came outside again and said to them,

O   Look, I am going to bring him out to you to let you see that I find no case.

N   Jesus then came out wearing the crown of thorns and the purple robe. Pilate said,

O   Here is the man.

N   When they saw him the chief priests and the guards shouted,

C   Crucify him! Crucify him!

N   Pilate said,

O   Take him yourselves and crucify him: I can find no case against him

N   The Jews replied,

C   We have a Law, and according to the Law he ought to die, because he has claimed to be the son of God.

N   When Pilate heard them say this his fears increased. Re-entering the Praetorium, he said to Jesus,

O   Where do you come from?

N   But Jesus made no answer. Pilate then said to him,

O   Are you refusing to speak to me? Surely you know I have power to release you and I have power to crucify you?

N   Jesus replied,

J   You would have no power over me if it had not been given you from above; that is why the one who handed me over to you has the greater guilt.

N   From that moment Pilate was anxious to set him free, but the Jews shouted,

C   If you set him free you are no friend of Caesar's; anyone who makes himself king is defying Caesar.

N   Hearing these words, Pilate had Jesus brought out, and seated himself on the chair of judgement at a place called the Pavement, in Hebrew Gabbatha. It was Passover Preparation Day, about the sixth hour. Pilate said to the Jews,

O   Here is your king.

N   They said,

C   Take him away, take him away. Crucify him!

N   Pilate said,

O   Do you want me to crucify your king?

N   The chief priests answered,

C   We have no king except Caesar.

N   So in the end Pilate handed him over to them to be crucified.

They then took charge of Jesus, and carrying his own cross he went out of the city to the place of the skull, or, as it was called in Hebrew, Golgotha, where they crucified him with two others, one on either side with Jesus in the middle. Pilate wrote out a notice and had it fixed to the cross; it ran: 'Jesus the Nazarene, King of the Jews.' This notice was read by many of the Jews, because the place where Jesus was crucified was not far from the city, and the writing was in Hebrew, Latin and Greek. So the Jewish chief priests said to Pilate,

C   You should not write 'King of the Jews', but 'This man said: I am King of the Jews'.

N   Pilate answered,

O   What I have written, I have written.

N   When the soldiers had finished crucifying Jesus they took his clothing and divided it into four shares, one for each soldier. His undergarment was seamless, woven in one piece from neck to hem; so they said to one another,

C   Instead of tearing it, let's throw dice to decide who is to have it.

N   In this way the words of scripture were fulfilled:

They shared out my clothing among them.

They cast lots for my clothes.

This is exactly what the soldiers did.

Near the cross of Jesus stood his mother and his mother's sister, Mary the wife of Clopas, and Mary of Magdala. Seeing his mother and the disciple he loved standing near her, Jesus said to his mother,

J   Woman, this is your son.

N   Then to the disciple he said,

J   This is your mother.

N   And from that moment the disciple made a place for her in his home.

After this, Jesus knew that everything had now been completed, and to fulfil the scripture perfectly he said:

J   I am thirsty.

N   A jar full of vinegar stood there, so putting a sponge soaked in vinegar on a hyssop stick they held it up to his mouth. After Jesus had taken the vinegar he said,

J   It is accomplished;

N   and bowing his head he gave up the spirit.

All kneel and pause a moment.

N   It was Preparation Day, and to prevent the bodies remaining on the cross during the sabbath – since that sabbath was a day of special solemnity – the Jews asked Pilate to have the legs broken and the bodies taken away. Consequently the soldiers came and broke the legs of the first man who had been crucified with him and then of the other. When they came to Jesus, they found that he was already dead, and so instead of breaking his legs one of the soldiers pierced his side with a lance; and immediately there came out blood and water. This is the evidence of one who saw it – trustworthy evidence, and he knows he speaks the truth – and he gives it so that you may believe as well. Because all this happened to fulfil the words of scripture:

Not one bone of his will be broken,

and again, in another place scripture says:

They will look on the one whom they have pierced.

After this, Joseph of Arimathaea, who was a disciple of Jesus – though a secret one because he was afraid of the Jews – asked Pilate to let him remove the body of Jesus. Pilate gave permission, so they came and took it away. Nicodemus came as well – the same one who had first come to Jesus at night – time – and he brought a mixture of myrrh and aloes, weighing about a hundred pounds. They took the body of Jesus and wrapped it with the spices in linen cloths, following the Jewish burial custom. At the place where he had been crucified there was a garden, and in the garden a new tomb in which no one had yet been buried. Since it was the Jewish Day of Preparation and the tomb was near at hand, they laid Jesus there.

FIRST READING

Isa 52:13–53:12

See, my servant will prosper,
he shall be lifted up, exalted, rise to great
heights.

As the crowds were appalled on seeing him
– so disfigured did he look
that he seemed no longer human –
so will the crowds be astonished at him,
and kings stand speechless before him;
for they shall see something never told
and witness something never heard before:
'Who could believe what we have heard,
and to whom has the power of the Lord been
revealed?'

Like a sapling he grew up in front of us,
like a root in arid ground.
Without beauty, without majesty (we saw him),
no looks to attract our eyes;
a thing despised and rejected by men,
a man of sorrows and familiar with suffering,
a man to make people screen their faces;
he was despised and we took no account
of him.

And yet ours were the sufferings he bore,
ours the sorrows he carried.
But we, we thought of him as someone
punished,
struck by God, and brought low.
Yet he was pierced through for our faults,
crushed for our sins.
On him lies a punishment that brings
us peace,
and through his wounds we are healed.

We had all gone astray like sheep,
each taking his own way,
and the Lord burdened him
with the sins of all of us.
Harshly dealt with, he bore it humbly,
he never opened his mouth,
like a lamb that is led to the slaughter-house,
like a sheep that is dumb before its shearers
never opening its mouth.

By force and by law he was taken;
would anyone plead his cause?
Yes, he was torn away from the land of
the living;
for our faults struck down in death.
They gave him a grave with the wicked,
a tomb with the rich,
though he had done no wrong
and there had been no perjury in his mouth.
The Lord has been pleased to crush him
with suffering.

If he offers his life in atonement,
he shall see his heirs, he shall have a long life
and through him what the Lord wishes will
be done.
His soul's anguish over
he shall see the light and be content.
By his sufferings shall my servant
justify many,
taking their faults on himself.

Hence I will grant whole hordes for
his tribute,
he shall divide the spoil with the mighty,
for surrendering himself to death
and letting himself be taken for a sinner,
while he was bearing the faults of many
and praying all the time for sinners.

RESPONSORIAL PSALM

Ps 30:2, 6, 12-13, 15-17, 25 (Luke 23:46)

R̸. Father, into your hands I commend
my spirit.

In you, O Lord, I take refuge.
Let me never be put to shame.
In your justice, set me free.
Into your hands I commend my spirit.
It is you who will redeem me, Lord.

R̸. Father, into your hands I commend
my spirit.

In the face of all my foes
I am a reproach,
an object of scorn to my neighbours
and of fear to my friends.

R̸. Father, into your hands I commend
my spirit.

Those who see me in the street
run far away from me.
I am like a dead man, forgotten in men's
hearts,
like a thing thrown away.

R̸. Father, into your hands I commend
my spirit.

But as for me, I trust in you, Lord,
I say: 'You are my God.'
My life is in your hands, deliver me
from the hands of those who hate me.

R̸. Father, into your hands I commend
my spirit.

Let your face shine on your servant.
Save me in your love.
Be strong, let your heart take courage,
all who hope in the Lord.

R̸. Father, into your hands I commend
my spirit.

SECOND READING

Heb 4:14-16; 5:7-9

Since in Jesus, the Son of God, we have the
supreme high priest who has gone through to
the highest heaven, we must never let go of
the faith that we have professed. For it is not
as if we had a high priest who was incapable
of feeling our weaknesses with us; but we
have one who has been tempted in every way
that we are, though he is without sin. Let us
be confident, then, in approaching the throne
of grace, that we shall have mercy from him
and find grace when we are in need of help.

During his life on earth, he offered up
prayer and entreaty, aloud and in silent tears,
to the one who had the power to save him out
of death, and he submitted so humbly that his
prayer was heard. Although he was Son, he
learnt to obey through suffering; but having
been made perfect, he became for all who
obey him the source of eternal salvation.

FIRST READING
Gen 1:1–2:2

In the beginning God created the heavens and the earth. Now the earth was a formless void, there was darkness over the deep, and God's spirit hovered over the water.

God said, 'Let there be light,' and there was light. God saw that light was good, and God divided light from darkness. God called light 'day', and darkness he called 'night'. Evening came and morning came: the first day. God said, 'Let there be a vault in the waters to divide the waters in two.' And so it was. God made the vault, and it divided the waters above the vault from the waters under the vault. God called the vault 'heaven'. Evening came and morning came: the second day.

God said, 'Let the waters under heaven come together into a single mass, and let dry land appear.' And so it was. God called the dry land 'earth' and the mass of waters 'seas', and God saw that it was good.

God said, 'Let the earth produce vegetation: seed-bearing plants, and fruit trees bearing fruit with their seed inside, on the earth.' And so it was. The earth produced vegetation: plants bearing seed in their several kinds, and trees bearing fruit with their seed inside in their several kinds. God saw that it was good. Evening came and morning came: the third day.

God said, 'Let there be lights in the vault of heaven to divide day from night, and let them indicate festivals, days and years. Let them be lights in the vault of heaven to shine on the earth.' And so it was. God made the two great lights: the greater light to govern the day, the smaller light to govern the night, and the stars. God set them in the vault of heaven to shine on the earth, to govern the day and the night and to divide light from darkness. God saw that it was good. Evening came and morning came: the fourth day.

God said, 'Let the waters teem with living creatures, and let birds fly above the earth within the vault of heaven.' And so it was. God created great seaserpents and every kind of living creature with which the waters teem, and every kind of winged creature. God saw that it was good. God blessed them, saying, 'Be fruitful, multiply, and fill the waters of the seas, and let the birds multiply upon the earth.' Evening came and morning came: the fifth day.

God said, 'Let the earth produce every kind of living creature: cattle, reptiles, and every kind of wild beast.' And so it was. God made every kind of wild beast, every kind of cattle, and every kind of land reptile. God saw that it was good.

God said, 'Let us make man in our own image, in the likeness of ourselves, and let them be masters of the fish of the sea, the birds of heaven, the cattle, all the wild beasts and all the reptiles that crawl upon the earth.'

God created man in the image of himself, in the image of God he created him, male and female he created them.

God blessed them, saying to them, 'Be fruitful, multiply, fill the earth and conquer it. Be masters of the fish of the sea, the birds of heaven and all living animals on the earth.' God said, 'See, I give you all the seed-bearing plants that are upon the whole earth, and all the trees with seed-bearing fruit; this shall be your food. To all wild beasts, all birds of heaven and all living reptiles on the earth I give all the foliage of plants for food.' And so it was. God saw all he had made, and indeed it was very good. Evening came and morning came: the sixth day.

Thus heaven and earth were completed with all their array. On the seventh day God completed the work he had been doing. He rested on the seventh day after all the work he had been doing.

shorter reading

Gen 1:1, 26-31

In the beginning God created the heavens and the earth.

God said, 'Let us make man in our own image, in the likeness of ourselves, and let them be masters of the fish of the sea, the birds of heaven, the cattle, all the wild beasts and all the reptiles that crawl upon the earth.'

God created man in the image of himself, in the image of God he created him, male and female he created them.

God blessed them, saying to them, 'Be fruitful, multiply, fill the earth and conquer it. Be masters of the fish of the sea, the birds of heaven and all living animals on the earth.' God said, 'See, I give you all the seed-bearing plants that are upon the whole earth, and all the trees with seed-bearing fruit; this shall be your food. To all wild beasts, all birds of heaven and all living reptiles on the earth I give all the foliage of plants for food.' And so it was. God saw all he had made, and indeed it was very good.

RESPONSORIAL PSALM
Ps 103:1-2, 5-6, 10, 12-14, 24, 35 (Cf. v. 30)

℟. Send forth your spirit, O Lord, and renew the face of the earth.

Bless the Lord, my soul!
Lord God, how great you are,
clothed in majesty and glory,
wrapped in light as in a robe!

℟. Send forth your spirit, O Lord, and renew the face of the earth.

You founded the earth on its base,
to stand firm from age to age.
You wrapped it with the ocean like a cloak:
the waters stood higher than the mountains.

℟. Send forth your spirit, O Lord, and renew the face of the earth.

You make springs gush forth in the valleys:
they flow in between the hills.
On their banks dwell the birds of heaven;
from the branches they sing their song.

℟. Send forth your spirit, O Lord, and renew the face of the earth.

From your dwelling you water the hills;
earth drinks its fill of your gift.
You make the grass grow for the cattle
and the plants to serve man's needs.

℟. Send forth your spirit, O Lord, and renew the face of the earth.

How many are your works, O Lord!
In wisdom you have made them all.
The earth is full of your riches.
Bless the Lord, my soul!

℟. Send forth your spirit, O Lord, and renew the face of the earth.

or

Ps 32:4-7, 12-13, 20, 22 (5)

℟. The Lord fills the earth with his love.

The word of the Lord is faithful
and all his works to be trusted.
The Lord loves justice and right
and fills the earth with his love.

℟. The Lord fills the earth with his love.

By his word the heavens were made,
by the breath of his mouth all the stars.
He collects the waves of the ocean;
he stores up the depths of the sea.

℟. The Lord fills the earth with his love.

They are happy, whose God is the Lord,
the people he has chosen as his own.
From the heavens the Lord looks forth,
he sees all the children of men.

℟. The Lord fills the earth with his love.

Our soul is waiting for the Lord.
The Lord is our help and our shield.
May your love be upon us, O Lord,
as we place all our hope in you.

℟. The Lord fills the earth with his love.

SECOND READING
Gen 22:1-18

God put Abraham to the test. 'Abraham, Abraham,' he called. 'Here I am' he replied. 'Take your son,' God said 'your only child

287

Isaac, whom you love, and go to the land of Moriah. There you shall offer him as a burnt offering, on a mountain I will point out to you.'

Rising early next morning Abraham saddled his ass and took with him two of his servants and his son Isaac. He chopped wood for the burnt offering and started on his journey to the place God had pointed out to him. On the third day Abraham looked up and saw the place in the distance. Then Abraham said to his servants, 'Stay here with the donkey. The boy and I will go over there; we will worship and come back to you.'

Abraham took the wood for the burnt offering, loaded it on Isaac, and carried in his own hands the fire and the knife. Then the two of them set out together. Isaac spoke to his father Abraham, 'Father' he said. 'Yes, my son' he replied. 'Look,' he said 'here are the fire and the wood, but where is the lamb for the burnt offering?' Abraham answered, 'My son, God himself will provide the lamb for the burnt offering.' Then the two of them went on together.

When they arrived at the place God had pointed out to him, Abraham built an altar there, and arranged the wood. Then he bound his son Isaac and put him on the altar on top of the wood. Abraham stretched out his hand and seized the knife to kill his son.

But the angel of the Lord called to him from heaven. 'Abraham, Abraham' he said. 'I am here' he replied. 'Do not raise your hand against the boy' the angel said. 'Do not harm him, for now I know you fear God. You have not refused me your son, your only son.' Then looking up, Abraham saw a ram caught by its horns in a bush. Abraham took the ram and offered it as a burnt-offering in place of his son. Abraham called this place 'The Lord provides', and hence the saying today: On the mountain the Lord provides.

The angel of the Lord called Abraham a second time from heaven. 'I swear by my own self – it is the Lord who speaks – because you have done this, because you have not refused me your son, your only son, I will shower blessings on you, I will make your descendants as many as the stars of heaven and the grains of sand on the seashore. Your descendants shall gain possession of the gates of their enemies. All the nations of the earth shall bless themselves by your descendants, as a reward for your obedience.'

shorter reading
Gen 22:1-2, 9-13, 15-18

God put Abraham to the test. 'Abraham, Abraham,' he called. 'Here I am' he replied. 'Take your son,' God said 'your only child

Isaac, whom you love, and go to the land of Moriah. There you shall offer him as a burnt offering, on a mountain I will point out to you.'

When they arrived at the place God had pointed out to him, Abraham built an altar there, and arranged the wood. Then he bound his son Isaac and put him on the altar on top of the wood. Abraham stretched out his hand and seized the knife to kill his son.

But the angel of the Lord called to him from heaven. 'Abraham, Abraham' he said. 'I am here' he replied. 'Do not raise your hand against the boy' the angel said. 'Do not harm him, for now I know you fear God. You have not refused me your son, your only son.' Then looking up, Abraham saw a ram caught by its horns in a bush. Abraham took the ram and offered it as a burnt-offering in place of his son.

The angel of the Lord called Abraham a second time from heaven. 'I swear by my own self – it is the Lord who speaks – because you have done this, because you have not refused me your son, your only son, I will shower blessings on you, I will make your descendants as many as the stars of heaven and the grains of sand on the seashore. Your descendants shall gain possession of the gates of their enemies. All the nations of the earth shall bless themselves by your descendants, as a reward for your obedience.'

RESPONSORIAL PSALM
Ps 15:5, 8-11 (1)

R̶. Preserve me, God, I take refuge in you.

O Lord, it is you who are my portion and cup;
it is you yourself who are my prize.
I keep the Lord ever in my sight:
since he is at my right hand, I shall stand
    firm.

R̶. Preserve me, God, I take refuge in you.

And so my heart rejoices, my soul is glad;
even my body shall rest in safety.
For you will not leave my soul among the
    dead,
nor let your beloved know decay.

R̶. Preserve me, God, I take refuge in you.

You will show me the path of life,
the fulness of joy in your presence,
at your right hand happiness for ever.

R̶. Preserve me, God, I take refuge in you.

THIRD READING
Exod 14:15–15:1

The Lord said to Moses, 'Why do you cry to me so? Tell the sons of Israel to march on. For yourself, raise your staff and stretch out your hand over the sea and part it for the

sons of Israel to walk through the sea on dry ground. I for my part will make the heart of the Egyptians so stubborn that they will follow them. So shall I win myself glory at the expense of Pharaoh, of all his army, his chariots, his horsemen. And when I have won glory for myself, at the expense of Pharaoh and his chariots and his army, the Egyptians will learn that I am the Lord.'

Then the angel of the Lord, who marched at the front of the army of Israel, changed station and moved to their rear. The pillar of cloud changed station from the front to the rear of them, and remained there. It came between the camp of the Egyptians and the camp of Israel. The cloud was dark, and the night passed without the armies drawing any closer the whole night long. Moses stretched out his hand over the sea. The Lord drove back the sea with a strong easterly wind all night, and he made dry land of the sea. The waters parted and the sons of Israel went on dry ground right into the sea, walls of water to right and to left of them. The Egyptians gave chase: after them they went, right into the sea, all Pharaoh's horses, his chariots, and his horsemen. In the morning watch, the Lord looked down on the army of the Egyptians from the pillar of fire and of cloud, and threw the army into confusion. He so clogged their chariot wheels that they could scarcely make headway. 'Let us flee from the Israelites,' the Egyptians cried 'the Lord is fighting for them against the Egyptians!' 'Stretch out your hand over the sea,' the Lord said to Moses 'that the waters may flow back on the Egyptians and their chariots and their horsemen.' Moses stretched out his hand over the sea and, as day broke, the sea returned to its bed. The fleeing Egyptians marched right into it, and the Lord overthrew the Egyptians in the very middle of the sea. The returning waters overwhelmed the chariots and the horsemen of Pharaoh's whole army, which had followed the Israelites into the sea; not a single one of them was left. But the sons of Israel had marched through the sea on dry ground, walls of water to right and to left of them. That day, the Lord rescued Israel from the Egyptians, and Israel saw the Egyptians lying dead on the shore. Israel witnessed the great act that the Lord had performed against the Egyptians, and the people venerated the Lord; they put their faith in the Lord and in Moses, his servant.

It was then that Moses and the sons of Israel sang this song in honour of the Lord:

RESPONSORIAL PSALM
Exod 15:1-6, 17-18 (1)

R̷. I will sing to the Lord, glorious his
      triumph!

I will sing to the Lord, glorious his triumph!
Horse and rider he has thrown into the sea!
The Lord is my strength, my song, my
      salvation.
This is my God and I extol him,
my father's God and I give him praise.

R̷. I will sing to the Lord, glorious his
      triumph!

The Lord is a warrior! The Lord is his name.
The chariots of Pharaoh he hurled into the
      sea,
the flower of his army is drowned in the sea.
The deeps hide them; they sank like a stone.

R̷. I will sing to the Lord, glorious his
      triumph!

Your right hand, Lord, glorious in its power,
your right hand, Lord, has shattered the
      enemy.
In the greatness of your glory you crushed
      the foe.

R̷. I will sing to the Lord, glorious his
      triumph!

You will lead your people and plant them on
      your mountain,
the place, O Lord, where you have made
      your home,
the sanctuary, Lord, which your hands
      have made.
The Lord will reign for ever and ever.

R̷. I will sing to the Lord, glorious his
      triumph!

FOURTH READING
Isa 54:5-14

Now your creator will be your husband,
his name, the Lord of hosts;
your redeemer will be the Holy One of Israel,
he is called the God of the whole earth.
Yes, like a forsaken wife, distressed in spirit,
the Lord calls you back.
Does a man cast off the wife of his youth?
says your God.

I did forsake you for a brief moment,
but with great love will I take you back.
In excess of anger, for a moment
I hid my face from you.
But with everlasting love I have taken pity
      on you,
says the Lord, your redeemer.

I am now as I was in the days of Noah
when I swore that Noah's waters
should never flood the world again.

So now I swear concerning my anger with you
and the threats I made against you;

for the mountains may depart,
the hills be shaken,
but my love for you will never leave you;
and my covenant of peace with you will never
      be shaken,
says the Lord who takes pity on you.

Unhappy creature, storm-tossed, disconsolate,
see, I will set your stones on carbuncles
and your foundations on sapphires.
I will make rubies your battlements,
your gates crystal,
and your entire wall precious stones.
Your sons will all be taught by the Lord.
The prosperity of your sons will be great.
You will be founded on integrity;
remote from oppression, you will have nothing
      to fear;
remote from terror, it will not approach you.

RESPONSORIAL PSALM
Ps 29:2, 4-6, 11-13 (2)

R̷. I will praise you, Lord, you have rescued
      me.

I will praise you, Lord, you have rescued me
and have not let my enemies rejoice over me.
O Lord, you have raised my soul from
      the dead,
restored me to life from those who sink into
      the grave.

R̷. I will praise you, Lord, you have
      rescued me.

Sing psalms to the Lord, you who love him,
give thanks to his holy name.
His anger lasts but a moment; his favour
      through life.
At night there are tears, but joy comes
      with dawn.

R̷. I will praise you, Lord, you have
      rescued me.

The Lord listened and had pity.
The Lord came to my help.
For me you have changed my mourning
      into dancing,
O Lord my God, I will thank you for ever.

R̷. I will praise you, Lord, you have
      rescued me.

FIFTH READING
Isa 55:1-11

Thus says the Lord:
      Oh, come to the water all you who are
            thirsty;
      though you have no money, come!
      Buy corn without money, and eat,
      and, at no cost, wine and milk.

Why spend money on what is not bread,
your wages on what fails to satisfy?
Listen, listen to me, and you will have good
            things to eat
and rich food to enjoy.
Pay attention, come to me;
and your soul will live.

With you I will make an everlasting covenant
out of the favours promised to David.
See, I have made of you a witness to the
      peoples,
a leader and a master of the nations.
See, you will summon a nation you never
      knew,
those unknown will come hurrying to you,
for the sake of the Lord your God,
of the Holy One of Israel who will glorify
      you.

Seek the Lord while he is still to be found,
call to him while he is still near.
Let the wicked man abandon his way,
the evil man his thoughts.
Let him turn back to the Lord who will take
      pity on him,
to our God who is rich in forgiving;
for my thoughts are not your thoughts,
my ways not your ways – it is the Lord
      who speaks.
Yes, the heavens are as high above earth
as my ways are above your ways,
my thoughts above your thoughts.
Yes, as the rain and the snow come down
from the heavens and do not return without
watering the earth, making it yield and giving
growth to provide seed for the sower and
bread for the eating, so the word that goes
from my mouth does not return to me empty,
without carrying out my will and succeeding
in what it was sent to do.

RESPONSORIAL PSALM
Isa 12:2-6 (3)

R̷. With joy you will draw water from the
      wells of salvation.

Truly God is my salvation,
I trust, I shall not fear.
For the Lord is my strength, my song,
he became my saviour.
With joy you will draw water
from the wells of salvation.

R̷. With joy you will draw water from the
      wells of salvation.

Give thanks to the Lord, give praise to his
      name!
Make his mighty deeds known to the peoples,
declare the greatness of his name.

R̷. With joy you will draw water from the
      wells of salvation.

Sing a psalm to the Lord
for he has done glorious deeds,
make them known to all the earth!
People of Zion, sing and shout for joy
for great in your midst is the Holy One
    of Israel.

℟. With joy you will draw water from the
    wells of salvation.

SIXTH READING
Bar 3:9-15, 32–4:4

Listen, Israel, to commands that bring life;
hear, and learn what knowledge means.
Why, Israel, why are you in the country of
    your enemies,
growing older and older in an alien land,
sharing defilement with the dead,
reckoned with those who go to Sheol?
Because you have forsaken the fountain of
    wisdom.
Had you walked in the way of God,
you would have lived in peace for ever.
Learn where knowledge is, where strength,
where understanding, and so learn
where length of days is, where life,
where the light of the eyes and where peace.
But who has found out where she lives,
who has entered her treasure house?

But the One who knows all knows her,
he has grasped her with his own intellect,
he has set the earth firm for ever
and filled it with four-footed beasts,
he sends the light – and it goes,
he recalls it – and trembling it obeys;
the stars shine joyfully at their set times:
when he calls them, they answer, 'Here we
    are';
they gladly shine for their creator.
It is he who is our God,
no other can compare with him.
He has grasped the whole way of knowledge,
and confided it to his servant Jacob,
to Israel his well-beloved;
so causing her to appear on earth
and move among men.

This is the book of the commandments
    of God,
the Law that stands for ever;
those who keep her live,
those who desert her die.
Turn back, Jacob, seize her,
in her radiance make your way to light:
do not yield your glory to another,
your privilege to a people not your own.
Israel, blessed are we:
what pleases God has been revealed to us.

RESPONSORIAL PSALM
Ps 18:8-11 (John 6:69)

℟. You have the message of eternal life,
    O Lord.

The law of the Lord is perfect,
it revives the soul.
The rule of the Lord is to be trusted,
it gives wisdom to the simple.

℟. You have the message of eternal life,
    O Lord.

The precepts of the Lord are right,
they gladden the heart.
The command of the Lord is clear,
it gives light to the eyes.

℟. You have the message of eternal life,
    O Lord.

The fear of the Lord is holy,
abiding for ever.
The decrees of the Lord are truth
and all of them just.

℟. You have the message of eternal life,
    O Lord.

The are more to be desired than gold,
than the purest of gold
and sweeter are they than honey,
than honey from the comb.

℟. You have the message of eternal life,
    O Lord.

SEVENTH READING
Ezek 36:16-28

The word of the Lord was addressed to me
as follows: 'Son of man, the members of
the House of Israel used to live in their own
land, but they defiled it by their conduct
and actions. I then discharged my fury at
them because of the blood they shed in
their land and the idols with which they
defiled it. I scattered them among the nations
and dispersed them in foreign countries. I
sentenced them as their conduct and actions
deserved. And now they have profaned my
holy name among the nations where they have
gone, so that people say of them, "These are
the people of the Lord; they have been exiled
from his land." But I have been concerned
about my holy name, which the House of
Israel has profaned among the nations where
they have gone. And so, say to the House of
Israel, "The Lord says this: I am not doing
this for my sake, House of Israel, but for
the sake of my holy name, which you have
profaned among the nations where you have
gone. I mean to display the holiness of my
great name, which has been profaned among
the nations, which you have profaned among
them. And the nations will learn that I am

the Lord – it is the Lord who speaks – when I
display my holiness for your sake before their
eyes. Then I am going to take you from among
the nations and gather you together from all
the foreign countries, and bring you home to
your own land. I shall pour clean water over
you and you will be cleansed; I shall cleanse
you of all your defilement and all your idols.
I shall give you a new heart, and put a new
spirit in you; I shall remove the heart of stone
from your bodies and give you a heart of flesh
instead. I shall put my spirit in you, and make
you keep my laws and sincerely respect my
observances. You will live in the land which I
gave your ancestors. You shall be my people
and I will be your God."'

RESPONSORIAL PSALM
Ps 41:3, 5; 42:3, 4 (41:1)

℟. Like the deer that yearns for running
    streams,
so my soul is yearning for you, my God.

My soul is thirsting for God.
the God of my life;
when can I enter and see
the face of God?

℟. Like the deer that yearns for running
    streams,
so my soul is yearning for you, my God.

These things I will remember
as I pour out my soul:
how I would lead the rejoicing crowd
into the house of God,
amid cries of gladness and thanksgiving,
the throng wild with joy.

℟. Like the deer that yearns for running
    streams,
so my soul is yearning for you, my God.

O send forth your light and your truth;
let these be my guide.
Let them bring me to your holy mountain
to the place where you dwell.

℟. Like the deer that yearns for running
    streams,
so my soul is yearning for you, my God.

And I will come to the altar of God,
the God of my joy.
My redeemer, I will thank you on the harp,
O God, my God.

℟. Like the deer that yearns for running
    streams,
so my soul is yearning for you, my God.

or

Isa 12:2-6 (3)

R̠. With joy you will draw water from the
 wells of salvation.

Truly God is my salvation,
I trust, I shall not fear.
For the Lord is my strength, my song,
he became my saviour.
With joy you will draw water
from the wells of salvation.

R̠. With joy you will draw water from the
 wells of salvation.

Give thanks to the Lord, give praise to his
 name!
Make his mighty deeds known to the peoples,
declare the greatness of his name.

R̠. With joy you will draw water from the
 wells of salvation.

Sing a psalm to the Lord
for he has done glorious deeds,
make them known to all the earth!
People of Zion, sing and shout for joy
for great in your midst is the Holy One
 of Israel.

R̠. With joy you will draw water from the
 wells of salvation.

or

Ps 50:12-15, 18, 19 (12)

R̠. A pure heart create for me, O God.

A pure heart create for me, O God,
put a steadfast spirit within me.
Do not cast me away from your presence,
nor deprive me of your holy spirit.

R̠. A pure heart create for me, O God.

Give me again the joy of your help;
with a spirit of fervour sustain me,
that I may teach transgressors your ways
and sinners may return to you.

R̠. A pure heart create for me, O God.

For in sacrifice you take no delight,
burnt offering from me you would refuse,
my sacrifice, a contrite spirit.
A humbled, contrite heart you will not spurn.

R̠. A pure heart create for me, O God.

EPISTLE
Rom 6:3-11

When we were baptised in Christ Jesus we
were baptised in his death; in other words,
when we were baptised we went into the tomb
with him and joined him in death, so that
as Christ was raised from the dead by the
Father's glory, we too might live a new life.

If in union with Christ we have imitated
his death, we shall also imitate him in his
resurrection. We must realise that our former
selves have been crucified with him to destroy
this sinful body and to free us from the
slavery of sin. When a man dies, of course, he
has finished with sin.

But we believe that having died with Christ
we shall return to life with him: Christ, as we
know, having been raised from the dead will
never die again. Death has no power over him
any more. When he died, he died, once for all,
to sin, so his life now is life with God; and in
that way, you too must consider yourselves
to be dead to sin but alive for God in Christ
Jesus.

RESPONSORIAL PSALM
Ps 117:1-2, 16-17, 22-23

R̠. Alleluia, alleluia, alleluia!

Give thanks to the Lord for he is good,
for his love has no end.
Let the sons of Israel say:
'His love has no end.'

R̠. Alleluia, alleluia, alleluia!

The Lord's right hand has triumphed;
his right hand raised me.
I shall not die, I shall live
and recount his deeds.

R̠. Alleluia, alleluia, alleluia!

The stone which the builders rejected
has become the corner stone.
This is the work of the Lord,
a marvel in our eyes.

R̠. Alleluia, alleluia, alleluia!

FIRST READING
Acts 10:34, 37-43

Peter addressed Cornelius and his household: 'You must have heard about the recent happenings in Judaea; about Jesus of Nazareth and how he began in Galilee, after John had been preaching baptism. God had anointed him with the Holy Spirit and with power, and because God was with him, Jesus went about doing good and curing all who had fallen into the power of the devil. Now I, and those with me, can witness to everything he did throughout the countryside of Judaea and in Jerusalem itself: and also to the fact that they killed him by hanging him on a tree, yet three days afterwards God raised him to life and allowed him to be seen, not by the whole people but only by certain witnesses God had chosen beforehand. Now we are those witnesses – we have eaten and drunk with him after his resurrection from the dead – and he has ordered us to proclaim this to his people and to tell them that God has appointed him to judge everyone, alive or dead. It is to him that all the prophets bear this witness: that all who believe in Jesus will have their sins forgiven through his name.'

RESPONSORIAL PSALM
Ps 117:1-2, 16-17, 22-23 (24)

R̀. This day was made by the Lord;
we rejoice and are glad.
    or:
R̀. Alleluia, alleluia, alleluia!

Give thanks to the Lord for he is good,
for his love has no end.
Let the sons of Israel say:
'His love has no end.'

R̀. This day was made by the Lord;
we rejoice and are glad.
    or:
R̀. Alleluia, alleluia, alleluia!

The Lord's right hand has triumphed;
his right hand raised me.
I shall not die, I shall live
and recount his deeds.

R̀. This day was made by the Lord;
we rejoice and are glad.
    or:
R̀. Alleluia, alleluia, alleluia!

The stone which the builders rejected
has become the corner stone.
This is the work of the Lord,
a marvel in our eyes.

R̀. This day was made by the Lord;
we rejoice and are glad.
    or:
R̀. Alleluia, alleluia, alleluia!

SECOND READING
Col 3:1-4

Since you have been brought back to true life with Christ, you must look for the things that are in heaven, where Christ is, sitting at God's right hand. Let your thoughts be on heavenly things, not on the things that are on the earth, because you have died, and now the life you have is hidden with Christ in God. But when Christ is revealed – and he is your life – you too will be revealed in all your glory with him.

or:

1 Cor 5:6-8

You must know how even a small amount of yeast is enough to leaven all the dough, so get rid of all the old yeast, and make yourselves into a completely new batch of bread, unleavened as you are meant to be. Christ, our Passover, has been sacrificed; let us celebrate the feast, by getting rid of all the old yeast of evil and wickedness, having only the unleavened bread of sincerity and truth.

SEQUENCE
Victimae paschali laudes
Christians, to the Paschal Victim
    offer sacrifice and praise.
The sheep are ransomed
    by the Lamb;
and Christ, the undefiled,
hath sinners to his Father reconciled.

Death with life contended:
    combat strangely ended!
Life's own Champion, slain,
    yet lives to reign.

Tell us, Mary:
    say what thou didst see
    upon the way.
The tomb the Living did enclose;
I saw Christ's glory as he rose!

The angels there attesting;
shroud with grave-clothes resting.
Christ, my hope, has risen:
he goes before you into Galilee.

That Christ is truly risen
    from the dead we know.
Victorious king, thy mercy show!

Gospel

John 15:1-8

Jesus said to his disciples:
'I am the true vine,
and my Father is the vinedresser.
Every branch in me that bears no fruit
he cuts away,
and every branch that does bear fruit he prunes
to make it bear even more.
You are pruned already,
by means of the word that I have spoken to you.
Make your home in me, as I make mine in you.
As a branch cannot bear fruit all by itself,
but must remain part of the vine,
neither can you unless you remain in me.
I am the vine,
you are the branches.

Whoever remains in me, with me in him,
bears fruit in plenty;
for cut off from me you can do nothing.
Anyone who does not remain in me
is like a branch that has been thrown away
– he withers;
these branches are collected and thrown on the fire,
and they are burnt.
If you remain in me
and my words remain in you,
you may ask what you will
and you shall get it.
It is to the glory of my Father that you should bear much fruit,
and then you will be my disciples.'

FIRST READING

Apoc 12:10-12

I, John, heard a voice shout from heaven,
'Victory and power and empire for ever have
been won by our God, and all authority for his
Christ, now that the persecutor, who accused
our brothers day and night before our God,
has been brought down. They have triumphed
over him by the blood of the Lamb and by the
witness of their martyrdom, because even in
the face of death they would not cling to life.
Let the heavens rejoice and all who live there.'

RESPONSORIAL PSALM

Ps 125 (5)

R̰. Those who are sowing in tears
will sing when they reap.

When the Lord delivered Zion from bondage,
it seemed like a dream.
Then was our mouth filled with laughter,
on our lips there were songs.

R̰. Those who are sowing in tears
will sing when they reap.

The heathens themselves said: 'What marvels
the Lord worked for them!'
What marvels the Lord worked for us!
Indeed we were glad.

R̰. Those who are sowing in tears
will sing when they reap.

Deliver us, O Lord, from our bondage
as streams in dry land.
Those who are sowing in tears
will sing when they reap.

R̰. Those who are sowing in tears
will sing when they reap.

They go out, they go out, full of tears,
carrying seed for the sowing;
they come back, they come back, full of song,
carrying their sheaves.

R̰. Those who are sowing in tears
will sing when they reap.

Gospel (cont.)
John 21:1-19

After the meal Jesus said to Simon Peter, 'Simon son of John, do you love me more than these others do?' He answered 'Yes Lord, you know I love you.' Jesus said to him, 'Feed my lambs.' A second time, he said to him, 'Simon son of John, do you love me?' He replied, 'Yes, Lord, you know I love you.' Jesus said to him, 'Look after my sheep.' Then he said to him a third time, 'Simon son of John, do you love me?' Peter was upset that he asked him the third time, 'Do you love me?' and said, 'Lord, you know everything; you know I love you.' Jesus said to him, 'Feed my sheep.

'I tell you most solemnly,
when you were young
you put on your own belt
and walked where you liked;
but when you grow old
you will stretch out your hands,
and somebody else will put a belt round you
and take you where you would rather not go.'

In these words he indicated the kind of death by which Peter would give glory to God. After this he said, 'Follow me.'

Gospel
John 21:1-14

Jesus showed himself again to the disciples. It was by the Sea of Tiberias, and it happened like this: Simon Peter, Thomas called the Twin, Nathanael from Cana in Galilee, the sons of Zebedee and two more of his disciples were together. Simon Peter said, 'I'm going fishing.' They replied, 'We'll come with you.' They went out and got into the boat but caught nothing that night.

It was light by now and there stood Jesus on the shore, though the disciples did not realise that it was Jesus. Jesus called out, 'Have you caught anything, friends?' And when they answered, 'No,' he said, 'Throw the net out to starboard and you'll find something.' So they dropped the net, and there were so many fish that they could not haul it in. The disciple Jesus loved said to Peter, 'It is the Lord.' At these words 'It is the Lord', Simon Peter, who had practically nothing on, wrapped his cloak round him and jumped into the water. The other disciples came on in the boat, towing the net and the fish; they were only about a hundred yards from land.

As soon as they came ashore they saw that there was some bread there, and a charcoal fire with fish cooking on it. Jesus said, 'Bring some of the fish you have just caught.' Simon Peter went aboard and dragged the net to the shore, full of big fish, one hundred and fifty-three of them; and in spite of there being so many the net was not broken. Jesus said to them, 'Come and have breakfast.' None of the disciples was bold enough to ask, 'Who are you?'; they knew quite well it was the Lord. Jesus then stepped forward, took the bread and gave it to them, and the same with the fish. This was the third time that Jesus showed himself to the disciples after rising from the dead.

The Ascension of the Lord, 30 May 2019

SECOND READING
Heb 9:24-28; 10:19-23

It is not as though Christ had entered a man-made sanctuary which was only modelled on the real one; but it was heaven itself, so that he could appear in the actual presence of God on our behalf. And he does not have to offer himself again and again, like the high priest going into the sanctuary year after year with the blood that is not his own, or else he would have had to suffer over and over again since the world began. Instead of that, he has made his appearance once and for all, now at the end of the last age, to do away with sin by sacrificing himself. Since men only die once, and after that comes judgement, so Christ, too, offers himself only once to take the faults of many on himself, and when he appears a second time, it will not be to deal with sin but to reward with salvation those who are waiting for him.

In other words, brothers, through the blood of Jesus we have the right to enter the sanctuary, by a new way which he had opened for us, a living opening through the curtain, that is to say, his body. And we have the supreme high priest over all the house of God. So as we go in, let us be sincere in heart and filled with faith, our minds sprinkled and free from any trace of bad conscience and our bodies washed with pure water. Let us keep firm in the hope we profess, because the one who made the promise is faithful.

or

Eph 1:17-23

May the God of our Lord Jesus Christ, the Father of glory, give you a spirit of wisdom and perception of what is revealed, to bring you to full knowledge of him. May he enlighten the eyes of your mind so that you can see what hope his call holds for you, what rich glories he has promised the saints will inherit and how infinitely great is the power that he has exercised for us believers. This you can tell from the strength of his power at work in Christ, when he used it to raise him from the dead and to make him sit at his right hand, in heaven, far above every Sovereignty, Authority, Power, or Domination, or any other name that can be named, not only in this age, but also in the age to come. He has put all things under his feet, and made him as the ruler of everything, the head of the Church; which is his body, the fulness of him who fills the whole creation.

Pentecost Sunday, 9 June 2019

SECOND READING
Rom 8:8-17

People who are interested only in unspiritual things can never be pleasing to God. Your interests, however, are not in the unspiritual, but in the spiritual, since the Spirit of God has made his home in you. In fact, unless you possessed the Spirit of Christ you would not belong to him. Though your body may be dead it is because of sin, but if Christ is in you then your spirit is life itself because you have been justified; and if the Spirit of him who raised Jesus from the dead is living in you, then he who raised Jesus from the dead will give life to your own mortal bodies through his Spirit living in you.

So then, my brothers, there is no necessity for us to obey our unspiritual selves or to live unspiritual lives. If you do live in that way, you are doomed to die; but if by the Spirit you put an end to the misdeeds of the body you will live.

Everyone moved by the Spirit is a son of God. The spirit you received is not the spirit of slaves bringing fear into your lives again; it is the spirit of sons, and it makes us cry out, 'Abba, Father!' The Spirit himself and our spirit bear united witness that we are children of God. And if we are children we are heirs as well: heirs of God and coheirs with Christ, sharing his sufferings so as to share his glory.

SEQUENCE
Holy Spirit, Lord of light,
From the clear celestial height
Thy pure beaming radiance give.

Come, thou Father of the poor,
Come with treasures which endure;
Come, thou light of all that live!

Thou, of all consolers best,
Thou, the soul's delightful guest,
Dost refreshing peace bestow.

Thou in toil art comfort sweet;
Pleasant coolness in the heat;
Solace in the midst of woe.

Light immortal, light divine,
Visit thou these hearts of thine,
And our inmost being fill:

If thou take thy grace away,
Nothing pure in man will stay;
All his good is turned to ill.

Heal our wounds,
   our strength renew;
On our dryness pour thy dew;
Wash the stains of guilt away.

Bend the stubborn heart and will;
Melt the frozen, warm the chill;
Guide the steps that go astray.

Thou, on us who evermore
Thee confess and thee adore,
thy sevenfold gifts descend:

Give us comfort when we die,
Give us life with thee on high;
Give us joys that never end.

The Most Holy Body and Blood of Christ, *23 June 2019*

OPTIONAL SEQUENCE

Sing forth, O Zion, sweetly sing
The praises of thy Shepherd-King,
   In hymns and canticles divine;
Dare all thou canst, thou hast no song
Worthy his praises to prolong,
   So far surpassing powers like thine.

Today no theme of common praise
Forms the sweet burden of thy lays –
   The living, life-dispensing food –
That food which at the sacred board
Unto the brethren twelve our Lord
   His parting legacy bestowed.

Then be the anthem clear and strong,
Thy fullest note, thy sweetest song,
   The very music of thy breast:
For now shines forth the day sublime
That brings remembrance of the time
   When Jesus first his table blessed.

Within our new King's banquet-hall
They meet to keep the festival
   That closed the ancient paschal rite:
The old is by the new replaced;
The substance hath the shadows chased;
   And rising day dispels the night.
Christ willed what He Himself had done
Should be renewed while time should run,
   in memory of His parting hour:
Thus, tutored in His school divine,

We consecrate the bread and wine;
   And lo – a Host of saving power.

This faith to Christian men is given –
Bread is made flesh by words from heaven:
   Into his Blood the wine is turned:
What though it baffles nature's powers
Of sense and sight? This faith of ours
   Proves more than nature e'er discerned.

Concealed beneath the two-fold sign
Meet symbols of the gifts divine,
   There lie the mysteries adored:
The living body is our food;
Our drink the ever precious blood;
   In each, one undivided Lord.

Not he that eateth it divides
The sacred food, which whole abides
   Unbroken still, nor knows decay;
Be one, or be a thousand fed,
They eat alike the Living Bread
   Which, still received,
   ne'er wastes away.

The good, the guilty share therein,
With sure increase of grace or sin,
   The ghostly life, or ghostly death:
Death to the guilty; to the good
Immortal life. See how one food
   Man's joy or woe accomplisheth.

We break the Sacrament; but bold
And firm thy faith shall keep its hold;
Deem not the whole doth more enfold
   Than in the fractured part resides:
Deem not that Christ doth broken lie;
'Tis but the sign that meets the eye;
The hidden deep reality
   In all its fulness still abides.

The shorter form of the sequence begins here.

Behold the bread of angels, sent
For pilgrims in their banishment,
The bread for God's true children meant,
   That may not unto dogs be given:
Oft in the olden types foreshadowed;
In Isaac on the altar bowed,
And in the ancient paschal food,
   And in the manna sent from heaven.

Come then, good shepherd, bread divine,
Still show to us Thy mercy sign;
Oh, feed us still, still keep us Thine;
So may we see Thy glories shine
   In fields of immortality;

O Thou, the wisest, mightiest, best,
Our present food, our future rest,
Come, make us each Thy chosen guest,
Coheirs of Thine, and comrades blest
   With saints whose dwelling is with Thee.

FIRST READING
Isa 49:1-6

Islands, listen to me,
pay attention, remotest peoples.
The Lord called me before I was born,
from my mother's womb he pronounced
    my name.

He made my mouth a sharp sword,
and hid me in the shadow of his hand.
He made me into a sharpened arrow,
and concealed me in his quiver.

He said to me, 'You are my servant (Israel)
in whom I shall be glorified';
while I was thinking, 'I have toiled in vain,
I have exhausted myself for nothing';
and all the while my cause was with
    the Lord,
my reward with my God.
I was honoured in the eyes of the Lord,
my God was my strength.

And now the Lord has spoken,
he who formed me in the womb to be
    his servant,
to bring Jacob back to him,
to gather Israel to him:
'It is not enough for you to be my servant,
to restore the tribes of Jacob and bring back
    the survivors of Israel;
I will make you the light of the nations
so that my salvation may reach to the ends of
    the earth.'

RESPONSORIAL PSALM
Ps 138:1-3, 13-15 (14)

R̡. I thank you for the wonder of
    my being.

O Lord, you search me and you know me,
you know my resting and my rising,
you discern my purpose from afar.
You mark when I walk or lie down,
all my ways lie open to you.

R̡. I thank you for the wonder of
    my being.

For it was you who created my being,
knit me together in my mother's womb.
I thank you for the wonder of my being,
for the wonders of all your creation.

R̡. I thank you for the wonder of
    my being.

Already you knew my soul,
my body held no secret from you
when I was being fashioned in secret
and moulded in the depths of the earth.

R̡. I thank you for the wonder of
    my being.

SECOND READING
Acts 13:22-26

Paul said: 'God made David the king of our ancestors, of whom he approved in these words, "I have elected David son of Jesse, a man after my own heart, who will carry out my whole purpose." To keep his promise, God has raised up for Israel one of David's descendants, Jesus, as Saviour, whose coming was heralded by John when he proclaimed a baptism of repentance for the whole people of Israel. Before John ended his career he said, "I am not the one you imagine me to be; that one is coming after me and I am not fit to undo his sandal."

'My brothers, sons of Abraham's race, and all you who fear God, this message of salvation is meant for you.'

FIRST READING
Ezek 34:11-16

The Lord God says this: I am going to look after my flock myself and keep all of it in view. As a shepherd keeps all his flock in view when he stands up in the middle of his scattered sheep, so shall I keep my sheep in view. I shall rescue them from wherever they have been scattered during the mist and darkness. I shall bring them out of the countries where they are; I shall gather them together from foreign countries and bring them back to their own land. I shall pasture them on the mountains of Israel, in the ravines and in every inhabited place in the land. I shall feed them in good pasturage; the high mountains of Israel will be their grazing ground. There they will rest in good grazing ground; they will browse in rich pastures on the mountains of Israel. I myself will pasture my sheep, I myself will show them where to rest – it is the Lord who speaks. I shall look for the lost one, bring back the stray, bandage the wounded and make the weak strong. I shall watch over the fat and healthy. I shall be a true shepherd to them.

RESPONSORIAL PSALM
Ps 22 (1)

R̶. The Lord is my shepherd;
there is nothing I shall want.

The Lord is my shepherd;
there is nothing I shall want.
Fresh and green are the pastures
where he gives me repose.
Near restful waters he leads me,
to revive my drooping spirit.

R̶. The Lord is my shepherd;
there is nothing I shall want.

He guides me along the right path;
he is true to his name.
If I should walk in the valley of darkness
no evil would I fear.
You are there with your crook and your staff;
with these you give me comfort.

R̶. The Lord is my shepherd;
there is nothing I shall want.

You have prepared a banquet for me
in the sight of my foes.
My head you have anointed with oil;
my cup is overflowing.

R̶. The Lord is my shepherd;
there is nothing I shall want.

Surely goodness and kindness shall follow me
all the days of my life.
In the Lord's own house shall I dwell
for ever and ever.

R̶. The Lord is my shepherd;
there is nothing I shall want.

SECOND READING
Rom 5:5-11

The love of God has been poured into our hearts by the Holy Spirit which has been given us. We were still helpless when at his appointed moment Christ died for sinful men. It is not easy to die even for a good man – though of course for someone really worthy, a man might be prepared to die – but what proves that God loves us is that Christ died for us while we were still sinners. Having died to make us righteous, is it likely that he would now fail to save us from God's anger? When we were reconciled to God by the death of his Son, we were still enemies; now that we have been reconciled, surely we may count on being saved by the life of his Son? Not merely because we have been reconciled but because we are filled with joyful trust in God, through our Lord Jesus Christ, through whom we have already gained our reconciliation.

Saints Peter and Paul, Apostles, 30 June 2019

FIRST READING
Acts 12:1-11

King Herod started persecuting certain members of the Church. He beheaded James the brother of John, and when he saw that this pleased the Jews he decided to arrest Peter as well. This was during the days of Unleavened Bread, and he put Peter in prison, assigning four squads of four soldiers each to guard him in turns. Herod meant to try Peter in public after the end of Passover week. All the time Peter was under guard the Church prayed to God for him unremittingly.

On the night before Herod was to try him, Peter was sleeping between two soldiers, fastened with double chains, while guards kept watch at the main entrance to the prison. Then suddenly the angel of the Lord stood there, and the cell was filled with light. He tapped Peter on the side and woke him. 'Get up!' he said 'Hurry!' – and the chains fell from his hands. The angel then said, 'Put on your belt and sandals.' After he had done this, the angel next said, 'Wrap your cloak round you and follow me.' Peter followed him, but had no idea that what the angel did was all happening in reality; he thought he was seeing a vision. They passed through two guard posts one after the other, and reached the iron gate leading to the city. This opened of its own accord; they went through it and had walked the whole length of one street when suddenly the angel left him. It was only then that Peter came to himself. 'Now I know it is all true,' he said. 'The Lord really did send his angel and has saved me from Herod and from all that the Jewish people were so certain would happen to me.'

RESPONSORIAL PSALM
Ps 33:2-9 (5, alt 8)

R̰. From all my terrors the Lord set me free.
   Or: The angel of the Lord rescues those who revere him.

I will bless the Lord at all times
his praise always on my lips;
in the Lord my soul shall make its boast.
The humble shall hear and be glad.

R̰. From all my terrors the Lord set me free.
   Or: The angel of the Lord rescues those who revere him.

Glorify the Lord with me.
Together let us praise his name.
I sought the Lord and he answered me;
from all my terrors he set me free.

R̰. From all my terrors the Lord set me free.
   Or: The angel of the Lord rescues those who revere him.

Look towards him and be radiant;
let your faces not be abashed.
This poor man called; the Lord heard him
and rescued him from all his distress.

R̰. From all my terrors the Lord set me free.
   Or: The angel of the Lord rescues those who revere him.

The angel of the Lord is encamped
around those who revere him, to rescue them.
Taste and see that the Lord is good.
He is happy who seeks refuge in him.

R̰. From all my terrors the Lord set me free.
   Or: The angel of the Lord rescues those who revere him.

SECOND READING
2 Tim 4:6-8, 17-18

My life is already being poured away as a libation, and the time has come for me to be gone. I have fought the good fight to the end; I have run the race to the finish; I have kept the faith; all there is to come now is the crown of righteousness reserved for me, which the Lord, the righteous judge, will give to me on that Day; and not only to me but to all those who have longed for his Appearing.

The Lord stood by me and gave me power, so that through me the whole message might be proclaimed for all the pagans to hear; and so I was rescued from the lion's mouth. The Lord will rescue me from all evil attempts on me, and bring me safely to his heavenly kingdom. To him be glory for ever and ever. Amen.

Fourteenth Sunday in Ordinary Time, 7 July 2019

Gospel (cont.)
Luke 10:1-12,17-20

The seventy-two came back rejoicing. 'Lord,' they said 'even the devils submit to us when we use your name.' He said to them, 'I watched Satan fall like lightning from heaven. Yes, I have given you power to tread underfoot serpents and scorpions and the whole strength of the enemy; nothing shall ever hurt you. Yet do not rejoice that the spirits submit to you; rejoice rather that your names are written in heaven.'

or Luke 10:1-9

The Lord appointed seventy-two others and sent them out ahead of him, in pairs, to all the towns and places he himself was to visit. He said to them, 'The harvest is rich but the labourers are few, so ask the Lord of the harvest to send labourers to his harvest. Start off now, but remember, I am sending you out like lambs among wolves. Carry no purse, no haversack, no sandals. Salute no one on the road. Whatever house you go into, let your first words be, "Peace to this house!" And if a man of peace lives there, your peace will go and rest on him; if not, it will come back to you. Stay in the same house, taking what food and drink they have to offer, for the labourer deserves his wages; do not move from house to house. Whenever you go into a town where they make you welcome, eat what is set before you. Cure those in it who are sick, and say, "The kingdom of God is very near to you."

ALTERNATIVE RESPONSORIAL PSALM
Ps 18:8-11 (9)

℟. The precepts of the Lord
gladden the heart.

The law of the Lord is perfect,
it revives the soul.
The rule of the Lord is to be trusted,
it gives wisdom to the simple.

℟. The precepts of the Lord
gladden the heart.

The precepts of the Lord are right,
they gladden the heart.
The command of the Lord is clear,
it gives light to the eyes.

℟. The precepts of the Lord
gladden the heart.

The fear of the Lord is holy,
abiding for ever.
The decrees of the Lord are truth
and all of them just.

℟. The precepts of the Lord
gladden the heart.

They are more to be desired than gold
than the purest of gold
and sweeter are they than honey,
than honey from the comb.

℟. The precepts of the Lord
gladden the heart.

Gospel (cont.)
Luke 11:1-13

'So I say to you: Ask, and it will be given to you; search, and you will find; knock, and the door will be opened to you. For the one who asks always receives; the one who searches always finds; the one who knocks will always have the door opened to him. What father among you would hand his son a stone when he asked for bread? Or hand him a snake instead of a fish? Or hand him a scorpion if he asked for an egg? If you then, who are evil, know how to give your children what is good, how much more will the heavenly Father give the Holy Spirit to those who ask him!'

ALTERNATIVE RESPONSORIAL PSALM
Ps 94:1-2,6-9. (7-8)

℟. O that today you would listen to his voice!
Harden not your hearts.

Come, ring out our joy to the Lord;
hail the rock who saves us.
Let us come before him, giving thanks,
with songs let us hail the Lord.

℟. O that today you would listen to his voice!
Harden not your hearts.

Come in; let us bow and bend low;
let us kneel before the God who made us
for he is our God and we
the people who belong to his pasture,
the flock that is led by his hand.

℟. O that today you would listen to his voice!
Harden not your hearts.

O that today you would listen to his voice!
'Harden not your hearts as at Meribah,
as on that day at Massah in the desert
when your fathers put me to the test;
when they tried me, though they saw
      my work.'

℟. O that today you would listen to his voice!
Harden not your hearts.

Gospel (cont.)
Luke 12:32-48

Peter said, 'Lord, do you mean this parable for us, or for everyone?' The Lord replied, 'What sort of steward, then, is faithful and wise enough for the master to place him over his household to give them their allowance of food at the proper time? Happy that servant if his master's arrival finds him at this employment. I tell you truly, he will place him over everything he owns. But as for the servant who says to himself, "My master is taking his time coming", and sets about beating the menservants and the maids, and eating and drinking and getting drunk, his master will come on a day he does not expect and at an hour he does not know. The master will cut him off and send him to the same fate as the unfaithful.

'The servant who knows what his master wants, but has not even started to carry out those wishes, will receive very many strokes of the lash. The one who did not know, but deserves to be beaten for what he has done, will receive fewer strokes. When a man has had a great deal given him, a great deal will be demanded of him, when a man has had a great deal given him on trust, even more will be expected of him.'

or Luke 12:35-40

Jesus said to his disciples: 'See that you are dressed for action and have your lamps lit. Be like men waiting for their master to return from the wedding feast, ready to open the door as soon as he comes and knocks. Happy those servants whom the master finds awake when he comes. I tell you solemnly, he will put on an apron, sit them down at table and wait on them. It may be in the second watch he comes, or in the third, but happy those servants if he finds them ready. You may be quite sure of this, that if the householder had known at what hour the burglar would come, he would not have let anyone break through the wall of his house. You too must stand ready, because the Son of Man is coming at an hour you do not expect.'

SECOND READING
Heb 11:1-2, 8-19 *(cont.)*

It was by faith that Abraham, when put to the test, offered up Isaac. He offered to sacrifice his only son even though the promises had been made to him and he had been told: It is through Isaac that your name will be carried on. He was confident that God had the power even to raise the dead; and so, figuratively speaking, he was given back Isaac from the dead.

or Heb 11:1-2, 8-12

Only faith can guarantee the blessings that we hope for, or prove the existence of the realities that at present remain unseen. It was for faith that our ancestors were commended.

It was by faith that Abraham obeyed the call to set out for a country that was the inheritance given to him and his descendants, and that he set out without knowing where he was going. By faith he arrived, as a foreigner, in the Promised Land, and lived there as if in a strange country, with Isaac and Jacob, who were heirs with him of the same promise. They lived there in tents while he looked forward to a city founded, designed and built by God.

It was equally by faith that Sarah, in spite of being past the age, was made able to conceive, because she believed that he who had made the promise would be faithful to it. Because of this, there came from one man, and one who was already as good as dead himself, more descendants than could be counted, as many as the stars of heaven or the grains of sand on the seashore.

FIRST READING
Apoc 11:19; 12:1-6, 10

The sanctuary of God in heaven opened, and the ark of the covenant could be seen inside it.

Now a great sign appeared in heaven: a woman, adorned with the sun, standing on the moon, and with the twelve stars on her head for a crown. She was pregnant, and in labour, crying aloud in the pangs of childbirth. Then a second sign appeared in the sky, a huge red dragon which had seven heads and ten horns, and each of the seven heads crowned with a coronet. Its tail dragged a third of the stars from the sky and dropped them to the earth, and the dragon stopped in front of the woman as she was having the child, so that he could eat it as soon as it was born from its mother. The woman brought a male child into the world, the son who was to rule all nations with an iron sceptre, and the child was taken straight up to God and to his throne, while the woman escaped into the desert, where God had made a place of safety ready. Then I heard a voice shout from heaven, 'Victory and power and empire for ever have been won by our God, and all authority for his Christ.'

RESPONSORIAL PSALM
Ps 44:10-12, 16 (10)

℞. On your right stands the queen,
in garments of gold.

The daughters of kings are among your
    loved ones.
On your right stands the queen in gold
    of Ophir.
Listen, O daughter, give ear to my words:
forget your own people and your
    father's house.

℞. On your right stands the queen,
in garments of gold.

So will the king desire your beauty:
He is your lord, pay homage to him.
They are escorted amid gladness and joy;
they pass within the palace of the king.

℞. On your right stands the queen,
in garments of gold.

SECOND READING
1 Cor 15:20-26

Christ has been raised from the dead, the first-fruits of all who have fallen asleep. Death came through one man and in the same way the resurrection of the dead has come through one man. Just as all men die in Adam, so all men will be brought to life in Christ; but all of them in their proper order: Christ as the first-fruits and then, after the coming of Christ, those who belong to him. After that will come the end, when he hands over the kingdom to God the Father, having done away with every sovereignty, authority and power. For he must be king until he has put all his enemies under his feet and the last of the enemies to be destroyed is death, for everything is to be put under his feet.

Gospel (cont.)
Luke 15:1-32

He also said, 'A man had two sons. The younger said to his father, "Father, let me have the share of the estate that would come to me." So the father divided the property between them. A few days later, the younger son got together everything he had and left for a distant country where he squandered his money on a life of debauchery.

'When he had spent it all, that country experienced a severe famine, and now he began to feel the pinch, so he hired himself out to one of the local inhabitants who put him on his farm to feed the pigs. And he would willingly have filled his belly with the husks the pigs were eating but no one offered him anything. Then he came to his senses and said, "How many of my father's paid servants have more food than they want, and here am I dying of hunger! I will leave this place and go to my father and say: Father, I have sinned against heaven and against you; I no longer deserve to be called your son; treat me as one of your paid servants." So he left the place and went back to his father.

'While he was still a long way off, his father saw him and was moved with pity. He ran to the boy, clasped him in his arms and kissed him tenderly. Then his son said, "Father, I have sinned against heaven and against you. I no longer deserve to be called your son." But the father said to his servants, "Quick! Bring out the best robe and put it on him; put a ring on his finger and sandals on his feet. Bring the calf we have been fattening, and kill it; we are going to have a feast, a celebration, because this son of mine was dead and has come back to life; he was lost and is found." And they began to celebrate.

'Now the elder son was out in the fields, and on his way back, as he drew near the house, he could hear music and dancing. Calling one of the servants he asked what it was all about. "Your brother has come" replied the servant "and your father has killed the calf we had fattened because he has got him back safe and sound." He was angry then and refused to go in, and his father came out to plead with him; but he answered his father, "Look, all these years I have slaved for you and never once disobeyed your orders, yet you never offered me so much as a kid for me to celebrate with my friends. But, for this son of yours, when he comes back after swallowing up your property – he and his women – you kill the calf we had been fattening."

'The father said, "My son, you are with me always and all I have is yours. But it was only right we should celebrate and rejoice, because your brother here was dead and has come to life; he was lost and is found."'

or Luke 15:1-10

The tax collectors and the sinners were all seeking the company of Jesus to hear what he had to say, and the Pharisees and the scribes complained. 'This man' they said 'welcomes sinners and eats with them.' So he spoke this parable to them:

'What man among you with a hundred sheep, losing one, would not leave the ninety-nine in the wilderness and go after the missing one till he found it? And when he found it, would he not joyfully take it on his shoulders and then, when he got home, call together his friends, and neighbours? "Rejoice with me," he would say "I have found my sheep that was lost." In the same way, I tell you, there will be more rejoicing in heaven over one repentant sinner than over ninety-nine virtuous men who have no need of repentance.

'Or again, what woman with ten drachmas would not, if she lost one, light a lamp and sweep out the house and search thoroughly till she found it? And then, when she had found it, call together her friends and neighbours? "Rejoice with me," she would say "I have found the drachma I lost." In the same way, I tell you, there is rejoicing among the angels of God over one repentant sinner.'

Gospel (cont.)
Luke 16:1-13

'And so I tell you this: use money, tainted as it is, to win you friends, and thus make sure that when it fails you, they will welcome you into the tents of eternity. The man who can be trusted in little things can be trusted in great; the man who is dishonest in little things will be dishonest in great. If then you cannot be trusted with money, that tainted thing, who will trust you with genuine riches? And if you cannot be trusted with what is not yours, who will give you what is your very own?

'No servant can be the slave of two masters: he will either hate the first and love the second, or treat the first with respect and the second with scorn. You cannot be the slave both of God and of money.'

or Luke 16:10-13

Jesus said to his disciples: The man who can be trusted in little things can be trusted in great; the man who is dishonest in little things will be dishonest in great. If then you cannot be trusted with money, that tainted thing, who will trust you with genuine riches? And if you cannot be trusted with what is not yours, who will give you what is your very own?

'No servant can be the slave of two masters: he will either hate the first and love the second, or treat the first with respect and the second with scorn. You cannot be the slave both of God and of money.'

All Saints, 1 November 2019

FIRST READING
Apoc 7:2-4, 9-14

I, John, saw another angel rising where the sun rises, carrying the seal of the living God; he called in a powerful voice to the four angels whose duty was to devastate land and sea, 'Wait before you do any damage on land or at sea or to the trees, until we have put the seal on the foreheads of the servants of our God.' Then I heard how many were sealed: a hundred and forty-four thousand, out of all the tribes of Israel.

After that I saw a huge number, impossible to count, of people from every nation, race, tribe and language; they were standing in front of the throne and in front of the Lamb, dressed in white robes and holding palms in their hands. They shouted aloud, 'Victory to our God, who sits on the throne, and to the Lamb!' And all the angels who were standing in a circle round the throne, surrounding the elders and the four animals, prostrated themselves before the throne, and touched the ground with their foreheads, worshipping God with these words: 'Amen. Praise and glory and wisdom and thanksgiving and honour and power and strength to our God for ever and ever. Amen.'

One of the elders then spoke, and asked me, 'Do you know who these people are, dressed in white robes, and where they have come from?' I answered him, 'You can tell me, my Lord.' Then he said, 'These are the people who have been through the great persecution, and they have washed their robes white again in the blood of the Lamb.'

RESPONSORIAL PSALM
Ps 23:1-6 (Cf. v. 6)

R̰. Such are the men who seek your face, O Lord.

The Lord's is the earth and its fulness, the world and all its peoples. It is he who set it on the seas; on the waters he made it firm.

R̰. Such are the men who seek your face, O Lord.

Who shall climb the mountain of the Lord? Who shall stand in his holy place? The man with clean hands and pure heart, who desires not worthless things.

R̰. Such are the men who seek your face, O Lord.

He shall receive blessings from the Lord and reward from the God who saves him. Such are the men who seek him, seek the face of the God of Jacob.

R̰. Such are the men who seek your face, O Lord.

SECOND READING
1 John 3:1-3

Think of the love that the Father has lavished on us,
by letting us be called God's children;
and that is what we are.
Because the world refused to acknowledge him,
therefore it does not acknowledge us.
My dear people, we are already the children of God
but what we are to be in the future has not yet been revealed,
all we know is, that when it is revealed
we shall be like him
because we shall see him as he really is.
Surely everyone who entertains this hope
must purify himself, must try to be as pure as Christ.

All Souls, 2 November 2019

FIRST READING
Isa 25:6-9

On this mountain,
the Lord of hosts will prepare for all peoples
a banquet of rich food.
On this mountain he will remove
the mourning veil covering all peoples,
and the shroud enwrapping all nations,
he will destroy Death for ever.
The Lord will wipe away
the tears from every cheek;
he will take away his people's shame
everywhere on earth,
for the Lord has said so.
That day, it will be said: See, this is our God
in whom we hoped for salvation;
the Lord is the one in whom we hoped.
We exult and we rejoice
that he has saved us.

RESPONSORIAL PSALM
Ps 26:1, 4, 7-9, 13-14 (1 or 13)

R℣. The Lord is my light and my help.
    or:
R℣. I am sure I shall see the Lord's goodness
in the land of the living.

The Lord is my light and my help;
whom shall I fear?
The Lord is the stronghold of my life;
before whom shall I shrink?

R℣. The Lord is my light and my help.
    or:
R℣. I am sure I shall see the Lord's goodness

in the land of the living.

There is one thing I ask of the Lord,
for this I long,
to live in the house of the Lord,
all the days of my life,
to savour the sweetness of the Lord,
to behold his temple.

R℣. The Lord is my light and my help.
    or:
R℣. I am sure I shall see the Lord's goodness
in the land of the living.

O Lord, hear my voice when I call;
have mercy and answer.
It is your face, O Lord, that I seek;
hide not your face.

R℣. The Lord is my light and my help.
    or:
R℣. I am sure I shall see the Lord's goodness
in the land of the living.

I am sure I shall see the Lord's goodness
in the land of the living.
Hope in him, hold firm and take heart.
Hope in the Lord!

R℣. The Lord is my light and my help.
    or:
R℣. I am sure I shall see the Lord's goodness
in the land of the living.

SECOND READING
Rom 5:5-11

Hope is not deceptive, because the love of
God has been poured into our hearts by the
Holy Spirit which has been given us. We were
still helpless when at his appointed moment
Christ died for sinful men. It is not easy to
die even for a good man – though of course
for someone really worthy, a man might be
prepared to die – but what proves that God
loves us is that Christ died for us while we
were still sinners. Having died to make us
righteous, is it likely that he would now fail
to save us from God's anger? When we were
reconciled to God by the death of his Son,
we were still enemies; now that we have been
reconciled, surely we may count on being
saved by the life of his Son? Not merely
because we have been reconciled but because
we are filled with joyful trust in God, through
our Lord Jesus Christ, through whom we have
already gained our reconciliation.

Thirty-Second Sunday in Ordinary Time, 10 November 2019

Gospel
Luke 27, 34-38

Some Sadducees – those who say that there is no resurrection –
approached Jesus and they put this question to him.

Jesus replied, 'The children of this world take wives and husbands,
but those who are judged worthy of a place in the other world and
in the resurrection from the dead do not marry because they can no
longer die, for they are the same as the angels, and being children of
the resurrection they are sons of God. And Moses himself implies that
the dead rise again, in the passage about the bush where he calls the
Lord the God of Abraham, the God of Isaac and the God of Jacob.
Now he is God, not of the dead, but of the living; for to him all men are
in fact alive.'

Thirty-Third Sunday in Ordinary Time, 17 November 2019

Gospel (cont.)
Luke 21:5-19

'But before all this happens, men will seize you and persecute you; they will hand you over to the synagogues and to imprisonment, and bring you before kings and governors because of my name – and that will be your opportunity to bear witness. Keep this carefully in mind: you are not to prepare your defence, because I myself shall give you an eloquence and a wisdom that none of your opponents will be able to resist or contradict. You will be betrayed even by parents and brothers, relations and friends; and some of you will be put to death. You will be hated by all men on account of my name, but not a hair of your head will be lost. Your endurance will win you your lives.'

St. Andrew, Apostle and Martyr, Patron of Scotland, 30 November 2019

FIRST READING
Wis 3:1-9

The souls of the virtuous are in the hands
    of God,
no torment shall ever touch them.
In the eyes of the unwise, they did appear
    to die,
their going looked like a disaster,
their leaving us, like annihilation;
but they are in peace.
If they experienced punishment as men see it,
their hope was rich with immortality;
slight was their affliction, great will their
    blessings be.
God has put them to the test
and proved them worthy to be with him;
he has tested them like gold in a furnace,
and accepted them as a holocaust.
When the time comes for his visitation they
    will shine out;
as sparks run through the stubble, so
    will they.
They shall judge nations, rule over peoples,
and the Lord will be their king for ever.
They who trust in him will understand
    the truth,
those who are faithful will live with him
    in love;
for grace and mercy await those he
    has chosen.

RESPONSORIAL PSALM
Ps 30:3-4, 6, 8, 17, 21 (6)

℟. Into your hands, O Lord,
I commend my spirit.

Be a rock of refuge for me,
a mighty stronghold to save me,
for you are my rock, my stronghold.
For your name's sake, lead me and guide me.

℟. Into your hands, O Lord,
I commend my spirit.

Into your hands I commend my spirit.
It is you who will redeem me, Lord.
As for me, I trust in the Lord:
let me be glad and rejoice in your love.

℟. Into your hands, O Lord,
I commend my spirit.

Let your face shine on your servant.
Save me in your love.
You hide them in the shelter of your presence
from the plotting of men.

℟. Into your hands, O Lord,
I commend my spirit.

SECOND READING
Rom 10:9-18

If your lips confess that Jesus is Lord and if you believe in your heart that God raised him from the dead, then you will be saved. By believing from the heart you are made righteous; by confessing with your lips you are saved. When scripture says: those who believe in him will have no cause for shame, it makes no distinction between Jew and Greek: all belong to the same Lord who is rich enough, however many ask his help, for everyone who calls on the name of the Lord will be saved.

But they will not ask his help unless they believe in him, and they will not believe in him unless they have heard him, and they will not hear him unless they get a preacher, and they will never have a preacher unless one is sent, but as scripture says: The footsteps of those who bring good news are a welcome sound. Not everyone, of course, listens to the Good News. As Isaiah says: Lord, how many believe what we proclaimed? So faith comes from what is preached, and what is preached comes from the word of Christ.

Let me put the question: is it possible that they did not hear? Indeed they did; in the words of the psalm, their voice has gone out through all the earth, and their message to the ends of the world.

APPENDIX B

Lectionary Pronunciation Guide

Lectionary Word	Pronunciation	Lectionary Word	Pronunciation	Lectionary Word	Pronunciation
Abilene	AB-bih-layn	Ephraim	EH-fraym	Penuel	PEN-yoo-ehl
Abishai	AB-bih-shai	Ephrathah	EHF-ruh-tah	Pharisees	FARry-seez
Abram	AY-bram	Ephron	EH-fronn	Philemon	fai-LEE-monn
Alphaeus	Al-PHAY-uhs	Epiphanes	eh-pi-FAH-neez	Philippi	FILL-ih-pai
Amos	AY-moss	Gehazi	geh-HAH-zih	Philistines	FILL-ih-stainz
Ampliatus	am-plee-AH-tous	Gilead	GIHL-ih-add	Phinehas	FINN-ee-ass
Andronicus	an-DRON-ih-kuhs	Habakkuk	HAB-ba-kuck	Phoenicia	fuh-NEE-she-uh
Antioch	AN-tih-ock	Hagar	HAY-gar	Pi-Hahiroth	PAI-HAH-hih-rott
Antiochus	an-tih-OCK-uhs	Hebron	HEB-ronn	Pithom	PAI-thomm
Apollos	ap-POL-oss	Hezron	HEHZ-ronn	Pontius	PONN-shus
Aram	AR-ram	Hophni	HOFF-nee	Pontus	PONN-tus
Arameans	ar-ra-MAY-uhns	Hosea	ho-ZAY-uh	Priscilla	prih-SIHL-ah
Areopagus	ar-rih-OP-puh-gous	Isaiah	ai-ZAI-yuh	Quirinius	kwih-RIHN-ih-uhs
Arimathea	ar-ri-muh-THAY-uh	Iscariot	ihs-CARry-uht	Raamses	RAM-zeez
Asaph	ASS-aff	Ituraea	ih-too-REE-ah	Rabbouni	ra-BOH-nih
Baal-shalishah	BAHL-SHALL-ih-shah	Jabbok	DZHAB-ock	Ramah	RAH-muh
Baal-Zephon	BAHL-ZEH-fon	Jairus	DZHAI-ruhs	Ramathaim	rah-muh-THAI-yeem
Barabbas	Ba-RAB-buhs	Javan	DZHAV-uhn	Rebekah	reh-BEHK-uh
Barak	BA-rack	Jehoiakim	dzheh-HOI-uh-kihm	Rehoboam	reh-ho-BO-am
Barsabbas	bar-SAB-buhs	Jehoshaphat	dzheh-HOSH-uh-fat	Salim	SAH-leem
Bartholomew	bar-THOLL-uh-myoo	Joppa	DZHO-puh	Salu	SAHL-yoo
Bartimaeus	bar-tih-MAY-uhs	Joshua	DZHOSH-yoo-ah	Samaritan	suh-MARry-tuhn
Baruch	BAH-rook	Leah	LAY-uh	Sanhedrin	SAN-heh-drihn
Bashan	BASH-an	Lycaonian	laik-ah-O-nih-uhn	Sarai	SAH-rai
Cenchreae	KENG-kree-ay	Lysanias	lai-sa-NAI-ass	Scythian	SIH-thee-uhn
Cephas	SEE-fass	Machir	MAH-kihr	Seba	SEE-bah
Chaldeans	chawl-DEE-uhnz	Malchus	MAL-kuhS	Shaalim	shah-LEEM
Chorazin	KOR-uh-zihn	Mamre	MAM-ray	Shadrach	SHAD-rack
Deuteronomy	dew-tuh-RON-o-mee	Megiddo	MEG-ih-doh	Shalishah	SHAH-lee-shah
Dionysius	dai-oh-NAI-see-ous	Mene	MEH-nee	Shaphat	SHAF-at
dromedaries	DROM-uh-dher-eez	Meribah	meh-REE-bah	Shechem	SHEH-kehm
Ebed-melech	EH-behd-MEH-lehk	Mishael	MEESH-ah-yehl	Shittim	SHEE-tihm
Elamites	EH-luh-maitz	Mizpah	MIHZ-pah	Silvanus	sihl-VAH-nuhs
Eleazar	ehl-ee-ADZ-uh	Mosoch	MO-sock	Sirach	SIH-rak
Eli Eli Lema	AY-lee AY-lee LAH-mah	Mysia	MIH-see-uh	Sodom	SOD-uhm
Sabachthani	sah-bahk-TAH-nee	Naaman	NAH-muhn	Solomon	SO-lo-muhn
		Nahshon	NAH-shuhn	Sosthenes	SOS-theh-neez
Eliab	EH-lee-ab	Naomi	NAY-o-mih	Stachys	STACK-ihs
Eliezer	ehl-ih-EH-zer	Naphtali	NAF-tuh-lih	Succoth	SUCK-ott
Elim	EH-lihm	Nathanael	nuh-THAN-ih-ehl	Syrophoenician	SAI-ro feh-NEE-shun
Elimelech	eh-LIHM-eh-lehk	Nazarene	NAZ-ah-reen	Terebinth	TEHR-eh-bihnth
Elisha	eh-LAI-shuh	Nebuchadnezzar	neh-book-uhd-NEHZ-er	Thaddeus	tha-DAY-uhs
Eliud	EH-lee-uhd			Theophilus	thee-OFF-ih-luhs
Elizabeth	eh-LIHZ-uh-bth	Nehemiah	neh-heh-MAI-uh	Theudas	THYOO-dass
Eloi Eloi Lama	AY-lo-ee AY-lo-ee LAH-mah sah-bakh-TAH-nee	Nicanor	NICK-a-nor	Thyatira	thai-uh-TEE-ruh
Sabechthani		Olivet	OLL-ih-veht	Timaeus	tih-MAY-uhs
		Omega	OH-meg-guh	Timon	TEE-mon
ephah	EH-fah	Ophir	O-fear	Tohu	TO-hoo
Ephah	EH-fah	Paphos	PAFF-oss	Tubal	TOO-b'l

Lectionary Word	Pronunciation	Lectionary Word	Pronunciation	Lectionary Word	Pronunciation
Ur	oor	Wadi	WOD-ih	Zarephath	ZAH-reh-fath
Urbanus	oor-BAH-nuhs	Zacchaeus	zak-KAY-uhs	Zebulun	ZEH-boo-loun
Uzziah	uh-ZAI-uh	Zadok	ZAY-dock		